Human choice and climate change

Human choice and climate change: an international assessment

EDITED BY

Steve Rayner & Elizabeth L. Malone

VOLUME ONE

The societal framework

VOLUME TWO

Resources and technology

VOLUME THREE

The tools for policy analysis

VOLUME FOUR

"What have we learned?"

Human choice and climate change

VOLUME THREE
The tools for policy analysis

EDITED BY
Steve Rayner
Elizabeth L. Malone

Pacific Northwest National Laboratory

Battelle Press

DISCLAIMER

Funding for the publication of this volume and funding for a portion of the research discussed in this volume were provided by the United States Department of Energy (DOE). The views and opinions of the authors expressed herein do not necessarily state or reflect those of the DOE. Neither the DOE, nor Battelle Memorial Institute, nor any of their employees, makes any warranty, expressed or implied, or assumes any legal liability or responsibility for the accuracy, completeness, or usefulness of any information, apparatus, product, or process disclosed, or represents that its use would not infringe privately owned rights. Reference herein to any specific commercial product, process, or service by trade name, trademark, manufacturer, or otherwise, does not necessarily constitute or imply its endorsement, recommendation, or favoring by the DOE or Battelle Memorial Institute. Trademarks belong to their various owners, and are not specifically identified herein. The DOE encourages wide dissemination of the technical information contained herein, with due respect for Publisher's rights regarding the complete work.

PACIFIC NORTHWEST NATIONAL LABORATORY
Operated by
BATTELLE MEMORIAL INSTITUTE for the
UNITED STATES DEPARTMENT OF ENERGY
Under contract DE-AC06-76RLO 1830

Library of Congress Cataloging-in-Publication Data
Human choice and climate change / edited by Steve Rayner and Elizabeth L. Malone.
p. cm.
Includes bibliographical references and index.
Contents: v. 1. The societal framework – v. 2. Resources and technology – v. 3. The tools for policy analysis – v. 4. What have we learned?
ISBN 1-57477-045-4 (hc: alk. paper). ISBN 1-57477-040-3 (softcover: alk. paper)
1. Climatic changes—Social aspects. 2. Human ecology. 3. Environmental policy. I. Rayner, Steve, 1953–. II. Malone, Elizabeth L., 1947–
QC981.8.C5H83 1998
363.738'74—dc21
97-49711
CIP

	Hardover	Softcover
Four Volume Set	1-57477-045-4	1-57477-040-3
Volume 1: The Societal Framework	1-57477-049-7	1-57477-044-6
Volume 2: Resources and Technology	1-57477-046-2	1-57477-041-1
Volume 3: The Tools for Policy Analysis	1-57477-047-0	1-57477-042-X
Volume 4: What Have We Learned?	1-57477-048-9	1-57477-043-8

Printed in the United States of America.

Battelle Press
505 King Avenue
Columbus, Ohio 43201-2693
614-424-6393 or 1-800-451-3543
FAX: 614-424-3819
E-Mail: press@battelle.org
Home page: www.battelle.org/bookstore

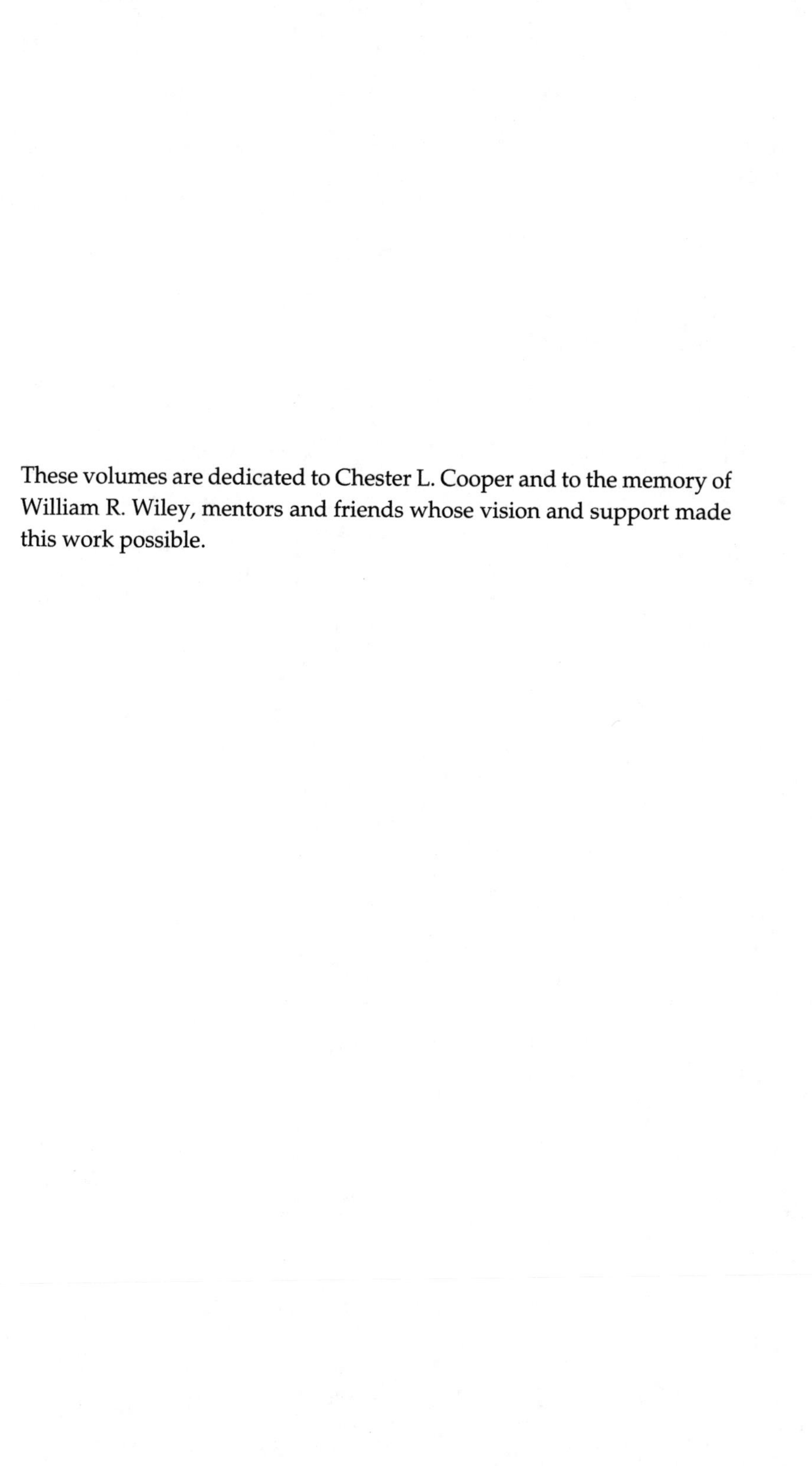

These volumes are dedicated to Chester L. Cooper and to the memory of William R. Wiley, mentors and friends whose vision and support made this work possible.

Contents

Foreword

The International Advisory Board

In contrast to other state-of-the-art reviews of climate change research, this project sees the world through a social science lens. This focus is reflected not only in the subject matter, but also in the authors' approach. It is a fundamental assumption of the project that the social sciences have ways of defining and analyzing the issues grouped under the term *global climate change* that are distinct from, yet potentially complementary to, those used in the natural sciences, and that social science analyses can generate findings of relevance to the policymaking community. The unique contributions that a social science story of global climate change can make include the awareness of human agency and value-based assumptions; a willingness to grapple with uncertainty, indeterminacy, and complexity; the consideration of social limits to growth; and the distinctiveness of an interdisciplinary social science approach.

We have been involved with this project from its early stages and have met to consider various aspects of the product on several occasions. The importance of social science research in formulating policies that are realistic and implementable can hardly be overstated. Thus, we have insisted that *Human choice and climate change* be policy-relevant. We hope that it will stimulate new scientific approaches to the processes involved in reaching and adhering to environmental agreements. Climate change impacts will be felt regionally and locally, and responses to these changes will be effected at these levels as well. Therefore, widespread understanding of the issues and potential choices is extremely important; focusing on the social dimension is critical for understanding them.

A social science framing of global climate change will help to make both natural and social science more relevant and more effective contributors to the policymaking process. Reflexive interdisciplinary research that recognizes the rich array of human motivations, actions, and perspectives can supply information that will better support the challenges of decisionmaking under sustained conditions of indeterminacy such as those surrounding global climate change.

We are pleased to have been associated with this project and hope its products promote the same level of thoughtful consideration that they did during our meetings and discussions of these challenging and significant issues.

The International Advisory Board

Dr Francisco Barnes
The Honorable Richard Benedick
Professor Harvey Brooks
Dr Jiro Kondo
Professor the Lord Desai of St Clement Danes
Professor George Golitsyn
Pragya Dipak Gyawali
The Honorable Thomas Hughes
Dr Hoesung Lee
Professor Tom Malone
The Honorable Robert McNamara
Professor Richard Odingo
Professor Thomas Schelling

Preface

When the Pacific Northwest National Laboratory (PNNL) established the Global Studies Program in 1989, I initiated an agenda to develop an integrated understanding of the important new linkages between human and natural systems, linkages that are affecting the evolution of both systems. To this end, the program encompassed the full range of the climate issue, focusing particularly on a sensible coupling between an understanding of the climate system itself and the human decisions that might affect it. This led a decision to assess the state of the art of the social sciences, in terms of their contribution to research on, and understanding of, the climate change issue. Thus, in the winter of 1993, as part of the Global Studies Program effort, the program launched the enterprise that, in due course, became *Human choice and climate change.*

This effort focused on what the social sciences have contributed to the climate change debate and on their potential to contribute more. My hope was that, at a minimum, the work would contribute to the development of a social science research agenda based on more than a call for funding parity with the physical sciences. I was also concerned that the finished document be directed not only to the academic community but also to the policy community.

From the very outset, the object was not to seek the creation of a consensus document of the kind developed by the Intergovernmental Panel on Climate Change, but rather the individual points of view on the climate issue from our 120 authors and contributors, representing a score of countries. Through their direct participation and from a host of peer reviewers, we now have a snapshot of the social sciences in the mid-1990s commenting not only on climate change but also on many aspects of sustainable development.

It is clear from these volumes that economics is by no means the only social science discipline that has relevant things to say about the issue of climate change. Despite the academic language and perspective, the pages of this document have put a human face on the climate change issue.

Some of the authors address social science itself as an issue, rather than social science contributions to climate change research. Indeed, a superficial reading of this material might cause some to question the credibility of social science in addressing climate change issues. For example, rather than speaking directly to the question of human behavior and climate change, the social sciences seem to have a penchant for placing climate change within a larger context, to consider climate change together with many other issues on the social agenda.

Human choice and climate change also reveals the social sciences to be a heterogeneous set of research programs, in which climate change research varies from being a peripheral issue to a highly refined subdiscipline with strong interdisciplinary connections to the natural sciences.

While the physical and natural sciences have been pursuing the questions of how much humans might affect climate, how fast these changes might take place and what the regional effects of these changes might be, our authors have added another question: even if we knew how climate were to change, what could we do about it and how would we decide to do it? Our assessment is that this question, among others, reveals a lack of fundamental knowledge of how society operates, and merits addition to the climate change research agenda.

The enterprise has borne fruit in ways that could not have been foreseen. It addressed the state of the art of the social sciences with regard to the climate change issue, but it also brought together social scientists in the pursuit of a collective goal; it has spotlighted strengths and weaknesses in social science research programs dealing with climate change; and it has laid the foundation for a substantive program of future climate change research.

The editors have conscientiously attempted to reflect the views of the many authors without endorsement or censure. PNNL is pleased to have provided a forum for the expression of a wide range of views and diverse, sometimes even contradictory, conclusions. We thank the International Advisory Board for its wise guidance. The editors, authors, contributors, and peer reviewers deserve substantial credit for striving to bridge and link fields of inquiry that have grown up in isolated traditions.

Gerald M. Stokes
Associate Director
Pacific Northwest National Laboratory

Why study human choice and climate change?

Steve Rayner & Elizabeth Malone

Why the concern with climate change?

Time and again over the course of the past decade, climate change has been described by scientists, environmentalists, and politicians as a threat unprecedented in human experience. Tolba's (1991: 3) statement is representative of such concerns: "We all know that the world faces a threat potentially more catastrophic than any other threat in human history: climate change and global warming." Many reasons and combinations of reasons are advanced for this claim, especially the potential rapidity of temperature rise, the irreversibility of change once the forces are set in motion, the geographical scale of the threat, the complexity and nonlinearity of the natural systems involved, the ubiquity and strength of human commitment to combustion technologies, and the political challenges of global cooperation that climate change seems to demand. The real danger, say many, lies in the potential for catastrophic surprise.

Similarly, several candidate causes have been identified. Emissions of greenhouse-related gases from human activities constitute the proximate cause, of course. In the background lurk possible underlying causes: population growth, overconsumption, humans' inability to control the technologies they have created, their inability to implement environmentally benign technologies, their unwillingness to spend current wealth to benefit future generations, their powerlessness to forge effective international agreements and abide by them. Whatever the cause, climate change is framed as a problem, which admits the possibility of solution.

Solutions come in many forms and approach the problem from different angles. Solutions to scientific problems take the form of improved knowledge, understanding, and predictability of natural systems. Solutions to technological problems require innovation and commitment of resources. Solutions to problems of societal cooperation and coordination are offered in the form of international treaties and policy instruments such as taxes or emissions controls. However, all solutions imply choices that must be made, consciously or unconsciously, enthusiastically or reluctantly, and with levels of information that may be satisfactory or unsatisfactory to the choosers.

Why the concern with human choice?

The possibility of human choice, albeit constrained, underlies all of these discussions; that is, humans can choose to respond to the prospect of climate change and can decide, with undetermined and perhaps undeterminable degrees of freedom, what steps to take. However, choice does not merely underlie any possible solution to climate change; it also underlies the problem itself. Increasing global greenhouse gas concentrations are the result of myriad choices that compose the history and contemporary operation of industrial society. Any attempt to change the course upon which human society appears to be embarked requires not only new choices about future actions, but also understanding of past choices—the existing social commitments that have set the world on its present course. The possibility, indeed the inevitability, of choice lies at the core of the climate change issue.

Everyone makes choices about accepting participation in any sort of society (even rebelling against it). Much of human life is devoted to negotiating within families, laboratories, firms, communities, nations, and other institutions the particular balance of independence and interdependence that each person is willing to accept. This tension, characteristic of all forms of social existence, is thrown into stark relief by the controversies that rage and the choices that must be made about the potential for climate change. Questions of choice, therefore, lie at the heart of not only the climate change issue but also the social sciences.

Possible choices with reference to climate change can be grouped into three broad categories, which can be combined in various ways:

- Do nothing. Some say that concern about climate change is unwarranted; the science is unproven, based on speculation bolstered by models so inaccurate they cannot reproduce historical shifts in climate. Others believe that impacts will be gradual, easily accommodated through technology, or insignificant on a global scale. If climate change does occur, then piecemeal adaptation will suffice. Even some who do believe that climate change is likely and may be disruptive suggest that the aggregate benefits of allowing climate change to run its course would outweigh the costs.
- Mitigate, that is, lessen emissions to reduce the magnitude of climate change. If one is convinced that anthropogenic emissions are giving rise to climate change, the obvious direct solution to the problem is to reduce

net emissions. Motivations for preferring this option include not only its directness but also, perhaps more importantly, that it can be conjoined with favored solutions to other perceived problems, such as population growth or the income disparities between industrialized and less industrialized nations.

- Anticipate and adapt; that is, change crops and growing regions, retreat from or defend coastal areas, prepare for population shifts and health impacts. Advocates of anticipatory adaptation also regard it as an opportunity to develop policies and technologies that would be beneficial in any event, such as infrastructure that is more resilient to extreme weather events.

For all three strategies, or any combination of them, it makes sense to invest in new knowledge. Improving the accuracy of climate forecasting may confirm that humans need not take any concerted action. Mitigation may require developing new technologies that will allow economic development while reducing the anthropogenic contributions to climate change. Society could invest in geoengineering techniques or large-scale removal of carbon dioxide from the atmosphere. Anticipatory adaptation will require foresight about impacts and new technological and social developments to respond to them.

But who should choose among the possible responses and combinations of responses to climate change? Since it is a global issue, the obvious decision-makers are the governments of nation states who have enjoyed legitimacy as the arbiters of high policy throughout the modern era. People habitually turn to their governments to choose goals (such as emissions reductions) and policy instruments (e.g., a carbon tax). Often climate change research among the social sciences focuses on the macro level of national and international political choice. Certainly the knowledge of how choice processes and mechanisms operate at these levels is valuable in framing issues and conducting negotiations.

However, research at the macro level may reduce important dimensions of social choice to simple instrumental issues. For example, the fundamental concept of fairness, as the glue holding societies together, may be reduced to an instrumental factor affecting the efficient implementation of the goal of emissions reduction. Furthermore, who chooses when the nation state or the market fails to produce a solution? The slogan, "Think globally—act locally" expresses the widespread recognition that choices are made at the micro level, by individuals and groups in particular places. Even in the context of national or international regulations, firms, families, communities, and citizens choose how to respond to incentives and sanctions. Moreover, other institutions, such as environmental organizations, can choose to respond in more robust ways and to try persuasive strategies so others will act voluntarily to comply with or even exceed statutory requirements.

Behind all such questions about choices associated with climate change lurk general questions about how societies and institutions choose the choosers and confer legitimacy upon their decisions. These are problems of collective choice. Choices are embedded and intertwined in social institutions of all kinds, including interest groups, pressure groups, lobbies, elected officials, citizens, and so on. Choices are often so deeply entrenched in societal norms that people will resist persuasion and coercion aimed at changing their behavior.

In part, the role of the social sciences is to probe these background choices by providing the capability to continually examine and re-examine our assumptions, that is, to provide what social scientists call "reflexivity" about societal choice. In the case of climate change, the social sciences remind us to question assumptions and propositions that those who are already committed to a course of action may take for granted. For instance, the conscious choice of responses arises only after we have chosen which issues to take seriously. How do people choose from among a large set of possible problems to work on as scientists, activists, entrepreneurs, homemakers, or politicians? How do individual choices influence what happens at a societal level? What roles do cultural and institutional processes play? How did the choice set of possible or potential issues come to be framed? How did other issues get to be excluded or incorporated into others? With regard specifically to climate change, various questions about choice are intertwined, for example:

- How do scientists choose to study climate change? How do they form a scientific consensus?
- How do people decide that climate change is worthy of attention?
- How do people attribute blame for climate change and choose solutions?
- How do people choose whom to believe about climate change and at what level of risk do they or should they choose to act?
- How do people and institutions mobilize support for (or against) policy action on climate change?
- What is the relationship between resource management choices and climate change?
- How do governments establish where climate change stands in relation to other political priorities?
- How are climate change policy instruments chosen?
- Why and how did the international community choose to address climate change?
- How do societies select technologies that cause, mitigate, or assist adaptation to climate change?
- How can research on social or collective action be useful to the global climate change debate?

Understandably, those who are unshakably convinced, either that climate change is an urgent and impending catastrophe or that talk of climate change is merely, to quote one US Congressman, "liberal claptrap," are likely to be impatient with such questions. For almost everyone else concerned about the issue, such questions may be the starting point from which society can work to make wise decisions about its future.

Different disciplines approach the kinds of questions that we pose from different perspectives, frequently simply modifying or fine-tuning the tools already in hand to account for choice. Issues of human needs and wants, the social bases for cultural or institutional choices, uncertainty, imperfect knowledge, and irrationality are often elided because they are too difficult to represent in equations and computer models.

As we venture among the social sciences, we run into rival prescriptions about how such choices ought to be made (e.g., by experts, by majority vote, by consensus, by preferences revealed in the marketplace) as well as the criteria to be used (e.g., the greatest happiness of the greatest number, or safeguarding individual or majority rights). In this sense, the social sciences reflect the diversity and the unity of human societies, institutions, and individuals on the issues of human choice facing the prospect of climate change.

The problem of collective choice has usually been framed as one of aggregation or of coercion:

- how to aggregate individual preferences into a collective preference, or
- how to persuade individuals to conform with normative requirements of corporations and governments, as implemented by the decisionmakers who are their officials.

Arrow (1951) has famously demonstrated the impossibility of aggregating individual preferences into a collective one in a way that satisfies certain minimal conditions of rationality and transitivity. For Arrow, the dictatorial social welfare function is the only one possible. However, dictatorship is incompatible with democracy. We seem to be caught in a bind. But Arrow's analysis assumes that preferences are inherently individual. If we use another set of assumptions—for example, that preferences are inherently relational (that is, expressions of social solidarity)—we change the nature of the problem from being one of aggregating individuals to discerning the structure and dynamics of social solidarity, which in turn may open up a new solution space for the problem of collective action.

Social science has long been confronted with the central issues of choice and constraint, and, thus, climate change is far from being a unique problem for the social sciences. Moreover, the individual–society tension within the social sciences often reflects a theoretical and methodological gap between the mindsets and methods of various social science disciplines. Even within disciplines, social science paradigms differ in their views of collective action. The problem of understanding and choosing a course of action with respect to climate change is that of articulating choices and consequences across the local and global levels.

For some analysts, social choice is an issue of aggregating individual preferences (from citizens to nations), whereas for others it is rather a problem of decomposing national or communal preferences into appropriate units of social solidarity, such as the household, the village, or the firm. It is pointless to ask which approach is right and which is wrong. Like wave and particle explanations of light, each offers insights that the other cannot reproduce. The characteristics of light's wave and particle properties cannot be simultaneously measured, yet both sets of properties are essential to understanding the behavior of light. Similarly, it is important to understand the sources and consequences of the divergent social science approaches to explaining human behavior so that climate change researchers and practitioners can capitalize on the strengths of that diversity.

The conceptual architecture of this assessment

Human choice and climate change is a climate-oriented assessment firmly rooted in the social sciences. That is, it takes as its starting point human social conditions around the world. Instead of examining the physical and chemical processes of climate change, this assessment looks at climate change in the broader context of global social change. Analysis of climate change needs to be conducted in the context of mainstream social science concerns with human choice and global (not just environmental) change. A global developmental and environmental perspective can be helpful to policymakers and scholars for at least two reasons:

- Social systems intersect and interact with several natural systems simultaneously and interdependently. Human activity therefore represents a crosscutting system constituting major linkages among natural cycles and systems. Hence, changes in human activity stimulated by interaction with one such system tend to influence others in potentially significant ways.
- The scale and rate of change in social systems may well outpace the scale and rate of climate change for the foreseeable future. For example, even vulnerable populations and vulnerable natural resources may plausibly be more directly affected by general economic conditions than by climate change over the course of the next hundred years.

The entry point of a global social science perspective allows us to set our bounds very widely. For instance, in the social sciences, the topic of "climate change" encompasses people's perceptions and behavior based on the threat (or, in a few cases, the promise) of such change, as well as the causes, processes, and prospective impacts of the change itself. In *Human choice and climate change*, we broaden our scope beyond that of the Intergovernmental Panel on Climate Change (IPCC) Working Group on the Economic and Social Dimensions of Climate Change (Bruce et al. 1996) to include research that, although relevant, is not focused specifically on climate change itself. At the same time, we have retained the orientation of climate change as an important policy issue that can act as a touchstone or reference point for theories and research.

Just as the same physical object confronted from different angles may present very different appearances to an observer, so can the same problem be very differently defined when viewed from different paradigms. One strategy for our assessment would have been to accept the conventional framing of the human dimensions of climate change in terms of proximate causes and impacts. Most extant texts concerned with the human dimensions of climate change or, more broadly, of global environmental change begin with a summary of the way that the natural sciences describe the changes that are occurring on the land and in the atmosphere and oceans (e.g., Jacobsen & Price 1991, Stern et al. 1992). These assessments draw directly on the natural sciences to frame the issues for social science inquiry. However, the authors and contributors to this project opted for a riskier approach of attempting to define climate change and, by extension, global environmental change from a thoroughgoing social science perspective.

We seek to learn from approaching the natural sciences from a social science viewpoint rather than through what has been the more orthodox approach of wading into the social science waters from the conventional terra firma of the natural sciences. In so doing, we do not seek to subvert the findings of the natural sciences or discover some social pretext to dismiss societal concern about climate. Rather, we seek to provide an additional footing from which the intellectual landscape of the climate change issue can be viewed. We have tried to complement the natural science perspective, not to replace it with another single vantage point.

Human choice and climate change is presented in four volumes. In the first three volumes, our goal is twofold: to create a text that could serve as an overview of social science relevant to global climate change for researchers with backgrounds in the natural sciences or in the social sciences but not as those backgrounds relate to global climate change; and to provide a reference work for both scholars and practitioners as they perform research, conduct negotiations, or plan and implement policies. To accomplish this goal, the assessment seeks to:

- Represent the range of social science research applicable to global climate change
- Provide insights into the world as viewed through the lens of social

science topics, tools, and data
- Review what is currently known, uncertain, and unknown within the social sciences in relation to global climate change
- Assemble and summarize findings from the international research communities of industrialized, less industrialized, and newly democratic nations
- Report these findings within diverse interdisciplinary frameworks
- Relate research results to policy issues and problems.

The fourth volume provides an editorial overview of the first three, reflexively focusing on the challenges that climate change issues present to the intellectual organization of social science, the lessons that the social sciences can bring to understanding climate change issues, and the implications of all of this for policymakers.

In each volume, we have sought to present the subject at a level of detail and theoretical sophistication to make the assessment useful as a reference work for scholars. We have also attempted to tie the material to practical issues useful to decisionmakers and their advisors. We are acutely aware that in aiming the assessment at two audiences we run the risk of pleasing neither. To the first audience we may seem simplistic, even instrumental in our approach. We may strike the second audience as excessively abstract and academic. However, it is our hope that the dual focus of this assessment can be fruitful in pointing to convergence between scholarship and action.

Human choice and climate change, volume 1: the societal framework

Volume 1 of *Human choice and climate change* begins our inquiry into social science perspectives and climate change with an assessment of the state of the Earth's social, cultural, political, and economic systems, which provide the context that supports and consists of the activities that contribute to the emissions of greenhouse gases and within which:
- climate change is perceived and debated
- the impacts of change will be experienced
- human beings will make the critical choices about their future, including choices about how to confront the prospect of changing climate in a changing world.

Climate change is occurring in a complex and rapidly changing framework of human choices that shapes people's perception of it and the opportunities for human response. The social context of climate change and knowledge about it are usually taken for granted. Subjecting it to social science analysis reveals the extent to which our understanding of the science, diagnoses of underlying causes, and views of appropriate action are not merely technical judgments, but embody deep-seated social commitments that provide the context for response options.

"Science and decisionmaking," the first chapter, examines the social processes by which technical knowledge about climate change (and other science-based issues) is created by scientists and communicated to policymakers. The authors begin with four interlocking questions that remained unasked, even unacknowledged, in earlier assessments of social science and climate change:

- How do scientists and their societies identify and delimit distinct problems related to climate change that are considered amenable to scientific resolution?
- How do scientists come to know particular facts and causal relationships regarding climate change and to persuade others that their knowledge is credible?
- How do conflicts over risk arise, and how are responses to them handled in a world of conflicting and plural political interests?
- How do human societies and their designated policy actors draw upon scientific knowledge to justify collective action on a worldwide scale?

The authors describe the role that the production and dissemination of scientific knowledge have played in the elevation of climate change to a topic of worldwide interest and political concern. Their analysis reveals how the normal model of the relationship between science and policy, which has been termed "speaking truth to power," assumes that the two domains are and should be largely distinct. However, social science analysis indicates a level of interdependence between science and politics so strong as to constitute a process of co-production of relevant knowledge, which most often occurs unrecognized by either scientists or policymakers.

Science and technology studies demonstrate how scientists build on local experiments and knowledges in laboratories and field studies to formulate generally accepted methods, facts, and theories. Through a process of standardization and network building, scientific knowledge can attain a universal validity, as climate change science has through the deliberations of the IPCC. Applying insights from studies of the social processes of scientific inquiry, the chapter examines the implicit assumptions embedded in theories and models used to study interactions between the biogeophysical and social systems. Making these assumptions explicit provides an opportunity to question them and to examine their validity in the specific situations to which the theories and models are being applied. This reflexivity is important because scientific research that fails to engage in such self-examination risks becoming irrelevant to the world beyond the laboratory or academy walls. Perhaps worse, it leaves science susceptible to political backlash against scientific consensus on climate change—just as has happened in the US Congress. Policymakers who rely on data from unreflexive research risk errors in their decisionmaking that may cost them (and the societies in whose name they act) dearly, whether financially, politically, or socially.

The interdependence between scientists and policymakers constitutes a process of co-production of knowledge seldom recognized by either.

"Population and health" and "Human needs and wants," the next two chapters, demonstrate that neither of the standard diagnoses of the underlying causes of climate change—overpopulation and overconsumption—can be justified by social science research. Chapter 2, "Population and health," lays out the world's changing sociodemographic profile, the social science controversies about the role of population in climate and other environmental change, and the micro-scale factors that shape peoples' preferences about family size and spacing of children. Although the authors find that rapid population growth has a negative effect on the development of many, albeit not all, less industrialized countries, the extent of this effect is difficult to quantify, or even to demonstrate on a global scale because of the complexity and multiplicity of relationships involved and the variability of local circumstances. The authors conclude that population policy has too often been based on the easy, specious logic "You would be happier if you had fewer children," which cannot be justified by rigorous social science evidence. The real underlying logic is often "I would be happier if you had fewer children."

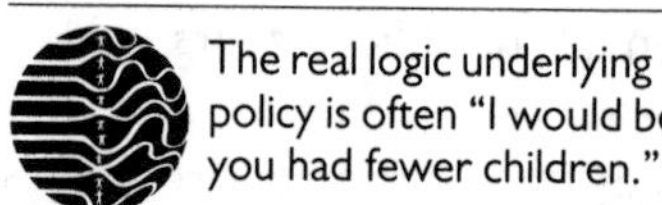

The real logic underlying population policy is often "I would be happier if you had fewer children."

Population, as such, is not the issue shaping climate change or other environmental degradation. The appropriate question is how are population factors mediated through institutional and social structures to affect natural resources and the environment? In some areas population makes a big difference to environmental impacts; in others it does not. Where it does make a difference, the costs and benefits of intervening directly to affect population must be weighed against the costs and benefits of policies designed to loosen institutional rigidities that prevent families from responding flexibly to the pressures of population growth. The people most vulnerable to impacts of climate change tend to be members of impoverished populations living in environmentally fragile zones of less industrialized countries. These populations already adapt very flexibly to the impacts of extreme climatic fluctuations, such as storms and droughts, albeit at considerable cost of human life and suffering. But climate change may overstretch their coping capacity. Although it is quite unlikely to change the big picture of world population size, rate of growth, and age structure, climate change will have an impact on mortality, fertility, and migration at regional and local levels.

If the impact of population is less than straightforward, what can be said about consumption? What justification is there for distinguishing consumption for survival from luxury consumption? Chapter 3, "Human needs and wants," evaluates the attempts of various disciplines to establish human needs as the basis for climate policies compatible with individual fulfillment and societal development. The authors show that the concept of basic human needs has universal rhetorical appeal, but it cannot made operational coherently in a way that helps policymakers to define climate policy goals. Everyone may agree that clean air, access to potable water, a minimum ration of calories and protein—even entitlements to atmospheric carbon sinks—are all somehow basic human needs, but in practice it is impossible to devise universally standardized measures for their operationalization. How clean is clean? How pure is potable? What constitutes access? What is the age and level of activity of the individual to be fed?

Only by understanding the essentially social character of needs, wants, and their satisfaction through consumption can analysts and policymakers lay the basis for behavioral change.

Furthermore, needs and wants cannot be usefully distinguished. Needs turn out to be wants that someone is unwilling to give up. So long as social scientists and policymakers continue to treat wants as private appetites, they cannot understand how wants come to be standardized in society and how those standards change. The issue of how societal preferences change is a critical one for long-term modeling and for policy interventions that seek to alter either the scale of consumer demands (including demands for small or large families) or the technologies by which demands are satisfied. If consumption choices are recast—not as private preferences but as public statements establishing or confirming community identity, group membership, or social solidarity—then fundamental changes in consumption patterns are likely to require very basic changes in the kinds of society people live in. Only by understanding the essentially social character of needs, wants, and their satisfaction through consumption can analysts and policymakers lay the basis for behavioral change.

The authors of Chapter 3 focus attention on the emergence of new models of wealth, based on the notion of social capital, that includes the levels of social support that people can expect from the communities and institutions to which they belong (rather than focusing on dollars per individual). Criteria for measuring social capital are being explored; however, they have not yet reached the level of development or received the recognition already being given to the valuation of natural capital and so-called green accounting.

. . . debate about climate change is often a surrogate for a broader, so-far intractable political discourse about population, lifestyles, and international development.

The broader "Cultural discourses" about climate are the subject of the fourth chapter, which probes deeper into societal controversy over diagnoses and prescriptions and exposes the social commitments that underlie the range of opinions and political positions. In the course of debating climate change at home, at work, in the media, or in the halls of power, experts and lay people alike diagnose the underlying human causes of climate change as lying in population growth, profligate consumption, or incorrect pricing and property rights allocations. In response to these diagnoses, participants in these cultural discourses seek prescriptions to remedy climate change while protecting competing principles for procedural fairness as well as distributional and intergenerational equity. Disagreements about the underlying human causes of climate change and proposed solutions to it are deeply rooted in competing institutional narratives about nature as well as rival principles of fairness. The chapter illustrates that debate about climate change is often a surrogate for a broader, so-far intractable political discourse about population, lifestyles, and international development.

In elucidating the various voices of experts and lay people in the climate change debate, the chapter demonstrates that the basis for such discourses is essentially institutional. The authors make a strong claim that social relationships, rather than individual preferences, stabilize the public expression of values about what is natural and what is right. How people bind themselves to each other simultaneously shapes the way they bind themselves to nature. Social and cultural variables of network density, interconnectedness, and rule sharing account more effectively for variations in environmental perceptions and behavior than do standard demographic variables such as age and sex. To guide the reader through this novel landscape, the authors present a conceptual map of human values to help social scientists identify and track the strength of support for alternative positions and to help policymakers identify opportunities for effective intervention in the debates.

Public information campaigns that assume that discrepancies between lay and experts accounts of climate change are simply attributable to knowledge deficiencies are bound to fail.

The social science perspective represented in this chapter suggests that public information and education campaigns to change people's energy use or other environmentally relevant behavior fail because changing behavior is not simply a problem of removing exogenous barriers to the natural flow of knowledge. The social science perspective redirects efforts at communication from simply overcoming ignorance to creating shared frames of reference and opportunities for shared action. Public information campaigns that assume that discrepancies between lay and experts accounts of climate change are attributable simply to knowledge deficiencies are bound to fail.

Climate discourses are complex and turbulent. Many voices join in, and they are often inconsistent, even self-contradictory, but not randomly so, nor in a way that can simply be ascribed to naked self-interest. By labeling the present state of affairs as disorderly, each voice seeks to legitimate the reordering of society along its own preferred institutional principles. How these institutional arrangements are structured and operate in the climate change arena is the topic of Chapter 5, "Institutions for political action," which ties the value commitments of climate discourses to the institutional arrangements that human beings use for making collective choices about society and the environment.

The growing prominence of global environmental issues as matters of high politics is itself a sign that the nation state retains an important and powerful position. However, the character and the role of the state are changing rapidly in fundamental aspects of its international and domestic roles. Political influence and real power is diffusing to international and domestic policy networks in which governments and their agencies interact directly with social movements, firms, and communities. The notion of unitary national interest is increasingly difficult to sustain. The rising importance of nonstate actors and the emergence of aspects of a global civil society, in the light of global climate change, are now garnering much attention from sociologists and international relations scholars alike.

The real business of responding to climate concerns may well be through smaller, often less formal, agreements among states; states and firms; and firms, nongovernmental organizations, and communities.

The new landscape of world politics—and global environmental politics in particular—has given voice to those formerly marginalized or excluded from political dialogue. The authors conclude that, although the Framework

Convention on Climate Change represents an important expression of worldwide concern about climate and the persistent issues of global development that are inextricably bound up with it, the real business of responding to climate concerns may well be through smaller, often less formal, agreements among states; states and firms; and firms, nongovernmental organizations, and communities.

However, this response process is likely to be messy and contested—not that messiness or contestation are to be disparaged. Patterns of interest-group mobilization and representation help to sustain a bias in favor of activities that lead to increasing greenhouse gas emissions. The status quo is insulated from fundamental change by the influence of routines, established procedures, and traditional and close ties among economic and political elites. Climate policies as such are bound to be hard to implement. Simply incorporating climate change into existing political agendas is unlikely to produce the desired outcomes. Similarly, presenting climate change measures as ways of achieving higher taxation or welfare expenditure is also likely to meet significant opposition. True win–win solutions prove to be elusive. Effective actions designed to mitigate or respond opportunistically or adaptively to climate change are likely to be those most integrated into general policy strategies for economic and social development.

Volume 1 places climate change in the dynamic context of a changing societal landscape that shapes changes in the atmosphere. Here the responses of political and social institutions are crucial, and human choice must be taken into account. Sometimes the separation of the biogeophysical systems from the social systems has led global climate change researchers to focus on climate change as if it were the most important issue facing the sustainable development of human society. Yet sustained consideration of one issue can be maintained only at the cost of excluding others. Decisionmakers need to consider the opportunity costs as well as the benefits of directing their present attention to climate change. Furthermore, for most of humankind, climate change is not life's most pressing issue, certainly not on a day-to-day basis. A social science framing of the problem introduces a more complex view by asking what else is going on in the development of human society and how climate change will affect and be affected by these societal changes. Volume 2 looks at climate change in relation to human resource use, and opportunities to reduce human impacts on the climate and climate impacts on humans, particularly through a broadly defined conception of technological change.

Human choice and climate change, volume 2: resources and technology

Volume 2 of *Human choice and climate change* anchors both the climate change issue and social science approaches to it in the context of the Earth's resources: climate, land, water, energy sources, and materials used in technologies. Climate change is the result of fundamental human choices about the conversion of energy and human occupation of the Earth's surface. These activities have been identified as both the proximate causes of greenhouse-related emissions and the sites of primary impacts on human activity.

Chapter 1, "The natural science of climate change" summarizes the present state of the international scientific consensus about climate change, drawing on the findings of the Second Assessment Report of the IPCC, as well as on other research. The social processes that go into producing and standardizing this kind of scientific consensus are described in the first chapter of Volume 1. Current scientific claims about climate change and its impacts introduce Volume 2 because it focuses on the major resource systems, or human support systems, that enable people to live as they do on the Earth: that is, land use, occupation of coastal zones, energy production and use, and the processes of technological change. As human systems, these are no less institutional systems than the ones examined in Volume 1. However, each is perhaps more directly dependent on constraints and opportunities presented by natural systems than (with the possible exception of population) the frameworks presented in Volume 1. Thus, it is appropriate at this point to introduce material from the natural sciences that social scientists should be aware of in analyzing and understanding the human dimensions of climate change.

This chapter explains the greenhouse effect, the results of greenhouse gas emissions on radiative forcing, and the mechanisms by which forcing translates into climate change. The complexities of these processes are further compounded by emissions of aerosols, the role of clouds, and interactions of gases in the atmosphere. Furthermore, the natural variability of climate is an undisputed fact, so the possible human contributions must be analyzed in the context of natural changes.

The current scientific consensus is that the global mean surface temperature has increased by 0.3–0.6° Kelvin (K) over the past century. The global temperatures in recent years have been among the warmest in historical records and probably one of the warmest periods in the past six hundred years. However, the warming is not uniform over the globe, with some areas even experiencing a cooling. The understanding of this climatic change is a high priority in the natural science community. Although the signal is still emerging from the noise of natural variability, recent studies suggest that the current changes in climate are indeed related to human activities, including the emissions of carbon dioxide and other radiatively important gases and aerosols.

The chapter goes on to outline the potential effects of changes in various climatic factors, specifically sea level rise, human health, agriculture and food supplies, water resources, and nonagricultural ecosystems. Although knowledge is improving in these areas, many aspects of climate change remain highly uncertain. In particular, the regional changes in climate expected from global climate change are poorly understood, as are the impacts on humanity and the biosphere.

Although the signal is still emerging from the noise of natural variability, recent studies suggest that the current changes in climate are indeed related to human activities.

The next four chapters trace the origins of climate change in human behavior at aggregated and disaggregated levels and focus on the potential impacts of climate change on fundamental human systems of productivity.

Chapter 2, "Land and water use," examines human activities that increase greenhouse gas emissions from the use of land and water resources. It also assesses the potential impacts of climate change and climate change policies on land and water use for the production of food, energy, fiber, and construction material, as well as for recreation, aesthetic and spiritual satisfaction, and creation of a sense of identity.

The intensification of land and water use has been a global trend during the five centuries of the colonial, industrial, and postindustrial periods. Today, every accessible hectare and waterway are managed (or deliberately not managed) for human ends. The most remote tundra in the Arctic North and the most forbidding reaches of the Sahara Desert are subject to human management decisions of one sort or another.

Land use and and water use are important to global climate change in at least three ways. First, land use affects the exchange of carbon dioxide, methane, and other greenhouse-related gases between the Earth and its atmosphere. Second, agriculture, forestry, and other land-based productive activities depend crucially on surface energy and water balance, which are closely linked to climate. Hence, they are more likely than other human activities to be affected by climate change. Third, projected growth in both population and resource-demands presents important challenges to land and water use in coming decades, whether climate changes or not. Discussions of global environmental change have tended to subjugate the issues of sustainable development of land and water resources to the globally systemic changes of ozone depletion and climate change. Analysts seek to identify no-regrets strategies that would enhance sustainability and at the same time help to prevent or adapt to climate change. Many opportunities exist for sequestering carbon or limiting emissions, although they require a searching analysis of their full social and environmental repercussions.

The chapter concludes that climate change is by no means necessarily the most important challenge to the sustainability of land and water resources. The connections between land use and climate change are important, but should not be allowed to set the land-use research agenda. There is room for serious concern about the adequacy of land and water resources to meet current and likely future demands locally and globally, whether climate changes or not. Around the world, increasing misuse of land and water resources already threatens human welfare in the near to medium term. The apparent failure in these regions of management to forestall such threats underlines the need to study land-use and water-use adaptation strategies, regardless of any efforts toward reducing greenhouse-related emissions. Responses that can address these issues while addressing the challenges of climate change should be a priority for research.

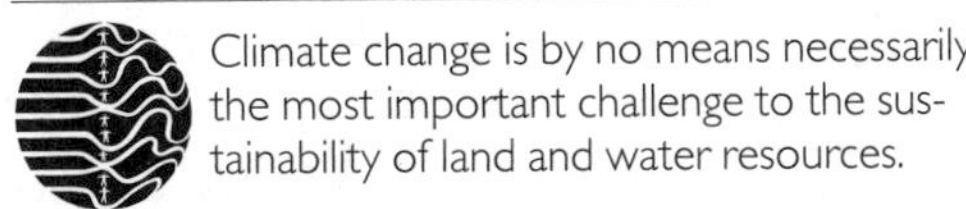
Climate change is by no means necessarily the most important challenge to the sustainability of land and water resources.

Measures encouraging adaptation to climate change may likewise offer collateral gains in other areas, improved agricultural research being an important case in point, and institutional strengthening to facilitate adaptive shifts in land and water use another. The key lesson of social science analysis is that the constraints on and opportunities for successful response are not only technical, and that influencing land and water use in desired ways requires a sound understanding of how and why these resources are used.

Similar themes emerge from Chapter 3, "Coastal zones and oceans." Coastal regions are particularly important because of high concentrations of human population living close to the sea and their particular vulnerability to potential climate impacts.

Coastal zones have historically generated economic activities that allowed societies to flourish. Many coastal problems now being encountered worldwide result from many people's use of the terrestrial and aquatic resources over a long period of mostly unrestricted development of coastal areas. These problems include the accumulation of contaminants in coastal areas, shoreline erosion, and the rapidly accelerating decline of habitats and natural resources. Population growth and migration associated with economic development places additional demands on coastal areas and resources, posing another threat to the sustainability of these areas. The impacts of unsustainable and often uncoordinated coastal development are likely ultimately to result in the degradation of natural systems that provide protection against the sea, habitat for many species, and food for many people. These impacts could pose significant risks to public health and welfare.

With or without climate change, coastal zones will see further growth in urban areas and increased tourism. The growing population density along the coasts will put further pressure on the resource base, including ocean fishing, wetlands-dependent products, and unique ecosystems and species. This pressure will probably result in deteriorating living conditions for many inhabitants, especially in less industrialized countries. Hence, there are strong imperatives to adopt integrated coastal zone management strategies that will combine responses to growing demands on coastal and ocean resources and the threat of climate change. Local knowledge will be essential to the success of these strategies. The adaptive coping abilities of coastal, often rural, and often nonliterate people have enabled their survival under stress. They have detailed knowledge of local conditions and past responses, as well as the complex and varied patterns of ownership and use of marine and coastal resources. In the policy hierarchy they seldom get their due recognition. Consultative and participatory approaches that include local stakeholders offer challenges and opportunities for both analysis and decisionmaking.

The adaptive coping abilities of coastal, often rural, and often nonliterate people have enabled their survival under stress. In the policy hierarchy they seldom get their due recognition.

The fourth chapter in Volume 2, "Energy and industry," examines global and regional patterns of greenhouse-related emissions arising from the production of goods and services. Over the twentieth century, energy use has become the most important human-generated source of greenhouse gases, especially carbon dioxide produced by fossil-fueled energy generation. Most analyses predict steady increases in worldwide energy consumption over the next several decades. Thus, any attempt to limit greenhouse gas concentrations in the atmosphere must focus on energy supply and demand and the costs associated with reducing greenhouse-related emissions from fossil fuel combustion. There is considerable uncertainty about what the levels of energy use and associated carbon dioxide emissions will be over the next century. Worldwide emissions of carbon from fossil fuel combustion are currently about 6 billion tonnes per year. In the absence of new policy initiatives, emissions projections range from a modest decrease to an increase by a factor of 15 over the next century.

Three complementary methods have been used to forecast the evolution of these changes:

- a top-down economic approach, relating aggregate energy use to fuel prices, labor and capital prices, and various measures of economic activity
- a bottom-up approach, employing engineering calculations on a technology-by-technology basis
- a social-psychological approach, focusing on how and why decisions regarding energy use are made at a more micro level than the top-down approach and embodying a more human-behavioral approach than the bottom-up approach.

In the absence of new policy initiatives, emissions projections range from a modest decrease to an increase by a factor of 15 over the next century.

A decade ago top-down and bottom-up approaches produced dramatically different projections. Since then it has become evident that each approach has its strengths and weaknesses, and various hybrid approaches have been proposed. Assumptions regarding the characteristics and likely rate of penetration of new technologies have been developed, and researchers have started sorting through the various explanations for slower than expected adoption of new technologies. There is still some debate about whether some of these explanations describe market failures or simply reflect indirect costs not typically included in the engineering estimates of using a new technology, but that debate has shifted from one about the analytic method to one about the fundamental assumptions employed.

All analyses point towards a much greater rate of growth in greenhouse gas emissions in the less industrialized countries than in the highly industrialized countries for at least three reasons:

- much higher rates of population growth
- higher rates of economic growth driven by technology transfer from the industrialized countries
- a propensity to pursue development through very rapid increases in the output of the heavy industries required to construct the facilities and infrastructure required to modernize economies.

Despite the greater importance of the presently less industrialized countries in shaping the greenhouse-related gas emissions and concentrations of the next century, analysis of these countries has been seriously undertaken only recently.

Two major research directions would greatly improve the usefulness of the analysis to policymakers:

- more intensive study of the less industrialized countries, where most of the growth in emissions is expected to occur
- improved integration between the economic, engineering, and social-psychological approaches.

The second of these is the topic of Chapter 5.

Whereas Chapter 4 concentrates on modeling energy production and use at the macro level, Chapter 5, "Energy and social systems," scrutinizes energy-related institutional decisionmaking about production and consumption at the level of the firm and household behavior. The chapter highlights the meaning and evolution of energy-consuming practice in everyday life. The authors advocate moving beyond conventional policy-oriented research, focused on the beliefs and behaviors of individual end users, to a focus on people as social actors operating within households, offices, government departments, or other institutions. Such a shift entails viewing energy-related decisions as processes of social negotiation rather than as the result of personal attitudes or enthusiasms. Rather than focusing on energy in isolation, or on the services that energy provides, energy-related practices are instead addressed as forms of consumption, much like any other.

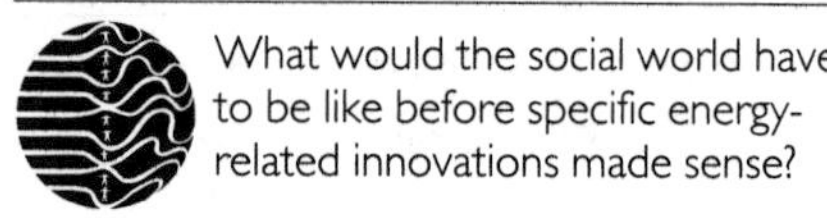

Instead of taking the social goals and purposes of energy consumption for granted, the approaches explored in this chapter call those ends into question. The rationalistic notion that technologies are neutral problem-solving devices gives way to the view that problem and solution are, as it were, joined at the hip. The authors challenge researchers and policymakers to rethink the relationship between policy and energy demand and the way in which energy analysts and policymakers conceptualize the future. Instead of trying to predict the future, the authors advocate efforts to specify the sociotechnical preconditions for a range of possible futures. Rather than seeking to model people's impact on future energy demand, the question would be, what would the social world have to be like before specific energy-related innovations made sense?

Much of the research reviewed in this chapter emphasizes the extent to which the future is already inscribed in existing practices, infrastructures, and cultural arrangements that limit the scope for doing things differently. Together these suggest that, even in the most favorable of circumstances, policy levers that focus on end-users are unlikely to modify the web of interests and histories that surround their choices and habits. But conventional tools and forms of policy analysis configure the conceptual landscape and the perception of possible courses of action, just as the tools and technologies of energy consumption configure their users. Discussion of the human dimensions of energy and global environmental change is currently embedded in a policy paradigm that contains within it a somewhat limited and restricting theory of social and technological change.

The dynamics of technological change have important implications for the expectation of many researchers and policymakers that such change will be important to resolving the issues of climate change. The final chapter in Volume 2, "Technological change," brings these issues into the foreground, illustrating how individuals, institutions, and societies select and reject technological opportunities. The chapter focuses on the important issues surrounding the dynamics of technical change and their outcomes, particularly in relation to attempts to orient technological developments.

"Technological change" begins with the fundamental question, "What is technology?" The answer is that the social sciences conceptualize technology in different ways, ranging from concrete artifacts and skills to more abstract, less nuts-and-bolts notions of technology as material culture or as sociotechnical landscapes.

Artifacts are black boxes that work; they are black boxes because users cannot see beyond their functions to their inner workings or their energy sources. Technological regimes, such as the hydrocarbon-based energy regime, consist of many commitments, sunk investments, and institutionalized practices that evolve in their own terms and are hard to change. Sociotechnical landscapes are the patterns of physical infrastructures, artifacts, institutions, values, and consumption patterns—the material culture of our societies—and the backdrop against which specific technological changes are played out. It is important to include all three levels of understanding technology, because its implication in climate change is as much through sociotechnical landscapes and technological regimes as through particular artifacts such as steam generators or internal combustion engines.

Thus, the conventional technology policy model of technology describes artifacts emerging from research and development establishments and subsequently transferred to the marketplace. However, this model tells only part of the story of technology in society. Other aspects include the processes and conditions of novelty creation, the messiness of implementation and introduction, and the aggregation of myriads of little decisions that underlie the development and embedding of technology in society. All of these elements are part of successful technological transformations that involve growing irreversibility and interdependence among social, economic, and material components of the sociotechnical landscape and that make it very difficult (but not impossible) to consciously direct technological change to meet climate policy ends.

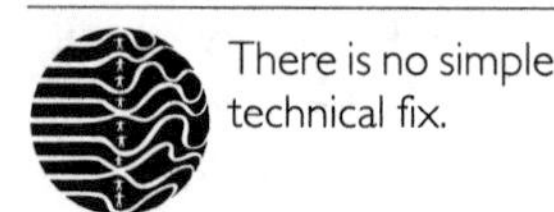

There is no simple technical fix.

In exposing the societal embeddedness of technical systems and highlighting the opportunities and constraints for changing the ways in which humans use energy and the Earth's surface, the final chapter of this volume drives home the fact that there is no simple technical fix. What tools do we have? This question is the topic of the chapters assembled in Volume 3.

Human choice and climate change, volume 3: the tools for policy analysis

Public policy and private decisionmakers often look to the simplifying frameworks of formal tools of analysis to guide their decisions. The third volume of *Human choice and climate change* evaluates the adequacy of the conventional tools of policy analysis for supporting or making prudent human choices in the face of climate change.

Chapter 1, "Economic analysis," describes the strengths and limitations of the most widely applied toolkit of contemporary industrialized society and a substantial contributor to the current state of understanding climate change. "Economic analysis" seeks to explain how the wants of a population interact with the technical means for their satisfaction to produce demand for goods and services; what the scale of that demand, expressed as economic growth, implies for the global environment; and what constraints on growth might result from climate change policies. Proposed policies may be evaluated from a variety of perspectives; a mainstream approach usually includes growth-oriented economic analyses of the costs and benefits. Costs of mitigation in the near and medium term are weighed against often diffuse and uncertain benefits in the very long term, and must account for countries whose economic development may depend upon emissions-generating activities and who may thus be unwilling to trade off growth for emissions reductions. The result of most studies employing cost–benefit analysis is that relatively modest near-term actions are required, although the degree of intervention grows over time.

Global climate change is part of a class of problems that tend to exacerbate the shortcomings of the mainstream approaches to economics,

Other issues for economic analysis include valuing nonmarket (environmental) goods and nonmonetary transactions and assets; global efficiency, trade, and the implications of inequities in the global distribution of income; handling surprises; and the choice of time-cost discount rates, which must be based on social criteria that lie outside of the framework of economic analysis. Global climate change is part of a class of problems that tend to exacerbate the shortcomings of the mainstream approaches to economics, although economic analysis remains a powerful tool to evaluate candidate policy options.

Policymakers have readily adopted the economics approach to analyze future prospects for growth in greenhouse-related emissions and the consequences of attempts at intervention. This useful, if somewhat narrow, focus has been criticized from within and without the economics paradigm for ignoring shortcomings in the assumptions and methodology of economic growth, as well as the insights available from other fields of social science. Confronted with environmental degradation and resource exhaustion, growth practitioners have added depreciation of these resources to the depreciation of capital stock depicted in their models, thus reducing sustainability to a constraint in the optimizing problem of maximizing per capita income. Other practitioners have devised means of valuation for nonmarket effects and nonuse values. These values can be included in the conventional calculus of cost–benefit analysis, where they lose their visibility and are often discounted if they grow too large for comfort.

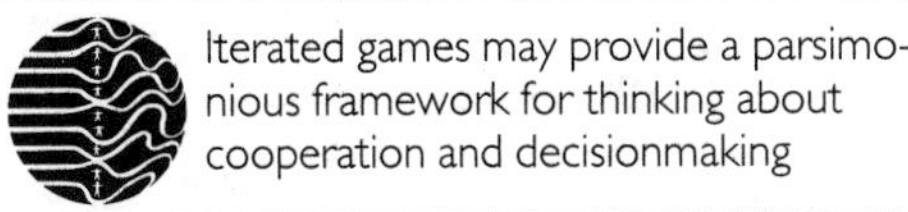

Even in its expanded forms, the economic paradigm is essentially based on the concept of the rational individual decisionmaker—the rational actor paradigm. Chapter 2, "Games and simulations," describes frameworks for explicitly exploring the interactions among multiple decisionmakers, in this case nation states, each acting out of self-interest. The authors argue that, although one-shot games are recognized as having very limited application to continuing relations among states, iterated games may provide a parsimonious framework for thinking about cooperation and decisionmaking in situations that fall between the levels of a single benevolent dictator and an anonymous market populated by many well-behaved individuals.

Game theoretic approaches preserve the idea of uniform or universal rationality. Often they do not take account of tensions among rival viewpoints and values within a state that can cause it to change course during negotiations in ways that cannot be predicted. Where two-level games have been developed (nesting intrastate games within interstate games), internal differences within states are still framed using the same assumptions about the universality of individual rationality. Simulations, involving human actors representing diverse experiences as well as interests within teams of players representing national actors, are one way of confronting this limitation. Simulation games, particularly when formal models are used within the simulation, can support focused communication among analysts and decisionmakers. Although significant risks accompany these benefits, principally bias and overgeneralization from small samples, simulation-gaming methods have potential value as devices for policy assessment, as supplements to conventional forms of analysis or sober critical reflection.

Both game-theoretic and simulation-gaming approaches move beyond atomistic rationality, but continue to rely on two core assumptions:

- Parties rationally perceive and act on self-interest.
- All of the participants share the same standards of rationality.

Generations of researchers have elaborated this universalistic notion of individual rationality to high levels of sophistication. One of its most prominent features is the rigid separation of reason and values. Chapter 3, "Decision analysis" explores the implications of this separation for global climate policy-making.

The separation of reason and values is deeply entrenched, not only in social science research but actually in the fabric of contemporary culture. Indeed, it has been suggested that the pervasiveness of behavioral sciences based on individualistic rationality derives from their role as *folk sciences*, providing security and guidance to their clientele, largely independent of their effectiveness in practice.

Beginning with the problem of climate risks from the viewpoint of a single decisionmaker who is able to control global greenhouse-related emissions, the authors of this chapter delve into the problems of multiple actors and multiple rationalities. The chapter surveys various social science approaches to the perception, communication, and management of technological and environmental risks, and assesses the potential role of risk assessments and decision rules in formulating climate change policy. In place of individual rationality, many of these approaches emphasize an analytic framework of social rationality in which collective or societal preferences are not merely aggregated from pre-existing individual preferences, but are collectively formulated in daily life and stabilized by institutional arrangements of social solidarity, rather than by the atomized choices of individual human agents.

Embedding the expertise of risk professionals in a broader social discourse requires appropriate forms of public participation

The authors argue that the basic problem of risk management, global and local, could be tackled in the emerging field of integrated assessment. For this purpose, advanced tools for integrated assessment need to combine the knowledge of experts, decisionmakers, stakeholders, and citizens. Such tools would reintegrate the faculty of reason with the intuition and emotional intelligence rooted in life experience and craft skills. Taking advantage of a broader range of human experiences in the integrated assessment of global climate change requires a critical appraisal of the historical process by which the rational actor paradigm has established an exclusive professional claim for objective knowledge in risk management. Embedding the expertise of risk professionals in a broader social discourse requires appropriate forms of public participation. This would profoundly move the role of science in society toward what is variously described as vernacular, civic, or postnormal science.

Predicting the degree of climate change, even quite accurately, is inadequate for deciding how important its consequences will be for human societies and what, if anything, should be done about it.

New forms of scientific collaboration engaging universal specialists (scientists) with local specialists (citizens) will require more than a broader decisionmaking framework. Such collaboration will also require more inclusive ideas of evidence and information. For example, Volume 1, Chapter 1 describes how climate change scientists tend to base much of their argument on mathematical modeling. On the other hand, citizens and politicians tend to draw more heavily on a holistic approach of reasoning by analogy (see for example, Gore 1992). This set of decisionmaking tools is explored in Chapter 4, "Reasoning by analogy." Past experience is a natural, inevitable source of human management strategies. All decisionmakers tend to compare present situations with past experience and adopt similar strategies for seemingly similar situations. Drawing on information about the past relationships between climate and society, researchers attempt to construct guidelines about possible future states, impacts, and coping strategies. The authors find that past climate and society interactions repay the attention of those seeking to understand the human dimensions of global climate change. Historically, the impact of climate as a hazard and a resource has been directly dependent on the adaptive capability of the society affected. It follows that predicting the degree of climate change, even quite accurately, is inadequate for deciding how important its consequences will be for human societies and what, if anything, should be done about it. It also suggests that changes in the characteristics of societies over time will alter the consequences of climate changes, and researchers should be very cautious about projecting potential long-term climate impacts onto the world as it is known today.

These useful insights notwithstanding, significant methodological difficulties arise in drawing rigorous analogies from past human experience of adaptation to climate. Although it is an enormously suggestive resource, the holistic philosophy of reasoning by analogy, almost by definition, makes it very difficult to draw valid comparisons across cases. Valid comparisons of future scenarios require greater formality than is provided by the analogue approach alone. Such formality turns inquiry back in the direction of simplifying models, although not necessarily so simple as the economic models discussed in the first chapter of the volume.

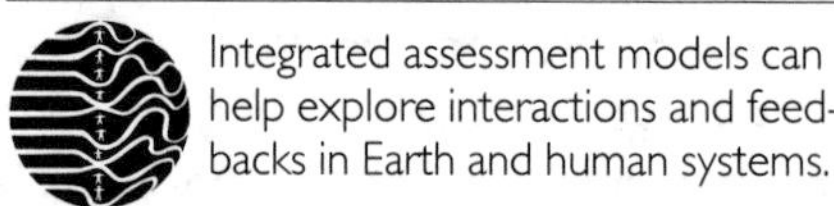

The final chapter of Volume 3, "Integrated assessment," examines the current state of the various modeling tools that contribute to our understanding of the human dimensions of climate change and the operation of climate change policies. Integrated assessment is an issue-oriented approach to research that knits together diverse knowledge from many disciplines to focus holistically on climate change processes. Integrated assessment includes model-based systems, simulation gaming, scenario analysis, and qualitative studies. At present, the dominant integrated assessment activity is computer-based modeling, which draws on multiple disciplines to focus on climate change processes. In that sense, integrated assessment models attempt to emulate the holism of analogies within the more formalized frameworks of (predominantly economic) modeling. Integrated assessment models can help explore interactions and feedbacks in Earth and human systems, function as flexible and rapid simulation tools, foster insights (sometimes counterintuitive) that would not be available from a single disciplinary approach, and provide tools for mutual learning and communication among researchers and policymakers.

Integrated assessment has contributed to the climate change debate by exploring impacts of climate change, mitigation and abatement strategies, issues in cooperative implementation, the likely equity effects of candidate policies, and complicating factors such as aerosols. Models have also provided information on balancing the carbon budget and on various integrated aspects of land use.

However, existing models leave considerable room for improvement. In particular, more satisfactory and representative models of social dynamics and ecological systems, as well as improved treatments of uncertainty, are needed before integrated assessment models can be made more realistic. There is also a need to focus on the factors that shape policymakers' decisions and to include policymakers and other stakeholders in the design and exercise of the models as advocated in Chapter 3.

As scientists develop modeling tools that are more open and flexible, policymakers will be able to use the model results and other insights from different integrated assessment approaches to inform decisions that bear on global climate change and on the social context in which climate change issues are to be considered.

A broad-based approach to integrated assessment embedded in a pluralistic and participatory decision process promises to be the best available guide to policymaking

As a whole, Volume 3 describes the existing toolkit of rational analysis and planning techniques available to scientific researchers and political elites. In so doing, the volume reveals a series of important shortcomings of the toolkit in the face of large complex problems facing multiple stakeholders over intergenerational timeframes. Under such conditions, the mainstream social science tools are presently incapable of providing a reliable basis for rational goal setting and policy implementation. They are overly dependent on a narrow concept of rationality and an approach to policy as the means for making the real world conform to a rational model. The dominant rational-actor approach is in many respects a normative framework masquerading as an analytic one. Social scientists have yet to develop any clearly superior alternatives, but a broad-based approach to integrated assessment embedded in a pluralistic and participatory decision process promises to be the best available guide to policymaking.

Human choice and climate change, volume 4: what have we learned?

The task of preparing *Human choice and climate change* has confirmed the conviction with which we started out, that a variety of social science theories, tools, and techniques, along with different ways of combining them, are essential to move climate change analysis and decisionmaking onto a robust foundation. In this fourth volume, we move into the realm of editorial commentary. We stress that responsibility for these interpretations belongs with the editors alone, although we are confident that all of our authors and contributors endorse most of our selections and emphases.

Our editorial chapters address three questions:

- How does climate change challenge the ability of social science to produce useful knowledge?
- What does social science have to say about global climate change and the debates that surround it?
- What might decisionmakers do differently in the light of our present knowledge of social science and climate change?

"The challenge of climate change for social science" sets out to explore how the intellectual organization of social science and its location in the larger framework of human intellectual inquiry may be constraining the ability of social scientists to realize the full potential of their contribution to climate change research and policy debate. The reasons may lie in the division of intellectual labor that has dominated Western science since the Enlightenment. In the social sciences, this division of labor has resulted in the emergence of two distinctive approaches to subject matter, research methods, and explanatory frameworks. We label these the descriptive and interpretive approaches. Although each potentially adds essential ingredients to humanity's understanding of climate change and related issues, the descriptive and interpretive practitioners of social science seldom communicate with each other, let alone integrate their insights.

Of the two approaches, the descriptive approach is usually considered to be more appealing to policymakers because of its apparent technical neutrality and its ability to generate a numerical bottom line. For example, quantitative analyses of responsiveness to tax rates or the effectiveness of regulation can, in principle, be directly translated into a set of policy choices about whether to implement a carbon tax or appliance efficiency standards and even at what level taxes or standards should be set. Interpretive social science tends to be less readily embraced by policymakers as lacking this potential to provide practical guidance.

But, in fact, the bottom-line solution provided by descriptive research is seldom adopted by policymakers, who actually use such studies to provide background or understanding to their own interpretations and decisionmaking inclinations. Hence, neither kind of social science has any real practical advantage. They merely provide different insights from different standpoints. Making space for both descriptive and interpretive social science in the process of reforming the relationship between scientific research and policymaking offers many advantages.

In "Social science insights into climate change," we draw on the whole of *Human choice and climate change* to elucidate some significant crosscutting themes in social science research related to global climate change. The research and analysis that underpins these themes is developed in detail in the earlier chapters—sometimes in several chapters, as they cover the same issues from different standpoints.

In the grand scheme of things, climate change is probably not the deciding factor in whether humanity as a whole flourishes or declines. The resilience of human institutions and their ability to monitor and adapt to changing conditions seems to be more important. However, changes in regional patterns of habitability are likely to harm poor populations in environmentally fragile areas. Although aggregated global effects may be negligible, regional effects may be severe, including violent storms, inundation caused by sea level rise, and formerly fertile land becoming unsuitable for agriculture.

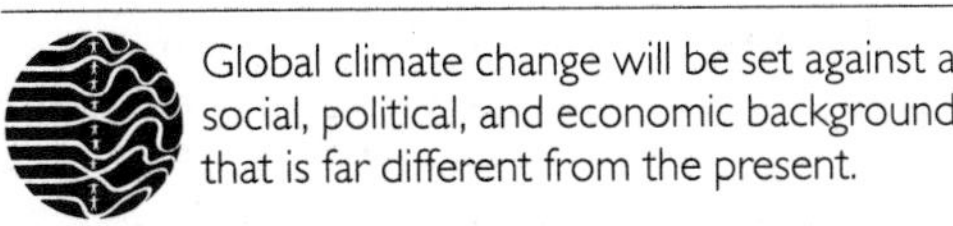

Global climate change will be inexorable, but also incremental, and will be set against a social, political, and economic background that is far different from the present. In fact, social and political structures and processes will probably change faster than the IPCC projects for climate. This difference in rates of change may lead policymakers to delay taking action to mitigate or adapt to climate change until disaster overtakes them. However, the same difference also offers the potential to allow societies to stay ahead of climate change, that is, to build in the capability to monitor, anticipate, and respond effectively to changes in many Earth systems resulting from climate change.

Whether or not humanity realizes the potential to get ahead and stay ahead of climate change impacts depends on what happens at the level of decision-making in households, firms, and communities. Diversity, complexity, and uncertainty will frustrate the search for top-down global policymaking and implementation. Social science research in all disciplines indicates that policymakers should attempt to reach agreement on high-level environmental and associated social goals, then look for local and regional opportunities to use policy in various ways appropriate to the institutional arrangements, cultural values, economic and political conditions, and environmental changes.

Overall we find that social scientists have contributed to climate change research by identifying human activities that cause climate change, highlighting environmental changes that affect human welfare, and examining the research process itself and its relationship to policymaking.

Finally, we conclude *Human choice and climate change* with 10 suggestions of ways in which decisionmakers concerned with climate change might modify their goals and approaches to climate policy.

1. View the issue of climate change holistically, not just as the problem of emissions reductions.
2. Recognize that institutional limits to global sustainability are at least as important for climate policymaking as environmental limits.

3. Prepare for the likelihood that social, economic, and technological change will be more rapid and have greater direct impacts on human populations than climate change.
4. Recognize the limits of rational planning.
5. Employ the full range of analytic perspectives and decision aids from the natural and social sciences and the humanities in climate change policymaking.
6. Design policy instruments for real world conditions rather than try to make the world conform to a particular policy model.
7. Integrate climate change concerns with other, more immediate policies such as employment, defense, economic development, and public health.
8. Take a regional and local approach to climate policymaking and implementation.
9. Direct resources into identifying vulnerability and promoting resilience, especially where the impacts will be largest.
10. Use a pluralistic approach to decisionmaking.

Human choice and climate change thus begins with describing the human landscape of the Earth and centers on the role of human choice in the development of climate change as an issue, the definition of causes and likely effects, and the analysis of possible responses. Along with natural science assessments and other related assessments, this social science assessment brings together a wealth of information—but *Human choice and climate change* is not just a report on the state of the social sciences as they have been applied to climate change. Performing an assessment broadens the research focus and generates new insights by the multifaceted analyses and approaches presented here. Theoretical and practical insights that have grown out of the process of producing this assessment can also enlarge the potential application of social science insights and methods to global change—for social scientists, policymakers, and natural scientists.

References

Arrow, K. 1951. *Social choice and individual values*. New York: John Wiley.

Bruce, J. P., H. Lee, E. F. Haites (eds) 1996. *Economic and social issues of climate change*. Cambridge: Cambridge University Press.

Gore, A. 1992. *Earth in the balance: ecology and the human spirit*. New York: Houghton Mifflin.

Jacobsen, H. & M. Price 1991. *A framework for research on the human dimensions of global environmental change*. Paris: International Social Science Council.

Stern, P. O. Young, D. Druckman 1992. *Global environmental change: understanding the human dimensions*. Washington DC: National Academy Press.

Tolba, M. K. 1991. Opening address. In *Climate change: science, impacts and policy*, J. Jaeger & H. L. Ferguson (eds). Cambridge: Cambridge University Press.

CHAPTER 1

Economic analysis

Robin Cantor & Gary Yohe

Contributors
Bayard Catron, Larry Boyer, Robert Costanza, Edward Crenshaw, Robert Deacon, Wayne Gray, Nick Hanley, Frank Hole, Craig Jenkins, Michael Lovell, Vernon W. Ruttan, P. R. Shukla, Clive Spash, John Whalley

The problem of climate change exists because the scale of human activity has expanded to the point where the unintended byproducts of those human activities, namely the emissions of greenhouse-related gases, have reached a magnitude at which they are significant compared with global-scale natural processes. The scale and composition of human activities will also frame the conditions under which an altered climate will be experienced. For example, the nature, extent, and distribution of resources risk, as well as those available to societies for coping with climate change, will be largely shaped by human choices.

The field of economics has made substantial contributions to the current understanding of climate change. Indeed, the policy community has relatively uncritically adopted the tools of economics to analyze prospects for greenhouse gas emissions and the consequences of potential emissions mitigation. In this chapter, we will review the state of the art with regard to the social science understanding of the foundations of economic activity and the associated tools of analysis. Although this understanding and the analytic tool kit come largely from the discipline of economics, the chapter will examine contributions from other social sciences and consider opportunities to deepen and extend our knowledge and tools.

We begin with the insight from economic history that human economic and social institutions coevolve in response to challenges posed by both the natural environment and human wants, by generating both technological and social innovations to satisfy these needs (these topic areas are the focus of Vol. 1, Ch. 3 and Vol. 2, Ch. 6.). Of particular interest is the historical relationship between climate, economy, and society. In modern economic thinking, innovation is usually linked with the idea of growth. However, throughout much of human history, economic growth has not been seen as inevitable. Both economic growth and the study of the causes of economic growth are relatively recent, and the models are still relatively simple.

In the second section, we deal with changes in the way economics has modeled the growth process, beginning with Malthus's observations on the growth of human population, with its demands on the natural environment and the constraints on growth imposed by the environment. From the point of view of economics, climate change and the overall environmental carrying capacity of the planet are really the latest in a long series of concerns about the constraints on human activity imposed by nature. The simple Malthusian view has undergone considerable revision, as appreciation of the roles of produced capital and human learning has advanced. But concern remains about the constraints imposed by nature and (perhaps less obvious) by social organization.

The third section of the chapter documents the tools and insights that are provided by standard economic analytic principles as they have been applied to the climate change problem, showing what has been learned about the issue itself and what could be the consequences of intervention.

The next section takes up the conceptual and measurement shortcomings of the standard economic paradigm as it has been applied to climate change, and discusses how resolving some of these shortcomings might affect the analysis.

The final section focuses the broad discussion in these previous sections on the current international process of studying climate change, which is tied to the Framework Convention on Climate Change (FCCC). In this context, the standard view of the economics paradigm, a view that regards climate as a constraint on economic development, may not be the best approach to achieving international agreement. However, expanding the standard view is likely to prove difficult, given the current situation in the international science and policy communities.

Historical perspective—climate, economy, and society

Humans have interacted with their environments and their climates for millennia, over which time the climate has been constantly subject to changes, although none so dramatic or rapid as that potentially to be encountered in the next centuries. What can humans learn from past experiences? What do they offer researchers and decisionmakers concerned with climate policy? Economic history records that human institutions have both prospered and declined as a result of climate. However, technological, social, and economic adaptations are extremely important intervening factors. A glimpse at the historical record demonstrates just how difficult it is even to correctly frame the issues involved in climate change. A little historical context can help researchers determine if they are even confronting the right set of questions. A few episodes are sufficient to show that most of the human economic activity has involved adapting to change, notably adaptations in agriculture:

- The systematic planting of crops first took place in the Near East around 8000 BC. Several authors, notably Byrne (1987), Blumler & Byrne (1991), and McCorriston & Hole (1991), have argued that this strongly seasonal Mediterranean climate, complete with mild and wet winters followed by rainless summers, was the key to the expansion of cereal agriculture in the Near East. Agricultural economies, in fact, expanded throughout the Near East and into regions of North Africa that today are too dry to support agriculture.
- Hole (1997) recorded that the sea rose rapidly from around 9000 BC until about 4000 BC, when it stabilized at approximately today's levels. A

simultaneous shift in climate patterns left the region essentially rainless, watered only by its rivers. Each response stimulated the growth of local and regional economies through new demand for, and access to, foreign commodities that could be acquired by overland and riverine routes as well as by sea. Indeed, Algaze (1989) remarked that this first internationalism saw the establishment of distant settlements along trade routes.

- As recounted in Holmes (1993) and Stanley & Warne (1993), farmers in both Egypt and Mesopotamia learned to irrigate and produced the world's first important food surpluses. Large cities grew, with specialist producers of different foods and manufactured goods coordinated not through markets but through patronage by temples, owners of diversified estates, and political leaders. The world's first system of bookkeeping to account for these goods and services was being written on clay tables by 3000 BC.
- An unusually sharp and prolonged period of drought apparently occurred about 2200 BC. The Nile floods failed in Egypt, and rainfed agriculture failed in the Near East. In fact, Bell (1975, 1979), Kemp (1983), Weiss et al. (1993), and Hole (1997) combine to describe a drought that extended at least from Greece to the Indus Valley and thereby contributed to the collapse of civilizations across a wide geographic span.
- The Roman Climatic Optimum dates from 300 BC to AD 300, when the mild Mediterranean climatic zone shifted north and then returned to its present position at the southern edge of Europe, allowing vineyards to thrive in England. Indeed, the cycle may have had a role in both the spread and fall of the agrarian-based Roman Empire.
- A subsequent climatic optimum affected the initially successful Norse settlement of Greenland. This was the Medieval Climatic Optimum, AD 900–1200, when Nordic warriors, traders, and settlers spread westward across the North Atlantic. McGovern (1994) reviewed the next several hundred years and portrayed thriving European communities in Arctic Greenland and sub-Arctic Iceland. Despite centuries of adaptation to this environment, however, the Greenland colonies died out by AD 1500.
- In the midst of potential starvation, one might have expected the Norse to engage in trade with Europe for needed foodstuffs. They embarked, instead, on a frenzy of church building, paying for imported liturgical accouterments with their only currency and praying for divine intervention. Norse Greenland did not decline exclusively because of changes in climate; their demise was a cultural phenomenon.

What is the value of such histories? One important guide to what is going to happen is to learn what actually has happened in the past—the climatic events, their frequencies, their duration, and their amplitudes or intensities; this is the focus explored in Chapter 4. For our current discussion, such historical vignettes illustrate a strong link between economic activity (based on agriculture) and climate. They demonstrate that favorable climate acts to spur economic activity, but unfavorable climatic change requires human management and productive response to avoid economic collapse. Finally, historical studies can offer a basis for prediction of economic effects. They tell what has happened, with what frequency, and what is possible. Furthermore, they can be used to identify productive and unproductive patterns of human response (Glantz 1988).

What can we say about the responses of systems? Some of the case studies noted above imply that excessive central direction puts a system at great risk. Managers may not respond quickly enough or appropriately to changes. They might depend upon the "this is how we have always done it" school of traditional decisionmaking. Moreover, they may tend to look first to their personal welfare and not that of the state. As a result, they may inhibit others from adopting alternative strategies.

Central direction can also distort agricultural production (or any type of production, for that matter) when foreign exchange is an issue. Excessive specialization at the expense of local subsistence can easily place a population at the mercy of international trade (Crumley 1994). Consequently, a strong diverse subsistence base, managed locally, is the most resilient.

Climate variability was a normal condition in premodern times; it was expected that agriculture would fail occasionally and that some proportion of a population would die of starvation, just as diseases also took their toll. Until this century, it was normal for family members to die and for people to attribute premature death to supernatural fate. Given such facts and attitudes, and the general lack of accurate weather records, people had difficulty even in determining whether there were weather trends or just normal fluctuations. Modern communication has made it possible to monitor productivity in real time, but in earlier societies, line of sight and word of mouth were the chief means. Even with modern communications and monitoring, the implication is clear: if a problem (meaning a situation out of the ordinary) is not perceived, no corrective measures will be taken. Or, if the problems are perceived to be not of human origin, people may resort to prayer rather than, say, to irrigation.

History does not suggest that there has generally been a pattern of sustained human development consistent with the modern growth paradigm. Rather, preindustrial populations grew, declined, and regrew to approximately the same levels repeatedly. When necessary economic conditions could not be sustained, the larger entities fragmented again into smaller units which were no longer under a protective umbrella and were free to shift for themselves. An age-old tactic was to disenfranchise peripheral segments of polities in an effort to sustain the life of the core. This is the political equivalent to the socially sanctioned infanticide and gerontocide sometimes practiced by populations living in marginal environments.

No doubt advantages and disadvantages of policies like these have always been considered, but the weights attached to their component parts must have varied greatly. It is therefore perhaps difficult to draw specific lessons from the experiences of the distant past that can inform the design of policy for modern economies facing the threat of anthropogenic global change. Analysts also do not fully understand the complex interactions between humans and the environment.

Global change policies are proposed, debated, analyzed, and sometimes adopted in the face of this complexity, enormous uncertainty, and century-long time horizons. For example, the Montreal Protocol limits the production and consumption of chloroflourocarbons worldwide. The Berlin Mandate calls for strengthening industrialized country commitment to limiting emissions of other greenhouse emissions; and further commitments are to be negotiated and prepared. It is, therefore, not possible simply to declare that the problem is too hard. Analysis must and will be undertaken to support negotiating positions and perhaps even policy development; and the question is how best to proceed in support of these initiatives.

Economic growth, population, and environmental constraints

Economic growth is a relatively recent phenomenon; there have been long periods in which the concept of sustained expansion in the level of economic output would never have occurred to anyone. Even after the beginning of the industrial age, the question of whether or not economic growth was sustainable had no clear answer. Malthus, for example, was profoundly pessimistic about the prospects for sustained economic growth.

We concentrate on the neoclassical economic growth model because, if we loosen its assumptions, a range of possible linkages can be considered. This section can, at best, aim to summarize only a few basic themes, and we have chosen to concentrate on links between population and the formation of physical and human capital.

The neoclassical economic model of population and the environment is essentially microeconomic in its foundations, but macroeconomics matters as well, with prices, tastes, and economic structures (and demands on the environment) evolving as living standards rise. Arguments have gone in two opposite directions concerning growth: more people at a higher living standard adversely affect the environment, including climate; or more people at a lower living standard have lower demands for environmental protection and will do more harm. The question thus in part involves whether population growth retards economic growth, enhances it, or is neutral. An additional question is whether population would continue to grow rapidly or fall toward replacement as economic growth proceeds. A vicious-circle view (see Vol. 1, Ch. 2) would be that, by stunting growth of demand for environmental quality and by perpetuating environmentally harsh economic structures, population growth places the global environment at greater risk.

The effects of population on physical capital formation, and thus on economic growth as it was traditionally understood, are ambiguous. In contrast, there is fairly strong evidence that, at the household level, high fertility stands in the way of human capital formation, which is now considered one of the keys to economic growth. However, reliable empirical studies (few as they are) suggest that, although significant, the causal role of high fertility in this vicious circle may be modest. In this section, we look at whether rapid population growth chokes off economic development. Population and economic development affect each other as well as climate change issues such as greenhouse-related emissions and capacity to mitigate impacts.

Pre-Malthusian views

The interpretation of population in economic rather than purely political or military terms is a surprisingly recent development in social thought. Both Plato (*The laws*) and Aristotle (*The politics*) argued that the population of the city state should be limited, but this was to avoid problems of governance arising from large populations. Roman authors regarded population in terms of the availability of soldiers and the maintenance of the elite class. As early as the reign of Augustus, low rates of marriage and fertility among the Roman aristocracy were a source of concern, leading to the propagation of laws to encourage unions among the nobility.

With the depopulation of Europe during the Dark Ages and the fourteenth-century Black Death as background, medieval writings not surprisingly stress the positive side of population growth. This strand of thought persisted through the Renaissance and found outlet in the mercantilist school, which emphasized the positive role of population growth in stimulating commercial demand.

Adam Smith (1776) was concerned with population in the context of the labor market. He observed that, when labor was scarce, the increase in wages would stimulate marriage and the survival of children, and vice versa when there was a glut of labor. The mechanisms through which population increase was regulated were two: age at marriage (and proportion never married) and infant and child mortality.

Malthus, environmental constraint, and climate

Malthus's *Essay on the principle of population*, to be distinguished from his more optimistic later writings, was published in 1798 and continues to exercise an enormous influence today. Malthus's principal interest was whether provision of relief to the poor would alleviate poverty or merely allow them to breed themselves back into destitution via earlier marriage and increased child survival as described by Smith. Economic activity (especially agriculture) and environmental limits (on food production) played crucial roles in Malthus's thinking, just as they play crucial roles in the climate change debate.

The Malthusian model is a macro-level economic–demographic vicious circle model. At its heart are the twin assumptions that, whereas increase in population *requirements* (Malthus thought in terms of food) are *linear* in population, *production* is characterized by diminishing marginal returns because the land base is fixed and, as more and more labor is applied to the same amount of land, the marginal product of labor will decline.

Europe escaped the Malthusian nightmare in three ways. First, the land base proved not to be fixed—Malthus never foresaw the opening up of the vast agricultural plains of North America, Russia, Australia, and Argentina. Second, despite the pervasive changes in agricultural technology that were going on around him, Malthus underestimated the possibilities for substituting capital and knowledge for land and labor. Similarly, he failed to anticipate improvements in storage facilities and transport networks. Finally, Malthus had no way of predicting that, during the nineteenth and early twentieth centuries, three factors—a shift in parents' attitudes toward children, followed and reinforced by changing assessment of the associated costs and benefits, and a mass acceptance of the legitimacy of fertility control—would combine to result in the Western fertility decline.

Nevertheless, the Malthusian view persists in updated form, couched in annual percentage change terms and generalized to incorporate capital formation and the demographic transition. In Figure 1.1 (from Todaro 1985), the vertical axis measures percentage change in population and income as a function of income per capita. At point A, population growth is slightly positive; it rises as death rates decline in the initial phase of the demographic transition and then falls as fertility rates eventually decline as well. The growth rate of income traces a similar path. It initially rises with output per capita because rising per capita income is, in its initial stages, associated with higher rates of saving and capital formation. Eventually, however, diminishing marginal returns to capital and fixed factors (such as land) lead to a deceleration in the rate of output growth. Note that environmental consequences, such as the impacts of climate change on productivity, could be included as a reason for decreasing marginal returns.

As drawn in Figure 1.1, point A represents the Malthusian poverty trap. To the left of A, output growth exceeds population growth and therefore the system will move to the right. To the right of A, population growth exceeds output growth and therefore per capita income will decrease. Point A is thus an equilibrium. What Figure 1.1 does allow, however, is a possibility of escaping the Malthusian trap. If output per capita is slightly displaced to the right of point A, it will return to its original position. However, a major shock—perhaps the discovery of a new technology or a public investment program—might cause a very large displacement, so that output per capita is displaced all the way to the right of point B. Since output growth exceeds population growth, output per capita will continue to grow until a new equilibrium is reached at point C. Thus, in this model two equilibria exist: a low-level trap and a high-level steady state.

One of the predictions of the model is that real wages should vary inversely with the labor:land ratio, and, thus, the rate of change in real wages should vary inversely with the rate of population growth, a proposition for which Lee (1980) and Weir (1991) found emphatic evidence in preindustrial Europe. However, evidence from contemporary less industrialized countries is sometimes contradictory (Evenson 1988, Boyce 1991).

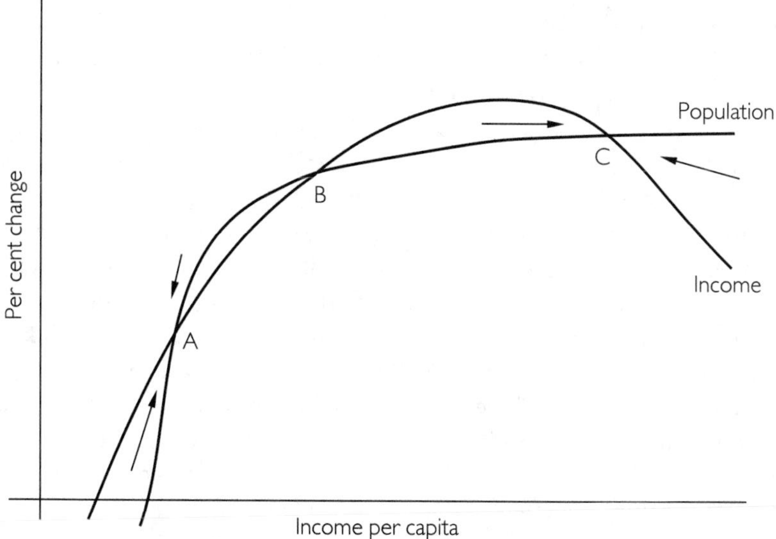

Figure 1.1 An updated Malthusian model and a way to avoid the Malthusian trap (*source:* Todaro 1985).

Various sources of economic growth have, of course, been the subject of intense study by economists for more than two centuries. Their interest has spawned a tradition that views economic growth as a process driven by a combination of basic elements, and the effects of policy on growth can therefore be traced through its effects on those drivers. Solow (1956, 1958) and Lucas (1988) contributed notably to this structure by highlighting specific drivers that explained much of the variation in aggregate economic performance observed across the industrialized and emerging economies. They both identified underlying technical change and innovation as sources of growth; and technological change and innovation are widely thought to have sustained 1.5 to 2.0 percentage points of growth per year across the countries of the Organisation for Economic Cooperation and Development (OECD) throughout the twentieth century.

Neoclassical growth models

Solow (1956) explained the OECD performance by constructing what has since been termed a neoclassical growth model. In his and other like models, labor was assumed to grow at a constant rate, and the models were asked to unveil and to analyze the properties of alternative growth paths for the economy. In some more recent models, though, the growth rate of labor was defined in quality terms to reflect the state of human capital improvement, so that attention could be paid to savings and asset accumulation. Optimal policies within these derivative neoclassical growth models subsequently explained large portions of the more recent and rapid growth across much of the Pacific Rim.

The neoclassical growth model has played an important role in climate change debates. First, the baseline projections (business-as-usual scenarios) assume a level of economic growth at the global level. Second, as climate change mitigation is expected to be a net cost, that cost is often expressed as forgone income or GDP. Third, the economic effects of climate change policies are modeled within a growth paradigm. Therefore, it is worthwhile to understand the economic model that underlies some central arguments in the debate.

The key to the neoclassical economic growth model is that capital is not in fixed supply as assumed by Malthus; rather, the stock of capital can be expanded by saving and investment. But if the rate of saving is not high enough to prevent a decline in the ratio of capital to labor, the productivity of labor, and hence per capita output, will fall. A key consideration with respect to the environment (including climate) is that investment in the environment in the simple neoclassical model does not increase the stock of capital or per capita income. In fact, it should decrease per capita capital stock since it represents a diversion of savings.

The key result of the neoclassical model may be stated thus: without productivity gains attributable to technical progress—that is, an exogenous increase in output independent of increase in inputs—output per capita eventually reaches an equilibrium level; output and population grow at the same rate in the long run. The more rapid the assumed rate of population growth, the lower the equilibrium level of per capita output. If technical progress grows at rate r, then, in the long run, output per capita will grow at rate r. In other words, barring a relationship between the rate of population and the rate of technical progress, the long-term equilibrium growth rate of output per capita is independent of the rate of demographic increase (but see Box 1.1 for further consideration of this issue).

Box 1.1 Is there an inverse correlation between population growth and economic growth?

If the neoclassical model is correct, then observations drawn from a population of economies on their equilibrium growth paths should reveal no correlation between the rate of population growth and the rate of per capita income growth. Theoreticians were thus long able to take comfort from the fact that the correlation between the rate of population growth and the rate of growth of per capita income was one of the most notorious nonrelationships in the social sciences. That is to say, when any number of researchers compared the per capita economic growth rates of countries with their population growth rates, there was no discernible relationship (see Blanchet 1991 for a summary of results and citations).

On the other hand, more recent correlation studies *have* found a significant inverse relationship for the 1970s and early 1980s, although not for earlier years and not always for the postwar decades considered as a whole. An econometric argument (Blanchet 1988) has it that the observations are being generated by an underlying Malthusian model which correlation analysis is only now starting to reveal. Another explanation is that poor countries were displaced from their steady-state growth paths during the troubled decades of the 1970s and 1980s and, failing to adjust to external shocks, remained displaced. This would be sufficient to lead to the emergence of a negative correlation; furthermore, it might be argued that countries with rapidly expanding populations found it more difficult to regain their steady-state paths than did countries with moderate rates of demographic increase. Complicating matters is the consideration that the current and lagged impacts of demographic increase may differ. Some statistical analyses (Ahlburg 1987, Bloom & Freeman 1988) have concluded that the rate of per capita economic growth is inversely correlated with the contemporaneous rate of population growth, but is positively correlated with the past—that is, lagged—rate of population growth, mostly via labor supply effects.

Implicit in this result is the key to the agnosticism that neoclassical economists have long expressed regarding rapid population growth and economic growth. Microeconomic theory posits a tradeoff between fertility and material standard of living, since both children and goods are sources of utility. If, therefore, rapid population growth is associated with lower per capita income at the macroeconomic level, this is merely the aggregation of utility-maximizing fertility decisions taken at the household level. Just as the unadorned microeconomic model gives no foundation for advising couples that they would be happier if they had fewer children, the macroeconomic growth model gives no foundation for advising national policymakers that they would be better off taking steps to encourage fertility decline. When such advice is extended, as it often is, the rationale must be found elsewhere than in the basic neoclassical economic model (Box 1.1).

Capital formation

Solow, Lucas, and others also saw the accumulation of factors of production, in both physical and human terms, playing a critical role in driving economic growth. In the rapidly growing Asian economies, for example, the accumulation of resources through high savings rates (30 percent or more) has long been thought to be one of the major determinants of the high growth of economies such as Korea, Taiwan, Hong Kong, Singapore, Thailand, China and, until ten years ago, Japan (see Balassa & Nolund 1988).

It is easy to imagine scenarios in which demographic increase would serve as an incentive for capital formation. By making labor more plentiful, population growth raises the return to capital relative to the real wage rate (Lee 1980, Weir 1991), thus favoring savings and investment. By temporarily threatening to reduce living standards, rapid population growth might even induce investment at both the national and household levels. Mortality decline should have an important accounting effect on investment decisions: by raising survival probabilities, reductions in mortality lengthen the horizon over which investment projects pay off. More important than accounting considerations may be a change in values accompanying mortality decline: less fatalistic persons are more likely to perceive and exploit profitable investment opportunities.

Human capital formation

Behrman (1990) coined the phrase "human-resource based development" to describe the contribution to economic growth of raising labor force quality via training, education, and indigenous research and development. However, the idea can usefully be broadened to include a wider range of human resource concerns: levels of health, literacy, adequacy of nutrition and housing, and so on. Moderate optimism concerning such effects can lead to strong and continuous growth in less industrialized countries (Box 1.2). In contrast to the ambiguity of the evidence regarding the effect of demographic parameters on savings and physical capital formation at the household level, rather strong evidence exists at the micro level that high fertility and large family size tend to depress children's living conditions and education and, as a result, give rise (with a lag) to low levels of human resource quality (MacKellar 1994 for citations). Recent

Box 1.2 Human resource quality and economic growth

Wheeler (1984) combined a human-resource quality approach with the neoclassical growth model of population and development. At the core of the model was a Cobb–Douglas production function in which the contribution of labor was a function of its quality as measured by the literacy rate and nutritional status. The investment rate depended on, among other things, life expectancy and literacy. Labor force participation rates were not included in the model, and the labor force was taken simply as the population over 15 years old. Calorie consumption depended largely on income growth and literacy on exogenous school enrolment rates.

Fertility was a function of income (positive), the crude death rate (positive; this embodies the quality/quantity tradeoff and its close relative, the child-replacement hypothesis), the availability of family planning services (itself a function of income) and an age-structure variable (women 25–34 as a proportion of women aged 15–49). Life expectancy was a function of income, calorie consumption and literacy. Mortality was a function of the number of doctors per capita and two age-structure variables, population younger than 15 and older than 50 as a proportion of the total population.

Wheeler did simulation runs to see if the model validated the existence of a Malthusian low-level trap. The answer, in brief, was no. If school enrolment rates were frozen at low initial-year levels and the family planning variable was set at a level consistent with no government promotion of family planning, the model traced a pessimistic scenario. However, when enrolment rates were assumed to rise in accordance with observed historical trends, and family planning was endogenized, the simulated growth path was satisfactory. For example, Africa was estimated to experience per capita growth of close to 3 percent per year over the very long term. Administering an extra upward boost to schooling improved results even more. In commenting on these results, Wheeler wrote (1984: 80):

> Is this all simple cockeyed optimism? Obviously, I cannot answer this question, but I take comfort in the fact that no one else can either. Pessimism has become so fashionable during the past decade that an attractive future for [less developed countries] under reasonable assumptions seems automatically suspect.

Wheeler hypothesized three investment scenarios with roughly equivalent costs—the first hypothesizing an increase of one percentage point in the baseline investment rate, the second hypothesizing the same amount of money invested in education, and the third hypothesizing equivalent resources invested in family planning. The alternative strategies were then ranked as to their effects on four quality-of-life indicators: income, literacy, life expectancy and nutrition. One striking conclusion emerged: for *no* indicator, including income, was the physical investment strategy dominant after roughly 15 years of age. In other words, in the medium term, investment in either schooling or family planning led to higher payoffs in income, literacy, life expectancy and nutrition, than did the traditional strategy of investment in physical capital.

advances in economic growth theory have emphasized the importance of precisely such effects. For example, Becker et al. (1990) elaborated a household-level growth model in which fertility and endowment of children with human capital are both endogenous variables and in which possibilities for intergenerational transfers exist. The model's solution is characterized by two stable equilibria: one with large family size and low endowment of human capital per child, the other with small family size and high endowment of human capital per child. The implication (practically, not formally, speaking) is that some exogenous push may be required to direct less industrialized countries away from the low-level steady state.

Technological change

A growing population might be expected to generate increasing demands for food and energy, with corresponding effects on greenhouse-related emissions. However, the population–emissions relationship is mediated by technology. Recent literature, exemplified by Romer (1986), has turned the focus to what has been termed *endogenous growth*. Modeling here focuses on the contribution of knowledge to growth through externality effects. The growth rate is thus determined endogenously in part by policies designed to harness economies of scale and other effects. Modern models therefore stress knowledge-based technologies, but they still focus attention on policies that might improve growth performance.

Role of climate change in growth models

In light of these complications, what can be said about the relationship between climate change and growth? One scenario suggests that climate change will probably induce policy attempts to slow or diminish climate change and that their effects will be largely once and for all. These scenarios see real income and production falling in the near term, but they also suggest that economies will eventually rebound, so that their potential will continue to expand.

A second view holds that mitigating policies will work to change the sequencing component of growth and thus the ability of economies to change the composition of their primary activities. Under such scenarios, climate change can retard growth over the short term and reduce its potential even over the long term, especially in less industrialized countries. Azimi (1994) noted, for instance, that China is already growing rapidly and is fast becoming a major user of carbon-based products in large measure because, in its national energy policies, it has a relatively low price policy toward carbon-based products. In fact, China currently accounts for perhaps 20–25 percent of global carbon emissions—a fraction that could grow to 40–50 percent of carbon emissions by the year 2010. Policies designed to slow carbon emissions certainly clash with this projected future for China.

Similar stories emerge from other Asian economies such as Indonesia, Malaysia, and Thailand. All of these countries have significant forest cover and export tropical lumber and associated products. To the extent that this component of their trade pattern and outwardly oriented development strategy is crucial to their growth, policies designed to limit this trade with the aim of affecting deforestation will have significant impacts on their abilities to grow.

Focusing attention on specific sectors should remind even the most rigid growth practitioner that resource reallocation issues have been central in most model-based analyses of the impacts of climate change. Reallocation issues arise, in part, because many analyses of climate change based on macro models do not focus on climate change as such, but rather on the impact of policies designed to lessen future climate change. Proposals to introduce large taxes on fossil fuels would be designed specifically to produce large resource re-allocations; and the very distortions that such policies would exploit to achieve their desired effects would dislodge the status quo in markets that span the globe and affect the ability of all countries to meet their performance objectives. Therein lies the problematic issue in designing policy; and policy debate hinges on weighing the economic costs, measured in terms of reduced economic performance in the near term, against a frequently diffuse and uncertain array of benefits sometimes distributed well into the future.

Insights from the standard economic paradigm

The standard economic paradigm provides key insights into the global change problem. Despite their shortcomings, simple economic models have yielded insights into how and where changes in economic activity are causing greenhouse gas emissions, how such crucial factors as international trade interact with growth and emissions, the potential costs and benefits of greenhouse gas emissions and their control (at least at an aggregate level), the effect of incentives for location decisions on emissions, and the effects of institutional structure and market adjustments on emissions and climate impacts.

Measurement of income, economic activity, and trade

If the costs and benefits of climate change policies are important, then a critical question in national and international environmental–economic policymaking is how to rate performance. Economics has done this historically by counting goods and services that are transacted through markets. In dealing with such issues as climate change, this way of approaching the world has limitations. Yet the standard paradigm has produced insights into the problem.

Measuring income

Each modern measure of aggregate economic performance has been devised to accommodate a specific economic complexity, but each can nonetheless be derived from the standard notion of gross national product (GNP). GNP is, quite simply, the current value of all of the final goods and services produced by a nation during some specified period of time (usually a year). It measures a flow of real economic value through an economy over a period of time, and it can be computed in one of three ways. The first sums personal consumption, domestic investment, government purchases and net exports; the second sums wages and other employee supplements, net interest, rental income paid to people, indirect business taxes, depreciation income to unincorporated enterprises, and corporate income before taxes. Most countries use a third approach: summing the net values of final output of the various sectors of the economy (output values from which the value of inputs have been subtracted). Understanding the nuances of all of the components of the three approaches is not necessary to see that their theoretically based equivalence can be employed not only to check and to validate GNP measures, when data are available to support more than one calculation, but also to provide at least one source of aggregate measurement when data are unavailable to complete one or the other of the requisite sums. Many of the categories in each sum might not be applicable to all countries. This can cause statistical problems in collecting data and comparing results across national boundaries, of course, but it does little violence to the conceptual notion of what is being measured.

Alternative measures of the flow of aggregate economic activity abound. One of the most popular, gross domestic product (GDP), represents the total value of output produced within a nation over a given time period. Importantly, in a world of increasing economic interdependence and multinational corporate activity, GDP is not the same as GNP. GNP captures only output produced from factors of production that are owned by the citizens of a nation in question; GDP includes output produced from any resources physically located within that nation, regardless of the nationality of their owners. GNP is conceptually the sum of GDP and net factor income from abroad, less income from worker compensation from abroad, interest payments on loans held domestically, and other factor payments made to residents from abroad (less corresponding payments to residents of other countries).

Historical trends in economic activity

Table 1.1 records several World Bank estimates of the per capita GNP achieved across a relatively complete listing of the nations of the world in four specific years: 1975, 1980, 1985, and 1990. Table 1.2 also draws from World Resources Institute (1995) to provide a more detailed portrait of the year 1991.

Table 1.1 Per capita GNP—selected years ($ US).

Country	1975	1980	1985	1990
Algeria	860	1950	2610	2350
Antigua and Barbuda			2570	4270
Argentina	1810	1970	2140	2380
Australia	7110	10500	11760	16670
Austria	4730	10000	9100	19050
Bahamas	2720	5840	9010	11550
Bahrain			8260	6830
Bangladesh	130	150	150	210
Barbados	1520	3140	4670	6450
Belgium	5930	12160	8290	17580
Belize	790	1170	1120	1960
Benin	200	390	290	360
Bermuda	6790	12040	18500	
Bhutan			130	190
Bolivia	360	490	430	630
Botswana	360	870	1040	2190
Brazil	1070	2070	1640	2710
Brunei		17220	17410	
Bulgaria			2060	2280
Burkino Faso	110	210	170	270
Burundi	100	200	250	210
Cambodia				170
Cameroon	310	760	830	950
Canada	7250	10610	14230	20210
Cape Verde	220	410	340	680
Central African Republic	170	320	270	400
Chad	150	160	130	180
Chile	850	2090	1410	1940
China	170	300	330	370
Columbia	550	1200	1280	1260
Comoros	170	340	300	480
Congo	530	850	1050	1000
Costa Rica	950	1900	1330	1780
Cote d'Ivoire	490	1160	660	760
Cyprus				8230
Czechoslovakia			2760	3190

Table 1.1 (cont'd) Per capita GNP—selected years ($ US).

Country	1975	1980	1985	1990
Denmark	6900	13150	11380	22440
Dominica	380	700	1230	2220
Dominican Republic	660	1090	800	820
Ecuador	540	1260	1180	940
Egypt, Arab Republic of	320	500	670	610
El Salvador	430	740	830	1010
Equatorial Guinea				340
Ethiopia	90	120	110	120
Faeroe Islands	4780	9850	10010	
Fiji	1030	1750	1650	1860
Finland	5390	10130	11040	24580
France	5980	11860	9810	19420
Gabon	2620	3840	3430	3550
The Gambia	210	350	250	340
Germany	6670	13270	10920	22360
Ghana	280	410	370	390
Greece	2370	4380	3700	5980
Grenada				2130
Guatemala	570	1130	1210	910
Guinea				440
Guinea-Bissau	190	130	180	180
Guyana	640	710	510	390
Haiti	150	260	320	370
Honduras	360	640	790	660
Hong Kong	2210	5220	6120	11890
Hungary		1930	1940	2780
Iceland	6350	13680	11810	22540
India	160	240	290	360
Indonesia	210	470	550	560
Iran	1310	1950	4030	2500
Iraq	1140	3030	2520	2140
Ireland	2640	5060	4940	10390
Israel	3880	5390	6610	11160
Italy	3690	7500	7750	16940
Jamaica	1250	1130	920	1580
Japan	4520	9840	11430	25840

Table 1.1 (cont'd) Per capita GNP—selected years ($ US).

Country	1975	1980	1985	1990
Jordan			1940	1290
Kenya	230	420	310	370
Kiribati			560	690
Korea, Republic of	580	1620	2340	5440
Kuwait	9040	17830	15110	
Lao, PDR				200
Lesotho	230	420	390	550
Liberia	410	580	480	
Libya	4630	9760	6810	
Lithuania				3110
Luxembourg	7460	14940	14080	29460
Madagascar	280	430	310	230
Malawi	120	180	170	230
Malaysia	820	1690	1980	2340
Mali	120	240	160	280
Malta	1540	3160	3410	6690
Mauritania	300	440	410	500
Mauritius	710	1190	1110	2310
Mexico	1430	2440	2300	2610
Morocco	500	930	620	970
Mozambique			180	80
Namibia			1090	1400
Nepal	110	130	170	180
Netherlands	6410	12310	9660	17850
New Zealand	4620	6960	6940	12770
Nicaragua	630	650	880	410
Niger	230	440	230	310
Nigeria	520	1100	1020	340
Norway	6600	12900	14560	22830
Oman	1280	3650	7410	5680
Pakistan	130	290	370	390
Panama	1090	1720	2090	1900
Papua New Guinea	530	770	750	860
Paraguay	550	1350	1180	1140
Peru	1000	990	940	1040
Philippines	340	650	540	730

Table 1.1 (cont'd) Per capita GNP—selected years ($ US).

Country	1975	1980	1985	1990
Poland			2100	1680
Portugal	1540	2380	1980	5190
Puerto Rico	2480	3460	4460	6050
Qatar	7550	31160	19190	14210
Romania				1670
Rwanda	90	240	280	320
São Tomé and Principe	440	480	340	410
St Kitts and Nevis			1720	3540
St Lucia				2350
St Vincent	350	580	1080	1710
Saudi Arabia	3280	10420	8700	7070
Senegal	350	510	380	720
Seychelles	800	2020	2580	5100
Sierra Leone	220	320	340	250
Singapore	2820	4820	7880	12430
Solomon Islands	290	400	530	730
Somalia	140	110	120	120
South Africa	1460	1710	2010	2450
Spain	2770	5370	4350	11010
Sri Lanka	290	260	390	470
Sudan	250	400	370	
Suriname	1340	2420	2420	3350
Swaziland	590	830	810	1030
Sweden	8300	14350	12020	23780
Switzerland	7940	17490	16340	32310
Syrian Arab Republic	860	1450	1750	1000
Tanzania	170	280	280	100
Thailand	360	670	810	1410
Togo	250	410	260	410
Tonga			750	1100
Trinidad and Tobago	1720	4620	6180	3460
Tunisia	710	1280	1180	1440
Turkey	830	1400	1080	1640
Uganda			170	180
United Arab Emirates	13240	30190	22360	19910
United Kingdom	3900	7980	8530	16020

Table 1.1 (cont'd) Per capita GNP—selected years ($ US).

Country	1975	1980	1985	1990
United States	7400	12040	16860	21910
Uruguay	1330	2720	1550	2600
Vanuatu			970	1160
Venezuela	2370	4120	3910	2670
Virgin Islands	4570	7510	9320	
Western Samoa			630	940
Yugoslavia	1380	3250	2060	2940
Zaire	400	590	260	220
Zambia	550	600	370	460
Zimbabwe	550	710	640	680

Source: World Bank (1993a).

Of course, enormous statistical difficulties present themselves in expressing international data in a common currency, so that they can be compared across national boundaries:

- problems in defining comparable and widely applicable reporting categories and procedures
- index number problems in deciding how to weight various activities and what prices to use
- exchange rate issues to be resolved so that local currencies can be converted to an international currency such as the US dollar.

To compensate, the World Bank reviews the national accounts of all countries to evaluate their collection and reporting and to make adjustments as necessary in the data. Wide differences between official and effective exchange rates are handled by creating conversion factors.

Indices based upon purchasing power parities (PPP—see Box 1.3) provide more reliable comparisons, although they are not used by the World Bank. PPP weights are designed to be more stable when exchange rates are volatile; using them can make a large difference to international comparisons (see the technical notes attached to table 15.1 in World Resources 1995). Notwithstanding the difficulties involved in using indices, or the conceptual problems with using per capita GNP or GDP as proximate measures of welfare, these and other data can provide some insight into how economic development and growth has been generated and distributed over the recent past. Large differences among economies can be identified and considered using GNP or GDP figures; but the researcher who tries to use them to support precise and quantitative measures of small differences is on very shaky ground.

Measured in either current exchange rates or PPP terms, governments use GNP or GDP figures to monitor their own economic performance both over time

Table 1.2 Gross national product and gross domestic product, 1991.

	Gross domestic product GDP										
	Gross national product GNP 1991[a]		Exchange rate based GDP 1991[b]		Purchasing power parity PPP 1991[c]		Average annual growth rate (%)		Distribution of GDP, 1991 (%)		
Continent and country	Total $US million	Per capita $US	Total $US million	Per capita $US	Total million $1	Per capita $1	GNP[d] 1980–91	GDP[e] 1980–91	Agriculture	Industry	Services
AFRICA											
Algeria	51060	1991	42993	1674	144627	5640	2.1	3.0	14.0[f]	50.0[f]	36.0[f]
Angola	×	×	8375	879	×	×	×	×	×	×	×
Benin	1854	389	1898	398	7151	1500[g]	2.1	2.4.	36.1	13.2	50.7
Botswana	3399	2666	3688	2893	5980	4690	9.3	9.8	5.5	58.5	36.0
Burkino Faso	2683	290	2753	298	6936	750	4.0	4.0	44.0[f]	20.0[f]	37.0[f]
Burundi	1230	218	1170	207	4072	720	4.3	4.0	55.0[f]	16.0[f]	29.0[f]
Cameroon	10174	858	11674	985	28457	2400[g]	2.1	1.4	23.0	29.4	47.6
Central African Republic	1258	407	1278	413	3368	1090	1.2	1.4	41.0[f]	16.0[f]	42.0[f]
Chad	1206	212	1297	228	4155	730	6.3	5.5	43.0[f]	18.0[f]	39.0[f]
Congo	2436	1060	2722	1185	6434	2800[g]	3.1	3.3	13.2	38.2	48.7
Cote d'Ivoire	8416	677	9503	764	18778	1510[g]	0.3	0.5	38.0[f]	22.0[f]	40.0[f]
Djibouti	×	×	445	982	×	×	×	×	×	×	×
Egypt	32783	611	32790	611	193072	3600[g]	4.5	4.8	18.0[f]	30.0[f]	52.0[f]
Equatorial Guinea	1124	345	131	363	×	×	5.8	×	×	×	×
Ethiopia	6313	123	6602	129	19010	370[g]	1.5	1.6	47.0[f]	13.0[f]	40.0[f]
Gabon	4643	3879	5435	4540	×	×	0.9	0.2	9.0	49.1	41.9

Gambia	324	367	341	386	×	×	3.2	×	28.5[h]	13.8[h]	57.6[h]
Ghana	6496	420	7000	452	30968	2000	3.1	3.2	51.1	16.9	32.0
Guinea	2952	498	3180	536	×	×	×	×	32.0	32.6	35.4
Guinea-Bissau	184	187	211	214	679	690	3.3	3.7	46.3	15.8	37.9
Kenya	8529	350	8261	339	32933	350[g]	4.1	4.2	27.0[f]	22.0[f]	51.0[f]
Lesotho	1042	582	601	336	3385	1890	2.7	5.5	14.0[f]	38.0[f]	48.0[f]
Liberia	×	×	×	×	×	×	×	×	×	×	×
Libya	×	×	×	×	×	×	×	×	×	×	×
Madagascar	2574	207	2673	215	8812	710[g]	0.5	1.1	33.0[f]	14.0[f]	53.0[f]
Malawi	1997	200	2192	220	7989	800[g]	3.5	3.1	35.0[f]	20.0[f]	45.0[f]
Mali	2387	251	2451	258	4565	480[g]	2.5	2.5	42.1	14.2	43.7
Mauritania	1042	500	1130	543	2895	1390	0.6	1.4	22.0[f]	31.0[f]	47.0[f]
Mauritius	2585	2380	2730	2514	12141	11180[g]	7.2	6.7	11.0[f]	33.0[f]	56.0[f]
Morocco	26530	1033	27653	1077	85795	3340[g]	4.3	4.2	16.8	32.8	50.4
Mozambique	1221	84	1328	92	8697	600	(1.1)	(0.1)	64.0[f]	15.0[f]	21.0[f]
Namibia	2354	1584	2278	1533	×	×	1.6	1.0	10.0[f]	28.0[f]	62.0[f]
Niger	2419	303	2328	291	6309	790	(0.9)	(1.0)	34.8	15.9	49.3
Nigeria	34226	305	34124	304	152418	1360[g]	1.4	1.9	37.0[f]	38.0[f]	26.0[f]
Rwanda	2052	282	1630	224	4944	680[g]	0.5	0.6	40.2	18.7	41.2
Senegal	5544	736	5639	749	12649	1680[g]	2.9	3.1	20.3	18.6	61.1
Sierra Leone	860	202	755	177	3409	800[g]	1.1	1.1	×	×	×
Somalia	×	×	×	×	×	×	×	×	×	×	×
South Africa	98854	2543	107437	2763	×	×	3.3	1.3	5.0[f]	44.0[f]	51.0[f]

Table 1.2 (cont'd) Gross national product and gross domestic product—1991.

Continent and country	Gross national product GNP 1991[a]		Gross domestic product GDP: Exchange rate based GDP 1991[b]		Gross domestic product GDP: Purchasing power parity PPP 1991[c]		Average annual growth rate (%)		Distribution of GDP, 1991 (%)		
	Total $US million	Per capita $US	Total $US million	Per capita $US	Total million $1	Per capita $1	GNP[d] 1980–91	GDP[e] 1980–91	Agriculture	Industry	Services
Sudan	×	×	7310	282	×	×	0.3	×	×	×	×
Swaziland	933	1210	942	1222	×	×	6.8	×	×	×	×
Tanzania	2561	95	3183	118	15332	570[g]	2.0	2.9	61.0[f]	5.0[f]	34.0[f]
Togo	1558	427	1637	449	4775	1310	1.8	1.8	33.0	22.2	44.8
Tunisia	12377	1504	13183	1602	38585	4690[g]	3.5	3.7	18.0	32.0	50.0
Uganda	2949	163	2566	142	20285	1120	5.9	×	51.0[f]	12.0[f]	37.0[f]
Zaire	×	×	×	×	×	×	×	×	×	×	×
Zambia	3508	418	3628	432	8473	1010[g]	0.7	0.8	18.2	45.3	36.5
Zimbabwe	6586	641	6324	616	22175	2160[g]	3.6	3.1	20.0[f]	32.0[f]	49.0[f]
ASIA											
Afghanistan	×	×	×	×	×	×	×	×	×	×	×
Bangladesh	23883	205	23394	201	135075	1160[g]	4.2	4.3	36.8	15.8	47.4
Bhutan	275	174	253	160	977	620	9.0	7.6	43.0[f]	27.0[f]	29.0[f]
Cambodia	1730	202	1965	230	×	×	×	×	48.9	12.4	38.6
China	425623	364	371455	317	1966771	1680[i]	9.4	9.4	28.4	38.8	32.8
India	284658	330	248583	288	992157	1150[g]	5.5	5.4	31.0[f]	27.0[f]	41.0[f]
Indonesia	111165	592	115878	617	512487	2730[j]	5.8	5.6	21.4	39.3	39.2

Iran	136348	2274	117190	1955	279957	4670[g]	2.5	2.2	21.0[f]	21.0[f]	58.0[f]
Iraq	×	×	×	×	×	×	×	×	×	×	×
Israel	59879	12293	63032	12940	65564	13460[j]	3.7	3.7	×	×	×
Japan	3326646	26824	3346486	26984	2404709	19390[k]	4.3	4.2	2.5	42.0	55.5
Jordan	3880	935	4082	984	20196	4870	0.6	(1.5)	7.0[f]	26.0[f]	67.0[f]
Korea, DPR	×	×	×	×	×	×	×	×	×	×	×
Korea, Rep.	274875	6277	282970	6462	364341	8320[g]	10.0	9.6	9.0	44.7	46.3
Kuwait	×	×	11199	5369	×	×	×	×	0.6	51.0	48.4
Lao People's Dem. Rep.	943	218	1033	238	8367	1930	4.2	×	×	×	×
Lebanon	×	×	4304	1546	×	×	×	×	×	×	×
Malaysia	45798	2479	47104	2568	135731	7400[l]	5.6	5.7	×	×	×
Mongolia	×	×	756	336	×	×	×	×	16.6	33.5	49.9
Myanmar	×	×	28278	662	×	×	×	×	×	×	×
Nepal	3420	170	3333	166	22681	1130	4.7	×	59.0[f]	14.0[f]	27.0[f]
Oman	9714	6148	10236	6479	14204	8990	9.3	7.9	3.3	57.7	39.0
Pakistan	46566	383	45294	373	239325	1970[g]	6.5	6.1	26.0[f]	26.0[f]	49.0[f]
Philippines	46466	728	45162	708	155718	2440[g]	1.2	1.1	22.1	34.9	43.0
Saudi Arabia	121452	7893	108640	7060	166949	10850	0.4	(0.2)	6.7	52.4	40.9
Singapore	39967	14263	40201	14677	43167	15760	7.1	6.6	0.3	37.4	62.3
Sri Lanka	8638	495	9054	519	46216	2650[g]	4.0	4.0	27.0[f]	25.0[f]	48.0[f]
Syria Arab Republic	14607	1141	17236	1346	×	×	1.4	2.6	29.8	23.4	46.8
Thailand	94022	1697	98261	1774	291921	5270[g]	7.8	7.9	12.7	39.7	47.6
Turkey	102495	1793	107842	1886	276683	4840[k]	5.4	5.0	18.0[f]	34.0[f]	49.0[f]

Table 1.2 (cont'd) Gross national product and gross domestic product—1991.

Continent and country	Gross national product GNP 1991[a] Total $US million	Per capita $US	Gross domestic product GDP: Exchange rate based GDP 1991[b] Total $US million	Per capita $US	Purchasing power parity PPP 1991[c] Total million $1	Per capita $1	Average annual growth rate (%) GNP[d] 1980–91	GDP[e] 1980–91	Distribution of GDP, 1991 (%) Agriculture	Industry	Services
United Arab Emirates	36137	22170	34323	21057	×	×	(1.8)	×	×	×	×
Vietnam	×	×	6970	102	×	×	×	×	38.6	23.7	37.7
Yemen	6746	557	8341	689	×	×	×	×	×	×	×
NORTH AND CENTRAL AMERICA											
Belize	422	2176	420	2165	×	×	5.3	×	21.9[h]	24.8[h]	53.3[h]
Canada	559825	20740	582000	21561	521505	19320[k]	3.1	3.1	3.0[m]	33.8[m]	63.2[m]
Costa Rica	5733	1841	5635	1810	15876	5100[j]	3.4	3.1	15.8	25.7	58.5
Cuba	×	×	×	×	×	×	×	×	×	×	×
Dominican Republic	6751	922	7148	976	22549	3080[j]	1.9	1.7	17.5	26.2	56.3
El Salvador	5740	1087	5915	1120	11143	2110[j]	1.1	1.0	11.2	23.3	65.5
Guatemala	8939	944	9353	988	30105	3180[j]	1.0	1.1	25.7	19.7	54.6
Haiti	2479	375	2641	399	8075	1220	(0.6)	(0.7)	×	×	×
Honduras	3112	587	3004	567	9642	1820[j]	2.6	2.7	20.0	23.5	45.6
Jamaica	3532	1446	3497	1431	8966	3670[l]	1.0	1.6	5.0	43.9	53.1
Mexico	256422	2971	286628	3321	618864	7170[l]	1.5	1.2	8.0	30.7	61.3
Nicaragua	1079	283	1736	456	9708	2550	(1.4)	(1.9)	31.1	20.0	48.9
Panama	5259	2133	5544	2248	12108	4910[j]	0.3	0.5	9.9	10.0	80.1

Trinidad and Tobago	4475	3793	4939	3948	10483	8380	(3.9)	(4.4)	2.5	38.6	58.9
United States	5645415	22356	5610802	22219[n]	5588356	22130[k,n]	3.1	2.6	2.0[o]	29.3[o]	68.6[o]
SOUTH AMERICA											
Argentina	129723	3966	189720	5800	167485	5120[j]	(0.2)	(0.4)	8.1	46.0	55.9
Bolivia	4808	654	5020	683	15941	2170[j]	0.5	0.3	×	×	×
Brazil	442698	2920	405771	2677	794394	5240[j]	2.5	2.5	10.0[f]	39.0[f]	51.0[f]
Chile	31582	2359	33977	2538	94512	7060[j]	3.4	3.6	×	×	×
Columbia	41207	1254	41700	1269	179421	5460[j]	3.2	3.7	16.1	36.5	47.4
Ecuador	10907	1010	11663	1080	44712	4140[j]	2.0	2.1	13.4	37.9	48.7
Guyana	242	302	349	435	×	×	(3.8)	×	×	×	×
Paraguay	5568	1266	6249	1421	15038	3420[j]	2.3	2.7	27.8	23.1	49.1
Peru	23434	1065	21899	996	68408	3110[j]	(0.4)	(0.4)	0.0	0.0	0.0
Suriname	1666	3874	1941	4513	×	×	(2.2)	×	11.1[h]	26.8[h]	62.1[h]
Uruguay	8971	2883	9804	3150	20757	6670[j]	0.2	0.6	11.3	32.1	56.6
Venezuela	53880	2728	53441	2705	160394	8120[j]	1.1	0.15	5.4	50.2	44.4
EUROPE											
Albania	×	×	1154	351	×	×	×	×	×	×	×
Austria	158054	20410	163992	21177	136991	17690[k]	2.3	2.3	3.2	36.1	60.7
Belgium	190140	19043	196873	19717	174837	17510[k]	2.2	2.1	1.8	30.1	68.1
Bulgaria	16316	1818	12687	1414	44696	4980	1.7	1.9	17.7	51.3	31.0
Czechoslovakia (former)	38810	2473	33172	2114	98565	6280	0.7	0.6	8.0[f]	56.0[f]	36.0[f]
Denmark	122484	23793	130277	25306	92046	17880[k]	2.2	2.3	50.0[f]	28.0[f]	67.0[f]
Finland	120326	24089	124542	24933	80569	16130[k]	2.9	3.0	6.0[f]	34.0[f]	60.0[f]

Table 1.2 (cont'd) Gross national product and gross domestic product—1991.

Continent and country	Gross national product GNP 1991[a]		Gross domestic product GDP: Exchange rate based GDP 1991[b]		Gross domestic product GDP: Purchasing power parity PPP 1991[c]		Average annual growth rate (%)		Distribution of GDP, 1991 (%)		
	Total $US million	Per capita $US	Total $US million	Per capita $US	Total million $I	Per capita $I	GNP[d] 1980–91	GDP[e] 1980–91	Agriculture	Industry	Services
France	1166992	20486	1199287	21053	1049865	18430[k]	2.3	2.3	3.4	29.0	67.6
Germany	1533932	19204	1574317	19709	1579168	19770[k]	2.3	2.3	1.5	38.7	59.8
Greece	66300	6530	70572	6951	77975	7680[k]	1.6	1.8	17.0[f]	27.0[f]	56.0[f]
Hungary	28436	2700	31593	3000	64035	6080[g]	0.5	0.6	12.6	32.4	55.0
Iceland	5994	23324	6490	25252	×	×	2.4	×	12.0[p]	29.0[p]	59.0[p]
Ireland	39279	11245	43432	12434	39925	11430[k]	2.4	3.5	11.0[f]	9.0[f]	80.0[f]
Italy	1703075	18588	1150517	19930	983702	17040[k]	2.4	2.4	3.2	33.3	63.5
Netherlands	283798	18858	290725	19319	253124	16820[k]	2.1	2.1	4.0	29.3	66.7
Norway	102684	24065	105922	24824	73264	17170[k]	2.5	2.7	3.1	35.6	61.3
Poland	68439	1787	78031	2037	172382	4500[g]	1.2	1.1	8.4	54.2	37.4
Portugal	58636	5944	65103	6599	93224	9450[k]	3.2	2.9	8.7[o]	37.1[o]	54.2[o]
Romania	32120	1380	27619	1187	160584	6900[l]	0.3	0.1	18.0	53.9	28.1
Spain	487150	12482	527284	13510	494485	12670[k]	3.2	3.2	5.3[m]	35.0[m]	59.7[m]
Sweden	217438	25254	236947	27520	150589	17490[k]	2.0	2.0	3.0[f]	34.0[f]	63.0[f]
Switzerland	228926	33850	232000	34304	147298	21780[k]	2.2	2.2	3.6[q]	35.5[q]	60.9[q]
United Kingdom	955828	16606	1009499	17538	940530	16340[k]	2.8	2.9	1.7[o]	36.3[o]	62.0[o]
Yugoslavia (former)	×	×	×	×	×	×	(0.7)	0.8	12.0[f]	48.0[f]	40.0[f]

USSR (former)											
Armenia	6583	1928	701	205	15739	4610[i]	2.9	×	×	×	×
Azerbaijan	8866	1232	×	×	26417	3670[i]	1.9	×	33.0	35.0	31.0
Belarus	33795	3288	×	×	70411	6850[i]	4.0	×	×	×	×
Estonia	6200	3914	×	×	12825	6090[i]	2.8	×	15.6	46.8	37.6
Georgia	9778	1788	×	×	20071	3670[i]	2.9	×	×	×	×
Kazakhstan	34227	2062	×	×	78850	4490[i]	2.1	×	×	×	×
Kyrgyzstan	5183	1163	6727	1509	14619	3280[i]	4.1	×	33.7	38.3	28.0
Latvia	10342	3850	×	×	20252	7540[i]	3.4	×	18.1	47.4	34.5
Lithuania	9046	2415	×	×	20266	5410[i]	3.4	×	27.7	43.3	29.0
Moldovia	7422	1700	14171	3246	20258	4640[i]	2.7	×	30.7	39.4	29.8
Russian Federation	515989	3469	×	×	1030851	6390[i]	2.0	×	17.0	49.0	34.0
Tajikistan	3793	697	×	×	11861	2180[i]	2.9	×	×	×	×
Turkmenistan	5419	1439	×	×	13328	3540[i]	3.2	×	×	×	×
Ukraine	114052	2191	168800	3243	269598	5180[i]	2.7	×	×	×	×
Uzbekistan	20510	978	×	×	58523	2790[i]	3.4	×	33.3	31.1	34.4
OCEANIA											
Australia	296051	17068	300900	17348	289315	16680[k]	2.8	3.1	3.3	30.9	65.8
Fiji	1423	1945	1475	2015	×	×	1.5	×	×	×	×
New Zealand	42106	12301	42233	12338	47819	13970[k]	1.0	1.5	8.4[m]	26.9[m]	64.8[m]
Papua New Guinea	3693	932	3787	955	7254	1830	1.7	2.0	29.0	30.4	40.6
Solomon Islands	226	684	217	656	×	×	6.7	×	×	×	×

Source: IMF (1995). *Data sources:* The World Bank and United National Population Division.
Notes: a. Current US dollars (Atlas methodology). b. Current 1991 US dollars. c. Current 1991 international dollars. d. Constant GNP. e. Constant GDP f. From the World Development Report 1993. g. Extrapolated from 1985 International Comparison Programme (ICP) estimates and scaled up by the corresponding US deflator. h. Data are for 1990. i. These values are subject to more than the usual margin of error. j. Extrapolated from 1980 ICP estimates. k. 1991 ICP estimates. q. Data are for 1985. r. Source: World Resources 1994–5, Table 15.1.
0 = less than half of the unit of measures; × = not available; negative numbers are shown in parentheses.

Box 1.3 Exchange rates, purchasing power parity and international comparisons

Currency exchange rates tend to be very volatile. They respond in the short run to changes in interest rates, political events, and other noneconomic events that cause expectations to fluctuate. Over the long run, however, exchange rates should be determined primarily by the relative prices of goods. They should work to equalize the cost of buying tradeable goods domestically and abroad. Accepting this theory, economists have designed and estimated purchasing power parity (PPP) rates of currency exchange to reflect this market-based tendency toward relative price equalization and to provide more stable conversion factors.

The PPP for any country is defined as the number of units of its currency that are required to purchase the same quantities of goods and services in the domestic market as US$1 would buy in the United States. There are obviously an infinite number of ways of spending a dollar, though, so the quantity bundles for each country comparison are based upon implicit quantities of goods and services that are drawn from national income accounts. The procedure is designed to give international comparisons the same sort of stable footing as is achieved over time by using constant dollars; and, as a result, intercountry comparisons of GDP can reflect differences in quantities of the goods and services that generate economic welfare without being distorted by intercountry price differentials.

Comparisons of the level of economic activity across national boundaries rely explicitly on the conversion of all statistics to a common currency, of course, and the more stable PPP rates are thought to be more reliable. The choice is, however, more than an academic artifact of little interest in the real world. The table below reports GDP statistics for a select group of countries computed in billions of dollars using average exchange and PPP rates. GDP in countries with relatively low incomes tends to be understated using exchange rates, and so they rank higher under the PPP conversion scheme. The reason is simple. Most of the output of these countries comes from nontradeable and labor-intensive services that are generally inexpensive in low income (i.e., low wage) economies. So, for example, China ranks far down the GDP list when exchange rates are used, but second in the world when PPP rates are used.

Comparison of GDP using market exchange and PPP rates.

Country	GDP using market exchange rates (billion US$)	GDP using PPP exchange rates (billion US$)
United States	6378	6398
China	520	2596
Japan	4260	2536
Germany	1869	1412
France	1257	1092
India	255	1045
United Kingdom	941	994
Mexico	391	633
Indonesia	139	616
Nigeria	30	178
Malaysia	63	171
Philippines	55	151

Source: DRI/McGraw-Hill adapted by Samuelson & Nordhaus (1995) for their table 21–2.

and relative to each other. Regardless of the environmental benefits involved, governments will carefully monitor the effects of climate change policies on GNP and GDP.

The impact of climate change policies on economic growth must be calculated relative to baseline growth rates and differences among countries in rates of growth. Different standard measurements may produce different results, thus altering the baseline comparisons.

Comparisons of the recent experiences of China and the United States can be a case in point. Per capita GNP and GDP (computed using exchange rates) both increased in China at an average annual rate of 7.2 percent over the decade from 1981 through 1991. Measured in terms of exchange rates, per capita GNP rose from US$179 to US$364 and per capita GDP rose from US$156 to US$317. By way of comparison, per capita GNP in the United States rose from US$18324 to US$22356 over the same period—an annual rate of 2.0 percent. GDP meanwhile climbed at an annual rate of 1.5 percent to grow from US$19154 to US$22219. The disparity in growth rates is enormous; China's growth over the decade of the 1980s exceeded that of the United States by more than 250 percent when measured in GNP (7.2 percent compared with 2 percent) and a staggering 380 percent in terms of GDP (7.2 percent vs 1.5 percent). Nonetheless, the absolute magnitude of the difference between per capita GNP and GDP in the United States and China increased by more than US$3800 and US$2900, respectively. These are comparisons whose qualitative import can survive any quarrel with the statistical accuracy of the data.

Historical trends in international trade

Trade among countries has grown dramatically over the past several decades—a trend reflected in the opening of domestic markets across the globe, a corresponding reduction in tariffs and other (nonprice) barriers to trade, and the explosive growth in multinational enterprises. Trade is a factor in computing emissions and in projections of energy-efficient mitigation paths; so, again, establishing a baseline is important.

Table 1.3 shows the trend from 1980 through 1990 in both exports and imports for the major geographic and economic regions and nations defined by the International Monetary Fund in its monthly publication, *International Financial Statistics*. The table shows that relatively stable flows of goods and services marked the beginning of the decade, but that increased trade took hold of the international marketplace in 1985. Indeed, more than 16 percent of total world economic activity of US$21196 trillion was exported across a national boundary in 1990. Clearly, international trade will play a vital role in global change as the future unfolds, and alternative regulatory strategies will need to be cast in the context of expanding internationalized sectors.

Table 1.3 Global exports and imports, 1980–90.

	EXPORTS										
	1980	1981	1982	1983	1984	1985	1986	1987	1988	1989	1990
World	1875 .9	1844 .0	1708 .5	1661 .9	1767 .7	1784 .5	2002 .9	2355 .3	2695 .0	2907 .3	3332 .0
Industrial countries	1239 .5	1218 .5	1155 .5	1139 .4	1214 .6	1258 .5	1485 .3	1735 .8	1985 .5	2126 .2	2457 .6
United States	220.8	233.7	212.3	200.5	217.9	213.1	227.2	254.1	322.4	363.8	393.6
Canada	67.7	72.7	71.2	76.5	90.3	90.6	90.3	98.2	116.6	120.2	131.7
Australia	22.0	21.8	22.0	20.6	24.0	22.8	22.6	26.5	33.0	37.7	39.8
Japan	130.4	151.5	138.4	147.0	169.7	177.2	210.8	231.3	264.9	273.9	287.6
New Zealand	5.4	5.4	5.6	5.4	5.5	5.7	5.9	7.2	8.8	8.9	9.5
Austria	17.5	15.8	15.6	15.4	15.7	17.2	22.5	27.2	31.0	31.9	41.3
Belgium–Luxembourg	64.7	55.7	52.4	51.9	51.9	53.7	68.8	83.1	92.1	100.0	117.7
Denmark	17.0	16.1	15.4	16.0	16.0	17.1	21.3	25.7	27.7	28.1	35.1
Finland	14.1	14.0	13.1	12.5	13.4	13.6	16.4.	20.0	21.7	23.3	26.6
France	116.0	106.4	96.7	94.9	97.6	101.7	124.9	148.4	167.8	179.4	216.6
Germany	192.9	176.1	176.4	169.4	171.7	183.9	243.3	294.4	323.3	341.2	410.1
Greece	5.2	4.2	4.3	4.4	4.8	4.5	5.6	6.5	5.4	7.5	8.1
Iceland	n/a	n/a	n/a	n/a	n/a	n/a	1.1	1.4	1.4	1.4	1.6
Ireland	8.4	7.7	8.1	8.6	9.6	10.4	12.7	16.0	18.7	20.7	23.7
Italy	77.7	75.3	73.5	72.7	73.3	79.0	97.2	116.7	127.9	140.6	170.3
Netherlands	73.9	68.7	66.3	64.7	65.9	68.3	80.3	92.9	103.3	107.8	131.8
Norway	18.5	18.2	17.6	18.0	18.9	20.0	18.1	21.5	22.4	27.1	34.0

Portugal	4.6	4.1	4.2	4.6	5.2	5.7	7.2	9.3	11.0	12.8	16.4
Spain	20.7	20.3	20.5	19.7	23.6	24.2	27.2	34.2	40.3	44.5	55.6
Sweden	30.9	28.7	26.8	27.4	29.4	30.5	37.3	44.5	49.7	51.5	57.6
Switzerland	29.6	27.0	26.0	25.6	25.9	27.5	37.5	45.5	50.7	51.2	63.8
United Kingdom	110.2	102.2	97.0	91.6	93.8	101.2	107.1	131.3	145.2	152.3	185.2
Less industrialized countries	616.7	603.0	531.0	497.4	523.7	495.3	517.6	619.5	709.5	781.1	874.4
Africa	95.3	78.8	62.2	59.8	61.1	62.5	54.7	63.7	61.9	61.9	73.7
Asia	144.3	153.9	153.5	155.3	179.9	179.9	227.0	295.3	363.9	406.5	453.6
Europe	42.8	45.2	46.0	46.0	48.2	49.6	66.7	71.1	76.5	74.8	71.1
Middle East	230.6	216.3	171.2	134.9	130.3	105.6	88.9	99.2	n/a	n/a	n/a
Western Hemisphere	103.7	108.3	97.6	97.7	103.7	98.4	80.6	91.6	104.6	117.4	127.8
IMPORTS											
World	1928 .1	1908 .2	1800 .4	1737 .6	1842 .7	1879 .3	2066 .2	2418 .1	2767 .6	3005 .6	3450 .0
Industrial countries	1369 .4	1298 .6	1219 .5	1200 .3	1309 .2	1361 .4	1545 .5	1829 .5	2067 .6	2238 .8	2571 .2
United States	257.0	273.4	254.9	269.9	341.2	361.6	382.3	424.4	459.5	492.9	517.0
Canada	62.8	70.3	58.4	65.1	79.8	81.1	85.5	92.6	112.7	119.8	122.0
Australia	22.4	26.2	26.7	21.5	25.9	25.9	26.1	29.3	36.1	44.9	42.0
Japan	141.3	142.9	131.5	126.4	136.2	130.5	127.6	151.0	187.4	209.7	235.4
New Zealand	5.5	5.7	5.8	5.3	6.2	6.0	6.1	7.3	7.3	8.8	9.5
Austria	24.4	21.0	19.5	19.4	19.6	21.0	16.9	32.7	36.2	39.0	49.1
Belgium–Luxembourg	71.9	62.5	58.2	55.3	55.5	56.1	68.6	83.2	92.4	98.5	119.7
Denmark	19.4	17.6	16.7	16.3	16.6	18.2	22.9	25.5	25.9	26.7	31.8
Finland	15.6	14.2	13.4	12.8	12.4	13.2	15.3	19.6	21.3	24.4	27.0

Table 1.3 (continued) Global exports and imports, 1980–90.

	IMPORTS										
	1980	1981	1982	1983	1984	1985	1986	1987	1988	1989	1990
France	134.9	121.0	115.7	105.4	103.7	108.3	129.4	158.5	178.9	193.0	234.4
Germany	188.0	163.9	155.4	152.9	153.0	158.5	190.9	228.4	250.5	269.7	346.2
Greece	10.5	8.8	10.0	9.5	9.4	10.1	11.4	13.2	12.3	16.2	19.8
Iceland	n/a	n/a	n/a	n/a	n/a	n/a	1.1	1.6	1.6	1.4	1.7
Ireland	11.2	10.6	9.7	9.2	9.7	10.0	11.6	13.6	15.6	17.4	20.7
Italy	99.7	91.1	86.2	80.4	84.2	91.1	99.4	125.7	138.6	153.0	182.0
Netherlands	78.0	67.2	63.8	61.7	62.3	65.2	75.5	91.3	99.5	104.3	126.1
Norway	16.9	15.7	15.5	13.5	13.9	15.5	20.3	22.6	23.2	23.7	26.9
Portugal	9.3	9.8	9.6	8.2	8.0	7.7	9.6	14.0	17.9	19.1	25.3
Spain	34.1	32.2	31.5	29.2	28.8	30.0	35.1	49.1	60.5	71.5	87.7
Sweden	33.4	28.8	27.6	26.1	26.4	28.5	32.7	40.7	45.6	49.0	54.4
Switzerland	36.3	30.7	28.7	29.2	29.5	30.7	41.1	50.7	56.4	58.2	69.7
United Kingdom	115.5	102.7	99.7	100.1	104.9	109.0	126.3	154.4	189.3	197.7	223.0
Less industrialized countries	538.9	588.4	562.1	516.9	511.4	497.9	520.7	588.6	699.0	766.7	878.7
Africa	82.8	89.7	79.6	69.1	64.9	55.9	54.2	57.6	64.0	64.8	72.1
Asia	160.8	177.6	174.0	178.8	192.3	200.8	231.3	293.7	367.2	418.0	473.3
Middle East	113.3	135.2	148.7	133.1	120.2	102.0	91.2	90.5	101.1	97.7	n/a
Western Hemisphere	113.8	119.2	94.4	75.9	74.9	72.2	71.8	81.3	91.1	100.6	111.5

Notes: In billions of US dollars using current exchange rates averaged over the cited year.
Source: IMF (1995).
Data source: International financial statistics, International Monetary Fund, 1980–95. Statistics for specific countries, as well as regional definitions, can be found in these publications.

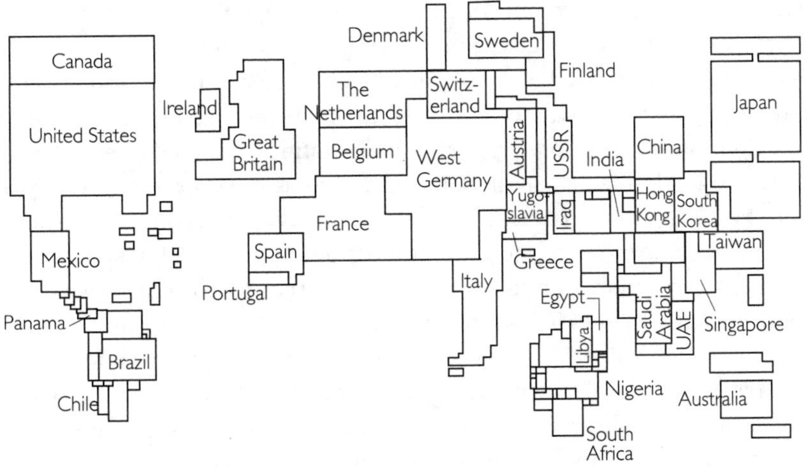

Figure 1.2 Countries of the world, scaled to their international trade. In this map, the area of each country is drawn proportional to its share of total world trade in 1985. Compare the size of the advanced industrial countries with that of Africa and Asia. (Adapted from M. Kidron & R. Segal, *The new state of the world atlas*. New York: Simon & Schuster, 1987.)

Figure 1.2 offers a graphic depiction of international trade patterns. The area of each country drawn there is proportional to its share of total world trade (exports) in 1991; and so it depicts not only the OECD nations that dominate the current international marketplace, but also Asian and African nations where the potential for future expansion and growth is the largest. Table 1.4 offers an

Table 1.4 Major categories of United States exports and imports (1993).

Commodity classification	Share of each commodity as percent of total: Exports	Imports
Industrial supplies		
Oil, coal, and other fuels	3	11
Food	10	5
Other	23	16
Manufactures		
Capital goods		
Computers and related equipment	13	11
Aircraft	9	3
Other	19	12
Motor vehicles	11	18
Consumer goods	12	24
Total	100	100

Source: Samuelson & Nordhaus (1995).

aggregated view of the composition of trade for the United States in 1993—one of the world's most advanced economies in a year of continued trade expansion. It reveals that the United States still exports a large volume of primary commodities, notably food and coal—evidence of an ample resource base. At the same time, the United States imports large quantities of capital-intensive manufactured goods such as automobiles and various types of electronic equipment. Perhaps most surprising, although actually quite typical of advanced economies, some industries (e.g., computers and motor vehicles) show sizable quantities of exports *and* imports. Similar data can be found routinely in another monthly International Monetary Fund publication, *Direction of trade statistics.*

The important question is, of course, what this expansion of international trade means for global climate change and for policies to deal with it. The standard economic models can provide some insights into the relationship of trade to economic growth and its implications for climate policy.

International trade can, for the most part, be explained in terms of conventional market constructions of supply and demand, but there are limits to economists' ability to straddle international borders with simple translations of domestic market analyses. International transactions must deal with multiple currencies, a variety of domestic policies that influence transactions in one but not all sovereign nations, and a complex litany of international trading restrictions, even as they seek to deliver the elusive gains from trade. However, the data suggest that international trade is growing, so the economic gains must be there for the taking.

Trade among nations reflects the diversity of tastes and productive possibilities that span the globe. On the supply side, different countries are endowed with different natural resources, so countries find it beneficial to trade the fundamental inputs of production. Countries also differ in their productive potential, so that they seek to exploit their economies of scale that lower the average cost of production of some good as the volume of output expands: they sell such goods abroad. On the demand side, tastes vary and drive any nation's citizens to seek expanded trading opportunities.

The result of all of this complication can still best be understood in terms of the Ricardian notion of comparative advantage—each country should benefit from trade if it tends to specialize in the production and potential export of those goods and services that it can offer to the world marketplace at relatively lower cost and import those goods and services which it finds both attractive and relatively costly to produce.

Comparative advantage has its limitations, though. It is based upon classical assumptions of smoothly working competitive markets within and between nations; and so it is based explicitly on the assumption that labor markets will adapt to any change to maintain full employment. But what if labor markets do not adapt, and trade causes dislocation and unemployment? Significant opposition to trade can emerge, and barriers to trade can be constructed. Even if labor market response can be anticipated, expanded trade does not mean that everyone will be better off unless some of the gains from the expansion are distributed to workers whose real wages might fall in its wake. The opening of trade tends to harmonize wages across national boundaries, in short, so that the gains from trade are not ubiquitous. Exchange rates muddle the workings of international markets even more.

The links between economic growth and international trade are complex and potentially very confusing. Indeed, even basic trade theory texts (e.g., Gray 1978) go to great lengths to explain that there is simply no straightforward correlation between one and the other. For example, economic growth might be expected to be an engine for expanded trade. However, this need not be the case. The correlation of trade and growth depends upon:

- the effect of growth on the relative (world) prices of exportables and importables (prices dubbed the "terms of trade" in the literature)
- the degree to which growth favors the domestic production of exportables over the domestic production of importables
- the degree to which growth increases domestic demand for exportables relative to the domestic demand for importables.

Scenarios in which growth works to retard trade and to produce a drag on future growth are just as easy to create as those in which growth works to promote trade and to ignite a second spurt of future growth. In the first scenario, growth in one country favors its exportables (so that they become relatively less expensive as world markets adjust to new supply conditions), turns the terms of trade against those exportables (so that importables become relatively more expensive), and nonetheless produces income effects that cause the demand at home for imports to rise even as the demand for exportables falls. In the second type of scenario, growth moves everything the other way.

Trade, growth, and the environment

How do these insights about economic growth and international trade relate to environmental concerns? The standard presumption in the political economy of international trade is that domestic environmental questions should remain in the hands of domestic policymakers. The argument is that any attempt to force a country to move in either direction from its self-selected environmental stance would be inefficient and would make that country worse off. This argument has been raised in the context of wage rates, where markets exist to facilitate adjustment, but the idea is the same: the harmonization of national environmental policies (by policy decree) can be just as weak as the harmonization of wages (by market adaptation). The fundamental question, then, is whether or not the argument against harmonization holds for regional pollutants and, perhaps more fundamentally, for global pollutants (Box 1.4).

Box 1.4 Harmonizing climate change policies

The European Union (EU) has since the early 1980s been engaged in a process of *harmonization* of economic and environmental goals, regulations, and practices.

The EU pursues its agenda of greater uniformity through two policy instruments. First is the EU Directive, which sets a goal (such as maximum permitted levels of nitrates in drinking water), but under the principle of *subsidiarity*, permits member states to determine how they will meet that goal.

The second category of instruments comprises uniform European regulations. For example, standards specify which varieties of fruits and vegetables may be offered for sale. Bans, such as a proposed ban on heavy motorcycles, prohibit the use of certain products within the entire EU. However, efforts to introduce community-wide taxes, such as an EU-wide carbon tax, have been defeated because of sovereignty concerns on the part of member states such as the United Kingdom.

One of the characteristics distinguishing the EU from other international organizations is its ability to adopt legislation that is directly binding on member states without further review or ratification by their national legislatures. Harmonization, particularly in relation to product and production standards, is widely viewed as essential to the EU's goal to establish a single market. However, there is considerable breadth of opinion about the effectiveness of such policies. For example, problems may arise from widespread variation in the institutionalized meanings of apparently common terminologies. In attempting the harmonize its handling of hazardous waste, the EU stumbled across a morass of different understandings even of the terms *hazard* and *waste*. On the other hand, the EU has adopted several hundred items of environmental legislation, most having a narrow technical content.

Nordhaus (1994b) reviewed the first principles of the economic paradigm as applied to international trade to argue that the answers to these questions are "yes" for regional pollutants and "no" for global pollutants. For the first case, the trade literature supports what many hold to be a contentious result. Nordhaus noted first that local or national pollutants can be viewed as nontradeable goods (bads) in the Ricardian sense that they cannot (do not, actually, by definition) move across national borders. Then, assuming that environmental quality is priced correctly within any nation or region and that the standard assumptions of classical trade theory hold, all of the apparatus of classical trade theory applies to show that the full set of internal, national competitive equilibria are optimal. Global efficiency in these cases therefore requires that countries do not harmonize their environmental policies. It follows that any attempt to do so (e.g., uniformly holding local emissions to 1990 levels) would reduce potential economic welfare. Any move toward harmonization would increase the economic cost of achieving any specific set of environmental objectives by forcing countries with high costs of meeting a given set of environmental objectives to meet the same requirements as countries with low costs.

This is a result that runs counter to the perspective of many who see harmonization as a nonnegotiable objective on grounds of simplicity or equity; and it also runs counter to the perspective of many who support free trade and see differential environmental standards as hidden barriers to trade.

The first group fundamentally questions whether or not local environmental quality can be correctly priced internally. To assume so rests on the notion that governments can be relied upon to value their environmental resources correctly from a social perspective; that is, that governments have both the desire and the wherewithal to try to maximize social welfare. To the extent that they do, the assumption stands; to the extent that governments fail, the assumption falters. However, this analysis begs the question of how to persuade governments to set internal prices correctly; and it does not offer any convincing argument that harmonized policies would do any better.

The supporters of free trade do not really question whether or not the classical assumptions required in the result hold. Rather, they worry that the power of these assumptions might be exploited by governments that would lower environmental standards in a race toward increased international competitiveness. To do so would, of course, be to pursue a "beggar thyself" policy that would be difficult to sustain over the long term. Another issue involves adjustment and the degree to which local or national competition might ultimately stimulate countries to find increasingly cost-effective ways of mitigating environmental damage (Box 1.5).

The case of global pollution is entirely different. Nordhaus is not alone in noting that global efficiency in controlling a global pollutant requires that countries harmonize their environmental policies in the sense of equalizing the marginal cost of emissions reductions across all sources. Why? Because to do otherwise would leave the most efficient solution unrealized. But this result does not support equal (proportional) quantity standards any more than the result for local pollution did. Although such policies have the advantage of simplicity, they are excessively costly even for a global pollutant, except in the improbable case in which the level and rates of growth of all marginal cost functions were identical.

Cost–benefit analysis applied to growth and climate

As suggested by even a casual reading of the Nordhaus (1994a,b) treatment of trade and the environment, economists like to evaluate the relative efficacy of

Box 1.5 Industrial location and the environment

The links between the location of economic activity and environmental issues run both ways. If economic activity generates localized pollution, then those areas with the most concentrated activity will tend to be more polluted. If environmental regulation imposes costs on business and regulations differ across locations, firms might choose to go where regulations are least strict. Economists have concentrated on the latter; the former appears to most to be more of an engineering question. Careful application of economic principles can nonetheless allow researchers to concentrate on the location decision.

As with most economic decisions, issues of location can be treated as optimal choice problems: many potential sites differ in terms of various characteristics (including environmental regulation), and a firm chooses the best location, where "best" is usually assumed to mean "profit-maximizing." The cost minimization procedures that produce cost curves are therefore implicitly assumed, and so environmental regulation could influence the location choice if regulatory stringency raises production costs. Firms will tend to leave high-regulation areas, or locate fewer new plants there, as long as any beneficial effects of regulation (e.g., a cleaner environment allowing the firm to attract better workers) are outweighed by the costs of complying with the regulation. Analyses of the respective costs and benefits might include concepts that would be familiar to a wide range of social scientists, but the economic perspective puts the greatest emphasis on dollar-denominated factors such as wages and taxes.

Considering the interactions among a variety of decisions broadens the applicability of the economic perspective. Oates & Schwab (1988), for example, identified the straightforward pressures on regulators to relax stringency in order to attract new businesses, leading to environmental standards that are too lax. In a more complex model, Markusen et. al. (1994) expanded the scope to three "players": two areas and a firm. Decisionmakers in each area must decide how stringent their regulations will be; decisionmakers in the firm wait to find out the level of stringency before deciding where to locate the firm's productive activities. The model captures the two opposing pressures on regulators: a desire to gain the jobs and income associated with the plant and a desire to avoid the associated pollution. Economic analyses show that regulators will tend to set excessively stringent standards, trying to encourage the firms to locate in the other area, if the pollution would be severe and/or very local. This is the classic NIMBY ("not in my back yard") response. However, if the pollution effects would be more general, standards would tend to be set too loosely, since the costs from the pollution are partially borne by the other area.

Empirical economic studies of location generally develop quantitative measures of actual location decisions and try to relate those measures to the measured characteristics of the areas chosen. These studies typically work with relatively large sample sizes (larger than the survey samples employed in other approaches, for example), but many have had trouble quantifying differences in environmental regulation across areas. Their results, therefore, may be very sensitive to the estimation method actually employed.

The most common statistical approach, for instance, uses plant-level data on locations of new plants to look at how differences in regulation across areas affect which area is chosen. It embraces the idea of competition between states for new plants, but it treats the number of new plants as given. As a result, an equal increase in regulation across all areas should have no impact on plant location, because the differences in regulation across areas are unaffected and, by assumption, so is the total number of new plants.

More direct regression analyses, and those based upon specific (e.g., Poisson) distributions for the creation of new firms, have the advantage of capturing the impact of a general increase in regulation, but they give up most of the sense of competition. In these approaches, an increase in regulation for a given area has the same impact on new plant location, regardless of whether or not other areas have the same increase in regulation.

Most studies seem to show some effect of regulation on plant location, but the estimated effect is generally small (especially compared to other economic factors such as wage differentials, unionization, or product demand). Direct measures of regulation (attainment status, enforcement activity, or indices of stringency) tend to show a more negative impact than do measures of regulatory spending (either by state regulators or by manufacturing firms). Studies using new plant openings in a conditional LOGIT framework seem less likely to find a significant impact. Some evidence shows a feedback effect of industrial location on air quality.

Although most of the empirical results to date are based on US data, there are implications for international differences in regulatory stringency. The results may suggest that it might make economic sense for developing countries to relax regulation. Poorer workers in poorer countries might place a high value on the jobs and a low value on the reduced pollution; and so, the argument goes, they might see some real advantage to such a trade. Calibrating this advantage so that the net global effect would be positive is, of course, difficult. Global insulation from the local cost would be certain only if the pollution were local, so that the same people who would reap the benefits lower regulation would bear the corresponding higher (environmental) costs. Aside from the ethical issues involved in endorsing such a trade, localized pollution is not universal. Researchers and decisionmakers seeking solutions to global environmental problems that require global regulatory solutions are thus warned that local incentives designed to influence industrial location decisions could easily hinder their ability to reach global regulatory goals.

many decisions, including decisions on how to manage the environment, in terms of their costs and benefits. Reaching beyond the traditional bounds of simple project analysis, modern cost–benefit analysis has investigated optimal provisions of public goods, the efficient level of ambient air and water quality, and other complex environmental issues. Many studies have been completed on these issues. The results of these studies would be reliable so long as they are guided by markets in their computation of costs and benefits and they have the welfare properties of competitive equilibria to use as benchmarks. Market demand and supply curves (or at least marginal cost schedules) support the specification of benefit and cost schedules, and decisions are made with an eye toward maximizing net benefits.

Cost–benefit analysis can lead the way toward allocations of resources that equate marginal costs with marginal benefits, just like a competitive market; and so the promise of improved if not maximized welfare is offered. The key assumption underlying this promise is that policies that produce benefits in excess of costs allow for the possibility of Pareto improvement; that is, enough economic surplus is created to permit full compensation of individuals who bear the cost of the policy by those who reap its benefits. Compensation schemes designed to accomplish this transfer are seldom part of the plan, of course; but it is enough for the paradigm that they could be.

The Intergovernmental Panel on Climate Change (IPCC) offered a chapter on cost–benefit analysis and its strengths and weaknesses (Munasinghe et al. 1996), which will not be repeated here. The cost–benefit analysis techniques can be adapted to a variety of types of data, with techniques varying from traditional project level cost–benefit analysis through cost effectiveness, multicriteria analysis, and decision analysis. Insights from such an expanded cost–benefit analysis are exemplified by the Richels & Edmonds (1995) findings that carbon dioxide stabilization could be achieved at a much lower cost if emissions were not stabilized immediately. The techniques of cost–benefit analysis, because they force at least semiquantitative thinking about climate policy, have highlighted the issue of uncertainty. Nordhaus (1994a) has used the framework to calculate the value of information on various aspects of the climate problem.

The integrated assessment community has, for the most part, adopted the cost–benefit paradigm in its portrayal of how best to design mitigation policy in the face of the threat of global change (see Ch. 5). At least ten models with varying degrees of sectoral detail and (dis)aggregation weigh global costs against global benefits to compute optimal mitigation policies. Each model sets marginal cost against marginal benefit and assumes that winners will compensate losers across international and intergenerational boundaries.

In dealing with global climate policy, some observers treat the emissions of greenhouse gases and the potential impacts of climate as if they were fixed physical relationships. For example, several vulnerability assessments of potential sea level rise have estimated potential damages as the (growing) value of resources placed at risk. A survey of such studies appears in Bijlsma et al. (1996). Yet standard economics reminds that markets and adaptive behavior can play a major role in modifying these effects through the real estate market. Economic damage that might be attributed to future sea level rise (in the absence of any decision to protect threatened property) must be calculated in terms of the value of that property at the (future) time of inundation. This value will include any adaptation that might have occurred naturally and efficiently prior to flooding and abandonment.

Satisfactory descriptions of how future development might affect coastline real estate values can be derived from empirical market analyses of driving socioeconomic variables such as population and real income. Changes in these variables will be reflected in fluctuations of real estate values over the same timeframe. Applied with care in the absence of any anticipated fundamental structural change in the real estate marketplace, the resulting development trajectories offer representative portraits of the evolving value of real estate vulnerable to sea level rise.

However, to determine the likely actual losses, this information must be combined with an assessment of how real estate markets actually work. Satisfactory descriptions of how real estate markets might respond on a more micro, local level in the face of threatened inundation from rising seas are difficult to create. Yohe (1990) provided some insight into how to proceed in his preliminary construction of vulnerability estimates for the United States. Yohe et al. (1995) later calculated economic cost. Land and structures had to be considered separately because the adaptation options open to the market differ. On the one hand, the value of the land lost to rising seas should, in most cases, be estimated on the basis of the value of land located far inland from the ocean. Any price gradient that placed higher values on parcels of land in direct correlation with their proximity to the ocean would, in a very real sense, simply migrate inland as shoreline property disappeared under rising seas.

Ignoring what could be significant transfers of wealth between owners, the true economic cost of inundation would be captured in most cases by the value of the land that was lost in an economic sense—interior land equal in area to the abandoned and inundated property. The exception to this procedure occurs when rising seas threaten a barrier island where the property value gradient encroaches from two sides. It is still possible to use the value of interior land to reflect costs, but care must be taken to note when interior values begin to reflect the higher values that define both gradients from the inside out.

In contrast to the case of lost land, the economic value of structures that might be lost to sea level rise would depreciate over time as the threat of impending inundation and abandonment became known. Structures would be lost at the moment of inundation, to be sure, but their true economic value at that point could be zero with enough advanced warning and with a complete understanding that the property would, indeed, be abandoned when the time came to retreat from the sea. Despite stories of individuals' reluctance to abandon threatened property in, for example, floodplains, the literature that records the results of investigations into how markets react to low probability and high cost events strongly supports the assertion that market-clearing real estate prices do indeed decline over time in response to the pending cost of a growing threat.

Brookshire et al. (1985) examined the validity of the expected utility hypothesis as a model of homeowner behavior in the face of low probability and high severity risk—earthquakes in this case. They found evidence to support the hypothesis in peoples' response to expert and legal descriptions of risk, even when the same people did not respond privately by purchasing disaster insurance. The Brookshire work was reinforced by MacDonald et al. (1987) after an analysis of homeowner behavior in the face of the threat of flooding. All of this work offers evidence to suggest that market values should accurately process information provided by experts on low probability natural hazards.

The assumption made in the sea level application extends that conclusion and argues that property prices should, over the very long term in the face of gradual manifestations of global warming, internalize the threat of rising seas, given some validating informational authority (provided perhaps as informally as some loosely documented history of sea level rise).

True economic depreciation (TED), modeled to start at some fixed time prior to inundation and to finish just when inundation would occur, is an appropriate representation of the maximally efficient market response to (known) risk of future sea level rise. TED is, by definition, a representation of how the value of an asset declines over time as it moves toward its retirement from service. Samuelson (1964) introduced the notion in a different context, but it applies equally well here. Its application to the cost of sea level rise supports the position that the true economic cost of structures lost to rising seas could be as low as zero, with sufficient warning.

Uncertain abandonment, caused by imprecise understanding of the rate of future sea level rise or a disbelief that existing property would actually be abandoned, would affect efficiency. Either a source of imperfect information or an incomplete reaction to the threat of rising seas could, for example, shrink the time period over which markets could react to the threat of rising seas. The value of lost structures under these conditions would not be zero; it would, instead, equal the remaining value of (shoreline) structure at the time of inundation. True economic depreciation takes a mirror-image trajectory over time, compared with the more familiar concept of accelerated depreciation. The actual trajectory depends upon the discount rate, but (for example) ten years of depreciation against a 30-year time horizon would, for all positive rates, mean that more than 67 percent of the true economic value of the structure would remain.

The worst case of imperfect information and uncertain abandonment would allow absolutely no warning and thus no time for any structural depreciation at all. Consideration of this case takes the lack of information to an extreme, caused more by a sudden realization that the policy of abandonment would be followed than a sudden realization that the oceans have risen. It would, however, capture the situation in which the cost attributed to rising seas would be maximized in either case.

The importance of taking efficiency-based adaptation actions can hardly be overstated. Table 1.5 replicates table 6 in Yohe et al. (1996). It shows that cost estimates for the United States along two selected sea level trajectories are a full order of magnitude lower than previous estimates based upon vulnerability calculations. However, these new estimates assume market adaptation in anticipation of inundation and protection decisions based upon a cost–benefit calculation that ignores the redistribution of wealth associated with the planned abandonment of property.

Table 1.5 The potential cost of sea level rise along the developed coastline of the United States (1990 billion US$).

Amount of sea level rise and source cited	Type of estimate	Amortized	Cumulative	Transient (2065)
4.6m				
Schneider & Chan (1980)	Vulnerability	n/a	$347	n/a
7.6m	Vulnerability	n/a	$474	n/a
Schneider & Chen (1980)				
100cm				
Yohe (1990)	Vulnerability	n/a	$321	$1.37
EPA (1989)	Protection	n/a	$73–$111	n/a
Nordhaus (1991)	Protection	$4.9	n/a	n/a
Cline (1992)	Protection	$1.2	$240	n/a
Fankhauser (1994a)	Protection	$1.0	$62.6	n/a
Yohe, et al. (1996)	Protection	$0.16	$36.1	$0.33
	Abandonment	$0.19	$45.4	$0.38
50cm				
Yohe (1990)	Vulnerability	n/a	$138	n/a
Cline (1992)	Protection	$3.6	$120	n/a
Fankhauser (1994b)	Protection	$0.57	$35.6	n/a
Yohe et al. (1996)	Protection and abandonment	$0.06	$20.4	$0.07

Note: All of the cumulative estimates but Fankhauser's are undiscounted; His are discounted effectively by the annual rate of growth of per capita GNP (expected to average approximately 1.6% for the US through 2100).
Source: Yohe et al. (1996).

Institutional structure and environmental consequences

The economic theory of how environmental resources are used centers on the notion of incomplete markets and externalities. Ordinary market activity uses natural resources, removing them from the natural environment for use as inputs, and then returns residual byproducts of production and consumption back to the environment. This process often degrades the quality of amenities and services that environmental media provide for their inhabitants. Such degradation is generally excessive, in the sense of imposing net costs that exceed the net benefits of degradation, because environmental costs are largely unrecognized in private economic decisions. They are unrecognized because the environmental resources affected are unowned—no owner can demand compensation when the service flow provided by an environmental resource is impaired. This theory prescribes the role for government as either to institute effective ownership, for example, by adopting regulations or marketable permit systems to regulate use, or to adopt policies that mimic the outcome a market would achieve, for example, by imposing a tax or fee on resource use.

This view of how environmental resources are used is incomplete, in large part because it does not recognize the imperfection and costliness of the enforcement process for ownership rights. Whether a particular environmental resource is owned, and hence whether the costs and benefits of using it are internal or external to the user, is taken as given, determined outside the policy analyst's model. One source of important variation, however, is in the form and stability of government from country to country, as the form of government is one determinant of the pattern of ownership in a country. More complete economic analysis has recognized that variation in government form and stability has implications for the policies that will be effective in controlling externalities. Policy prescriptions designed with country A's context in mind may make no sense in country B, either because they are not politically compatible with B's system of government or because they require a degree of policy continuity not present in B.

Empirical evidence relating to the effect of political regimes on environmental outcomes is scanty at best. It is consistent with anecdotes and casual observation of levels of environmental protection in the former Soviet bloc nations. Pollution control, a public good that generally benefits the population at large, was largely neglected by these regimes. One relevant statistical test was performed by Grossman & Krueger (1993) as part of a study of international variations in air pollution levels. The partial effect of a communist government was found to be statistically significant for sulfur dioxide and for one of the two measures of particulates. Moreover, the effect was large, ranging from one-third to four-fifths of the mean concentration level for the entire sample. A dummy variable for communism is, of course, only a rough measure of the degree of government representation.

Another hypothesis is that investments in manufactured capital and natural resource conservation will be most extensive in countries ruled by stable laws, precedent, and impersonal institutions, because ownership security is greatest (transactions costs associated with enforcement of ownership rights and contracts are lowest) in these circumstances. The idea here is that the incentive to invest or conserve is diminished if the individual who bears the cost of such actions cannot be sure of enjoying the ultimate payoff.

Ownership insecurity (whether individual or social) has implications for the use of forests, for example, because allowing a forest to grow and provide a stream of output or services in future years, rather than consuming it immediately, is a form of investment. Insecure ownership rights might induce short rotations on land used to grow timber or biomass for shifting cultivation, or eliminate incentives to replant land that has been cut over. Insecurity also weakens incentives to develop plantation forests and village wood-lots for timber and fuelwood—investments that would reduce pressure on natural forests. These considerations indicate a possible link between insecure ownership and loss of forest cover (see the discussion of land tenure in Vol. 2, Ch. 2). This is a significant issue for global change, because emissions from land clearing could increase, carbon uptake from forests could be reduced, and the resiliency of human and natural systems affected by climate change could be reduced.

The political factors that might be associated with ownership risk are arguably of two sorts. The first are instability and general lawlessness—indicators that government lacks the power, stability, and popular support to enforce ownership laws. Specific indicators might include the occurrence of guerrilla warfare, armed revolt, and the frequency of major constitutional changes. The second set would indicate whether a country is ruled by specific individuals and dominant elites rather than by laws and anonymous institutions. They might indicate whether the head of government is a military dictator, whether a legislature exists, and so forth. By hypothesis, the average citizen's ownership claim is weaker and less predictable when it depends on the favor of a specific individual, and upon the individual's grip on power, rather than the persistence of established (and more predictable) legal institutions.

A simple way to examine and test these hypotheses is to compare the political attributes of countries experiencing high versus low deforestation rates. Data on deforestation rates, investment rates, and political attributes were collected, and countries in the sample were partitioned in two ways. The first partition places countries into high versus low deforestation rates, depending on whether their percentage reduction in forest cover over the period 1980–85 was greater or less than 10 percent. The second partition depends on whether their investment was greater or less than 10 percent of GDP during 1980–1985.

Table 1.6 reports mean political attributes for both partitions. Twenty high-income countries were excluded from all comparisons to deflect the potential criticism that these nations are not comparable to less industrialized countries. All of the measures of government instability are higher in high deforestation countries (see Deacon 1994 for additional political measures). Three of the four instability measures also are higher in low investment countries. The single exception, more frequent government crises in the high investment group, has no ready explanation except that two countries (Bolivia and Liberia) dominated this political indicator during the period examined. Tests for associations with measures of nonrepresentation in government also are as expected—deforestation rates are high and investment rates low where the country's chief executive is a military dictator, where no legislature exists, and so forth.

These results reinforce findings from an extensive body of empirical research on the relationship between political insecurity, investment and economic growth. Barro (1991) examined crosscountry data and found certain measures of political turmoil to be negatively related to growth and investment rates, suggesting the influence of incomplete ownership in volatile political regimes. Persson & Tabellini (1990), Ozler & Rodrik (1992), Alesina et al. (1991), and

Table 1.6 Deforestation, investment and political attributes (means of political attributes, 1980–85).

	Deforestation rate		Investment rate	
	High	Low	Low	High
Measures of government instability				
Guerrilla warfare	.333*	.205*	.326	.184
Revolutions	.326*	.186*	.410*	.150*
Major government crises	.144	.068	.035*	.089*
Major constitutional changes	.114*	.070*	.118*	.064*
Indicators of nonrepresentation				
Government executive is military	.242*	.094*	.230*	.070*
Nonelected executive	.439	.318	.490*	.310*
Executive is not a premier	.614*	.412*	.640*	.370*
No legislature exists	.174	.141	.320*	.130*
Legislature is elected	.788	.842	.660*	.820*
Number of countries	22	78	24	86

*Difference in mean political attribute between high and low deforestation, or high and low investment countries, is significant at 10 percent.

Definitions:

Guerrilla warfare is the presence of any armed activity, sabotage, or bombings carried on by independent bands of citizens or irregular forces and aimed at the overthrow of the present regime. A *revolution* is an attempted illegal or forced change in top government elite, or armed rebellion intended to gain independence from the central government. A *major government crisis* is a rapidly developing situation that threatens to bring the downfall of the present regime–excluding revolt aimed at such overthrow. A *major constitutional change* is a basic alteration in a state's constitutional structure, e.g., adoption of a new constitution that alters roles of different branches of government (minor constitutional amendments are excluded.) *Government executive is military* indicates that the individual who exercises primary influence in shaping the country's major internal and external decisions is in the armed services. *Executive is not a premier* indicates that the executive is not drawn from the legislature of a parliamentary democracy. *Legislature is elected* indicates that a legislature exists and that legislators are chosen either by direct or indirect election. Other measures are self-explanatory.

others corroborated the importance of political factors in the investment behavior of countries. Keefer & Knack (1994) and Clague et al. (1995) have found significant associations between property rights measures and systems of government that are stable and representative.

These results also lend support to recent work on the role of nominal ownership rights in determining environmental outcomes. Southgate et al. (1991) showed that security of tenure, as measured by the prevalence of adjudicated land-claims, is negatively related to deforestation rates in Ecuador. Alston et al. (1994) presented evidence from Brazil that the existence of adjudicated land-claims enhances incentives for agricultural investments, and that land-claim adjudication is slower and less complete in areas where government jurisdiction is disputed. Pearce & Bann (1993) summarized other empirical research on the determinants of deforestation.

Limitations and critiques of the standard paradigm for climate policy analysis

Earlier sections have emphasized that the interpretation of economic activity is highly dependent on the organization and specification of particular economic models. Although these models are well established, they are not universally accepted, and they certainly have a long and rich history of controversy.

Global change is part of a class of policy problems that tend to exacerbate the shortcomings of the mainstream approach in economics. Examining policy in the context of global change brings attention not only to methodological or analytical component, but also to certain scope or domain considerations. The complex interactions of highly interdependent systems and the long-term nature of the decision problem are features that analysts have recognized as particularly important for global environmental problems. Concepts such as intergenerational equity, stewardship, and sustainability are often at odds with the growth and efficiency paradigm that has dominated the traditional models.

This section discusses various criticisms, and extensions to the traditional economic perspective that are particularly important for the type of complex, long-term, and far-reaching decision problems inherent in global change policies. The discussion emphasizes key model components that have been somewhat minimized in standard treatments and key extensions to the scope of the models that emerge from consideration of the relationships between economic and environmental systems.

For clarity, we separate the list of issues into two general categories: measurement problems, and concept and domain problems. The first category is one where we expect better methods and data might eventually lead to resolution of the problems. The second category, however, is more problematic, and we anticipate that resolving scope problems will require substantial theoretical and conceptual changes in the traditional approach.

Measurement problems

Many goods and services are traded or otherwise made available in every part of the world through nonmarket mechanisms. For example, neighborhoods populated by individuals who are excluded from formal market share developed trading and exchange systems for goods and services employing a variety of skills (Whyte 1955, Liebow 1967, Dow 1977). Studies of low-income neighborhoods showed that these trading networks serve to integrate the community and provide a social fabric of mutual aid and support (Lowenthal 1975, 1981). Other studies showed that not only the poor trade in informal exchange structures. Disillusion with established helping services and declines in the traditional systems of social support, such as the family, have led to expansion of nonmarket exchange structures that provide self-help and mutual aid among group members (Katz & Bender 1976, Robinson & Henry 1977).

Many important relationships, which are actually economic or have important economic attributes, are transacted through nonmarket institutions and arrangements. For example, the dominance of Hassidic Jews in the New York wholesale diamond market significantly reduces transaction costs to the extent that the entire business is conducted by passing packets of stones from trader to trader, tracked only by handwritten slips of paper. Although cheating would be easy, it would probably result in ostracism from the community, that is, social death. This gives rise to measurement problems because economic measurements are done best when those things measured are traded in markets.

Informal economic activity and national income accounting

The contributions of informal sectors to the economies of industrialized and less industrialized nations can be huge—often as large as the official sectors of some smaller nations. Consequently, informal sectors influence the transmission of macroeconomic policies and can sometimes cause those policies to produce contrary results. Global modelers and decisionmakers must begin to understand the workings of informal sectors and to incorporate their dynamics explicitly into an overall view of economic activity. This subsection will examine the problem in industrialized and less industrialized countries.

All activity that lies beyond the pale of official regulation and control is considered informal. In less industrialized nations, the informal economy also includes many activities in traditional and rural sectors that continue to lie outside the bounds defining systemic linkages with formal institutions. Searching over both sets of activities, researchers have identified four broad classes of informal economic activity:

- activities that generate goods, services, and income that are not recognized in the official estimates (such as subsistence agriculture)
- activities that are recognized for official accounts and are not intrinsically unlawful, but are nonetheless arranged so that no official record is reported (such as unlicensed and unrecorded extraction of coal from open-pit mines as far afield as Appalachia and India)
- illegal activities (such as narcotics trading, prostitution, or theft of electricity through illegal hookups and distribution networks)
- myriad activities in the rural traditional sector and in the urban periphery of less industrialized countries, activities that occur outside the domain of established institutions (such as fuelwood extraction from forests and woodlands).

Table 1.7 records some estimates of the size of the informal economy in several less industrialized countries and in some specific urban areas. The measures reported there are not exactly comparable, but their dimension is nearly as impressive as the diversity of the activity that they reflect.

Informal activities in urban areas include, for example, street trading, unregistered factories and shops, informal housing, self-employment in private transport, scavenging, casual labor transactions in urban construction, and domestic service. Traditional sectors meanwhile include activities such as artisan work, cattle tending, household employment by women (including collecting fuelwood, dung, and drinking water; see Cecelski 1991), irrigation transactions among farmers (see Kolavalli & Chicoine 1989 or Shah 1993), and subsistence agriculture. Table 1.7 also shows that informal financial markets can play a large role in less industrialized nations. Informal credit transactions take place between family members and friends, to be sure, but informal lending mechanisms provide significant credit to small enterprises and households across the less industrialized world.

Regardless of its form, informal activity in less industrialized countries can generally be viewed in terms of the response of economic agents to their economic environments. Informal markets serve varied purposes. Lowenthal (1975, 1981), for example, argued that informal markets integrate the community and provide a safety net. In the informal sector of less industrialized countries, moreover, the information embodied in the operation of product and factor markets is thin and the underlying institutional structure is weak. Consequently, the market does not resemble the smoothly operating institution

Table 1.7 The informal economy in less industrialized nations.

Country/location	Estimate	Year	Source
India	80% of GDP	1990	Bose (1993)
Zambia	95% of GDP	1990	" "
Argentina	98% of GDP	1990	" "
Calcutta	40–50% of employment	1971	Sethuraman (1981)
Jakarta	45% of employment	1976	" "
Bombay	45% of employment	1961	Heather & Joshi (1976)
Latin America	30–57% of urban employment	1975	Lubell (1982)
India	Black income = 51% of GDP	1987	Gupta (1992)
Cameroun	Informal institutions hold 58% of total savings	1988	Lubell (1982)
Sri Lanka	40% of credit informal	1980s	Montiel (1993)
India	40% of credit informal	1980s	" "
Bangladesh	33–67% of credit informal	1980s	" "
China	" " " "	1980s	" "
Malaysia	67–75% of credit informal	1980s	" "
Nepal	" " " "	1980s	" "
Pakistan	" " " "	1980s	" "
Thailand	" " " "	1980s	" "

Source: Shukla 1994

assumed by simple neoclassical economics. Geertz (1978) saw the resulting personalized and informal contracts as ways to deal with imperfect information and institutional gaps.

Cantor et al. (1992) noted that exchange rules of the traditional and informal economies are often different and deserve separate consideration. Traditional sectors in less industrialized nations are typically decentralized and isolated; the economic activities that they support are therefore performed within localized, mainly rural, and effectively isolated spheres. Linkages among these localized economies are weak, and so the exchange of goods, services, and technological innovations is minimal. Difficulties in establishing a credible and widely accepted currency, and feeble financial institutions act as barriers to the flow of finance across sectors and regions. Interest rates in traditional sectors are thus generally higher than in the formal sector, and so the penetration of efficient technologies is retarded even more. Characteristics of technological progress in traditional sectors of less industrialized nations must therefore be very different, both from their counterparts in the industrialized nations and from other more modern segments of their own economies. Inasmuch as the results of the models of energy and greenhouse gas abatement policy analysis currently in vogue depend critically on the assumptions about future technological progress and market penetration, the technological relationships assumed for less industrialized nations can be misleading.

Finally, informal economic activity is not confined to less industrialized economies. Several studies report estimates of the size and growth of the informal activity within a few industrial nations. The estimates recorded in Table 1.8 vary widely—owing in large measure to inaccurate data and differences in the ranges of activities included in the estimate.

Table 1.8 The informal economy in industrialized economies.

Country	Estimate (% of GNP, except USA)	Year	Source
United States	$270 billion	1988	IRS (1988)
Canada	10	1982	Mirus & Smith (1989)
Sweden	3.8–6/8	1988	Hansson (1989)
Italy	9.4	1977	Contini (1989)
France	6.7	1979	Barthelemy (1989)
Netherlands	1.8–9.1	1979	Broesterhuizen
United Kingdom	3	1977	Dilnot & Moris (1981)
	15	1979	Feige (1981)
	7.5–9.3	1982	Bhattachryya (1990)
West Germany	8–12	1980	Kirchgaessner (1983)
Japan	3.9	1980	Langfeldt (1989)
European Community	12	n/a	Manasian et al. (1987)

Source: Shukla (1994).

Measuring inequality in the global distribution of income

Much of global climate policy is concerned with equity—the measurement and sharing of the burdens of impacts and mitigation costs across countries, regions, and income and ethnic groups. For example, Bruce et al. (1996) recognized costs related to damages, to protection or adaptation, and losses from extreme events. They devote a chapter to equity considerations. The impacts of each of those sources of cost could be distributed quite differently across regions and groups, but the parties to the FCCC disagree concerning even the appropriate burden-sharing principles (see Vol. 1, Ch. 4). Social welfare analysis has not been attempted.

Measurement of equality or inequality across the distribution of any economic variable is a difficult problem under the best data conditions. There are enormous methodological difficulties to overcome, but these are only part of the problem of comparing international and intertemporal income inequality. Issues of scale, comparability of data, and quality all come into play in that arena.

Scalar measures of equity are popular and convenient, but they can also prove to be difficult to interpret. Sen (1975) argued that any single measure can conceal information about the structure of inequality and the way it might change over time and distance. Many others have observed that different measures are liable to produce different and potentially conflicting results.

The technical annex to *Investing in health* (the 1993 World Development Report) notes that different measures fail to produce similar results for magnitude and sometimes even the direction of changes in inequality, because they assign different weights to different parts of the income distribution. Three of the more widely applied measures are applied to historical data collected and analyzed by Berry et al. (1983) in Box 1.6. The measures are drawn from a Lorenz curve, which is a plot of the cumulative percentile share of national income against cumulative percentile share of population. If plotted as a 45° line, income is equally distributed.

The first measure, the Gini coefficient (GINI), is the ratio of the area between the plotted Lorenz curve and a 45° line, divided by the area under a 45° line (equal per capita income). GINI measures the degree of inequality. It is really a variance measure and is particularly sensitive to changes in the neighborhood of the modal income.

A second common approach tabulates the ratio of the income received by the wealthiest x percent of the population to the income received by the poorest y percent of the population. Growing inequality would be indicated by an expansion of the ratio, but interpretation of exactly what is going on is often difficult. In particular, ratio measures are extremely sensitive to small changes around the critical x and y percentage thresholds.

Box 1.6 Measuring inequality in the global distribution of income

Berry et al. (1983) constructed statistics from per capita GNP data, assuming that income for every resident in every country matched their country's per capita average and that imprecisely registered growth in the People's Republic of China was moderate over the 27-year period from 1950. Shares of world income received, and consumption enjoyed, by people were reported for a selection of years; consumption shares were recorded for 1950, 1960, and 1977. However, since all of the entries were constructed using national averages, inequality in the distribution of income within countries was omitted. There are, nonetheless, a few observations that can be drawn from even these restricted estimates.

First of all, the lowest 60 percent of the world's population saw their share of income fall from 1950 through 1977 by 1.3 percent, the upper-middle 30 percent of the population enjoyed a 1.8 percent increase, and the uppermost 10 percent of the population felt a 0.5 percent decline. The first change worsened the distribution of income, of course, but the second improved it so that no unambiguous conclusion can be drawn about the overall trend. However, the distribution of income did worsen unambiguously over the 2-year period from 1970 until 1972; the cumulative percentage of income received up through every decile was smaller in 1972 than in 1970. The consumption data tell the same discouraging story even over the longer term from 1950 through 1977. The upper 30 percent of the world's population increased its share of world consumption from 79.2 percent to 81.5 percent at the expense of the lower seven deciles—an unambiguous worsening of the overall distribution.

Berry et al. went further with their analysis of the data, looking empirically for explanations of the trends that they observed. It should be clear, however, that more sophisticated measures of inequality are required if summary data such as these are to be instructive. Studies of changes in the distribution of income, for example, rely heavily on the measures chosen to reflect that change. This is certainly true of any comparative methodology or analysis, but the difficulties posed by international and intertemporal comparisons of income inequality are particularly acute.

A third scalar, developed by many economists, including Sen (1974), deflates average per capita income by the Gini coefficient to produce a theoretically rooted measure of the economic cost of income inequality (essentially aggregate costs incurred by individuals because they may place poorly in future income distributions). Termed GINI2, this measure is technically equal to average per capita income multiplied by a factor that varies with the Gini coefficient. GINI2 equals zero under perfect inequality and average per capita income under perfect equality. Yitzhaki (1979) and Hey & Lambert (1980) showed that GINI2 is really a special case of a relatively general welfare function in which there is no correlation between the welfare achieved by any individual and the distribution of income across national boundaries. In other words, no one's welfare depends upon the opportunities offered to citizens in other countries. In addition, reliance on GINI2 means that the researcher is implicitly assuming that the value of the last dollar earned is the same for citizens of the poorest countries as it is for the citizens of the richest counties. These are obviously very strong assumptions, but they do provide the foundation for a benchmark measure that is distorted neither by jealousy and envy across national boundaries nor by the value judgments of researchers who might arbitrarily assign different weight to different changes in income.

Lovell (1994) used the *Penn world table* and *World development report* data to estimate, on the basis of GINI2, that the cost of inequality across the world was more than US$5400 per person in 1990—a value derived in equal proportion from inequality within and between nations and equal to more than 60 percent of the average world per capita GDP during 1981–90 .

Many other measures of income inequality can be developed axiomatically from a theoretical structure that relates welfare functionally to per capita income. Atkinson (1970) echoed some of the insights first offered by Dalton (1920). Gastwirth (1972), Sheshinski (1972), and Dagum (1992) made notable contributions to a body of highly technical literature based entirely on utility theory and the notion of aversion to risk. All of the competing measures still produce the same comparative results under the simple case that one society's income inequality is more severe than another's for the full range of population percentages (0–100 percent). When relative income inequality is worse only for some portion of population percentages, comparative results for two such countries can be contradictory—in part because of technical reasons embodied in the underlying functional forms and in part because they must deal with enormous differences in scale from one nation to another.

Lovell (1994) explored the scale dimension after noting that large inequality in the distribution of income does not necessarily mean lower welfare for even the least advantaged citizens. Disadvantaged citizens in wealthier countries may be better off than their counterparts elsewhere simply because they receive smaller shares of larger pies. He shows, for example, that it is better to be in the lowest quintile in the United States than it is to be in the same class in all but ten other countries, including some, such as Hungary, that have a more egalitarian distribution of income.

Broadening the perspective, Lovell also considered a concept termed *Pareto dominance*, which is based on the relative standing of income classes in two or more countries. Pareto dominance of one country by another seems to be most likely when there is a great difference between their respective average income levels; and Pareto dominance undermines the implications of some Lorenz curve comparisons. The US Pareto dominates 44 of the 55 other countries included in the Lovell analysis, whereas the US Lorenz curve lies unambiguously above only 15 different nations, indicating that the US distribution of income is unambiguously more egalitarian than these 15 countries only. In all other cases, results depend on what part of the income distribution is under discussion.

Studies concerning climate change effects on income mostly have concentrated on average effects or per capita income. Little has yet been done concerning the distribution of the costs and benefits of climate change among groups or the distribution of mitigation and adaptation costs (Banuri et al. 1996).

Additional concerns about the quality and the coverage of data have also been noted. Summers & Heston (1990), for example, offered subjective ratings of the quality of the data from 134 countries. Such overviews show that the data are, for the most part, not very good. Researchers can, as a result, rely on these data as perhaps the best available; but they should certainly be cautious to avoid overstating precision in making international comparisons or fine tuning modeling parameters.

Nonmarket valuation

To conduct policy analysis where standard signals of market value are missing or suspect, environmental economists have had to devise methods to derive values for many environmental resources and service flows. The resulting nonmarket values are sometimes taken to be those accruing to current users of a resource, but they are not usually confined to these individuals or to their individualistic motives. If climate change were to cause a wetland to deteriorate, for example, then those currently fishing or hunting in the wetland would certainly be affected; but other individuals might register losses, too. Some might want to fish some day, and that opportunity would be lost. Others might want their children to be able to fish the wetland in ten years' time, and they would feel a loss. So would people who just like knowing that high-quality wetlands exist. The US National Oceanographic and Atmospheric Administration (NOAA 1993) and Larson (1993) have been particularly forceful in their assertions that acknowledging the validity of adding these option and existence values to more standard use values has been a major step in nonmarket valuation.

Economists have followed two largely separate routes, dubbed direct and indirect valuation, in trying to estimate nonmarket values for the environment. A survey of methods can be found in Freeman (1993). For a rare example of a combining the two, see Adamowicz et al. (1994). In both methods, individuals are assumed to come to the table equipped with utility functions that include both market-valued private goods and nonmarket environmental goods, such as clean air and the stock of white rhinos. A central feature of this utility function is that the individual is assumed to be prepared, in principle, to trade more or fewer environmental goods against more or fewer market goods to maintain a certain level of utility. Stevens et al. (1991) and Spash & Hanley (1994) both provided counterexamples to this assumption, so care will need to be taken to investigate when it makes sense, when it does not, and whether it will matter much.

In direct valuation, individuals are asked, in a carefully structured way, to specify the greatest amount that they would give up to secure more of an environmental good or to prevent a loss of the environmental good. This is their maximum *willingness to pay* (WTP) for environmental gains and losses respectively. In other cases, individuals are asked to specify the least they would willingly accept in compensation to forgo an increase or to accept a decrease in the environmental good; this is their minimum *willingness to accept compensation* (WTAC). Either question is usually framed so that individuals are paying or receiving money income to offset the environmental change and hold them on a constant level of utility. *Contingent valuation, contingent ranking,* and *stated preferences* are all methods that have been devised to make direct valuation assessments.

Indirect valuation, on the other hand, seeks to infer environmental values from individuals' expenditures on marketed goods and standard assumptions about the complementarity or separability of environmental and market goods within their utility functions. For example, if it were necessary to spend money on a marketed good to offset an increase in pollution, then the change in expenditure on the marketed good might be used as a money measure of the cost of environmental change. If expenditure on travel were necessary to enjoy fishing on a salmon river in the Scottish Highlands, then this cost might be used to value a day's salmon fishing. If it were known that forest planting would cause the number of salmon to fall, then an economist would know how to place a money estimate on this cost. Principal indirect valuation methods include the *travel method, hedonic pricing, averting expenditure,* and *dose–response models.*

Valuations produced by the methods of environmental economists seem likely to take more and more prominence in public decisions over environmental management. Assessment of how accurate and reliable these values are is a subject for debate. For example, Morey (1994) noted unresolved difficulties over the valuation of travel time, multipurpose trips and the unit of activity being valued in the travel cost approach. Hedonic pricing suffers from heavy data demands, statistical problems over the choice of functional form, multicollinearity, and the unconvincing assumption that housing markets are always in equilibrium for each environmental characteristic. Finally, averting expenditure only measures welfare changes accurately if this expenditure is a perfect substitute for the environmental good in question and if it generates no other benefits. But how likely is that to be the case?

Most empirical methods in the social sciences are problematic in use, and cataloging shortcomings for one particular set of methods does little to help assess the validity of the results. Hanley & Spash (1993) have proposed three criteria that might be used more productively in that assessment:

- How repeatable are results gained from any method?
- How valid are these results?
- In what esteem are the methods held by the academic community?

Loomis (1989) and Laughland et al. (1991) have used repeatability as a test for the *contingent valuation method* (CVM), and their results have, by and large, been encouraging. Testing repeatability in travel cost models has proven to be more difficult, but some encouraging evidence can be found in the meta-analysis of travel cost studies presented by Smith & Kaoru (1990). Validity can be interpreted in several ways. *Convergent validity* compares the valuation results from one method with results from another method; d'Arge & Shogren (1989) and Smith & Desvouges (1986) are examples. By way of contrast, *theoretical validity* can be claimed if empirical results are in line with theoretical predictions, but that is only as good as the theory. Carson & Mitchell (1993) noted clearly and accurately, for example, that one group of economists claims that empirical evidence that confirms the embedding hypothesis undermines CVM, since theory suggests that it should fail. Meanwhile, a second group claims that the success of the embedding hypothesis supports CVM, because theory suggests that it should be so. Obviously, the two camps rely on different theory, but which is correct? Finally, *construct validity* refers to how well the method's results can be explained statistically. In CVM, this involves estimating an equation relating WTP to those variables thought a priori to influence it. If this equation has the right parameter values and explains well (in terms of the goodness of fit), then the construct validity criterion is satisfied.

At the present time, however, whether nonmarket values can be shown to be repeatable and valid or not is not really the heart of the issue. The real question still remains: should society use nonmarket values in making decisions over the environment? Using nonmarket values implies accepting the philosophical basis that underlies them: that anthropocentric values are all that matter and that they can be represented effectively in a utilitarian framework. The utilitarian framework comes into play because it lies at the heart of the cost–benefit structure into which nonmarket values are thrust, and so even the incorporation of nonuse values builds on the notion that individuals are prepared to trade off environmental goods against other goods or income. Spash & Hanley (1994) noted all of this, and warned that using nonmarket values might be wrong if this is not how individuals think about the environment. Traditional economic reasoning counters their cautionary note by asserting that making decisions on environment issues necessarily involves making tradeoffs so that cost–benefit analysis does little more than force those tradeoffs into the open.

Although environmental valuation makes decisionmaking through cost–benefit analysis more efficient by making it more inclusive, it does not guarantee that environmental quality will be improved or even maintained. Some analysts argue that including environmental values into the cost–benefit calculus elevates them to the same level of importance as more conventional costs and benefits (such as labor costs and the value of electricity). Nonmarket valuation also reduces environmental values to the common currency metric, so no special treatment is necessarily accorded to the environment. Environmental quality is treated in the same way as labor hours, kilowatt hours, and bags of cement. Listing environmental impacts as intangibles in the past may have led to their being ignored or downgraded in the eyes of policymakers, but that might not have been the case. Keeping environmental impacts out of the cost–benefit calculus might have allowed them to retain a special status, which could make their safeguarding more likely.

Concept and domain problems

One of the difficulties of much of the work done on the policy of climate change is that it has assumed a single decisionmaker with a rational view of the benefits and costs of climate change (see Ch. 3 for additional discussion of the rational actor paradigm). The reality is much more complex and it undermines the standard paradigm. The non-economics social science literature suggests some approaches that take account of this more complex reality and expand on the standard approach.

Methodological individualism and aggregation

The discussion of nonmarket valuation raises the issue of grounding environmental decisionmaking in individual or societal preferences. Neoclassical welfare economics and the cost–benefit framework derived from it are grounded in the principle of consumer sovereignty. The implication for a normative theory of government behavior is that the government is merely an agent of its citizens. Institutional or societal preferences have no role in the welfare calculation, except perhaps to the extent that they may influence individual preferences.

Formal conditions and particular behavioral assumptions establish the fundamental linkages among individual preferences, individual utility, and social welfare, based on the view that self-interested individuals employ a rational decision process over final wealth states and personal changes in utility. The philosophical positions of consumer sovereignty and the rational pursuit of self-interest in consumer decisionmaking have stimulated many theoretical and empirical debates in the social sciences. Many of these debates turn on the validity of the behavioral assumptions. Others rest on the ethical proposition that social decisions should always be grounded in individual preferences. Both sources of criticisms are particularly relevant for addressing the role of government in global environmental problems.

In conventional microeconomics, rationality involves two major components: the basic motivation for action and the decisionmaking process by which actions are selected. The first component, the motivation underlying choice, refers to whether or not economic agents are motivated primarily by self-interest in their decision behavior. Alternative motivations would be altruism and malevolence (i.e., the presence of purposeful maliciousness in actions). The underlying assumption of motivation is important, since it bears directly upon the perceived gains from choice. Analytical approaches characterized by self-interest assumptions emphasize the influences of perceived personal and social payoffs from behavior and choice. Not surprisingly, health risk and costs for one's descendants are a significant part of what people fear in the absence of environmental protection (Hays 1987). Kempton (1991) found that his subjects defined most environmental value in economic and anthropocentric terms.

Economists have preferred the self-interest assumption on the grounds that the other explanations can be made consistent with it by redefining gain. Although recognizing the tautological implications of this position, Aaron (1994) argued that the central issue for economic modeling of behavior is not the assumption of self-interest, but rather how interests are defined and conveyed in the modeling of preferences and utility. Accordingly, economists have felt much more challenged by concerns about the second component of rationality: the decisionmaking process by which people maximize their self-interest. This component directly addresses the relationships among preferences, utility, and choice. Global environmental change is problematic for the standard behavioral assumptions about decisionmaking because it reflects an unusually complex and uncertain decisionmaking problem. In economics, such problems are commonly studied within a framework that relies on the *expected utility theory* (EUT) of decisionmaking under uncertainty (see also Ch. 4).

Although the EUT model does fairly well in predicting common decisions under risk where consequences are well understood and the decisions repeated often, it performs poorly at predicting the results of rare or complex decisionmaking (Schoemaker 1982, Harless & Camerer 1994). Consequently, EUT seems particularly ill suited to describe decisionmaking behavior for problems like global environmental change (see also Munasinghe et al. 1996).

More recent models of decisionmaking under uncertainty have emerged that build upon the parsimony of EUT models and psychological insights into rationality. In general, these economic–psychological models reflect subjective probability–consequence estimates elicited from individuals or individuals' heuristics (editing practices) for dealing with very high or low probability events. In spite of their greater attention to actual risk behavior and less stringent axioms of rationality, the focus of economic–psychological models has remained on numerical assessments of risk by individual decisionmakers. Therefore, without rejecting the self-interest paradigm, risk modelers have concentrated their efforts on developing models that are less mathematically elegant than the EUT model but more empirically based for assumptions of rational behavior. One example is Kunreuther et al. (1990), who contrasted a benefit–cost model with one that explicitly includes several psychometric factors.

Another approach to making models more responsive to exotic or highly complex decisionmaking problems involves enlarging the scope of possible costs and benefits to include irreversibilities and morbidity health effects. If greater concerns about environmental risks are linked to greater perceived costs, individuals should be willing to pay some amount to reduce their risk of exposure. However, this modification may continue to indicate risk preferences poorly. Gardner & Gould (1989) showed that expanded definitions of perceived benefits and costs account for no more than a third of the variance in risk preferences. As another example of this approach, Fischer et al. (1991) used a phased procedure to elicit important risk concerns and WTP amounts from respondents. Although environmental risk was mentioned most often by the 460 respondents, it evoked the smallest WTP amount. On the other hand, health risks, which are very directly tied to self-interest but mentioned only half as often as environmental risk, evoked the highest WTP value.

In addition to the arguments about economic rationality and its role in actual decisionmaking, Sagoff (1988) argued that the links between unobservable preferences and operative utility functions are tenuous at best, and, for many environmental risks, nonexistent. Behavioral research strongly challenges the underlying assumptions of a single, stable set of preferences over many environmental goods, especially where there is little personal familiarity with the good in or outside of markets (Fischhoff 1991). Psychologists reject the notion of stable and well-ordered preferences in favor of models that view preferences as adaptable and constructed as needed in particular contexts (Kahneman et al. 1993).

These criticisms have led to something of a crisis for the welfare paradigm. If individuals have labile or constructed preferences for many environmental goods, then it is unlikely that the technical conditions tying preferences to individual welfare will be met. Under these circumstances, results from economic models of behavior and choice seem a particularly inappropriate source of information about improvements to social welfare. Aaron (1994) rescued the welfare paradigm by suggesting that the crisis is not about utility maximization, but rather about assumptions regarding the utility function. He argued that a more realistic model of human behavior is based on a pluralism of motivations that lead to separate utility responses that must be weighed by the individual decisionmaker. Aaron's argument preserves the relationship between preferences and individual welfare, by suggesting a much richer view of utility, that is, multiple sets of preferences that reference personal satisfaction, self-reference, altruism, spite, and the regard of others, a view consistent with Sen (1977) and Schelling (1984).

Another criticism on aggregate welfare was made by Sagoff (1993), who disputed that social welfare is measured or varied by the satisfaction of individual preferences. Although preference satisfaction comprises the core of utilitarianism, Sagoff suggested that "happiness depends more on the quality of our desires than on the degree to which we satisfy them" (1993: 5). Social norms often shape perceptions of satisfaction from the acquisition of wealth, producing a constraint on wants that Marshall (1961) called "material plenty," with a low standard of living, or what Sahlins (1972) called the "zen road to affluence." Like hunter–gatherers, the Amish Mennonite communities of Pennsylvania restrict the wants of their members, with respect to consumer goods, both to maintain group solidarity and to guarantee availability of capital for essential resources (Hostetler 1963). Social groups are able to shape the utility functions of their members even when they are constantly exposed to the wide range of goods that entice members of neighboring communities (Cantor et al. 1992). The variety and pervasiveness of such norms would seem to support Sagoff's position. A related argument was raised by Berndt (1985), whose analysis of the energy theory of value suggested that there may be a collective preference to limit the use of individual preferences for certain policy areas.

Similarly, preferences of economists for market-based incentive solutions to environmental regulation often clash with preferences of environmentalists, who favor a stronger signal about the moral illegitimacy of polluting behavior (Kneese & Schulze 1985). Which preference actually dominates in a welfare sense is a question that has not been addressed empirically.

In summary, many arguments raise questions about the role of consumer sovereignty and the welfare view:

- conceptual shortcomings in the preference–utility–social welfare linkages in the case of complex and uncertain environmental problems
- the absence of explicit treatment for social norms or welfare that is greater than the sum of the parts
- evidence that social preferences predominate over individual preferences.

However, consumer sovereignty remains at the core of the neoclassical framework.

A technical reality of the welfare paradigm is that individual preferences and societal preferences are not likely to coincide in the presence of market failures. Most environmental problems are permeated by market failures, generally involving public goods, health and safety externalities, intergenerational consequences, and high levels of government intervention. Thus, it would be unrealistic to assume that individual and collective preferences coincide for most environmental problems.

Economists have responded to the problem of missing or incomplete markets by relying on implicit or explicit valuations of hypothetical scenarios. On the other hand, Sagoff (1993) argued that applying the welfare model and substituting hypothetical preferences for actual choices is in fact an imposition by economists of institutional sovereignty on the policy model.

Welfare economists have long been perplexed by the problem of social decisionmaking and representing individual preferences with a social decisionmaking rule. Arrow (1951) demonstrated that the principle of consumer sovereignty cannot be satisfied with a single rule that reflects the preferences of all individuals for all options in the choice set. Realistically, social decisions that impose institutional or expert sovereignty are made all the time, some with little or no public conflict.

Recognizing the many drawbacks of the pure individualistic framework, analysts have developed other frameworks for social decisionmaking that, although falling short of satisfying the Arrow criteria, appear reasonable compromises. Common to all these frameworks is the process of using a subset of the population to decide an issue for the larger group.

For example, Keeney & Raiffa (1976) suggested using the supra-decisionmaker approach. In this approach, the preferences of a small set of public decisionmakers are used to represent the societal preferences and the public interest. The preferences of the decisionmakers can be combined by using a multiattribute utility model, where attributes are weighted by rankings elicited from the public decisionmakers. This approach has been extended as a process to capture the objectives, values, and weights that characterize different stakeholders in an environmental decision problem (for a summary, see von Winterfeldt 1992).

Another approach to construct the social decisionmaker is to use social preferences as revealed by past policy decisions. This approach is consistent with decisionmaking in judicial processes that rely heavily on the precedent of past rulings. In the United States, court rulings have stated that current risk acceptance levels should be determined by reference to past regulatory decisions that deemed a particular chemical or hazard as safe (NRDC 1987).

A third approach to social preferences is to use collective preferences as revealed in social decisionmaking processes (Cox 1986). Such processes include voting, arbitrated negotiation and settlement, and tort-law adjudication. The value of this approach is that it is a distributional rather than point decision framework. Social decisions are not evaluated in isolation, based on the costs and benefits of each alone; rather, each decision is seen as part of a sequence of decisions generated by a socially beneficial decision process or mechanism, possibly involving implicit compromises in which those who lose on one round win on the next, and all win on average in the long run. Fairness and efficiency are evaluated for the sequence, rather than for each decision in it (Cox 1986).

Approaches that reject consumer sovereignty either explicitly or implicitly vary greatly in theoretical sophistication and methodological development. It would be naïve, however, not to recognize the pervasiveness of their use in actual decisionmaking in public policy as well as business and household contexts. In fact, decision processes that violate the spirit of consumer sovereignty are probably the rule and not the exception. One of the more intriguing approaches to bridge the individual and social influences on welfare is the substitution of such concepts as well-being for utility (see Vol. 1, Ch. 3).

Social and cultural influences

In stark contrast to methodological individualism, sociology reminds us that societies are complex ecosystems in their own right, and these societies may be every bit as fragile as tropical rainforests or the delicately balanced atmosphere. Simplistic formulations of the interface between these human ecosystems and the biosphere implicitly assume that society can and must change rapidly to avert disaster, but this assumption renders them inappropriate and perhaps useless.

The real problem here involves the unit of analysis. Although human–ecological frameworks (e.g., Ehrlich & Holdren 1971) and other such schemes apparently focus on society-level effects, in fact they are reductionist in their approach to society. According to this dominant view, population impacts the environment because each person makes sustenance demands on the environment. Affluence and technological development are important because they allow excessive individual consumption of natural resources, greatly increasing the social carrying capacity and thus the population while producing wasteful (and sometimes poisonous) byproducts. Unfortunately, nowhere in this framework can we find an appreciation of sociological forces that both shape our consumption and elimination of resources and mediate our personal relationships to the natural environment. That is, the most important variable that intervenes in the interactions among population, affluence, technology, and environmental impact is poorly represented in the equation: social structure or, more broadly, *social organization*.

Not only are population and economic growth indirectly related to environmental impacts via social organization, but also (net of population and economic development level) social organization exerts a direct (or unique) impact on such phenomena as the global climate or biodiversity. Social organization reflects the institutional and demographic matrix that constitutes any society. Social stratification and the social division of labor; population size, density, and demographic regime; the spatial distribution of human activities; and complex political economy are among the properties of social organization. None of these properties can be attributed to individual human beings, but all shape individual consumption and regulate our personal connection to the environment.

However, most contemporary analysts in this area ignore sociology (the study of social organization), and this may cripple the policy relevance of research on environmental degradation for two reasons. First, a concentration on proximate determinants as an explanation for atmospheric pollution (e.g., the influence of energy consumption on carbon dioxide emissions) is a valid model of the situation, but its policy relevance is limited, since policy actually must affect social, economic, and political processes that in turn affect the proximate determinants. Phenomena such as infrastructural inertia (e.g., sunk investments in "automotive" urban configurations), political or class alliances (e.g., working classes wedded to energy-intensive, state-owned industries), or patterns of social mobility that demand a certain energy regime (e.g., quaternary-services economies) may render both the visible and invisible hands (governments and markets) impotent to change a nation's impact on natural ecology. That is, energy consumption is a symptom of a fundamental set of social processes that heavily condition both the political and economic calculations of rational actors. Climate policy analysis, if it is to prove useful, must begin to gauge (quantitatively, if possible) the degree of influence of these sociological phenomena and analyze their malleability to policy instruments.

A severe decline in a society's key functions (perhaps through a severe energy crisis or ecological disaster) may be met with unemployment, an outward rippling of economic decline, and (eventually) a smaller population. This serves to lower the social carrying capacity permanently in many unpredictable ways. No one chooses the fall of civilization; decline is seldom manageable or predictable, as is demonstrated by the histories of the Mesopotamians, Mayans, or Easter Islanders.

Time, effects across generations, and discounting

Discounting is the technique designed by economists to make tradeoffs, not only between goods in the present and goods in the future but also between the aggregate personal satisfaction of having those goods in the two time periods. For long time periods, researchers are dealing with the problem of overlapping, or perhaps even mutually exclusive, generations. In other words, in addition to a concern that goods are delivered at various points in time, a more challenging modeling complication involves wholly changing economic conditions.

One reason that discounting techniques do not work well over long time periods is an artifact of the mathematics involved: since the present value of future net benefits declines exponentially with time, a large benefit enjoyed 100 years (let alone 1000 or 10000 years) from now can have a negligible present value. To illustrate the point dramatically, a complete loss of the today's world GDP in a hundred years would be worth about a million dollars if discounted at something close to the present prime rate of interest (6–7 percent); the loss of 100 percent of the GDP that the world might support in a hundred years would, however, be worth much more. The choice of the discount rate used also makes a great difference: Employing the usual formula, US$1 billion received two hundred years in the future discounted with a 1 percent discount rate has a present value of US$137 million; at a 10 percent discount rate, the present value is only US$5.27.

Several arguments claim that discounting is ethically inappropriate for decisions that affect future generations. Spash (1994) has argued that climate change could have serious impacts upon future generations while actually benefiting their predecessors. The standard application of cost–benefit analysis to the greenhouse effect, even if all costs and benefits could be calculated from individual preferences, would give the impression that the future is almost valueless, largely because of discounting. Nordhaus (1991) argues that, in the case of high costs, low damages, and high discounting, no greenhouse gas control is justified; whereas, with no discounting and high damages, the efficient degree of control is 30 percent of greenhouse gas emissions. Cost–benefit analysis as commonly applied would use a positive social discount rate. For closely reasoned arguments among economists on the appropriateness of discounting, the effects of long time horizons, appropriate discount rates, and environmental consequences, see Lind (1982), Cline (1992), Nordhaus (1994a), Schelling (1995), Toth (1995), Manne (1995), Bruce et al. (1996), and especially Lind (1995), who addressed several of the objections raised in this section.

Spash (1993) emphasized four common assumptions being made within the standard model that are critical to the normative case for giving less weight to the expected future damages of long-term environmental pollution, than to the same damages in the present. These assumptions address who constitutes the electorate, uncertainty over future preferences, the extinction of the human race, and uncertainty over future events.

In contrast, Adams (1989) opined that our responsibilities to future generations for global climate change are alleviated by higher material standards of living from current investments in technology, capital stocks, and other infrastructure. However, future generations being better off is not equivalent to societies consciously deciding to compensate the future. Undertaking investments with the express purpose of compensating future generations for climate change would imply that the extent to which the future will be better off has in some sense been balanced against all environmental damages. Each case of long-term damage implies compensation that is distinct from catering to the general needs of future individuals.

Yet the suggestion has been made that spreading the costs of climate change equitably across generations is an acceptable solution (Crosson 1989). This approach relies upon the economic view that changes in units of welfare are equivalent, regardless of their direction. However, doing harm is not necessarily canceled out by doing good. If an individual pays to have a road straightened and saves two lives a year, he or she cannot shoot one motorist a year and simply calculate an improvement (Barry 1983). This argument can be extended beyond the right to life. For example, assume individuals of a nation have an accepted right to live in their own homeland. If the Maldavians are relocated and compensated for greenhouse-gas-induced sea level rise that destroys their homeland, this right has been violated.

The appeal to the *safe minimum standard* can be viewed as an example of constraining economic tradeoffs by introducing rights. In the case of climate change, Batie & Shugart (1989) argued that the safe minimum standard would support emission reductions despite apparently high costs. However, tradeoffs are still allowed once costs become too high.

Along these lines of thought, the literature on discounting contains several suggestions for addressing intergenerational equity and stewardship. According to Howarth (1993), all projects that affect future generations should be examined under the conditions of the precautionary principle before discounting occurs. As articulated by Howarth (1993: 40), this principle holds that "inhabitants of today's world are morally obligated to take steps to reduce catastrophic risks to members of future generations if doing so would not noticeably diminish their own quality of life." Perrings (1989) advocated using the precautionary principle when both the level of fundamental uncertainty and the potential cost or stakes are high—where science is inadequate and ethical judgments are ubiquitous.

Following Howarth's advice, the first question to be addressed is: "Will the project impose catastrophic risks or damages on another generation?" In the case of no catastrophic risk, Burton (1993) advocates a method whereby different intergenerational and intertemporal discount rates are applied to material/commercial and ecological benefits and costs. However, in the case where there is catastrophic risk, then another question must be asked: "Can we take steps to substantially reduce risk without compromising our well-being?" If the answer is yes, we may proceed as above. If the answer is no, then serious consideration should be given as to whether the project should be undertaken and whether discounting or cost–benefit procedures should be used at all.

Others believe that intergenerational discounting is acceptable under some circumstances. Farber & Hemmersbaugh (1993) believed that society's concern should focus on the well-being of future persons, being careful not to expose them to serious deprivation. Even in this case, however, economists disagree about the magnitude and type of discount rate to use (e.g., social discount rate or the shadow price of capital). Nordhaus (1994a) offered a succinct description of the normative economic approach to determining the appropriate discount rate. Using the Ramsey optimal growth model, he derived the discount rate on goods and services (more precisely the real rate of interest) from a combination of time discounting, aversion to inequality, and growth in per capita consumption.

Many discussions of discounting ignore the distinction between discounting goods and discounting utility. The concept of discounting growth follows from a recognition that, if future generations are wealthier than the current one, then current consumption is, in a sense, more precious. It further follows that current costs and benefits should be weighed more heavily than future ones. Arguments suggesting that it is inappropriate to discount significantly the welfare of future generations are based on the position that social rates of time preference (the tradeoff between current and future welfare) should be low. However, this does not imply that the discount rate to be employed in cost–benefit analyses for discounting goods and services should be low. A risk averse society that is growing could still support a large discount rate for goods; low time discounting would simply combine with high discounting for growth to support such a rate.

Burton's (1993) discounting technique incorporated a personal discount factor for the present generation's concerns, and a generational discount factor for matters affecting future generations. Both factors are incorporated in calculations and they interact, producing an lower overall discount factor.

A question that has not been adequately answered is whether, as a result of adopting a widely held environmental ethic, the market-determined discount rates would decline toward the rate preferred by those advancing the stewardship agenda. The question of the impact of the use of a positive discount (or interest) rate on resource exploitation decisions is somewhat more complex than is often implied in the literature. High rates of resource exploitation can be consistent with either high or low interest rates (Norgaard 1991, Price 1991). As an alternative to lower discount rates, Mikesell (1991) suggested taking resource depletion into account in project cost–benefit analysis. (For a useful commentary on the debate about the effects of high and low interest rates on sustainability, see Lipton 1991.) Or it may be necessary to impose sumptuary regulations that constrain current consumption, in an effort to induce society to shift the income distribution more strongly toward future generations.

Many observers clearly feel that, in most countries, efforts to achieve sustainable growth must involve some combination of higher contemporary rates of saving—that is, deferring present in favor of future consumption—and more rapid technical change—particularly the technical changes that will enhance resource productivity and widen the range of substitutability among resources. Norgaard & Howarth (1991) and Norgaard (1991) argued that decisions regarding the assignment of resource rights among generations should be made on equity grounds rather than efficiency grounds. When resource rights are reassigned between generations, interest rates will change to reflect the intergenerational distributions of resource rights and income.

We can interpret these arguments as saying that, if present generations adopt an ethic that causes them to save more and consume less, the income distribution will be tilted in favor of future generations. However, this is not the end of the story. A decline in marginal time preference has the effect of lowering the interest rate. Improvement in investment opportunities resulting, for example, from technical change will have the effect of increasing the demand for investment and thus raising interest rates (Hirshleifer 1970). But will this be enough?

What should be done, given the inability of economic theory to provide satisfactory tools to deal analytically with obligations toward the future? One answer is that we should take a strategic approach to the really large issues—how much should be invested to reduce the probability of excessive climate change, for example. At the same time, we can continue to employ conventional cost–benefit analysis to answer the smaller questions, such as when to develop the drainage systems needed to avoid excessive buildup of waterlogging and salinity in an irrigation project.

Sociopolitical views of growth

Traditional development theories that relate social structure to industrial development have given little attention to ecological impact. Only the neo-Malthusians have made this a central concern. Some argue that development sociology and economics are irrelevant and that a "new sociology" has to be created before these problems receive the attention they require. Other disciplines, which emphasize different frames of reference (sociopolitical or environmental) provide critical insights into some of the climate-related problems that macroeconomics is trying to solve. In some cases, the problem is completely redefined. An alternative approach is to modify existing development theories to address ecological impact, thereby building on existing knowledge. There are five major approaches to development: neo-Malthusianism, modernization theory, dependency/world-systems theory, ecological evolutionary ideas, and state-centered approaches.

The core neo-Malthusian contention (discussed in more detail above) is that population growth is outstripping ecological limits and hence is the key source of greenhouse gas emissions, but studies such as Bongarts' (1992) analysis shed doubt on this assertion. Population growth may have a simple additive effect, but economic development is more central. However, increased energy consumption tied to development may be offset by increased efficiency which works against the thesis of a development multiplier.

The relationship between population and development suggests the need for macrosocial theory linking the two. The first, the convergence theory of modernization, posits the driving forces of development to be industrialization and global diffusion (Rostow 1960, Moore 1978). Following the painful accumulation of capital necessary for initial industrial takeoff, technological progress forces a gradual shift in the division of labor from primary to secondary sectors and, with the era of high consumption and the huge increase in labor productivity (which expands carrying capacity), the growth of tertiary or service industries. Less industrialized countries develop primarily by global diffusion, that is, borrowing and adapting technologies and the social structures and social psychologies that go along with them. Educational expansion and the building of modern institutions (especially schools, the mass media, and the state) are central facilitators of this process. The logic of industrialism is therefore viewed as the great transformer of traditional societies. Following productivity gains in agriculture, agricultural labor becomes redundant and several changes occur:

- Population shifts from rural to urban residence.
- Social organization becomes more complex and formal.
- Social psychologies evolve to grasp "modernity" (e.g., cause-and-effect).
- Demographic transition occurs as children become less economically essential to the family.

This theory offers several hypotheses. First, energy usage may be a symptom of sectoral evolution. As economies mature, the need for heavy industrial products (e.g., iron and cement) decreases, so infrastructural maturity may place lower stress on the natural environment. Second, sectoral evolution entails a shift from heavy to light industrialization and services, with concomitant shifts in energy requirements. That is, postindustrial societies have passed their dirty industrial stages and should therefore generate lower per capita greenhouse gas emissions. Third, modernization is usually associated with market economics. As economies increase in complexity, competition forces producers and consumers to minimize factor costs, one of which is energy. Complex markets should therefore encourage technological progress that is less hostile to the environment. Fourth, industrial societies are urban societies, and cities can be viewed as economic engines that help producers and consumers enjoy efficiencies of agglomeration. Accelerated communications, centralized consumer and labor markets, and reduced transport and warehousing costs (Henderson 1988) are among the benefits of urbanization that should reduce natural resource extractions and toxic byproducts over time, so highly concentrated space economies should reduce stress on the ecosystem relative to equally developed but less concentrated systems. Finally, modern individuals enjoy high levels of education, private resources, and social proximity to others (via urbanization and telecommunications). Political mobilization in the form of environmental social movements should therefore be much more prevalent in advanced industrial or postindustrial societies. Moreover, given the much greater level of social surplus, these movements should also be more successful, as producer elites can afford to comply with environmental regulations.

Evidence for these hypotheses is scattered, and little of it has been interpreted in the light of modernization theory. The idea of an inverted U-curve of energy intensity is well documented, however. Newly industrialized countries and those at middle levels of industrialization have lower greenhouse efficiency (greenhouse-related emissions per unit of GNP) than their less industrialized and fully industrialized counterparts, whether the analysis be normalized per capita or on GDP (Minzter 1990, Owata 1990). Studies of particular industries and technologies have also found that energy intensity and carbon emissions are greater in heavy industries (especially energy production and cement manufacture) that are strategic to early industrialization (Schipper et al. 1992). Dietz & Rosa (1994) also found an inverted U-curve for development in their cross-sectional analysis of carbon dioxide emissions. Ameen et al. (1994) found negative effects of literacy and urbanization on the growth of industrial energy intensity. Of course, the central criticism of modernization theory is its neglect of sustainability. Traditional modernization ideas have assumed that economic growth is potentially infinite with no ecological limits. The central question is therefore whether modernization processes produce effects that offset environmental impacts. Clearly, much more research needs to be done on the socioeconomic "metabolism" of nations and how this relates to ecological degradation.

In many respects, world systems and dependency theories offer an alternative framework. The central idea is of a global stratification system shaped by uneven political and economic power, with the industrialized countries (the *core*) at the top and underindustrialized countries (the *periphery*), controlled by coercion, international measures, and the inherent logic of capitalism at the bottom (Frank 1967, Wallerstein 1974, Bornschier & Chase-Dunn 1985). A set of newly industrialized countries (the *semiperiphery*) is undergoing a distorted form of development shaped by the core. A central premise is that world capitalism has a developmental logic characterized by unequal exchange, uneven development, and growing ethnoracial and class inequalities. Hence, social structure is largely determined by capitalist relations, which determine the effects of technology, population, and ecological constraints. Like modernization theory, this approach assumes an unlimited ecosystem but, unlike it, places primary emphasis on economic rather than technological determinism.

The theory focuses on the impact of world capitalism on less industrialized countries, and several hypotheses can be derived about the ecological impact of international stratification. First, this approach encourages the view that core countries control the capital and technology and treat less industrialized countries as simple production inputs whose costs must be minimized (i.e., they are "dependent") This means that less industrialized countries have to make economic concessions to attract foreign investment, such as relaxing environmental regulations or providing energy subsidies to multinational corporations (Repetto 1985). A critical precondition is that less industrialized countries have more need for economic integration than industrialized countries have need for resources, or else that the costs of coercion to the industrialized countries are less than the benefits they receive.

Extending this, greater integration of less industrialized countries into the world capitalist system implies weaker environmental controls and greater subsidies to multinational corporations, both of which should reduce their greenhouse efficiency. By this logic, middle income countries should have fewer environmental controls than their poorer neighbors. Second, peripheral economies often experience distorted development, or economic disarticulation. Such economies exhibit a small, modern export sector atop a much larger preindustrial subsistence sector, and this mismatch truncates multiplier effects, lowers mobility across economic strata, and therefore produces a poorer overall rate of national–regional integration (Amin 1976). Ironically, then, some versions of dependency theory might posit lower levels of greenhouse-related emissions in response to lagging industrialization, but higher levels of phenomena such as deforestation as poor populations struggle to obtain subsistence through primary commodity extraction. According to this view, equalizing access to technology and wealth could reduce deforestation and similar phenomena, and allow more rapid and high-quality industrialization earlier (bypassing the dirty early development phase of industrialization).

Little systematic research has been conducted on these questions. Ameen et al. (1994) found that commodity concentration in exports slowed the growth of energy intensity. In another study, Grimes et al. (1994) claimed that a country's position in the world system is indeed related to greenhouse efficiency in an inverted U-shaped curve, which is to say that semiperipheral societies generate on average more greenhouse gas emissions per unit of GNP than do core and peripheral societies. This study is flawed, however, because the authors do not control for industrialization. Their findings support the modernization hypothesis that societies at intermediate levels of industrialization (the heavy industrial stage) emit higher per capita greenhouse gas emissions. In other words, Grimes et al. provided no critical experiment to differentiate world systems theory from modernization theory. Finally, there is the historical thesis that noncore countries were forcibly incorporated into the world system, thus creating severe inequalities that continue to shape social structures and institutions. Peasant "land hunger" is partially a result of this legacy, leading to deforestation pressures. A close-grained analysis in the Amazon basin showed that severe land inequality was a factor that could be traced to earlier colonialism, although current settlement regulations could be blamed just as easily (Rudel 1989).

A third theory of economic development is ecological evolutionary theory. It can be viewed as complementary to modernization and world systems theories in that it posits the existence of preindustrial social structures that facilitate industrial takeoff and incorporation into the world economy. The adoption of plow agriculture and the resulting increased population densities gave old agrarian societies an evolutionary advantage that facilitated their ready adoption of industrial technology (Lenski & Noland 1984, Nolan & Lenski 1985). These societies had agricultural surpluses that allowed population growth. This, in turn, led to greater urbanization, occupational specialization, administrative growth, and social integration between rural and urban areas, which in turn predisposed these societies toward rapid development once world industrialization was under way (Crenshaw 1992). Rapid industrialization also facilitates occupation of labor-intensive industrial niches within the international division of labor, allowing countries to be upwardly mobile within the world system.

Existing research indicates that agricultural density (net of development) contributes to energy efficiency and thus lowered greenhouse gas emissions. Ameen et al. (1994) found that agrarian population density raised energy efficiency in both manufacturing and services. Jenkins & Crenshaw (1992) also demonstrated in cross section how population densities reduce carbon dioxide emissions per capita. Obviously, much more research is needed on the institutional and demographic inheritances of contemporary nation states. Greater predictive power in forecasting which regions are likely to experience more rapid economic growth, accelerated adoption of new technologies, and concomitant effects on the natural ecosystem might allow some degree of policy intervention.

The fourth set of arguments focuses on the state. Research on the role of different types of state regimes is limited, yet this factor is critical to understanding the social structural constraints on environmental change. Many ideas about the state role are eclectic, some arguing that strong and politically responsive states increase economic efficiency and, by implication, greenhouse efficiency. Others argue that states shelter dominant groups against market competition, reducing economic (and thus energy) efficiency. Recent empirical research suggests that the political regime may have profound implications for environmental concerns, as illustrated by Table 1.6 above.

One line of argument is that stronger states (in the sense of having more centralized authority, decisionmaking power, and enforcement powers) contribute to economic development, thus promoting economic and energy efficiency (Rueschemeyer & Evans 1985, Migdal 1988). This should translate into greater greenhouse efficiency. A related idea centers on the policy responsiveness of the state. Political opportunities facilitate the mobilization of groups to press their interests, including protection from environmental risks. In a comparative study of the nuclear power industry, Kitschelt (1986) argued that strong responsive states provided the greatest possibilities for environmental protection, since the state is able to implement policies and is also responsive to citizen concerns about environmental risks. Strong but unresponsive states, such as France, have weak environmental movements and large, inefficient, and risky energy sectors, whereas weak (decentralized federal system) but responsive states, such as the United States, have strong environmental movements but cannot get the state to effectively provide protection. For Kitschelt, the German state represents the best mix, strong enough to intervene and also responsive. These propositions could be seen as further specifying the political side of modernization theory or as capturing the repressiveness of peripheral states.

A competing line of argument focuses on the inefficiencies created by state interventions. The older and more institutionalized the state, the more it has been captured by organized groups that use the state to protect themselves against market competition (Olson 1982). This means greater inefficiency, which should lead to greenhouse inefficiency. No direct research bears on this question, but the extensive evidence on comparative energy efficiency strongly suggests that state subsidies and market protections reduce energy efficiency (Bates 1993, Schipper et al. 1992, Kosmo 1987). The former Soviet Union exposed its citizens to major environmental risks and still displays one of the world's lowest energy efficiencies at its level of industrialization (Goldman 1972, Owata 1990). Repressive peripheral states among the less industrialized countries have displayed many of the same features, protecting large inefficient industries against market forces (Bates 1993, Kosmo 1987).

In summary, little systematic research has attempted to sort out the importance of different macrosocial theories of development. The best evidence bears on energy efficiency, which is assumed to be a strong determinant of greenhouse efficiency. Although neo-Malthusian ideas and some of the modernization and world system hypotheses have attracted scrutiny, very little work on the ecological evolutionary or state-centered ideas has yet been done. It is too early to forecast what such research might suggest, but it seems obvious that a more complex model of the social structural sources of global change will eventually develop, incorporating the insights from multiple theories. One of the most promising lines of inquiry may be the interplay among state economic policies, industrialization, and energy paths, as these shape greenhouse efficiency. Existing theories present clear rival hypotheses, suggesting the need for critical tests. They also present points of possible convergence and hence possible synthetic models.

Sustainability ideas

A significant distinction for sustainability concepts is the one between *growth* and *development*. Growth refers to the quantitative increase in the scale of the physical dimension of the economy, the rate of flow of matter and energy through the economy, and the stock of human bodies and artifacts; whereas development refers to the qualitative improvement in the structure, design, and composition of physical stocks and flows, improvements that result from greater knowledge, both of technique and of purpose (Daly 1987). The potential for a more efficient use of natural resources, recycling, and reduction of waste and pollutants means a potential for economic progress based on development (qualitative improvement) rather than growth (quantitative improvement)—an economic progress that is not at the expense of the environment. On the contrary, this concept of progress tries to fit economic activity and human skills into biogeochemical cycles and adjust the economic system within the framework of the overall finite global life-supporting environment (Gilliland & Kash 1994, Viederman 1994).

Sustainability has become a transdisciplinary field of study that addresses the relationships between ecosystems and economic systems in the broadest sense, in order to develop a deep understanding of the entire system of humans and nature. In particular, ecological economics views the socioeconomic system as a part of the overall ecosphere, emphasizing carrying capacity and scale issues in relation to the growth of the human population and its activities, and the development of fair systems of property rights and wealth distribution (Carson 1991). The belief of many that humans can continue on the same path of expansion, that technological progress will eliminate all energy, resources, and environmental limits, and that infinite substitutability can be made between human-made and natural capital is considered by ecological economists to be a dangerous one. Blind faith in technology is viewed as similar to the situation of the man who fell from a ten-story building, and when passing the second story, concluded, "So far so good, so why not continue?"

The emergent paradigm of ecological economics seeks to address the distinction between growth and development, while retaining many of the useful features of neoclassical economics, such as the clarity with which arguments can be made; the emphasis on opportunity costs, and price and profit signals; and the rent-seeking literature. The main features of this new approach, according to Klaasen & Opschoor (1991), are co-evolution, an emphasis on physical limits to recycling and technological improvements (limits that derive from the first and second laws of thermodynamics), and community values that count for more than individual preferences.

Solow (1991) placed sustainability in the context of development by referring to two distinct cases of future economic activity that allow future generations the opportunity to be as well off as their predecessors. The first involves unique resources: irreplaceable assets that should be preserved for their own sake. The second case refers to more mundane assets, and sustainability here does not impose the requirement to bequeath to posterity any particular asset. Sustainability holds each generation to endowing the future with whatever it takes to achieve a standard of living that is at least as good as its own. No generation can consume "humanity's capital," but that capital needs to be defined in its broadest sense. The economic definition of that sense is clear. Except for the unique assets of the first case noted above, resources are not valued for what they are. They are, instead, valued for the goods and services that they provide; and once that perspective is accepted, then the debate over what to do is conducted in the context of ordinary substitutions and tradeoffs.

Key to distinguishing the cases of unique resources from those involving mundane assets is scientific knowledge about the role of technology in widening the substitutability among natural resources and between natural resources and reproducible capital. Economists and technologists have traditionally viewed technical change as widening the possibility of substitution among resources—of fertilizer for land, for example (Solow 1974, Goeller & Weinberg 1976). The sustainability community rejects the "age of substitutability" argument. The loss of plant genetic resources is viewed as a permanent loss of capacity. The elasticity of substitution among natural factors and between natural and manmade factors is viewed as exceedingly low (James et al. 1989, Daly 1991). Considering the production of a particular commodity—for example, the substitution of fertilizer for land in the production of wheat—is an argument over the form of the production function. But substitution also occurs through the production of a different product that performs the same function or fills the same need—of fiber-optic cable subsitituted for conventional copper telephone wire or the replacement of coal by fuels with higher hydrogen-to-carbon ratios, for example.

The argument about substitutability, although inherently an empirical issue, is typically argued on theoretical or philosophical grounds. Historical experience or advances in futures modeling may lead toward some convergence of perspectives. But the scientific and technical knowledge needed fully to resolve disagreements about substitutability will always lie in the future. The issue is exceedingly important. If a combination of capital investment and technical change can continuously widen opportunities for substitution, imposing constraints on present resource use could leave future generations less well off. If, on the other hand, real output per unit of natural resource input is narrowly bounded, that is, it cannot exceed some upper limit which is not too far from where we are now, then irreversible damage, or perhaps even catastrophe, is unavoidable.

A well-known operating principle for researchers at the interface of ecology and economics is that the scale and rate of throughput of energy and matter passing through the economic system is subject to an entropy constraint. Intervention is required because the market by itself is unable to reflect this constraint accurately (Pearce & Turner 1990). Daly (1984) found no more reason to expect the market to find the optimum scale than there is to expect it to find the optimum income distribution. Just as the market adjusts to ethical constraints imposed on income distribution, so the market will adjust to ecological constraints imposed on the scale of throughput. Daly's analogy with the Plimsoll line on a boat clearly illustrates this. Suppose economists want to maximize the load that a boat carries. If they place all the weight in one corner of the boat, it will quickly sink or capsize. They need to spread the weight out evenly and, to do this, invent a price system. The higher the waterline in any corner of the boat, the higher the price for putting another kilogram in that corner, and the lower the waterline, the lower the price. This is the internal optimizing rule for allocating space (resources) among weights (alternative uses). This pricing rule is an allocative mechanism only. With lack of information and true uncertainty, the rule keeps on adding weight and distributing it equally until the optimally loaded boat sinks to the bottom of the sea. What is lacking is a limit (albeit dynamic) on scale, a rule that says "stop when total weight is one ton, or when the waterline reaches the red mark" (Daly 1984).

Figures 1.3, 1.4, and 1.5 illustrate this concept in relationship to two other prevalent visions of the future. Figure 1.3 shows the conventional economic optimistic view of ever-continuing growth (in terms of the above definitions) of the human-made components of capital at the expense of natural capital. Environmentally minded individuals within the conventional camp argue that this growth can be used to fund preservation of some of the remaining natural capital, but only as a luxury, since natural capital is not necessary to operate the economy and could be driven to zero without causing collapse of the economy. Figure 1.4 illustrates a more realistic (but pessimistic) view that shows overexpansion of the human economy, causing collapse of the ecological life-support system and ultimately collapse of the economy that depends on it. The collapse may be more or less severe and allow for recovery afterward, but this is still not a very desirable vision of the future. The third vision (Fig. 1.5) indicates the distinction between growth and development, the ecological "Plimsoll line" (including uncertainty) and the possibility for continued development (in terms of the above definitions), if the physical dimensions of the economy are maintained below the planet's carrying capacity. This vision of the future encapsulates the essential characteristics of ecological economics.

Ecological economists speak of natural capital, human capital (and/or cultural capital), and manufactured capital when categorizing the different kinds of stocks that produce the range of ecological and economic goods and services used by the human economy (Daly 1994, Berkes & Folke 1994). The latter two are sometimes referred to together as human-made capital (Costanza & Daly 1992). These three forms of capital are interdependent and to a large extent complementary (Daly 1994). As a part of nature, humans with our skills and manufactured tools not only adapt to but modify natural capital, just like any other species in self-organizing ecosystems (Ehrlich 1994, Holling 1994, Jansson & Jansson 1994).

Ecological economists argue that natural capital and human-made capital are largely complements (rather than substitutes), and that natural capital is increasingly becoming the limiting factor for further development (Costanza & Daly 1992, Daly 1994). Therefore, to sustain a stream of income, the natural capital stock must be maintained. This does not mean an unchanged physical stock, but rather an undiminished potential to support present and future human generations. A minimum safe condition for sustainability (given the huge uncertainty) is to maintain the total natural capital stock at or above the current level (Turner et al. 1994). An operational definition of this condition for sustainability means that (Barbier 1989, Costanza & Daly 1992):

- the physical human scale must be limited within the carrying capacity of the remaining natural capital
- technological progress should be efficiency increasing rather than throughput increasing
- harvesting rates of renewable natural resources should not exceed regeneration rates
- waste emissions should not exceed the assimilative capacity of the environment
- nonrenewable resources should be exploited, but at a rate equal to the creation of renewable substitutes.

Carrying capacity depends on the resilience of ecosystems and the behavior of the economy–environment system as a whole (Common & Perrings 1992, Perrings 1994, Holling 1992, 1994, Jansson & Jansson 1994, d'Arge 1994, Costanza 1991).

In the context of biological conservation and human welfare, the major challenge from the ecological economics perspective is to maintain the amount

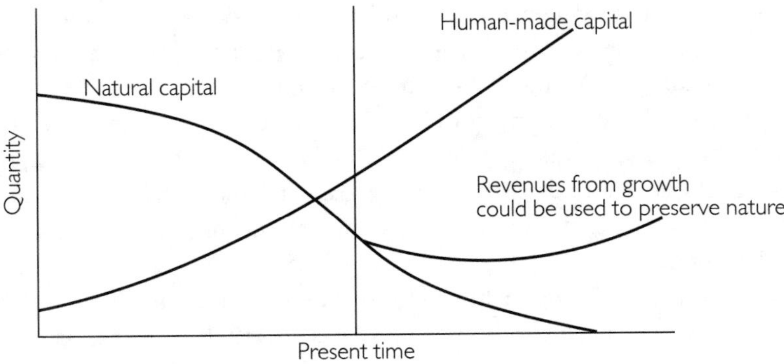

Figure 1.3 The economic optimist vision.

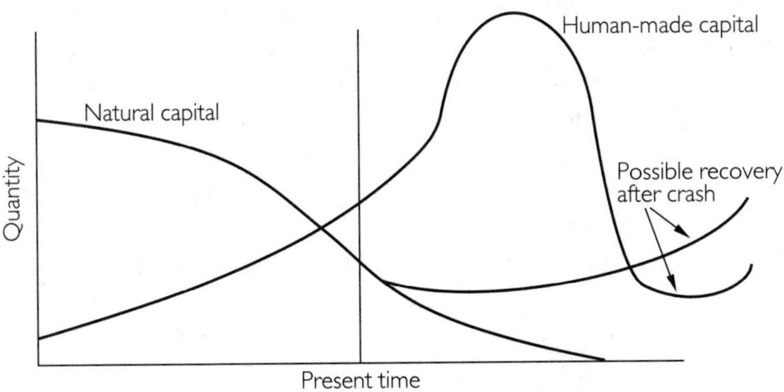

Figure 1.4 The environmental pessimist vision.

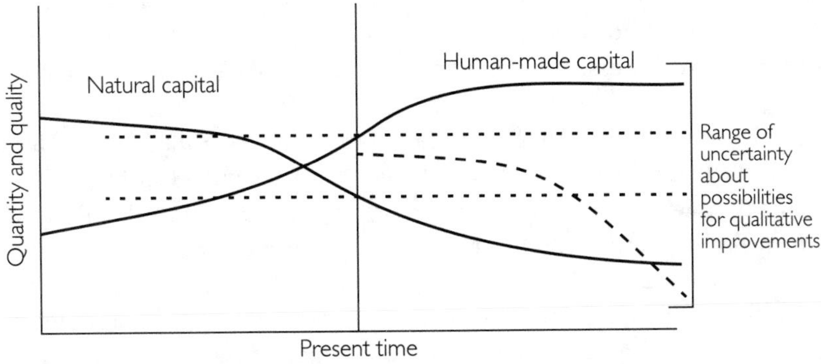

Figure 1.5 The ecological economic vision.

of biodiversity that will ensure the resilience of ecosystems, and thereby the flow of crucial renewable resources and ecological services to human societies (Perrings et al. 1992, Perrings 1994). This perspective maintains the importance of ethical and moral concerns for biodiversity conservation (Norton 1986) or people's preference value for particular species even when they do not know the species' role in the system (d'Arge 1994). Such a hierarchy of values has to be explicitly stressed in discussions of biodiversity conservation and sustainable development.

In economic modeling, a hierarchy of values is relevant for estimating opportunity costs. Ecological economists assert that natural capital is rapidly becoming scarcer, and it is inappropriate to calculate the net benefits of a project or policy alternative by comparing it with unsustainable options. The economic allocation rule for attaining a goal efficiently (maximize present value) cannot be allowed to subvert the goal of sustainability that it is supposed to be serving (Daly & Cobb 1989). When project appraisal raises development versus conservation conflicts, decisionmakers may require that cost–benefit analysis be used to choose between alternatives only within a choice-set bounded by sustainability (ecosystem stability and resilience) constraints (Bishop 1993, Turner et al. 1994).

In addition, Solow (1991) noted the recent attention paid by many economists to the depletion of nonrenewable resources and recurring threats to the very existence of other environmental assets. He has joined others to suggest also how a new *net national product* (NNP) might be constructed by subtracting a measure of their depreciation. He noted that the logic of the economic theory of capital allows construction of a net national product, but he has taken this argument a step further by suggesting that the creation of such a measure of net economic activity might provide the sound logic upon which to base the more elusive notion of sustainability. Solow argued that calls for sustainability must amount to injunctions to preserve productive capacity for the indefinite future if they are to be more than emotional slogans that rapidly lose intellectual and practical content. For Solow, the calculation that produces an adjusted net national product is essential for placing a strategy of sustainability on a firm footing.

Tobin & Nordhaus (1972) advocated an approach called *new economic welfare* (NEW), which would subtract items such as the unmet cost of pollution and the disamenities of urbanization. More recent attention paid to the environment has suggested adding the value of environmental services and the appreciation of natural resources (e.g., carbon fixing in forests) and subtracting government expenditure for preserving environmental assets, defensive expenditures by households against environmental threats, environmental damage more broadly defined, and the depreciation of natural resources

(Serageldin & Steer 1994, US NRC 1994).

Proper accounting, in other words, would turn any nation's capital stock into an indefinite retirement annuity for the future. If reasonably accurate measures of the value of each year's depletion of nonrenewable resources were available, then economies could see that they owed themselves a certain volume of investment to compensate for that year's withdrawal from the inherited stock. The appropriate policy would then generate an economically equivalent amount of net investment so that the broadly defined capital stock would be sustained for another year.

Table 1.9 provides insight into more aggregate measures that speak directly to national sustainability. It shows estimates of the proportion of national income devoted to saving in select economies (private plus public saving), the proportion of income devoted to depreciation on human-made capital (the NNP adjustment), and estimates of the proportion of income reflected in damage or depreciation to natural resources or the environment. If the computed net savings rate is positive for an economy, then it can be judged by this measure to be sustainable; the conclusion is opposite if savings turn out to be negative.

No real surprises in the locations of the various nations are recorded in Table 1.9. Highly industrialized countries populate the sustainable category, although not exhaustively; and less industrialized countries come up short. The United States is listed as sustainable, but only to a limited degree because its base savings rate is relatively low. High savings are no guarantee, though. Indonesia saves proportionately more than the United States and the same as Brazil, but the Indonesian economy falls below the line. Comparing the United States and Indonesian cases with other countries therefore shows clearly that this is entirely an economic measure. The likelihood of sustainability can be improved by either preserving natural resources and the environment or by maintaining a high national savings rate, and the linearity of the sustainability index implicitly assumes that the two are perfect substitutes in its calculation.

Ecological economics stresses that uncertainty is fundamental, large, and irreducible, and that particular processes in nature are essentially irreversible (Clark & Munro 1994, Costanza 1994). Instead of locking the world in development paths that may ultimately lead to destruction and despair, humans need to conserve and invest in natural capital, in the sense of keeping life support ecosystems and interrelated socioeconomic systems resilient to change (Hammer et al. 1993, Holling 1994, Jansson & Jansson 1994, Perrings 1994).

One of the primary reasons for the problems with current methods of environmental management is the issue of scientific uncertainty—not just its existence, but the radically different expectations it engenders and the ways that have been developed to deal with it. If people are to successfully manage the environment, they must understand and expose differences about the nature of

Table 1.9 Sustainability of selected national economies.[a]

Economies	S/Y –	δ_M/Y –	δ_N/Y =	Z
Sustainable				
Brazil	20	7	10	+3
Costa Rica	26	3	8	+15
Czechoslovakia	30	10	7	+13
Finland	28	15	2	+11
Germany (pre-unification)	26	12	4	+10
Hungary	26	10	5	+11
Japan	33	14	2	+17
Netherlands	25	10	1	+14
Poland	30	11	3	+16
United States	18	12	4	+2
Zimbabwe	24	10	5	+9
Marginally sustainable				
Mexico	24	12	12	0
Philippines	15	11	4	0
Unsustainable				
Burkina Faso	2	1	10	–9
Ethiopia	3	1	9	–7
Indonesia	20	5	17	–2
Madagascar	8	1	16	–9
Malawi	8	7	4	–3
Mali	–4	4	6	–14
Nigeria	15	3	17	–5
Papua New Guinea	15	9	–7	–1

Note: S = national savings; Y = national income; δ_M = depreciation on manmade capital; δ_N = depreciation and damage to natural resources and the environment; Z (weak) = sustainability.
Source: Pearce (1993).

uncertainty and design better methods to incorporate it into the policymaking and management process (Costanza & Cornwell 1992, Costanza 1994).

To understand the scope of the problem, analysts must distinguish between risk (which is an event with a known probability, sometimes referred to as *statistical uncertainty*) and true uncertainty (which is an event with an unknown probability, sometimes referred to as *indeterminacy*).

Risks and uncertainties abound in reducing natural capital because of very imperfect understanding of the life-support functions, the inherently limited predictability of ecosystems and social systems (Holling 1994), and a limited capability to invent technical substitutes for natural functions. Such complex systems as ecological and economic systems are fundamentally evolutionary and nonlinear in causation and of limited predictability (Costanza 1991, Holling 1994). Therefore, policies that rely exclusively on social or economic adaptation to smoothly changing and reversible conditions lead to reduced options, limited potential, and perpetual surprise.

Ecological economists stress the need to remember that substituting for natural capital in one place requires natural capital from elsewhere, and that losses of life-support functions are often irreversible. In the face of uncertainty and irreversibility, the approach favors conserving natural capital and designing management instruments that are adaptive, flexible, and acknowledge uncertainty as a sound risk-averse strategy (Pearce & Turner 1990, Ludwig et al. 1993, Costanza 1994, Duchin & Lange 1994, Arrow et al. 1995).

However, we are very far from being able to design either an adequate technological or institutional response to the issue of how to achieve sustainable growth in economic development—or how to achieve sustainable growth in both the sustenance and the amenity components of consumption.

For example, in spite of the large literature in agronomy, agricultural economics and related fields, no package of technology is available for transfer to producers that can assure the sustainability of growth in agricultural production at a rate that will enable agriculture, particularly in less industrialized countries, to meet the demands that are being placed on them (Board on Agriculture, US NRC 1991, 1992, Rosenberg & Eisgruber 1992). The value to be placed on such studies is limited by the absence of clarity about the concept of sustainable agricultural development, suggesting that researchers approach the issue of technological and institutional design pragmatically.

Sustainability is appropriately viewed as a guide to future agricultural research agendas rather than as a guide to practice (Ruttan 1994). As a guide to research, a useful definition would include the development of technology and practices that maintain or advance the quality of environmental resources, improve the performance of other production inputs, and facilitate the substitution of nonpolluting technology for less environmentally benign technology. The research agenda on sustainability needs to explore what is biologically and technically feasible without being excessively limited by present economic constraints.

At present, the sustainability community has not been able to advance a program of institutional innovation or reform that can provide a credible guide to the organization of sustainable societies. Humans have yet to design the institutions that can ensure intergenerational equity. Few would challenge the assertion that future generations have rights to levels of sustenance and amenities that are at least equal to those enjoyed (or suffered) by the present generation. They also should expect to inherit improvements in institutional capital—including scientific and cultural knowledge—needed to design more productive and healthy environments.

Forecasting the future

Past and present experiences are of little use in studying issues of global change unless they offer some insight about what the future might hold. Indeed, a full array of methodological approaches has emerged with which to confront the problem. Given what we know (or what we think) happened over the past decades (or centuries), what can we say about what might happen over the next several decades (or centuries)? Some of these efforts have chosen to exercise aggregate economic models typical of the top-down approach. Other research has focused on the detailed workings of microeconomic phenomena in taking a bottom-up approach. In both, however, the more-is-better foundation of economic analysis has concentrated attention on economic growth, growth accounting, and efficiency. Cost–benefit analysis has been applied widely, both in evaluating global mitigation strategies and in contemplating adaptive strategies. Other researchers are beginning to go beyond the economic paradigm to explore how a wider range of social scientific knowledge and perspective might change expectations about the trend and character of future economic activity. Alternative futures abound.

Offering portraits of economic progress over the long term is difficult, to be sure; but concentrating research effort exclusively on handling those difficulties may be dangerous. Most of the diversity reflected in the previous section can be expected to pass the "So what?" test, so alternative approaches to projecting future economic activity, based perhaps on alternative objectives for social and economic policy, should be able to offer widely varying but nonetheless credible portraits of what might happen. This additional diversity in approach will add variety to our set of portraits, not only because different researchers will make different assumptions about the major economic parameters that define their scenarios, but, perhaps more importantly, because different researchers will have entirely different views of what will be most important in determining what the future holds and will apply completely different norms in evaluating those futures.

This section will begin to make this point with a brief review of a well-known set of projected futures, the IPCC scenarios in 1992 (IS92) endorsed in the 1996 *Second assessment report*. These scenarios are thought to provide adequate coverage of possible uncontrolled emissions trajectories, but they nonetheless fall short of providing adequate vehicles upon which to evaluate alternative policy options. Even so, they have focused attention on smooth trajectories of emissions. As a result, conventional wisdom now holds that the economics of efficiency and growth support only minimal intervention along such trajectories, in part because most of the emissions are derived from energy consumption and in part because the associated costs, taken in the context of adaptation to smooth and gradual change, are likely to be small in the industrialized world.

Expanding the paradigm allows exploration of alternative approaches to the policy problem, thereby admitting that this sort of economic analysis might not capture the entire picture. Alternative approaches will allow researchers to search for sources of potential surprise from within the boundaries of social science. They will allow researchers to test the credibility of the underlying economic scenarios. Most importantly, though, they will allow researchers to explore and to advance alternative means with which to evaluate prospective long-term policy responses that must be crafted under enormous uncertainty.

Standard scenario development

Table 1.10 provides enough information to see why the six IS92 scenarios offered by the IPCC produce such different views of the future; see Leggett et al. (1992) and Pepper et al. (1992) for more detailed descriptions. Each scenario includes the London Amendments to the Montreal Protocol, the (then) most recent World Bank and United Nations population forecasts, political and economic changes in the former Soviet Union, eastern Europe and the Middle East, and the (then) most recent data on tropical deforestation as well as other sources and sinks of greenhouse gases.

The data recorded in the last column of the table support at least a casual comparison of the six IPCC scenarios in terms of carbon emissions. They differ in large measure because they incorporate different assumptions about driving socioeconomic variables and not because they portray fundamentally different sociopolitical futures. IS92a adopts intermediate assumptions about population and economic growth, and IS92b adds some information about 1992 commitments of several OECD countries to stabilize their carbon emissions. Scenario IS92c is a limiting case on the low side with low population and economic growth assumptions; IS92d adopts only low population growth. On the high side, scenarios IS92e and IS92f capture high-side deviations in the same variables. Taken together, the six easily differentiated alternatives reflect the vast range of current opinion, at least in terms of global carbon emissions. Indeed, as noted in Alcamo et al. (1994), associated carbon emissions dominated by energy consumption span much of the 1.2 gigatonnes of carbon (GtC) to 60 GtC range found in the published literature through the middle of 1994. However, the distribution of expert opinion, as well as variance across the IS92 scenarios, is relatively tight over the short term, even though it grows dramatically over the longer term.

Alcamo et al. evaluate the IS92 scenarios in terms of their usefulness in meeting four different purposes. Because they span the range of expert opinion

Table 1.10 Summary of assumptions for the six IPCC alternative scenarios.

Scenario	Population	Economic	Growth (%)	Energy supplies	Other	CFCs	C emissions in 2100 (GtC/yr)
IS92a	World Bank 1991 11.3 B by 2100	1990–2025 1990–2100	2.9 2.3	12000 EJ conventional oil	Legally enacted internationally agreed controls on SO_2, NO_x, and NMVOC emissions Efforts to reduce emissions of SO_2, NO_x, and CO in less industrialized countries by middle of next century	Partial compliance with Montreal Protocol Technological transfer resulting in gradual phaseout of CFCs in non-signatory countries by 2075	19.8
IS92b	World Bank 1991 11.3 B by 2100	1990–2025 1990–2100	2.9 2.3	Same as "a"	Same as "a" plus commitments by many OECD countries to stabilize or reduce CO_2 emissions	Global compliance with scheduled phaseout of Montreal protocol	18.6
IS92c	UN medium-low case 6.4 B by 2100	1990–2025 1990–2100	2.0 1.2	8000 EJ conventional oil 7300 EJ natural gas Nuclear costs declining by 0.4% annually	Same as "a"	Same as "a"	4.6
IS92d	World Bank 1991 11.3 B by 2100	1990–2025 1990–2100	2.7 2.0	Oil and gas same as "c" Solar costs fall to $0.65 per kWh 272 EJ of biofuels available at $50 per barrel	Emission controls extended worldwide for CO, NO_x, NMVOC, and SO_2 Deforestation halted Capture and use of emissions from coal mining and gas production and use	CFC production phaseout by 1997 for industrialized countries Phaseout of HCFCs	9.9
IS92e	UN medium-high case 17.6 B by 2100	1990–2025 1990–2100	3.5 3.0	18400 EJ conventional oil Gas same as "a" Phaseout nuclear by 2075	Emission controls that increase fossil energy costs by 30%	Same as "a"	34.9
IS92f	UN medium-high case 17.6 B by 2100	1990–2025 1990–2100	2.9 2.3	Oil and gas same as "e" Solar costs fall to $0.083 per KWh Nuclear costs increase to $0.09 per KWh	Same as "e"	Same as "a"	25.9

Source: Leggett et al. 1992

reasonably well, the six taken together are thought to be an adequate source of input for evaluating the consequences of nonintervention strategies. They are not, however, thought to be very useful in:

- evaluating the consequences of intervention
- examining the feasibility and cost of mitigation across regions and over time
- supporting negotiation over emissions reduction trajectories across regions and over time.

Other sets of scenarios have therefore been developed, based on specific modeling efforts but nonetheless cast against the IS92 nonintervention trajectories to validate their context in the sphere of uncontrolled trajectories.

Results from these efforts have been cascading into the literature for almost a decade, and it is dangerous to try to summarize their content. Several general observations can, however, be offered. Review of the most recent Energy Modeling Forum (EMF-14 1996) survey of modeler-preferred scenarios (whose uncontrolled emissions trajectories span the IS92 range) shows, first of all, that most analyses of optimal mitigation strategies exhibit very similar (and very modest) control trajectories and emissions reductions over the near term (through, say, the year 2020) even though they disagree wildly over the long term. This tendency also appears in the results of probabilistic analyses published by Nordhaus (1994a) or Yohe et al. (1996).

Second, as noted in Richels et al. (1996), reductions of up to 90 percent can be achieved (in the present value of the cost of reducing global emissions according to the prescriptions of the Berlin Mandate) by designing control strategies that take advantage of interregional and/or intertemporal efficiencies. Cast more generally, the lesson of this work is that applying the foundations of economic efficiency to the construction of global policy can produce dramatic results, even if the prescribed policy targets are drawn from outside what might be supported by the economic paradigm.

Third, Mendelsohn et al. (1996) reported that including economically efficient adaptation in the context of future economic activity can significantly reduce the cost of smoothly emerging global change in a industrialized economy (specifically the United States). Indeed, Mendelsohn and his coauthors found that the economic cost schedule is U-shaped in temperature and that there are regions in the United States for which current temperatures are actually too low; that is, higher temperature would actually improve welfare through most of the next century. Although the conditions that support negative net costs are not ubiquitous across the country, the net effect on the United States of gradual change through the next century of the sort reflected in the IS92 scenarios is actually positive.

In addition, Manne (1996), Yohe & Wallace (1996), and Yohe et al. (1996)

suggested that moving the growth-and-efficiency based paradigm to the extremes in terms of climate sensitivity and economic cost can have an effect on optimal near-term control strategies, but only if the subjective likelihood of some sort of high consequence event over the next 50 years or so climbs into the 5 percent range. Stepping back from optimality, moreover, Yohe & Wallace (1996) also showed that uncertainty over future emissions and concentration targets has little effect on near-term policies.

Finally, some researchers have questioned the validity of mainstream cost–benefit analyses of policy drawn from the IS92 scenarios, because they tend to miss the potential efficiency gains of using carbon-tax revenues to reduce the distortionary effects of other taxes. Ekins (1994) looked to an analysis of the UK economy to suggest that distribution of carbon tax revenue could combine with tax-based incentives for innovation to produce economic benefit rather than cost. Ekins (1995) offered further evidence that the cost of mitigation might be systematically overestimated by standard models when he surveyed their underlying modeling assumptions. The economics of second best is dangerous water, of course; but these are questions that are likely to be raised repeatedly within the paradigm as international negotiations move toward setting targets and timetables.

Effects of expanding the perspective

Perhaps the most significant lesson to be drawn from the recent work on the impact of global change and global change policy on economic activity is that most of the real potential for harm lies in the potential for surprise. The global climate system, expanded appropriately in its domain to include human activities of all kinds, is enormously complex. It is certainly capable of delivering some sort of nonlinear impact on the natural science side that could produce an irreversible effect of enormous consequence; and if that occurs, all of the policy bets made against smoothly emerging futures will be off. Therefore, researchers will be wise to begin systematic exploration of global change within paradigms of the sort described earlier to:

- expand the range of objectives beyond the growth and efficiency prescriptions of economics
- explore the broader systems consistency of futures that researchers contemplate
- increase the likelihood that surprise will be discovered before it is too late.

We have offered some insight into alternative objectives and different perspectives. The potential for systems inconsistency can be suggested by bringing the notion of equity to bear on the IS92 scenarios.

Edmonds et al. (1993) used their underlying income and population assumptions to add some consistent regional detail to the six IS92 scenarios. Yohe & Palmer (1994) worked with the Edmonds et al. results to compute Gini coefficients for the resulting distribution of income under the assumption that each resident in every region recovers the per capita income computed by the model for his or her region. As a result, the coefficients mask the potentially enormous interregional and intraregional differences in income. Moreover, they depend entirely upon the dynamics of trade and economic activity portrayed by Edmonds and his colleagues for the nine regions into which they divided the globe. Other modeling efforts, including more recent work by Edmonds and his colleagues to divide the globe into more regions, might produce different results; but the body of research supports these qualitative insights.

Most striking among the derivative results is a remarkable improvement in the distribution of income that develops (at least eventually) along every scenario. It is most dramatic in the IS92e scenario, where the Gini coefficient falls from 0.6 in 1990 to 0.5 in 2050 and to almost 0.4 in 2100. The IS92e is perhaps the most favorable IPCC scenario; it is driven by high economic growth rates and medium population growth, but it is constrained by 18400 exajoules of conventional oil and emissions controls that increase fossil fuel costs by 30 percent. Even along scenario IS92c, the least favorable growth story with slow population growth and limited oil and natural gas supplies, the Gini coefficient falls to 0.53 in 2050 and well below 0.5 by 2100. Both (in fact, all) therefore show Lorenz-dominant improvement over time at rates that far exceed historical experience.

These scenarios suggest that the less industrialized world rapidly adopts industrialized country technology (leading to increases in labor productivity and per capita income), while the industrialized world itself advances more slowly. This is consistent with a catching-up phase of development for the less industrialized world, but omits the possibility of further dramatic technological breakthroughs in the OECD. Is this reasonable—from economic, political, and social perspectives? What happens if the improvement does not materialize? Is it consistent with sustainable development globally? Regionally? On a national level for members of the OECD? For rapidly industrializing nations? For currently less industrialized nations? What is implied about food demand and the agricultural production base in each region, or the efficiency of the energy delivery and transportation infrastructure?

Some simple diagnostics display how the improvement occurs and add some context for these questions. The percentage of world GDP attributed to the upper 10 percent of the distribution holds (or actually increases in some cases) through 2050, but it declines quite precipitously in the second half of the next century. Movement toward equality through 2050 therefore comes mostly from redistribution of something like 50 percent of global income among the lower 90 percent of the population. Modest improvement in (formerly) centrally planned Asia, Latin America, and Africa at the expense of the (formerly) centrally planned countries of eastern Europe is typical. These regions, including eastern Europe, all improve more rapidly when the share devoted to the upper 10 percent begins its decline from its 1990 level—around 2050 along IS92e, after 2050 along IS92a, and after 2075 along IS92c. Most of the improvement in the distribution of income appears to come from reallocations among the lowest nine deciles for many years to come. Is this something that can be sustained over a half a century, or will resultant political and social pressures cause a discontinuity in business as usual? What do social and political science suggest about the consequences of sustained income inequality and perceived legitimacy of systems? Will different relative distributions of income cause different fertility rates over time, and with what demographic consequences?

The details of the analysis notwithstanding, the questions clearly stand. Economics must play a role in their consideration, but they are questions that the economic paradigm itself will not necessarily raise. Only concern about equity and the sustainability of dramatically uneven distributions of income lead to them directly; and their potential significance increases when it is understood that the distribution of income improves less quickly along scenarios that track lower carbon emissions and slower growth in the context of more restrictive controls directed at other environmental problems.

Meanwhile, the correspondence between global change and the distribution of income goes in two directions. The previous observations clearly show that increased attention needs to be paid to the effects of change and any response that might be forthcoming on the distribution of income. It should be equally clear that changes in the distribution of income driven by other conditions could easily have significant effects on the direction, size, and speed of global change.

For example, the Berry et al. (1982) data recorded above can provide a highly speculative taste of the dimension of these potential effects. Those data showed that a 1.8 percent increase in the per capita income received by the upper-middle three deciles from 1950 through 1977 was "financed" by a 1.3 percent decline in the per capita income of the lowest 6 deciles and a 0.5 percent decline in the average income of the wealthiest 10 percent of the world's population. Even without concern for changes in the distribution of income within nations, these relatively small trends would certainly affect total energy consumption. Assuming a unitary income elasticity of demand for energy (a restrictive assumption requiring that percentage changes in per capita energy consumption exactly match percentage changes in per capita income, a low estimate for less industrialized countries and a high one for industrialized countries, these trends would push global per capita energy consumption up by something on the order of 0.7 percent. If this speculative arithmetic suggests a number that can believed at least for illustrative purposes, then total carbon emissions in 1977 were more than 35 million tonnes higher than they otherwise would have been had the distribution of income not changed. Historically, the Gini coefficient actually has risen, not fallen as it is projected to do. What differences are implied that make the future so different?

Prospects for expanding the perspective

A broader view of the story might ask for a list of options that neither the economist nor the policy analyst has so far considered. Narrowly focused research paradigms can miss extraordinarily important social (and research) agendas; and so researchers should guard against excessive focus. Is that a real issue? Two observations suggest that it is.

The International Council of Scientific Unions (ICSU), working through its sponsorship of the International Geosphere–Biosphere Program (IGBP), has devised a set of research protocols that are extraordinarily rigid. These protocols require that their major international research programs develop detailed science plans by progressing through a multiyear process of international consultation, drafting, and peer review. The process is designed to be inclusive in its early stage so that all options and associated issues can be aired. However, the resulting science plans set the research agendas for IGBP Core Projects; and these plans include only issues deemed to be most significant by the participants of the science committees who are assigned to craft them.

This procedure may or may not be appropriate for natural science, in which controlled experiments are possible. Where agreement on central problems is relatively widespread, the IGBP certainly has an impressive record in sustaining good work through its science plan process. However, it is less obvious that the procedure can be applied equally well in defining the research agendas for the social science of global change. A case can certainly be made that the social science issues are so fluid that it cannot. The Human Dimensions Program (HDP) of the International Social Science Council (ISSC) is the social science analogue of IGBP, and it has recently accepted co-sponsorship by ICSU and ISSC. Discussions proceed, but pressure is mounting for complementary HDP Core Programs to emerge from the same science plan protocol with the same underlying criteria. If that happens, then the process is likely to focus attention only on the sorts of social science that interface well with the natural science base and that produce output with which the policy community can comfortably deal. For example, research suggesting that climate control would lead to redistributions of income and power large enough to spark chronic political revolution in industrialized countries almost certainly would be unwelcome.

The more narrow focus of this chapter is the second observation. The economic paradigm has its limits, and they have been recognized by practitioners for many years. However, most practitioners have been reluctant to accept alternative perspectives and to help bring their insights to the policy community. Confronted with environmental degradation and the exhaustion of environmentally based resources, growth practitioners have simply added depreciation of those resources to depreciation in the capital stock to their models. Cast that way, sustainability can simply be a constraint in the optimization problem of maximizing per capita income (discounted or steady state) rather than a separate and significant dimension to the problem. Confronted with nonmarket impacts and other market failures, other practitioners have devised means of valuation so that their nonmarket effects and nonuse values can be incorporated into the conventional calculus of cost–benefit analysis. There, they lose their identity and are frequently discounted if they grow large.

The problems notwithstanding, the research focus stays within the economic paradigm because it has an established role to play in policy evaluation and because the policy community has come to understand how to deal with the results that it produces. In a world where all of the action will come with dimensions not currently foreseen, though, narrow focus may mean missing the action.

Conclusions

Economic activities depend upon climate, as well as on natural resources and on human labor and technology. Changes in the types and scale of human activities in the modern age are the proximate cause of anthropogenic climate change. Further, the prospect for continued increases in scale imply continued increases in greenhouse-related emissions, although such increases are not inevitable. Policies may be devised to reduce greenhouse-related emissions, to mitigate climate change in other ways, and to adapt.

Proposed policies may be evaluated from a variety of perspectives; a mainstream approach usually includes growth-oriented economic analyses of the costs and benefits. Costs of mitigation in the near and medium term are weighed against often diffuse and uncertain benefits in the very long term, and must account for countries whose economic development may depend upon emissions-generating activities and who may thus be unwilling to trade off growth for emissions reductions. The consensus result of studies employing cost–benefit analysis is that relatively modest near-term actions are required, although the degree of intervention grows over time.

Issues for economic analysis include valuing nonmarket (environmental) goods and nonmonetary transactions and assets; global efficiency, trade, and the implications of inequities in the global distribution of income; the handling of surprises (economic tools remain crude for this purpose); and the application of a discount rate, which is economically unresolvable. Global climate change is part of a class of problems that tends to exacerbate the shortcomings of the mainstream approaches to economics, although economic analysis remains a powerful tool to evaluate candidate policy options.

References

Aaron, H. J. 1994. Distinguished lecture on economics in government: public policy, values, and consciousness. *Journal of Economic Perspectives* **8**, 3–21.

Adamowicz, W., J. Louviere, M. Williams 1994. Combining revealed and stated preference methods for valuing environmental amenities. *Journal of Environmental Economics and Management* **26**, 271–92.

Adams, R. M. 1989. Global climate change and agriculture: an economic perspective. *American Journal of Agricultural Economics* **71**, 1272–9.

Ahlburg, D. 1987. The impact of population growth on economic growth in developing nations: the evidence from macroeconomic-demographic models. In *Population growth and economic development: issues and evidence*, D. G. Johnson & R. Lee (eds). Madison: University of Wisconsin Press.

Alcamo, J., A. Bouwman, J. Edmonds, A. Grübler, T. Morita, A. Sugandhy 1995. An evaluation of the IPCC IS92 emission scenarios. In *Climate change 1994: radiative forcing of climate change and an evaluation of the IPCC IS92 emission scenarios* [IPCC Special Report], J. T. Houghton, L. G. M. Filho, J. Bruce, H. Lee, B. A. Callander, E. Haites N. Harris, K. Maskell (eds). Cambridge: Cambridge University Press.

Alesina, A., S. Ozler, N. Roubini, P. Swagel 1991. Political instability and economic growth. Cambridge, Massachusetts: National Bureau of Economic Research.

Algaze, G. 1989. The Uruk expansion: cross-cultural exchange as a factor in early Mesopotamian civilization. *Current Anthropology* **30**, 571–608.

Alston, L. J., G. D. Libecap, R. Schneider 1994. *An analysis of property rights, land value, and agricultural investment on two frontiers in Brazil*. Unpublished paper, University of Illinois at Urbana–Champaign.

Ameen, A., E. Crenshaw, J. C. Jenkins 1994. *The structural determinants of energy intensity*. Unpublished paper, Department of Sociology, Ohio State University, Columbus.

Amin, S. 1976. *Unequal development*. New York: Monthly Review Press.

Arrow, K. J. 1951. *Social choice and individual values*. New York: John Wiley.

Arrow, K. J., B. Bolin, R. Costanza, P. Dasgupta, C. Folke, C. S. Holling, B. O. Jansson, S. Levin, K. G. Mäler, C. Perrings, D. Pimentel 1995. Economic growth, carrying capacity, and the environment. *Science* **268**, 520–21.

Atkinson, A. B. 1970. On the measurement of inequality. *Journal of Economic Theory* **2**, 244–63.

Azimi, A. M. 1994. Greenhouse gas options and issues in Asia region. In *Climate change: policy instruments and their implications*, A. Amano, B. Fisher, M. Kuroda, T. Morita, S. Nishioka (eds). Proceedings of the Tsukuba Workshop of IPCC Working Group III, Center for Global Environmental Research, Tsukuba, Japan.

Balassa, B. & M. Nolund 1988. *Japan in the world economy*. Washington DC: Institute for International Economics.

Banuri, T., K. Goran-Maler, M. Grubb, H. K. Jacobson, F. Yamin 1996. Equity and social considerations. See Bruce et al. (1996).

Barbier, E. B. 1989. *Economics, natural-resource scarcity and development: conventional and alternative views*. London: Earthscan.

Barlow, R. 1967. The economic effects of malaria eradication. *American Economic Review* **57**(2), 130–57.

Barro, R. 1991. Economic growth in a cross section of countries. *Quarterly Journal of Economics* **61**, 407–444.

Barry 1983. Intergenerational justice in energy policy. In *Energy and the future*, D. MacClean & P. G. Brown (eds). Washington DC: Resources for the Future.

Barthelemy, P. 1989. The underground economy in France. See Feige (1989).

Bartik, T. J. 1988. The effects of environmental regulation on business location in the United States. *Growth and Change* **19**(3), 22–44.

Bates, R. W. 1993. The impact of economic policy on energy and the environment in developing countries. *Annual Review of Energy and Environment* **18**, 479–505.

Batie, S. S. & H. H. Shugart 1989. The biological consequences of climate changes: an ecological and economic assessment. In *Greenhouse warming: abatement and adaptation*, N. J. Rosenberg, W. E. Easterling, P. R. Crosson, J. Darmstadter (eds). Washington DC: Resources for the Future.

Bhattacharyya, D. K. 1990. An econometric method of estimating the "hidden economy", United Kingdom (1960–1984): estimates and tests. *The Economic Journal* (September), 703–717.

Becker, G., K. Murphy, R. Tamura 1990. Human capital, fertility and economic growth. *Journal of Political Economy* **98**(5), S12–S37.

Behrman, J. 1990. *Human resource-led development?* Geneva: International Labour Office.

Bell, B. 1975. Climate and history of Egypt: the Middle Kingdom. *American Journal of Archaeology* **79**, 223–69.

——1979. The Dark Ages in ancient history, I: the first Dark Age in Egypt. *American Journal of Archaeology* **75**, 1–26.

Berkes, F. & C. Folke 1994. Investing in cultural capital for sustainable use of natural capital: the ecological economics approach to sustainability. See Jansson et al. (1994).

Berndt, E. 1985. From technocracy to net energy analysis: engineers, economists, and recurring energy theories of value. In *Progress in natural resource economics*, A. Scot (ed.). Oxford: Oxford University Press.

Berry, A., F. Bourguignon, C. Morrison 1982. Changes in the world distribution of income between 1950 and 1977. *Economic Journal* **93**, 331–50.

Bijlsma, L., C. N. Ehler, R. J. T. Klein, S. M. Kulshrethsa, R. F. McLean, N. Mimura, R. J. Nicholls, L. A. Nurse, H. Pérez Nieto, E. Z. Stakhiv, R. K. Turner, R. A. Warrick 1996. Coastal zones and small islands. See Watson et al. (1996).

Bishop, R. C. 1993. Economic efficiency, sustainability and biodiversity. *Ambio* **22**, 69–73.

Blanchet, D. 1988. A stochastic version of the Malthusian trap model: consequences for the empirical relationship between economic growth and population growth in LDCs. *Mathematical Population Studies* **1**(1), 79–99.

——1991. Estimating the relationship between population growth and aggregate economic growth in developing countries: methodological problems. In *Consequences of rapid population growth and aggregate economic growth in developing countries*, G. Tapinos, D. Blanchet, D. E. Horlacher (eds). New York: Taylor & Francis.

Bloom, D. & R. Freeman 1988. Economic development and the timing and components of population growth. *Journal of Policy Modeling* **10**(1), 57–82.

Blumler, M. A. & R. Byrne 1991. The ecological genetics of domestication and the origins of agriculture. *Current Anthropology* **12**, 23–54.

Board on Agriculture and Board on Science and Technology for Development, National Research Council, National Research Council, National Research Council 1992. *Sustainable agricultural development in the humid tropics*. Washington DC: National Academy Press.

Board on Agriculture, National Research Council 1991. *Sustainable agriculture research and education in the field*. Washington DC: National Academy Press.

Bongarts, J. 1992. Population growth and global warming. *Population and Development Review* **18**, 299–319.

Bornschier, V. & C. Chase-Dunn 1985. *Transnational corporations and underdevelopment*. New York: Praeger.

Bose, S. A. 1993. *Money, energy, and welfare: the state and the household in India's rural electrification policy*. Delhi: Oxford University Press.

Boyce, J. 1989. Population growth and real wages of agricultural labourers in Bangladesh. *Journal of Development Studies* **25**(4), 467–85.

Branson, W. 1989. *Macroeconomic theory and policies*. London: Harper & Row.

Broesterhuizen, G. A. A. M. 1989. The unrecorded economy and the national income accounts in the Netherlands: a sensitivity analysis. See Feige (1989).

Brookshire, D., M. Thayer, J. Tschirhart, W. Schulze 1985. A test of the expected utility model: evidence from earthquake risks. *Journal of Political Economy* **93**, 369–89.

Bruce, J. P., H. Lee, E. F. Haites (eds) 1996. *Climate change 1995: economic and social dimensions of climate change*. Cambridge: Cambridge University Press.

Burton, P. S. 1993. Intertemporal preferences and intergenerational equity considerations in optimal resource harvesting. *Journal of Environmental Economics and Management* **24**, 119–32.

Byrne, R. 1987. Climatic change and the origin of agriculture. In *Studies in the Neolithic and urban revolutions*, L. Manzanilla (ed.). Oxford: BAR International Series.

Cantor, R., S. Henry, S. Rayner 1992. *Making markets: an interdisciplinary perspective on economic exchange*. Westport, Connecticut: Greenwood Press.

Carson, R. T. & R. C. Mitchell 1995. Sequencing and nesting in contingent valuation. *Journal of Environmental Economics and Management* **28**(2), 155–73.

Cassen, R. (ed.) 1994. *Population and development: old debates, new conclusions*. Washington DC: Overseas Development Council.

Cecelski, E. W. 1991. Practical strategies and approaches to addressing gender issues at planning stages in the energy and water sectors: lessons from international experience. Presented at the Seminar/Training Workshop on Women in Water and Energy Development, Kathmandu, Nepal.

Clague, C., P. Keefer, S. Knack, M. Olson 1995. Property and contract rights under democracy and dictatorship. IRIS [online system], University of Maryland.

Clark, C. W. & G. R. Munro 1994. Renewable resources as natural capital: the fishery. See Jansson et al. (1994).

Cline, W. 1992. *The economics of global warming*. Washington DC: Institute for International Economics.

Common, M. & C. Perrings 1992. Towards an ecological economics of sustainability. *Ecological Economics* **6**, 7–34.

Contini, B. 1989. The irregular economy of Italy: a survey of contributions. See Feige (1989).

Costanza, R. 1991. *Ecological economics: the science and management of sustainability*. New York: Columbia University Press.

—— 1994. Three general policies to achieve sustainability. See Jansson et al. (1994).

Costanza, R. & L. Cornwell 1992. The 4P approach to dealing with scientific uncertainty. *Environment* **34**, 12–20.

Costanza, R. & H. E. Daly 1992. Natural capital and sustainable development. *Conservation Biology* **6**, 37–46.

Cox Jr, L. A., 1986. Theory of regulatory benefits assessment and expressed preference approaches. In *Benefits assessment: the state of the art*, J. D. Bentkover, V. T. Covello,

J. Mumpower (eds). Dordrecht: Reidel.

Crenshaw, E. 1992. Cross-national determinants of income inequality. *Social Forces* **71**, 339–63.

Crosson, P. R. 1989. Climate change: problems of limits and policy responses. In *Greenhouse warming: abatement and adaptation*, N. J. Rosenberg, W. E. Easterling, P. R. Crosson, J. Darmstadter (eds). Washington DC: Resources for the Future.

Crumley, C. L. 1994. The ecology of conquest. In *Historical ecology*, C. L. Crumley (ed.). Santa Fe, New Mexico: School of American Research.

d'Arge, R. C. 1994. Sustenance and sustainability: how can we preserve and consume without major conflict. See Jansson et al. (1994).

d'Arge, R. C. & J. Shogren 1989. Non-market asset prices: a comparison of three valuation approaches. In *Valuation and policy making in environmental economics*, H. Folmer & E. van Ireland (eds). Amsterdam: Elsevier.

Dagum, C. 1990. On the relationship between income inequality measures and social welfare functions. *Journal of Econometrics* **43**, 91–102.

Dalton, H. 1920. The measurement of inequality of incomes. *Economic Journal* **30**, 348–61.

Daly, H. E. 1984. Alternative strategies for integrating economics and ecology. In *Integration of ecology and economics: an outlook for the eighties*, A. M. Jansson (ed.). Stockholm: Department of Systems Ecology, Stockholm University.

——1987. The economic growth debate: what some economists have learned but others have not. *Journal of Environmental Economics and Management* **14**, 323–36.

——1991. Allocation, distribution, and scale: towards an economics that is efficient, just, and sustainable. *Ecological Economics* **6**, 185–94.

——1994a. Alternative strategies for integrating economics and ecology. In *Integration of ecology and economics: an outlook for the eighties*, A. M. Jansson (ed.). Stockholm: Department of Systems Ecology, Stockholm University.

——1994b. Operationalizing sustainable development by investing in natural capital. See Jansson et al. (1994).

Daly, H. E. & J. B. Cobb 1989. *For the common good: redirecting the economy toward community, the environment and a sustainable future*. Boston: Beacon Press.

Deacon, R. T. 1994. Deforestation and the rule of law in a cross section of countries. *Land Economics* **70**, 414–30.

——1996. Deforestation, investment, and political stability. In *The political economy of conflict and appropriation*, M. Garfinkel & S. Skaperdas (eds). Cambridge: Cambridge University Press.

Dietz, T. & E. A. Rosa 1994. *Effects of population and affluence on CO_2 emissions*. Unpublished paper, Department of Sociology, George Mason University.

Dilnot, A. & C. N. Morris 1981. What do we know about the black economy in the United Kingdom? *Fiscal Studies* **2**, 237–50.

Dow, L. M. 1977. High weeds in Detroit. *Urban Anthropology* **6**, 111–28.

Duchin, F. & G-M. Lange 1994. Strategies for environmentally sound economic development. See Jansson et al. (1994).

Edmonds, J., H. Pitcher, D. Barns, R. Baron, M. Wise 1993. Design for the Global Assessment Model – GCAM. In *Papers of the international workshop on integrated assessment of mitigation, impacts and adaptation to climate change*. Laxenburg, Austria: International Institute of Applied Systems Analysis.

Ehrlich, P. R. 1994. Ecological economics and the carrying capacity of Earth. See Jansson et al. (1994).

Ehrlich, P. R. & J. P. Holdren 1971. Impact of population growth. *Science* **171**, 1212–17.

Ekins, P. 1994. The impact of carbon taxation on the UK economy. *Energy Policy* **22**, 571–9.

——1995. Rethinking the costs related to global warming: a survey of the issues. *Environmental and Resource Economics* **6**, 231–77.

Energy Modeling Forum (EMF-14) 1996. *Models for second round scenario results*. Unpublished

paper, Stanford University.
Evenson, R. 1988. Population growth, infrastructure and real income in North India. In *Population, food and rural development*, R. Lee, B. Arthur, A. Kelley, T. N. Srinivasen (eds). New York: Oxford University Press.

Fankhauser, S. 1994. *Valuing climate change: the economics of the greenhouse effect*. London: Earthscan.
Farber, D. A. & P. A. Hemmersbaugh 1993. The shadow of the future: discount rates, later generations, and the environment. *Vanderbilt Law Review* **46**(2), 267–304.
Feige, E. L. 1981. The UK's unobserved economy? *Challenge Magazine* (November/December), 5–13.
——(ed.) 1989. *The underground economies: tax evasion and information distortion*. Cambridge: Cambridge University Press.
Fischer, G., M. G. Morgan, B. Fischhoff, I. Nair, L. Lave 1991. What risks are people concerned about? *Risk Analysis* **11**, 303–314.
Fischhoff, B. 1991. Elicitation: is there anything in there? *American Psychologist* **46**, 835–47.
Frank, A. G. 1967. *Capitalism and underdevelopment in Latin America*. New York: Monthly Review Press.
Freeman, A. M. 1993. *The measurement of environmental and resource values: theory and methods*. Washington DC: Resources for the Future.

Gardner, G. & L. Gould 1989. Public perceptions of the risks and benefits of technology. *Risk Analysis* **9**, 225–42.
Gastwirth, J. L. 1972. The estimation of the Lorenz curve and Gini index. *Review of Economics and Statistics* **54**, 306–316.
Geertz, C. 1978. The bazaar economy, information and change in peasant marketing. *American Economic Review* **68**, 28–31.
Gilliland, M. W. & J. P. Kash 1994. Economic conversion, engineers, and sustainability. See Jansson et al. (1994).
Glantz, M. H. (ed.) 1988. *Societal responses to climate change: forecasting by analogy*. Boulder, Colorado: Westview.
Goeller, H. E. & A. M. Weinberg 1976. The age of substitutability. *Science* **191**, 683–9.
Goldman, M. I. 1972. *The spoils of progress*. Cambridge, Massachusetts: MIT Press.
Gray, H. P. 1978. *International trade, investment and payments*. Boston: Houghton Mifflin.
Grimes, P. E., J. T. Roberts, R. L. Manale 1994. *Social roots of environmental damage: a world-system analysis of global warming and deforestation*. Unpublished paper, Department of Sociology, Johns Hopkins University.
Grose, P. (ed). The Marshall Plan and its legacy (Special Section). *Foreign Affairs* **76**(3), 159–221.
Grossman, G. & A. B. Krueger 1993. Environmental impacts of a North American Free Trade Agreement. In *US–Mexico free trade agreement*, P. Garber (ed.). Cambridge, Massachusetts: MIT Press.
Gupta, S. 1992. *Black income in India*. New Delhi: Sage.

Hammer, M., A. M. Jansson, B. O. Jansson 1993. Diversity change and sustainability: implications for fisheries. *Ambio* **22**, 97–105.
Hanley, N. & C. Spash 1993. *Cost–benefit analysis and the environment*. Cheltenham, England: Edward Elgar.
Hansson, I. 1989. The underground economy in Sweden. See Feige (1989).
Harless, D. & C. F. Camerer 1994. The predictive utility of generalized expected utility theory. *Econometrica* **52**, 1251–89.
Hey, J. D. & P. Lambert 1980. Relative deprivation and the Gini coefficient—comment. *Quarterly Journal of Economics* **95**(3), 567–74.
Hays, S. 1987. *Beauty, health, and performance: environmental politics in the United States, 1955–85*. Cambridge: Cambridge University Press.

Heather, J. & J. Vijay 1976. *Surplus labour and the city: a study of Bombay*. Delhi: Oxford University Press.

Henderson, J. V. 1988. *Urban development: theory, fact and illusion*. New York: Oxford University Press.

Hirshleifer, J. 1970. *Investment, interest and capital*. Englewood Cliffs, New Jersey: Prentice-Hall.

Hole, F. 1997. Evidence for mid-Holocene environmental change in the western Habur drainage, northeastern Syria. In *Third millennium BC abrupt climate change and old world social collapse*, H. N. Dalfes, G. Kukla, H. Weiss (eds). New York: Springer.

Holling, C. S. 1992. Cross-scale morphology, geometry and dynamics of ecosystems. *Ecological Monographs* **62**(4), 447–502.

—— 1994. New science and new investments for a sustainable biosphere. See Jansson et al. (1994).

Holmes, D. L. 1993. Rise of the Nile delta. *Nature* **363**, 402–440.

Hostetler, J. A. 1963. *Amish society*. Baltimore: Johns Hopkins University Press.

Howarth, R. B. 1993. Environmental risks and future generations: criteria for public policy. In *Clean water and the American economy*, Publication 800-R-93-0013, US Environmental Protection Agency, Office of Water, Washington DC.

IMF 1995. *International financial statistics*. Washington DC: International Monetary Fund.

IRS [US Internal Revenue Service] 1988. *Income tax compliance research, supporting appendixes to Publication 7285*. Washington DC: Department of Treasury.

James, D. E., J. Nijkamp, J. B. Opschoor 1989. Ecological sustainability in economic development. In *Economy and ecology: toward sustainable development*, F. Archibugi & P. Nijkamp (eds). Dordrecht: Kluwer.

Jansson, A. M. & B. O. Jansson 1994. Ecosystem properties as a basis for sustainability. See Jansson et al. (1994).

Jansson, A. M., M. Hammer, C. Folke, R. Costanza (eds) 1994. *Investing in natural capital: the ecological economics approach to sustainability*. Washington DC: Island Press.

Jenkins, J. C. & E. Crenshaw 1992. *The globalization of environmental degradation*. Department of Sociology, Ohio State University.

Kahneman, D., I. Ritov, K. Jacowitz, P. Grant 1993. Stated willingness to pay for public goods: a psychological perspective. *Psychological Science* **4**, 310–15.

Katz, A. & E. Bender 1976. *The strength in us: self-help groups in the modern world*. New York: Franklin Watts.

Keefer, P. & S. Knack 1994. Property rights, inequality and growth. IRIS [online system], University of Maryland.

Keeney, R. L. & H. Raiffa 1976. *Decisions with multiple objectives: preferences and value tradeoffs*. New York: John Wiley.

Kemp, B. J. 1983. Old Kingdom, Middle Kingdom and Second Intermediate Period *c.* 2686–1552 BC. In, *Ancient Egypt: a social history*, B. E. Trigger, B. J. Kemp, D. O'Connor, A. B. Lloyd (eds). Cambridge: Cambridge University Press.

Kempton, W. 1991. Lay perspectives on global climate change. *Global Environmental Change* **1**, 183–208.

Kirchgaessner, G. 1983. Size and development of the West German shadow economy. *Zeitschrift für die Gesamte Staatswissenschaft* **139**, 197–214.

Kitschelt, H. 1986. Political opportunity structure and political protest. *British Journal of Political Science* **16**, 58–95.

Klaasen, G. & J. Opschoor 1991. Economics of sustainability or the sustainability of economics. *Ecological Economics* **4**, 93–116.

Kneese, A. V. & W. D. Schulze 1985. Ethics and environmental economics. In *Handbook of natural resource and energy economics* (vol. 1), A. V. Kneese & J. L. Sweeney (eds). Amsterdam: Elsevier.

Kolavalli, S. & D. Chicoine 1989. Groundwater markets in Gujarat, India. *Water Resources*

Development **5**(1), 38–44.

Kosmo, M. 1987. *Money to burn? The high cost of energy subsidies*. Washington DC: World Resources Institute.

Kunreuther, H., D. Easterling, W. Devousges, P. Slovic 1990. Public attitudes toward siting a high-level waste repository in Nevada. *Risk Analysis* **10**, 469–84.

Langfeldt, E. 1989. The underground economy in the Federal Republic of Germany: a preliminary assessment. See Feige (1989).

Larson, D. 1993. On measuring existence values. *Land Economics* **69**, 377–88.

Laughland, A., W. Musser, L. Musser 1991. *An experiment on the reliability of contingent valuation*. Staff Paper 202, Department of Agricultural Economics, Pennsylvania State University.

Lee, R. 1980. A historical perspective on economic aspects of the population explosion: the case of preindustrial England. In *Population and economic change in developing countries*, R. Easterlin (ed.). Chicago: University of Chicago Press.

Leggett, J., W. J. Pepper, R. J. Swart 1992. Emissions scenarios for the IPCC: an update. In *IPCC climate change 1992: the supplemental report to the IPCC scientific assessment*. Cambridge: Cambridge University Press.

Lenski, G. & P. Nolan 1984. Trajectories of development. *Social Forces* **63**, 1–23.

Liebow, E. 1967. *Talley's Corner: a study of Negro corner men*. Boston: Little, Brown.

Lind, R. C. 1982. *Discounting for time and risk in energy policy*. Baltimore: Johns Hopkins University Press.

——1995. Intergenerational equity, discounting, and the role of cost–benefit analysis in evaluating global climate policy. *Energy Policy* **23**(4/5), 379–89.

Lipton, M. 1991. Accelerated resource degradation by Third World agriculture: created in the commons, in the West, or in bed? In *Agricultural sustainability, growth and poverty alleviation: issues and policies*, S. A. Vosti, T. Reardon, W. von Urff (eds). Washington DC: International Food Policy Research Institute.

Loomis, J. 1989. Test–retest reliability of the contingent valuation method: a comparison of general population and visitor responses. *American Journal of Agricultural Economics* **71**, 77–84.

Lovell, M. 1994. *Inequality within and among nations*. Unpublished paper, Department of Economics, Wesleyan University.

Lowenthal, M. 1975. The social economy in urban working class communities. In *The social economy of cities*, G. Gappert & H. Rose (eds). Beverly Hills, California: Sage.

——1981. Non-market transactions in an urban community. In *Informal institutions*, S. Henry (ed.). New York: St Martin's Press.

Lubell, H. 1991. *The informal sector: in the 1980s and 1990s*. Paris: Development Centre Studies, Organisation for Economic Cooperation and Development.

Lucas, R. E. 1988. On the mechanics of economic development. *Monetary Economics* **22**, 3–42.

Ludwig, D., R. Hilborn, C. Walters 1993. Uncertainty, resource exploitation, and conservation: lessons from history. *Science* **260**, 20–36.

MacDonald, D., J. Murdoch, H. White 1987. Uncertain hazards, insurance, and consumer choice: evidence from housing markets. *Land Economics* **63**, 361–71.

MacKellar, L. 1994. Population and development: assessment in advance of the 1994 World Population Conference. *Development Policy Review* **12**(June), 1–28.

Manisan, D., L. Bruce, L. Bernier, R. Ingersol, L. Pilarski, C. Reed, P. Mollett, R. Skole 1987. Europe's booming black economy. *International Management* **42**, 24–30.

Manne, A. S. 1995. The rate of time preference: implications for the greenhouse debate. *Energy Policy* **23**(4/5), 391–4.

Manne, A. S. 1996. *Hedging strategies for global carbon dioxide abatement: a summary of poll results*. EMF-14 Subgroup on Analysis for Decisions under Uncertainty, Stanford University.

Markusen, J. R., E. R. Morey, N. Olewiller 1994. Noncooperative equilibria in regional environmental policies when plant locations are endogenous. *Journal of Public Economics* **41**, 261–76.

Marshall, L. 1961. Sharing, talking, and giving: relief of social tensions among !Kung Bushmen. *Africa* **31**, 231–49.
Mason, A. 1988. Saving, economic growth and demographic change. *Population and Development Review* **10**(2), 177–240.
McCorriston, J. & F. Hole 1991. The ecology of seasonal stress and the origins of agriculture in the Near East. *American Anthropologist* **93**, 46–69.
McGovern, T. H. 1994. Management for extinction in Norse Greenland. In *Historical ecology*, C. L. Crumley (ed.). Santa Fe, New Mexico: School of American Research.
Mendelsohn, R., J. Callaway, B. Hurd, B. McCarl, W. Morrison, K. Segerson, J. Smith, B. Sohngen, G. Yohe 1996. The market impacts of climate change in the United States. Paper presented to the Third International Workshop on Integrated Assessment of Mitigation, Impacts and Adaptation to Climate Change, International Institute of Applied Systems Analysis, Laxenburg, Austria.
Migdal, J. 1988. *Strong societies and weak states*. Princeton, New Jersey: Princeton University Press.
Mikesell, R. F. 1991. Project evaluation and sustainable development. In *Environmentally sustainable economic development: building on Brundtland*, R. Goodland, H. Daly, E. S. Serafy (eds). Environment Working Paper 46, World Bank, Washington DC.
Minzter, I. M. 1990. Energy, greenhouse gases, and climate change. *Annual Review of Energy* **15**, 513–50.
Mirus, R. & R. Smith 1989. Canada's underground economy. See Feige (1989).
Montiel, P., P. R. Agenos, N. Haque 1993. *Informal financial markets in developing countries – a macroeconomic analysis*. Oxford: Basil Blackwell.
Moore, W. 1978. *World modernization*. New York: Elsevier.
Morey, E. 1994. What is consumers' surplus per day of use, when is it a constant independent of the number of days of use, and what does it tell us about consumers' surplus? *Journal of Environmental Economics and Management* **26**, 257–70.
Morgan, G., M. Kandikar, J. Rishbey, H. Dowlatabadi 1996. *Why conventional tools for policy analysis are often inadequate for problems of global change*. Unpublished paper, Department of Engineering and Public Policy, Carnegie Mellon University.
Munasinghe, M., P. Meier, M. Hoel, S. W. Hong, A. Aaheim 1996. *Applicability of techniques of cost–benefit analysis to climate change*. See Bruce et al. (1996).

NOAA [US National Oceanographic and Atmospheric Administration] 1993. *Federal Register* 58 FR 4601.
Nolan, P. & G. Lenski 1985. Technoeconomic heritage, patterns of development, and the advantage of backwardness. *Social Forces* **64**, 341–58.
Nordhaus, W. D. 1991. To slow or not to slow: the economics of the greenhouse effect. *Economic Journal* **101**, 920–37.
——1994a. *Managing the global commons: the economics of climate change*. Cambridge, Massachusetts: MIT Press.
——1994b. *Locational competition and the environment*. Discussion Paper 1079, Cowles Foundation, Yale University.
Norgaard, R. B. 1991. *Sustainability as intergenerational equity: the challenge to economic thought and practice*. Report DP7, World Bank, Washington DC.
Norgaard, R. B. & R. B. Howarth 1991. Sustainability and discounting the future. In *Ecological economics, the science and management of sustainability*, R. Costanza (ed.). New York: Columbia University Press.
Norton, B. G. 1986. *The preservation of species*. Princeton, New Jersey: Princeton University Press.
NRDC [Natural Resources Defense Council] 1987. *Natural Resources Defense Council, Inc. v. Environmental Protection Agency* **824**(F.2nd), 1146 (DC Cir.).

Oates, W. E. & R. M. Schwab 1988. Economic competition among jurisdictions: efficiency enhancing or distortion inducing? *Journal of Public Economics* **35**, 333–54.

Olson, M. 1982. *The rise and decline of nations*. New Haven, Connecticut: Yale University Press.
Owata, Y. 1990. Economic activity and the greenhouse effect. *The Energy Journal* **12**, 23–35.
Ozler, S. & D. Rodrik 1992. *External shocks, politics, and private investment: some theory and empirical evidence*. Working Paper 3960, National Bureau of Economic Research, Cambridge, Massachusetts.

Pearce, D. W. 1993. *Economic values and the natural world*. Cambridge, Massachusetts: MIT Press.
Pearce, D. W. & K. Turner 1990. *Economics of natural resources and the environment*. London: Harvester Wheatsheaf.
Pearce, D. W. & C. Bann 1993. *North–South transfers and the capture of global environmental value*. Unpublished paper, Centre for Social and Economic Research on the Global Environment, University College London.
Pepper, W. J., J. Leggett, R. Swart, J. Wasson, J. Edmonds, I. Mintzer 1992. *Emissions scenarios for the IPCC: an update—assumptions, methodology, and results*. Geneva: Intergovernmental Panel on Climate Change
Perrings, C. A. 1989. Environmental bonds and environmental research in innovative activities. *Ecological Economics* **1**(1), 95–110.
——1994. Biotic diversity, sustainable development, and natural capital. See Jansson et al. (1994).
Perrings, C., C. Folke, K-G. Maler 1992. The ecology and economics of biodiversity loss: the research agenda. *Ambio* **21**, 201–211.
Persson, T. & G. Tabellini 1990. Is inequality harmful for growth? Working Paper, Department of Economics, University of California, Los Angeles.

Repetto, R. 1985. *The global possible*. New Haven, Connecticut: Yale University Press.
Richels, R. & J. Edmonds 1995. The economics of stabilizing atmospheric CO_2 concentrations. *Energy Policy* **23**(4/5), 373–8.
Richels, R., J. Edmonds, H. Gruenspecht, T. Wigley 1996. *The Berlin mandate: the design of cost-effective mitigation strategies*. Palo Alto, California: Electric Power Research Institute.
Robinson, D. & S. Henry 1977. *Self-help and health: mutual aid for modern problems*. Oxford: Martin Robertson.
Romer, P. M. 1986. Increasing returns and long-term growth. *Journal of Political Economy* **94**, 1002–1037.
Rosenberg, E. & L. M. Eisgruber 1992. *Sustainable development and sustainable agriculture: a partially annotated bibliography with emphasis on economics*. Working Paper 92-101, Graduate Faculty of Economics, University of Oregon.
Rostow, W. W. 1960. *The stages of economic growth*. New York: Cambridge University Press.
Rudel, T. K. 1989. Population, development and tropical deforestation. *Rural Sociology* **54**, 327–38.
Rueschemeyer, D. & P. Evans 1985. The state and economic transformation. In *Bringing the state back in*, P. Evans, D. Rueschemeyer, T. Skocpol (eds). New York: Cambridge University Press.
Ruttan, V. W. 1994. Constraints on the design of sustainable systems of agricultural production. *Ecological Economics* **10**, 209–210.

Sagoff, M. 1988. *The economy of the Earth*. New York: Cambridge University Press.
——1993. Environmental economics: an epitaph. *Resources* **111**, 2–7.
Sahlins, M. 1972. *Stone age economics*. Chicago: Aldine–Atherton.
Samuelson, P. A. 1964. Tax deductibility of economic depreciation to insure invariant valuations. *Journal of Political Economy* **72**(4), 604–606.
Samuelson, P. A. & W. D. Nordhaus 1995. *Economics*, 15th edn. New York: McGraw–Hill.
Schelling, T. C. 1984. *Choice and consequence*. Cambridge, Massachusetts: Harvard University Press.
——1995. Intergenerational discounting. *Energy Policy* **23**(4/5), 395–401.

Schipper, L., S. Meyers, R. Howarth, R. Steiner 1992. *Energy efficiency and human activity*. New York: Cambridge University Press.

Schmidt-Hebbel, K., S. Webband, G. Corsetti 1992. Household saving in developing countries: first cross-country evidence. *World Bank Economic Review* **6**(3), 529–47.

Schneider, S. & R. Chen 1980. Carbon dioxide warming and coastline flooding: physical factors and climatic impact. *Annual Review of Energy* **5**, 107–140.

Schoemaker, P. 1982. The expected utility model: its variants, purposes, evidence, and limitations. *Journal of Economic Literature* **20**, 529–63.

Sen, A. K. 1974. Informational bases of alternative welfare approaches: aggregation and income distribution. *Journal of Public Economics* **21**, 387–403.

——1975. *On economic inequality*. New York: Norton.

——1977. Rational fools: a critique of the behavioral foundations of economic theory. *Philosophy and Public Affairs* **6**, 317–44.

Serageldin, I. & A. Steer (eds) 1994. *Valuing the environment*. Washington DC: The International Bank for Reconstruction and Development/The World Bank.

Sethuraman, S. V. 1981. *The urban informal sector in developing countries: employment, poverty and environment*. Geneva: International Labour Office.

Shah, T. 1993. *Groundwater markets and irrigation development: political economy and practical policy*. Bombay: Oxford University Press.

Sheshinski, E. 1972. Relation between a social welfare function and the Gini index of inequality. *Journal of Economic Theory* **4**(1), 98–100.

Shukla, P. R. 1994. *Informal and traditional sector dynamics: a missing dimension in the global greenhouse gas (GHG) abatement policies*. Paper submitted as input to the IPCC Second Assessment Report (Working Group III, Writing Teams 6 and 7), Intergovernmental Panel on Climate Change, Geneva.

Smith, J. B. & D. Tirpak (eds) 1989. *The potential effects of global climate change on the United States* [report to Congress]. Washington DC: Environmental Protection Agency.

Smith, V. K. & W. Desvouges 1986. *Measuring water quality benefits*. Boston: Kluwer–Nijhoff.

Smith, V. K. & Y. Kaoru 1990. Signals or noise? Explaining the variation in recreation benefit estimates. *American Journal of Agricultural Economics* **72**, 419–33.

Solow, R. M. 1956. A contribution to the theory of economic growth. *Quarterly Journal of Economics* **70**, 56–94.

——1958. Growth theory and after. *American Economic Review* **78**(3), 307–317.

——1974. The economics of resources or the resources of economics. *American Economic Review* **64**, 1–14.

——1991. Sustainability: an economist's perspective. J. Seeward Johnson Lecture, Marine Policy Center, Woods Hole Oceanographic Institution, Massachusetts.

Southgate, D., R. Sierra, L. Brown 1991. The causes of tropical deforestation in Ecuador: a statistical analysis. *World Development* **19**, 1145–51.

Spash, C. L. 1993. Economics, ethics and long-term environmental damages. *Environmental Ethics* **15**, 117–32.

——1994. Double CO_2 and beyond. *Ecological Economics* **10**, 27–36.

Spash, C. & N. Hanley 1994. *Preferences, information and biodiversity preservation*. Discussion Papers in Ecological Economics 94/1, Department of Economics, University of Stirling.

Standing, G. 1978. *Labour force participation and development*. Geneva: International Labour Office.

Stanley, D. J. & A. G. Warne 1993. Sea level and initiation of predynastic culture in the Nile delta. *Nature* **363**, 435–8.

Stevens, T., J. Echeverria, R. Glass, T. Hager, T. More 1991. Measuring the existence value of wildlife. *Land Economics* **67**, 390–400.

Summers, R. & A. Heston 1990. The Penn World Table (Mark 5): an expanded set of international comparisons, 1950–1988. *The Quarterly Journal of Economics* **106**, 327–52.

Teitelbaum, M. & J. Winter 1989. *The fear of population decline*. New York: Academic Press.
Tobin, J. & W. Nordhaus 1972. Is growth obsolete? In *Fiftieth anniversary colloquium* V, National Bureau of Economic Research. New York: Columbia University Press.
Todaro, M. P. 1985. *Economic development in the third world*, 3rd edn. New York: Longman.
Toth, F. L. 1995. Discounting in integrated assessments of climate change. *Energy Policy* **23**(4/5), 403–409.
Turner, R. K., P. Doktor, N. Adger 1994. Sea-level rise and coastal wetlands in the UK, mitigation strategies for sustainable management. See Jansson et al. (1994).

United Nations 1993. *Interpolated National Populations: 1950–2025*. New York: United Nations.
US NRC [United States National Research Council] 1994. *Assigning economic value to natural resources*. Washington DC: National Academy Press.

Viederman, S. 1994. Public policy: challenge to ecological economics. See Jansson et al. (1994).

Wallerstein, I. 1974. *The modern world system*. New York: Academic Press.
Watson, R. T., M. C. Zinyowera, R. H. Moss (eds) 1996. *Climate change 1995: impacts, adaptations, and mitigation of climate change: scientific–technical analyses*. Cambridge: Cambridge University Press.
Weir, D. 1991. A historical perspective on the economic consequences of rapid population growth. In *Consequences of rapid population growth in developing countries*, G. Tapinos, D. Blanchet, D. E. Horlacher (eds). New York: Taylor & Francis.
Weiss, H., M. A. Courty, W. Wetterstrom, F. Guichard, L. Senior, R. Meadow, A. Curnow 1993. The genesis and collapse of third millennium north Mesopotamian civilization. *Science* **261**, 995–1004.
Wheeler, D. 1984. *Population, human resources and economic growth in developing countries*. Oxford: Oxford University Press.
Whyte, W. F. 1955. *Street corner society*. Chicago: Chicago University Press.
Willig, R. 1976. Consumer's surplus without apology. *American Economic Review* **66**, 589–97.
Winterfeldt, D. von 1992. Expert knowledge and public values in risk management: the role of decision analysis. In *Social theories of risk*, S. Krimsky & D. Golding (eds). Westport, Connecticut: Praeger.
World Bank 1992. *World Bank tables*. Washington DC: World Bank.
——1993a. *World Bank tables*. Washington DC: World Bank.
——1993b. *World development report*. Oxford: Oxford University Press.
World Resources Institute 1995. *World resources*, select years including 1995.

Yitzhaki, S. 1979. Relative deprivation and the Gini coefficient. *Quarterly Journal of Economics* **93**, 321–4.
Yohe, G. 1990. The cost of not holding back the sea: toward a national sample of economic vulnerability. *Coastal Management* **18**, 403–431.
Yohe, G. & A. Palmer 1994. The distribution of income across the IS92 scenarios. Unpublished paper, Department of Economics, Wesleyan University.
Yohe, G. & B. Garvey 1995. Incorporating uncertainty and nonlinearity into the calculus of efficient response to the threat of global warming. *International Journal of Energy Issues* **7**, 34–47.
Yohe, G., J. Neumann, H. Amaden 1995. Assessing the economic cost of greenhouse-induced sea level rise: methods and application in support of a national survey. *Journal of Environmental Economics and Management* **29**, S78–S97.
Yohe, G., J. Neumann, P. Marshall, H. Amaden 1996. The economic cost of greenhouse induced sea level rise for developed property in the United States. *Climatic Change* **32**(3), 387–410.
Yohe, G. & R. Wallace 1996. Near term mitigation policy in response to global change under uncertainty. *Environmental Modelling and Assessment* **1**, 47–57.

CHAPTER 2

Games and simulations

Edward A. Parson & Hugh Ward

In the previous chapter we saw how economic discussions of decisionmaking are deeply rooted in methodological assumptions of atomistic rationality; that is to say, they tend to treat decisions as if they are made by a unitary actor based on rational expectations. Hence, as Chapter 3 describes, the kind of information that is generated to help societal decisionmaking about climate change (or, indeed any other issue of public policy concern) is often structured as if addressed to a benevolent dictator seeking to make the most efficient decision on behalf of us all. In this chapter, we begin to explore the limitations of analysis based on this kind of assumption. We use game theory and simulations to introduce the problem of how multiple decisionmakers acting in their own self-interest may or may not produce an outcome that is rational from a global standpoint.

The first half of the chapter discusses this problem from the standpoint of formal game theoretic analyses. This body of social science research and writing explores decisionmaking among limited numbers of unitary rational actors. In game-theoretic explorations of international relations, these actors are nation states. Although one-shot games are recognized as having very limited application to ongoing relations among states, iterated games do provide a parsimonious framework for thinking about cooperation and decisionmaking at levels between the benevolent dictator, on the one hand, and the anonymous market characterized by many well-behaved individuals, on the other.

However, notwithstanding efforts to develop nested or two-level games (e.g., Putnam 1988), game-theoretic approaches are generally not so well adapted to explore the effect on decisionmaking of nonunitary actors; that is, they do not take account of the tensions among rival viewpoints and values within a state that can cause it to change course during negotiations in ways that cannot be predicted within the parameters of the game. This is one of the issues that is used in the second half of the chapter to justify supplementing formal game theoretic analyses with actual simulations involving human actors representing diverse interests within teams of players representing national positions in iterated cooperation games.

Game theoretic approaches to international cooperation

Global environmental change issues raise the question of international cooperation and collaboration to overcome the problems associated with them. In contrast to local environmental questions that affect specific regions or countries, global environmental change results from activities by individuals, firms, social groups, or entire countries—activities that have global consequences. This is true in particular for climate change, where local emissions of greenhouse gases, resulting from a variety of human activities, have global effects: the mixing of these gases in the atmosphere is so thorough that they may contribute to global climate change by increasing the greenhouse effect on the Earth. This process means that there is no a priori relation between the quantity of greenhouse gases that a region or a country emits and the climate change consequences that it experiences as a result of these emissions.

Hardin's metaphor of the "tragedy of the commons" (1968), in which self-interest and the lack of any constraints on access lead to the overexploitation of open access grazing seems, at first sight, to be a useful way of thinking about the dilemma faced by the international community on global climate change.

Stabilization of the global climate system can be conceptualized as a relatively pure international public good: nations not paying for the cost of stabilizing emissions cannot be excluded from the benefits of a stable climate; climate stability is a good in joint supply, because all countries can enjoy it without prejudice to others' consumption (Weale 1992). Framed thus, the problem is that, because the benefits cannot be limited to those who pay for stabilization, countries may rationally free ride, that is, take advantage of the benefits produced by sacrifices (made by other nations) at no cost to themselves.

National self-interest seems to pressure many nations toward free riding, so that we are currently failing by a wide margin to do what may be required for long-run stability of greenhouse-related emissions. However, just as many small communities over the millennia have developed institutions that have prevented the tragedy of the commons from occurring (Berkes 1989, Ostrom 1990), many hope that the international community will develop the necessary institutions and agreements to restrain the pursuit of national interests.

Game theoretic models offer a way to examine issues of international cooperation, negotiation, and bargaining—especially in the context of international public goods. One of the assumptions included in the practical use of game theoretic models is that participants in international interactions (either nations, or subnational or transnational groups) can be viewed as unitary actors making choices between strategies so as to maximize their expected payoffs. This assumption is made mostly for practical reasons. Elaborated game theoretic models can be constructed from the bottom up, starting with individuals or small groups, and then generate preferences for large groups as well as national preferences. However, because of their size and complexity, models constructed in this way would be excessively difficult to handle.

Generally, a nation's payoff from adopting a particular strategy will vary, depending on the strategies chosen by other nations. To make a rational choice among strategies, a nation has to be able to predict the responses of other nations. The simplest models assume that nations know not only their own payoffs but also those of all the other nations or groups. Also, they assume that all nations are rational and known to be rational. Thus, nations can predict the responses that others will make to any strategy that they choose. An *equilibrium* is a strategy vector where each nation's strategy is a best response to what the others are doing. The prediction is that rational actors will play strategies corresponding to one of the equilibria of the game because, in an equilibrium, no country has an incentive unilaterally to change strategy.

The game theoretic conception outlined above includes the assumption of a priori knowledge of the payoff structure. Clearly, however, in the area of climate change such an assumption is not warranted, since the benefits of greenhouse gas emission restrictions are very difficult to evaluate. The latter occurs, in part, because the effects (damages) associated with global climate change are not yet well known. It has even been suggested that some countries or regions might actually benefit from global climate change (see Oberthür 1993). Therefore, payoffs can only be evaluated in a probabilistic rather than deterministic fashion and conceived of as expected utilities. In principle, resorting to expected utilities to define payoffs and assuming a risk-averse attitude (i.e., emphasizing the dangers and uncertainties of global climate change) should reinforce the precautionary principle and lead actors to cooperate in taking emission reductions. However, the precautionary principle is contested by a school of thought that stresses the importance of uncertainty and the variance associated with the expected outcome, and not just its mean realization (which is implicitly the way the concept of expected utility works).

Including estimated variance as well as averages to evaluate the likelihood of an outcome is part of the conception put forward by Allais (1953) to assess risky situations. In particular, Allais asserts that individuals avoid outcomes associated with large uncertainties, even if they appear more rewarding than outcomes with little or no uncertainty. The risk-averse nature of actors has also been questioned at the individual level by the studies made by Kahneman et al. (1982), who have noticed sudden reversals in risk preferences. It is unclear how group preferences evolve as a result of risky, uncertain, and potentially detrimental outcomes. If there are as many differences among groups as there are among individuals, their perceptions of risk and uncertainty might strongly affect bargaining strategies and thus outcomes of attempted international cooperative arrangements.

In summary, two major cooperative problems emerge at the international level concerning the environment, in general, and climate change, in particular:

- International cooperation is often needed to achieve a collective good and to create a particular institutional framework to keep free riding from occurring. The collective or public good problem to be solved is similar to a Prisoner's Dilemma situation, in which a detrimental equilibrium is obtained in a one-shot situation but where mutually beneficial cooperation can emerge over time as a result of successful threat of retaliation strategies.

- International cooperation often consists of enforcing rules of mutual restriction, such as the reduction of greenhouse-related emissions. This leads to the dilemma of common aversion outlined below and exemplified by the game of Chicken, which contains several equilibria. Paradoxically, such a situation might be more difficult to solve because of the ineffectiveness of retaliation threats (see Ward 1993). The question of international cooperation is complicated further by the fact that the two categories for collaboration outlined above often cannot be separated in the analysis of concrete situations. The creation of an international climate change regime involves both the creation of a public good and the establishment of rules for mutual restriction in order to avoid a mutually detrimental outcome.

Game theory has been used by several authors to theorize about the possibilities of international environmental cooperation (e.g., Taylor & Ward 1982, Livingston 1989, Livingston & von Witzke 1990, Maler 1990, Hoel 1991, Ward 1993, Soroos 1994). However, relatively little has been written with specific and detailed application to global climate change. In the following, we will present a simple iterated model from a game theoretic perspective, *supergame*, apply it to global climate change, relate the model to the debate between realism and institutionalism about the role of institutions, and finally raise some issues of institutional design.

One-shot games are widely recognized to be inadequate models of international cooperation, although they provide metaphors for certain failures of collective actions at the international level (Keohane 1984, Snidal 1986). Even if an international agreement has been signed, the possibilities remain that some countries may overtly break away from it or, more or less covertly, fail to implement it. Thus, nations should be pictured as having repeated opportunities over time to make decisions about whether or not to cooperate. They play so-called *supergames* in which they repeatedly play a one-shot game—with the number of rounds being infinite or uncertain. For clarity of presentation, we assume in formal approaches that cooperation refers to positions favoring greenhouse-related emissions reductions and vice versa.

The basic idea of the model is that the players choose strategies so as to maximize the sum of their own supergame payoffs through time. In calculations of this sum, future payoffs weigh less heavily, that is to say, they are time and cost discounted. A supergame strategy consists of a plan of how to play in each future round, given every pattern of play that would have preceded that round. For a formal statement of the supergame model, see Box 2.1.

The key to cooperative collective action in supergames is the possibility of

Box 2.1 The supergame model

The game matrix in Figure 2.1 may represent row and column's payoffs whether they have Prisoner's Dilemma, Chicken, or Assurance preferences. For Prisoner's Dilemma the ordering of the payoffs is as shown in the diagram. If $x>y$ and $w>z$, the player has Assurance preferences. There are two versions of Assurance, depending on whether $w>y$ or $y>w$. If $y>x>z>w$ and $y'>x'>z'>w'$, the game is Chicken.

The players play an infinite number of rounds of the game, discounting future payoffs. For row from the perspective of round 1, a payoff of P gained in round t is worth dtP, a smaller value of d meaning heavier discounting of future payoffs. Column's discount parameter is d'. Players aim to maximize the discounted sum of their payoffs in each round, taken over the infinite number of *rounds*. Thus, for example, if both players cooperated in each round, row's Supergame payoff is

$$\lim_{t\to\infty} \sum_{t=1}^{t=t^*} (dx + d^2x + d^3x\ldots + d^{t^*}x) = dx1/(1-d)$$

and column's Supergame payoff is $d'x'/(1-d')$.

making the choice of cooperation conditional on the past cooperation of others (Taylor 1987). If others did not cooperate in the past, this triggers retaliation in the form of refusal to continue to cooperate in the future. Conditionally cooperative strategies of this sort embody threats. If the penalty is large enough, it may pay others conditionally to cooperate. In the context of global climate change, an example of such a strategy might be that the European Union would press ahead with cutting its greenhouse-related emissions so long as the other major industrialized economies do the same; but if they fail to cooperate in this way, the European Union would switch its strategy; that is, it would abandon its plan to make further emissions cuts. It is important that the threat built into conditional strategies is credible; credible threats place restrictions on plausible strategies and equilibria (Fudenberg & Tirole 1991).

To illustrate these conclusions, it is assumed that negotiations are bilateral or that two groups of countries contemplate the merits of mutually beneficial agreements (Fig. 2.1). We call the groups or blocs "rows" and "columns". Each side has two strategies: to cooperate in some measure which it is believed will help stabilize the global climate, or not to cooperate. Suppose for the moment

	C	NC
C	x, x'	z, y'
NC	y, z'	w, w'

where $y>x>w>z$ and $y'>x'>w'>z'$

Figure 2.1 The one shot Prisoner's Dilemma Game payoff matrix.

that both countries favor noncooperation over cooperation regardless of the strategy chosen by the other country and the game is played only once—a one-shot game. The resulting equilibrium for this Prisoner's Dilemma game is where both players choose noncooperation. *Pareto-efficient* outcomes are such that there is no alternative that is better for one side without making the other side worse off. Thus, the outcome is not efficient in this sense. As in Hardin's tragedy of the commons (Hardin 1968), the failure of collective action, which is conceived of as the rational pursuit of individual interests, leads to an inefficient outcome. Although this kind of game theoretic analysis is often applied at the national level, it can also be carried out at the group or political movement level. For instance, Hillman & Ursprung (1992) showed how policy coordination between environmentalist green movements can take the form of a Prisoner's Dilemma game and how this inefficient outcome can sometimes be overcome.

In a so-called Chicken game, row may rationally choose noncooperation if column chooses to cooperate, and cooperation if column chooses noncooperation. Column has the same preference pattern. Pure strategies have two equilibria and, in each of these, one side decides to cooperate and the other side decides not to. Each side has an incentive to commit to noncooperation in order to hijack the other side into cooperation (Schelling 1960). Each side can be expected to be tempted toward brinkmanship, swerving only at the last minute, if at all, away from the strategy of noncooperation. One side may swerve, so that the equilibrium is reached where one side free rides and the other cooperates. However, the danger is that both sides cannot reverse commitments from noncooperation to cooperation, again leading to a failure of collective action. It has been argued that Chicken is an example of a dilemma of common aversion in which the key problem is that of coordinating strategies, so that one of the equilibria—which all sides agree is better than both sides not cooperating—emerges (Stein 1982). Although coordination is crucial, to characterize Chicken and related games with multiple equilibria in this way ignores the potential dangers of commitment tactics and brinkmanship.

Beside the Prisoner's Dilemma and Chicken games discussed above, other one-shot games have also been found helpful in general discussions of international cooperation (Oye 1986). One important alternative to Prisoner's Dilemma and Chicken is Assurance, in both variations of which it is rational to choose cooperation if the other side chooses to cooperate, and to choose not to cooperate if that is also the choice of the other side. In the one-shot game, we say that a player has the following preferences:

- Prisoner's Dilemma if it always prefers noncooperation—no matter what the other side does
- Chicken if it prefers noncooperation if the other side chooses cooperation, and cooperation if the other side chooses noncooperation

- Assurance if it prefers noncooperation when the other side chooses noncooperation, and cooperation when the other side chooses cooperation.

One-shot games in which the two sides have different preference patterns are plausible, too (Taylor 1987). For instance, one side might have Chicken preferences and the other side Prisoner's Dilemma preferences.

The one-shot game underlying the supergame may take various different forms when each player has either Prisoner's Dilemma, Chicken, or Assurance preferences. Nevertheless, perpetual cooperation can typically be sustained only by conditional strategies. (The exception is the case in which both players have Assurance preferences.) Consider a case where players are conditionally cooperating. Suppose one side considers free riding by not cooperating in some round. In some subsequent rounds, the other side would punish it by changing its strategy to noncooperation. Whether it would choose to stick with its original strategy of conditional cooperation in the face of this threat depends on:

- the short-term benefits from free riding

versus

- the long-term costs to itself if cooperation breaks down.

In turn, the long-term costs depend on how much weight is attached to the future payoffs relative to current payoffs, that is, they depend on how heavily future payoffs are discounted. There will be an equilibrium in which everyone conditionally cooperates if three conditions are satisfied:

- Gains from short-term free riding are low.
- Penalties per round from the breakdown of cooperation are high.
- Payoffs in future rounds are not too heavily discounted.

Variation in these factors across issue areas and across time may help explain differences in levels of international cooperation (Lipson 1984, Axelrod & Keohane 1986). For example, it is often suggested that cooperation was easier to achieve in relation to stratospheric ozone depletion than it will be in relation to climate change, because the total economic costs of abatement are much higher in the second case.

The conditionally cooperative equilibrium is never the only one. For instance, if the game being repeated is Prisoner's Dilemma, noncooperation is always an equilibrium; and if the game being repeated is Chicken, the picture is not fundamentally altered, since the two possible patterns in which one side free rides on the other through time are always equilibria. In fact, if any Pareto-efficient outcomes are equilibria, there will generally be an infinity of equilibria.

Suppose that two blocs of countries repeatedly play the Prisoner's Dilemma game shown in Figure 2.1. Then the feasible payoffs for the supergame all lie within the shaded region of Figure 2.2 (Fudenberg & Tirole 1991). The average payoff per round if both blocks always fail to cooperate is w for row and w' for column. These payoffs are the security levels of each side. No matter what

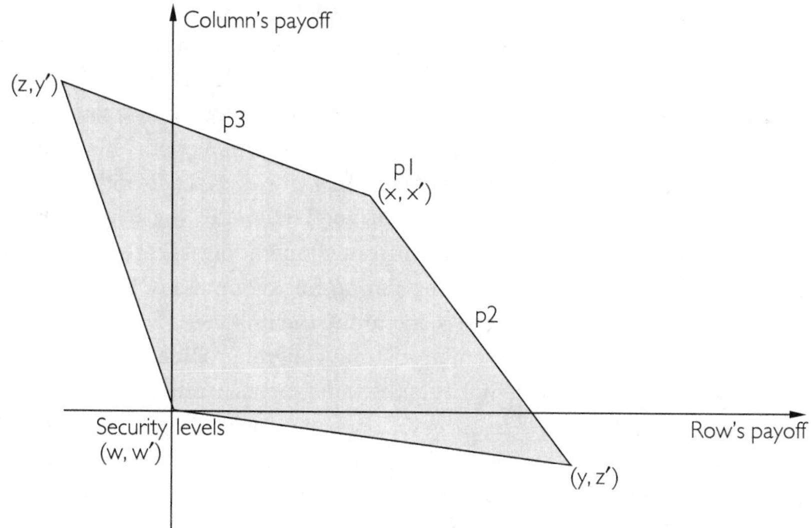

Figure 2.2 Feasible average payoffs.

happens, a bloc can never get a lower payoff even if the other side is carrying out a threat against its countries because of their failure to cooperate. The *folk theorem* (so called because no one can recall who first proved it) shows that each payoff point in the shaded region can be equilibrium as long as each bloc puts a high enough weight on future payoffs and each side gets more than its security level (see Fudenberg & Tirole 1991). The intuition is that, so long as sufficient weight is placed on future payoffs to make the punishment substantial and the game lasts long enough, then the threat to drive payoffs down to the security level will deter both sides from breaking away from any pattern of play.

For some commentators, the existence of multiple equilibria calls into question the explanatory power of game theoretic approaches. It may be necessary to resort to an institutional or sociological account of equilibrium selection (see, for instance, Keohane 1988, Sebenius 1992). For other analysts, the existence of multiple equilibria gives explanatory insights into bargaining tactics. The existence of multiple equilibria and conflict of interest over which of those equilibria may combine to produce incentives to use *commitment tactics*. Just as in a one-shot Chicken game, each actor will try to reach an equilibrium with the highest possible payoff. This can be illustrated as follows. Point $p1$ of Figure 2.2 is associated with each side cooperating in every round, getting average payoffs of x and x' for row and column respectively. At $p2$, row cooperates less often. For instance, it might start cooperating after column does, free riding for several rounds on column's actions before it is willing to resume to cooperate. At $p3$, column gets a higher payoff than at $p1$. Row prefers $p2$ to $p1$ to $p3$; column prefers *p*3 to *p*1 to p2. Suppose each of these payoff points can arise in equilibrium. Then row might try to get *p*2 and column might try to get *p*3, each side committing to delaying cooperation until after the other moved. The threats implicit in these strategies of both sides may be triggered, resulting in a worse-all-around outcome in which only security level payoffs of *w* and *w′* are enjoyed. This is analogous to the collision that occurs in one-shot Chicken games when both sides are committed to noncooperation. It has been argued that repeating an underlying Chicken game increases the dangers of noncooperation, because it creates incentives to build and maintain a reputation for toughness (Oye 1986). The same arguments apply to other cases, including the Prisoner's Dilemma game.

Besides the general commitment problem, a general problem of *distrust* also enters in iterated games of qualitatively the same sort as in one-shot Assurance games (Sen 1969, Ward 1989). In order to cooperate, each side has to be assured that the other will also do so. If either believes that there is a large enough probability that the other will not, the first may rationally choose noncooperation rather than risking the worst outcome in which one side cooperates and the other side free rides. Distrust on both sides may be so high that each plays safe by choosing noncooperation. In the supergame, the same problem arises. Assurance may be lacking, because it is suspected that the other side's declarations of intent to cooperate are a tactic to lure the other actor into cooperation with a view to getting a short-term free ride. For instance, the outcome in which both sides always defect must be an equilibrium if the underlying game is Prisoner's Dilemma. Even if players suspect that cooperation in every round is stable, distrust may prevent cooperation from occurring (Ward 1989). The general problem of distrust can arise in other cases, too. Relatively uncooperative equilibria may exist that are worse all round than more cooperative equilibria, and distrust may lead to failure of collective action.

Applying the supergame model to global climate change

Despite its simplicity, the supergame model provides useful insights into global climate change. Many of the conclusions carry over when the model is made more realistic. For instance, there are clearly multiple levels at which nations could cooperate in relation to global climate change, so that the choice is not the binary one of cooperate versus not cooperate. Emission levels could range from further increases, through a freeze, the 20 percent cuts discussed at the Toronto Conference, to the 60 to 80 percent cuts that the IPCC suggests would be required to achieve atmospheric stabilization. In addition, nations might agree to varying degrees of resource transfers to facilitate monitoring and joint implementation, or varying degrees of transfer of control of policy implementation to international agencies. Yet the problems of short-termness, commitment, and distrust identified in the binary choice supergame model continue so long as the following conditions are all fulfilled:

- There are several discrete levels of cooperation.
- The outcome where all sides cooperate to a high degree is among the efficient outcomes.
- The outcome where all sides cooperate to a high degree is not necessarily an equilibrium.

One interpretation of the current state of play in relation to global climate change politics is that collective action has failed. On paper, signatories to the Framework Convention on Climate Change appear to have moved beyond the cooperative zero point. Moreover, some nations will probably go further, developing policies actually to cut their emissions of greenhouse gases. Even supposing that nations intend to carry out their current commitments, the equilibrium is one where the level of cooperation is generally low, and a case can be made that all-around cooperation at a higher level would be a good collective insurance policy against the risks of global warming. Also, many nations seem to be forgoing national benefits from no-regrets energy efficiency policies. This seems irrational at first sight, yet it may be explained by the desire to gain a reputation for doing little with a view to getting an outcome closer to the national interest in the long term.

The supergame model identifies heavy discounting of future payoffs and uncertainty about benefits as likely causes of the low level of cooperation. Politicians discount future payoffs particularly heavily, because their focus is on the short-run dynamics of support and the reaction of capital markets in which heavy discounting of future investment returns are the norm. The problem of short-termness is exacerbated by a time pattern in which the financial and other benefits from current cooperation arise in the future. Also, uncertainty about the level of future benefits makes risk-averse decisionmakers even less prone to take gambles.

While recognizing the limitations of the FCCC, some see it as a first step to a solution—analogous to the process leading ultimately to the Montreal Protocol. The hope is that levels of cooperation will gradually be increased as scientific certainty and trust between nations increase (e.g., Lang 1993). Distrust is clearly a problem in relation to climate change, just as it was in the case of stratospheric ozone depletion (Ward 1993). From the viewpoint of supergame analysis, a strategy to gradually reduce tension (e.g., Osgood 1979, Ward 1989) may be a way to get from the status quo to a more efficient equilibrium. Nations may be willing to increase their level of cooperation once they see others actually reciprocating cooperation at the current level. Theory suggests that it may pay to make cooperative probes, pushing somewhat further than others to gain valuable information about whether they will reciprocate (Ward 1989). The unilateral policy initiatives to cut greenhouse-related emissions, entered into by some states, may be interpretable in this way, although playing to domestic electoral sentiment and seeking energy efficiency gains are alternative explanations.

Comparing the likely direct abatement costs measured, for simplicity, as the share of gross domestic product (GDP) committed to emission reductions, some nations are currently cooperating more than others. This might result from the unilateral pursuit of no-regrets policies by some and the lack of such easy gains for others. However, the supergame model suggests another explanation: researchers and decisionmakers ought to observe nations committing themselves to relatively low levels of cooperation, both

- to try to bring about a pattern where they currently do relatively little
- to build and to maintain a reputation for tough bargaining.

The actual case of commitment tactics lends some support to this idea (Ward 1993). For instance, while the CANZ group (Canada, Australia, and New Zealand) was willing to take the first steps of setting targets and timetables for stabilizing emissions of greenhouse gases in the late 1980s, the Bush administration in the United States (as part of a block which then included Japan and the former Soviet Union) argued that there was insufficient scientific evidence to justify commitments to emissions reductions, thus ensuring that no specific timetables were written into the FCCC. Even under the more environmentally proactive Clinton administration, the difficulty of steering anything but the most anodyne legislation through Congress effectively binds the United States to relative inaction, even though the administration proposed a plan for stabilization within a definite timeframe. The member states of the European Union may move more rapidly. However, there have been difficulties in the European Union over burden sharing and the carbon tax, partly because of the United Kingdom's refusal to pick up the burden of poorer member states. Again, the Rio Earth Summit saw potentially important actors, such as Brazil, China, and India, committing themselves to inaction unless the North paid a substantial part of the abatement costs. Thus, one incentive to build a reputation for toughness is, over time, to remain part of a larger bloc which can avoid major abatement costs.

The worse the collision outcome resulting from noncooperation (relative to joining in cooperation), the more likely a nation is to back down by switching to cooperation. Nations that stand to lose little from failure, or can make others believe they see things in this way, are in a powerful bargaining position. No matter how much or little climate change affects less industrialized countries, the bargaining power of this group will be enhanced if the strenuous attempts it made in the process of negotiating the FCCC to convince others that it was relatively unconcerned about failure actually work.

Game theory, international regimes of cooperation, and dilemmas of institutional design

Game theory can help to elucidate the various schools of international relations theory and the concept of regimes (Vol. 1, Ch. 6). While some *institutionalists* come close to seeing international law as binding, others have moved closer to the realist assumption that the world is in some sense anarchic (Waltz 1979, Oye 1986, Grieco 1988). However, even if the international system is anarchic, states can cooperate with the assistance of international regimes. Regimes of cooperation consist of formal and informal institutions, shared principles, norms, rules, rights, and decisionmaking procedures. Regimes can provide more favorable circumstances for the existence of conditionally cooperative equilibria, even though they cannot enforce binding agreements. Realists agree that regimes help solve collective action problems, but they are generally more pessimistic about the extent and stability of cooperation (Grieco 1988, Baldwin 1993).

Regimes constrain interdependent decisionmaking by coordinating actions and fostering various forms of collaboration in a way that makes efficient outcomes more likely (Stein 1982). First, regimes may alter the incentives to free ride by threatening to reduce the payoffs for free riders (Axelrod & Keohane 1986, Oye 1986). Second, they provide an institutional context within which a reputation for trustworthy cooperation and for carrying out threats can be built up and then cashed in, both in future rounds and related bargaining forums (Young 1989). Third, monitoring arrangements are typically built into the regime (Levy et al. 1993), and this encourages conditional cooperation by making free riding more visible (Oye 1986, Lipson 1984). Fourth, diplomatic activity on the part of the secretariats of institutions associated with regimes may help to dispel distrust and increase the capacity of nations actually to meet commitments (Levy et al. 1993). Even if a regime has no current value, nations may maintain it because the regime may be useful in the future or because it has attained legitimacy in its own right (Stein 1982, Keohane 1984, Young 1989).

At first sight, a major difference appears to divide realists and institutionalists, because the former emphasize payoff differentials, whereas the latter emphasize absolute payoffs (Powell 1991). Realists argue that institutionalists are too optimistic about the possibilities of cooperation, because they ignore relative gains (Grieco 1988). However, the relative gains perspective opens up difficult issues of interactor comparison of utilities, which might be better treated in the form of a classical but noncooperative gain perspective. Although some have argued that negotiations over environmental problems do not involve relative assessments of payoffs (e.g., List & Rittberger 1991), this seems implausible to realists in the light of the economic and strategic implications of the very large flows of resources involved in moving away from a fossil fuel economy. One argument is that relative payoffs count, because they translate into differentials in future power capacities to remain secure and to alter outcomes (Waltz 1979, Powell 1991). Thus, they affect long-run absolute payoffs. The weight placed on relative payoffs goes up in times of uncertainty and insecurity (Grieco 1988), an argument that may well become pertinent if the fears of some authors about the adverse effects of climate change on international security are realized (Homer-Dixon 1991).

Too much can be made of the apparent differences between the two sides over relative gains. Institutionalists regard regimes as normative orders (Jervis 1988, Weale 1992) in which considerations of fairness have a major impact on states' behavior (Stein 1982, Krasner 1982). This inevitably implies that comparisons of payoffs and relative deprivation matter to nations. Albeit for different reasons, realists and institutionalists game theory suggests that both need to take the relative gains issue seriously.

As relative payoff differences become more and more important, the conditions under which conditionally cooperative equilibria generally exist become more restrictive (Powell 1991, Nicholson 1994; but see also Snidal 1991). As time goes by, an asymmetric equilibrium in which some nations are perceived as cooperating to a much greater extent than others will provoke greater concern for relative gains. It will eventually become apparent that some nations do not honor their obligations. As in the case of burden sharing in the North Atlantic Treaty Organization (Olson & Zeckhauser 1966), there may be growing domestic perceptions of unfairness in nations who shoulder a large part of the collective burden.

This argument suggests that it is important to try to design international regimes in such a way that they steer attention away from asymmetric equilibria and toward equilibria in which no major player gains in relative terms. Bounded rationality (Simon 1982) may make it difficult if not impossible for players to know what the full range of equilibria is or what the best response to others' current strategy is. If institutionalists are right to suggest that international regimes can steer the agenda in relation to problems in the global commons (Keohane et al. 1993, Weale 1992), they may also be able to produce equilibria in which the relative gains perspective is not as much of a problem as a focal point for bargaining (Schelling 1960, Levy et al. 1993, Weale 1992). Although formal theory illuminates the problems here, the question of what ought to be, or might actually be, considered a fair outcome is treated in more detail in Volume 1, Chapter 5.

Despite the prominence of the North–South split in the politics of global climate change, there are arguably more than two bargaining blocs, and there is evidence that the coalition structure shifted both before and during the Earth Summit (Paterson & Grubb 1992, Nilsson & Pitt 1994, Mintzer & Leonard 1994). A split emerged in the Northern bloc between the United States and other nations, the picture being further complicated by the fact that the United Kingdom, to name one example, often seemed to be close to the United States position. Also, newly developed economies with large fossil fuel reserves and forests, such as China, Brazil, the Organization of Petroleum Exporting Countries (OPEC), and India took a tougher line than others in the South, notably the Association of Small Island States.

However, the conclusions reached from supergame analysis tend to be strengthened if there are more than two blocs of players. First, the commitment problem seems to be even more likely to arise. When the underlying game is a version of Prisoner's Dilemma (Taylor 1987) or a version of Chicken, there is typically a multiplicity of equilibria where some players always free ride and some cooperate in every round. There are additional dangers in attempts by nations to free ride permanently by using commitment tactics when increased numbers make the commitment scramble even more chaotic. Increased numbers also pose difficulties for regimes: problems of distrust are more likely to arise as the numbers of players goes up, because:

- the amount of information necessary to be assured that a nation's cooperation will be reciprocated increases
- it becomes more complex and difficult to apply conditional sanctions (Axelrod & Keohane 1986, Oye 1986)
- transaction costs in deal making rise (Oye 1986)
- the second-order collective action problems surrounding who should punish defectors become harder to solve (Axelrod & Keohane 1986)
- underprovision of compliance mechanisms becomes more likely (Young 1989).

Another reason for pessimism about the chances of collective action in relation to global climate change as compared to the stratospheric ozone depletion problem is the relatively large number of major players in the climate change game. The arguments relating numbers of players to successful collective action make it tempting to go for a less inclusive regime than the one constructed at Rio—or a *fast track* option within the existing convention. Relatively small numbers of like-minded countries (probably members of the OECD, with the United States being a less plausible member of the group) could push cooperation among themselves to relatively high levels (Andresen & Wettestad 1992, Sebenius 1994). One possible assumption underlying this strategy is that once a high level of cooperation is firmly institutionalized, other countries would be pulled in. However, a game theoretic perspective provides no good reason to suppose that the coalition would eventually grow to include all the significant players, as assumed. Given likely equilibria where some nations cooperate and others never cooperate, a point will be reached where it does not pay additional nations to join the group of ambitious emissions reducers. It might be possible to break such a pattern of the nongrowth of the cooperative group by using trade sanctions against those outside the cooperative coalition (Sebenius 1994), but this would require an amendment of the General Agreement on Trade and Tariffs or the World Trade Organization. Once asymmetric cooperation appears permanent, the relative gains effect may arise, leading to the erosion of the cooperative coalition. With more than two players, conditionally cooperative strategies are liable indiscriminately to punish both defectors and cooperators, so that their activation may provoke a general breakdown in cooperation (Oye 1986). The dilemma for institutional design is:

- short-term progress is highly desirable given irreversibilities in the damage being done to the global commons
- such progress may be more likely with less inclusive deals among like-minded countries
- stable cooperation in the long run may require taking the grave risk of holding out for an inclusive deal where all major players are perceived as pulling their weight.

Realists and institutionalists also disagree about the role of leadership in regimes. Although some realists associate leadership with superpower hegemony and see hegemony as a necessary condition for cooperation, for some institutionalists leadership can be provided even in the absence of a hegemonic power in the international system, and leadership is just one factor among others increasing the likelihood of cooperation (Keohane 1984, Snidal 1985, Young 1991, Weale 1992). Both sides accept that leadership is potentially important to the success of regimes. Leaders may provide or distribute selective incentives which go only to other countries which cooperate (Young 1991). Regimes typically produce an array of private goods as well as public goods, and these can be selectively directed to ensure compliance, either by leaders or by regime institutions (Young 1989, Levy et al. 1993). In the context under discussion, these private goods might include technology transfers, payment of monitoring costs, and loans to fund transitions to less polluting technologies. Also, leaders with entrepreneurial skills can put together attractive packages of policies across different issue areas (Young 1991). The idea is that players with different perceptions of the importance of issues can be induced to trade concessions on areas that are of relatively low salience to themselves for a better deal on an issue dimension that they consider important. Commentators on global climate change have already noted dilemmas of institutional design associated with trading concessions across issues. Despite its potential benefits in facilitating progress, such issue trading may result in the agenda becoming impossibly crowded, leading to transaction cost increases and the sort of long delays observed when the Law of the Sea was being negotiated.

The package deal implicitly proposed at Rio by countries in the South (whereby they concede on global climate change if their demands about the international economic order and development are met) may provoke the emergence of a blocking coalition in the North (Andresen & Wettestad 1992, Sebenius 1994). It may be crucial to success that deals are put together which prevent the emergence of blocking coalitions (Sebenius 1991, Sebenius 1994). Also, power differentials affect the ability of states to get outcomes on the Pareto frontier which asymmetrically favor their interests (Krasner 1991, Sebenius 1992). Ideas about winning and blocking coalitions receive more formal treatment in theories of weighted games (Ordeshook 1986). According to this approach, winning coalitions are inherently unstable when trading concessions across different issue dimensions is possible, because members can be seduced away by a sweeter deal, no matter what the current deal that has been struck (Peterson & Ward 1995). The practical consequences of this are inaction, with negotiations being limited only by nations' rational capacity and information to put together new deals and coalitions.

Game theorists acknowledge that institutional rules and decisionmaking structures may keep issues apart and defuse this problems (e.g., Shepsle & Weingast 1975). The thrust of game theory is, then, further to strengthen the arguments for designing the climate regime, so that it deals sequentially with well-defined issues and encourages package deals only when this seems unlikely to destabilize the whole edifice (Sebenius 1994).

Institutionalists' understanding of regimes places them in a constitutive or mutually constitutive position (Krasner 1982) with respect to the actions of nation states, while realists regard regimes as derivative. For institutionalists, regimes are seen as constraints, facts of life facing nations that may not be dispensed with or ignored, even when there are incentives to do so (Keohane 1988, Young 1989). They are able to alter states' worldview and their preferences (Keohane 1988, Young 1991, Levy et al. 1993). From this perspective, cooperation can literally become a matter of socialization or policy habit, rather than something continually scrutinized for its costs and benefits (Stein 1982, Young 1989). These arguments also make institutionalists more optimistic about the chances of regimes bringing about stable cooperation at relatively high levels over global climate change. They also begin to call into question the utility of formal approaches such as game theory.

The contribution of game theory

Although the supergame model can provide useful insights into international cooperation, in general (Snidal 1986), and global climate change, in particular, its limitations need to be acknowledged. First, supergame analysis has not been extended to cover the cases where players' level of cooperation can vary continuously over several dimensions (Jervis 1988, Sebenius 1992) or current-round payoffs depend on past choices, as they may do in a world where certain forms of environmental damage are irreversible. The ability of nations to rationally pursue national self-interest may be severely limited by distortions in dealing with information and bounds on rational capacity to process it (Jervis 1988). Because of this, some have raised doubts about states' abilities to articulate, communicate, and carry through even simple conditionally cooperative strategies (Lipson 1984, Oye 1986), suggesting the need to further develop models of collective action which assume bounded rationality (Keohane 1984).

Game theory cannot constitute a freestanding explanation, because it takes states' preferences, beliefs, and strategic opportunities as given (Jervis 1988). Existing attempts formally to model how nations' preferences over global climate change arise from domestic political competition (e.g., Ward 1993) are poorly integrated with the structural and systemic basis of states' interests that concern realists (Waltz 1979, Jervis 1988, Lang 1993). In defense of game theory, it can be argued that this approach does not even attempt to explain where preferences, beliefs, and strategic opportunities originate. However, there seems to be no clean break empirically between strategic choice and the processes that mold the underlying parameters of the game. For example, preferences may change during the bargaining process.

In practice, game theorists rarely attempt to model the internal divisions within particular governments, but these sorts of differences are important in negotiating the FCCC (List & Rittberger 1991). This suggests a need to take further and to formalize Putnam's idea (1988) of two-level games, in which national political games are developed within an international game (e.g., Dupont 1994). Presently, internal division is represented more frequently in simulation games where representative national teams can be assembled to include diverse actors (see p. 124 on simulation gaming).

Although arguments about commitment and trust seem empirically relevant to the analysis of negotiations, the supergame model tells us little about the patterns of offer and counteroffer observed in negotiations and the coalitional structures that emerge. One problem is that there are many competing formal models of the bargaining process and associated accounts of coalition formation (e.g., Coddington 1968, Ordeshook 1986), most of which assume quite implausibly that binding agreements can be struck and that the efficient outcomes are known (Sebenius 1992). Although some progress has been made by using formal bargaining models (Hoel 1991), the most fruitful approaches to bargaining dynamics are likely to be those that are both

- informed by empirical observation and experimental work as well as by game theoretic ideas, and
- do not stick rigidly to standard assumptions, such as perfect information and perfect rational capacity to make decisions (e.g., Raiffa 1982, Sebenius 1992, Sjostedt 1993).

Scholars of international relations have adopted different conceptual lenses to study international cooperation and coordination among countries. In particular, they focus on a variety of levels of analysis and variables of interest articulation, and differ about what information and knowledge base they consider decisive for decisionmaking.

Formal game theoretic analysis shows that efforts at international collaboration will not bring about a unique optimal solution satisfying all countries involved. In particular, as the number of bargaining blocs increases in international negotiations, the more difficult it will become to overcome collective action problems. From a practical standpoint, it may appear to be important to prevent blockage of international negotiations by a single country (under anonymity rules). By analogy to revisions of domestic constitutional law, qualified majority voting might enhance the likelihood of getting effective agreements and avoid weak compromises satisfying the most obstructionist country.

If a country takes the lead in promoting international collaboration to limit greenhouse-related emissions, others may try to resist such moves or even to exploit the position of the leading country. However, a government may rationally adopt such a leadership position for reasons of crucial domestic support and pressures (e.g., from environmental NGOs and business interests) and, in addition, to persuade others to join forces. If the latter case materializes, the joint gains lead to an improved cost–benefit balance for all. As a consequence of organized domestic political pressures, groups of countries (mostly economically well developed and with democratic forms of interest representation) are likely to act as leaders in the international arena of decisionmaking on global environmental accords. Paradoxically, countries having important marginal agricultural sectors and, therefore, being most vulnerable to climate change, are often too weak and too preoccupied with the management of their economies to initiate international cooperation in this area. Given the diversity of factors influencing national positions across countries, we are unlikely to find quick agreements favoring the mobilization of major resources in order to prevent or actively adapt to the likely challenges posed by global climate change. Instead, we should expect the emergence of a cooperative framework lacking precise and costly obligations.

Game theory can provide insight into the bargaining around the FCCC. Game theory cannot stand alone, but it may have a symbiotic relationship with other approaches. It poses important questions about institutional design. Although it does not propose clear-cut solutions to these questions, it can add to the rigor of the debate about these vital issues.

Simulation gaming and its applications

Most formally modeled approaches to human choices cope with multiple decisionmakers in one of two ways: either individual choices are aggregated into market equilibria, subject to the usual assumptions as suggested in Chapter 1; or policy choices are assumed to be made by a unitary national decisionmaker as described already in this chapter. But real policy choices are made neither by absolute and unitary national authorities nor by actors so numerous and well behaved that their collective decisions can appropriately be modeled as markets. Rather, outcomes are often shaped by a combination of institutional, political, strategic, and negotiation processes that involve a few major actors or many. These actors' values and preferences may be unclear or contested, particularly as regards outcomes that are multiattribute, risky, or distant in time. Over matters that require joint decisions, parties' interests may be partly common and partly conflicting. Finally, the range of parties' feasible choices may be ambiguous, poorly known, or changing.

When some of these conditions hold, the most basic uncertainties about a problem may concern behavior, values, preferences, or strategic interaction of choices. In assessing such uncertainties, simulation gaming methods can serve as supplements or alternatives to formal analysis of rational actors in negotiations or markets. Like formal analyses, these methods can help shed light on problems that are both too novel to be dealt with by simple reasoning from precedent or analogy and too high-stakes to be dealt with by ad hoc decisionmaking. Unlike formal economic models or game theoretic analysis, these methods introduce decisionmaking by actual people into the assessment, through the use of human participants who deliberate, negotiate, and act within a simulated decision context that represents the issue or policy problem to be investigated. In other words, the moves in the game are actually decided by various players representing distinct decisionmaking entities and their bounded rationalities, rather than by a single gamemaster or analytic entity externally constructing the rational behavior of each party to a negotiation. The objectives of simulation methods are those of integrated assessment (see Ch. 5): to assemble and interpret knowledge from varied domains to serve the needs of policy and decision. They have been exercised extensively in other fields; their application to environmental problems is relatively new, but growing.

Problems can most usefully be investigated with simulation gaming when an intermediate amount of knowledge is available—enough to represent its basic structure or building blocks (actors, their interests, authority, relationships, and knowledge, plus relevant knowledge about the world), but not so much that conventional, cheaper, or simpler methods can effectively inform policymaking, making the expense and difficulty of simulations superfluous. Examples of problems well suited to simulation gaming include those in which many complex organizational routines must work together smoothly, particularly under conditions of crisis such as arise in military operations and emergency response (Bracken 1990); and major institutional innovations affecting many actors, such as reform of healthcare systems or developing new institutions for managing global environmental problems.

Simulation gaming methods share two basic characteristics. First, they are all representations of a complex system by a simpler one with relevant behavioral similarity (Brewer & Shubik 1979). The behavioral similarity permits learning about the complex system by manipulating the simpler one. Second, they use participants' reasoning, decisionmaking, and action to represent the reasoning, decisionmaking, and negotiation of the individuals, organizations, or governments whose actions are at issue.

Other aspects of simulation gaming methods can vary widely. Participants' choices must be defined, supported, and constrained in a way that fills in the representation of the policy issue in question. Ways of accomplishing this can include the following:

- textual scenarios that describe the decision setting, focus attention on essential elements, and provide a sense of realism and importance for the proceedings
- an expert control team, whose judgments determine the consequences of participants' decisions
- formal models, which can supplement or replace a control team in this job
- specific analytic tools or general information resources to support participants' deliberations, planning, and negotiations.

Applicability of simulation gaming to global environmental change

Problems of global environmental management exhibit precisely circumstances under which formal economic modeling and game theoretic analysis can provide essential but only partial insights. Important decisions are made interactively in international negotiations. There is substantial disagreement and uncertainty regarding the values at stake, as well as the magnitude, locus, and character of potential threats. Decisions have long consequences. And the most important uncertainties may not based in biophysical knowledge, but rather concern values, behavior, and strategy.

Given these characteristics, simulation gaming assessment methods offer several potential advantages over formal approaches alone:

- They support integration of knowledge from a broader set of domains, including disciplinary knowledge and knowledge embedded in formal models, as well as intuition or judgment of multiple experts
- They investigate questions that are primarily behavioral or strategic, such as processes for developing and maintaining cooperation, coalition formation, and the robustness of strategies to uncertainty or surprise.
- They investigate problems for which preferences and values are contested or obscure (and not easily reconcilable through formal devices such as game theory or multiattribute utility theory).
- They promote more effective communication between assessment and policymaking.

Simulation gaming exercises that incorporate formal models can help improve models' utility and relevance by bringing them into a demanding policy-relevant setting for focused scrutiny and use by their intended audiences.

Major approaches to simulation gaming

Simulations come in various forms, and have been applied to a variety of policy domains. Whereas the term "simulation" refers to any representation, including formal models, simulation gaming always involves human participants, possibly augmented by formal models. Simulations that combine human participants with formal models (*person–machine simulations*) can permit more sophisticated representation of technical, scientific, or economic aspects of a problem, and hence may have advantages in investigating environmental issues. These can also be used to educate participants in the modeled phenomena, or to critique and test the plausibility and usefulness of formal approaches. *All-person simulations* emphasize the decision, negotiation, communication, and information-processing aspects of the problem. These are less able to represent the behavior of complex systems, but offer greater play for judgment and discussion on the feasibility, utility, and potential consequences of particular combinations of decisions.

A few basic dimensions capture much of the relevant variation of design among simulation gaming exercises:

- choice of boundaries: how much of the real problem is included in the simulation, and how much of that is represented by the participants and how much by formal models or rules.

- how tightly participants are constrained, trading off the benefits of a sharply focused simulation addressing a very specific question when participants have limited freedom against the benefits of encouraging creative solutions and insights when participants are allowed wide latitude to improvise or challenge the games' presumptions.
- intensity of time pressure and role identification, which can both be varied to promote a character ranging from calm, detached reflection to intense, engaged crisis decisionmaking.
- representation of simulated time, which can be fast or slow and can either traverse a single path through simulated time or multiple paths under different presumed conditions (Toth 1988a)
- treatment of uncertainty: whether participants see explicit uncertainty when considering their choices; whether the development of events in the simulation is stochastic (or is asserted to be); and whether the equivalent decision situations are faced more than once under different realizations of uncertain events.
- the expertise and seniority of participants, and how closely their simulation roles correspond to their real-life responsibilities.

War games and political–military exercises

The earliest simulations used to inform complex decisions were war games, either played on real battlefields or through representations on scaled playing surfaces. Postwar simulations moved beyond strictly military uses to include related diplomatic and political issues, in pursuit of a synoptic-scale representation of foreign-policy crises. The earliest such diplomatic simulations used teams of players to represent national governments, with a referee team ruling on the plausibility of proposed moves. Later developments included teams representing particular national and subnational organizations, and allowed both diplomatic interactions and the playing out of military confrontations. Similar free-form scenario-based simulations modeling foreign-policy crises are still in use (Goldhamer & Speier 1959, Paxson 1963, Mandel 1985, Kahan et al. 1985, Allen 1987).

The structures of all such simulations are similar. A text *scenario* describes the history and context, defines participants' objectives and resources, establishes the essential focus of the simulation, and provides a vivid, engaging setting in which participants can immerse themselves. Players, in two (usually) or more teams, make decisions on behalf of the organizations, groups, or nations they represent, over a period of several days. Simulated time normally stops while teams deliberate over their decisions, and jumps discretely between decisions. The control team, which normally includes the exercise designers and scenario writers, manages the simulation and determines the consequences of teams' decisions—in effect representing the underlying causal structure of the simulation, plus other actors not represented by teams, and nature. In contrast to earlier war-game traditions, the game's assumptions and the control team's decisions are normally open to challenge and discussion (Jones 1985), particularly during the intensive debriefing that follows the play. The control team's ability to maintain a plausible, vivid, evolving history that responds to participants' choices is crucial to these exercises. As such exercises have developed, the control team has increasingly been assisted by formal models (Bracken 1984).

The primary function of such simulations is to stress and test a complex system of organizations, technology, and routines, a system that cannot anticipate every kind of challenge that it may be called upon to face. Simulations permit critical, reflective examination of system response to hypothetical challenges, including crises that would happen too fast to allow such examination, or even considered responses, while they were happening.

Simulations of politics and international relations

From 1956 to 1972, a project at Northwestern University conducted research on person–machine simulations of politics and international relations (Guetzkow & Valadez 1981). These simulations, although inspired by the practical and operational political–military exercises, sought to develop and test theory, coupling international security relations with domestic political processes. Over time, the project's simulations came to include more actors and more issues, and to make increasing use of formal models—including some large all-machine simulations.

The project's first major simulation was the InterNation Simulation (INS), a simulated five-nation, two-bloc world in which national teams' decisions determined national welfare and security, and political change, through a set of programmed rules that took the place of a control team (Guetzkow 1968, 1981, Modelski 1970, Smoker 1972, Bloomfield 1984, Alker 1985). Later project simulations moved in two directions: toward richer and more detailed person–machine formats, and toward pure computer simulations without human participants (Valadez 1981). Principal among the former was the International Process Simulator (IPS), with roles for national governments, national and multinational industry, international NGOs, and international governmental organizations (Smoker 1981). Programmed (admittedly rudimentary) rules simulated trade and investment, research and development, and popular and labor unrest, whereas domestic politics was represented by teams playing opposing elites. Subsequently, the GLOBUS project sought to combine IPS's political and economic modeling with systems-dynamic models of resource, energy, and pollution constraints (Bremer 1987).

Adaptive environmental assessment and management

The simulation approaches summarized above use formal models to represent the physical world and hence define and constrain the participants' decision environment. Adaptive environmental assessment and management (AEAM) reverses this relationship between participants and models. AEAM is a process for bringing dispersed expertise to bear on complex and contentious decision problems, particularly concerned with natural-resource management. Participants, including both substantive experts and stakeholders, collaborate to construct a simulation model of the system under dispute, with staff support from a group of modelers and facilitators. The process serves two potential purposes: integrating dispersed knowledge and making it accessible to decisionmakers; and encouraging participants to enter a constructive dialog by focusing their attention on the demanding (and interesting) job of building a representation of the system under dispute. In many cases, the value of the exercise comes entirely from the focused discussion among protagonists that takes place around the modeling exercise, rather than from the model itself (Holling 1978, Sonntag 1986).

Policy exercises

A new class of simulation methods to study complex policy problems, including environment and development issues, has been developed, initially at the International Institute for Applied Systems Analysis (IIASA), under the name *policy exercises*. These share with the political–military exercises the emphasis on prior scenario development, and the structure of playing teams and one control team, but differ in the following respects:

- Policy exercises do not normally represent situations of strong intergroup conflict; in fact, some applications are to problems with no salient conflict, and hence use only one team, or parallel teams engaged in identical or complementary tasks.
- Teams' jobs are normally to create and analyze future or counterfactual

histories, with less active control-team intervention than is typical of political–military exercises.

- The exercises typically cover timescales of years to decades, rather than short-term crisis response.
- They represent time flexibly; rather than simply stepping forward in simulated time, they may work forward to or backward from a specified future endpoint, or go over the same period repeatedly under different conditions.

Policy exercises seek to integrate isolated pieces of knowledge, to build communication bridges between the academic and policy communities, and to encourage longer term, less constrained, and more creative thinking (Brewer 1986, Sonntag 1986, Toth 1988a,b, 1994). Obtaining useful results, as in political–military exercises, normally depends on the use of senior, expert policy participants. Policy exercises have been used to study comprehensive synopses of future world histories (Svedin & Aniansson 1987); to develop scenarios for regional impacts of global climate change (e.g., Jäger et al. 1991); and to study regional and forest-industry response to European acid rain (Duinker et al. 1993).

Stockholm Environment Institute (SEI) Greenhouse Policy Exercise

Following a suggestion made at the 1985 Villach Conference (WMO 1986), the Stockholm Environment Institute sponsored a global climate-change policy exercise in September 1990 at Bad Bleiberg, Austria (Jäger et al. 1991). The 25 participants were experts in climate and environmental policy, although none held a senior policy position at the time of the simulation.

The exercise focused on scenarios of the world in the year 2050. It used no computer models, and no gaming through which interactions of participant decisions determined outcomes. Rather, each of three teams worked in parallel to develop future histories leading from the present to an endpoint scenario that specified either large or small anthropogenic climate change in 2050. Teams did this job twice. The first time, each team's scenario was fixed in advance: while each one stated that sustainable development had been achieved by 2050 (defined by level and distribution of world income, rising life expectancy, and reversal of net deforestation and desertification), each specified a different combination of high or low climate change in Europe and in Southeast Asia. In the second round, each team chose its own 2050 endpoint, from a menu that combined different levels of climate change and of world equity, but did not specify particular regional results.

The results of this exercise served primarily to illuminate the participants' assumptions and heuristics about climate change, and the confidence with which these were held. In particular, all teams equated high or low climate change in 2050 with high or low anthropogenic emissions, neglecting other sources of uncertainty. In particular, every group with a low-climate-change future assumed that this came about through strong emission limits, and so described how major new international commitments and institutions were developed beginning in the 1990s. Every high-climate-change group described much more delayed changes in policies and institutions, which were eventually driven by grassroots political and religious movements reflecting public response to major climatic shocks of the next century.

RIVM simulation gaming and strategic planning exercises

A project of the National Institute for Public Health and the Environment (RIVM) of the Netherlands is developing simulation gaming exercises for global environment and climate change that draw on RIVM's formal integrated assessment models.

A major exercise under development, the Global Environmental Strategic Planning Exercise (GESPE) (de Vries et al. 1993) includes national teams making sequential decisions setting national investment, energy prices, energy conservation and alternative supply options, recycling, and reforestation. Teams' decisions are taken to represent a combination of government policy and aggregate social response. The structure of participants' decisionmaking will be constrained according to a model of decision processes developed by Mintzberg et al. (1976), while consequences will be determined by a set of dynamic computer models. Preliminary development of GESPE has used the systems dynamics model World 4.0, and it is planned to integrate this exercise with one of RIVM's formal integrated assessment models, either IMAGE 2.0 or TARGETS (see Ch. 5).

Preliminary exercises have been conducted using the simpler model SusClime (de Vries 1995), which presents a two-country world undergoing demographic and energy transitions. Nations manage these transitions by trading energy, by exchanging loans or aid, and, most importantly, by allocating current production among five investment alternatives: goods-producing capital; energy capital for fossil, renewable, and conservation; and population capital, which provides for current consumption and welfare, and at sufficiently high levels brings down population growth rates. New energy sources exhibit learning, while accumulating atmospheric carbon dioxide eventually degrades capital productivity. More tightly or more loosely constrained scenarios can be defined by varying the size of fossil resources, and the intensity of climate change impacts.

The primary objective of this project is to convey information embedded in the models—about dynamics, uncertainties, and interdependencies of global climate change, and related demographic and energy transitions—to policy participants. Work with SusClime has also explored the dynamic behavior associated with players adopting various simple heuristic strategies for their allocation choices.

IIASA climate change policy exercise

A series of policy exercises developed at IIASA seek to combine the advantages of scenarios and formal models in simulated decision environments. A test run of the first exercise involved 25 participants in four national teams, negotiating decisions over national emissions commitments plus associated measures for implementation, in scenarios set in 2005 and 2020. Each team had access to the reduced-form integrated assessment model MiniCAM, through a simple spreadsheet-based graphical interface, to design and execute custom model runs to examine the long-term consequences of their choices.

Test-run behavior and results highlighted the negotiation of obligations, rather than using model projections to evaluate long-run strategies, or design implementation details. The exercise generated sharply focused, cogent arguments illuminating current policy disputes over the form of national targets, the use of punitive sanctions, and joint implementation; generated a few policy proposals of moderate novelty; and, most centrally, provided methodological insights into opportunities and pitfalls of simulation design for global environmental change. Subsequent exercises will focus more narrowly on the relationship between emission obligations and financial transfers, and will use an episodic structure in which participants are sometimes organized into partisan national negotiating teams, and sometimes into neutral expert teams (Parson 1996a).

Uses of simulation gaming in integrated assessment

A conventional dichotomy divides potential uses of simulation methods into research and teaching. Some, although not all, potential uses of simulation gaming for integrated assessment can be categorized as research and teaching. In both domains, the potential value of simulation gaming is clear, but carries significant limitations and risks. Using simulation methods to test general research hypotheses about the behavior of people, organizations, or governments poses serious validation problems, because the simulation's contextual richness normally implies that they involve too many potentially confounding variables and admit insufficient replication (Parson 1996b). But strikingly similar phenomena that sometimes arise in diverse simulations, settings, and participant groups suggest plausibly generalizable patterns. Schelling, for example, reports that it is very difficult to keep a crisis at the boil in any simulation and offers a plausible (and testable) general explanation: that team members differ in how belligerently they wish to act, and that teams accommodate these differences by ordering their possible actions, doing the softest ones immediately and postponing the hardest ones to be contingent on other teams' actions. Consequently, teams normally see only the softest end of their counterparts' range of proposed actions; each thinks the others less belligerent than they actually are, and hence never reveals its own belligerence (Schelling 1987). Such generalizable behavior patterns can arise in simulations, although simulation games alone cannot validate them.

Simulation games can also be powerful vehicles for conveying insights to policymakers, although such use presumes that simulation designers or modelers have indeed discerned deep, important truths that should guide policy decisions. This is a bold presumption, and great caution is warranted before assuring policymakers that there are good grounds for confidence that the insights to be conveyed are true, important, enduring, and not liable to misinterpretation.

Other potential contributions of simulation gaming to complex, ill-posed, and imperfectly understood policy problems do not fit cleanly into the categories of research or teaching. Merely by providing a structured vehicle for critical reflection and dialogue, a simulation exercise can change the way participants think about the problem: help to clarify their views of its scope or importance; shake up preconceptions; or identify plausible and overlooked risks, innovations, contingencies, consequences, or responses (Parson 1996c). Simulation exercises can exhibit new, collective-level outcomes that no individual would have thought of alone, bringing the benefit of a list of things researchers might never have thought of (Schelling 1964). By drawing out concrete implications of key uncertainties, simulation exercises can provide a more thorough identification and more practical ranking of policy-relevant uncertainties than formal analyses alone.

Simulation games, particularly when formal models are used within the simulation, can also support focused communication between analysts and decisionmakers. Immediate benefits of this interaction may take the form of educating the policy community in insights embedded in models, or educating modelers to the needs and priorities of policymakers, hence helping to test or improve the policy relevance and legitimacy of formal models. General improvement of such communication may also bring substantial value of a more diffuse and long-term nature.

Significant risks accompany these benefits, principally bias and overgeneralization from small samples (Levine 1964). Subtle bias in simulation design is an ever-present risk that can push results in particular, predictable directions and diminish the heuristic value of the exercise. Both participants and designers are at risk of overgeneralizing, making too much of a sample of one experience, particularly because simulation experiences can be vivid and compelling. However, this risk may be no more serious than the widespread tendency to do the same thing from small samples of vivid real-life experiences. Both kinds of risks can be greatly mitigated by the use of simulation debriefing, in which participants and designers can question the simulation's relevance and generalizability, present other possibilities, and reflect critically on their experience. These risks are also unlikely to be severe when simulations are used to bound issues, clarify relevant preferences or values, or identify overlooked issues.

In summary, simulation gaming methods have potential value as devices for integrated assessment, as supplements to conventional forms of analysis or sober critical reflection, but not as replacements for them. Simulation methods are immature and developing. Their most evident contributions are as scoping devices, to clarify preferences and values, to promote creative thinking, and to identify overlooked issues. Simulation methods merit further exploration and experimentation, to elaborate and define their potential contributions, to make their contributions more reliable and to permit critical professional evaluation of the contribution of particular simulation exercises and approaches. In pursuing this development it will be important to avoid excessive claims and vain hope of certainties, predictions, or strong verifications that simulation methods cannot hope to achieve.

Conclusion

Thus, game theoretic and simulation gaming approaches both move analysis beyond the atomistic rationality of formal models of individual and market behavior, to encompass small numbers of multiple actors with differing perceptions and incentives. Of the two approaches, formal game theoretic analysis remains closer to the paradigm of universal rationality, and accordingly permits the analyst to predict moves based on his or her analysis of the actor's perception of self-interest. In the simulation gaming approaches, players actually represent social entities larger than their individual selves; this dimension injects a larger human element of complex behaviors into the execution of the game. However, although both approaches move beyond atomistic rationality, they continue to rely on two assumptions:

- that parties rationally perceive and act upon self-interest
- that, because rationality is universal, the decisions or actions of a game analyst or of a player in a simulation are reasonably representative of another player faced with the same information and incentives.

We will explore the basis of both of these assumptions in Chapter 3.

References

Alker Jr, H. R. 1985. Global modeling alternatives: the first twenty years. In *Theories, models, and simulations in international relations: essays in honor of Harold Guetzkow*, M. D. Ward (ed.). Boulder, Colorado: Westview.

Allais, M. 1953. Le comportement de l'homme rational devant de risque: critique des postulats et axiomes de l'école américaine. *Econometrica* **21**, 503–546.

Allen, T. B. 1987. *War games*. New York: McGraw-Hill.

Andresen, S. & J. Wettestad 1992. International resource cooperation and the greenhouse problem. *Global Environmental Change* **2**(4), 277–91.

Axelrod, R. & R. O. Keohane 1986. Achieving cooperation under anarchy: strategies and institutions. See K. Oye (1986).

Baldwin, D. A. 1993. *Neorealism and neoliberalism: the contemporary debate*. New York: Columbia University Press.

Berkes, F. (ed.) 1989. *Common property resources: ecology and community-based sustainable development*. London: Pinter (Belhaven).

Bloomfield, L. 1984. Reflections on gaming. *Orbis* **27**(4), 783–90.

Bracken, P. 1984. Deterrence, gaming, and game theory. *Orbis* **27**(4), 790–802.

—— 1990. Gaming in hierarchical defense organizations. In *Avoiding the brink: theory and practice in crisis management* A. C. Goldberg, D. Van Opstal, J. H. Barkley (eds). London: Brassey.

Bremer, S. A. (ed.) 1987. *The GLOBUS model: computer simulation of worldwide political and economic developments*. Frankfurt: Campus.

Brewer, G. D. 1986. Methods for synthesis: policy exercises. In *Sustainable development of the biosphere*, W. C. Clark & R. E. Munn (eds). Cambridge: Cambridge University Press.

Brewer, G. D. & M. Shubik 1979. *The war game: a critique of military problem solving*. Cambridge, Massachusetts: Harvard University Press.

Coddington, A. 1968. *Theories of the bargaining process*. London: George Allen & Unwin.

Duinker, P. N., S. Nilsson, F. L. Toth 1993. *Testing the "Policy Exercise" in studies of Europe's forest sector: methodological reflections on a bittersweet experience*. Working Paper WP-93-23, Laxenburg, Austria: International Institute for Applied Systems Analysis (IIASA).

Dupont, C. 1994. Domestic politics and international negotiations – a sequential bargaining model. In *Game theory and international relations: preferences, information, and empirical evidence*, P. Allan & C. Schmidt (eds). Cheltenham, England: Edward Elgar.

Fudenberg, D. & J. Tirole 1991. *Game theory*. Cambridge, Massachusetts: MIT Press.

Goldhamer, H. & H. Speier 1959. Some observations on political gaming. *World Politics* **12**(October), 71–83.

Grieco, J. M. 1988. Anarchy and the limits of cooperation: a realist critique of the newest liberal institutionalism. *International Organization* **42**, 51–8.

Guetzkow, H. 1968. Some correspondence between simulations and realities in international relations. In *New approaches to international relations*, M. Kaplan (ed.). New York: St Martin's Press.

—— 1981. International relations theory: contributions of simulated international processes. See Guetzkow & Valadez (1981).

Guetzkow, H. & J. J. Valadez (eds) 1981. *Simulated international processes: theories and research in global modelling*. Beverly Hills, California: Sage.

Hardin, G. 1968. The tragedy of the commons. *Science* **162**, 1243–8.

Hillman, A. L. & H. W. Ursprung 1992. The influence of environmental concerns on the political determination of trade policy. In *The greening of world trade issues*, K. Anderson & R. Blackhurst (eds). London: Harvester Wheatsheaf.

Hoel, M. 1991. Global environmental problems: the effects of unilateral action taken by one country. *Journal of Environmental Economics and Management* **20**, 55–70.

Holling, C. S. (ed.) 1978. *Adaptive environmental assessment and management*. Chichester, England: John Wiley.

Homer-Dixon, T. F. 1991. On the threshold: environmental change and violent conflict. *Scientific American* **16**, 76–116.

Jäger, J., N. Sonntag, D. Bernard, W. Kurz 1991. *The challenge of sustainable development in a greenhouse world: some visions of the future* [report of a policy exercise at Bad Bleiberg, Austria, September 2–7, 1990]. Stockholm: Stockholm Environment Institute.

Jervis, R. 1988. Realism game theory and cooperation. *World Politics* **40**, 317–49.

Kahan, J. P., W. M. Jones, R. E. Darilek 1985. *A design for war prevention games*. Rand Note N-2285-RC, Rand Corporation, Santa Monica, California.

Kahneman, D., P. Slovic, A. Tversky 1982. *Judgment under uncertainty: heuristics and biases*. Cambridge: Cambridge University Press.

Keohane, R. O. 1984. *After hegemony: cooperation and discord in the world political economy*. Princeton, New Jersey: Princeton University Press.

——1988. International institutions: two approaches. *International Studies Quarterly* **32**, 379–96. [Reprinted in *International institutions and state power*, R. O. Keohane (ed.). Boulder, Colorado: Westview, 1989.]

Keohane, R. O., P. M. Haas, M. A. Levy (eds) 1993. The effectiveness of international institutions. In *Institutions for the Earth: sources of effective international environmental protection*, P. M. Haas, R. O. Keohane, M. A. Levy (eds). London: MIT Press.

Krasner, S. D. 1982. Structural causes and regime consequences: regimes as intervening variables. *International Organization* **36**, 185–205.

——(ed.) 1983. *International regimes*. Ithaca, New York: Cornell University Press.

——1991. Global communications and national power: life on the Pareto frontier. *World Politics* **43**(3), 336–66.

Lang, W. 1993. International environmental cooperation. In *International environmental negotiations: process issues and contexts*, S. Sjostedt et al. (eds). Stockholm: Swedish Council for Planning and Coordination of Research and the Stockholm Institute of International Affairs.

Levine, R. A. 1964. Crisis games for adults. Internal Research Memorandum, Rand Corporation, circulated summer 1964 and published in *Crisis games 27 years later: plus c'est déja vu?* P-7719. Santa Monica, California: Rand Corporation.

Levy, M. A., R. O. Keohane, P. M. Haas 1993. *Improving the effectiveness of international environmental institutions*. In *Institutions for the Earth: sources of effective international environmental protection*, P. M. Haas, R. O. Keohane, M. A. Levy (eds). Cambridge, Massachusetts: MIT Press.

Lipson, C. 1984. International cooperation in security and economic affairs. *World Politics* **37**, 1–23.

List, M. & V. Rittberger 1991. Regime theory and international environment management. In *The international politics of the environment*, A. Hurrell & B. Kingsbury (eds). Oxford: Oxford University Press.

Livingston, M. 1989. Transboundary environmental degradation: market failure, power and instrumental justice. *Journal of Economic Issues* **23**, 79–91.

Livingston, M. & H. von Witzke 1990. Institutional choice in transboundary pollution. *Society and Natural Resources* **3**, 159–71.

Maler, K. 1990. International environmental problems. *Oxford Review of Economic Policy* **6**, 80–108.

Mandel, R. 1985. Professional-level war gaming: a critical assessment. In *Theories, models and simulations in international relations: essays in honor of Harold Guetzkow*, M. D. Ward (ed.). Boulder, Colorado: Westview.

Mintzberg, H., D. Raisinghani, A. Theoret 1976. The structure of unstructured decision processes. *Administrative Science Quarterly* **21**, 246–75.

Mintzer, I. & J. A. Leonard 1994. *Negotiating climate change: the inside story of the Rio Convention*. Cambridge, Massachusetts: Cambridge University Press.

Modelski, G. 1970. Simulation, realities and international relations theory. *Simulation and Games* **1**(June), 111–34.

Nicholson, M. 1994. Interdependent utility functions: implications for cooperation and conflict. In *Game theory and international relations: preferences, information, and empirical evidence*, P. Allan & C. Schmidt (eds). Cheltenham, England: Edward Elgar.

Nilsson, S. & D. Pitt 1994. *Protecting the atmosphere: the Climate Change Convention and its context*. London: Earthscan.

Oberthür, S. 1993. *Politik im Triebhaus: die Entstehung des internationalen Klimaschutzregimes*. Berlin: Edition Sigma.

Olson, M. & R. Zeckhauser 1966. An economic theory of alliances. *Review of Economics and Statistics* **48**, 266–79.

Ordeshook, P. C. 1986. *Game theory and political theory*. Cambridge, Massachusetts: Cambridge University Press.

Osgood, C. E. 1979. GRIT for MBFR: a proposal for unfreezing force-level postures in Europe. *Peace Research Reviews* **8**, 77–92.

Ostrom, E. 1990. *Governing the commons: the evolution of institutions for collective action*. Cambridge: Cambridge University Press.

Oye, K. 1986. *Explaining cooperation under anarchy: hypothesis and strategies*. Princeton, New Jersey: Princeton University Press.

Parson, E. A. 1996a. *A global climate-change policy exercise: results of a test run*. IIASA Working Paper WP-96-90, International Institute for Applied Systems Analysis, Laxenburg, Austria.

——1996b. What can you learn from a game? In *Wise choices: decisions, games, and negotiations*, R. J. Zeckhauser, R. L. Keeney, J. K. Sebenius (eds). Boston: Harvard Business School Press.

——1996c. *How should we study global environmental problems? A plea for unconventional methods of assessment and analysis*. IIASA Working Paper WP-96-157, International Institute for Applied Systems Analysis, Laxenburg, Austria.

Paterson, M. & M. Grubb 1992. The politics of climate. *International Affairs* **68**, 293–310.

Paxson, E. W. 1963. *War gaming report*. RM-3489, Santa Monica, California: Rand Corporation.

Peterson, J. & H. Ward 1995. Coalitional stability and the new multidimensional politics of security: a rational choice argument for US–EU cooperation. *European Journal of International Relations* **1**(2), 131–56.

Powell, R. 1991. Absolute and relative gains in international relations theory. *American Political Science Review* **85**, 1303–320.

Putnam, R. D. 1988. Diplomacy and domestic politics: the logic of two-level games. *International Organization* **42**(3), 427–60.

Raiffa, H. 1982. *The art and science of negotiation*. Cambridge, Massachusetts: Harvard University Press.

Schelling, T. C. 1960. *The strategy of conflict*. Cambridge, Massachusetts: Harvard University Press.

——1964. An uninhibited pitch for crisis games. Internal Research Memorandum, RAND Corporation, circulated Summer 1964 and published in *Crisis games 27 years later: plus c'est déjà vu*, P-7719, Rand Corporation, Santa Monica, California.

——1987. The role of war games and exercises. In *Managing nuclear operations*, A. B. Carter,

J. D. Steinbruner, C. A. Zraket (eds). Washington DC: Brookings Institution.

Sebenius, J. K. 1991. Designing negotiations towards a new regime: the case of global warming. *International Security* **15**, 110–48.

——1992. Challenging conventional explanations of international cooperation: negotiation analysis and the case of epistemic communities. *International Organization* **46**, 323–65.

——1994. Towards a winning climate coalition. In *Negotiating climate change: the inside story of the Rio Convention*, I. Mintzer & J. A. Leonard (eds). Cambridge: Cambridge University Press.

Sen, A. 1969. A games-theoretic analysis of collectivism. In *Growth and choice*, T. Majumdar (ed.). Oxford: Oxford University Press.

Shepsle, K. A. & B. R. Weingast 1975. Structure-induced equilibrium and legislative choice. *Public Choice* **23**, 503–519.

Simon, H. A. 1982. *Models of bounded rationality*. Cambridge, Massachusetts: MIT Press.

Sjostedt, G. 1993. Special and typical attributes of international environmental negotiations. In *International environmental negotiations: process, issues and contexts*, G. Sjostedt et al. (eds). Stockholm: Swedish Council for Planning and Coordination of Research and the Stockholm Institute of International Affairs.

Smoker, P. 1972. International relations simulations. In *Simulation in the social and administrative sciences*, H. Guetzkow, P. Kotler, R. L. Schultz (eds). Englewood Cliffs, New Jersey: Prentice-Hall.

——1981. The international process simulation. See Guetzkow & Valadez (1981).

Snidal, D. 1985. The limits of hegemonic stability theory. *International Organization* **39**(4), 579–614.

——1986. *The game theory of politics*. See Oye (1986).

——1991. Relative gains and the pattern of international cooperation. *American Political Science Review* **85**, 701–727.

Sonntag, N. C. 1986. Commentary. In *Sustainable development of the biosphere*, W. C. Clark & R. Munn (eds). Cambridge: Cambridge University Press.

Soroos, M. S. 1994. Global change, environmental security, and the Prisoner's Dilemma. *Journal of Peace Research* **31**, 317–32.

Stein, A. 1982. Coordination and collaboration: regimes in an anarchic world. *International Organization* **36**, 299–324.

Svedin, U. & B. Aniansson, (eds) 1987. *Surprising futures: notes from an international workshop on long-term world development*. Report 87-1, Stockholm, Sweden: Swedish Council for Planning and Coordination of Research.

Taylor, M. 1987. *The possibility of cooperation*. Cambridge: Cambridge University Press.

Taylor, M. & H. Ward 1982. Chickens, whales and lumpy public goods: alternative models of public-goods provision. *Political Studies* **30**, 350–70.

Toth, F. L. 1988a. Policy exercises: objectives and design elements. *Simulation and Games* **19**(3), 235–55.

——1988b. Policy exercises: procedures and implementation. *Simulation and Games* **19**(3), 256–76.

——1994. Practice and progress in integrated assessments of climate change: a review. In *Integrative assessment of mitigation, impacts, and adaptation to climate change*, N. Nakicenovic, W. D. Nordhaus, R. Richels, F. L. Toth (eds). Proceedings of a workshop held on 13–15 October 1993. Laxenburg, Austria: IIASA.

Valadez, J. 1981. Generational developments in modeling. See Guetzkow & Valadez (1981).

Vries, H. J. M. de 1995. SusClime: a simulation game on population and development in a resource- and climate-constrained two-country world. GLOBO Report Series 11, National Institute of Public Health and Environmental Protection [RIVM], Bilthoven, the Netherlands.

Vries, H. J. M. de, T. Fiddaman, R. Janssen. 1993. Outline for a Global Environmental Strategic

Planning Exercise (GESPE Project). GLOBO Report Series 2, National Institute of Public Health and Environmental Protection [RIVM], Bilthoven, the Netherlands.

Waltz, K. N. 1979. *Theory of international politics*. London: Addison–Wesley.
Ward, H. 1989. Testing the waters: taking risks to gain reassurance in public goods games. *Journal of Conflict Resolution* **33**, 274–308.
——1993. Game theory and the politics of the global commons. *Journal of Conflict Resolution* **37**, 203–235.
Weale, A. 1992. *The new politics of pollution*. Manchester: Manchester University Press.
WMO [World Meteorological Organization] 1986. *Report of the international conference on the assessment of the role of carbon dioxide and of other greenhouse gases in climate variations and associated impacts*. Conference Report WMO 661, World Meteorological Organization, Villach, Austria.

Young, O. R. 1989. *International cooperation: building regimes for natural resources and the environment*. Ithaca, New York: Cornell University Press.
——1991. Political leadership and regime formation: on the development of institutions in international society. *International Organization* **45**, 281–308.

CHAPTER 3

Decision analysis and rational action

Carlo C. Jaeger, Ortwin Renn,
Eugene A. Rosa, Tom Webler

Contributors
Robin Cantor, Ottmar Edenhofer, Silvio O. Funtowicz, Gavan McDonell,
Jerome R. Ravetz, Steve Rayner, Galina Sergen

For helpful discussions we are indebted to Hadi Dowlatabadi, Larry Goulder, Jean-Charles Hourcade, Ray Kopp, Irene Peters, Jan Rotmans, and Matthias Waechter. A more extensive elaboration of the theoretical argument made in the chapter will be developed in a forthcoming book by the principal authors.

Climate change is representative of a class of issues that raise tough challenges for individual and collective decisionmaking. It is perhaps surprising, therefore, that the fundamental conceptual framework for climate change decisionmaking has received so very little scrutiny in such a large literature.

An exception is Arrow et al. (1996a: 62) who adumbrated the fairly restrictive set of assumptions under which standard decision analytic perspectives and tools operate. They include a unique decisionmaker faced by a limited number of alternatives which can be compared by an unambiguous quantitative criterion. Of course, it is widely recognized that these conditions will not be perfectly satisfied for most real-world decisions. Provided that the violations are minor, decision analysis may still offer a solution close to the optimal outcome desired by a rational actor. What is less generally agreed upon is the problem of how to distinguish which violations are minor and which are major, as well as what level of cumulative minor violations synergize to invalidate the approach.

For climate change, the same authors recognize significant violations. In particular, there is no single decisionmaker. Differences in values and objectives prevent collectives of decisionmakers from using the same selection criterion for decision alternatives—so decision analysis cannot yield a universally preferred solution. Moreover, uncertainties in climate change are so pervasive and far reaching that the tools for handling uncertainty provided by decision analysis are no longer sufficient.

The problem of multiple decisionmakers leads Arrow and his coauthors to recommend a less formal approach to the choice of climate policy at the intergovernmental level: a structured incremental negotiation framework designed to produce a solution acceptable to multiple parties, rather than an impossible optimum. This framework embodies various formal decision analytic techniques designed to maintain the rationality of the decision process. The extent to which such processes of structuring negotiations violate the assumptions of decision theory is not explored in detail, raising the question of whether sustaining the relevance of formal decision analysis in spite of significant violations is a prudent preservation of insights from a potentially powerful tool or, rather, a misleading procedure somewhat akin to looking for one's keys under a street lamp because that is where the light is.

In the context of the Intergovernmental Panel on Climate Change and the negotiations that it is designed to serve, the parties to decisionmaking are not citizens but national governments. "Decision analysis suffers fewer problems when used by individual countries to identify optimal national policies" (Arrow et al. 1996a: 65). However, the authors were not explicit about how it is that an intergovernmental decision involving fewer than 200 decisionmaking parties poses greater problems for applying decision analysis than the shaping of national policy by governments representing millions of households, thousands of firms and nongovernmental organizations, hundreds of communities, dozens of economic sectors, and multiple regions. Even the legislatures of most countries have more members than there are parties to the Framework Convention on Climate Change. The presumption of a unitary national interest seldom withstands close scrutiny, particularly in a world of economic, political, and cultural interdependence across national boundaries.

Furthermore, it is clear that decision analytic perspectives and tools continue to be applied uncritically by a large segment of the technical community that advises government decisionmakers. The climate policy literature almost universally shares the fundamental assumption underlying the application of rational analysis and decision analytic tools: that climate change can be decomposed into a conceptually simple (if still practically challenging) problem, for which a rational solution can be constructed and implemented within the existing framework of political power and technical expertise. In other words, climate change can be distilled down to the problem of controlling greenhouse-related emissions, the relevant actors are national governments, and the relevant action required is coordinated regulation (through whatever policy instruments) of the emission of greenhouse-related gases by firms and households at an optimum level from the standpoint of the general welfare, expressed as a proportion of gross domestic (or global) product.

This persistence of analysts in using conventional decision analytic perspectives, and the continued focus on optimization where no optimum can exist, suggest that the fundamentals of decision analysis are worth a closer look to get a handle on how to decide where and when decision analytic insights are useful or misleading, as well as to investigate possible alternative or supplementary approaches that currently may be underutilized.

As uncertainty is a salient feature of climate change, the tools of risk analysis need special attention here. Combined with the issue of uncertainty, however, are additional difficulties. In particular, decisions relating to climate change are not oriented by a unique consistent value system. Even a single actor may be influenced by several value systems that contradict each other. The classical result by Arrow (1951) on the impossibility of a general procedure for aggregating given individual preferences in a democratic fashion is exacerbated by such conditions (see Sen 1995 for a recent discussion). Obviously, aggregation may be performed by a technocratic rule system, but this is neither a desirable nor a reliable institutional setting for climate policy.

Democratic institutions aggregate individual preferences by enabling individuals to modify their preferences through the combination of voting procedures and public debate. The role of public debate reminds us of the need for interpretive approaches such as that of the Frankfurt School (Bottomore 1984), to complement the reductionist analysis of conventional mathematical methods. Interpretive approaches open the way to a social rationality, and to the fruitful interaction of reason and values, which are essential elements of a matured theory of decisionmaking in problems such as those of climate change.

The tension between a purely individualistic notion of rationality and an understanding of social rationality shows that the problem with using decision analysis in climate policy has important ramifications. Conventional decision analysis is a particular instance of a much larger conceptual framework, the rational actor paradigm. We will argue that successful climate policy needs to advance beyond the limits of this paradigm, and that such a move raises challenging research questions.

The move from individualistic to social rationality looks like a classic instance of a paradigm shift, a scientific revolution. There may be even more at stake, however. The very understanding of scientific inquiry as the autonomous production of knowledge on which decisionmakers can and must base their action becomes questionable. Social rationality may require a different role for science, a role in which the embeddedness of scientific activities in larger social contexts is seen not as an imperfection to be minimized but as a precondition of meaningful scientific inquiry. Rather than providing answers for elite decisionmakers, the study of climate change may help decisionmakers, including a broadly defined public, to clarify and resolve their own concerns. By such a process, climate change analysis and decisionmaking would be moved from technical arguments in narrow, elite circles to the realm of political judgments in democratic institutions.

We will investigate the meaning and possibility of rational action with regard to climate change step by step. First, we consider the problem of climatic risks from the point of view of a single decisionmaker who is able to control global greenhouse-related emissions. We then discuss some major difficulties that arise with such a solipsistic approach to risk analysis, and introduce a plurality of actors who are engaged in processes of exchange and negotiation in the face of climatic risks. However, these actors will still be of a remarkably homogeneous character insofar as they all operate as optimizing automata who are not very interested in communicating with each other. We move on to consider a more pluralistic setting where different actors may display very different kinds of behavior, including intense communication about shared and contested meanings. This introduces the themes of social rationality and non-optimizing choices. The conclusion spells out some implications for future research and action.

The rational actor paradigm

A single decisionmaker, or benevolent planner seeking an optimal climate policy, would be searching for nothing less than the optimal amount of anthropogenic climate change. Several sophisticated models have been built with the explicit purpose of computing this magnitude (e.g., Nordhaus 1994, Manne & Richels 1995; see also Ch. 5). Such studies are mathematical in form, and their authors must necessarily employ some quantity as a surrogate for the complex process of global change. Such bold simplification cannot be avoided; the only choice is which indicator to use. Some employ the atmospheric concentration of greenhouse gases (which is closer to the physical processes causing the phenomenon), whereas others employ the global mean temperature (which is closer to the climate and, therefore, human effects). The relationship between the two, beyond the range of events already recorded, is not fully known.

The use of quantitative indicators for environmental welfare is also problematic, particularly with respect to the manipulation and suppression of crucial uncertainties. The construction of a unique numeraire for measuring economic welfare is well embedded in traditional practice; but its extension to the environment for evaluating natural goods raises difficult issues (Funtowicz & Ravetz 1994). Despite these difficulties, gross national product (GNP) or gross domestic product (GDP) is widely used as the relevant variable. Recently, efforts have been made to incorporate into the measurement of GNP some estimate of nonmarket impacts, and we will assume that modification in our use of the term here. To compare values of GNP realized at different moments in time, some decision has also to be taken about discounting (Broome 1992). (See the discussions of discounting in Chs 1 and 5.)

The claim that there might be such a thing as an optimal amount of climate change is based on the idea that there is a need to balance the costs that result from the environmental impacts of climate change and the benefits that result from the use of fossil fuels and similar activities (e.g., Manne & Richels 1995; see also Munasinghe et al. 1996). Total GNP is seen as the potential GNP that could be obtained if there were no negative impacts of climate change, less the social costs that result from such change. So long as climate change is small, the negative impacts of additional climate change are assumed to be small as well. At the same time, the benefits to be gained from incurring some additional climate change—that is, the goods and services whose provision results in the emission of greenhouse gases—are assumed to be substantial. However, if climate change is already large the marginal costs of additional climate change are expected to be large as well. Under the same circumstances of substantial climate change, the marginal benefits resulting from additional climate change are supposed to be rather small. It is a trivial property of the mathematical representation of net benefit (the difference between costs and benefits) that, when the net benefit is at a maximum or minimum, the marginal costs and marginal benefits are equal. (This is not at all the same as saying that equality of those marginal effects is sufficient for an optimal net benefit.)

Whether cost–benefit analysis should be applied to environmental problems such as climate change is a subject of debate (Arrow et al. 1996b). However, the issue is not simply cost–benefit analysis. This methodology is just one example of the much larger class of optimizing procedures. Cost–benefit theory arose out of engineering economics and its goal for increased efficiency. Cost–benefit analysis seeks to establish the optimum alternative within any given situation, by employing a criterion of efficiency based on the objective measurement of advantages and disadvantages to individuals, the aggregate of which is then compared to derive a measure of the collective good (Merkhofer 1984, Smith 1986).

Problems arise, of course, when markets fail. Private property rights are not well defined for many environmental resources, for example; so, no market prices exist with which to impute their value in the cost–benefit calculus. Prices do exist in other cases, but they might not fully reflect either the true and complete marginal social cost of using a resource or the true and complete marginal social benefit of having more of something desirable. To overcome these difficulties, environmental economists have devised methods with which to value many environmental resources and service flows (see Ch. 1). The resulting values are referred to as nonmarket values and are sometimes taken to be those accruing to current users of a resource, but the values are not usually confined to these individuals or to their individualistic motives.

For the problem of climate change, Figure 3.1 may be used as a condensed representation of different options. An option consists in a time path of climate change. Each path can be characterized by the amount of climate change realized in some target year in the future, say, 2050. Of the different paths leading to the same amount of climate change in 2050, we consider only those that yield the highest possible welfare. For the sake of the argument, welfare is measured as the sum of discounted values of GNP between now and the target year. (The argument can be further generalized to an infinite future.) Point S marks a small amount of climate change, with points Sc and Sb indicating the costs and benefits associated with that amount of climate change. An analogous situation is represented for a large amount of climate change. In between lies the optimal amount.

If the benevolent planner has direct control over global greenhouse gas emissions, the problem is now solved. Models of this kind actually compute an optimal amount of climate change. Where do they place it? Interestingly, they suggest that for the next 10 or 20 years a business-as-usual strategy would be

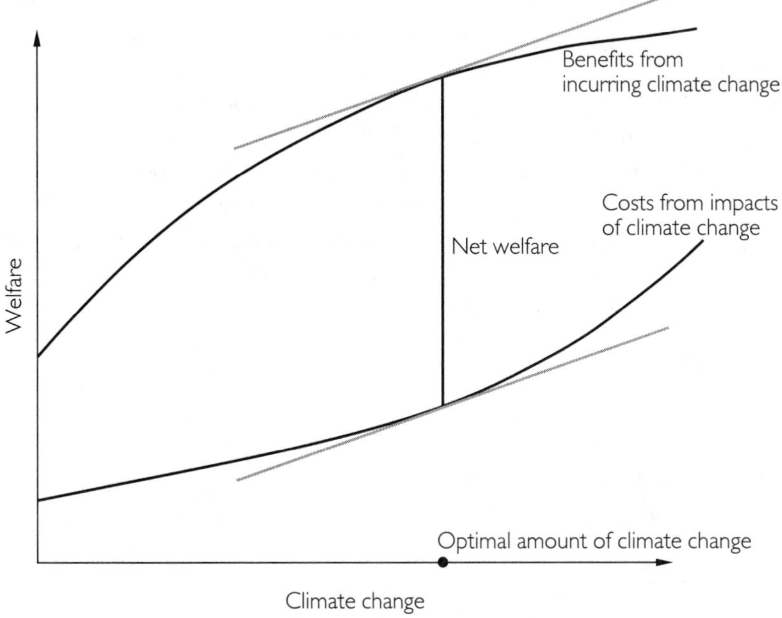

Figure 3.1 A simple view of climate change and welfare change.

very close to an optimal path (Wigley et al. 1996). Only later on would an optimal strategy require some reduction in comparison with a business-as-usual strategy, but, even then, increasing climate change would be optimal for at least another century (Nordhaus 1994). Obviously, exploring optimal time paths in detail requires an explicit dynamic analysis that goes beyond the representation of Figure 3.1.

In the framework of optimizing rationality, the problem of climate change arises because the operation of the world economy is not equivalent to the decisionmaking by a benevolent planner. In fact, greenhouse gas emissions are controlled by a multitude of individual agents who are individually rational without being socially rational. How can this happen? The benevolent planner optimizes the difference between the welfare gain from incurring climate change and the costs of climate change that the planner attributes to society as a whole. The latter may be called the social costs. However, individual agents may be unaffected by costs to other agents, which they generate via climate change. Under these circumstances, individual costs differ from social costs. If an individual agent increases his contribution to climate change, his individual costs increase less than social costs. Therefore, individually optimizing agents will generate greater climate change than is socially optimal (Fig. 3.2).

When individual and social costs differ, individual and social rationality diverge as well, and the individual agents are trapped in a social dilemma. It is important to notice that now the individual cost curve depends on the actions of the other agents. In other words, climate change involves external effects. Because the other agents behave differently at the social optimum than at the individual optimum, there are two different individual cost curves for each of these two points. At the social optimum, the individual cost curve leads an optimizing agent to increase climate change. At the individual optimum, the individual cost curve leads an optimizing agent to settle at the corresponding level of climate change, even if the social optimum would require a smaller level.

If the benevolent planner has no direct control over greenhouse gas emissions but has the power to raise taxes, the planner can redress the situation by levying a tax on activities that contribute to climate change. The level of the tax must be such that, in the social optimum, marginal individual costs are identical to marginal social costs (Nordhaus 1994). The social optimum then is an individual optimum, too (in Fig. 3.2, the two curves would have the same slope in the social optimum.) This is the rationale of the proposals to tackle the problem of climate change by introducing a carbon tax.

There is a striking similarity between the benevolent planner and a less friendly figure: Hobbes's *Leviathan*. In the *Leviathan* (1651) Hobbes took the existence of a wide variety of desires and aversions as a fact of human life. And

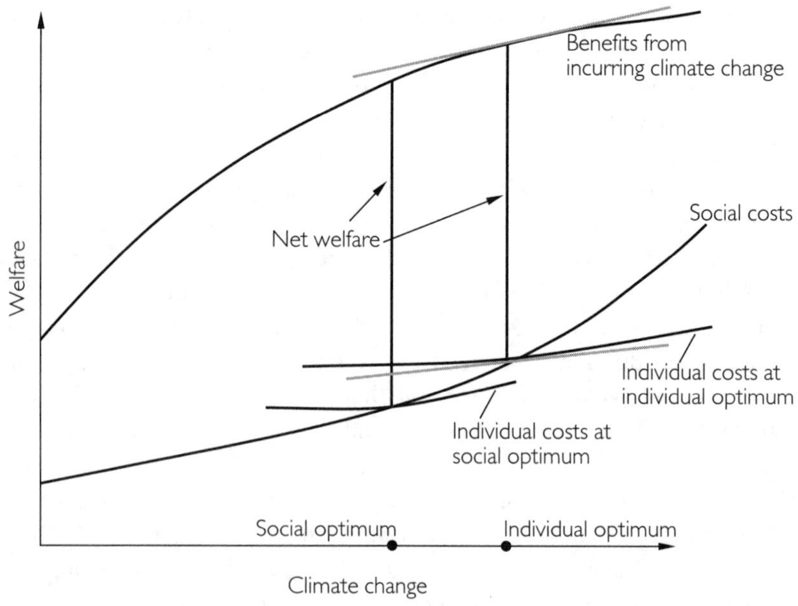

Figure 3.2 Divergence between individual and social optimum.

he considered that human individuals try to fulfil their desires with whatever means are at their disposal. In particular, if many individuals possess arms of similar power, they will use these arms in attempts to rob and subjugate each other. As a result, they will live in a rather unpleasant situation and will miss the opportunity of enjoying the personal security provided by a peaceful society. In other words, they are trapped in a social dilemma. If, however, one of them possesses arms of overwhelming superiority, he can assume the role of the Leviathan. He can establish state power characterized by a monopoly of physical violence. For all the other individuals, using physical violence now becomes unattractive. As a result, individual and social rationality are harmonized and the social dilemma is solved.

With this analysis, Hobbes laid the foundations for a view of human affairs that had a profound influence on the social sciences in particular and on contemporary society in general. We call this view the *rational actor paradigm*. It has become the most widely accepted paradigm in the social sciences for the explanation of human behavior. Its main ideas can be characterized by four statements:

- Rational actors can choose between different possible actions.
- Rational actors can order the different consequences of possible actions according to their preferences.
- The possible actions available to different rational actors depend on parameters of their joint situation.
- Rational actors choose a possible action which, according to their preferences, is optimal given the parameters of the situation.

A crucial feature of the rational actor paradigm may be called atomistic rationality. Every individual is supposed to deliberate alone until reaching a decision. This is closely related to the explanation of human behavior in terms of self-interest (Lasswell 1958, March & Simon 1958, Easton 1965). This concept underlies the economist's account of the search for profit and the political scientist's analysis of the quest for power.

Hobbes acknowledged that a person may hold different desires, or values, that are incompatible under given circumstances. He did not clarify how a human agent could make a rational choice among such desires. Bentham (1789) proposed a solution by claiming that what people actually desire is happiness, and that the contribution of an object to a person's happiness can be described as a quantitative variable. With such a concept of utility, the theory of rational choice could become an exercise in constrained maximization, and human agency became amenable to description with the mathematical means of the calculus.

Bentham's concept of utility prepared the ground for later developments in mathematical economics. But the immediate consequences were of a more philosophical nature. Bentham treated utility much like a physical substance such as water: he considered that quantities of utility could be added together both for a single individual and for a society as a whole. Technically speaking, he assumed a cardinal utility, which allowed for interpersonal comparisons. This remarkable assumption led straightforwardly to a utilitarian approach to ethics. If everyone tries to maximize utility, ethical judgment should be focused on the consequences of human actions and institutions for the utility enjoyed by human beings.

With the assumption of cardinal utility, it is very plausible to argue that increasing quantities of a good lead to diminishing marginal utilities. However, this has severe consequences for distribution conflicts: as a rule, total utility (as well as utility per head) will decrease if wealth is transferred from the poor to the rich. A recent study (Daly & Cobb 1989) has shown how changes in income distribution in the United States have produced just such an effect. Such an argument is quite relevant for the distribution issues raised by climate policy. However, this embarrassing property of the rational actor paradigm was neutralized early on with the discovery that the rational actor paradigm requires only an ordinal concept of utility (Robbins 1932). Edgeworth (1881), Pareto (1906), Hicks (1939), and many others showed that utility functions could be reinterpreted as simply a shortcut description of preference orderings. To say that for an actor the utility of a car is greater than the utility of a bicycle is simply another way of saying that the actor in question prefers a car to a bicycle. And with ordinal utility, interpersonal comparisons of utility become pointless.

Bentham's notion of cardinal utility presented a serious measurement problem. It is easy to talk about diminishing marginal utility, but it is hard, often impossible, to measure the utility of specific events to specific agents. Ordinal utility, on the other hand, avoided this problem. Specifying preferences of a specific agent is often easy, and when this can be done it is usually trivial to formulate them in terms of ordinal utilities. Any monotonic transformation of a utility function that is consistent with the specified preferences will do. When ordinal utilities refer to possibilities of action available to the agent in question, the machinery of the rational actor paradigm can be used to analyze his decisions.

With ordinal utility, the insight behind the idea of diminishing marginal utility can still be expressed with the well-known device of indifference curves. Basically, convex indifference curves yield the same behavior as the hypothesis of diminishing marginal utility. For example, a rational actor may be able to invest a fixed amount of money in several activities whose extension can be varied and which can be combined with each other. The optimal action will then usually involve a combination of activities rather than a single activity. If any differentiable representation of ordinal utilities is chosen, the optimal action will be such that the investment of an additional dollar in any activity yields the same marginal utility. For climate policy, therefore, one should usually expect a policy mix to yield better results than a pure policy (for a similar result with regard to the Montreal protocol, see Fernando et al. 1993).

Optimization, however, does not necessarily involve the computation of a numerical difference between costs and benefits. A set of preferences geared to a set of possible actions is all that is required for optimizing rationality to operate. If utility analysis is to be grounded in preference orderings, then there must be simple preferences that cannot be further reduced to advantages and disadvantages of different options. If someone prefers the present climate to a potentially changed future climate, then he may be said to maximize his utility even if it makes little sense to try to distinguish relative costs and benefits of these two options.

The cardinal difference of benefits and costs refers to a special, if very important, case of rational action. Basically, the distinction arises with the development of economic enterprises. Such enterprises follow practices of accounting, which establish a distinction between costs and revenues. Revenues may be seen as benefits, and profits as the difference between benefits and costs. When economic enterprises are considered as rational actors, it is reasonable to say that, with a given stock of capital, they prefer larger profits to smaller ones. In this sense, the decisions of enterprises may be said to result from a cost–benefit analysis.

On the basis of the partial analogy with economic enterprises, cost–benefit analysis is presented as a decision tool for public authorities. Decisions by such bodies often generate costs, economic and otherwise, for other agents. In a democratic setting, these costs require some kind of justification. Hopefully, a governmental decision that is costly for some agents also leads to benefits, although not necessarily for the same agents. If the benefits generated by a decision can be expressed in monetary terms, they can be compared to the costs generated by the same decision. A decision may then be justified by claiming that benefits exceed costs.

The conceptual device of the benevolent planner has the analytical advantage of bypassing all questions about the appropriateness of cost–benefit analysis where multiple agents are involved. One simply assumes that costs and benefits for society as a whole are meaningful concepts and can be measured quantitatively. In the case of climate change, this assumption is often used to develop the kind of analysis presented above (see Box 3.1). So far, however, we have assumed that the benevolent planner is gifted with perfect foresight. Next, we confront the benevolent planner with risk.

Box 3.1 Designing a Global Marshall Plan: the optimization approach

The literature on the costs of emissions reduction makes two major claims relevant to any intergovernmental agreement to reduce total greenhouse gas emissions to some specific level:

- In any country, the costs of reducing emissions by an additional unit increase with the total amount of reduction. (This also implies that the total costs of emissions reduction increase with the total amount of reduction.)
- According to that literature, the costs of reducing emissions by an additional unit are much higher in industrialized countries than in most less industrialized countries.

The difference in costs is greatly amplified if reductions are computed not from present levels but from an expected baseline scenario—simply because emissions are expected to raise by much greater amounts in less industrialized countries than in those that have already industrialized.

Current economic theory implies that under such circumstances each country should reduce emissions to the point where the marginal abatement costs of all countries are equal. With any other distribution of emissions reductions, total costs will be unnecessarily increased. In practice, this means that money for emissions reductions should be spent primarily in less industrialized countries rather than in the industrialized world. On the other hand, both widely accepted notions of fairness and the idea that external effects of economic activities should be internalized suggest that the money for emissions reductions should be collected mainly from the industrialized nations. Therefore, some scheme for substantial financial transfers seems warranted.

With his call for a Global Marshall Plan, Gore (1992) envisaged a scheme of that sort. The Global Environmental Facility (Gan 1993) may be considered as a prototype upon which further efforts in that direction can build. Within the framework of the rational actor paradigm, the design of a Global Marshall Plan can be approached as an exercise in constrained optimization. It may be solved by an international emissions trading agreement, as advocated by the Economists' Statement on Climate Change (1997). This would rely on a two-tiered approach. At the global level, national governments would trade emissions permits with each other and possibly with other partners. Initial quotas would be set so that industrialized nations are bound to contribute substantial emissions reductions. The permits trade would then enable industrialized countries to realize these reductions in less industrialized countries, in line with the philosophy of joint implementation. At the national level, governments would implement the resulting emissions quota via carbon taxes or auctions of emissions permits. Obviously, many different variants may be considered. The main point is to collect money in the industrialized world and transfer it to the less industrialized world so as to finance emissions reductions there.

However, this design is faced with at least three major difficulties:

- It may be very difficult to secure the necessary support in many industrialized countries for major financial transfers to less industrialized countries.
- It is hard to imagine how national emissions quotas could be enforced. Is it realistic to expect Brazil to stop deforestation if it lacks the permits for emitting greenhouse gases from burning the rainforest?
- The whole approach requires a binding agreement about emissions reductions to start with. Although such an agreement may emerge, if at all, as the outcome of a long-lasting negotiation process, it will not happen as its starting point (Jaeger et al. 1997).

Because of these difficulties, we will further explore the design of a Global Marshall Plan in subsequent boxes.

Rational risk management

Despite significant advances in scientific knowledge over the past decade, climate policy will continue for the foreseeable future to require decisionmaking under conditions of significant and complex uncertainty (see Vol. 2, Ch. 1). Indeed (as discussed in Vol. 1, Ch. 1), some of this uncertainty may be irreducible in principle. As formulated by the former chairman of the IPCC, the issue of climate change is properly framed as a problem of risk management (Bolin 1995):

> The issue at stake is not to agree on policies for decades into the next century but rather to adopt a strategy whereby needed actions could be formulated as more knowledge becomes available. The climate change issue will in any case be with us for decades to come and the adequacy of the commitments under the Convention should be judged in that perspective.

And

> It is important to realize that uncertainty about the details of a potential climate change (that is, regional and local climate change) does not diminish risks; it merely makes it more difficult to assess them quantitatively.

Sociologist Beck (1986) commented on the emergence of a *risk industry*, consisting of *risk professionals* (Dietz & Rycroft 1987) dedicated to the rational management of dangerous uncertainty. The conception of risk within this modern industry has been profoundly shaped by the rational actor paradigm (Jaeger et al. 1995). In this view, risk is seen as involving two principal components. The first is the threat of possible unwanted consequences and loss; the second is the uncertainty that surrounds the nature and extent of the threat (Rowe 1977).

The first step in the provision of a scientific basis for the risk industry was made in the seventeenth century with the development of probability theory as an intellectual tool to handle gambling situations (Hacking 1975). Later on, this tool played a pivotal role in the development of institutions providing insurance, in both the private and public sectors. Insurance is still an important social institution for the professional handling of danger. Including the notion of probability into the rational actor paradigm led to the concept of a lottery as a crucial metaphor for decision theory. A lottery in this sense is a set of possibilities that represent feasible courses of action. The second step was the combination of probability and utility in the expected utility model (Box 3.2). According to this model, a rational actor should be indifferent between a lottery

Box 3.2 Expected utility theory

The notion that individuals reveal their preferences about risks and benefits through their choices among goods and services is well established in the economics literature (Smith 1986). In economic theory, risk-acceptance problems are commonly studied with a framework that relies on the expected utility theory (EUT) of decisionmaking under uncertainty. The EUT model, as it was first proposed, arose out of the analysis of gambling behavior over risky lotteries in Von Neumann & Morgenstern's *Theory of games* (1947). The model was not developed to describe how people actually perceive risk and behave, but how they should behave if they desired to follow the axioms of rational choice. In spite of this qualification, the model is used widely to describe or predict how people make decisions under uncertainty.

Five axioms of rational choice underlie the EUT model:

- First, preferences for lotteries are complete (lotteries can be ranked or the player is indifferent about them) and transitive (if lottery A is preferred to B, and B is preferred to C, then A is preferred to C).
- Second, if outcome *X* is preferred to *Y* which is preferred to *Z*, then we can find a probability, *p*, such that the player is indifferent between receiving *Y* for certain or receiving a lottery paying *X* with probability *p*, and *Z* with probability $(1-p)$.
- Third, if the player is indifferent between outcome X and Y, then he/she is also indifferent between a lottery A (paying *Z* with probability (*p*) and *X* with probability $(1-p)$) and lottery B (paying *Z* with probability (*p*) and *Y* with probability $(1-p)$). This is the famous independence axiom.
- Fourth, in lotteries with identical outcomes, a player will always prefer the lottery that offers the largest expected value.
- Fifth, a player views a compound lottery (i.e., one where the outcomes are also lotteries) as equivalent to the simple lottery that could be derived from multiplying probabilities according to standard probability theory.

and a single possibility with the same utility as the expected utility of the lottery.

The expected utility model laid the foundations for applying advanced statistical and mathematical methods to the optimization of operational problems. The whole approach was first put to strategic use in the work of British naval intelligence in combating U-boat attacks on Atlantic convoys during the Second World War and was closely linked to the field of operational research. This framework was later extended to air defense, strategic bombing, and other problems of military operations, and was particularly useful for deciding what levels of losses, from various convoy strategies, for example, would be tolerated or *acceptable*. These techniques were goal directed; that is to say, their solution consisted in finding the maxima or minima for some mathematical expression, the *objective function*. These methods were given extensive military application during the period of the Cold War (Blackwell & Grishik 1954, Koopmans 1951); the techniques of the transportational problem and other linear programming and mathematical methods were taken to an advanced stage in the work that was carried out by Robert McNamara in the Ford company and later in the US

Department of Defense in the 1960s. A related strand of application ran through the development of the chemical and pharmaceutical industries during the same period. With rapid economic and technological growth, policymakers and regulatory agencies in those countries where innovation and production in the chemical and related fields were particularly important (such as the United States, United Kingdom, and Germany) were pressing to produce standards and procedures for the control of dangerous processes and products (Curtiss Priest 1988)

After the developments in choice and decision theory during the 1940s and 1950s, risk analysis was used to examine more closely the role of public perceptions in risk decisionmaking and problem solving. Starr's controversial article, "Social benefit versus technological risk" (1969), set in motion the systematic study and analysis of public perceptions of risk. Clearly, Starr saw technological risk as part of the costs that have to be incurred to realize social benefits.

A related view of climate change considers an emissions path of greenhouse gases, of which some effects will increase GNP by 20 percent with a probability of 90 percent, and of which other effects will reduce GNP by 40 percent with a probability of 10 percent. If GNP is a measure of utility, such an emissions path can be calculated as equivalent to the option of increasing GNP by 14 percent ($0.2\times0.9-0.4\times0.1 = 0.18-0.04 = 0.14$). A recent example of this kind of computation is the work by Manne & Richels (1995). These authors used an integrated assessment model to discuss an emissions path of greenhouse gases that, as in the example just discussed, could lead to two different levels of GNP. This enabled them to discuss optimizing strategies in the face of climatic risks. Technically speaking, these risks are represented as lotteries, and GNP is used as the utility measure that represents preferences between these lotteries.

Risk preferences

Preferences among lotteries inevitably have two different aspects: preferences between the various possible outcomes involved and risk preferences. Sometimes people behave as risk seekers, be it in mountain climbing or industrial markets. On other occasions they are risk averse, be it in keeping to a diet or buying insurance. Given the considerable uncertainties in climate change, accounting for risk preferences is essential for any theory of choice in climate policy.

Arrow (1953, 1970, 1984) and Pratt (1964) developed an influential way of representing risk preferences (Fig. 3.3). If one can indicate probabilities for the different possible GNP values in a lottery involving GNP, the lottery as a whole can be characterized by its expected value of GNP. The expected utility of the

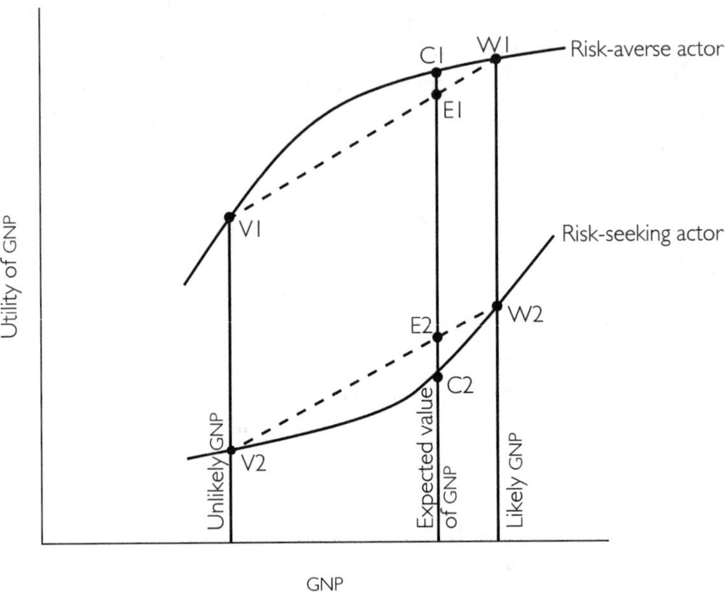

Figure 3.3 Expected utility and risk preferences.

lottery is the weighted average of the utilities associated with the single possibilities, weighted with the respective probabilities. We can then distinguish between simple utilities, which refer to single outcomes, and expected utilities, which refer to lotteries involving several possible outcomes. In Figure 3.3, simple utilities for three events assessed under the assumption of risk aversion and risk seeking are represented as points V1, C1, W1, and V2, C2, and W2. Expected utilities for a lottery assessed under the same assumptions are represented by the points E1 and E2.

Risk aversion will lead an actor faced with the lottery in question to prefer the expected value of GNP for sure rather than the lottery. This can be represented by a utility C1 of the expected value which is greater than E1. Under conditions of risk seeking, the inverse situation results, with C2 smaller than E2. In this representation, the preferences between individual outcomes are expressed by points V, C, and W, whereas risk preferences are expressed by the difference between points C and E. Under conditions of perfect risk neutrality, the utility function would be represented by a straight line and the difference between points C and E would vanish. In many cases, it is sensible to assume risk seeking for lotteries with a low expected value, risk aversion for lotteries with a high expected value, and risk neutrality at the transition between these two ranges (Friedman & Savage 1952).

This line of argument is of immediate relevance to climate change. If GNP is used as cardinal measure of utility, then the utility function in Figure 3.3 becomes a straight line. This directly implies risk neutrality with regard to levels of GNP. If the preferences of the benevolent planner are to represent some kind of shared interest of humankind, however, then this must hold not only for preferences between single outcomes but also for risk preferences. With regard to future GNP, humankind plausibly would be rather risk averse than risk neutral or risk seeking. Therefore, some function of GNP is required as a measure of utility. What degree of risk aversion should the benevolent planner take into account? This question can be discussed only by considering the multitude of actors that the benevolent planner is supposed to represent. (We will discuss multiple actors below.)

In Figure 3.3, risk aversion is represented by the shape of the utility function. This means that utility is no more an ordinal concept, because with a concept of ordinal utility the shapes of the two utility functions in Figure 3.3 would be equivalent. There are two ways of interpreting this situation. The first, which goes back to Bernoulli (1738), analyzes choices between lotteries on the basis of cardinal utility for single outcomes. But if cardinality is introduced at the level of single outcomes, the shape of the utility function is already given. Introducing risk aversion then requires the introduction of a second utility function. The other approach, which goes back to von Neumann & Morgenstern (1947), uses ordinal utilities for single outcomes and introduces cardinality to represent risk aversion. The ordinal utility function for single outcomes is, so to speak, stretched and squeezed until it has the shape required to represent risk preferences, too. Von Neumann & Morgenstern showed that, if the preferences of an actor faced with a set of lotteries satisfy certain axioms, a cardinal utility function can be found which represents both the preferences between simple outcomes and risk preferences.

In the professional analysis and management of risk, the distinction between cardinal and ordinal utility interacts with the distinction between objective and subjective probability. No risk professional will doubt that the probabilities of getting heads or tails when tossing a coin are both about 50 percent. These probabilities are treated as objective figures because they can be checked by experiment. Similarly, many disagreements about probability estimates used in the natural sciences, in engineering, and even in the social sciences, can be resolved by empirical checking. The whole argument developed so far about optimizing choice under uncertainty can be applied to objective probabilities of this kind.

However, in many decision situations involving uncertainty, objective probabilities are unavailable. Following Knight (1921), sometimes the word "risk" is even reserved for situations that can be characterized by objective probabilities. Uncertainty proper is then said to arise in situations that cannot be so characterized. We do not follow this terminology, however, because the rational actor paradigm has found ways to deal with both objective and subjective probabilities.

The study of subjective probabilities has been developed by Bayes (1763), De Finetti (1974), Savage (1954) and others. This work has shown how subjective probabilities can be improved in a systematic fashion, thanks to additional information. One can then distinguish between the priors, that is, the probability judgments made before additional information is available, and the amended probability judgments. If some stochastic process obeying an objective probability distribution is observed by a rational actor who starts with arbitrary priors, his probability judgment may well converge toward the objective probability distribution. Very often, risk professionals see their role as providing additional information that will lead the subjective priors of lay persons to converge toward the objective probabilities that the professionals know.

With regard to many important decision problems, however, the risk professionals themselves often have only subjective probabilities at their disposal (Morgan & Henrion 1990). This holds not only in management and policy decisions involving human beings, but also with regard to problems of engineering and of the natural sciences, including the problem of climate change (Pahl-Wöstl et al., in press; Morgan & Keith 1994). In the specific case of climate change, hundreds of global change experiences lasting for tens of thousands of years would be needed to achieve a convergence of subjective probabilities toward objective values. Therefore, it is important to know how far the rational actor paradigm can handle decisions under true uncertainty, where no objective probabilities are available.

Two approaches are relevant here. Savage (1954) has shown how the rational actor paradigm can deal with decisions involving only subjective probabilities, for example, in considering the preferences of an actor faced with a set of lotteries without objective probabilities. If these preferences satisfy certain axioms, a cardinal utility function can be found which represents both the preferences between simple outcomes and risk preferences. As scientists make great efforts to identify objective probabilities, however, the approach pioneered by Anscombe & Aumann (1963) may be more instructive here. In this approach, both objective and subjective probabilities are considered. In climate research, for example, one might use subjective probabilities to express the uncertainty about future climatological conditions in a specific region and try to combine them with objective probabilities for precipitation patterns in that region.

If the preferences of an actor faced with such situations obey certain axioms, the preferences of a rational actor may be represented by a utility function. The resulting utility function can be decomposed into several components: first, the simple ordinal utilities of the single outcomes; second, the objective probabilities that under given circumstances a given outcome will result; third, the expected utilities of the lotteries involving only objective probabilities; fourth, the subjective probabilities that various circumstances will arise; fifth, the subjective expected utility of the lotteries involving both subjective probabilities for the circumstances and objective probabilities for specific outcomes. Because of the explicit role for subjective probabilities, this approach is known as an instance of subjective expected utility theory.

We have already characterized the rational actor paradigm by four statements. These statements carry over to the investigation of decisionmaking under uncertainty provided that the following specification is added:

- The consequences of a possible action consist either in a unique atomistic event (in case of certainty) or in a set of such events (in case of uncertainty).

For example, with regard to climate change, efficiently implementing tradeable permits for a fixed quantity of greenhouse gas emissions will lead to emissions which do not exceed that quantity. On the other hand, emitting a specific quantity of greenhouse gases will lead to one of a whole set of possible outcomes. The treatment of uncertainty that is content with the specification of preferences between sets of possibilities is called the state-preference approach. This approach was introduced by Debreu (1959) in his seminal work on general equilibrium theory. It shows that the statement according to which neoclassical economics presupposes perfect information is inaccurate: preferences can easily refer to uncertain prospects. The treatment of uncertainty within the rational actor paradigm, however, is not limited to the state-preference approach, because an additional statement leads to a wealth of additional insights:

- If a given action has several possible consequences, these may depend on possible events that the actor cannot influence. In these cases, the actor can order possible events by judgments of likelihood. The relative likelihood of consequences then establishes a link between preferences among specified consequences and preferences among actions with uncertain consequences.

To see the relevance of this statement for climate change, we can consider a benevolent planner faced with two possible actions: business as usual versus introducing tradeable permits for energy use. In comparison with a business-as-usual strategy, introducing such permits may lead to reduced GNP, but it may also induce technical change to an extent that actually increases GNP. Suppose that the benevolent planner prefers higher GNP to lower GNP and that without additional information prefers business as usual to energy permits. If the planner now learns that the economy has many more possibilities to increase energy efficiency than previously thought, planning preferences may shift toward introducing energy permits.

However, decisions about climate change clearly will not be made by a benevolent planner, but through political negotiations and market mechanisms. The contemporary world is shaped to a very large extent by economic processes, and the rational actor paradigm provides the only widely used description and interpretation of these processes. Under these circumstances, it would be awkward to discuss the problems of multiple control with regard to climatic risks without taking into explicit account the possible contributions of the rational actor paradigm. Therefore, we now say farewell to the benevolent planner and look at interactions between multiple rational actors.

Rational negotiations

Obviously, a drastic effort to reduce greenhouse gas emissions by, say, the United States, would have very different effects, depending on the actions of other governments, such as that of China. The reverse is also true. This kind of situation can be represented with the tools of game theory (see Ch. 2). Each actor has a set of possible actions available, and the consequences of each action depend on the actions of all other actors. In the case of climate change, for many governments, significant greenhouse gas emissions reductions may well be quite costly. On the other hand, the benefits of such reductions are shared by all governments. This implies that the costs depend on the government in question only, whereas the benefits depend on all other governments as well. As a result, every government has an obvious interest in seeing the other governments reducing emissions while keeping its own reduction efforts as low as possible. This is exactly the situation of diverging individual and social optimum depicted in Figure 3.2.

The scheme that von Neumann & Morgenstern (1947) developed for representing preferences about uncertain events with cardinal utilities could be used for the treatment of uncertainty about the world in general. This is what has happened with much work in risk analysis. Besides the uncertainty about natural events such as a thunderstorm, an earthquake, or a harvest resulting from good weather, there is the uncertainty about the actions of other human beings. This kind of uncertainty raises peculiar problems for the rational actor paradigm, because each actor needs to take into account the choices of the other actors.

With game theory, a way was found to use the rational actor paradigm, not only in the analysis of uncertainty about states of the world but also in the analysis of uncertainty about other rational actors. The basic idea can be conveyed by considering just two actors, Ego and Alter. The consequences of Ego's actions are evaluated according to Ego's cardinal utility, which blends his simple preferences with his attitude toward risk. These consequences, Ego's payoffs, now depend on Alter's actions, as well as the other way round. This introduces the problem that in sociology is known as *double contingency*: at first sight, no actor can act unless the other one does. More precisely, Ego needs to assign subjective probabilities to Alter's action in order to be able to make an optimizing choice about his own actions. But Ego knows that the same is true for Alter.

Interestingly, Ego can describe not only the actions of Alter but also his own actions, by means of subjective probabilities: if he wants to take a specific action, he can assign probability one to that action and probability zero to all other actions. Actions that can be characterized by probabilities are often called strategies. In repeated games, each actor may actually mix several pure strategies according to some self-assigned probability. Game theory handles the problem of double contingency by assuming that each actor uses the same standards of rationality for him- or herself as for all other actors. As a result, the actor can look for a set of subjective probabilities which yield some kind of optimal action for all actors involved.

It is now time to take stock of the treatment of uncertainty by the rational actor paradigm discussed so far. We have first characterized the rational actor paradigm by four statements, which for convenience we repeat here:

- Rational actors can choose between different possible actions.
- Rational actors can order the different consequences of possible actions according to their preferences.
- The possible actions available to different rational actors depend on parameters of their joint situation.
- Rational actors choose a possible action that according to their preferences is optimal given the parameters of the situation.

To these we have then added two statements which refer specifically to decisionmaking under uncertainty:

- The consequences of a possible action consist either in a unique atomistic event (in case of certainty) or in a set of such events (in case of uncertainty).
- If a given action has several possible consequences, these may depend on possible events that the actor cannot influence. In these cases, the actor can order possible events by judgments of likelihood. The relative likelihood of consequences then establishes a link between preferences between specified consequences and preferences between actions with uncertain consequences.

Now we add a final statement to take into account the specific uncertainty that results from the presence of several actors:

- The consequences of an action may depend on the choices of other actors. In this case, a rational actor can try to order the possible actions of each actor, including him- or herself, by subjective probabilities. In so doing, the actor can identify constellations where each actor reaches an optimum.

What does optimality mean in a situation of multiple control? Two different answers are possible. One answer focuses on individual action, the other on social optima.

The first answer says that a strategy is optimal for an individual actor if the actor in question cannot obtain a better payoff unless at least one other actor changes his strategy. That is, a strategy is optimal given the strategies of all other actors. One can then ask whether there is a situation where all actors choose a strategy that is individually optimal for each of them. Such a situation is a Nash equilibrium. In games that admit mixed strategies, the existence of at least one Nash equilibrium is usually trivial. However, if multiple equilibria are possible, and it is unclear what an optimizing rational actor can do. In fact, we will argue that the inevitability of multiple equilibria requires a notion of social rationality that enables human beings to take nonoptimizing decisions.

The second answer has to do with the idea of a social optimum. The sociologist Pareto introduced the distinction between situations where all actors can improve their payoffs and situations where no actor can improve his payoff without at least one other actor being worse off. The latter case is called a Pareto optimum. This may be considered as a social optimum. Again, the existence of at least one Pareto optimum is usually trivial in game theory. However, there may be more than one, and Pareto optima may not coincide with Nash equilibria. When a Nash equilibrium is not Pareto optimal, rational actors may be trapped in a social dilemma. If they find themselves in such a Nash equilibrium, none of them has an individual incentive to move out of that situation, although all would be better off if they did.

International negotiations about climate policy can be analyzed as attempts to overcome a social dilemma. The starting point is a Nash equilibrium that is not Pareto optimal, and the goal is to reshape the game in such a way that a Pareto-optimal Nash equilibrium can be reached. In the absence of a benevolent planner with the capacity to reshape the game in this way, are processes of social learning possible in which the various actors move out of the social dilemma in which they are trapped?

This line of thought has gained prominence thanks to Axelrod's (1984) research on the evolution of cooperation. He used computer simulations to study under which conditions a multitude of actors threatened by a social dilemma can learn to avoid it without relying on a benevolent planner. Meanwhile, a significant literature on the subject has emerged. The more specific results are hard to generalize to cases such as climate policy, but two robust insights emerge. First, cooperative solutions can evolve without the intervention of a benevolent planner. Second, if this happens, totally selfish rational actors are displaced by actors who keep a balance between selfishness and solidarity.

With this kind of research, game theory itself is being transformed. From a tool to include uncertainty about other rational actors into the fabric of the rational actor paradigm, a new approach is beginning to take shape. In evolutionary game theory, preferences may or may not cover all conceivable alternatives in a consistent fashion, and agents may or may not make decisions according to an optimization algorithm. Together with preferences, constraints, and optimization—the toolbox of the rational actor paradigm—other phenomena come into play, including memories and expectations, cultural rules and social networks. Interactions between different agents can be studied without the heroic assumption that each agent is able to check the hypothetical consequences between all possible combinations of actions. Agents may argue with each other about their preferences, and they may use these preferences to assess the quality of an argument.

Market solutions

The single most important reason for the dominance of the rational actor paradigm in the contemporary social sciences lies in its analysis of market mechanisms. The rational actor paradigm describes many economic phenomena, but above all interpretations how a market economy works. This interpretation is based on the metaphor of the invisible hand. Since the days of Pythagoras and Plato, mathematics has been used to convey metaphor, and rarely has this been more influential than in the case of the invisible hand. The metaphor comes in two versions, large and small. The small one (e.g., Marshall 1890) refers to a multitude of rational actors, each characterized by given preferences, and each owning given amounts of two goods, say fish and money, which they can exchange on a market. To these actors we now add an imaginary figure, call the invisible hand, the market, or the auctioneer. The invisible hand sets a price for fish, and thereby sets a parameter which affects all actors in the game. Preferences are such that, if the price for fish increases, the offer of fish will increase while demand for fish will fall. If supply and demand match, trade takes place; otherwise, the invisible hand tries a new price. It is then relatively easy to show that for each conceivable price one or more patterns of offers and demands form a Nash equilibrium, but that only one Nash equilibrium can be a Pareto optimum. The efficiency of the market mechanism provides a way of aggregating heterogeneous preferences in an overall outcome with high social legitimacy.

The large version of the metaphor was elaborated in a huge effort beginning with Adam Smith (1776), unfolding with Walras (1926), and completed by Arrow & Debreu (1954). It runs very much along the lines of the small one, but now there are many goods and the actors can use given technologies to produce new goods. Under these circumstances, it can still be shown that under suitable assumptions at least one Nash equilibrium exists which is also a Pareto optimum. But now one should expect multiple equilibria even under very restrictive assumptions (Kirman 1992). If assumptions about technologies are made more realistic than usual by introducing increasing returns to scale, multiple equilibria become even more common (Arthur 1994).

In both versions, uncertainty can be dealt with according to the state-preference approach discussed above. Therefore, the market system also provides an institutional mechanism to aggregate heterogeneous risk preferences into an outcome of considerable social legitimacy. The uncertainties about climatic risks give rise to two problems, one widely recognized, one less so.

First, the right to pollute the atmosphere with greenhouse gases is a free good in the contemporary world economy. As some people already do care, and many more probably will care, about the greenhouse effect, the well-being of these people is affected by every activity that emits greenhouse gases. This effect, however, is not visible in the market system, as no price is paid for it: it is an external effect. It can be shown that external effects imply a dissociation between Nash equilibria and Pareto optima, even where supply and demand match. The basic reasoning follows from Figure 3.2. This analysis leads to the well-known proposals for carbon taxes or tradeable emissions permits to internalize the external effect in question.

The second problem consists in the absence of futures markets for all kinds of goods hundreds of years from now. Where futures markets do exist, they draw on the subjective probabilities and the risk preferences of the market participants. Futures prices then can bring about an efficient way of taking these expectations and preferences into account. Where futures markets do not exist, the market system needs some kind of stopping rule to discard uncertainties about the future that may be relevant for humankind, but are irrelevant for existing markets. This stopping rule is provided by discounting future events according to market rates of interest. The rate of interest itself is arguably an expression of the time preference of the various actors. However, this holds only as far as futures markets do exist. Together with existing futures markets for various assets, monetary authorities and various other factors heavily influence rates of interest. It is neither possible nor desirable to install futures markets for all kinds of goods centuries into the future. Therefore, uncertainty about climate change cannot be handled efficiently by the market system alone.

At that stage, governmental authorities need to enter the picture, but no more in the role of the benevolent planner. For the moment, we look at a single government which somehow has resolved its uncertainties about climate change and has decided to invest a given amount of resources in climate policy.

However, now a new problem arises: given the uncertainty about the consequences of various policies, which policy should be chosen? If several policies are available, the rational actor paradigm would suggest looking for a policy mix where the marginal utility of each dollar invested in various policies is roughly equalized.

Two insights are useful here, one from financial markets and one from corporate restructuring. In financial markets, an efficient portfolio is based on maximal diversification. The reason is simple, even if the realization may be highly sophisticated. Investing in assets whose risks are uncorrelated, or even negatively correlated, lowers the overall risk, and for risk averse investors this is a gain. In corporate restructuring, an efficient organization seems characterized by the very opposite strategy of clear focus on core activities. Again the reason is simple, although the realization may be an art. Within a common organization, compatibility problems may arise between different activities (Milgrom & Roberts 1992). For climate policy, this has an interesting consequence. Governments should design their policy so as to focus on core activities within their own organizational setting. At the same time they should provide incentives for other actors to engage in a wide variety of activities which suit the goals of climate policy (see Box 3.3 for an example).

These two strategic orientations may well prove to be more efficient than a schematic use of cost–benefit analysis. In principle, they should be equivalent, as both are based on the idea of equalizing marginal utilities across a spectrum of activities. In practice, however, cost–benefit may prove an inferior approach because it identifies utility functions with monetary magnitudes. As cost–benefit analysis is widely used and is often considered the obvious way to proceed, it is important to emphasize that in practice its own costs have to be carefully balanced against its benefits in each specific situation.

Basing social decisions on aggregate net benefits, cost–benefit analysis only considers total societal welfare and is somewhat insensitive to the distribution of that welfare throughout society (Hanley 1992). The focus of cost–benefit analysis and the underlying theory is on the consequences of the decision required at hand; how the decisions are reached or the way in which preferences are formed are not part of the accounting process. In this respect cost–benefit analysis is weaker than more sophisticated tools of risk management based on the rational actor paradigm, such as portfolio analysis and identification of core activities. It also shares the deeper shortcomings of the rational actor paradigm in that it ignores equity and fairness and does not allow for the intricacies of trust, liability, and consent, interwoven in a risk situation. In effect the rational actor paradigm acknowledges only one facet of the multifaceted reality that risk situations present and is not capable of addressing the cultural diversity that policymakers are finding they must acknowledge.

Box 3.3 Designing a Global Marshall Plan: learning from the original

It is instructive to compare current ideas for how to organize the financial flows required by an effective climate policy with the experience of the Marshall Plan in the wake of the Second World War (see Simon 1976, for a thoughtful analysis of this experience and Grose 1997 for a recent discussion). The reconstruction of the German economy in the framework of the Marshall Plan was not based on simple financial transfers across the Atlantic. It was based on a financial institution that was endowed with dollars, but which gave credits in Deutschemarks to German entrepreneurs. These credits enabled German entrepreneurs to invest in American equipment, which the intermediate institutions purchased with dollars. This arrangement was designed to enable entrepreneurs to repay their credits in local currency. This mechanism enabled the whole scheme to achieve three things:

- It enabled German entrepreneurs to invest in new equipment and to use technologies developed in America.
- It boosted American exports.
- It enabled the German economy to pick a path of sustained internal growth. Eventually, the Deutschemarks paid back for the credits were sufficiently valuable to compensate for a substantial part of the initial dollar transfers.

From the standpoint of the rational actor paradigm, this scheme represents an unnecessary detour. Free currency markets are supposed to lead to equilibrium exchange rates at which there is no difference between an implementation of financial transfers based on dollars and one involving local currency along the lines sketched above. But this notion of equilibrium presupposes that economic agents are able to develop mutually compatible expectations about the future path of the global economy and that these expectations will turn out to be accurate, at least in a probabilistic sense. At least three reasons make it impossible for agents operating according to the rational actor paradigm to develop such expectations:

- Futures markets spanning a time horizon of at least a century would be required for such agents to be able to coordinate their expectations via market processes in the present. In the absence of futures markets, these agents lack the mechanism that they would need to assure mutual consistency of their expectations.
- Even if such futures markets did exist, increasing returns to scale (which are common in many economic activities) imply that multiple equilibria can arise. There is no way that agents confined to individualistic rationality could calculate which one of these will be realized by the joint decision of all agents.
- Even with the required futures markets and without increasing returns to scale, systems of more than two interdependent markets may easily display multiple equilibria (Jaeger & Kasemir 1996).

If individualistic rationality is embedded in social rationality, however, the emergence of shared expectations is no mystery anymore. Social rationality provides the basis of shared expectations because it enables human beings to follow socially shared rules and to modify these rules in processes of communication. After the Second World War, the victory over Nazism and the fear of Stalinism provided a frame of shared expectations in which decision-makers could design the original Marshall Plan. It was not based on optimization, but on political judgment, and it did not rely on the fairy tale of a unique equilibrium on interdependent markets, but on the reality of currency markets driven by shared expectations about the economies involved.

Here we are entering the transition zone between the rational actor paradigm and a way of looking at human affairs that is not yet well defined but which in the foreseeable future may put the rational actor paradigm into a new perspective. Presently, the rational actor paradigm is the only widely used framework for the study of economic phenomena and the most influential framework for the study of many other phenomena, including those of risk and uncertainty. However, future research may lead to a broader view which will overcome important paradoxes of atomistic rationality by embedding the insights of the rational actor paradigm in a different framework.

Paradoxes of atomistic rationality

Risk analysis based on the rational actor paradigm provided a highly effective framework for the activity of the risk professionals. However, the smooth formation of this body of theory was interrupted by a series of objections from Allais (1953), according to which the activity of risk taking as conducted by humans in everyday life could not conform to the axioms of what he called "the American school," namely, expected utility theory. In a rather unusual note, the editor of *Econometrica* remarked (Allais 1953: 503):

> The problem discussed in Professor Allais' paper is of an extremely subtle sort and it seems to be difficult to reach a general agreement on the main points at issue. I had a vivid impression of these difficulties at the Paris colloquium in May, 1952. One evening when a small number of the prominent contributors to this field of study found themselves gathered around a table under the most pleasant exterior circumstances, it even proved to be quite a bit of a task to clear up in a satisfactory way misunderstandings in the course of the conversation.

Among other things, Allais showed that for perfectly reasonable people a difference in probabilities between 0 percent and 1 percent matters much more than a difference between, say, 33 percent and 34 percent. No technically satisfactory way of reconciling this paradox with the axioms of expected utility theory could be found at the time. To most researchers involved in risk studies, however, this looked like an irritating, but basically minor puzzle which would be solved somehow sooner or later.

Whereas the Allais paradox was based on objective probabilities, a decade later, Ellsberg (1961) produced another paradox related to the difference between objective and subjective probabilities. He argued that reasonable people try to avoid the uncertainty involved in subjective probability as long as they can stick to objective probabilities. Again, this paradox could not be reconciled with the axioms of subjective expected utility. Several other paradoxes were formulated in the literature, until about two decades later Machina (1982), Fishburn (1988) and others found weaker axioms that enabled them to take these paradoxes into account in a rational actor framework.

By then Kahneman & Tversky (1979) had already produced experimental evidence about framing paradoxes. These experiments showed that reasonable people, including professional specialists, made different choices about mathematically identical lotteries, depending on the wording and graphical presentation of these lotteries. No theory restricted to the mathematical structure of the lotteries involved had a chance of describing this behavior (described in more detail below).

These paradoxes presented a heavy challenge to conventional risk analysis. One response was an intensification of empirical research about how people actually think about risks. In this vein, psychometric studies, derived from the seminal work of Fischhoff et al. (1978), investigated subjective risk judgments to understand the cognitive structure and the sociopsychological factors that shape the perceived magnitude and acceptance of risks (Slovic 1992). Although the focus is very much on human cognition, this literature provided the empirical base and evidence to extend the scope of risk analysis beyond its historically technical and physical domains to a multidimensional concept (Mitchell 1992). Since the mid-1980s, the number of studies using the psychometric approach has grown dramatically (Rohrmann 1991).

In general, psychometric studies ask subjects to judge various hazard sources according to a list of risk ratings. Key ratings may be magnitude, in some probability or consequence sense, and acceptability. After initial ratings are obtained, subjects are asked to rate risks on the basis of various risk characteristics that shape risk perceptions. Using a factor analysis, Slovic et al. (1980) produced the now well-known representation of 90 risk sources according to the dread and familiarity factors (Fig. 3.4). Over time, the literature has generated an extensive list of attributes that are claimed to affect risk perceptions. Covello et al. (1989) summarized the major insights regarding factors that influence risk comparisons and acceptability (Table 3.1). The psychometric factors that are well supported by the literature are dread, familiarity, catastrophic potential, and reversibility. However, Roth et al. (1990) suggested that the relevance of these factors in risk comparisons is limited.

Psychometric factors have been linked to discussions of environmental vulnerability, but few psychometric studies have been focused on global change. An explicit psychometric study of ecological risk, including the risks of global change, was provided by McDaniels et al. (1995). However, most psychometric studies further explore some subset of the 90 risk sources first investigated by

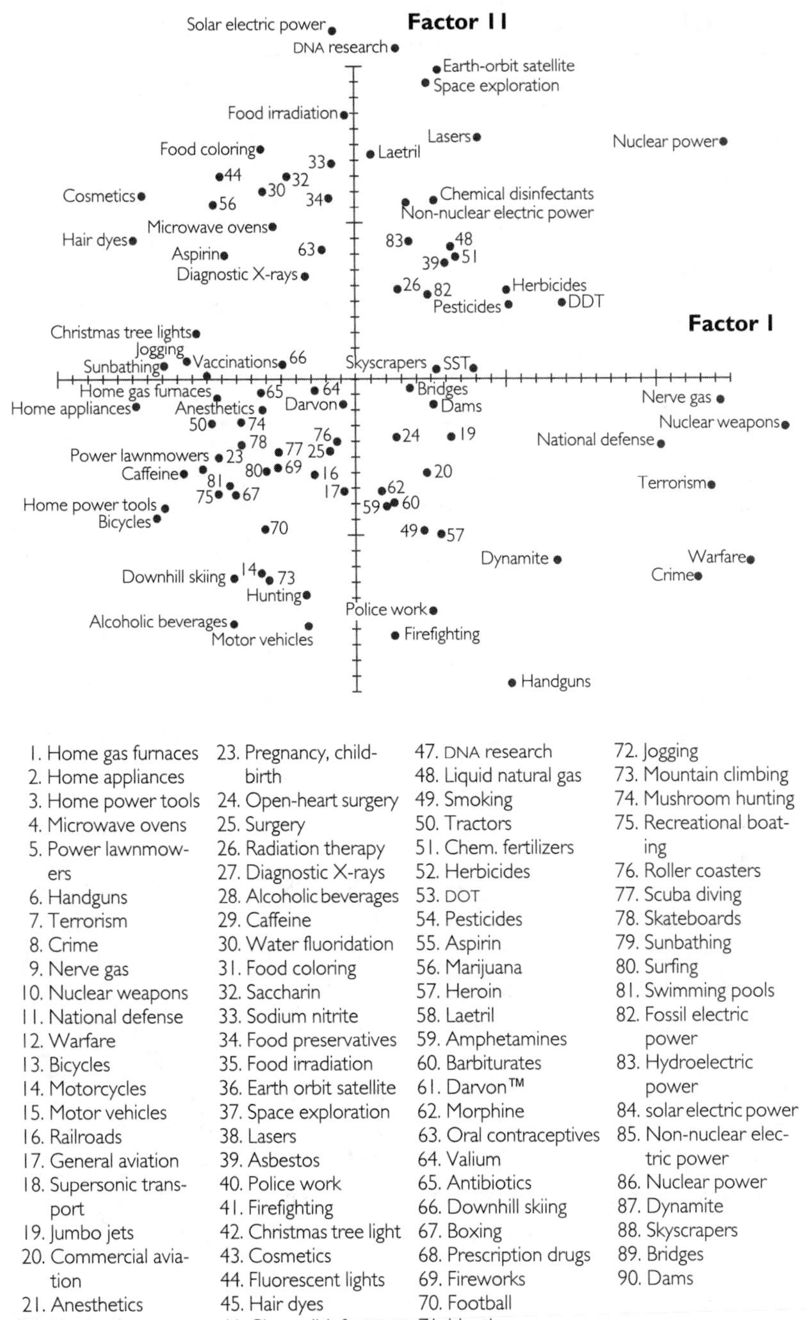

Figure 3.4 Risk sources arranged by (I) dread and (II) familiarity factors (*source:* Slovic et al. 1980).

Table 3.1 Qualitative factors affecting risk perception and evaluation.

Factor	Conditions associated with increased public concern	Conditions associated with decreased public concern
Catastrophic potential	Fatalities and injuries grouped in time and space	Fatalities and injuries scattered and random
Familiarity	Unfamiliar	Familiar
Understanding	Mechanisms or process not understood	Mechanisms or process understood
Controllability (personal)	Uncontrollable	Controllable
Voluntariness of exposure	Involuntary	Voluntary
Effects on children	Children specifically at risk	Children not specifically at risk
Effects manifestation	Delayed effects	Immediate effects
Effects on future generations	Risk to future generations	No risk to future generations
Victim identity	Identifiable victims	Statistical victims
Dread	Effects dreaded	Effects not dreaded
Trust in institutions	Lack of trust in responsible institutions	Trust in responsible institutions
Media attention	Much media attention	Little media attention
Accident history	Major and sometimes minor accidents	No major or minor accidents
Equity	Inequitable distribution of risks and benefits	Equitable distribution of risks and benefits
Benefits	Unclear benefits	Clear benefits
Reversibility	Effects irreversible	Effects reversible
Origin	Caused by human actions or failures	Caused by acts of nature or God

Source: Covello et al. (1989)
Note: In selecting risks to be compared, it is helpful to keep these distinctions in mind. Risk comparisons that ignore these distinctions (e.g., comparing voluntary and involuntary risks) are likely to backfire unless appropriate qualifications are made.

Slovic et al. (1980), who did not address global change risks explicitly. Fischer et al. (1991) found that people perceive less personal control relative to social control over large, ecological risks and less control overall relative to other risks mentioned by respondents as concerns. This finding is significant for the evolution of perceptions, since controllability has consistently emerged as an important factor in technology and hazard studies, although its influence is mixed across studies (Rohrmann 1991). Schmidt & Gifford (1989) also addressed global environmental impacts and distinguished between environmental risks for humans and risks for the state of the environment. In particular, changes to the ozone layer are perceived as a significant threat to self and the environment among 24 environmental hazards, but neither threat is correlated with controllability.

Building on psychometric studies, mental model approaches have emphasized how and where these factors fit in the cognitive structure, that is, intuitive ways of thinking, that people use to represent risks. The objective of the mental model approach "is to learn how people think about their particular situation, what they know, and what they misperceive about the facts and processes" (Lave & Lave 1991: 260). Mental modeling follows the tradition of cognitive bias research in that it extends the notion of judgmental errors to misconceptions about risks. However, being knowledge based, this approach allows the subjects to define the salient information about risk perceptions which is contrasted with an expert representation. Additional information on sociodemographics and experiences is also collected from subjects to interpret mental model results.

As described in Volume 1, Chapter 4, mental model research has produced some results for global climate change. First, there is an overall tendency to use the terms and concepts *weather* and *climate* interchangeably (Kempton 1991, Bostrom et al. 1994, Read et al. 1994). Extreme weather events may then have a significant effect on perceptions of climate change. Second, one of the more salient concepts linked to global warming is stratospheric ozone depletion (Kempton 1991, Löfstedt 1991, Bostrom et al. 1994, Read et al. 1994). This further implies disagreement with the "expert" influences and sources of global warming or appropriate responses. Finally, a concern for future generations seems to be an important reference for environmental values.

What does this kind of research demonstrate about the validity of the rational actor paradigm? In many situations people seem to judge specific risks on the basis of rather well-defined preferences and judgments of likelihood. Moreover, people sometimes try to improve the quality of their judgments of likelihood as well as the consistency among these judgments and various preferences. Therefore, wholesale dismissal of the rational actor paradigm would be inappropriate. Decision analysts are acting prudently in their desire to retain the insights of decision analysis, even in the face of significant violations of its fundamental assumptions, as in much of the analysis of climate change.

On the other hand, the intricate pattern of preferences and probabilities presupposed by expected utility models is incompatible with important empirical results, especially with those concerning framing effects. The rational actor paradigm is clearly deficient as a tool for describing and interpreting human decisions under uncertainty. Moreover, the rational actor paradigm is deficient as a normative tool. Many situations of uncertainty are simply too complex to be handled in the way proposed by the rational actor paradigm. Human beings have a finite lifespan, and the time of a human life would be insufficient to check all the possibilities involved even in a single baseball game. As Simon (1955) has argued, the rational actor paradigm ignores the burden it places on a person's ability to reason and use information. Thus, a more realistic approach is that individuals intend to be rational but are limited in their abilities to be so (Simon 1961), especially when faced with uncertain conditions.

Another kind of objection to the rational actor paradigm must be taken into consideration. The rational actor paradigm does not explain the formation of preferences, technological constraints, and judgments of likelihood. These objections are fundamental because they suggest that the rational actor paradigm misses one of the most interesting feature of human beings, namely consciousness. With regard to preference formation, for example, consciousness implies the possibility of second-order intentions: humans may have the intention to change their intentions, as when a smoker decides to stop smoking. Humans do reflect on their preferences and on the results of their actions. In particular, such questions as are dealt with in public policy typically concern the ends or objectives of rational, social behavior; and the theory, strictly speaking, has nothing to say about ends.

At first blush, the second kind of objection does not really challenge the rational actor paradigm, because such objections merely point out limitations that any reasonable practitioner of the rational actor paradigm could easily acknowledge. Such objections seem to imply that the rational actor paradigm may be a necessary but not sufficient conceptual tool for practical decisionmaking. And there the matter is usually allowed to rest. Seldom do policymakers ask for more, and seldom do policy analysts attempt to provide more. But the question arises: If the rational actor paradigm is necessary but not sufficient, what else is required for sound societal decisionmaking? Furthermore, if the rational actor paradigm is essentially the province of technical experts, what are the implications for societal decisionmaking in a democratic society?

Technical assessment and societal evaluation

Risk professionals generally respond to the second question by advocating the separation of technical assessment from societal evaluation of risk (US NRC 1982). However, we know that selections of assessment criteria are themselves driven by the analysts' value frameworks (see Vol. 1, Ch. 1). Furthermore, risk professionals themselves tend to enlarge the domain of reason, where they may claim a superior competence. With regard to subjective probabilities, this is done in two steps. First, the expert can provide additional information to people holding subjective probabilities. Bayesian learning should then nudge these subjective probabilities toward the objective probabilities, about which the expert knows more than the lay person. Second, the Harsanyi doctrine claims that rational actors having access to the same information need to come up with the same subjective probabilities (Aumann 1987). So, if lay persons have subjective probabilities different from those of experts, this must be attributable to differences in information. And experts usually think that they are better informed.

Implicit in this view is the idea that risk assessment should be left to the experts, who should not be influenced by the political values of risk managers. These experts should be left alone to calculate the risks associated with the project or technology involved, which can then be communicated to risk management decisionmakers. Risk management is defined as the political realm of public concerns, perceptions, and conflict, whereas risk analysis is only possible by experts who have access to the objective, true nature of the risks. This approach toward risk situations is strictly technical, with the delineation of management and analysis made according to a hierarchy of scientific expertise. This approach perceives and presents risk assessment as a technical issue, within which the probabilities and consequences are assessed scientifically.

In risk management, a distinction is often made between *objective* risk and *perceived* risk. The former is the so-called true risk, as calculated or at least estimated by risk assessment procedures; the latter is the distorted or uninformed view of risk often held by the public or others not exposed to good risk assessment analysis. In the implicit model a one-way flow of neutral scientific information occurs, through which the public and the politicians will become educated about what the risks are.

In this context, the idea of acceptable risk became a highly influential tool (McDonell 1991). It was popularized, for example, in Lowrance's book, *On acceptable risk* (1976). Since all life is risky and dangers lurk on every side, there must be some level of risk, it was argued, which in everyday life is taken as normal or *acceptable*, and this, if it could be measured, could be taken as an index of the risks we take and against which abnormal or unacceptable situations could be compared. Thus, it was assumed, the chances of an liquefied natural gas tank exploding, of a particular concentration of chemical being carcinogenic, and of an equipment failure causing a leak of toxic chemicals, could be related to some benchmark level of everyday risks. This level could be assessed by making measurements, in particular by showing from revealed preference studies the levels of risk that people actually tolerate in their daily lives, for example, in traveling by car or by public transport, by smoking, and by working at their daily occupations.

The idea of some base level of measurable acceptable risk which would be used as an objective regulatory index fits with empiricist views of society. For example, the report of the Royal Society Study Group on Risk Assessment (1983: 17), while bowing in the direction of the importance of social and political processes, strongly argued for the applicability to risk management of standardized measures of acceptable risk levels:

> Particularly at the more strategic levels, risk management is thus an essentially political process, performed by technical estimates. Increasingly, it becomes necessary to consult representatives of the public, or even the

> public as a whole, and to make publicly available the necessarily imperfect quantitative estimates of risk. While it is clearly not possible to set single quantitative guidelines on risk acceptability, some broad indicators of the current position can be noted. The average expectation of life is 70–75 years and the imposition of a continuing annual risk of death to the individual of 1/100 seems unacceptable. At 1/1000 it might not be totally unacceptable if the individual knows of the situation, and enjoys some commensurate benefit, and everything reasonable has been done to reduce the risk. At the other extreme, there are levels of assumed annual risk so low that the manager or regulator can regard them as trivial. The study group judges this figure to be commonly about 1/1000000 and an annual risk ten times as great, 1/100000, in traveling by train, does not cause the ordinary traveler any concern. It is principally in between these upper and lower levels that risk management should consist of comparing risks, detriments, costs and benefits. (p. 17)

These procedures of quantitative risk management have been in vogue (US NRC 1983, Royal Society 1983) and are still widely adopted, although with less enthusiasm than heretofore. They have been widely criticized (Douglas 1985, Wynne 1987, Ronge 1982, Schaffer 1988). The principal criticism to be noticed here concerns the implication associated with the term acceptable risk: that it corresponds to a social entity, regarded as objective and that can be measured, however imperfectly. Risks arising in the context of scientific and technological processes are not "out there" in the same sense as we regard natural phenomena such as falling meteorites, unstable hillsides, or spontaneously combustible gases, as being hazards to life and limb. Risks arising from the spread of a rogue virus, the explosion of an energy receptacle, the spilling of an industrial chemical, or the emission of greenhouse-related gases, are the result of unintentional human action performed through organizational and political processes. Most of the technologies we call risky, for the management of which regulatory agencies interpret statistics and develop measures of acceptability, are socially produced; the conditions of their production are socially constructed. Those who manage these technologies must understand and interpret the action that produces them in the context of the moral and political world of the society in which, for some social purpose, that action takes place.

In many cases, especially in the areas where risk management based in the rational actor paradigm has been most conspicuously applied, the separation of assessment and evaluation seems to have been ineffective and, at times, counterproductive, leading to more opposition and distrust over time, instead of less. The result has been a challenge to major public policy decisions about risk issues such as nuclear power and chemical wastes. Uncertainty and indeterminacy inherent in new technologies set against a background of techno-fiascos—such as Three Mile Island, Seveso, thalidomide, Bhopal, Chernobyl, and Sandoz—have made the lay public increasingly aware of risks and wary of conventional risk analysis. The policymaking process often includes contradictory studies and arguments, all apparently based upon good scientific analysis of risk. It often seems as if the more science is used to help support such decisions, the more controversy is generated (Robinson 1992).

A sophisticated elaboration of the view of risk assessment as a technical specialty still perceives risks as inherent in the physical world, but regards their successful management as dependent upon coherent strategies adopted by the human actors. Understanding the positions of both the risks and the humans is crucial to this perspective. This view uses psychological constructs and strategies as risk communication tools with which to correct the misperceptions held by the lay public about the true nature of the risk concerned. It thus allows for social perceptions and concerns to be incorporated into the expert risk management process.

This view of risk highlights the importance of the relationship between risk assessors and managers, and the public, thus leading to substantial growth in the subfield of *risk communication* (Cohen 1985, Leiss & Krewski 1989, US NRC 1989, Robinson 1992). The change is toward analyzing public perceptions of risk; they have to be taken into account since they influence risk management decisions and affect policy efficiency. The basic procedure is to access the views of the lay public via a survey sample intended to be representative of the wider population. The views the members of the sample have toward the risk are analyzed and assessed for their degrees of accuracy or fit with the expert delineation of the risk. Risk communication methods are then devised to educate the lay public more efficiently, to correct the misperceptions they hold.

Risk communication relies in part on research into cognitive bias in risk perception. Observed psychological and behavioral consequences of decision-making under uncertainty stimulate for investigations into heuristics and biases. Of primary concern is how people interpret alternative, probable conditions and make selections across uncertain outcomes. Experimental research on risk-taking behavior (Kunreuther et al. 1978) suggests that individuals make judgments about risk that consistently err with respect to the laws of probability.

Kahneman & Tversky (1979) proposed a systematic approach to these distortions in terms of prospect theory. This theory involves subjective decision weights that do not obey the axioms of probability theory. Decision weights can rescale probabilities along the lines identified by Allais (1953), but they can also represent the common behavior of neglecting small departures from the extreme probabilities of one and zero. Prospect theory does not explain decision weights; it takes them for granted and tries to describe their influence. In particular, decision weights may depend on a reference state with which possible events are compared. In many cases, people need such a reference state to make a decision. In these cases, gains are usually attributed smaller weights than losses. A famous example refers to a comparison between two strategies to deal with a deadly disease. In one frame, deaths are emphasized and recoveries are treated implicitly. In the other frame, recoveries are emphasized and deaths are treated implicitly. Empirical results show very clearly that the choice between the two strategies depends on the frame in which they are presented. More generally, the way in which a problem is framed often defines the reference state, and different reference states can lead to different decisions. Framing effects obviously play a major role in debates about many risk issues, including those of climate change. For example, the discount rate to be used in cost–benefit analyses of climate change is arguably frame dependent.

The authors of prospect theory identified heuristics and biases that are characteristic of the decisionmaking process under uncertainty and that are easily elicited in experimental settings (Tversky & Kahneman 1974, Kahneman et al. 1982):

- *Representativeness* This tendency is generally expressed by overweighing similarities of events in the probability judgment. Thus, the heuristic propagates stereotypes to make risk judgments, even to the exclusion of relevant prior information about the risk or information about sample size.
- *Availability* This tendency is expressed by overweighing events that can be easily imagined or recalled. Availability is common where information about an event is readily retrieved but the sources of information have little to do with the attributes of the risk. This heuristic is consistent with an excessive reaction to current information and an underestimation of future uncertainties.
- *Adjustment and anchoring* People may anchor risk judgment to some starting point in the assessment (e.g., the last point on a time series), and their adjustments from the initial position often ignore subsequent evidence. This heuristic plays an important role in eliciting judgments from people correctly.
- *Certainty effect* This tendency is expressed by a preference for certain outcomes or treating events as if they are certain when they are not.
- *Editing and isolation* This tendency is expressed often in problems of low-probability events, either to edit choice parameters or isolate mutually exclusive parameters.
- *Calibration and overconfidence* People are often over- or underconfident regarding their judgments, depending on the difficulty of the assessment.

For moderate or extremely difficult assessments, people with general knowledge are often overconfident (Lichtenstein et al. 1982). Overconfidence means that people believe their judgments about assessing risks to be more accurate than they actually are, even if this confidence cannot be supported by statistical evidence.

Fischhoff & Furby (1983) provided a discussion and a research agenda that addressed the significance of the heuristics and biases for climate change. They suggest that the more important heuristics for climate change judgments are overconfidence, editing, availability, and anchoring. Research on cognitive biases emphasizes cognitive structure, sociopsychological factors, anxiety, experience, and intuitive ways of thinking to structure the risk perceptions of subjects. Slovic et al. (1979: 14) captured a common motivation for the approach: "People respond to the hazards they perceive. If their perceptions are faulty, efforts at public and environmental protection are likely to be misdirected." The notion that alternative framings of risk are merely corrigible misperceptions leads to risk communication procedures through which risk assessment findings are channeled to the public or to special interest groups, so that their misperceptions can be corrected and they can make decisions based upon scientific risk assessments undertaken outside the risk management process.

This kind of research has been criticized, however, for beginning with the phenomenon of technical risk and then seeking the misconceptions, errors, limitations, confusions, and inaccuracies of subjects in their assessments of risk sources (Rayner 1984, Bradbury 1989). As we describe below, such a view ignores or dismisses the validity of local knowledge about social or natural systems that the risk professionals may have passed over. Furthermore, appearing to include individuals in the decisionmaking process creates an expectation that the process is consensual when it remains arbitrary (Otway & Wynne 1989). This has led to distrust between expert scientists and concerned lay people and has exacerbated the divide between the two (Wynne 1989a,b).

Global risks in a pluralistic society

We have discussed approaches to climatic risks based on the rational actor paradigm, which assumes that society can be identified with a unique optimizing decisionmaker. We have discussed some major difficulties of these approaches and have looked at the consequences of dropping the societal optimizing assumption. This has led us to the consideration of multiagent models, with regard to both negotiation processes and market mechanisms. In such models, the problem of uncertainty about global environmental change is compounded by each actor's uncertainty about the other actors. The assumption of rationality offers important ways of dealing not only with the former but also with the latter kind of uncertainty. However, several problems arise:

- The paradoxes of atomistic rationality now hold not just for a unique benevolent planner, but for every single rational actor.
- Each actor is assumed to handle a bewildering complex of possibilities when choosing the optimal course of action.
- Under standard assumptions the interaction between rational actors usually leads to multiple equilibria. As each of them results from optimizing behavior, optimization is of no help in selecting among this set of equilibria.

The issue of multiple decisionmakers raises questions not only about applying decision techniques based on the assumption of unitary decisionmakers with access to full information, but also about identifying the relevant decisionmakers. Integrated assessment and decision science have seldom addressed what climate change means at the level where its causes and impacts are likely to be most direct.

For the most part, governments do not directly emit greenhouse-related gases; firms and households do. Similarly, governments do not directly experience impacts of climate variability; farmers, foresters, and hoteliers do. Ultimately, it is not governments that will pay the price of climate policies or their failure; citizens as consumers and taxpayers will. Thus far, decision analysis has addressed climate risks at their most aggregated (and, thus, abstract) level as government policy. What can decision analysis, and the social sciences more broadly, tell us about how human choices will be made, and can be made, about the myriad concrete risks that climate change presents to individual, household, community, commercial, and governmental decisionmakers? In other words, what do the social sciences have to say about risk management at the level of everyday decisionmakers—those who actually emit greenhouse-related gases and will sustain impacts?

Spectacular dangers from climate change tend to capture popular attention for short periods, for example, catastrophic sea level rise resulting from the detachment of the West Antarctic ice sheet. However, such high-consequence events are generally agreed among scientists to be of very low probability. More likely consequences are those affecting mundane actions on the part of significant segments of the human population. For example, Table 3.2 lists a series of potential climate change risks identified by the US Office of Technology Assessment (1993). Alongside each of these risk categories we have indicated some kinds of institutional or individual decisionmakers that are likely to encounter such changes and be forced to manage the uncertainty associated with them.

In the light of this decentralized set of risk problems as well as in relation to

Table 3.2 Summary of potential climate change risks for various systems.

Potential risks	Potential risk managers
Forests/terrestrial vegetation	
• migration of vegetation • reduction of inhabited range • altered ecosystem competition	• forest product companies • logging communities • tourist industry • ecologists
Species diversity	
• loss of diversity • migration of species • invasion of new species	• pharmaceutical industry • indigenous communities • farmers and foresters
Coastal wetlands	
• inundation of wetlands • migration of wetlands	• environmental and wildlife groups • indigenous communities
Aquatic ecosystems	
• loss of habitat • migration to new habitats • invasion of new species	• fishermen • tourist industry • environmental and wildlife groups • indigenous communities
Coastal resources	
• inundation of coastal development • increased risk of flooding	• city and transportation planners • tourist industry • householders
Water resources	
• changes in supplies • changes in droughts and floods • changes in water quality and hydropower production	• utility companies • public health professionals • farmers
Agriculture	
• changes in crop yields • shifts in relative productivity and production	• farmers and farming communities • agribusiness
Human health	
• shifts in range of infectious diseases • changes in heat-stress and cold-weather afflictions	• householders • medical and public health professions • women and the elderly
Energy	
• increase in cooling demand • decrease in heating demand • changes in hydropower output	• householders • industrial producers • utility companies • environmental groups
Transportation	
• fewer disruptions of winter transportation • increased risk for inland summer navigation • risks to coastal roads	• transportation infrastructure planners • trucking and railroad companies • barge operators

Source: Based upon US Office of Technology Assessment (1993).

the role of stakeholders in formulating government policies, we now consider a series of approaches that, in various ways, try to transcend the limits of the standard view of rationality in dealing with issues of risk and uncertainty.

We will discuss four approaches, which may be characterized with the following labels: social amplification of risk, sociology of science, arena theory, and the cultural theory of risk. Other classifications would have been possible, but the main point of this section would be the same: there are several attempts to overcome the limits of the rational actor paradigm in risk analysis by emphasizing the social dimensions of human behavior in the face of risk and danger. They do not yet offer a coherent approach to risk analysis and their relations to the rational actor paradigm still require considerable clarification. Nevertheless, they already provide valuable help in analyzing risk issues and in designing policies to deal with such issues.

Social amplification theory

In the case of climatic risks, scientific information about possible hazards interacts with psychological, social, institutional, and cultural processes in ways that amplify or attenuate public perception of these risks. Kasperson et al. (1988) proposed an influential conceptual framework that is relevant for such situations. It links risk analysis based on the rational actor paradigm with psychological, sociological, and cultural perspectives of risk perception and risk-related behavior (Renn et al. 1992, Machlis & Rosa 1990). Response patterns generate secondary social or economic consequences and may increase or decrease the social process triggered by a risk event. Secondary effects may instigate demands for additional institutional responses and protective actions, or impede risk management actions. The social structures and processes of risk experience, the resulting repercussions on individual and group perceptions, and the effect of these responses on community, society, and economy compose a general phenomenon that Kasperson et al. described as the social amplification of risk. (The authors have subsequently made it clear that *amplification* may refer to a process of reducing the risk as perceived, as well as increasing it.)

Amplification occurs at two stages: in the transfer of information about risk and in the response mechanisms of society. Signals about risk arise through direct personal experience with risk events or through receipt of information about risk events. They are then processed by individual and social amplifiers, including the scientist who communicates the risk assessment, the news media, cultural groups, interpersonal networks, and others. Kasperson et al. (1988: 181–2) suggested that the key amplification steps consist of the following:

- filtering signals (only a fraction of incoming information is processed)

- decoding signals
- processing risk information (for example, using a cognitive heuristic to draw inferences)
- attaching social values to information, drawing implications for management and policy
- interacting with cultural and peer groups to interpret and validate signals
- forming behavioral intentions to tolerate the risk or act against the risk or risk manager
- engaging in group or individual actions to respond to the risk.

The amplified risk leads to behavioral responses, which result in secondary impacts. Secondary impacts can include individual responses, for example, people forming enduring mental images and attitudes, such as alienation from the physical environment or antitechnology attitudes. There may be local impacts on businesses, political and social pressure, even social disorder. Institutions may respond by providing training or education about the risk, changing risk monitoring or regulation, or increasing liability and insurance costs.

Another stage of amplifications may occur to produce third-order impacts. Impacts may spread, or ripple, to other parties, distant locations, or future generations (Fig. 3.5).

Since very little of our information about global environmental change arises from direct experience, what Kasperson and his colleagues theorized about the amplification of indirect signals is particularly pertinent to climatic risks. Networks of friends, family, and colleagues, or the media become important sources of information when direct personal experience is limited. Information flow is a key factor in public response and amplification. Other key information factors are volume, the degree to which information is disputed, the extent of dramatization, and the symbolic connotations of the information. Kasperson et al. point out that the news media have received the bulk of attention for their critical role in public opinion formation and community responses to risk; however, information communication networks may be equally important.

Kasperson et al. claimed that "Signals arise through direct personal experience with a risk object" (p. 181), but the theory does not attempt to explain how the receiver was tuned to receive signals on one frequency and not another, and how it selected a particular subset from various signals coming in on the same wavelength. That is to say, the theory elides the issue of signal (or risk) selection (Rayner 1988).

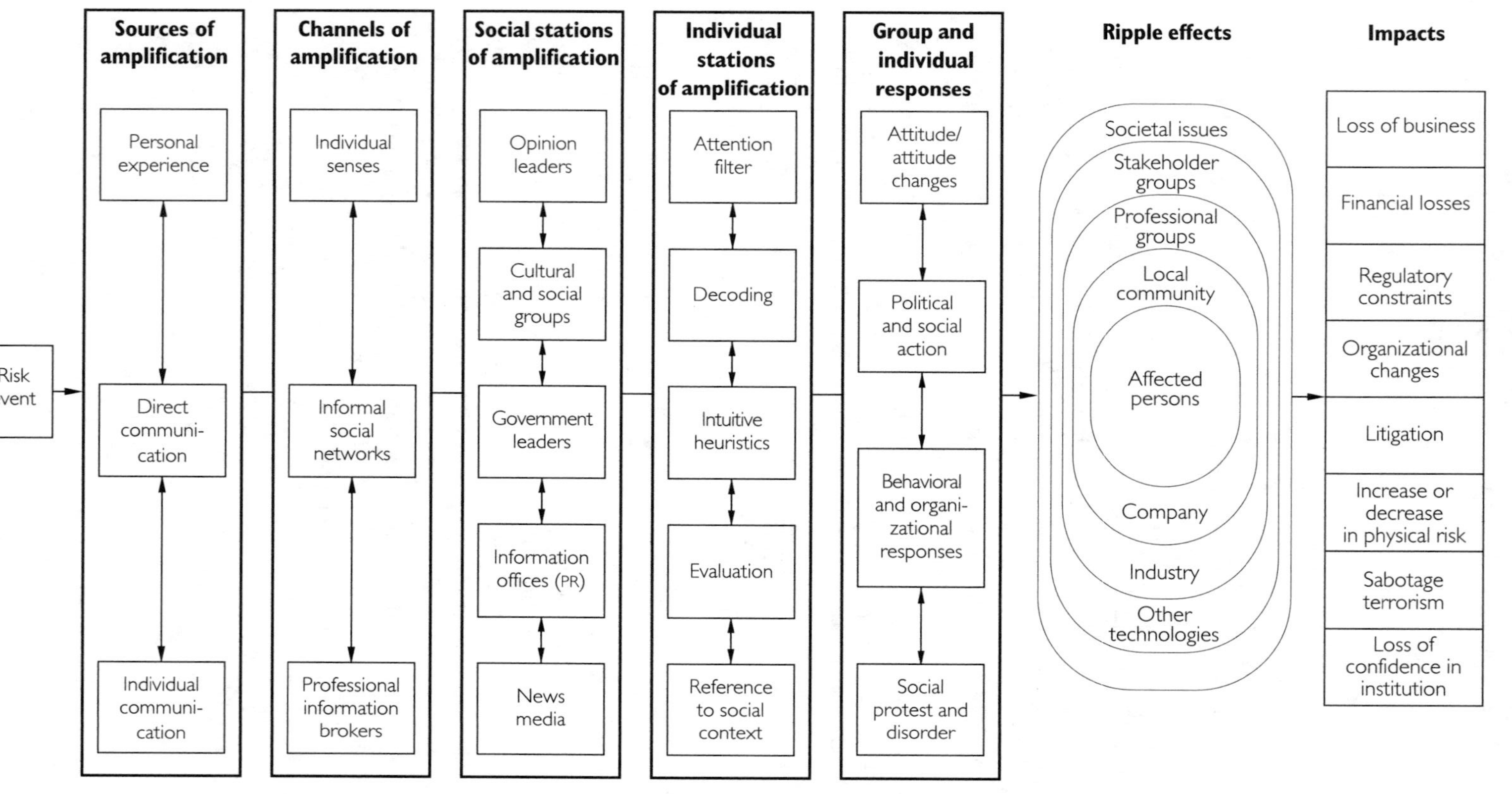

Figure 3.5 Detailed conceptual framework of social amplification of risk (source: Kasperson et al. 1988).

Sociology of science

The amplification metaphor retains the notion of an initial risk signal which can be identified objectively by means of scientific rationality. Over the past decade, however, critics of traditional approaches to risk issues have begun to articulate a perspective that focuses on the very concepts of rationality and science underlying the risk debate (Wynne 1982, 1989a,b,c, Winner 1986, Rayner & Cantor 1987, Otway 1992, Otway & von Winterfeldt 1992). Rooted in the contemporary sociology of science, their views represent a fundamental challenge to the claims that the problems of climate change are the physical risk problems, and that science can provide us with objective measures of the nature of risk.

With respect to the first of these issues, this view suggests that much of the current risk debate is misconstrued, that describing social choices about technology as risk issues distorts their nature by singling out only one aspect of the problem for attention. To the extent that this is so, risk debates are not fundamentally about risk, at least not as conventionally defined, but are instead about issues such as social and technological choice, trust, credibility, power, legitimacy, and control. In Wynne's words (1987: 10), risk "is artificially abstracted by analysts from people's multidimensional social experience of issues, technologies, and decisionmaking institutions. We propose instead that people rationally react to their (past and current) social experience of decisionmaking relationships, in which physical risk defined by analysts is inextricably embedded as only one element."

In other words, far from perceived risk being a simplified, distorted, and usually inaccurate version of objective risk, it is the broader and more inclusive view from which objective risk is abstracted. Objective risk represents only the technical dimension of a much more complex set of decisionmaking problems. Insofar as measures of objective risk are taken to be measures of the risk problem as a whole, such measures seriously distort that problem. Certainly there is a scientific dimension to risk issues; however, this dimension is rather limited, not addressing many crucial issues about control, legitimacy, trust, credibility, and appropriate decisionmaking processes. From this point of view, calls for more science and more scientific literacy do not solve the problem but deflect attention from these larger dimensions. In fact, they may well make the problem worse by further mystifying the issue and creating more distrust on the part of those who resent having their concerns reduced to technical risk issues and who resent being told they have distorted views of the problem.

The expert/lay dichotomy emphasized by contemporary sociology of science has been regarded by some as public antipathy toward science. Palmlund (1992: 199) suggested that, "the social interaction over risk has strong roots in existential anxiety and in the needs we have to exert control over the unknown and the uncontrolled." Management and resolution of the types of conflict that arise when these social beliefs and ways are threatened has led to studies that look in depth at the different values held by the lay public and scientific expertise (Nelkin 1979, Nelkin & Pollack 1980, Wynne 1989a,b, Otway 1992, Otway & von Winterfeldt 1992). In particular, these studies focused on the extent to which different perceptions, worldviews, and social beliefs have contributed to generating controversy, either through poor communication or blind sides that prevent a cooperative approach to the problem.

The case of British sheepfarming after Chernobyl (Wynne 1989b) illustrated clearly the politicized nature of scientific expertise in juxtaposition to less highly regarded lay (indigenous) knowledge. Favoring a purely technocratic approach over a more holistic one increased the problems for the farmers and the policymakers attempting to contain the situation. The farmers' level of frustration, distrust, and unwillingness to cooperate steadily increased, while the scientists systematically ignored farmers' concerns about the way the radiation contamination was spreading and concentrating in the flocks.

Case study comparisons provided by sociologists, cultural anthropologists, historians, and philosophers of science provide empirical evidence of the differences between expert and indigenous knowledge. Fieldwork such as that done by Nelkin & Pollack (1980), Jasanoff (1982), Rayner (1986), Wynne (1992), and Bradbury et al. (1994) showed the importance of accounting for different types of knowledge in risk analysis.

Very often the clash of expert and lay biases underlies a risk dispute (Wynne 1991). Researchers have addressed this by emphasizing expertise as another key factor in the expert/lay distinction. Expert knowledge may differ from local expertise and may differ among experts with different expertise. A commonly used approach to understanding differences between expert and lay judgment relies on the cognitive bias literature, in particular the work of Slovic et al. (1980). Studies that use this approach attempt to uncover how personal values, experiences, and cognitive biases influence expert judgment in much the same ways as these factors influence lay judgment. However, the approach also incorporates the self-interest bias, since the approach calls attention to what some see as the alarming role of scientists as part of a political elite in the risk management process, and it challenges the legitimacy of scientific assessments in controversial risk problems (Barke & Jenkins-Smith 1993).

Empirical evidence supports the claim that experts, like lay persons, treat risk as a multidimensional concept and are subject to many judgment errors for complex risk magnitudes. However, the biases that dominate expert and lay judgments may be very different, since experience is an important factor. Experts may be particularly susceptible to bias from unstated assumptions and mindsets, the way a problem has been structured for analysis, personal reputation consequences, overconfidence, anchoring, and availability (Otway & von Winterfeldt 1992). For example, Stewart & Glantz (1985) used the expert bias approach to reject expert predictions on climate change, because no attempt has been made to control for biases systematically.

Often, expert bias does not lead to a homogeneous scientific consensus, but to a variety of contradicting claims defended by different experts. This creates not only opportunities but also serious problems for decisionmakers. Different social groups expect decisionmakers to base their judgment on scientific evidence, but the plurality of evidence does not give them a justifiable rule to select an alternative as the best. In this dilemma, policymakers define exclusion rules not for expertise but for experts. Some would like to establish science courts or to produce meta-science rules for selecting people who can serve as science advisors. But neither the logic of legal systems nor the philosophy of knowledge provides generally acceptable rules for distinguishing good from bad science.

Therefore, policymakers try to find those scientists who are in agreement with their basic political views and legitimize their choice by formal positions, such as research experience or status within the scientific community. However, this status has been attained through the same type of networks that provides positive rewards for those who produce what the policymakers demand.

The problem with the attempt to approach risk studies through the establishment of one privileged expert consensus lies in the possibility that more than one view of a specific risk may be perfectly defensible. Although this possibility runs against the thrust of traditional philosophy of science, it is easy to understand even from the perspective of the rational actor paradigm. If the definition of risks is a matter of utility functions and subjective probabilities, there is no reason to expect a single definition to be superior to all other ones. Perfectly rational people may hold different utility functions and different probability judgments, and this will lead them to differ in what they consider as relevant, acceptable, or desirable in dealing with risks like those of climate change.

Moreover, one can make a case that scientific rationality as such always depends on the fulfillment of the conditions embedded in a particular knowledge model. When considering a specific risk, one should expect a whole set of different, but equally legitimate, descriptions of the risk in question. Under such conditions, risk management becomes an exercise in social learning (Wynne 1992). This need not be seen as a second-best solution in comparison with a simple expert consensus. The dialogue between actors holding different legitimate conceptions of a specific risks may be seen as a process in which different social actors mutually create meaning and value (Tribe 1973). Rather than a simple negotiation in which instrumental rationality is employed to reach predefined goals, such a process may be seen as a form of social rationality which lies at the roots of democratic institutions.

Arena theory

Both the social amplification view and the approaches inspired by contemporary sociology of science emphasize the difference between experts and lay persons, albeit in very different ways. For the problem of climate risks many other distinctions are at least as important. Oil-producing and oil-importing countries, less industrialized countries and highly industrialized ones, firms with stakes in nuclear energy and reinsurance firms, nongovernmental organizations and the mass media—all these actors and many more play important roles in climate policy formation. Although game theory is certainly useful to analyze some aspects of multiactor interactions, it tends to neglect the process in which the rules of the game are changed as the game goes on (see Ch. 2).

An important framework to understand and analyze the dynamics of risk issues involving many agents is the concept of social arenas (Renn 1992). A social arena metaphorically describes the symbolic location of political actions that influence collective decisions or policies (Kitschelt 1980). Symbolic location means that arenas are neither geographical entities nor organizational systems. They describe the political actions of all social actors involved in a specific issue. Issues can be pending political decisions, such as the introduction of a carbon tax; social problems, such as the contrast between highly industrialized and less industrialized countries; or ideas, such as the concept of sustainability. The arena concept attempts to explain the process of policy formulation and enforcement in a specific policy field. Its focus is on the meso-level of society rather than on the individual (micro-level) or societal behavior as an whole (macro-level). It reflects the segmentation of society into different policy systems that interact with each other but still preserve their autonomy (Hilgartner & Bosk 1988).

The arena model incorporates only those actions of individuals or social groups that are intended to influence collective decisions or policies. Someone who merely believes in deep ecology and communicates the idea of equal rights of animals and humans to others is irrelevant for the social arena unless this person attempts to change environmental policies, reform hunting laws, or restrict current practices in agriculture and animal laboratories. Intentional behavior to affect policies is certainly not the only way that policies are affected by public input (examples of other possibilities are given by public opinion polls or by media coverage), but indirect effects are conceptualized as inputs into the arena rather than as elements of the arena.

Arena theory assumes that social groups in an arena intend to influence policies. This assumption is very important because it provides the yardstick for evaluating social constructs that groups may use to define their causes and to pursue their goals. Under this assumption, success and failure of group activities can be measured (intersubjectively) by the amount of influence that the specific group has been able to exert on the resulting decision(s) or policies. The reasons explaining why people feel motivated to become active or why they invest time and effort to become players in the arena are not in the focus of the arena concept. To refrain from motivational analysis of the actors involved in an arena does not mean that these motivations are irrelevant for political success or failure. Within arena theory, however, they are only of interest if they are part of the resource mobilization effort, in other words, if motivations are used to generate support.

The center stage of the arena is occupied by the principal actors—those groups in society that seek to influence policies. Some groups often focus on several issues at once and are hence involved in different arenas; others focus only on one issue in a single arena. Each arena is characterized by a set of rules: formal rules that are coded and monitored by a rule enforcement agency and informal rules that are learned and developed in the process of interactions among the actors. Among the formal rules are laws, acts, and mandated procedures; among the informal rules are regulatory styles, political climate of group interactions, and role expectations. In most cases the rules are external constraints for each single actor. Formal rule changes require institutional actions; informal changes occur as a result of trial and error and may happen according to whether or not rule bending is penalized. Several actors may join forces to change the rules, even if they disagree on the substance of the issue.

The rule enforcement agency ensures that the actors abide by the formal rules and it often coordinates the process of interaction and negotiation. In many arenas the rule enforcement agency is also the ultimate decisionmaker. In this case, all actors try to make their claims known to this decisionmaker and to convince the agency by arguments or through public pressure to adopt their viewpoint. In an adversarial policy style, which is typical for the United States (O'Riordan & Wynne 1987, Renn 1989), rule enforcement agencies regard themselves more as brokers or mediators than as sovereign administrators who are consulted by various social actors, which tends to be the European policy model (Coppock 1986).

Besides the principal actors and the rule enforcement agency, two other kinds of actors are particularly important: the *issue amplifiers* and the *audience*. The issue amplifiers are the professional theater critics who observe the actions on stage, communicate with the principal actors, interpret their findings, and report them to the audience. Through this communication process they influence the allocation of resources and the effectiveness of each resource to mobilize public support within the arena. The audience consists of other social groups who may be enticed to enter the arena and individuals who process the information and may feel motivated to show their support or displeasure with one or several actors or the arena as a whole. Part of the political process is to mobilize social support by other social actors and to influence public opinion.

In contrast to traditional role theory or the theater stage metaphor (Goffman 1959, Palmlund 1992), the arena concept does not picture the actions on stage as a play with a script or actors as performing role assignments. Arenas are more like medieval contests in which knights fought for honor and royal recognition according to specified arena rules that determined the conditions for the fight, but left to the actors the choice of their own strategies. Accordingly, modern arenas provide actors with the opportunity to influence the policy process and to direct their claims to the decisionmakers. Their behavior is not necessarily defined by behavioral roles and routines; actors may use innovative approaches to policymaking or use traditional channels of lobbying. However, arenas are regulated by norms and rules, which limit the range of potential options. Actors may decide to ignore some of the rules if they feel that public support will not suffer and if the rule enforcement agency is not powerful enough to impose sanctions on actors who violate the rules.

The outcome of the arena process is undetermined. On one hand, various actors may play out different strategies that interact with each other and produce synergistic effects (game theoretical indeterminacy). Strategic maneuvering can even result in an undesired outcome that does not reflect the stated goal of any actor and may indeed be suboptimal for all participants. This is the situation of a social dilemma. On the other hand, interactions in the arena change the arena rules (structural indeterminacy). Novel forms of political actions may evolve as actors experience the boundaries of tolerance for limited rule violations. Therefore, arenas often behave like indeterministic or nonlinear systems: small changes in strategies or rules are capable of producing major changes in conflict outcomes. It is also difficult to predict who is going to benefit from potential rule changes induced by trial and error. Both characteristics of arenas limit the use of arena theory for predictions, but do not compromise its value for explanation and policy analysis.

The social arena concept clearly has its limitations, however. It leaves the impression of politics as a game in which players want to win and spectators want to be entertained. Although some political debates support this impression, others certainly do not. Many debates are characterized by a good faith effort of all actors to improve a situation or to resolve a conflict. The emphasis on social resources may obscure the fact that not all political actions are strategic and that people often mean what they say. In addition, the division between actors and spectators seems to support a concept of democracy in which elites fight for power and influence and the masses are used as instruments for these elites to gain relative advantages.

Cultural theory

Another vein of research, the cultural theory of risk, addresses issues such as equity and trust through different social perspectives on risk (Douglas & Wildavsky 1982, Rayner 1984, 1992, Douglas 1985, Schwarz & Thompson 1990, Thompson et al. 1990). As an introductory example, Jacobs (1992) claimed that in contemporary society two basic cultural orientations coexist. One places great emphasis on loyalty, is determined to enforce the law, values classical virtues such as prudence and courage, and operates in a hierarchical setting with a clear distinction between insiders and outsiders. This is the orientation cultivated in large government bureaucracies; it is represented by civil servants. Jacobs calls it the orientation of the *guardians*. The second orientation emphasizes the art of the deal, the development of extended social networks without clear-cut boundaries, the combination of different specialized competencies. It is represented by the world of commerce and markets. Jacobs calls it the orientation of the *merchants*.

At one level, the distinction between these two orientations corresponds to the distinction between a political and an economic sphere, although, as Saul (1992) pointed out, most contemporary firms are actually run by bureaucratic structures rather than by entrepreneurs. According to cultural theory the contrast between open-ended networks and strongly transitive hierarchies rather than the sphere of activity (government or trade) is the focus for understanding the worldviews that predominate in any institution.

Indeed, a distinctive feature of cultural theory is its insistence on including forms of social organization that are usually excluded by conventional social science dichotomies, such as *markets* and *hierarchies* (Williamson 1975) and *politics* and *markets* (Lindblom 1977). Cultural theory also focuses on forms of social organization that are largely ignored by political scientists and economists alike. These are *egalitarian collectivism* and *atomized individualism*. The four basic types are generated by consideration of the compactness of social interaction and networks (group) and the extent of social differentiation governing the mode of interaction (grid). The evaluation of each of these variables as high or low strength gives rise to the four prototypes of social organization. In a further elaboration, Thompson (1982) introduced a fifth category, the hermit. However, for the analysis of public policy debates, cultural theorists will often follow the example of arena theorists in restricting themselves to the three kinds of social organization that actively give voice to their positions, that is the *hierarchist*, the *entrepreneur*, and the *egalitarian* (see, for example Rayner 1991 and Ch. 4, Vol. 1).

But cultural theory is not just a typology of social organization. Its central hypothesis is that, in the active process of building, maintaining, and dismantling any type of social organization, people call each other to account for their actions and justify their own actions within a social organizational frame of reference (Douglas 1978). For example, hierarchists and egalitarians may be susceptible to pressure to act explicitly for the common good of the institution. Entrepreneurs are more likely to be persuaded to act by arguments that focus on their ability to obtain competitive advantage. Alternatively, egalitarians and entrepreneurs are less likely than hierarchists to expect people to constrain their social interactions in accordance with ascribed characteristics, such as age, gender, color, or social class.

Rayner (1992) explicitly noted that this is not a psychological theory that accounts for private preferences, but a sociological view of culture that is concerned with what can be said in social conversations. Authors working in the cultural theory of risk accept that the different cultures of hierarchists, individualists, and egalitarians are all essential parts of modern society (Schwarz & Thompson 1990, Rayner 1991). They study how these cultures interact and interfere with each other and to what kinds of risk management such interaction may lead.

Cultural analysis of risk looks behind the perception of physical risks to the social norms or policies that are being attacked or defended. Of all the things that people can worry about, they will be inclined to select for particular attention those risks that can be used to reinforce the solidarity of their institutions. Cultural theory differs from behavioral approaches to risk perception in that it focuses not on the individual but on an institution that is driven by organizational imperatives to select risks for management attention or to suppress them from view.

According to cultural theory, risks are not defined on the basis of individual preferences, as assumed by the rational actor paradigm, but rather as a function of sociocultural necessities. Cultures define those actions that threaten basic assumptions of the culture in question as unacceptable risks—quite independently from the consequences for the single actor. The cultural theory of risk proposes an analysis of the distinction between acceptable and unacceptable risks. Acceptable risks are the ones that do not pose a threat to a given culture. In these cases, a comparison between costs and benefits for individual actors may guide the decisions by these actors. There are, however, also risks that put a whole social fabric at risk by undermining the cultural presuppositions of human life in a given community. These risks are unacceptable for the sociocultural fabric as a whole, and no individual actors are allowed to decide about them on the basis of their particular assessment of costs and benefits.

Hierarchists tend to be especially concerned with threats to the orderly and efficient maintenance of the social system. On the other hand, health risks for individuals, as well as commercial risks for firms, are acceptable as long as they can be managed within well-established formal procedures. For entrepreneurs, the true risks lie elsewhere, namely in the lack of business opportunities and the danger of bankruptcy. Entrepreneurs react to the volatility of financial markets by engaging in sophisticated hedging operations. Hierarchists tend to see these operations as an amplification of the original volatility and look for regulations to avoid a financial meltdown. In a similar vein, hierarchists develop regulations to limit what they perceive as the risks of complex technologies and environmentally harmful activities. Entrepreneurs tend to see these regulations as making problems worse and try to reduce the risks of industrial and environmental accidents by technical and organizational innovations. Moreover, entrepreneurs tend to see risk taking as a highly attractive course of action, because risks are generally seen as closely tied to opportunities. The egalitarian culture treats risks as unacceptable when they are not evenly distributed, either within a generation or between generations. The latter point is of obvious relevance to environmental risks and has meanwhile led to the debate about sustainable development. At least with regard to environmental and technological risks, the egalitarian culture seems to be much more risk averse than the logic of both merchants and guardians.

In addition to being proactive, management strategies in cultural theory include various coping and adaptive behaviors that tend to be discounted in conventional approaches (O'Riordan & Rayner 1990). Finally, risk communication in cultural theory emphasizes creation of shared meaning and trust over the transfer of quantitative information or the articulation of risk benefits or tradeoffs (Rayner 1992).

Cultural theorists have proposed that contemporary environmental debates can be understood in the context of people's invoking differing mythologies of the workings of nature to support their various political and moral beliefs (Rayner 1984, Douglas 1985, Schwarz & Thompson 1990). The climate change issue provides ample evidence that there are abiding and sometimes contradictory views of nature and philosophies of risk management—in short, plural rationalities (Rayner 1991). Cultural theory suggests that different cultural orientations are geared to different myths of nature which have been discussed in the literature on environmental management (Holling 1986, see also Vol. 1, Ch. 4). According to this hypothesis, individualists see nature as robust; egalitarians see it as fragile. Hierarchists may see nature as resilient; fatalists view it as capricious. Each myth is supposed to lead to a particular moral imperative, preference in response strategy, and type of social organization.

This typology is a heuristic device; few individuals should be expected to hold to these extreme positions consistently. However, cultural theory does suggest that the social organization of institutions, including political parties, government agencies, environmental groups, and scientific laboratories may lead them to frame their internal discourse in such a way that one or another of these strategies will tend to set the terms of the discussion. This is because the organizational framework within which a discussion occurs places certain constraints on the intelligibility and credibility of propositions and arguments that can be advanced in debate.

In practice, cultural models offer powerful interpretive schemes, but are difficult to test systematically. Gross & Rayner (1985) provided an early design for operationalizing cultural theory for the purposes of empirical research. It has found little application, however, mainly because it required a nearly prohibitive amount of research effort. Meanwhile, a series of empirical studies relying on cultural theory have been carried out (Wildavsky & Dake 1990, Dake 1991, 1992, Dake & Wildavsky 1991, Dake & Thompson 1993, Jenkins-Smith & Smith 1994, Sjöberg 1995, Marris et al. 1996, Earle & Cvetkovich 1998). They show that meaningful operationalizations of cultural theory are possible. By and large, the results of these studies are consistent with main assertions of the theory. However, many results can easily be interpreted in other ways, too. In some operationalizations using questionnaires, perception of environmental risk seems to depend less on cultural orientation than on political attitudes. In some other studies, environmental risks can be as well described along a one-dimensional continuum, ranging from egoistic individualism to solidarity with other humans and living beings. An interesting opportunity for such inquiries is given by recent applications of cultural theory in the construction of integrated assessment models (Rotmans et al. 1994, Rotmans 1995, van Asselt & Rotmans 1995, Pahl-Wöstl et al. in press).

Beyond studies that try to interpret empirical data directly in terms of cultural orientations, inquiries have not been pursued to determine whether models including intermediate variables would establish more complex links between theory and data. Among these intermediate variables, trust, liability, and consent may play a prominent role. Trust emerges as a significant factor in several studies of risk where other cultural variables are not investigated (Bord & O'Connor 1990, Slovic et al. 1991). Together with trust, liability and consent have been proposed as relevant variables by Rayner & Cantor (1987; see also Rayner 1987, 1992). Different forms of social organization are likely to have different ways in which trust is established, liability is characterized, and consent is obtained.

Rayner (1992) characterized the interplay of probability (*P*), damage (*D*), trust (T), liability (*L*), and consent (*C*) in determining risk with the metaphoric formula:

$$R = P \times D + T \times L \times C$$

The formula is useful because it points to further research needs. In empirical terms, it emphasizes the need to find robust indicators for trust, liability, and consent, and to define reasonable scaling procedures so that these indicators can be combined with each other and with the usual variables used in quantitative risk assessment. In theoretical terms, it emphasizes the possibility and the need to clarify the relations between the rational actor paradigm and cultural theory. First, the relations between the *TLC* variables and the *PD* variables are more subtle. In the rational actor paradigm, the product of probability and damage is summed up over all single risk events to characterize the overall risk of a specific course of action. The *TLC* variables characterize primarily a risky prospect as a whole, rather than single-risk events. Moreover, they may well influence the *PD* variables themselves: for example, low trust may lead to high subjective probabilities for threatening possibilities, low consent to extremely low subjective utilities for the same possibilities.

Second, the role of cultural orientations needs to be specified. One may try to define a different utility function and different subjective probabilities for each cultural orientation. At first sight, cultural theory then becomes an extension of the rational actor paradigm by providing additional explanations for the variables employed by it. There is an important difference, however. In the rational actor paradigm, actors are characterized by a unique utility function. Cultural theory would consider actors as actively selecting one of several utility functions depending on circumstances. But this selection is not simply a matter of utility maximization; it is rather a human choice of a nonoptimizing kind that demands some understanding of how to embed optimizing rationality in a broader framework of social rationality. Although this need is widely acknowledged, it remains a task for future research.

Social rationality and nonoptimizing choices

We have discussed a series of approaches that explicitly try to overcome the limitations of the dominant style of risk analysis based on the rational actor paradigm and risk management. Although there are major differences between these approaches, a common theme emerges: the emphasis on cultural and social realities, which cannot be reduced to individual choices. This leads to a better understanding of the difficulties met by conventional risk management. It also leads to the danger of a sterile dilemma (Funtowicz & Ravetz 1985). One horn of the dilemma would consist of a naïve subjectivism, which believes that rational actor paradigm is sufficient to handle the theoretical and practical problems of risk and uncertainty. The other horn would consist of a reductionism, which tends to believe that debates about environmental and technological risks are just disguised debates about cultural and social orientations. In the present section, we will consider three steps which may help to avoid this dilemma.

The first step consists of developing an awareness of the changing role of science in the face of global environmental change. This is especially relevant for the emerging field of integrated assessment, which in many respects may become the framework for dealing with the unsettled problems of risk analysis.

The second step consists of blending the tools of integrated assessment modeling with the tradition of stakeholder involvement in environmental impact assessment. This leads to remarkable opportunities of public participation. The interpretive approach of critical theory may be helpful for identifying and seizing such opportunities.

The third step may well be the most difficult one. It consists of a patient effort to integrate the wealth of insights provided by the rational actor paradigm in a broader framework of social rationality. The difficulty is twofold. First, most social scientists are trained in the realm of either the rational actor paradigm or the varieties of interpretive approaches that emphasize social rationality. And second, considerable amendments of the latter approaches, as well as of analyses based on the rational actor paradigm, will be required if their combination is to be helpful in dealing with the problems of global change.

Issues for integrated assessment

From the viewpoint of an enlightened aristocrat observing the young American democracy, de Tocqueville (1840) emphasized a peculiar problem with the concept of truth. If truth is something that human beings can grasp to a greater or lesser degree, then the notion of truth establishes something like an aristocracy of the mind. And if one wants political decisions to be based on true beliefs, then it might be important to make sure that such decisions are influenced primarily by those with an exceptional ability to grasp the truth about the problem at hand. However, democracy emphasizes everybody's right to hold whatever beliefs he pleases, and also everybody's right to shape political decisions on the basis of those beliefs. This problem is of obvious relevance to scientific institutions, as they are widely trusted to perform exceptionally rigorous checks on the truth of the beliefs that they are willing to defend. According to this view, in a sense scientific experts represent an aristocracy of the mind. What then should their role be in a democratic society?

Funtowicz & Ravetz (1985, 1992, 1993) provided a fruitful approach to the expert judgment question by developing a model of the production of scientific knowledge. They emphasized two variables: systems uncertainty and decision stakes (Fig. 3.6). Whereas systems uncertainty contains the three elements of

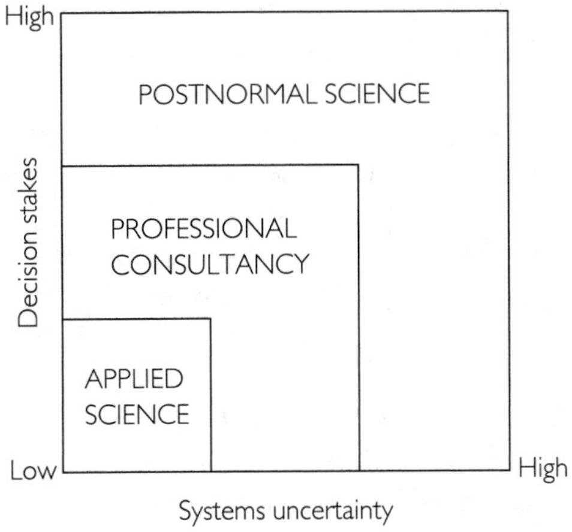

Figure 3.6 Three kinds of science (based on Funtowicz & Ravetz 1985, 1992).

inexactness, uncertainty, and ignorance encountered in technical studies, decision stakes involve the costs or benefits of the various policy options to all interested parties. They use this scheme to distinguish three kinds of science, each with its own style of risk assessment.

Low systems uncertainty and decision stakes describe *applied science* situations in which databases are large and reliable, the opportunities and dangers associated with various decisions are limited, and the technical community largely agrees on appropriate methods of investigation. When both systems uncertainty and decision stakes are considerable, a different style of activity is expected, the mode of *professional consultancy*. This kind of activity involves the use of quantitative tools of risk analysis, supplemented explicitly by experienced qualitative judgment. Professional consultancy is highly relevant in the management of technical and environmental risks, as well as in the management of financial risks.

When decision stakes and systems uncertainty are high, Funtowicz & Ravetz described a scientific style they termed *postnormal science* (earlier on, they used the label *total environmental assessment*). This kind of activity is permeated by qualitative judgments and value commitments. Inquiry, even into technical questions, takes the form largely of a dialogue, which may be in an advocacy or even an adversary mode. Although the proportion of risk assessments that fall into this category is only a limited proportion of the whole, they often are those of greatest political significance.

The idea of postnormal science is closely related to the practice of integrated assessment, which is currently evolving in the field of climate change, as in other fields. So far, integrated assessment has taken mainly two forms. In the first form, large interdisciplinary efforts try to integrate results provided by a variety of scientific disciplines in a process that blends procedures of peer review with political negotiations. A very influential example of this approach is provided by the IPCC process. Peer review is clearly necessary to maintain the credibility of scientific expertise, but it is not sufficient to provide the required integration. The mechanism of peer review is based on specialization by disciplines; integration across disciplines needs additional procedures of quality control. Whether negotiations involving scientists and policymakers will be sufficient for this purpose remains to be seen. They have already helped to launch major interdisciplinary efforts (Stern 1992).

The second form of integrated assessment is the provision of computer models that try to represent problems like those of climate change in an integrated format (see Ch. 5). This means that results from all kinds of disciplines may be used to represent relevant phenomena and possibilities. The problems of quality control met by the first kind of integrated assessment are at least as severe in this case. An additional difficulty arises because every question requiring expertise from a specialized discipline is now intertwined with issues of computer science. Again, combinations of peer review with political negotiations seem to offer an interesting prospect for future efforts in the field. The experience of the RAINS model (Alcamo et al. 1990) clearly suggests that such combinations can be of considerable practical value. However, much remains to be done before viable forms of quality control will have been established in the field of computer-based integrated assessment.

The two forms of integrated assessment that have been developed so far may well be combined, and in the IPCC process such combinations have already begun to take shape. However, both approaches to integrated assessment remain in the mode of professional consultancy. The challenge of postnormal science has not yet been met. As Rayner (1987) noted, although cost–benefit analysis and other decision analytic methodologies are wholly appropriate for the domain of normal science, postnormal science provides a plausible opportunity for applying a cultural perspective. Sociocultural processes are highly relevant to situations of high systems uncertainty and high decision stakes. At the same time, the use of sophisticated computer technology in integrated assessment should facilitate a creative use of insights based on mathematical models in the rational actor paradigm. Integrated assessment, therefore, provides a remarkable opportunity to overcome the dilemma between naïve subjectivism and cultural reductionism (see Ch. 5).

If science is to be helpful in the design of climate policy, it has to find new forms of contributing its insights and doubts to democratic debates about not only the means but also the goals of such policy. How then can science make appropriate contributions?

Opportunities for public participation

An interesting starting point for such a development is given by experiences of public participation in risk assessment. Several formats have been developed for this purpose. For our present purposes, the following possibility is particularly instructive (Renn et al. 1991, 1993). An authority which is preparing a decision involving environmental risks declares that it will follow the consensual results of a public participation procedure in well-specified aspects of its overall decision. If no consensus emerges, however, the authority in question will take an autonomous decision. Next, several discussion groups of ordinary citizens are drawn from the population affected by the decision in question. A set of possible courses of actions is given to each group, together with the following task. First, it should specify the criteria which it deems relevant for the decision to be taken. Second, it should assess the consequences of the various courses of action with regard to these criteria. For this step, each group may hold hearings with scientific experts of its own choice. Third, it should select a course of action on the basis of the preceding steps (for a related procedure, see Dienel 1992).

This procedure blends elements of the rational actor paradigm with an emphasis on social rationality in a promising way. The rational actor component is given by the distinction between alternative courses of action, decision criteria (which correspond to preferences), assessment of consequences (where the main uncertainties have to be dealt with), and the selection of a specific action. Social rationality comes into play with a methodological choice which is very much in line with the well-established practice of using focus groups in marketing and public opinion research. In this case, however, social rationality is used to generate preferences as well as judgments about how to handle uncertainty.

Much further research is needed to assess how and how well this specific procedure works and how it could be further modified for purposes of integrated assessment. Similar procedures deserve the same attention. They include the US National Environmental Policy Act (NEPA) experience (Hildebrand & Cannon 1993), comparative risk projects (Minard et al. 1993), as well as work with citizen advisory committees in different settings (Lynn & Busenberg 1995). All these experiences suggest that advanced integrated assessment requires an iterative process in which citizens, experts, various stakeholders, and policymakers develop a shared system of social learning (Robinson & Timmerman 1993).

Research on advanced integrated assessment may use insights from critical theory to analyze the working of public participation (O'Hara 1996, Habermas 1984, 1991). Central to the critical theory of both Habermas and the early Frankfurt School is the idea that people have contradictory patterns formed by their interests and actions, and that they must and can reflect upon these in the definition of authentic personal and collective needs. One basic tenet of critical theory is that blind pursuit of effective means, without due reflection and justification for the validity of the chosen ends, is potentially exploitative and morally irresponsible. People can ask: How does what we do contradict what we want and need? Critical theory takes seriously the fact that individuals living together need to discuss norms, interests, and values (preferences) in a reasonable way.

Habermas realizes that his claim stands or falls on his ability to provide a convincing explanation of how people can argue in a rational way about normative issues. Here the main element of his argument (and that of cultural theory) comes into play; rationality is a property not of individuals but of social relations. The rational actor paradigm clearly treats rationality as a property of individuals, and so does most modern thinking since the days of the Enlightenment. If this were adequate, decisionmaking could be analyzed and organized in a basically atomistic fashion. However, if rationality is a property of social relations, it is essential to ask what kind of social setting is most conducive to good decisions with regard to specific problems. Where scientific knowledge needs to be combined with moral and aesthetic judgment, a social setting that fosters nonspecialized dialogue is much more appropriate than the setting of applied science or professional consultancy. In this view, the inclusion of the ordinary citizen in schemes of public participation is vital to enhance the level of rationality in the debate in question.

This version of critical theory presents an attractive proposal for how groups of autonomous individuals could rationally and cooperatively select among ends. This theory can be used to explain not only how collective choices about norms and preferences are made, but how they should be made. This is not the same as saying which preferences should be accepted. Preference formation has always been a difficult area for the rational actor paradigm. It cannot explain seemingly irrational behavior, for example risk aversion to some things (nuclear power) and voluntary risk exposure to others (cigarettes) (Slovic 1987). Critical theory may achieve a plausible explanation of preference formation because its conception of rationality is much broader than that of the rational actor paradigm.

Challenges of combining atomistic and social rationality

Generations of researchers have elaborated the atomistic notion of rationality to astonishing levels of sophistication. The separation of reason and values is deeply entrenched, not only in social science research but actually in the fabric of contemporary culture. Indeed, one might be tempted to explain the pervasiveness of behavioral sciences based on atomistic rationality in terms of their functioning as *folk sciences*, providing security and guidance to their clientele, largely independently of their effectiveness in practice (Ravetz 1994–5). In this sense, they serve elites rather like astrology did in the past, when the framework of plausibility was of an enchanted cosmos rather than a universe of billiard-ball atoms (material or personal). Work on social rationality has a remarkable tradition, too, but in comparison it still looks tenuous.

The crucial difference lies in the treatment of economic phenomena. In this area, the rational actor paradigm has a wealth of insights to offer, and it is able to integrate them into a coherent picture with the help of powerful ideas. So far, research about social rationality has tended to accept rational actor views about economic affairs wholesale, and to insist that these views should be complemented by other arguments referring to other topics. This stance can be quite useful in those instances of risk analysis where the weight of economic factors is limited. But in the case of climate change the weight of economic factors is overwhelming. Fossil fuels drive a huge part of the world economy, so much so that they have become a major geopolitical factor.

If the idea of social rationality is to be of real help in dealing with climatic risks, therefore, it needs to be applicable not only to the subtleties of social discourse in various institutional settings but also to the reality of oil prices and global markets. Twenty years ago, such a suggestion would have sounded absurd. Economic reality was to be explained in terms of self-interest and relative scarcities, of competition and the equilibrium of supply and demand. Today, things look different. Various researchers have emphasized the need to study economic phenomena in a more comprehensive framework than the one provided by the rational actor paradigm (Nelson & Winter 1982, Anderson et al. 1988, Burt 1992, Granovetter 1992, Drucker 1993).

In a recent microeconomics textbook, Kreps (1992: 773) concluded his treatment of conventional tools of economic analysis:

> The techniques we have are useful in some contexts, but they are potentially dangerous in others, and even when they are useful, we don't have the complete story why. It remains to develop the tools necessary for the bigger picture and to place the smaller picture properly in that bigger picture.

More specifically, he advances the notion that the solution to the problem of multiple equilibria lies in the individual's strategic expectations, and social and normative environment. This idea has major implications for the analysis of climate change. We will briefly discuss these implications with regard to optimization behavior and to the role of price signals.

We have stressed that the interaction of a multitude of rational actors may easily allow for multiple equilibria, both in the general context of game theory and in the specifically economic setting of general equilibrium theory. This conclusion is hard to grasp as long as one stares at a diagram representing the intersection between a rising supply curve and a falling demand curve. How could there be more than one intersection? The answer has two parts.

The first part refers to situations where the relevant preferences and the available technology lead to a rising supply and a falling demand curve as long as only one price is allowed to vary. In these situations, multiple equilibria can arise out of the interdependence of markets. As soon as there are many supply and demand schedules, each curve starts to move around whenever conditions on other markets change (like a computer screen with a window for each market). Supply and demand of oil are not independent from supply and demand for dollars, and so on for the whole system of markets. In the immediate surroundings of each equilibrium, supply and demand schedules can be drawn in the usual way, but the whole system may have many such equilibria.

The second part of the answer refers to situations where supply and demand curves do not have the familiar slopes. This is especially relevant with regard to supply curves under conditions of increasing returns. Such situations greatly amplify the possibilities for multiple equilibria.

Optimization under conditions of multiple equilibria requires an explicit distinction between their local and global contexts. Local and global here refer to the range of prices and quantities traded on different markets, not to geographical distance. In the local context of a given equilibrium, rational actors may keep optimizing much as they would do in a world with a unique equilibrium. When the global context of a given equilibrium becomes relevant, however, optimization breaks down as a guide for rational action. Technically speaking, individual optimization is of no help in selecting one out of several Nash equilibria. In these situations, the ability to engage in nonoptimizing behavior becomes indispensable. Social rationality is relevant here because it enables interacting agents to select a possible equilibrium by developing mutually compatible expectations (Box 3.4).

The distinction between local and global contexts is crucial for the problem of uncertainty, too (Jaeger & Kasemir 1996). In the local context of a given equilibrium, familiar techniques of dealing with risk and uncertainty may be perfectly adequate. When the global context is relevant, however, uncertainty acquires much greater weight. It may be perfectly reasonable to use cost–benefit analysis to assess the utility of small initiatives in climate policy and to reject its use when it comes to major initiatives. The reason is that small initiatives may nudge the system within a basically unchanged local context, and major initiatives may drive it out of that local context in a situation whose parameters

Box 3.4 Designing a Global Marshall Plan: the relational approach

The design of the original Marshall Plan relied on a social context of rules and expectations which enabled the relevant decisionmakers to proceed without much consideration for the dynamics of public opinion. Political leaders implemented a financial mechanism designed to foster economic reconstruction, and public opinion followed, with a little help from governmental public relations efforts. A global Marshall Plan could not work along these lines. The diplomatic process leading to the Framework Convention on Climate Change would never have happened without the pressure of public opinion increasingly worried about the state of the planet. Public participation is certainly not a sufficient condition, but it is a necessary ingredient of successful international environmental diplomacy in this area. The relationships among science, policy, and public opinion would need careful attention if a Global Marshall Plan were to emerge. In fact, a climate policy based on social rationality would need to follow a thoroughly relational approach.

The relationships among industrialized and less industrialized countries are an essential concern for the design of a Global Marshall Plan. Several aspects need explicit consideration here. The privileged situation of industrialized countries is particularly pronounced when it comes to technological innovation. Industrialized countries have much greater capacity to generate such innovations. Moreover, it is harder for innovations from less industrialized countries to diffuse into the industrialized world than vice versa. Both the generation and the diffusion of innovations involve increasing returns to scale, and therefore lead to path-dependent multiple equilibria. At the same time it is impossible to know what innovations would have happened if history had taken a different turn at some stage. This is why a pure optimization approach is of limited help in designing a Global Marshall Plan. If industrialized countries do not invest a substantial fraction of their innovative capacity in emissions reductions, nothing much will happen. If they do, however, the global economy will follow a different path with its own optima and equilibria. Optimization makes sense along such a path, not for the choice of the path.

Clearly, this does not mean that the self-interest of the parties involved should be ignored; quite the opposite (Edenhofer 1996). The relevant parties must develop the expectation that their self-interest will be fulfilled to a reasonable degree by an effective climate policy if they are to support it. This is especially important for relations with the financial community (Schmidheiny & Zorraquín 1997). It may be achievable with a Global Marshall Plan based on a financial mechanism similar to the one of the original (Box 3.3). Such a mechanism could make technological innovations from industrialized countries quickly available to less industrialized countries, it could trigger economic growth in less industrialized countries, and it would create new export opportunities for industrialized countries. In financial terms, it would generate a flow of resources from industrialized countries to less industrialized countries, with short-run business and employment opportunities for industrialized countries and a long-run prospect of reverse flows of finance once the transition to sustainability has been achieved. These could be obtained without disrupting financial markets with wild swings of exchange rates. Rather it might stabilize them by generating shared expectations of economic growth.

If a Global Marshall Plan depends on the emergence of shared expectations between a multitude of actors with partially conflicting interests, one should not expect this to happen quickly. It will take a long process of social learning for the required trust and competence to evolve, and it will involve structures of governance with new procedures of public participation. Such a process requires many small steps with possibly very limited success, but with one common feature: they should keep the process going, build trust relations, accumulate experience in problem solving. A workable international scheme of tradeable emission permits may stand at the end of the process; it will hardly form its beginning. Still, individual nations or coalitions of nations may implement permit schemes as tools for climate policy, just as others will experiment with carbon taxes and other instruments. Partial success of such policies may foster innovations in technology and lifestyle, leading to lower emisssions, and such innovations may diffuse across national boundaries. If such experiences are brought to resonate with both environmental diplomacy and public opinion, a global Marshall Plan can gradually become a realistic prospect.

cannot all be known in advance. Again, atomistic rationality may be appropriate to deal with the uncertainties inherent in a given local context, whereas social rationality is required to deal with the uncertainties of the global context.

The emerging concept is that of atomistic rationality as embedded in social rationality. Atomistic rationality is a special case appropriate either for theoretical analysis or for real-life situations based on extremely simple decision units. It comes into play whenever a system of interlocked actors is stabilized in such a way as to constitute a self-reproducing pattern of well-defined preferences and opportunities. These conditions are met in the local context of an economic equilibrium. However, social rationality is not limited to non-economic phenomena; it is relevant within the economy whenever the global context of economic equilibria matters.

This picture is reminiscent of Adam Smith's (1776) distinction between market prices and what he called natural prices. Normal prices might be a better label, as Smith referred to shared expectations about what the long-run price of a commodity should be. (In contemporary marketing research, reference prices sometimes play a similar role.) Market prices fluctuate in the neighborhood of a pattern of normal prices. Price theory can then be used to analyze the deviations of market prices from normal prices. As for normal prices, Smith tried to explain them in terms of historically given technologies and consumption patterns. In today's highly innovative economy, this is less than satisfactory as an explanation. It seems more realistic to consider normal prices as social norms which evolve in mutual interaction with technologies and consumption patterns (Jaeger 1994). Prices are part of the social and normative environment that shapes the individual's strategic expectations.

This analysis is highly relevant for the dynamics of oil prices. Over more than a century, oil prices have been remarkably stable despite major shifts in technology and consumption patterns. Over the past two decades, oil prices have been subject to dramatic fluctuations. Nevertheless, these fluctuations have not led to a permanent shift in the normal price of oil. The introduction of a sizeable carbon or energy tax is bound to shake up the pattern of normal prices in the energy sector. This would seriously affect the strategic expectations of major players in the global oil market. They may well take countermeasures to re-establish the normative environment on which they have relied for several generations.

Although normal prices are part of the normative environment that enables economic agents to form mutually compatible expectations, the same is not true of quantities of production. This does not deny that there are social norms referring to quantities. In a specific firm, for example, a manager may be fired because he misses some threshold level of output. However, normal prices are equally relevant for the single firm, for the market in question, and for the economy as a whole. This is not the case for quantities of production, because the quantity produced by a firm is only a fraction of total production.

This asymmetry is highly relevant for the choice between policies affecting prices and policies affecting quantities. The seminal work of Coase (1960) established that a discrepancy between social and individual optimum may be eliminated not only by taxation, but also by the introduction of new property rights. Older analyses of environmental externalities were focused on private property of natural resources. Newer analyses emphasize the possibility of usufructual rights. Tradeable emission permits, for example, would not constitute private property of the atmosphere as such, while they would constitute rights to use the atmosphere for well-defined purposes. In a one-equilibrium economy, taxation and tradeable permits would be basically equivalent. The policy problem of choosing the right level of taxation could be framed as an optimization problem, and the problem of choosing the right amount of emission permits would then be the mathematical dual of that problem. In an economy with multiple equilibria and normal prices, however, this symmetry disappears.

As soon as taxation drives the economy out of the local neighborhood in which it was placed before, major players may start to counteract the taxation scheme in order to maintain their familiar normative environment. One should take quite seriously the possibility that some alliance between OPEC, the United States, and the global oil industry would seek to avoid any major carbon tax scheme. The experience of the oil market suggests that things are different with a quantity target. After all, OPEC did limit global oil production in the past. A quantity target may be set by political decision and implemented by tradeable permits or other means. After a period of transition, the target may be met in another equilibrium with similar normal prices. Although major shifts in consumption patterns and technology are unavoidable, the normative environment constituted by the existing pattern of normal prices can remain quite stable in the long run.

To a large extent, the enormous flexibility of market economies in dealing with technical progress and shifts in demand may depend on its ability to reproduce patterns of normal prices under changing conditions. However, the choice of an emissions target could not be based on an optimization procedure, because the relevant alternatives would go beyond the local environment of the pre-existing situation (Kasemir et al. 1996). Social rationality would be necessary to deal with the uncertainties involved in that decision.

Conclusion

We have seen how the rational actor paradigm deals with such problems as the one of climate change. First, there is the model of a single benevolent planner with perfect knowledge who strives to reach the optimal amount of climate change. For this purpose, the planner needs to correct situations where individual actors can reap the benefits of emitting greenhouse gases without paying for the corresponding costs. Next, the model is modified by introducing some degree of uncertainty. The benevolent planner now acts on the basis of subjective or objective probabilities associated with different possible outcomes. These outcomes are measured in utility units, which express how risk averse the benevolent planner is with regard to climate change. Finally, the fiction of the benevolent planner is dropped with the introduction of multiple actors. They may still realize suboptimal amounts of climate change, but now one should expect many social optima.

Optimizing rationality is unable to select a member of this set. Obviously, one may try to introduce a social welfare function that orders the various multiple equilibria. But this brings us back to the benevolent planner who can achieve consistency only by becoming dictatorial. We have discussed additional difficulties of the rational actor paradigm, in particular the series of paradoxes that arise in conventional risk analysis. We have stressed the practical failures to which these difficulties can lead in risk management, especially with regard to such huge and intractable problems such as climate change. Before this background, we have looked at several approaches to risk analysis which emphasize nonoptimizing, social rationality. These approaches emphasize phenomena such as trust, negotiation, misunderstanding, and communication. In particular, we have looked at the approaches to risk associated with the social amplification of risk, with the sociology of science, with the arena theory of risk, and with the cultural theory of risk. There can be little doubt that risk management in the field of climate change, as in other fields, has much to gain from the awareness of social rationality fostered by these approaches.

We have then looked for ways to avoid the sterile dilemma between blind faith in the explanatory power of the rational actor paradigm and wholesale dismissal of the paradigm in the name of a poorly understood social rationality.

We have argued that this basic problem of current risk studies could be tackled in the emerging field of integrated assessment. For this purpose, advanced tools for integrated assessment need to combine the knowledge of experts, decision-makers, stakeholders, and citizens. By so doing, tools would reintegrate the faculty of reason with the emotional intelligence rooted in the passions, without one being the slave of the other. First experiences along these lines have been collected in a variety of situations dealing with local risks. Taking advantage of these experiences in the integrated assessment of global risks such as climate change requires a critical appraisal of the historical process which has established a professional claim for objective knowledge in risk management. The scientific basis for this claim has been provided by the rational actor paradigm. By now, however, it is necessary and possible to embed the activities of risk professionals in a broader social discourse providing appropriate forms of public participation. This would profoundly affect the role of science in society, in a direction which is sometimes discussed with the concept of postnormal science (Funtowicz & Ravetz 1992).

Perrow (1984) argued that the well-known concept of bounded rationality is an initial step in overcoming the limits of the rational actor paradigm in risk management. Perrow emphasized, however, that the real task is to embed the rational actor paradigm in an understanding of social rationality. Dietz (1994) provided an instructive proposal for such an embedding. He observed that cost–benefit analysis is the standard tool recommended by the rational actor paradigm for decision support in environmental policy. He then claimed that the rational actor paradigm is appropriate for the study of economic phenomena, whereas the study of other phenomena requires a more general theory. He presented some remarkable arguments to the effect that an evolutionary-linguistic model of human agency would be appropriate for that task, but for our present purposes any theory of social rationality could be considered. Finally, he argued that, beyond the legitimate scope of the rational actor paradigm, such a broader theory would favor procedures of public participation rather than cost–benefit analysis.

The strong part of this argument is the revitalization of a basically Aristotelian understanding of democratic policy as the exercise of social rationality. Both means and ends can be fruitfully discussed in democratic debate, and by appropriate procedures agreement about reasonable decisions can be reached. However, the argument is unsatisfactory in its treatment of the rational actor paradigm. If the paradigm were an adequate description of modern economic reality, invoking the ideal of democratic debate would be a helpless gesture in the face of the contemporary global economy. It seems more appropriate to see the rational actor paradigm as a reasonable description of social situations where a set of agents is interlocked in such a way that individual optimization is possible and necessary for each of them. Such situations arise in economic affairs as elsewhere. At the same time, situations where optimizing rationality is of little help abound in economic affairs as elsewhere, too. Therefore, embedding the rational actor paradigm in a broader understanding of social rationality will require a twofold research effort. First, procedures of public participation and stakeholder involvement need to be carefully developed in order to gain a better understanding of their potential and limitations. Second, models of human–environment systems need to be developed so as to gain a better understanding of economic reality than the one provided by the rational actor paradigm.

This will not lead to the dismissal of the rational actor paradigm in favor of some theory of social rationality. Rather, our understanding of social rationality will be enhanced by a critical appraisal of the insights contributed by the rational actor paradigm. As a small, but instructive, example, a client might ask his bank to optimize his portfolio according to state-of-the-art techniques. The bank would confront the client with a schedule of different degrees of risk and ask him to set a limit to what risks he considers acceptable. The client will likely discuss his choice with relatives and friends; he may also ask his bank for additional information, but eventually the choice will be his own. It is only after the lay person has taken that nonoptimizing choice that the sophisticated techniques of optimizing risk management become appropriate.

We should not expect the risks and uncertainties involved in anthropogenic climate change to provide a larger scope for optimizing risk management than the reality of financial markets. Only after basic nonoptimizing decisions have dealt with the huge uncertainties involved in the choice of climate policies do optimizing procedures make sense. This corresponds to the design of the Framework Convention on Climatic Change, which in this respect is sounder than blind believers in optimization may claim.

If all the risks and uncertainties of anthropogenic climate change are fed into optimizing procedures, no solution can be found. Optimization fails where multiple solutions are available, and this is the case here as in many other fields. The frustration about forms of risk management that seem rational in theory but are ineffective in practice threatens the complex pattern of trust relations engendered by a highly differentiated society. This is no minor issue, as trust relations are vital to maintain a sense of *ontological security* (Giddens 1984), without which human beings are prey to despair. The risk society (Beck 1986) is marked by failures to handle specific risks, which end up putting the social fabric itself at risk (Short 1984, Horlick-Jones & De Marchi 1995).

Optimizing risk analysis and management is based on notions of atomistic rationality, whereas nonoptimizing choices are based on capabilities of social rationality. Although a complex interplay of incompatible rationalities may be essential for pluralistic societies, this is not the issue here. It would be sterile to construe an opposition between atomistic and social rationality. The real task is to understand how the former is embedded in the latter. It will take much research until this question is settled.

Such research will investigate the interplay of individual expectations and normative settings in policymaking as well as in the world of business. By so doing, it will clarify the relations between atomistic and social rationality. It will be able to draw on a rich tradition in the investigation of atomistic rationality. As for social rationality, its investigation will lead researchers to create new interfaces between science and a pluralistic society. These interfaces will engage scientists and policy in new forms of dialogue with lay persons. Social rationality is not only part of reality out there, ready to be discovered, described, and interpreted. It is also a possibility that researchers can help to identify and to realize. Through a common dialogue, in which particular contradictions are explored and made the basis of a social learning process, passion can be brought into the definition of goals and evaluation of means, as the true complement of reason. The analysis of climate change and climate policy choices will have much to gain from such an enriched perspective on the process of human choice.

References

Alcamo, J., R. Shaw, L. Hordijk (eds) 1990. *The RAINS model of acidification: science and strategies in Europe.* Dordrecht: Kluwer.

Allais, M. 1953. Le comportement de l'homme rational devant le risque: critique des postulats et axiomes de l'école américaine. *Econometrica* **21**, 503–546.

Anderson, P. W., K. J. Arrow, D. Pines (eds) 1988. *The economy as an evolving complex system.* Redwood City, California: Addison–Wesley.

Anscombe, F. & R. Aumann 1963. A definition of subjective probability. *Annals of Mathematical Statistics* **34**, 199–205.

Arrow, K. J. 1951. *Social choice and individual values.* New York: John Wiley.

——1953. Le rôle des valeurs boursières pour la répartition la meilleure des risques. *Econométrie* **11**, 41–7. [Reprinted as "The role of securities in the optimal allocation of risk bearing"; see Arrow 1984.]

——1970. *Essays in the theory of risk bearing.* Amsterdam: North Holland.

——1984. *Collected papers of Kenneth J. Arrow, 3: individual choice under certainty and uncertainty.* Cambridge, Massachusetts: Harvard University Press (Belknap).

Arrow, K. J. & G. Debreu 1954. Existence of an equilibrium for a competitive economy. *Econometrica* **22**, 265–90.

Arrow, K. J., J. Parikh, G. Pillet, M. Grubb, E. Haites, J. C. Hourcade, K. Parikh, F. Yamin 1996a. Decision-making frameworks for addressing climate change. In *Climate change 1995: economic and social dimensions of climate change,* J. P. Bruce, H. Lee, E. F. Haites (eds). Cambridge: Cambridge University Press.

Arrow, K. J., M. L. Cropper, G. C. Eads, R. W. Hahn, L. B. Lave, R. G. Noll, P. R. Portney, M. Russell, R. Schmalensee, V. K. Smith, R. N. Stavins 1996b. Is there a role for benefit–cost analysis in environmental, health, and safety regulation? *Science* **272**, 221–2.

Arthur, B. W. 1994. *Increasing returns and path dependence in the economy*. Ann Arbor: University of Michigan Press.

Asselt, M. B. A. van & J. Rotmans 1995. *Uncertainty in global modelling: a cultural perspective-based approach*. GLOBO Report Series 9, National Institute of Public Health and Environmental Protection [RIVM], Bilthoven, the Netherlands.

Aumann, R. 1987. Correlated equilibrium as an expression of Bayesian rationality. *Econometrica* **55**, 1–18.

Axelrod, R. M. 1984. *The evolution of cooperation*. New York: Basic Books.

Barke, R. P. & H. C. Jenkins-Smith 1993. Politics and scientific expertise: scientists, risk perception, and nuclear waste policy. *Risk Analysis* **13**, 425–39.

Bayes, T. 1763. Essay towards solving a problem in the doctrine of chances. *Philosophical Transactions of the Royal Society of London* **58**, 24–87.

Beck, U. 1986. *Die Risikogesellschaft: auf dem Weg in eine andere Moderne*. Frankfurt: Suhrkamp.

Bentham, J. 1789. *An introduction to the principles of morals and legislation*. London: Athlone Press.

Bernoulli, D. 1738. Specimen theoriae novae de mensura sortis. *Commentarii Academiae Scientiarum Imperalis Petropolitariae* **5**, 175–92. [Translated in 1954 by L. Sommer in *Econometrica* **22**, 23–36.]

Blackwell, D. & M. A. Grishik 1954. *Theory of games and statistical decisions*. New York: John Wiley.

Bolin, B. 1995. Statement to the first session of the Conference of the Parties to the UN Framework Convention on Climate Change. Mimeo, Conference Secretariat, Berlin.

Bord, R. & R. O'Connor 1990. Risk communication, knowledge, and attitudes: explaining reactions to a technology perceived as risky. *Risk Analysis* **10**, 499–506.

Bostrom, A., M. G. Morgan, B. Fischhoff, D. Read 1994. What do people know about climate change? Part 2: mental models. *Risk Analysis* **14**(6), 959–70.

Bottomore, T. 1984. *The Frankfurt School*. London: Routledge & Kegan Paul.

Bradbury, J. A. 1989. The policy implications of differing concepts of risk. *Science, Technology, and Human Values* **14**, 380–99.

Bradbury, J. A., K. M. Branch, J. H. Heerwagen, E. Liebow 1994. *Community viewpoints of the Chemical Stockpile Disposal Program*. Washington DC: Battelle, Pacific Northwest National Laboratories.

Broome, J. 1992. *Counting the cost of global warming*. Cambridge: White Horse Press.

Burt, R. S. 1992. *Structural holes: the social structure of competition*. Cambridge, Massachusetts: Harvard University Press.

Coase, R. A. 1960. The problem of social cost. *Journal of Law and Economics* **3**, 1–44.

Cohen, B. 1985. A reply to Dr Otway. *Risk Analysis* **5**, 275–6.

Coppock, R. 1986. *Regulating chemical hazards in Japan, West Germany, France, the United Kingdom, and the European Community: a comparative examination*. Washington DC: National Academy Press.

Covello, V., B. McCallum, M. Pavlova (eds) 1989. *Effective risk communication, contemporary issues*. New York: Plenum.

Curtiss Priest, W. 1988. *Risks, concerns and social legislation: forces that led to laws on health, safety, and the environment*. Boulder, Colorado: Westview.

Dake, K. 1991. Orienting dispositions in the perception of risk. An analysis of contemporary worldviews and cultural biases. *Journal of Cross-Cultural Psychology* **22**, 61–82.

—— 1992. Myths of nature: culture and the social construction of risk. *Journal of Social Issues* **48**, 21–37.

Dake, K. & A. Wildavsky 1991. Individual differences in risk perception and risk taking preferences. In *The analysis, communication and perception of risk*, B. J. Garrick, & C. Gekler (eds). New York: Plenum.

Dake, K. & M. Thompson 1993. The meanings of sustainable development: household strategies for managing needs and resources. In *Human ecology: crossing boundaries*, S. D. Wright, T. Dietz, R. Borden, G. Young, G. Guagnano (eds). Fort Collins, Colorado: Society for Human Ecology.

Daly, H. E. & J. J. Cobb 1989. *For the common good*. Boston: Beacon Press.

De Finetti, B. 1974. *Theory of probability*. New York: John Wiley.

Debreu, G. 1959. *Theory of value, an axiomatic analysis of economic equilibrium*. New York: John Wiley.

Dienel, P. C. 1992. *Die Planungszelle*. Opladen: Westdeutscher.

Dietz, T. 1994. What should we do? Human ecology and collective decisionmaking. *Human Ecology Review* **1**, 301–309.

Dietz, T. & R. Rycroft 1987. *The risk professionals*. New York: Russell Sage Foundation.

Douglas, M. 1966. *Purity and danger: concepts of pollution and taboo*. London: Routledge & Kegan Paul.

——1978. *Cultural bias*. Occasional Paper 35, Royal Anthropological Institute, London. [Reprinted in *In the active voice*, M. Douglas. London: Routledge, 1982.]

——1985. *Risk acceptability according to the social sciences*. New York: Russell Sage Foundation.

Douglas, M. & A. Wildavsky 1982. *Risk and culture: an essay on the selection of technical and environmental dangers*. Berkeley, California: University of California Press.

Drucker, P. F. 1993. *Post-capitalist society*. New York: HarperCollins.

Earle, T. C. & G. Cvetkovich 1998. Social trust and culture in risk management. In *Social trust: advances in concepts and research*, G. Cvetkovitch & R. Löfstedt (eds). London: Earthscan.

Easton, D. 1965. *A framework for political analysis*. Englewood Cliffs, New Jersey: Prentice-Hall.

Economists' Statement on Climate Change 1997. [Electronic document.] San Francisco: Redefining Progress (e-mail: info@RProgress.org).

Edenhofer, O. 1996. Das Management globaler allmenden. In *Umweltsoziologie*, A. Diekmann & C. Jaeger (eds). *Kölner Zeitschrift für Soziologie und Sozialpsychologie* **36**, 390–419 [special issue].

Edgeworth, F. Y. 1881. *Mathematical psychics*. London: Kegan Paul.

Ellsberg, D. 1961. Risk, ambiguity, and the savage axioms. *Quarterly Journal of Economics* **75**, 643–69.

Fernando, C. S., P. R. Kleindorfer, M. Munasinghe 1993. *Economic design for implementing the Montreal Protocol: country plans and global efficiency*. Divisional Working Paper 1993-41, Environment Department, World Bank, Washington DC.

Fischer, G., M. G. Morgan, B. Fischhoff, I. Nair, L. Lave 1991. What risks are people concerned about? *Risk Analysis* **11**, 303–314.

Fischhoff, B. & L. Furby 1983. Psychological dimensions of climatic change. In *Social science research and climatic change: an interdisciplinary appraisal*, R. S. Chen, E. Boulding, S. H. Schneider (eds). Dordrecht: Reidel.

Fischhoff, B., P. Slovic, S. Lichtenstein, S. Read, B. Combs 1978. How safe is safe enough? A psychometric study of attitudes toward technological risks and benefits. *Policy Sciences* **9**, 127–52.

Fishburn, P. C. 1988. *Nonlinear preference and utility theory*. Baltimore: Johns Hopkins University Press.

Friedman, M. & L. J. Savage 1952. The expected utility hypothesis and the measurability of utility. *Journal of Political Economy* **60**, 463–75.

Funtowicz, S. O. & J. R. Ravetz 1985. Three types of risk assessment: a methodological analysis. In *Risk analysis in the private sector*, C. Whipple & V. T. Covello (eds). New York: Plenum.

——1992. Three types of risk assessment and the emergence of post-normal science. In *Social theories of risk*, S. Krimsky & D. Golding (eds). Westport, Connecticut: Praeger.

——1993. Science for the post normal age. *Futures* **25**, 739–56.

——1994. The worth of a songbird: ecological economics as a post-normal science. *Ecological Economics* **10**, 197–207.

Gan, L. 1993. The making of the Global Environmental Facility: an actor's perspective. *Global Environmental Change* **3**(3), 256–75.
Giddens, A. 1984. *The constitution of society: outline of the theory of structuration*. Cambridge: Polity.
Goffman, E. 1959. *The presentation of self in everyday life*. New York: Free Press.
Gore, A. 1992. *Earth in the balance: ecology and the human spirit*. Boston: Houghton Mifflin.
Granovetter, M. 1992. Economic institutions as social constructions: a framework for analysis. *Acta Sociologica* **35**, 3–11.
Gross, J. L. & S. Rayner 1985. *Measuring culture*. New York: Columbia University Press.

Habermas, J. 1984. *The theory of communicative action* [2 vols]. Boston: Beacon Press.
—— 1991. *Moral consciousness and communicative action*. Cambridge, Massachusetts: MIT Press.
Hacking, I. 1975. *The emergence of probability: a philosophical study of early ideas about probability, induction and statistical inference*. Cambridge: Cambridge University Press.
Hanley, N. 1992. Are there environmental limits to cost–benefit analysis? *Environmental and Resource Economics* **2**, 33–59.
Hicks, J. R. 1939. The foundations of welfare economics. *Economic Journal* **49**, 696–712.
Hildebrand, S. G. & J. B. Cannon (eds) 1993. *Environmental analysis: the NEPA experience*. Boca Raton, Florida: Lewis.
Hilgartner, S. & C. L. Bosk 1988. The rise and fall of social problems: a public arenas model. *American Journal of Sociology* **94**, 53–78.
Hobbes, T. 1651. *Leviathan*. London: A. Crooke. [Reissued, edited by C. B. Macpherson. Harmondsworth, England: Penguin, 1968.]
Holling, C. S. 1986. The resilience of terrestrial ecosystems: local surprise and global change. In *Sustainable development of the biosphere*, W. Clark & R. Munn (eds). Cambridge: Cambridge University Press.
Horlick-Jones, T. & B. De Marchi 1995. The crisis of scientific expertise in fin de siècle Europe. *Science and Public Policy* **22**, 139–45.

Jacobs, J. 1992. *Systems of survival: a dialogue on the moral foundations of commerce and politics*. New York: Vintage Books.
Jaeger, C. C. 1994. *Taming the dragon: transforming economic institutions in the face of global change*. Yverdon, Switzerland: Gordon & Breach.
Jaeger, C. C., O. Renn, E. A. Rosa, T. Webler 1995. *Risk, uncertainty, and rational action*. Unpublished paper, Swiss Federal Institute for Environmental Science and Technology [EAWAG], Zürich.
Jaeger, C. C. & B. Kasemir 1996. Climatic risks and rational actors. *Global Environmental Change* **6**, 23–36.
Jasanoff, S. 1982. Science and the limits of administrative rule making: lessons from the OSHA cancer policy. *Osgood Law Journal* **20**, 536–61.
Jenkins-Smith, H. C. & W. K. Smith 1994. Ideology, culture, and risk perception. In *Politics, policy and culture*, D. J. Coyle, & R. J. Ellis (eds). Boulder, Colorado: Westview.

Kahneman, D. & A. Tversky 1979. Prospect theory: an analysis of decision under risk. *Econometrica* **21**, 503–546.
Kahneman, D., P. Slovic, A. Tversky (eds) 1982. *Judgment under uncertainty: heuristics and biases*. Cambridge: Cambridge University Press.
Kasemir, B., C. C. Jaeger, O. Edenhofer 1996. Structures of complementarity, benefit–cost analysis and integrated environmental assessment. Paper presented to the "Ecology, society, economy – in pursuit of sustainable development" conference, Paris, 23–25 May.
Kasperson, R. E., O. Renn, S. Slovic, H. Brown, J. Emel, R. Goble, J. Kasperson, S. Ratick 1988. The social amplification of risk: a conceptual framework. *Risk Analysis* **8**, 177–87.
Kempton, W. 1991. Lay perspectives on global climate change. *Global Environmental Change* **1**, 183–208.

Kirman, A. P. 1992. Whom or what does the representative individual represent? *Journal of Economic Perspectives* **6**, 117–36.
Kitschelt, H. 1980. *Kernenergiepolitik: Arena eines gesellschaftlichen Konflikts*. Frankfurt: Campus.
Knight, F. H. 1921. *Risk, uncertainty and profit*. Boston: Houghton Mifflin.
Koopmans, T. C. (ed.) 1951. *Activity analysis of production and allocation*. New York: John Wiley.
Kreps, D. M. 1992. *A course in microeconomic theory*. New York: Harvester Wheatsheaf.
Krimsky, S. & D. Golding (eds) 1992. *Social theories of risk*. Westport, Connecticut: Praeger.
Kunreuther, H., R. Ginsberg, L. Miller, P. Sagi, P. Slovic, B. Borkan, N. Katz 1978. *Disaster insurance protection: public policy lessons*. New York: John Wiley.

Lasswell, H. 1958. *Politics*. Cleveland, Ohio: Meridian.
Lave, T. & L. Lave 1991. Public perception of the risks of floods: implications for communication. *Risk Analysis* **11**, 255–67.
Leiss, W. & D. Krewski 1989. Risk communication: theory and practice. In *Prospects and problems in risk communications*, W. Leiss (ed.). Waterloo, Ontario: University of Waterloo Press.
Lichtenstein, S., B. Fischhoff, L. D. Phillips 1982. Calibration of probabilities: the state of the art to 1990. See Kahneman et al. (1982).
Lindblom, C. 1977. *Politics and markets: the world's political and economic systems*. New York: Basic Books.
Löfstedt, R. 1991. Climate change perceptions and energy-use decisions in northern Sweden. *Global Environmental Change* **1**, 321–4.
Lowrance, W. W. 1976. *On acceptable risk: science and the determination of safety*. Los Altos, California: William Kaufman.
Lynn, F. M. & G. J. Busenberg 1995. Citizen advisory committees and environmental policy: what we know, what's left to discover. *Risk Analysis* **15**, 147–62.

Machina, M. 1982. Expected utility analysis without the independence axiom. *Econometrica* **50**, 277–323.
Machlis, G. E. & E. A. Rosa 1990. Desired risk: broadening the social amplification of risk framework. *Risk Analysis* **10**, 161–8.
Manne, A. & R. Richels 1995. The greenhouse debate: economic efficiency, burden sharing and hedging strategies. *The Energy Journal* **16**, 1–37.
March, J. & H. Simon 1958. *Organizations*. New York: John Wiley.
Marris, C., I. Langford, T. O'Riordan 1996. *Integrating sociological and psychological approaches to public perception of environmental risks*. Working Paper GEC 96-07, Centre for Social and Economic Research on the Global Environment [CSERGE], University of East Anglia.
Marshall, I. A. 1890. *Principles of economics*. New York: Macmillan.
McDaniels, T., L. J. Axelrod, P. Slovic 1995. Characterizing perception of ecological risk. *Risk Analysis* **15**, 575–88.
McDonell, G. 1991. Intellectual sources of the idea of "acceptable risk". *Public Policy* **GE15**(1), 69–75.
Merkhofer, M. 1984. Comparative analysis of formal decision making approaches. In *Risk evaluation and management*, V. T. Covello, J. Menkes, J. Mumpower (eds). New York: Plenum.
Milgrom, P. & J. Roberts 1992. *Economics, organization and management*. Englewood Cliffs, New Jersey: Prentice-Hall.
Minard, R., K. Jones, C. Paterson 1993. *State comparative risk projects: a force for change*. South Royalton, Vermont: Northeast Center for Comparative Risk.
Mitchell, J. 1992. Perception of risk and credibility at toxic sites. *Risk Analysis* **12**, 19–26.
Morgan, G. M. & M. Henrion 1990. *Uncertainty: a guide to dealing with uncertainty in quantitative risk and policy analysis*. Cambridge: Cambridge University Press.
Morgan, G. M. & D. Keith 1994. Climate change: subjective judgments by climate experts. *Environmental Science and Technology* **29**, 468–76.

Nelkin, D. (ed.) 1979. *Controversy: politics of technical decisions*. Beverly Hills, California: Sage.

Nelkin, D. & M. Pollack 1980. Consensus and conflict resolution: the politics of assessing risk. In *Technological risk: its perception and handling in the European Community*, M. Dierkes, S. Edwards, R. Coppock (eds). Cambridge, Massachusetts: Oelgeschlager, Gunn & Hain.

Nelson, R. R. & S. G. Winter 1982. *An evolutionary theory of economic change*. Cambridge, Massachusetts: Harvard University Press.

Neumann, J. von & O. Morgenstern 1947. *Theory of games and economic behaviour*. Princeton, New Jersey: Princeton University Press.

Nordhaus, W. D. 1994. *Managing the global commons: the economics of climate change*. Cambridge, Massachusetts: MIT Press.

O'Hara, S. U. 1996. Discursive ethics in ecosystem valuation and environmental policy. *Ecological Economics* **16**, 95–107.

O'Riordan, T. & B. Wynne 1987. Regulating environmental risks: a comparative perspective. In *Insuring and managing hazardous risks: from Seveso to Bhopal and beyond*, P. R. Kleindorfer & H. C. Kunreuther (eds). Berlin: Springer.

O'Riordan, T. & S. Rayner 1991. Risk management for global environmental change. In *Global Environmental Change* **1**(2), 91–108.

Otway, H. 1992. Public wisdom, expert fallibility: toward a contextual theory of risk. See Krimsky & Golding (1992).

Otway, H. & D. von Winterfeldt 1992. Expert judgement in risk analysis and management: process, context and pitfalls. *Risk Analysis* **12**, 83–93.

Otway, H. & B. Wynne 1989. Risk communication: paradigm and paradox. *Risk Analysis* **9**, 141–5.

Pahl-Wöstl, C., C. C. Jaeger, S. Rayner, C. Schaer, M. B. A. van Asselt, D. Imboden, A. Vckovski in press. Integrated assessment of climate change and the problem of indeterminacy. In *Climate and environment in the Alpine region—an interdisciplinary view*, P. Cebon, H. Davies, D. Imboden, C. C. Jaeger (eds). Cambridge, Massachusetts: MIT Press.

Palmlund, I. 1992. Social drama and risk evaluation. See Krimsky & Golding (1992).

Pareto, V. 1906. *Manuale di economica politica, con una introduzione alle scienze soziale*. Milano: Societa Editrice Libraria.

Perrow, C. 1984. *Normal accidents: living with high-risk technologies*. New York: Basic Books.

Pratt, J. W. 1964. Risk aversion in the small and in the large. *Econometrica* **32**, 122–36.

Ravetz, J. 1994–5. Economics as an elite folk science: the suppression of uncertainty. *Journal of Post Keynesian Economics* **17**, 165–84.

Rayner, S. 1984. Disagreeing about risk: the institutional cultures of risk management and planning for future generations. In *Risk analysis, institutions and public policy*, S. G. Hadden (ed.). Port Washington, New York: Associated Faculty Press.

——1986. Management of radiation hazards in hospitals: plural rationalities in a single institution. *Social Studies of Science* **16**, 573–91.

——1987. Risk and relativism in science for policy. In *The social and cultural construction of risk*, B. B. Johnson & V. T. Covello (eds). Dordrecht: Reidel.

——1988. Muddling through. From metaphors to maturity: a commentary on Kasperson et al., "The social amplification of risk." *Risk Analysis* **8**, 21.

——1991. A cultural perspective on the structure and implementation of global environmental agreement. *Evaluation Review* **15**, 75–102.

——1992. Cultural theory and risk analysis. See Krimsky & Golding (1992).

Rayner, S. & R. Cantor 1987. How fair is safe enough? The cultural approach to societal technology choice. *Risk Analysis* **7**, 3–13.

Read, D., A. Bostrom, M. G. Morgan, B. Fischhoff, T. Smuts 1994. What do people know about climate change, part 2: survey studies of educated lay people. *Risk Analysis* **14**, 971–82.

Renn, O. 1989. Risikowahrnehmung—psychologische Determinanten bei der intuitiven

Erfassung und Bewertung von technischen Risiken. In *Risiko in der Industriegesellschaft*, G. Hosemann (ed.). Nürnberg: Universitätsbibliothek.

——1992. The social arena concept of risk debates. See Krimsky & Golding (1992).

Renn, O., T. Webler, B. Johnson 1991. Citizen participation for hazard management. *Risk Issues in Health and Safety* **3**, 12–22.

Renn, O., W. Burns, J. X. Kasperson, R. E. Kasperson, P. Slovic 1992. The social amplification of risk: theoretical foundations and empirical applications. *Journal of Social Issues* **48**, 137–59.

Renn, O., T. Webler, H. Rakel, P. C. Dienel, B. Johnson 1993. Public participation in decision making: a three-step-procedure. *Policy Sciences* **26**, 189–214.

Robbins, L. 1932. *An essay on the nature and significance of economic science*. London: Macmillan.

Robinson, J. B. 1992. Risks, predictions and other optical illusions: rethinking the use of science in social decision making. *Policy Sciences* **25**, 237–54.

Robinson, J. B. & P. Timmerman 1993. Myths, rules, artifacts and ecosystems. In *Framing the human dimensions of global change*, S. D. Wright, T. Dietz, R. Borden, G. Young, G. Guagnano (eds). Colorado: Society for Human Ecology.

Rohrmann, B. 1991. *A survey of social-scientific research on risk perception*. Studies on Risk 6, Communication Research Center, Jülich, Germany.

Ronge, V. 1982. Risks and the waning of compromise in politics. In *The risk analysis controversy: an institutional perspective*, H. Kunreuther & E. Leys (eds). Laxenburg: IIASA.

Roth, E., M. G. Morgan, B. Fischhoff, L. Lave, A. Bostrom 1990. What do we know about making risk comparisons? *Risk Analysis* **10**, 375–87.

Rotmans, J. (ed.) 1995. *TARGETS in transition*. Bilthoven, the Netherlands: National Institute of Public Health and Environmental Protection [RIVM].

Rotmans, J., M. B. A. van Asselt, A. J. de Bruin, M. G. J. den Elzen, J. de Greef, H. Hilderink, A. Y. Hoekstra, M. A. Janssen, H. W. Köster, W. J. M. Martens, L. W. Niessen, H. J. M. de Vries 1994. *Global change and sustainable development: a modelling perspective for the next decade*. GLOBO Report Series 4, National Institute of Public Health and Environmental Protection [RIVM], Bilthoven, the Netherlands.

Rowe, W. D. 1977. *An anatomy of risk*. New York: John Wiley.

Royal Society, Study Group on Risk Assessment 1983. *Risk assessment: a study group report*. London: Royal Society.

Saul, J. R. 1992. *Voltaire's bastards: the dictatorship of reason in the West*. Toronto: Penguin.

Savage, L. 1954. *The foundations of statistics*. New York: John Wiley [Revised and enlarged edn, New York: Dover Publications, 1972.]

Schaffer, S. 1988. The risk conspiracy. *The Times Literary Supplement* (April 8–14), 392, 404.

Schmidheiny, S. & F. Zorraquin 1996. *Financing change*. Cambridge, Massachusetts: MIT Press.

Schmidt, F. & R. Gifford 1989. A dispositional approach to hazard perception: preliminary development of the environmental appraisal inventory. *Journal of Environmental Psychology* **9**, 57–67.

Schwarz, M. & M. Thompson 1990. *Divided we stand: redefining politics, technology and social choice*. Philadelphia: University of Pennsylvania Press.

Sen, A. K. 1995. Rationality and social choice. *American Economic Review* **85**(1),1–24.

Short, J. F. 1984. The social fabric at risk: toward the social transformation of risk analysis. *American Sociological Review* **49**, 711–25.

Simon, H. A. 1955. A behavioral model of rational choice. *Quarterly Journal of Economics* **69**, 99–118.

——1961. *Administrative behaviour*, 2nd edn. New York: Macmillan.

——1976. *Administrative behavior*, 3rd edn. New York: Free Press.

Sjöberg, L. 1995. Explaining risk perception: an empirical and quantitative evaluation of cultural theory. Paper presented at the Annual Meeting of the Society for Risk Analysis (Europe), "Risk analysis and management in a global economy", Forum Ludwigsburg, Stuttgart, Germany.

Slovic, P. 1987. Perception of risk. *Science* **236**, 280–85.
——1992. Perception of risk: reflections on the psychometric paradigm. See Krimsky & Golding (1992).
Slovic, P., B. Fischhoff, S. Lichtenstein 1979. Rating the risks. *Environment* **21**(3), 14–39.
——1980. Facts and fears—understanding risk. In *Societal risk assessment*, R. C. Schwing & W. A. Albers (eds). New York: Plenum.
Slovic, P., M. Layman, J. Flynn 1991. Risk perception, trust and nuclear waste: lessons from Yucca Mountain. *Environment* **33**, 6–11, 28–30.
Smith, A. 1976 (1776). *An inquiry into the nature and causes of the wealth of nations*, R. H. Campbell, A. S. Skinner, W. B. Todd (eds). Oxford: Oxford University Press.
Smith, V. K. (ed.) 1986. Benefit–cost analysis and risk assessment. In *Advances in applied micro-economics*, vol. 4: *Risk, uncertainty, and the valuation of benefits and costs*. Greenwich, Connecticut: JAI Press.
Starr, C. 1969. Social benefit versus technological risk. *Science* **165**(September), 1232–8. [Reprinted in *Environmental risks and hazards*, S. L. Cutter (ed.). Englewood Cliffs, New Jersey: Prentice-Hall, 1994].
Stern, P. 1992. *Global environmental change: understanding the human dimensions*. Washington DC: National Academy of Sciences.
Stewart, T. & M. Glantz 1985. Expert judgment and climate forecasting: a methodological critique of "Climate Change to the Year 2000". *Climate Change* **7**, 159–83.

Thompson, M. 1982. A three-dimensional model. In *Essays in the sociology of perception*, M. Douglas (ed.). London: Routledge & Kegan Paul.
Thompson, M., R. Ellis, A. Wildavsky 1990. *Cultural theory*. Boulder, Colorado: Westview.
Tocqueville, A. de 1945(1840). *De la démocratie en Amérique* [translated by P. Bradley as *Democracy in America*]. New York: Knopf.
Tribe, L. H. 1973. Technology assessment and the fourth discontinuity: the limits of instrumental rationality. *Southern California Law Review* **46**, 617–60.
Tversky, A. & D. Kahneman 1974. Judgement under uncertainty: heuristics and biases. *Science* **185**, 1124–31.

US NRC [US National Research Council] (Committee on Risk and Decision Making) 1982. *Risk and decision making: perspectives and research*. Washington DC: National Academy Press.
——(Committee on the Institutional Means for Assessment of Risks to Public Health) 1983. *Risk assessment in the federal government: managing the process*. Washington DC: National Academy Press.
——(Committee on Risk Perception and Communication) 1989. *Improving risk communication*. Washington DC: National Academy Press.
——1996. *Understanding risk in a democratic society*. Washington DC: National Academy of Sciences.
US Office of Technology Assessment 1993. *Preparing for an uncertain climate: summary*. Washington DC: Office of Technology Assessment, United States Congress.

Walras, L. 1926. *Eléments d'économie politique pure ou théorie de la richesse sociale*, 4th edn. Paris: Pichon.
Wigley, T. M. L., R. Richels, J. A. Edmonds 1996. Economic and environmental choices in the stabilization of atmospheric CO_2 concentrations. *Nature* **379**, 240–43.
Wildavsky, A. & K. Dake 1990. Theories of risk perception: who fears what and why? *Daedalus* **119**, 41–60.
Williamson, H. 1975. *Markets and hierarchies: analysis and antitrust implications*. New York: Free Press.
Winner, L. 1986. Risk: another name for danger. *Science for the People* **18**, 5–11.
Wynne, B. 1982. *Rationality and ritual: the Windscale Inquiry and nuclear decisions in Britain*. Chalfont St Giles, England: British Society for the History of Science.

——1987. *Risk management and hazardous waste: implementation and the dialectics of credibility.* New York: Springer.
——1989a. Building public concern into risk management. In *Environmental threats: perception, analysis and management*, J. Brown (ed.). London: Pinter (Belhaven).
——1989b. Sheepfarming after Chernobyl: a case study in communicating scientific information. *Environment* **31**, 10–15, 33–9.
——1989c. Frameworks of rationality in risk management: towards the testing of naïve sociology. In *Environmental threats: perception, analysis and management*, J. Brown (ed.). London: Pinter (Belhaven).
——1991. Knowledges in context. *Science, Technology, and Human Values* **16**, 111–21.
——1992. Risk and social learning: reification to engagement. See Krimsky & Golding (1992).

CHAPTER 4

Reasoning by analogy

William B. Meyer, Karl W. Butzer, Thomas E. Downing,
B. L. Turner II, George W. Wenzel, James L. Wescoat

Researchers can assess the novel challenges and opportunities that global climate change may present to human beings and activities by examining how similar challenges and opportunities already posed have been met. Using the experiences of individuals, groups, and places in other times and in the contemporary world as analogues for climate change may help to refine our sense of how important such climate changes would be, help "to determine how flexible (or rigid) societies are or have been in dealing with climate-related environmental changes," and "help us to identify societal strengths and weaknesses in coping . . . so that we can reinforce those strengths and reduce the weaknesses" (Glantz 1988: 3–4). Reasoning by analogy has dangers and limitations as well as uses. That analogues are likely to be employed in discussions of climate change makes an assessment of the method all the more important.

Innumerable past situations may be compared or contrasted to aspects of global climate change and its human dimensions. Chapters in this assessment invoke specific analogues ranging from the demographic transition in Europe (Vol. 1, Ch. 2) to past diffusion of new technologies (Vol. 2, Ch. 5) to experience with international agreements and successes and failures with the use of particular regulatory control instruments (Vol. 2, Ch. 5). The possible scope of a chapter on analogues is enormous. For the sake of manageability and of thematic unity, the actual scope of this chapter is much narrower, focusing on past human interactions with climate and environmental realms closely related to it. The chapter further homes in on integrated assessments—that is, on studies that deal with the interaction of areas ordinarily treated by topical specialists in different fields—and on studies primarily qualitative in method and regional or local in scale. (More formal methods of integrated assessment are dealt with in Ch. 5.)

Bounding the topic of climate change analogues in this way still encompasses a large literature and the bulk of what the human sciences have said about actual human interaction with climate and its variations to date. We examine that literature with two goals in mind. The first is to illustrate the uses and limitations of reasoning by analogy as a method for assessing global climate change. The second is to present such lessons about climate and society relevant to global climate change as can be derived from the analogies that we examine.

Climate, human affairs, and the human sciences

The climate and society literature that we review in this chapter consists of two bodies of work. Some studies explicitly draw analogies between the material analyzed and the human dimensions of global climate change. Others analyze the material in ways that permit such analogies to be drawn. The former literature is much smaller than the latter, but neither is as large as it might be. An inventory of climate and society analogues does not have a rich or well-tested body of work on which to draw, because the social sciences during the twentieth century have paid little attention to climate–society interaction.

Most disciplines have done so deliberately rather than by mere neglect. The trend of Western sociological theory and research during most of the twentieth century has been, on principle, to exclude the biophysical environment ever more thoroughly from consideration (Catton & Dunlap 1980, Guterbock 1990). In development economics, early excesses of climatic determinism gave way by mid-century to a tendency to reject climate a priori as a significant factor (Myrdal 1968). Seasonality in economic data is not necessarily attributable to climate but is a good place to look for climatic influences; forsaking earlier traditions (e.g., Kuznets 1933), however, macroeconomists after mid-century devoted much more effort to removing seasonal trends from data than to accounting for them (Barsky & Miron 1989). Even in geography, the social science most attentive to climate and the biophysical world, an early school of thought that assigned them a large role in controlling human affairs provoked a reaction that discouraged any attention to the environmental dimensions of human activity (Rostlund 1956, Lewthwaite 1966, Hewitt & Hare 1973). Although social scientists clearly showed the biophysical environment to be less overwhelmingly important in human affairs than environmental determinists had painted it, they did not show conclusively that it was unimportant. In geography, "environmentalism was not disproved, only disapproved" (Rostlund 1956). There appear to be two main reasons for its banishment: the first was a desire to claim a subject matter for the social sciences independent of the natural sciences; the second was a widespread distaste for what many took to be the reactionary, racist, or imperialist implications of asserting the environment's importance, and particularly that of climate (Guterbock 1990, Bassin 1992).

The general trend notwithstanding, climate–society interactions remained of interest to many individuals and even subfields in the mid-twentieth-century human sciences, such as the Annales school in history, crop–climate modeling in agricultural economics, cultural ecology in anthropology and geography, and multidisciplinary research on natural hazards. A wider interest became evident during the 1970s. Schneider & Mesirow (1976) and Bryson & Murray (1977) warned of the threat that climate change and instability might pose to society. Several major syntheses of existing research appeared early in the next decade. Rotberg & Rabb (1981) and Wigley et al. (1981) took stock of the methods, findings, and further agenda of work on prehistoric and historic climate–society interactions. Kates et al. (1985) reviewed the application of diverse impact assessment methods to climate variation as a natural hazard. Chen et al. (1983) assembled overviews of the state of knowledge in the major social science disciplines specifically relevant to the challenges of climate change.

The work reviewed in all of these volumes offers useful analogues for climate change. In a further development, Glantz & Ausubel (1984) pioneered the explicit use of analogy as a method of research into global climate change and society. It has been pursued since by international collaborative research efforts (Glantz 1988, 1992, Schmandt & Clarkson 1992, Kammen et al. 1994) as well as by individual researchers. Contributors to Glantz (1988) examined North American cases of various climate-related environmental challenges—aquifer drawdown, river and lake-level variation, agricultural and urban drought, and frost—as analogues for impacts of and responses to change.

In the following sections, we assess studies explicitly drawing analogies between other events and global climate change, and also climate–society research allowing such analogies to be made. We first examine the concept, the uses, and the limits of analogues, and illustrate by considering the use of the urban climate as an analogue for global climate change. Then, in succession, we review archaeological analogues, historical and contemporary analogues of climate as hazard, and historical and contemporary analogues of climate as resource. We conclude by summing up the lessons drawn and suggesting avenues for research.

Analogues and climate–society research

Distinguishing between formal and heuristic analogies is useful (Hesse 1966). A *formal* argument by analogy typically depends upon evidence of one individual having several properties, yielding inference of unknown properties in another individual known to be similar to the first in key respects. Less rigorous *heuristic* analogies between past and future climate–society relations or between those in different places are far more common. They are heuristic because they are too complex or too contextually different to be formally specified. The analyst draws upon them selectively to develop a chain of ideas about climate–society relations, and valuable lessons may be learned from the process of drawing the analogy. By and large, the analogues discussed or drawn in this chapter are heuristic rather than formal.

We might also distinguish between temporal and spatial analogues: those comparing sequences of events and those comparing characteristics of places. In the latter vein, Ullman (1967) proposed a *geographical analogue method* as a way to assess the consequences of introducing in one place something that is already present in another and otherwise similar place. The approach has not been systematically developed as a method within social science, although versions of it are sometimes used ad hoc. They have long been used in decisionmaking, with varying degrees of success. Early settlers of North America made the costly mistake of supposing that latitude–climate relationships in western Europe would hold true on the other side of the Atlantic, and therefore that crop choices appropriate in Old World locations could be duplicated at the same parallels in the New (Kupperman 1982). Agricultural development in early and mid-twentieth century Morocco was guided more successfully by an explicit analogy with agriculture in California, which was seen as representing a similar biophysical environment offering similar opportunities and constraints (Swearingen 1987). The analogues discussed or drawn in this chapter tend to mix the temporal and spatial, but with an emphasis on the former. They principally take the approach of qualitative examinations of particular episodes, events, and communities: historical narratives, anthropological ethnographies, theoretically informed case studies.

Heuristic analogies can offer illumination in various ways. Differences as well as similarities between cases can be sources of insight; Turner (1988) argued that one of the principal aims of analogy is to shake up conventional categories of thought by making associations with unlike categories. Analogues can increase awareness of possible surprises and of response options that have been neglected or ignored, and they can sensitize researchers to the extent and character of real-world variations from idealized models. They can also be a means of translating scientific understanding into terms meaningful to the lay public (Kearney 1994). Their concrete character gives them a compelling vividness in scientific and popular discourse alike; their basis in actual experience can give them an advantage in plausibility over modeled quantitative scenarios. Even if they do not offer explicit guidance they can admirably serve the purpose of enlightenment, which may indeed be the most useful actual contribution of social science to policy.

Analogies have been widely used in scientific, popular, and policy discussions of global climate change. The term *greenhouse effect* itself is an analogy (and a faulty one). So is the description of human release of greenhouse gases to the atmosphere as a large-scale geophysical experiment (e.g., Revelle & Suess 1957). The hot and dry summer of 1988 in the United States was taken by many lay and some scientific observers as representative of a future under global climate change (Ungar 1992). Weather events, such as unusual heat and runoff patterns, are linked in everyday conversations in Delhi and Islamabad with global change; so, increasingly, are longer term flood and drought hazards. Addressing the causes of climate change, Ahuja (1992), among others, cited the historical experience of western European and North American societies that cleared forests and industrialized, using fossil fuels as an analogue that might justify contemporary developing societies in doing the same, while noting that differences in scale and context might invalidate the parallel.

If analogies are used to judge the nature and significance of an unfamiliar phenomenon, choosing different analogues may lead to different conclusions. How important would be the net global temperature changes forecast for the next century by general circulation models? A US National Academy of Sciences report noted that the estimated climate change over the next century "is much smaller than that from day to night, from summer to winter, or between airports one might leave and reach in an hour" (US NRC 1992: 635). Smil (1990: 10) observed that in the United States "many millions of people have migrated voluntarily from the microthermal climate of the Snow Belt to mesothermal and megathermal climates of the Sun Belt, where the annual average temperatures are 10–14 degrees Celsius higher and the summer maxima are 5–10 degrees Celsius above the more northerly means." Mathews (1991: 45) contested the use of such analogies by observing that "the fact that one can move with ease from Vermont to Miami has nothing to say about the consequences of Vermont acquiring Miami's climate." She argued using a different yardstick that, because the change expected "is unprecedented in the experience of the human species," adaptation may be difficult and prevention the wiser course. To similar effect, Botkin (1992) used the range and rate of natural environmental variation as a standard for the degree of human perturbation that can safely be allowed, and found that the global greenhouse warming forecast by general circulation models fails the test.

Observers sometimes claim that analogies do not drive the reasoning of actors and analysts but are chosen merely to justify results reached by other means. The most thorough review and case study bearing on the issue in political science (Khong 1992) dealt with the use of historical analogies by decision-makers in the United States' intervention in Vietnam in 1965. It cautiously argued that analogies can be selected to illustrate conclusions, as well as being the analytic basis for new conclusions. Whether the choice of analogies is, or is not, driven by their apparent lessons, analysts of different outlooks or from different cultures might be expected to invoke different analogues to clarify the issues of climate change and society. They might also deny the relevance of the analogues invoked by the others. The tendency of conservative thinkers to dwell upon, and liberal ones to resist, stories of unintended consequences that illustrate the perversity, jeopardy, or futility of purposeful reform has often been noted (Hirschman 1991). But it greatly complicates the search for the lessons of history that analysts of different persuasions can invoke the same events and episodes as analogues because they understand them differently. The difficulties of interpreting historical climate–society interactions are considerable (Anderson 1981, de Vries 1985). Intelligent and scholarly inquiries into a single episode may reach radically different conclusions.

The Dust Bowl of the 1930s on the US Great Plains is a case in point. It is often cited as an episode of classical significance in environment–society interaction and its lessons are often invoked (Riebsame 1990), but what are its lessons? Three influential interpretations of the Dust Bowl represent almost perfectly the three major perspectives identified by cultural theory (see Vol. 2, Ch. 4). A received view of sorts, evident in much of the literature written at the time and since, exemplifies the hierarchist position in seeing the lesson of the 1930s as the need for a stronger role for government planning and management informed by scientific expertise (e.g., Great Plains Committee 1937, Hurt 1981, Lockeretz 1978). For Malin (1947, 1956) and Bonnifield (1981), by contrast, the Dust Bowl represented a temporary setback experienced by settlers in an unfamiliar environment, from which they soon recovered, thanks to their adaptive ingenuity. Government intervention, in this view, did much more to hinder than to help them in recovering: an individualist account. Worster (1979, 1986, 1992) has judged both the managerialists and the individualists superficial in their handling of the fundamental crisis on the Plains in the 1930s—that of capitalism's inherently unsustainable relations with nature. He suggests that only a more just and less exploitative system of social and economic relations can avert many more environmental disasters of the same sort. (For a detailed comparison of two of these views, see Cronon 1992.)

Interpretations of the Sahel droughts of the 1970s and 1980s, perhaps the Dust Bowl's only rival for notoriety among episodes of climate–society interaction, cover as wide a range. Some analysts have asserted a lessening of drought impacts over time, some an increase. Causal agents held responsible for loss have ranged from isolation from wider exchange networks to incorporation into them, from the persistence of traditional technologies unsustainable in new conditions to the adoption of unsustainable new ones, from the survival of traditional resource tenure systems to their disruption (see, for example, Comité Information Sahel 1974, Picadi & Seifert 1976, Franke & Chasin 1980, Garcia 1981, Kates 1981, Giri 1983, 1989, Watts 1983, Dumont 1986, Mortimore 1989, Pegeau 1989a,b, Hill 1990). So recent an episode as the California drought of 1987–91 has already been interpreted as showing the state's water supply system to be fragile, to be resilient, and to be resilient within limits that are being approached (Rogers 1994). Even cases on which less divergence of opinion seems to exist may appear to be matters of consensus only because fewer authors have written about them. Were they to receive more attention, they too might be plausibly interpreted in conflicting ways. There is no way to judge conclusively what the lessons of a given analogue are, nor which is the better of two analogues to use for a given question.

Past uses of analogues themselves deserve attention. Explicit reasoning by analogy has sometimes led to outcomes widely regarded as disastrous (for examples, see Neustadt & May 1986, Khong 1992). If the dangers of failing to learn from history are real enough to have become proverbial, so are those of "always fighting the last war": of blindly repeating courses of action suited to other times and places under significantly different circumstances. Nineteenth-century American common law judges, seeking guidance from analogy in obedience to the norm of precedent, likened groundwater, oil, and gas to wild animals, which by longstanding doctrine could not be regarded as property until physically captured. The rule obstructed the establishment of property rights in subsurface pools and, by imposing a regime of free access, created conditions for their wasteful depletion (Posner 1995). British colonial officials in the 1930s and 1940s unsuccessfully applied lessons drawn from the American Dust Bowl to land-use policy in Africa (Anderson & Grove 1987).

Many limitations of analogies in climate–society research have been noted (e.g., Glantz 1988, 1992, Jamieson 1988, Wescoat 1991), as those of analogies have been noted more generally. Several are especially pertinent to issues of global climate change:

- Because analogies between cases are never perfect, the lessons that analogues generate (even if not contested in their home domain) may not prove compelling or convincing when applied elsewhere. Analysts can always find differences among cases in the rate, magnitude, character, and context of the climate changes, and in the character, scale, and context of the social systems affected, and it can always be argued that those differences invalidate the analogy advanced.
- Such differences may indeed make an analogy inappropriate. Studies of past interaction with climate fluctuations, largely over the scale of years to decades, may have little to say about future interactions with longer term climate change. For example, irrigation, may be a successful adaptation to brief droughts, but may also be an ineffective response to protracted droughts or permanent climate change that depletes the water supply (Liverman 1990). Studies of coping with recurrent hazards may teach little about coping with novel ones. Results from studies at one spatial scale may not apply at others. Past analogies may be poor guides to contemporary problems altogether if current and prospective changes are unprecedentedly *global* in two senses: the worldwide scale on which they operate and the range and variety of systems that they affect. To the extent that global climate change would be unique in human experience, any analogue from past climate–society experience can do no more than shed light on parts of it.
- A review of existing studies of society–climate interactions will likely overrepresent disasters and striking and unusual events. Routine expe-

rience and successful coping with climate challenges and opportunities are apt to be scanted. Parry (1978, 1981, Parry et al. 1988) advanced and has carried out a research agenda focusing on the impact of climate variation on agriculture and settlement in regions already physically marginal for them. If climate variation and change matter much, as he argued, their effects will be most apparent in such areas. Yet an unintended effect of such a focus may be to increase further the overrepresentation in the literature of cases in which climate change or variation led to more than ordinarily large consequences. Judgments under uncertainty tend to be made according to what is called the *availability heuristic*, whereby the approximate likelihood of an event is judged by the share of cases in which it appears that can be readily recalled (Kahneman et al. 1982). If the climate–society literature deals disproportionately with disasters, maladaptation, and climate-sensitive activities, a thorough review of it may make society seem more vulnerable to climate than it is. This is not to say that valuable lessons cannot be drawn from a literature in which failures to adapt are overrepresented, only that caution is required in drawing lessons.

Analogues illustrated: the urban climate

Global climate change would involve a human-induced warming of several degrees Celsius, affecting precipitation and possibly also extreme weather events, over a timespan of decades to centuries. According to these criteria, a close parallel in human experience to date is the urban heat island (Changnon 1992). Urban warming may thus offer, carefully handled, a useful analogue for social interaction with changes resulting from human emissions of greenhouse gases.

The METROMEX study (Changnon 1981) of the St Louis metropolitan area (Missouri, United States) is the only sufficiently thorough study of human-induced change in the urban climate, the impacts of the change, and the perception of and responses to it to offer an integrated analogue for global climate change. The METROMEX researchers identified a heat island displaying, in the city center, an average departure of +1.9°C from the areal mean temperature. Many downwind effects, most marked in summer, were traced to increased convection from the heat island. They included increased rainfall and increased occurrence of heavy rainstorms, hail, wind gusts, and thunder (Fig. 4.1). Further research documented the consequences of the precipitation changes, both positive and negative, for human activities (Table 4.1).

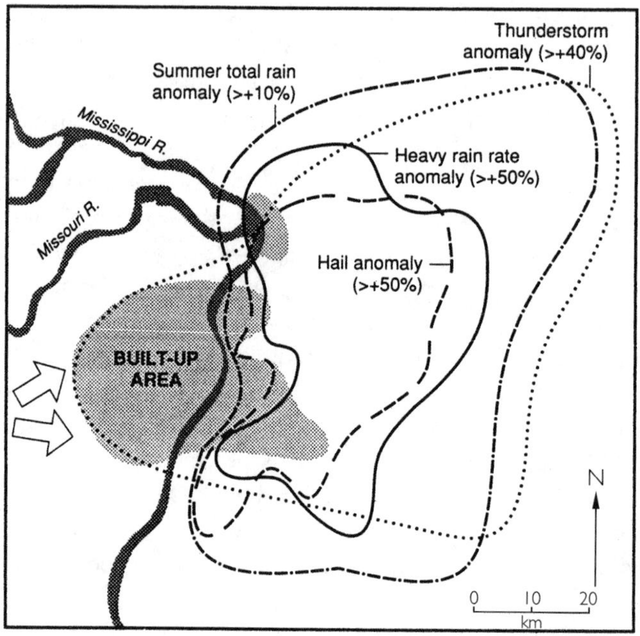

Figure 4.1 Areal extent and magnitude of major precipitation anomalies associated with the St Louis (Missouri) urbanized area. Arrows show the prevailing direction of storm systems in summer. (*Source:* Jäger & Barry 1990; redrawn from Barry & Chorley 1987, after Changnon.)

Several general suggestions emerge from the use of urban change as an analogue for global warming (Changnon 1992). First, societies can absorb, or adjust to, a physically significant climate change in a variety of ways. Adjustment may not require accurate perception or understanding of the change, for most of the actors in the St Louis region did not notice the climate trends by which they were affected. Scientists have long recognized the existence of urban heat islands and have suggested ways of moderating them (Landsberg 1973, Meyer 1991, McPherson 1994). However, the responses documented in the METROMEX region have involved adaptation—shifts in land use and location and the absorption of losses and gains—rather than mitigation or geoengineering to prevent climate change. The region has experienced a substantial change in climate without significant upheaval or massive loss, while being transformed to far greater extent by other processes. Given that "much of our population has adjusted to comparable climate changes over periods of 50 to 150 years, successful adjustment to considerable future climate change is at least possible" (Changnon 1992: 622). Second, human activities are so diverse and the pathways of adjustment and response so complex (Fig. 4.2) that there will

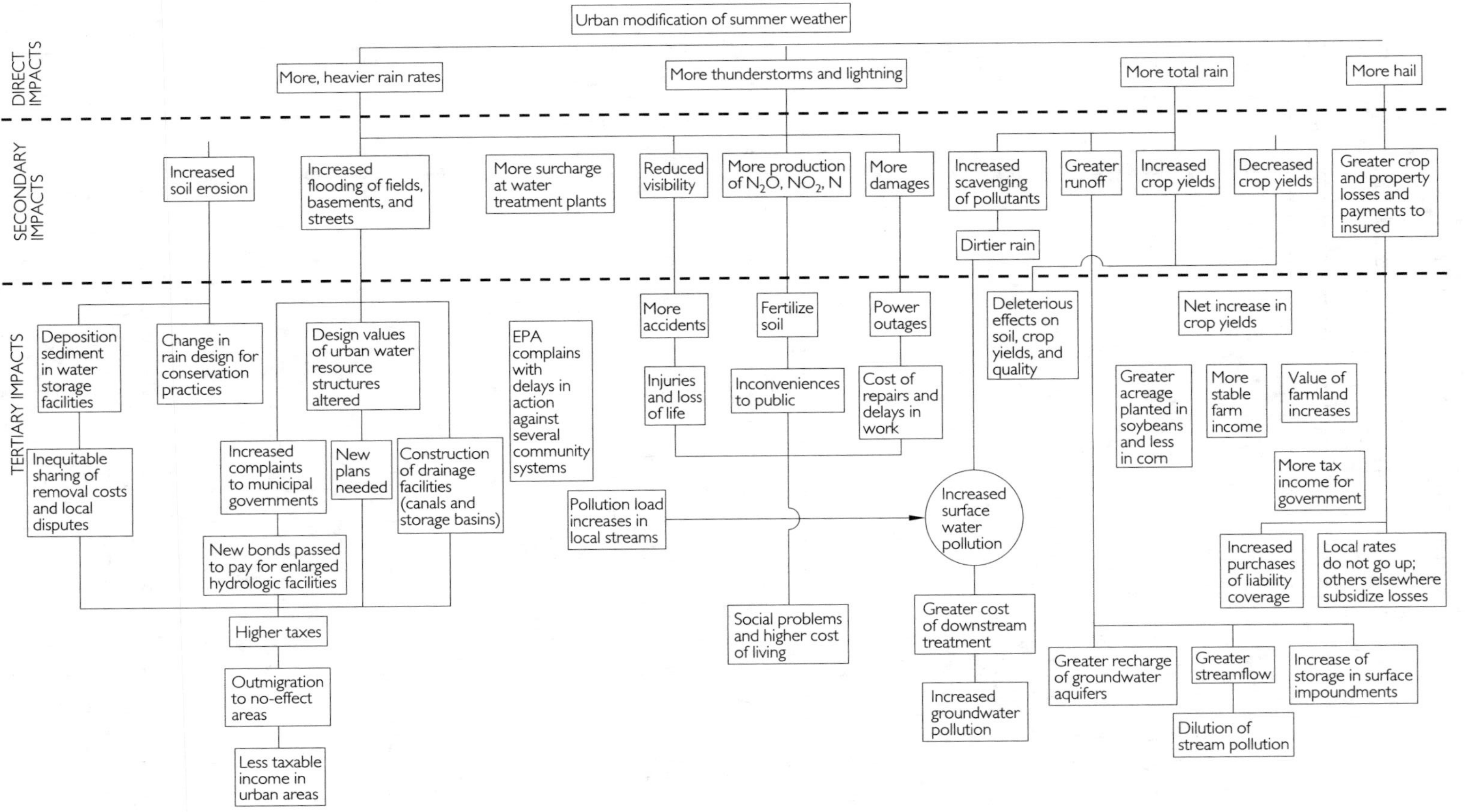

Figure 4.2 Interrelated impacts of certain urban-induced precipitation anomalies at St Louis (after Changnon et al. 1977; source Changnon 1981).

Table 4.1a Impacts of more total summer rainfall and pollutants (after Changnon et al. 1977; source Changnon 1981).

Impacts	Effect[1]	Change (%)[2]
Increased summer runoff	B	+11
Increased storage in lakes and ponds	B	+10
Increased groundwater supplies	B	+5
Dilution of water pollutants	B	Unknown
Altered low flow levels and water quality regulations exceeded	D	+97
More pollutants in streams	D	+1 to –200[3]
More deposition of pollutants	D	+15
More pollutant damage to buildings	D	Unknown
Increased groundwater pollution	D	+10
Increases in corn yields	B	+3
Increases in corn yields in dry years	B	+7
Increases in soybean yields	B	+4
Increases in soybean yields in dry years	B	+6
Increased pollution effect on crop yields	N	Unknown
Greater farm income and more stable income	B	Unknown
More acreage in soybeans	N	+6
Less acreage in corn	N	–16
Higher value of agricultural lands	B	+3
Increased tax income to government rural areas	B	+5

1. Effect classed as benefit (B), disbenefit (D), and neutral (N), good and bad.
2. Percent change, plus or minus, or unknown, based on the most common, area-wide value if several were available.
3. Range shown reflects differences found with varying pollutants, including 1 percent for potassium, 100 percent for zinc, and 200 percent for sulfates.

Table 4.1b Impacts of higher rain rates and more heavy rainstorms attributable to St Louis effects on the climate (after Changnon et al. 1977a; source Changnon 1981).

Impacts	Effect[1]	Change (%)[2]
More bypasses of sewage treatment plants	D	+40
More fluctuations in groundwater levels	D	+100
More frequent urban flooding	D	+100
Increased automobile accidents	D	+20
Increased soil erosion in uplands	D	+34
Increased sedimentation of streams	D	+1 to +30[3]
Sedimentation of floodplain facilities	D	Unknown
Added operations and management of floodplain water facilities	D	>100
Added drainage systems	D	Unknown
Altered design for hydrologic structures	D	Unknown
Added soil losses on crop production	D	Unknown
Delays and danger to air transportation	D	Unknown
Decreased visibility and increased crime	D	+30
Inequitable local taxing for water management facilities	D	Unknown
Higher costs to government agencies for water management, treatment, and planning	D D	Unknown
More acreage in soybeans	D	Unknown

1. Effect classed as benefit (B), disbenefit (D), and neutral (N), good and bad.
2. Percent change, plus or minus, or unknown, based on the most common, area-wide value if several were available.
3. Range reflects differences found in various streams.

probably be both gains and losses from climate change, even within small areas experiencing essentially the same conditions. Downwind of the St Louis metropolitan area, for example, farmers and (through taxes) local governments gained from increased crop production and cropland values; sources of loss for nonfarmers included more automobile accidents, less outdoor leisure time, and increased storm damage (see Table 4.1). The fact that impacts and adaptations must be traced through such a complex network of human interactions points up a final and key lesson: that the consequences of a climate change cannot simply be calculated from its physical characteristics alone, but also depend on the characteristics of the society experiencing it.

The imperfections of the analogue are as important to note as its lessons. The METROMEX study, although extensive, was not exhaustive in its coverage. It dealt almost exclusively with the consequences of precipitation changes, which have the disadvantage of being less solidly documented and less well understood than the thermal changes in the city climate. The possible direct consequences of the heat island itself are important: for mortality in summer heatwaves, which the urban climate may significantly exacerbate (Buechley et al. 1972, Clarke 1972); for mortality in winter, which it may lower; for energy demand for space heating and cooling. In a study of the London climate, Chandler (1965) estimated a 20 percent reduction in home heating costs in the central city as a consequence of the heat island. Air conditioning costs, however, are bound to increase in summer. Urban residential patterns will probably cause all of these gains and losses to be unequally distributed among different social groups.

Other limitations inhere in the urban analogue and its differences from global climate change. That of scale is the most obvious. The problems posed by global warming cannot fail to differ significantly from those posed by change at the metropolitan level. A focus on urban and near-urban impacts excludes most climate-sensitive human activities (notably rural land and water use) and climate-sensitive environmental realms (e.g., sea level and unmanaged biodiversity). Save in a few significant areas—transportation, construction, energy use, water supply, recreation, and health—cities are relatively climate insensitive. Both METROMEX specifically and any urban analogue more generally will understate the significance and probably the net cost of a global climate change (Changnon 1992). Nonetheless, further and comparative studies of this sort represent a promising area of integrated assessment that can cast light on all of the key human dimensions of climate change: its impacts, vulnerability to those impacts, perception of the change and impacts, and responses to them. Both in its lessons and in its limitations, the urban heat island comparison illustrates well the nature of analogies in climate research.

Archaeological analogues: climate and society in prehistory

Other things equal, an analogue for contemporary and future society–climate relations is less plausible the more remote in time it is. The most compelling and the most valuable analogues are likely to be from modern experience (Jamieson 1991). Yet archaeological and premodern cases are often invoked, in public forums as well as in scientific discussions of contemporary global change, sometimes to show that human societies are inherently vulnerable to climate variation (e.g., Gore 1992), sometimes to argue from the experience of past civilizations that global warming would be beneficial (Moore 1995). The examples most often cited are of drastic societal transformations attributed to climate change. They offer images so striking as to compel attention as analogues for current dilemmas, whatever their flaws as such, and, because they receive such attention, an examination of their uses and limitations is important. Moreover, if (as is sometimes supposed) premodern societies were less vulnerable to climate change than contemporary ones are because they were more flexible, a collapse by such a less vulnerable society in the face of change would carry a sobering lesson for modern societies; if (as is also sometimes supposed) premodern societies were more vulnerable because they were poorer in resources and capacity for response, a finding that few failed to cope successfully would have very different implications.

Even without reference to modern issues, the archaeological literature is replete with efforts to explain sociopolitical discontinuities by climate change. For most such cases, climate has been proposed as a cause. In studies of prehistoric civilizations and their climates, integrated societal analysis becomes a virtue born of necessity. Finer interactions are hard to distinguish in the archaeological record. Relations of cause and effect are complex, and multicausal explanations are already difficult enough to construct, in data-rich contemporary settings. For historical and prehistoric cases, the danger of attributing change too simplistically to climate is greater, since external triggering events may be more conspicuous in the surviving data but not more important than a complex web of underlying socioeconomic problems, accentuated or dampened by political factors and events. In prehistoric settings, that is, cases where direct contemporaneous testimony is unavailable—researchers can rarely do more than correlate climate trends and events with population shifts or political disjunctures. Possible concatenations of factors can seldom be deciphered, so that "conclusions" are little more than models generally not amenable to satisfactory testing.

Claims for the role of climate in the archaeological record should be carefully scrutinized from several perspectives: the validity of the climatic inference per se; the supposed synchronicity of climate anomalies over extensive areas, and their match with particular historical events and processes; and the ecological, socioeconomic, demographic, and political context as a source for other rationales. Hypotheses cannot be proven correct, but their acceptance depends on the validity of the supporting data, some or all of which can conceivably be shown to be false or capable of alternative explanations. Some of the key considerations that arise in particular cases are illustrated below by three examples of climate change explanations for major archaeological disjunctures.

Abrupt climate change and civilizational collapse c. *2200* BC*?*

Between 2300 and 2000 BC much of the Near East and the Aegean world was engulfed in a "time of troubles" that brought an end to the Early Bronze Age. Many if not most urban states from the Balkans to Mesopotamia and Palestine were abandoned, destroyed, or greatly reduced in size; early states such as the Akkadian Empire and Old Kingdom Egypt collapsed *c.* 2230 BC. Mysterious invaders, such as Indo-Europeans or Semitic pastoralists, have long been conjured up (in two waves, if necessary) to explain these widespread discontinuities, with some sort of climatic deterioration suspected or invoked to account for an apparently synchronous time of troubles from Spain to China.

Based on excavation of the urban mound of Tell Leilan, northeastern Syria, Weiss et al. (1993) invoked an abrupt climate change—desiccation—to explain the abandonment of this and other adjacent urban tells, located in what is now a marginal environment for rainfed agriculture. Abandonment of these sites, forming part of the Akkadian imperial state, signaled the agricultural ruin of a key province, sharply cutting state revenues at a time of Euphrates discharge in the Akkadian heartland (Weiss et al. 1993, Weiss 1994). The state crumbled and nomadic groups moved in. The presence of wind-borne volcanic glass particles at Leilan and adjacent sites is attributed to the cataclysmic eruption of a volcano, probably in Anatolia, possibly causing a "volcanic winter" that destabilized global climate (Weiss et al. 1993, Courty 1994). Here, then, is the prime mover invoked to explain political devolution in Mesopotamia, synchronous with climate change and collapse in the Aegean, Egypt, Palestine, and the Indus (Weiss et al. 1993).

Published recently in a rigorously refereed journal, this argument requires critical scrutiny from several perspectives:

- Are the empirical climate data valid?
- If so, was the climate anomaly effective and synchronous across the area?
- Did sociopolitical unrest or collapse everywhere follow upon climate change, in a form consistent with greater aridity?
- Do the archaeological and historical sources provide demographic,

socioeconomic, and political information that supports different explanations?

The post-Leilan collapse strata represent a volcanic and edaphic sedimentary horizon, documenting a catastrophic biological event rather than an abrupt climate change in the strict sense of the term. The local settlement hiatus coincided with a devegetated, biologically arid period (which is what happened 100–200 km downwind of the more familiar, ash-spewing eruption of Mt St Helens, where 100 cm or more of volcanic dustfall blanketed and choked the vegetation). Stream behavior immediately after the event (see Courty 1994: figs 10, 13–15) did not change notably, except for a much greater sediment supply. A thin mantle of volcanic silt spread out over the farm lands of a marginal environment would constitute an agricultural disaster. If local rainfed agriculture was already marginal and under stress, abandonment given these new conditions may have seemed a reasonable choice to the local societies. The scenario of a volcanic winter finds no support. There is no evidence of a globally effective eruption in this general time range from the published ice corings from Greenland (Hammer et al. 1985), and deep-sea cores from the eastern Mediterranean fail to record volcanic materials from this period (Guichard & Courty 1994). The Leilan volcanic glass represents a regional, not a global event, and its environmental impact would have been limited to the direct biological repercussions of a dust and ash mantle.

There are other clues to change. A pollen core from Lake Zeribar in the Zagros Mountains (Van Zeist & Bottema 1991) indicates an abrupt decline of oak and corresponding increase of grass and other ground cover plants *c.* 2200 BC. Oxygen-18 isotopes from Lake Van varve (layers of sediment) chronologies (Schoell 1978) suggest reduced dilution of the lake waters by runoff, which would imply reduced Euphrates discharge in Mesopotamia. In short, there is indeed evidence for a drier climate in the upper Euphrates Basin and the Zagros Mountains during the last centuries of the third millennium. Synoptically, the case for environmental stress c.2200 BC is reasonably good, but it was limited to eastern Anatolia and Mesopotamia. There is no discernible evidence of vegetation change in western Anatolia, southeastern Europe, Syria, or Palestine (Beug 1967, Bottema 1984, 1994, Baruch 1990, Bottema & Woldring 1990, Jahns 1991). How the abandonment of large local tells—concurrent with rapid growth in towns on the adjacent floodplain of the Euphrates River, liable to flood irrigation—would have affected the Akkadian state is a matter for conjecture. Carried by a usurping dynasty and an alien ethnic group, established upstream of the old Sumerian city states, Akkad may have been unstable for various reasons.

In the larger picture, the political discontinuity experienced over a very wide area was real. In detail, however, there was as much sociocultural continuity as there was change in Greece (Forsén 1992), for example, and destruction—as opposed to abandonment—is only rarely evident at many settlement sites that disappeared. There was no general climate change, no evidence of invaders, and any local decreases in population were brief. Widespread political devolution can be readily explained by more appealing models. Imperial states consume considerable revenue that is generated through either the windfall profits of conquest or the income derived from commerce. Areas far from their boundaries can also profit and accumulate wealth from that trade until it is somehow interrupted. At that point both the state and its distant suppliers can become impoverished and metastable. The collapse of one state within a chain of commercially integrated regions (a small-scale *world system*) can have repercussions for all the others. Times of troubles are perhaps better considered as the failure of systemic relationships (Butzer 1994), without recourse to mysterious prime movers.

Nile failure and the collapse of New Kingdom Egypt

A second case indicates the significance that environmental perturbations could have for a society highly vulnerable to them. Ancient Egypt, with its dense population and intensive irrigation agriculture, was inextricably linked to the Nile River. Running through a barren desert, the Nile's plain was annually watered by life-giving floods derived from distant East Africa, an environment particularly prone to abrupt climate change. With the simple technologies of the period, Egyptian subsistence was highly vulnerable to famine and the sociopolitical repercussions that major food shortfalls can provoke. Egyptian history is divided into three epochs—the Old, Middle, and New Kingdoms—which represent cycles of political integration and devolution. The Egyptians themselves tied the collapse of the Old Kingdom *c.* 2200 BC to a period of Nile failures and social disintegration (Bell 1971), and there is reason to believe that the Middle Kingdom was badly weakened by decades of excessive and destructive Nile floods, before the Hyksos invasion *c.* 1670 BC (Bell 1975). Devolution of the New Kingdom (1153–1070 BC) came at the end of another widespread time of troubles, a time that saw the collapse of other states in the Near East and that has generated its own literature of climatic causation (e.g., Weiss 1982).

The collapse of the New Kingdom is a good case for study because there is clear evidence of falling Nile floods, coupled with unusually good contemporary detail on food prices and social unrest (Butzer 1976, 1980a, 1984). Upstream in Nubia, a segment of the valley heavily settled during the thirteenth century BC, when flood levels were 1 m higher than today, there was total abandonment after about 1200 (Trigger 1965). Dune sands spread over the floodplain, and a lack of subsequent flooding allowed salts to build up (Heinzelin 1964). At the same time, the royal capital in the Nile Delta, located on a failing Nile distributary, was abandoned in favor of a new site on another, more central distributary (Bietak 1975). A significant decline of Nile discharge is supported by a dramatic fall of East African lake levels at about this time, in response to a major shift of climatic equilibrium in the Upper Nile watershed (Butzer 1980b).

Egypt had been able to provide grain to the Hittite state during a famine in Anatolia in 1210 BC (Faulkner 1975), and Egyptian grain prices remained stable until 1170. They then began to increase rapidly, fluctuating to as much as eight times the normal price, even though the value of precious metals, services, and livestock remained unchanged (Černy 1933, Janssen 1975). In 1153 BC, the food supply failed, so that the royal workmen in the capital rioted. The best efforts of the prime minister turned up barely half of the wheat needed (Faulkner 1975), indicating that the temple granaries were empty (Butzer 1976). Ramesses III, a strong Pharaoh, was apparently assassinated two years later, and the subsequent reigns of weaker kings were short. Five further food strikes or riots are documented during 1151–1105 BC, and in 1130–1125 BC wheat prices fluctuated to as much as 24 times their earlier level, with barley and oil prices also high (Janssen 1975). Taxation pressures during this time of poor harvests then led to massive rural flight and depopulation (Caminos 1954, 1977). Although food prices stabilized at about 1110 BC and began to fall after 1100 BC, the last king of the dynasty (Ramesses XI, 1099–1070 BC) was explicitly disenfranchised by the priesthood as the divine provider of life and safeguard of the cosmic order, being demoted to a simple agent of the supreme Egyptian god, Amun (Černy 1975).

It is tempting to see this usurpation of power as an indictment of the dynasty's failure to guarantee nature and thus the livelihood of Egypt. The cemetery record indicates widespread impoverishment and, possibly, a declining population. The new, priestly dynasty after 1070 BC was unable to hold the country together or to stave off Libyan or Ethiopian–Sudanese invasion and control. High Nile floods were recorded again only after 868 BC, and the country was reunified under a new Egyptian dynasty in 656 BC. During the 450 years following the death of Ramesses III, Egypt lacked effective central authority, political–economic structures were strongly simplified, and both subsistence and population were reduced to significantly lower levels.

It would, however, be simplistic and contrary to the historical context to attribute this devolution to a protracted decline and repeated failure of Nile floods between 1170 and 1100 BC. Egypt had fended off a powerful coalition of barbarian peoples in three costly battles in 1207, 1177, and 1171 BC. Unlike other Near Eastern kingdoms, it survived intact, but its Asiatic provinces were lost and its external exchange system destroyed. Moreover, the priesthood of the god Amun had been competing with the Pharaoh for power since about 1400

BC. Significantly, the end of the environmental crisis did not reverse the continuing shift of power to the priesthood. Again, a new trend to a favorable hydrological regime of the Nile, during the mid-ninth century, preceded political reintegration by a full 200 years. Finally, the Egyptian state had been characterized by a top-heavy sociopolitical structure (Butzer 1980a) since the late fifteenth century, with increasing energy expenditure for system maintenance, and accelerating demands on the agricultural substrate during the course of the thirteenth century. Sociopolitical structures were already metastable before the succession of Ramesses III, and systemic disintegration set in immediately after his death. In this setting, severe environmental stress reinforced economic stagnation, sociopolitical instability, dynastic weakness, and foreign pressures. It was one potent factor in a concatenation of negative processes in the demise of the New Kingdom. Stress was maintained for 50–70 years, and consequently must have contributed significantly to the forces already undermining the political structure of Egypt. The fact that Egypt was both a complex society and an imperial state, with extensive international linkages, underscores the fact that medium-term environmental stress can contribute to dramatic changes.

A comparison with the European historical record helps to clarify the ways in which Egypt was vulnerable to such stress. The traditional European economy was considerably more diversified, in terms of field crops, orchard produce, and livestock, and it was variably adjusted to a much more complex environmental mosaic. Egypt had a population density four to ten times greater and was almost completely dependent on its grain produce, which in turn was dependent on a single ecological variable, the Nile flood. The Egyptian adaptive system lacked risk-reducing complementarities and had a lower threshold of instability than the much less specialized European economic subsystems.

The classic Maya collapse

Efforts to link a third case of civilizational discontinuity with climate change illustrate the difficulties often encountered in correlating the two and also the insufficiency of the latter, even when demonstrated, as an adequate explanation of the former. Sometime between AD 800–1000 the Classic Lowland Maya civilization of the greater Yucatan peninsular region collapsed and most of its homelands were dramatically depopulated (Culbert 1973, Culbert & Rice 1990). The role of climate change in this collapse and depopulation has been regularly invoked since first proposed by Huntington (1917). Until recently, however, direct evidence for such a role was slim and supported mainly by inferences from Maya settlement patterns.

Recent sustained work on the paleohistory of the Maya lowlands has produced a considerable body of evidence indicating major biophysical changes in the area (Bloom et al. 1983, Brenner et al. 1990, Rice 1993). Some of this evidence, particularly that of the geochemistry of lake cores in the Maya area (Hodell et al. 1995), points to possible climate changes during Maya occupation. For the most part, however, it is extremely difficult to distinguish climate change from human-induced changes in the paleorecord, because of the length and magnitude of ancient Maya occupation (Turner 1985). To sustain a massive population for the greater part of a millennium before the collapse required large-scale and extensive landscape changes (Turner 1993). Around the middle of the first millennium BC, the Maya began to manipulate and then transform their lowland tropical habitat. They denuded upland forests for large-scale settlement and agriculture; erected stone walls on slopelands, to control soil moisture and preserve soil on the slopes; reconfigured wetlands to permit cultivation; and managed flora for species useful to the population. By the middle of the first millennium AD, the Maya lowlands were well manicured, with little left relatively untouched. The paleorecord abounds with evidence of this transformation, playing havoc with the detection of climate change per se, although geochemical evidence for such change is mounting.

Long-term intensive alteration of the landscape may have made the Maya economy and environment sensitive to climate fluctuations or change, such that a shift to sustained wetter, drier, or more extreme seasonal conditions could have triggered systemic changes throughout, weakening the resource base and leading to cultural and demographic demise (Sabloff 1990, Lowe 1985). This kind of scenario based on climate (warming or desiccation?) has been invoked through analogy to hydrological regimes of the Rio Candelaria (Gunn et al. 1983). The possible agency of climate change cannot be adequately evaluated at this time, given the speculative nature of the evidence, yet such changes as may have occurred do not seem to represent a sufficient cause for collapse inasmuch as they appear to have been within the capacity of the Maya to manage so long as the socioeconomic and political atmosphere necessary to do so was maintained (Turner 1993). Desiccation possibly associated with the collapse (Hodell et al. 1995) drives this point home. It is thought to have been most severe in the northern Maya lowlands, precisely the area retaining a large population into historic times. The long-term depopulation of the central and southern Maya lowlands after the collapse had little basis in climatic or environmental deterioration. The regional environment subsequently recovered, sometime after AD 1000 (the collapse), but long before it was first observed by Europeans in the sixteenth century (Turner & Butzer 1992).

Conclusion

The appeal of prehistoric examples as striking analogues for greenhouse-gas-induced climate change notwithstanding, researchers cannot identify unambiguous examples of ancient societies that collapsed because of climate shifts. What emerges from the examples reviewed here and from the wider archaeological literature is, rather, some situations where the intervention of climate change in societal processes bears close consideration. The list could be extended into the historical period by considering (see below) the abandonment of marginal environments in highland Britain and in Scandinavia. Even where the database has been drastically simplified by the erosion of time, simple explanations will not account for these abandonments. Even when climate change has been established and adequately correlated with sociopolitical transformation, conclusions of the form "it got cold/hot/dry/wet and they died/fluoresced/migrated/intensified" (McGovern 1991: 78) still mistake the identification of a temporal coincidence for a full causal link.

The archaeological analogues suggest the need for caution in positing even the occurrence and character of particular climate and related events in prehistory. Their clearest and most useful lesson is that the significance and consequences of a climate event, once documented, are not direct functions of its physical characteristics. The consequences, rather, vary with the ways in which a society has organized its relations to its resource base, its relations with other societies, and the relations among its members. A climate event is not a sufficient cause for a societal collapse if the failure of the society to deal adequately with it has not been accounted for. In archaeological—as well as historical and contemporary—studies, the most promising research strategy is:

> . . . explicitly to focus attention on the processes of adaptation—or, on the other hand, of failure to adapt—that partly condition the impact of climatic stress in particular societies . . . cases in which societies appear to have been seriously damaged by, or even totally succumbed to, climatic stress should not be taken to demonstrate the determining influence of climate. It is essential to consider ways in which these societies might have coped better, and to focus on the political, cultural, and socio-economic factors which inhibited them from doing so. (Ingram et al. 1981: 37; see also Tainter 1988)

McGovern's (1991) reexamination of the extinction of the Greenland settlements is an exemplary study straddling archaeology and history (see next section). Modeling the resource use system, he found that the stress imposed by climate shifts was indeed severe, but was within the theoretical ability of the colonies to have coped with by means that documentary evidence shows were available to them. Why they failed to employ those means emerges as the key question, still incompletely answered, in explaining the collapse: "It did get cold and they did die out, but why?" (McGovern 1991: 94). Intervening between the physical events and the social consequences is the vulnerability of the society and its different groups, activities, and individual members.

Climate as hazard: vulnerability

The historic and contemporary case studies that offer the most plausible analogies with global climate change come from the multidisciplinary areas of environmental hazards, climate impact assessment, and climate history. They offer integrated assessments of the social consequences of and response to harmful variations in precipitation and temperature, addressing two major themes: vulnerability and response. (On the related contributions of risk , see Ch. 3.)

Among geophysical agents, weather and climate are by far the most lethal to humankind worldwide. Together flood, hurricane, and drought account for 75 percent of the world's natural disasters. Only earthquakes exact a comparable toll (Burton et al. 1993). However, during the twentieth century global losses of life from disasters, more broadly defined, have been overwhelmingly the result of civil strife and famine—the latter sometimes related to, but not simply caused by, drought—rather than geophysical events (Blaikie et al. 1994).

Studies of social interaction with climate hazards and change offer analogues for global climate change on the premise that experience with weather and climate in the historical and recent past can aid the understanding of climate change in the future. The dissimilarities among kinds of events, of course, may make unprofitable the use of some as analogues for others. When atmosphere-related hazards are classified by duration, speed of onset, area affected, and other physical characteristics (Burton et al. 1993), drought appears the one most akin to the longer term challenges of climate change. We emphasize drought here as an analogue, and deal with other hazards (e.g., temperature variations and floods) as appropriate; studies of extreme weather events may also be relevant if the claim is correct that they will become significantly more frequent in the future with climate change.

Researchers have reached a broad consensus that

> Hazards always result from interactions of physical and human systems. To treat them as though they were wholly climatic . . . or political or

> economic is to risk omission of components that must be taken into account if sound solutions for them are to be found. (Burton et al. 1993: 188; see also Blaikie et al. 1994, Tricart 1994)

The elements that are omitted when climate impacts are treated as wholly climatic are those characteristics of societies, individuals, groups, places, systems, and activities that cause them to lose or gain to differing degrees from particular weather and climate events. Knowing the physical attributes of a climate variation or change is never adequate for understanding or predicting its consequences for human society. Such is the case for climate hazards; it may reasonably be assumed by analogy to be the case for global climate change. The intense concentration of research effort to date on projecting the physical attributes of a climate change thus scants an equally essential task: clarifying what they mean and for whom. Attention to the concepts and approaches of hazards research offers useful guidance in that task.

Human activities and groups are sensitive to climate to the degree that they can be affected by it, and vulnerable to the degree that they can be harmed. Only the latter term incorporates a human judgment of value. *Sensitivity* refers to the elasticity between different processes or states, *vulnerability* to the potential for negative outcomes or consequences. A *resilient* system, activity, or population is one with low vulnerability, being either resistant to hazard effects or readily capable of coping with and recovering from them. Both sensitivity and vulnerability should also be distinguished from *hazards*—denoting either events threatening people and things that they value, or the probability of the occurrence of such events. *Impacts,* finally, are the actual consequences (losses or, conceivably, gains) resulting from a biophysical event. Negative impacts are the product of hazard events and vulnerability. A focus on vulnerability, then, is a partial one that addresses the sensitivity of human systems, not only to the threats but also to the opportunities (Burton 1992), presented by particular climate events and by the human activities with which they interact. There are few studies of gains from climate variation and of human activities vulnerable to climate that compare the losses to the overall gains from the activity. Yet "the use of resources of a hazardous area almost always leads to social benefits as well as social costs. It is essential to identify the tradeoffs between the benefits and the costs in the broadest sense" (Burton et al. 1993: 188).

The vulnerability of populations and activities is the most widely used umbrella concept for those factors that mediate between geophysical events and human losses. Because vulnerability and its causes play an essential role in determining impacts, understanding the dynamics of vulnerability is as important as monitoring and predicting climate change and variation. Vulnerability is a composite concept, incorporating environmental, social, economic, political, cultural, and psychological factors, describing in integrated terms "the capacity to be wounded" (Kates et al. 1985: 17). It draws attention to "what amplifies or mitigates the impacts of climate change and channels them toward certain groups, certain institutions, and certain places" and "emphasizes the degree to which the risks of climate catastrophe can be cushioned or ameliorated by adaptive actions that are or can be brought—within the reach of populations at risk" (Downing 1991: 380).

As two aspects of differential vulnerability, researchers distinguish between differences in physical exposure to the hazardous agent and in ability to cope with its impacts (Chambers 1989). The former are closely associated with biophysical, and the latter with socioeconomic, differentiation, but by no means perfectly. Aspects of the biophysical environment may be important sources of coping ability, for instance, and differences in exposure to hazards may be the consequence of socioeconomic differences. No standard framework exists for identifying the fundamental sources of differential vulnerability, but clearly they are numerous and complex. One classification focused on vulnerability to hunger distinguishes three dimensions:

- those of human ecology, or the specific relations of social groups to the physical environments they inhabit
- expanded entitlements, or the "commodity bundles" (Sen 1990: 36) that people acquire through production, market exchanges, and participation in social and political institutions
- and the political economy that forms the wider context within which these relations are embedded (Bohle et al. 1994).

Poverty is generally recognized as one of the most important correlates of vulnerability to hazard, but it is also recognized as being neither necessary nor sufficient for it. The very young and the old are often identified as especially vulnerable. Other categories widely invoked are differences in health, gender, ethnicity, education, and experience with the hazard in question (Dow 1992; see also Liverman 1990). Empirical local-level studies reveal such complex mosaics of vulnerability as to cast doubt upon attempts to describe patterns and estimate trends at the global or even the regional scale (Liverman 1990, Downing 1991, Dow 1992). Vulnerability to global climate change is likely to be as complex.

Still, analysts have tried to identify overall trends causing increased or decreased vulnerability to, and losses from, environmental hazards globally over time. Torry (1979) and Lamb (1982), for example, asserted that the world is becoming more vulnerable, for reasons including a greater rigidity of resource use and response, a claim that Blaikie et al. (1994) cautiously endorsed; Bain & Otway (1979) found more plausible the opposite assertion, that overall vulnerability is declining. Ausubel (1991b) described a world that has through technological adaptation grown steadily less vulnerable to climate and its vagaries. Dotto (1988: 38) on the other hand, reported "every reason to believe that the complex nature of modern societies renders them more susceptible" than earlier societies to collapse through environmental perturbations. Larger systems are sometimes argued to be more capable of dealing with small fluctuations, but more vulnerable to catastrophe through large ones. The implications of the different positions are evident; presumably a world increasingly vulnerable to climate hazards is a world more vulnerable to greenhouse-gas-induced change than would be one becoming less sensitive to climate hazards. Such claims might be fruitfully assessed by modeling, for various times in the past—say, 1850, 1900, and 1950, and perhaps much earlier dates as well—the food supply, health, and other global social consequences of climate changes similar to those projected for the future.

Not only overall trends but even the partial effect on hazard vulnerability of particular changes is often in dispute. Many general assertions, often conflicting, are advanced in the literature about what specific social processes and patterns mean for the vulnerability of society and societal elements to climate fluctuation and climate change. Most of them, viewed as analogues, hold clear implications about the prospect of global climate change. Because of their policy implications, it is important to examine how well they hold in practice and what limits exist to their generality, a task to which integrated case studies are well suited. These generalizations will most likely not apply always and everywhere; the very fact that many contradict others indicates that each probably holds true under some circumstances. Theoretical expectations are generally modified or disappointed in concrete contexts. Because of the composite nature of vulnerability, any social change may well make individuals or activities more vulnerable in some ways and less in others, and/or increase vulnerability for some and lessen it for others.

Population growth is one prominent variable (see Vol. 1, Ch. 2). Neo-Malthusians (and others) can argue that more people place added stress on the environment, increasing vulnerability to natural hazard, as well as, of course, increasing the total population at risk; from the opposite point of view, more people reduce vulnerability, because a more populous society possesses greater resources with which to cope. The parallel views obtain regarding affluence. The net effect of technological change, it has been suggested, has been to climate-proof human societies to ever-greater degrees over time (Ausubel 1991b); case studies, on the other hand, point to instances where technological modernization has displaced practices better adapted to climate variation (e.g., Johnson 1976, Wilken 1987). Integration into market (also communication/transportation) networks has been regarded as reducing vulnerability by increasing the efficiency of resource use and by making available external sources of trade or assistance (e.g., Crosson & Rosenberg 1993). Such integration has also been seen as increasing vulnerability by increasing socioeconomic differentiation and by undermining preexisting risk-minimization strategies of resource use and traditional social institutions that provided support during crises (Susman et al. 1983, Waddell 1983). Particular common-property systems have been identified as both more (e.g., Liverman 1990) and less (e.g., Runge 1992, Thompson & Wilson 1994) vulnerable to climate variation than private ones. A major comparative study of two regions found a tendency to lessening of impacts from climatic stresses over time, but without being able to rule out the possibility that vulnerability to catastrophe from major stress was increasing (Bowden et al. 1981).

Other assertions are less often contested: for example, that agricultural economies are more vulnerable to climatic hazards than industrialized ones, and that vulnerability is greatest (other things being equal) for regions that are geographically, economically, or politically marginal and for groups and individuals (e.g., the poor, women, children, the elderly, ethnic minorities) who are socially, politically, or economically marginal. It is a plausible and popular assertion that regions in institutional transition, for example, from nonmarket to market relations (Ingram et al. 1981, Burton et al. 1993), are particularly vulnerable, although the concept of transition remains loosely defined, and in the absence of a clear definition most regions can in some sense be said to be undergoing it.

Vulnerability is a potential quality, and measures for it are best assessed through measures of impacts recorded as a result of a hazard event. Quantitative indices of impact often used include absolute and proportional numbers for lives lost, persons injured, persons displaced, property damage, involuntary transfers of property, and production and income shortfalls. Statistics on all leave much to be desired, however, and slow pervasive hazards such as drought in particular present problems of distinguishing climate-related impacts from impacts of other nonclimate factors operating simultaneously. Qualitative assessments of social disruption are also often used. It cannot be assumed that all indices will point in the same direction. More explicit statements as to what is meant by vulnerability and impact may help to reconcile some differences of opinion as to how and why they are changing. To take a simple illustration, as a society increases in affluence, it may be in absolute terms more vulnerable, having a greater stock of property capable of being damaged, yet higher total losses for it may represent declining shares of its total stock with less impact on well-being and functioning. A society becoming poorer may lose less in absolute terms from one hazard event to the next, but suffer more from those losses. As vulnerability can be defined only relative to a particular hazard, moreover, it may at the same time be increasing and decreasing with reference to different hazards. However, even with respect to a single hazard assessment of what the impacts have been may differ; certain risks and losses, for example, will be viewed as tolerable by some actors but not by others (Kasperson & Dow 1991, Dow 1992).

To illustrate vulnerability to weather and climate hazards in a variety of social and physical settings, we examine experiences of some regions that have been well studied in the published literature. The first two—medieval and early modern Europe and the North American Arctic—involve the impacts of temperature fluctuation, largely considered at the societal level. A long-term perspective on each region shows how societal transformations have greatly altered the significance of recurrent weather and climate events for human activities. The next two—the US Great Plains and the Brazilian Northeast—are industrialized- and industrializing-world areas of recurrent drought that have displayed over the past century substantially contrasting trajectories and complicated mosaics of hazard vulnerability. Finally, we review the literature on two large world regions—South Asia and sub-Saharan Africa—both regions of high vulnerability to recurrent weather and climate stresses, both further illustrating how vulnerability has varied over time and space over the past century for reasons other than variations in physical exposure to hazard events.

Subsistence crises and climate: medieval and early modern Europe

The relations between climate and subsistence in western Europe during the past millennium can be examined at different scales of resolution: the long and the short to medium term. Two long-term climatic trends are commonly recognized: the Little Ice Age of AD 1550–1900 (Grove 1988) and (less unanimously) the Medieval Warm Epoch or Little Climatic Optimum of AD 1000–1200 (Lamb 1982). Dates vary according to the proxy climate record emphasized—the Alpine glacial record, dendroclimatological data, and the date of the opening of the wine harvest are the most commonly used for the area in question. In semiquantitative terms, the cold intervals had summers averaging on the order of 0.5–0.8°C colder than the warm intervals, but in Scandinavia 12 summers from 1100 to 1150 and 13 summers from 1600 to 1650 were at least 1°C colder (Briffa et al. 1990, Pfister 1984). The deviations of the cold periods largely resulted from a higher incidence of cool summers, making the growing season and harvest weather less reliable. Conversely, during the peak of the Little Optimum, July–August temperatures rose 2°C or more above the long-term average at least once per decade (Pfister 1988).

Did these anomalies and trends have a marked effect on the macroeconomic history of western Europe? The social effects of the cold periods is very difficult to gauge because of the systemic interrelationship of demography, agricultural productivity, and prices (Abel 1974, 1980, Slicher van Bath 1977, Le Roy Ladurie & Goy 1982). The key problem in trying to unravel the possible input of climate is that the western European population overexpanded *c.* 1200–1315 and *c.* 1520–1590, leading to demographic stagnation or decline in 1315–1520 and 1600–1700, exacerbated by the Black Death and its echoes after 1348 (Grigg 1980, Wrigley & Schofield 1981, Galloway 1986, Butzer 1990). Such stagnation by itself provokes a range of symptoms, characteristic of agricultural recession: falling grain prices, declining crop yields, increasing wages for unskilled labor, disintensification, and rural abandonment (Slicher van Bath 1977). The database is incomplete and the interdependencies too complex to allow unraveling of the multiple feedbacks. In the last analysis, such broad cyclic trends are more likely to be related to the growth and crises of world system economies (Abu-Lughod 1989, Braudel 1979) than they are to climate variation.

The most tempting linkage of the Little Ice Age and other cold intervals is with widespread settlement abandonment of marginal lands, specifically in Central Europe, upland Scandinavia, highland Britain, and Greenland. In Germany, over 40000 of 170000 settlements were abandoned, primarily between the 1340s and 1500 (Abel 1976). Most had been founded during the thirteenth century by forest clearance on poor soils, commonly in wet mesoclimates. Anomalously cool and wet summers would certainly have reduced productivity, but high labor costs and rents, combined with lower prices for grains, provide by themselves a sufficiently convincing explanation. In Scandinavia there were two main episodes of rural abandonment, primarily in areas highly marginal for agriculture as well as stockraising; the first is poorly dated to the fourteenth century, the second *c.* 1600–1800 (Müller-Wille 1965, Lunden 1974, Grove & Battagel 1983). In Norway, direct climate impacts are verified during the seventeenth century, but royal edicts to prevent rural to urban migration were already posted in 1250. For highland Britain, seventeenth-century climate deterioration increased the probability of harvest failures from one year in twenty to one year in three (Parry 1978, Parry & Carter 1985). The late Medieval desertions were much more widespread, even on moderately good soils in lowland Britain (Beresford & Hurst 1973), and are much more difficult to attribute to poor weather. They were part of a much wider phenomenon of desertions in other parts of Europe, with different climatic controls over harvest success.

More dramatic was the disappearance of the Norse farming communities in Greenland, implanted on the margins of the glaciated landmass in the tenth century, and successively "lost" between AD 1350 and 1500. Summers became shorter and wetter, and colder waters offshore changed the patterns of marine resources, while increasingly extensive ice along the coast cut off contacts with Europe by 1408. Analysis of the archaeological evidence shows clearly that the Norse settlers were placed under great stress by the climate shift, but they also failed for reasons embedded in their social structure to adapt their livestock, farming, and foraging strategies to the changing circumstances, while the more versatile Thule Eskimo expanded southward along the western coastline, taking advantage of new game and fishing opportunities and coping with the change (McGovern 1981, 1991).

The potential role of sharp climate anomalies and longer trends for settlement retraction or abandonment in marginal environments seems intuitively evident, but it cannot be demonstrated other than as a covariable, given the complexity of human decisionmaking, the variety of push and pull factors, and the stabilizing and mobilizing elements embedded in a socioeconomic system.

Lower-order feedbacks can be shown to have responded to climate inputs over shorter timespans. Specific harvest failures can be linked to short-term weather crises, typically cold springs followed by cool, wet summers, within a region (with considerable covariance) between Britain and northern Italy, and from France to Germany (and not generally including Scandinavia, east-central Europe, or typically Mediterranean environments). In general, the larger the region affected by major food shortage, the more severe the harvest loss; similarly, the longer the period of dearth, the larger the area eventually affected. Among the major episodes of famine since AD 1000 (as documented by Curschman 1900, Abel 1974, 1980, Alexandre 1986, Appleby 1979, 1980, Grigg 1980, Le Roy Ladurie 1972, Pfister 1984, Schofield 1985), the most disastrous appear to have been those of 1315–17, 1438–39, the 1590s, and 1816–17. Several that are particularly well documented will be examined briefly.

The most important famine of Medieval Europe was that of 1315–17 (Curschman 1900, Abel 1980, Grigg 1980). The winter of 1315–16 was cold and wet in northwestern Europe, and excessive rainfall from the summer of 1315 continued through 1316. Harvests were locally halved and livestock disease subsequently became rampant. Northwestern Europe had enjoyed an almost unbroken sequence of mild weather from 1170 to 1310, and agricultural activity had expanded steadily as technology improved, bringing demographic growth, so that resources were stretched thin. High mortality resulted in epidemic disease combined with acute nutritional stress, with a loss of a tenth to a third of the population in some areas. Growth in much of Europe came to a standstill, followed a generation later by the catastrophic Black Death. The harvest failures of 1315–17 precipitated a crisis that led to a major "correction" in the demographic history of western Europe.

Harvest failures during the next two centuries had little impact on decennial grain prices (Abel 1980, Day 1987) or on demographic trends. The next noteworthy crisis dates to 1569–73, when a series of exceptionally long and cold winters, heavy spring frosts, and cool, unrelentingly wet summers brought unprecedented social crises to western and northern Europe (Clark 1985,

Utterstrom 1955). Following 50 to 75 years of rapid population growth, agricultural resources were already overstressed, despite a regular, massive import of Baltic grains. As the crisis expanded to the Baltic and Scandinavia, food prices skyrocketed and all grain imports stopped, cities competing fiercely for food supplies. A desperate flight of paupers from the cities spread epidemic disease, contributing to high mortalities. Governments responded to popular disorders by introducing poor relief: establishing public granaries, poor houses, and organized grain imports, features that significantly reduced the scope and frequency of later famines in Europe.

With soil fertility and crop yields already declining, the famine of the 1590s reinforced shifts to new, intensified or diversified forms of agriculture in England, the Netherlands, Switzerland, and southern France (Clark 1985, Pfister 1984; also Lunden 1974, Chambers & Mingay 1966). Demographic growth rates were drastically cut and, by the 1620s, populations were either stable or declining, with sharp reductions in life expectancy (Galloway 1986), falling industrial employment and production, and growing poverty among rural folk and urban craftsmen. The agrarian boom and price revolution of the sixteenth century came to an abrupt end, and the Renaissance states were shaken to their roots. In conjunction with plague, fierce and recurrent religious wars, and a declining flow of New World treasure, Europe embarked upon the new century with frugal fiscal policies more appropriate to recession; economic recovery was delayed until the end of the 1600s, when exports of slave-produced Caribbean sugar began to boom. The disastrous weather and famines of the 1590s did not cause the seventeenth-century recession, but they contributed to the second Malthusian correction in three centuries and to a drastic switch to new economic policies and patterns.

As a result of greater and beneficial government intervention in appropriating and redistributing food staples (de Vries 1976, 1980, Abel 1974), weather-related famines and epidemics became increasingly uncommon during the seventeenth and eighteenth centuries, although the events of the 1690s (Lindgren & Neumann 1981) and 1740–41 (Post 1985) were serious enough. Local shortfalls, however, were more commonly the result of market manipulation (Hufton 1985). Close study of French peasant society in the 1780s shows that rural society was well adapted to dealing effectively with recurrent poor harvests (Sutherland 1981), and the bread crisis in Paris at the outset of the French Revolution in 1789 (Tilly 1975) was artificial rather than meteorological.

Europe's last catastrophic weather-related famine came in 1816–17. The Northern Hemisphere was already in the throes of the last great glacial readvance of the Little Ice Age when the volcanic peak of Tambora Island in Indonesia exploded in April 1815, injecting the largest quantity of sulfur in Holocene time into the stratosphere (Clausen & Hammer 1988). The summer of 1816 averaged at least 1–2°C colder than normal (Briffa et al. 1988, Harington 1991). Switzerland experienced the worst growing season in over 500 years of records (Pfister 1984). Floods and destructive hail were commonplace, crops were blighted by disease, and in western Germany the immature potato crop froze in the ground in November and subsequently rotted. Even in Southern Europe the grape and olive harvests were ruined by late summer cold and rains.

In some Swiss cities, mortality rates were two or three times the normal. Hardest hit was the Rhenish Palatinate, where tens of thousands of the destitute crowded into Mainz (Abel 1974, Post 1977). Widespread theft led to police repression and in turn to riots and unrest and to attempts at mass migration. However, worse scenarios were avoided by the well-organized relief and food reallocation efforts of the Prussian and French governments, and eventually the crisis passed. Subsequent European history has shown a much lessened vulnerability to weather fluctuations, the result among other factors of the shift away from climate-sensitive primary production (Flohn & Fantechi 1989), although severe storms can still take a large economic toll.

At this scale, and with the historical documentation that supports it, the role of climate in the pre-nineteenth century economic story of Europe is clear and unassailable. Through the agency of catastrophic famine, it severely impacted population growth, stimulated shifts in agricultural strategies, and provoked modifications in economic policies and patterns and greater economic intervention by the state. Equally clear is the way in which subsequently social transformations have lowered the region's vulnerability to similar meteorological events.

North American Arctic

Researchers from disciplines as diverse as climatology, physical oceanography, and biology (Vasari et al. 1972, Andrews & Andrews 1979) have long recognized that even apparently minor temperature variations in the climatic regime of the Arctic have produced large positive feedbacks in the environment and had dramatic impact on other physical and biological subsystems (see also Vibe 1967, Koerner 1977, Barry et al. 1977, Andrews & Miller 1979). Successful and long-term occupation and use of the North American Arctic by human populations, and most notably the Inuit (Dekin 1969, 1972, Maxwell 1985) has been intimately linked to their climate-related adaptive adjustments. Two areas are of particular interest regarding the possible consequences of climate amelioration in the Arctic: the ecology and exploitation by the Inuit of northern renewable resources and the pattern of human settlement established at present across the North American Arctic.

Because of the continuing nutritional and socioeconomic importance of terrestrial and marine wildlife to modern Inuit, any climate-induced disruption in the numbers, range, or availability of key species is of concern. That a warming may affect the ecological relations of Inuit and various prey species is well established by paleoclimatic and zooarchaeological evidence. Vibe (1967) provided the most detailed analysis of the effects in the historical period of episodes of warming and cooling on Northern biota and on the Inuit hunting economy. Using a nearly 150-year database, he identified the influence of climate on winter sea ice, the critical habitat element in ringed seal ecology, as a primary determinant of seal availability to polar bears, the other main winter marine resource, and to Inuit. Climatic amelioration often disrupts the stability of winter and spring sea ice, depriving ringed seals of feeding and breeding habitat and causing them to migrate (sometimes hundreds of kilometers) to areas where they can breed and find food. These seal-depleted areas are subsequently abandoned by polar bears. For Inuit, these two factors have serious socioeconomic consequences of a scale termed by Vibe (1967) as catastrophe.

The continued strong reliance on wildlife by the Inuit of Alaska (Burch 1985, Fienup-Riordan 1986), Greenland (Nuttall 1992), and Canada (Wenzel 1991) for much of their day-to-day subsistence suggests that Vibe's conclusions, although drawn from the historical record, retain impressive currency. Dunbar's work (1970; also Dunbar 1976, Dunbar & Thomson 1979) on the fisheries potential of the eastern Arctic makes clear that the commercial utilization of the north's marine resources is no more insulated from the effects of climate than is subsistence use. Although Inuit reliance on wildlife may mean high vulnerability to climate change, new technologies (e.g., snowmobiles, motorized boats, and even sonar) may prevent catastrophes. The summer conditions associated with warming, moreover, positively affect access to northern habitat for some other species (e.g., narwhal) and enhance Inuit opportunities to hunt them. However, exploitation of these opportunities is now strongly constrained by politics (game management regulations on protected or endangered animals). As ringed seal may represent as much as 80 percent (Wenzel 1991) of the edible biomass entering the summer subsistence of an Inuit community, any significant reduction in its share of the local harvest is likely to mean a net negative impact regardless of concurrent positive changes.

Settlement mobility is a second factor in changing vulnerability. Inuit in Alaska, Canada, and Greenland today live under greatly circumscribed conditions, their communities far more fixed than were those of even 50 years ago. Governments in all three Arctic regions have emphasized the development of permanent settlements with extensive residential, communication, and service infrastructures. Together, the 300 or more Inuit communities spread from southwest Alaska to Greenland represent the investment of several billion dollars by governments, Native corporations, and individual Inuit. The great majority of these communities lie at least partially within a few meters of present sea level. In extremely low areas such as the Yukon–Kuskokwim Delta and North Slope of Alaska, the Keewatin Barren Lands, and the Mackenzie Delta, an elevation of 4–5 m in sea level could mean marine incursions extending tens of kilometers inland. In the eastern portions of the North American Arctic, isostatic rebound may at least offset any rise in sea level, but, to the west, deglaciated much earlier, its effects are at best residual. As a result, some of the most densely populated parts of the Inuit world are at risk. Premodern Inuit settlements possessed an attribute—semi-permanence (Chang 1962)—that contemporary ones no longer have. Nearly a century of outside-directed development has placed today's population at an unprecedented disadvantage, which in all likelihood it lacks the resources to overcome. Virtually no Inuit group possesses the needed material or social resources to move or replace the elaborate permanent infrastructure that has arisen from the past 20 years of culture contact.

US Great Plains

Drought affecting agricultural production has been a significant hazard on the US Great Plains since White settlement beginning in the mid-nineteenth century. Changes in its aggregate consequences over that period appear to represent a case of declining societal vulnerability to climate. A major study covering the period from the late nineteenth to the mid-twentieth centuries found a marked lessening of local and regional impacts from droughts of comparable size (Warrick 1980, 1983, Bowden et al. 1981, Warrick & Bowden 1981). It examined, region wide and/or for representative counties, a variety of societal consequences of the four major modern droughts of the 1890s, the 1910s, the 1930s, and the 1950s (that of the 1930s was the most severe meteorologically and that of the 1950s the next most severe). No clear decline in drought impact on wheat yields was apparent. However, all of the other measures showed a marked lessening of outmigration as a proportion of population (Fig. 4.3), decline in farm income, farm foreclosures, and relief funds expended (beginning with the 1930s). The social disruption induced by droughts in the 1890s and 1910s far exceeded the impact in the 1950s of a more severe precipitation shortfall. Adaptation through technological change and institutional development—including both improved market integration and the emergence of a government role in crisis relief and in resource management—was identified as the cause of lessening. In a local case study, Riebsame (1981) identified several technological measures, crop insurance, diversification, and disaster relief as the most significant contributing factors.

The MINK study (Rosenberg 1993) examined the impacts an analogue climate representing the severe drought of 1931–40 would have on the Missouri–Iowa–Nebraska–Kansas region as it is at present and as it is projected to be in 2030. Substantial losses were envisioned in agriculture, forestry, and water resources, but the modeled impact on the regional economy overall was not found to be severe, the result of shifts in the regional economy away from climate-sensitive activities, of technological and institutional adaptation, and of interregional trade. The apparent decline in vulnerability to climate was further ascribed to the workings of an open economy, to the cultivation of research capacity informing adaptation, and to a flexible institutional structure, including a significant state role to correct market failures (Crosson & Rosenberg 1993), all recommended as key strategies for adapting to global climate change generally.

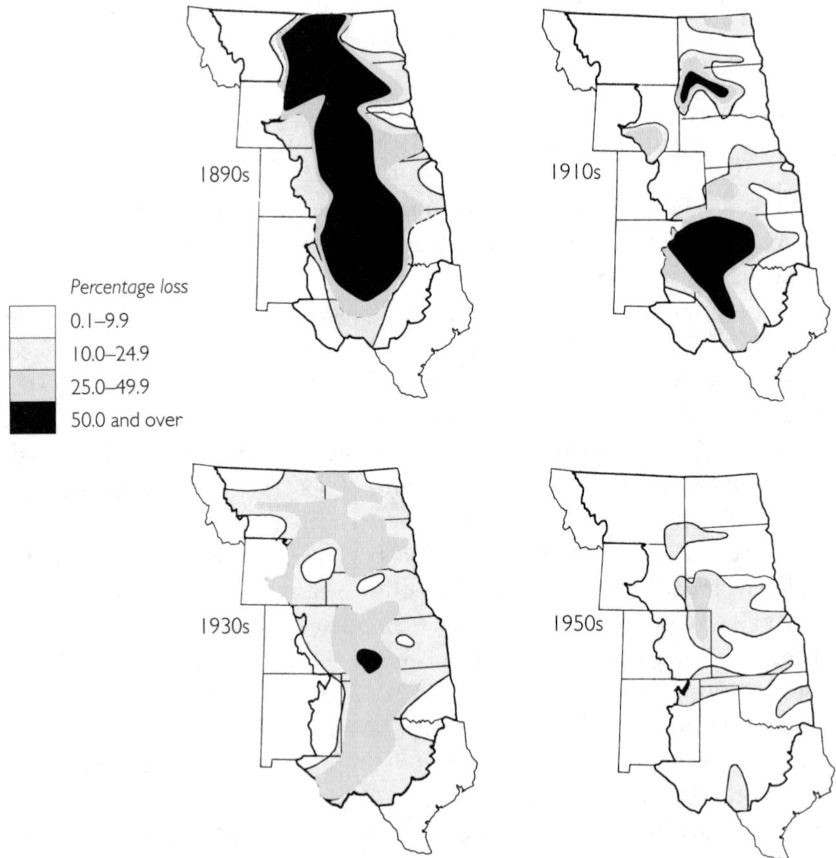

Figure 4.3 Population declines during major drought decades, US Great Plains (*source:* Warrick 1980).

The findings of these studies, however, warrant several caveats. The differences in impact among the four major past droughts studied may have had less to do with a trajectory of declining vulnerability to drought per se than with the economic context in which each occurred, for the 1890s and the 1930s, which saw the severest societal impacts, were also periods of severe national economic depression. The authors of the MINK study warn that synergisms not considered in the models might mean higher losses than the ones projected, and that conditions hotter and drier than those modeled might bring far higher losses (Crosson & Rosenberg 1993). On portions of the Great Plains, some of the insulation from the weather has been achieved by possibly fragile means—notably cheap energy and the mining of the Ogallala aquifer (Kromm & White 1992). Bowden et al. (1981) and Warrick (1983) accompanied their *lessening* hypothesis of decreased local losses on the Plains with a *catastrophe hypothesis*—although finding little support for it—that the national and global systems were at increasing risk from impacts displaced upward. A national-level study of the 1987–9 drought suggests that the capacity for loss remains as large as ever and has probably increased over the past few decades, despite technological advances in agriculture, forestry, and other natural resource areas that should lower vulnerability (Riebsame et al. 1991).

Just as the consequences of similar droughts varied over time, the consequences of individual ones have been markedly uneven. Region wide, tenant farmers, sharecroppers, and migrant laborers were among the hardest hit during the 1930s, while some more affluent cultivators may, in the aggregate, have benefited from the events of the decade (Warrick & Riebsame 1983). In southwestern Kansas during the 1930s, social impacts varied not only by the meteorological severity of the drought but by such socioeconomic determinants of coping ability as farm tenure status, farm size, family size and local kinship ties, race, citizenship status, and local off-farm employment opportunities (Riney-Kehrberg 1994).

Northeast Brazil

With a long history of severe drought, the Brazilian Northeast, like the US Great Plains, offers an opportunity to trace change over a century or more in the character and degree of impact of climate variation on human society (Hall 1978, Dias et al. 1986, Pessoa 1987, Magalhães et al. 1988, Correia de Andrade 1989, Magalhães 1992, 1993, Magalhães & Magee 1994). The Brazilian Northeast, like the Great Plains, illustrates the uneven character of drought impact on exposed populations; longitudinally, it shows less evidence than the Great Plains does of diminished vulnerability.

The region is subject to irregular failures of the winter (wet season) rainfall, particularly serious in the early months of the season. They have occurred with extreme severity a few times per century since the early 1800s and frequently in more moderate form. Geographically most exposed to water shortage within the Northeast are the *sertao* zone and the *agreste* zone on its fringe; they hold most of the region's rural population. Land use during the past century and a half has represented a mix of cash crops, subsistence crops, and livestock raising. Land ownership is so heavily skewed that large holdings (only 1 percent of farms) cover 44 percent of the total area, while smallholdings (56 percent of the farms) cover only 3 percent (Magalhães & Magee 1994). The population of the *sertao* and *agreste*, dense compared to that of Brazil as a whole, is substantially landless rural laborers, plus smallholders and large landowners. The growing urban population of the Northeast overall now exceeds the rural, which declined slightly during the 1980s to about 16 million (Magalhães 1993).

Judging by some measures of impact, regional vulnerability has decreased since the late nineteenth century. "Massive death" (Magalhães 1993: 189) was a prominent feature of the 1877–80 drought, "the most costly natural disaster in the history of the Western hemisphere," with an excess mortality estimated at several hundred thousand (Cunniff 1970), but is no longer evident. The development of urban and industrial sectors less sensitive than agriculture to drought has necessarily tended to reduce the vulnerability of the region as a whole. Nonetheless, in social and economic terms the rural sector is probably more vulnerable than before, as a consequence of population increase, land stress, and underdevelopment. Impacts of drought on agricultural production and productivity remain sharp (Table 4.2), and contemporary droughts of mild or medium severity have been judged by experts to have greater impact now than did events of comparable severity in earlier decades (Magalhães 1992, Magalhães & Magee 1994).

The impacts of drought also remain quite uneven among different groups. Rainfed subsistence agriculture is the most vulnerable activity. Irrigated cash-crop agriculture and livestock raising, practiced mostly on large holdings, are much less affected, and the activities of the urban centers and the industrial sector in the Northeast less still. Landless agricultural laborers and tenant farmers, who are likely to lose employment, are most vulnerable to drought. Smallholders may be obliged to sell land, usually to larger owners. Severe droughts may produce gains for the wealthiest inhabitants, who have a large and well-tested repertoire of responses at their disposal (Magalhães 1992, 1993), and the public sector swells in drought years from the influx of national relief aid.

Table 4.2 Planted area, production, and yield in Ceará state in nondrought or drought years.

Main products	Nondrought year (1978) Planted area (ha)	Production (tonnes)	Yield (tonnes per ha)	Drought year (1983) Planted area (ha)	Production (tonnes)	Yield (tonnes per ha)
Tree cotton	1200000	237600	0.198	675202	47264	0.07
Annual cotton	84000	27720	0.33	74367	17034	0.229
Rice	56000	60200	1.075	16292	30077	1.846[1]
Beans	400000	120000	0.3	167291	24811	0.148
Corn	480000	259200	0.54	146092	175310	0.12
Manioc (cassava)	175000	1575000	9.0	82974	442088	5.0

Source: Magalhães et al. (1988).
1. The increase in rice productivity in a drought year is probably attributable to the fact that production continued only in irrigated areas.

South Asia

Climate–society relations are of great importance in the populous, agrarian, monsoon region of South Asia, where climate-sensitive activities remain immensely important and where the climate displays a sharp seasonal character and high variation in space and time. Failure of the monsoon brings widespread hardship. A series of failures can threaten large-scale disaster for agricultural ecosystems and human populations. Intense monsoon rains, on the other hand, contribute to flood mortalities of massive proportions (Wescoat & Jacobs 1993). When drought or flood coincides with social and political instability, the risk of famine increases.

Despite the importance of the issues involved, research on the human dimensions of global change in the region to date is much less extensive than either the size of the population affected or its relative vulnerability warrants. Within the body of relevant research that does exist, use of historical–geographic evidence and approaches to climate–society and global change questions is most evident in research on what may be termed *critical resource problems*. Although easy to define in terms of the frequency, magnitude, and severity of physical events or social consequences, the concepts of criticality and vulnerability are only beginning to be defined in ways that examine causal links among natural and social processes (e.g., see South Asian case studies in Blaikie & Brookfield 1987, Jodha 1989, US NRC 1992, Kasperson et al. 1995).

Many representatives of South Asian countries assert that their concern about global climate change stems directly, and almost exclusively, from specific concerns about basic food supplies, water availability, and coastal inundation (Wescoat 1991). These basic practical concerns stem, in turn, from historical experience with famine, disease, and environmental disaster (Hewitt

1983). There are more than 100 years of modern scientific research on famine in South Asia, as well as abundant textual evidence from earlier periods (Currey & Hugo 1984).

Although catastrophic drought-related famines had occurred for many centuries, only from the late nineteenth century onward they have been extensively documented and debated. Especially severe ones occurred in the 1860s and 1870s, in 1896–7, in 1899–1900, and in 1943—the last, in Bengal, one of the worst food disasters in recent history (Sen 1981, Greenough 1982, Drèze 1990). (As in most famines, deaths were predominantly the result of malnutrition-related disease, rather than starvation per se.) One key question concerns the role of climate patterns and events relative to political and economic sources of vulnerability. Although Gregory (1989) has underscored the importance of drought frequency and duration as independent factors, it has been necessary to pay close attention to regimes, institutions, and economic policies to account for changing patterns of impact. In 1880 the British colonial government began to use the so-called Famine Codes to guide official response. Strongly influenced by the tenets of the classical economists, the codes emphasized the provision of public works employment at subsistence wages during emergency periods to create purchasing power, while discouraging direct intervention in the food trade through price controls, state supply, or other means.

This strategy, which with some modifications has remained the basis of Indian famine policy (Drèze & Sen 1989), worked better in some circumstances than others; it worked poorly in the 1890s when severe droughts may have reduced the absolute food supply within reach so much that even income support did not make it available for purchase (Drèze 1990). Economic integration, especially through improved transportation and interregional trade, has permitted both the import of food to drought-stricken areas and its export from such areas when higher price levels elsewhere so dictated. The Bengal famine of 1943 owed more to war, disorder, state-ordered appropriation of food stocks, and inadequate response to the onset of the crisis than to weather variation.

Interpretations of modern trends in vulnerability to drought exhibit little consensus. McAlpin (1983) argued that, in Western India, traditional political explanations centering on the role of colonialism in increasing vulnerability (e.g., Bhatia 1967) should be balanced by greater emphasis on conjunctions of agrometeorological variability and drought adjustments. She contended also that impacts of drought generally have diminished since the mid-nineteenth century because of the social and technological responses, such as interregional trade, credit, and government relief, that have come into play. Subbiah (1993) credited post-Independence government policy with markedly lessening vulnerability to drought. Others (e.g., Chen 1991) emphasized its persistence, with population growth and environmental stress countering the gains from technological advances and crisis relief overemphasized in policy over longer term *drought proofing*. Commercialization has relieved some forms of vulnerability but eroded some traditional protections against it.

Impacts of drought are far from uniform. Different states within India have shown markedly different capacities for responding to drought crises (Drèze 1990). Chen (1991) conducted a local level study of drought in 1985–7 in a village in Gujarat. She found that landless laborers, traditionally the most vulnerable class, were less affected in terms of decreased food consumption than some other groups were, such as peasant cultivators and shepherds, not well protected by the standard measures of state employment on public works. Such was the case only for droughts severe enough to evoke emergency measures; at other times, landless laborers were indeed disproportionately vulnerable. Shepherds, barred by caste mores and tradition from engaging in wage labor and thus unable to make use of relief employment, fared especially badly in 1985–7 (Chen 1991). Across all social groups, vulnerability was greater for households with no able-bodied adult males.

That India has in the past half-century avoided major famine despite the exposure of a highly vulnerable population to severe drought may be considered at least a qualified success story (Drèze 1990)—qualified because of the persistence of poverty and other conditions contributing to vulnerability. For the relative success of drought-response policy, Drèze & Sen (1989) credit both India's principal choice of instruments (aimed at protecting entitlements) and a democratic system able to pressure decisionmakers effectively to respond to crises. Yet the variety of cultural responses to drought—ranging from long-distance migration to sale of jewelry to religious conversion—reminds us of the complexity and specificity of such episodes. Nor may it be possible, or particularly useful, to try to make generalizations about whether vulnerability to climate change is increasing or decreasing on a regional or subregional scale. Many tools of coping, such as access to emergency credit and food redistribution, have on the whole become more available over the past 150 years. Some drought adjustments (e.g., weather forecasting and irrigation engineering) have become more effective, whereas others (e.g., traditional peasant agronomic practices and crop choices) may be waning or displaced by rural–urban and international migration.

The drought and famine literatures from South Asia in any case underscore the importance, perceived and real, of the political and cultural contexts of environmental crisis—both as causal factors and as constraints on adjustment. These political and cultural factors range in scale from household and village adaptability up to the political stability and capacity of national institutions. Their effects can be severe and short, as in the Bengal famine of 1943, or incremental and long. A long-term perspective on changes in South Asian political and cultural history reinforces the need for subnational as well as national assessments of global climate change. Both climate phenomena and vulnerability vary enormously across the region, owing in part to its demographic and cultural complexity. In some places with glaciated headwaters, such as the Indus River Basin, flood hazard may be a more likely consequence of greenhouse-gas-induced change than drought (Wescoat & Leichenko 1992). Historically conditioned complexity makes it very difficult to generalize about regional climate impacts, and the natural variability of the climate system makes it especially hard to distinguish short-term anomalies from long-term changes. And, as in many (or even most) parts of the world, political instabilities and uncertainties raise worrisome questions about the value of planning for sustainable development on timescales of decades to centuries. The variability of climate and society in South Asia calls for research that focuses on processes of dynamic adjustment in the face of major uncertainties and structural changes.

Sub-Saharan Africa

"African economies are currently based on a narrow range of economic activities, most of which are highly vulnerable to climatic variability and change" (Ominde & Juma 1991: 195). The most damaging climatic hazard in Africa is drought, and vulnerability is dominated by food insecurity. Global climate change may increase the magnitude, duration, and frequency of drought, although this is highly uncertain. Vulnerability to food deficits, of which drought is one possible trigger, depends on a chain of failures in the human ecology of production, exchange entitlement through commercial markets, and political ecology of empowerment and enfranchisement (Bohle et al. 1994).

Four epochs of drought vulnerability may be distinguished in Africa: precolonial, colonial, postindependence, and contemporary. (This is a generalized perspective; see, for example, Ravallion 1987, Drèze & Sen 1989, Huss-Ashmore & Katz 1989, Bohle et al. 1991, Fischer et al. 1991, Field 1993.).

With independence, beginning with Ghana in 1957, the colonial patterns of administration persisted, although Africanized to various extents. The state continued to take a role in crises and sought to identify and achieve development targets that would prevent famine. One widespread result of independence was that control of the means of production shifted from foreigners to Africans; also, industries and trade became the focus of internal development. This period of transition, from largely self-provisioning rural economies to mixed systems, resulted in quite varied patterns of vulnerability. In some areas (e.g., the highlands of Kenya), farming systems based on coffee and tea were commercially successful, and drought and famine were no longer serious threats. In other places and for vulnerable groups, the transition resulted in enhanced vulnerability—with neither traditional production and kinship entitlements nor viable commercial enterprises. In the 1970s and 1980s climate also varied more than in the two decades before independence. Drought and famine in 1983–5 affected half of Africa's countries (Alexandratos 1988). The dominant state response was massive food aid.

Current vulnerability might be characterized as interdependence. For most of rural Africa, coping with climatic variations now depends on access to commercial markets. Effective responses are shared and multilevel: households require diversified incomes to ensure that they can purchase food when necessary (Farming Systems Research Unit 1994); nations must be prepared to import food and stabilize market prices; and the global market needs to have sufficient stocks for trade (Downing 1990). Effective markets spread and lessen the risk of drought from the household and village ultimately to the world. Additional responses are required to meet the needs of the especially vulnerable, however; they usually take the form of crisis interventions, which tend to be expensive, do little to reduce drought vulnerability, and often fail to prevent serious loss of life and welfare. The realization that disaster and development planning must be merged is not new, but it is receiving greater emphasis after a decade of emergency responses.

Current drought impact in Africa is affected at the global level by the availability and cost of grain imports (dependent on world markets) and the level and timeliness of international aid (a product of attention cycles and political agendas). Climate change impacts will likewise be related to global agricultural and commodity markets, international finance, investment and development assistance, and information systems, among other factors. A contextual factor lessening the impact of the 1984–5 drought and food crisis in Kenya was the relatively high world prices at the time for the major national export crops of tea and coffee, which allowed the government to import needed food reserves (Downing et al. 1989). At the world scale, agricultural prices continue to decline, as does donor investment in African agriculture (von Braun et al. 1993).

Vulnerabilities vary from group to group and change over time. During the Kenya drought of 1984–5, impacts varied substantially among regions, communities, households, and individuals, with results ranging from death and disability of family members to windfall profits from livestock and food trading (Rocheleau et al. 1994). Gender was one important dimension of vulnerability, with women more subject to loss than men; access to reliable off-farm employment was another crucial factor distinguishing those less and more hard-hit (Rocheleau et al. 1994, Downing et al. 1989). Targeted vulnerability assessments are required to identify dependent populations and to plan for their needs on a recurrent basis and even more so in times of emergency. Patterns of vulnerability today differ from rural smallholders to landless laborers to the urban poor, the destitute, and refugees. The situation for most smallholders may improve as they become more integrated into national and regional economies. In contrast, pastoralists are more likely to remain dependent on external aid. Perhaps the most significant recent changes have been large increases in the urban poor, destitute, and refugees, as a result of the deprivations of drought, structural adjustment, and ethnic conflict. Many depend on occasional and low-paying jobs and on begging and relief.

Research on Africa needs to integrate the human dimensions of vulnerability with climate and climate change impact assessment. Such research should focus on the nexus of vulnerability/resilience and coping strategies/adaptive responses, rather than repeating the dominant paradigm of predicting the impacts of scenarios of global change for the next 100 years against indeterminate projections of demographic and economic growth.

Conclusion

Documented impacts of climate hazards provide a useful though imperfect analogue for vulnerability to global climate change. The differential effects of climate hazards on human groups and activities teach valuable lessons about the prospective impacts of global climate change. "Too many people," it has been observed, "still believe that the impacts of disasters and climate change are determined solely by the physical characteristics of events . . . We can know very little about the social impacts of global change unless we work to understand, document, and communicate the nature of vulnerability" (Liverman 1990: 39).

The regional studies reviewed in this section illustrate that such analyses are indispensable for making sense of human interactions with climate variation and of the differences in impact among and within societies. They convey a simple but telling lesson about climate hazards, which can be extended by analogy to global climate change: that the significance of climate variation or change depends on both the change itself and on the characteristics of the society exposed to it. Although exposure to geophysical events is an important dimension of vulnerability, it is not the only one. The point is clear in studies of hazard effects over time: similar recurrent events in particular regions have had vastly different consequences because of societal transformations that occurred in between hazard events. It is equally clear in studies of the differential effects of hazards on groups and activities equally exposed to them; particular hazard events can be of vastly different consequence for those on whom they impinge because of differences in coping ability. The far higher losses of life from similar extreme weather events in the Third World than in the First World (Burton et al. 1993, Blaikie et al. 1994) illustrate the point at the global scale; rainfall and temperature fluctuations in western Europe have far milder effects on human well-being today than they did in the medieval and early modern periods.

A recurrent hazard such as drought in Northeast Brazil has consequences for different groups that cannot be understood simply from the meteorological character of the event, any more than their differences from drought impact on the US Great Plains can be. Vulnerabilities are in constant evolution, and the factors affecting them include many policies and trends not related to climate, as is apparent in several ways in the Canadian Arctic. Single-factor explanations of vulnerability and hazard impact have not proven adequate; attention is needed, in both hazards research and the human dimensions of climate change, to the ways in which relevant factors interact to affect the consequences experienced from natural events.

Climate as hazard: adaptation and response

A key contribution of vulnerability analysis is the way in which it:

> . . . expands the range of choices in responding to global change. For example, it demonstrates that we can reduce impacts of global change not just by slowing the rate of climate change or ozone depletion but also by reducing the vulnerability of populations to these changes. (Liverman 1990: 39)

The *range of choice* concept in the hazards field (Burton et al. 1993) calls attention to the possible existence of responses other than the ones usually considered or preferred by decisionmakers. Criticisms of the concept and of the ways in which it has been used (e.g., Emel & Peet 1989) view it as overly individualistic in application and emphasize the degree to which the choice of response for many actors is restricted and the selection of seemingly inferior responses the result of structural constraints rather than subjective choice. Attention to both the *range* and the *restriction* of responses to climate hazards illuminates choices about climate change.

The distinction between vulnerability and response is somewhat artificial. It is used here largely for convenience and because it reflects a frequent division in emphasis among studies of climate interaction. Obviously, vulnerability to climate variation is in part determined by the responses that have been taken or are available. Yet vulnerability is affected by many social changes whose relation to climate and climate impacts, though perhaps profound, may also be only incidental rather than deliberate. Separating responses to climate from other factors can help determine to what extent change in vulnerability has been the result of purposeful action.

Actions taken without reference to climate can affect vulnerability to it; actions taken primarily in response to a climatic challenge can either lower or increase impacts. Failure of response may occur through a misunderstanding of the situation: through the outside selection of response instruments poorly matched to the social system affected (for examples, see Torry 1979). Or response may fail to decrease vulnerability because such was not the principal concern of the decisionmakers. The history of response to drought in the Brazilian Northeast is a long and varied one, but the rural population remains highly vulnerable because the responses have not addressed the most important sources of vulnerability. They have instead emphasized relatively uncontroversial, but also relatively ineffective, technological solutions that have incidentally worked to the benefit of the regional elite (Hirschman 1963, Hall 1978, Boudon 1984, Magalhães & Magee 1994).

Studies of responses to natural hazards in the range of choice perspective (Burton et al. 1993) have developed a typology that can enrich the menu of geoengineering, abatement, and adaptation often used in discussions of global climate change (e.g., US NRC 1992). This response typology (Fig. 4.5) has the further advantage of simultaneously permitting description of those societal changes that, without being undertaken for reasons of their climate–society consequences, nonetheless have such consequences. Future research could profitably use the typology to compare the changes in vulnerability and impact produced by deliberate responses to those produced incidentally by changes acting through the same agencies; in each section below we offer some examples of the latter as well as the former. The categories in the typology most relevant to global climate change are: modify the event and thus prevent effects, change location, change use, or accept (share or bear) losses.

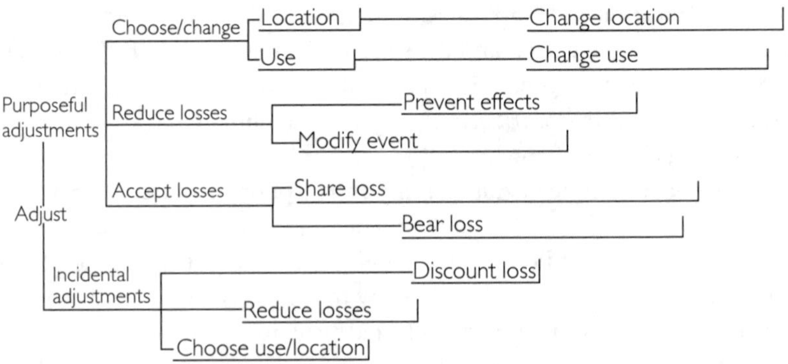

Figure 4.5 Choice tree of responses to natural hazards (adapted from Burton et al. 1993).

Modifying the event

Modifying the event—that is, controlling the climate—has frequently been proposed but has rarely been attempted beyond the local scale. Perhaps the largest project seriously considered, that of flooding a portion of North Africa lying below sea level to increase the region's rainfall, was long debated but never acted upon by the French government in the late nineteenth century. Opponents invoked three of the principal arguments available against climate-controlling schemes generally (Fuchs 1877, Heffernan 1990):

- it would not have the desired effects, or enough of them to justify the cost
- it would have disastrous unintended environmental consequences
- it was sociopolitically objectionable.

Initiatives toward weather modification in many countries since the end of the Second World War have been hampered by fears of the damage that such techniques might do and by apparent and potential conflicts of interest in weather among different users (Breuer 1980).

At the micro scale, modification has been widespread and effective. Peasant farmers have deployed such techniques as shelterbelt planting and earth mounding to improve the conditions within which their crops grow (Wilken 1972, 1987). Forms of microclimate modification used on commercial farms include windbreaks and shelterbelts (Caborn 1965, Rosenberg 1986). Rainmaking through magical or religious intervention has at least as long a history of use, if not of proven success. Its employment and perceived efficacy have declined as a result of changes that range in Tanzania, for example, from the diffusion of macro- and meso-scale weather maps and forecasts to the undermining by central authority of the rainmaker's status (Feierman 1990).

A commonplace of social theory since Merton (1949) has held that, although rainmaking ceremonies do not objectively affect the weather, they are not without consequences for the group performing them (a classic African case study is James 1972). Efforts at weather and climate control large enough to offer analogues for global geoengineering are few, but they too show how, even where there are few of the desired physical consequences, there may be significant social ones. The Timber Culture Act of 1873 in the United States was meant to encourage the development on the Great Plains of tree cover that would moderate temperatures and increase rainfall (Emmons 1971). Because of lax and corrupt administration, it had little effect on land cover, but it did facilitate the transfer of public land to private owners, particularly speculators (McIntosh 1975). The belief that cultivation would increase rainfall, although incorrect, stimulated settlement in the Plains in the late nineteenth century (Kutzleb 1968). Extensive private and state-supported cannonading of clouds in western Europe around the turn of the century failed in its purpose of preventing hailstorms, but did cause considerable injury and loss of life (Changnon & Ivens 1981). Brazilian government responses to the great drought of 1877–80 in the Northeast focused on the construction of reservoirs; evaporation from them was expected to make the atmosphere more humid and rainfall more regular (Cunniff 1970, da Cunha 1944). The policy structure thus established, with its focus on technical solutions, remained dominant through the mid-twentieth century, although the expectation of direct climatic benefit gradually faded. The policy did help maintain the socioeconomic structure of the region—itself a prime source of high vulnerability for most of the population—by furnishing relief employment on public works during droughts, contracts to politically powerful individuals, and water supply for livestock to wealthy landowners (Hirschman 1963, Magalhães 1993). Land-use regulation in many eighteenth- and nineteenth-century British and French colonies in South Asia and Africa was driven by a *desiccationist* thesis, attributing disastrous climate change to forest clearance. Policies controlling forest use by indigenous cultivators caused substantial hardship and widespread resistance, because such policies were incompatible with the land-use systems being regulated (Grove 1990, 1995).

Response to floods has often taken the related form of seeking to *control effects* by physically preventing inundation. Widely used where the resources are available, flood control works have often proved to be less suitable than other responses would have been. A classic example is the longstanding choice in the United States of expensive and relatively ineffective streamflow regulation and forestry projects (modify event), disaster relief, and subsidized insurance (share losses) over floodplain zoning (change location/change use) as a means of reducing flood losses. The preference apparently reflects both an aversion to land-use regulation and the imperatives of local economic development, but it has had the perverse effect of raising losses by encouraging occupation of floodplains (White et al. 1958, Montz & Gruntfest 1986). Bangladesh's Flood Action Plan, proposed after disastrous inundations in 1987 and 1988, relied heavily on the engineering solution of building embankments, and drew severe criticism on social, environmental, and efficiency grounds. Critics advanced alternative proposals aimed less at preventing flooding inundation than at reducing the vulnerability of the population to its effects (Haque & Zaman 1993, Zaman 1993).

As with climate control, the scientific basis on which flood control is planned or urged may be faulty. Flooding has been widely blamed on upstream forest clearance, and reforestation promoted as a solution, yet often on questionable grounds. That interpretation has sometimes—for example, in the early twentieth-century United States (Dodds 1969) and in contemporary South Asia (Chapman & Thompson 1995)—been compelling enough for political reasons to have achieved wide acceptance despite its weak scientific base in these cases.

Changing location

Changing location—that is, migration of people or activities induced by climate variation or by environmental degradation in other forms—has received some attention as an analogue for response to climate change (e.g., Jacobson 1988, Kritz 1990). Whether, in the aggregate, this option is more or less available than in the past—whether an increased physical ease of movement outweighs possibly increasing social barriers to it—is not clear. The North American Arctic case shows a growing stability imposed on populations by investment in settlement infrastructure; that of Northeast Brazil, on the other hand, an increased mobility promoted by construction of roads leading out of the region. Mobility, in the Brazilian case, has depended in part on the apparent availability of open land elsewhere, on the Amazonian frontier. However, open agricultural land is not essential to outmigration. The urban sector is an alternative destination, whether temporary, circulatory, or permanent, as it is for drought-affected cultivators in many parts of Africa and as it is for flood refugees in Bangladesh (Huq-Husain 1995).

Kritz (1990) reviewed case studies of climate-related migration and the attempts that have been made to draw lessons from them for global change. She drew a distinction between the industrialized and the less industrialized worlds. In the former, the influence of climate hazards on migration has been buffered to the point of economic insignificance by technology and public policy (as in the case of the US Great Plains or marginal land abandonment in medieval Europe as compared with the present). Climate-related relocation is now chiefly a search for amenity values rather than a flight from hazards. In the less industrialized world, climate variations, notably droughts and floods, sporadically swell or redirect population movements, but the role they play is markedly affected by the character of the social system with which they interact. Kritz (1990) cautioned that because most economists and sociologists concerned with migration have neglected the possible role of climate in migration, any conclusions that can be stated now rest on a weak base of research.

Governments have sometimes promoted migration as a response to drought and famine: in northeast Brazil, for example. In British India, such efforts had to overcome the strong reluctance of subsistence farmers to move (Drèze 1990, Hill 1991). By contrast, in late imperial China, relocation was one of the first responses of drought-afflicted peasants and the one most strongly and consistently discouraged by the state, which feared social disruption through large-scale population transfers (Will 1990).

Drought-induced migration may have adverse environmental consequences in the destination region; the Brazilian policy of building roads to facilitate outmigration from the Northeast has contributed to tropical deforestation through resettlement in Amazonia (Magalhães & Magee 1994). However, an overview of what is known about the environmental effects of refugee immigration in general found a complex picture, with examples of both degradation and improvement, that cannot be reduced to simple formulae; closer study is needed of "the many complex linkages between economic, social, political, and environmental change established in refugee-affected areas" (Black 1994: 273).

Government resettlement projects, many in association with large dam schemes, present a major archive of analogues for state-directed population movement. Success stories are much less apparent in the literature on resettlement than in cases where the social, economic, and health effects on the transferred populations have been severe and costly (for reviews, see Adams 1990, Gutman 1994). In the hazards field, Blaikie et al. (1994) identify relocation of populations as the worst option among responses to disaster. An equally discouraging analogue for global climate change is the experience of migrant populations in unfamiliar climates; inexperience with novel environments is often cited as a factor making regions of recent settlement highly vulnerable (e.g., Ingram et al. 1981, Butzer 1990). The adjustments employed by many new settlers in the Great Plains between the Civil War and the Dust Bowl—rainfed agriculture and dry farming techniques—proved ill suited to a region subject to recurrent severe drought and windstorms (Riebsame 1990). The concept of preadaptation (e.g., Jordan 1989), or the degree to which a group's repertoire of skills happens to include ones suited to a new environment into which the group migrates, may also be useful in characterizing differences in ability to cope with a new environment created by climate change.

Migrations not undertaken in response to climate variation can for other reasons affect vulnerability to it. The worldwide concentration of population near coastlines is one example of a major trend increasing physical exposure (although not necessarily increasing overall vulnerability) to hazards. Glantz (1994) proposed—and illustrated with case studies from nine regions in the First, Second, and Third Worlds—the thesis that drought follows the plow. He and his contributors argued that, as a result of population pressure, migration in search of new agricultural land (most prime lands having already been occupied) is increasingly bringing population and farming into marginal zones. There agriculture is highly exposed to drought, is likely to be low in coping ability, may be practised in ways unsuited to the new environment, and may inflict environmental degradation (e.g., desertification) of which it becomes the principal victim.

Changing use

Changing use to some activity less vulnerable represents the third category of hazard response. Ausubel (1991b: 652) argues that long-term changes in human activities have steadily reduced human vulnerability: "the trend is toward systems that are less vulnerable to climate," whether or not climate figured among the reasons for particular changes. Innumerable innovations—from the development of weather forecasting to the replacement of climate-sensitive energy sources and modes of transportation by climate-insulated ones—have lessened the significance of weather variations for human activities. The rapidity with which capital stock is replaced, moreover, means that societies possess a high degree of flexibility in adapting their activities to global climate change. Such insulation, though, has not been uniform across the world; less industrialized countries "may well lack the resources to apply such technologies to raise or maintain the quality of life in the face of changing climate" (Ausubel 1991b: 651). The overall global trend in production and employment from highly climate-sensitive sectors of agriculture, fisheries, and forestry to much less climate-sensitive ones implies the same overall trend, and the much greater share in the former sectors in less industrialized than in highly industrialized countries implies the same unevenness in sensitivity to climate. In Northeast Brazil, national government policy between 1954 and 1975 emphasizing development through industrialization, although not an unqualified success, proved more effective in insulating the regional economy from drought than had the preceding three quarters of a century's emphasis on reservoir construction and crisis relief (Magalhães et al. 1988).

Cases can also be cited where modern techniques have replaced more climate-adapted land uses; intercropping in indigenous cultivation is a case in point (Wilken 1987). It is not clear that such a change in use always represents a net increase in vulnerability. An exemplary case is that discussed by McCloskey (1976): medieval English farmers scattered their landholdings as a means of diversifying against climate risk, but ceased to do so when financial instruments for buffering against bad years became available and the usefulness of field scattering no longer outweighed the inconveniences. Field scattering has persisted elsewhere as a response to climate risk in the absence of the conditions that prompted its abandonment in England (e.g., Goland 1989).

Irrigation is perhaps the best-studied land-use response to climatic unreliability. It is often asked in the social science literature "whether irrigation as a sociotechnical activity, by its very nature, has certain organizational prerequisites" (Enge & Whiteford 1989: 10)—and also whether it has certain organizational consequences. The *hydraulic society* thesis, derived from the work of Wittfogel (1957; see also Mitchell 1973) linked large-scale irrigation and water management as cause and/or effect of a despotic centralized state. Worster (1986, 1993) recently sought to explain the development of the modern American West in these terms, although others have contested such an interpretation (Maass & Anderson 1978, Long 1995), documenting the capture of great hydraulic systems by local interest groups. That no necessary link exists between irrigation and such a state structure is acknowledged and is amply evident in the histories of many small-scale, self-governing, and long-persistent irrigation systems (Ostrom & Gardner 1993). That large-scale water systems may have certain such organizational requirements remains an inviting but controversial hypothesis.

In any case, water's qualities as a resource significantly constrain the ways in which societies can effectively organize its use (Bennett & Dahlberg 1990). In particular, the frequent collective good problems encountered in irrigation, large or small scale (see, for example, Ostrom & Gardner 1993), may make either state control or common-property arrangements more conducive to surface-water irrigation than free-market or individualist institutions. Privately developed groundwater irrigation on the US Great Plains, drawing on the Ogallala Aquifer, is increasingly regulated by government institutions that have developed with the threat of resource depletion (Kromm & White 1992).

Adverse environmental and social consequences of large-scale irrigation offsetting their reduction of climatic vulnerability have been documented in many integrated studies. Such experience cautions against unquestioning promotion of it as a buffer against climate change. Widely recorded impacts include soil and water degradation, disease, involuntary population displacement, and unequal partitioning of impacts and benefits (see, for example, Adams 1990, 1992). The physical provision of water even on a vast scale may also do little to reduce drought impacts on much of the population. During the 1960s the development of irrigation represented the focus of Brazilian government response to the drought hazard in the Northeast, but the benefits accrued mainly to the groups and individuals least vulnerable to drought to begin with (Hall 1978).

Share or bear losses

Human societies have long possessed a wide variety of instruments by which to buffer and spread losses imposed by the weather (Halsted & O'Shea 1989). The regions examined here show different mixes over time of such strategies and of the institutions—market, state, or society—predominantly entrusted with them. The existence has been documented in many peasant societies of a *moral economy*, whose norms create networks of obligations within communities and stipulate redistribution to guarantee minimal subsistence for the poorest members. However, the actual functioning of these norms in times of crisis has been questioned, and so has the degree to which modern famines can be attributed to their dissolution (Torry 1986); so too has the applicability of the term "moral economy" to actions, such as food riots, meant to maintain inequitable patterns of access to subsistence (Root 1990).

Eighteenth-century China has been contrasted with Europe of the same period (Will 1983, 1990, Wong 1983) regarding the roles played by state and market in response to the threat of famine. Late imperial China deployed a varied and pragmatic set of responses, including food provision from an elaborate granary storage system, loans, cash relief, transfer of grain between provinces, and controls on the food trade. In western Europe, despite an active state role, market mechanisms were given more responsibility than in China. The Chinese approach was, considering the magnitude of the challenges it faced, remarkably successful during the eighteenth century in alleviating the potentially catastrophic results of production shortfalls (Will 1990), but proved much less so in the next century when a variety of circumstances gravely weakened the imperial state's capacity. Europe, on the other hand, witnessed a gradual decline in vulnerability to weather and climate hazards, which stemmed from both market development and public intervention. Its experience offered cautionary examples when the market was given too wide or too narrow a role. Price controls and prohibitions on the transfer of food supplies in the face of subsistence crises often had the disastrously perverse effect of lessening food supplies by reducing incentives for their provision. An overly optimistic reliance on laissez-faire during periods in eighteenth-century France created localized food shortages when price levels dictated the export of grain from hungry regions. Popular unrest found expression in food riots and other disturbances (Tilly 1971, Hufton 1985).

The Indian Famine Codes transferred European experience and management preferences, further shaped by economic theorists, to South Asia. Their emphasis on upholding purchasing power in food markets through cash employment proved, as noted earlier, well suited to some circumstances and much less so to others. The important role open to public action (Drèze & Sen 1989) is underlined by some classic imperfections in market operation. Market and transportation development, if they create the capacity to bring food to areas where drought has created shortfalls in production, can also create or amplify famines by drawing food out of drought-affected areas if higher prices elsewhere so dictate. In present-day South Asia, speculation in response to uncertainty can significantly destabilize markets that are imperfectly integrated and informed and can amplify the price impacts of agricultural shortfalls (Ravallion 1987). Public action has principally taken the form of crisis relief, without, however—as in Northeast Brazil, India, and Africa—substantially altering the persistent vulnerability of many groups to recurrent climate variation, still less to harmful climate change. Programs of sustainable development increasing the resilience of the most vulnerable groups has been identified as the key to lessening drought impacts, and future climate change ones, in Northeast Brazil (Magalhães 1992, 1993) and elsewhere.

Formal crop insurance represents another means of dealing with weather-related risks and losses. Experience with it highlights several crucial features of such insurance—the prevalence of adverse selection (the disproportionate enrollment of high-risk operations) and moral hazard (the encouragement of risky behavior among those enrolled). These features have virtually everywhere required substantial government subsidy for such insurance, the problem of uncertainty alone making it an unappealing task for the market (Hazell et al. 1986). The need for subsidy in turn raises issues of efficiency (encouraging risky behavior) and equity (transferring wealth from some parties to others) and, in any case, limits the degree to which resource-poor governments will be able to finance insurance.

Conclusion

The hazards typology and criticisms of it illustrate, if they do not exhaust, the varied ways in which actors at different levels might respond to climate challenges. Several lessons emerge from case studies of response viewed in these terms. The first is that not all responses are equally available to all actors. The viability of crop insurance depends heavily on the degree of information, organization, and subsidy available to support it, for example, and the option of changing location in the face of hazard or environmental deterioration on conditions in the potential destination area. Many response strategies have become less available; many others, more so. Individual cultivator response to climate risk in India has long relied upon a diverse mix of strategies from land use to outside employment (sometimes requiring temporary migration) to reciprocal obligations for support; many of these strategies have been undermined by changes such as population pressure and government policy, without being fully replaced by others, illustrating the often-remarked vulnerability of regions and populations in transition (Jodha 1989, Gadgil et al. 1988). In Kenya, effective smallholder response to drought has shifted from traditional planting strategies to employment diversification, without necessarily becoming less effective (Downing et al. 1989).

Yet it is a pervasive theme in the hazards literature that "in only extremely rare circumstances is there solely one adjustment that merits adoption. Usually there are alternatives that may be as effective as or more viable than the conventional technique or the one that lends itself most easily to public action" (Burton et al. 1993: 188). It is an equally pervasive theme that rarely do people choose the best responses—the ones among those available that would most effectively reduce losses—often because of an established preference for, or aversion to, certain options. Attention to the wide range of responses illustrated in the hazards literature may broaden the perceived range of possible responses to global climate change. Certain policies may decrease vulnerability both to hazards and to climate change. Measures likely to reduce current sensitivity to climate variations in Africa are the same ones likely to reduce the threat of adverse impacts from climate change (Ominde & Juma 1991). Most analysts in the less developed countries believe that the urgent need, in the face of both climate variation and prospective climate change, is to identify policies that reduce recurrent vulnerability and increase resilience. Prescriptions for reducing vulnerability span drought proofing the economy, stimulating economic diversification, adjusting land and water uses, providing social support for dependent populations, and providing financial instruments that spread the risk of adverse consequences from the individual to society and over longer periods. For the near term, development targets should ensure that livelihoods are resilient to a range of perturbations.

Finally, comparative analyses of cases from varied settings have noted that responses to large environmental challenges tend to be incremental and ad hoc rather than fundamental. In all of the climate analogue cases examined by Glantz (1988: 408):

> ad hoc responses were favored over longer term planned responses. As a result, there has been a tendency to "muddle through." This has not necessarily been an inappropriate response, but it is probably more costly in the long term than putting a long-term strategy together in order to cope with climate-related environmental change.

In each case, moreover, action was not taken without a catalyst or trigger that dramatically indicated the seriousness of a threat (Glantz 1988). Other comparative studies support both findings (Russell et al. 1970, Wilhite et al. 1986, Glantz 1992, Kasperson et al. 1995). Both suggest that problems that demand early or long-term attention often fail to receive it, and the most efficient responses are not taken. That earlier action would have been more efficacious, however, presupposes that the best strategy was evident to the decisionmakers and that premature responses closing off useful options would not have been taken instead. The historical record richly illustrates the many, often unintended, further environmental and social consequences of particular responses; these must be taken into account in judging their overall effectiveness.

Climate as resource

Views of climate as a resource offer analogues for global climate change just as do views of it as a hazard. Both perspectives necessarily involve a social science component. Natural hazards are not purely natural but reflect the interaction of nature and society; so too, neutral physical stuff (Zimmermann 1951) becomes a natural resource only when made one by particular human wants and abilities.

To speak of climate in hazards terms indicates a focus on loss; to speak of it in resource terms, on gain. The distinction is real but not perfect. Concepts developed in the resource field address loss through resource degradation as well as gain through proper management. Studies of hazards have long noted how some individuals, groups, and places benefit from the occurrence of extreme events damaging to others. Drought in one area can mean higher returns for farmers elsewhere. Hurricanes often bring benefits as well as costs, such as replenishing a failing water supply. Postdisaster assistance can sometimes be so substantial as to produce a net financial gain (Dacy & Kunreuther 1969). That possession of resources, conversely, can itself be a hazard, in that it can retard economic or social development, is suggested by Auty's (1994, 1995) *resource curse thesis*, by Arnold Toynbee's model of *challenge and response*, and by a vein of theorizing going back to antiquity about the stimulation of harsh and barren surroundings and the enervating effects of bountiful ones (Glacken 1967).

Precisely that fear underlies the only concern raised around the turn of the century when a global climate change was first projected: a warmer world might be "less favorable to high civilization" (Van Hise 1910: 373). Otherwise, all of the consequences foreseen were gains: more productive agriculture, an expansion of habitable areas, lower fuel requirements for heating, and greater human comfort, along with a lessened likelihood of another Ice Age (Ekholm 1901, Van Hise 1904, 1910, Arrhenius 1908, Callendar 1938). Today, losses are emphasized over possible gains in assessments of such a change; hazards analogues thus predominate over resource ones. They may also predominate because more hazards analogues are available. Useful resource analogues are relatively few in the climate–society literature because, "Despite calls for better recognition of the natural resource attributes of climate . . . this theme remains rather ill defined and ambiguous. It awaits both further development of natural resource theory and the application of that theory to climate" (Riebsame 1985: 79). We examine briefly several resource perspectives on climate as analogues for global change.

Climate as input

Climate can be defined in resource terms as a series of deliveries of energy and water to actual or prospective human users (Ausubel 1980, Maunder 1986). The quantities of each may enter into the resource endowments possessed by particular locations for particular activities. Climate provides tremendous energy for the key processes of photosynthesis, ambient heating, and water purification and distribution through the hydrologic cycle, but many other activities also depend to some degree on climate inputs (Maunder 1986). The extent to which human activities exploit them may measure the opportunities for gain as well as the vulnerability to loss. If human activities have become steadily less dependent on climate (Ausubel 1991b), they may not only have become less vulnerable to hazards but also less able to take advantage of favorable shifts. If relatively climate-sensitive less industrialized countries are more vulnerable, so too they may have more opportunities to gain from climate change as a resource, although exploiting those opportunities may require means that they do not possess.

Climate's principal drawback as an input, as well its principal characteristic as a hazard, is its uncertainty. Such uncertainty could be lowered by better forecasting. Information about the weather and climate is of great economic value in various sensitive sectors (Maunder 1986). Forecasts of El Niño Southern Oscillation (ENSO) events have enabled agricultural planners in Peru and Brazil to choose crops and techniques for a coming season and to lessen losses from drought (Golnarighi & Kaul 1995). However, more accurately forecast weather and climate might not be conducive to efficiency everywhere; it would probably worsen the problem of peaking of use in outdoor recreation (Clawson 1966). Uncertainty can also be lowered by controlling the weather and climate—the goal of much experimentation in rainmaking since the 1940s. Across all major countries, research on the technical aspects of weather modification in the 1950s, 1960s, and 1970s was vastly better funded than research on the social consequences that were presumably its main justification (Breuer 1980). Nonetheless, the experience presented enormous problems to the orthodox resource analysis calculation of costs and benefits. The problems stem from the uncertainty of the effects produced and the varied roles and values of any given weather event as a resource and hazard for many different users having different and sometimes incompatible needs and wants (Sewell 1966, Breuer 1980).

Amenity

As Ullman (1954) forecast, environmental amenities, climate prominent among them, play an increasing role in regional growth in the industrialized world. Although "most studies of internal migration tend to focus on economic differentiation (wage and employment differentials) between sending and receiving areas," yet "the few scholars who have looked at the effects of climate . . . on migration" have concluded that it is a factor of real significance, and "when climate measures are introduced into econometric models, explanatory power tends to increase" (Kritz 1990: 7). The share of migration attributed to climatic differentials can be viewed as a manifestation of revealed preference for certain kinds of climates over others, and those preferences can be used to judge the desirability of certain climate changes. Within the industrialized world, migrants have been attracted to regions of moderate warmth, moderate seasons generally, and low humidity (Svart 1976, Cushing 1987, Kritz 1990, Perry 1993). As with studies of climate and migration in the industrializing world, however, the paucity of research requires that any conclusions reached be handled with care until better substantiated. Migration and amenity research has not been widely invoked in discussions of climate change, but it was considered relevant during the 1970s to assessing the impacts of the opposite change. When stratospheric flight was thought likely to induce a global temperature drop, "the largest estimated cost" in American expert studies (Nordhaus 1993: 17; see also Ausubel 1991a):

> . . . was the amenity effect of cooling, determined through regional wage differentials. This topic was completely ignored in the EPA studies [of global warming in the late 1980s]. One is tempted to say that environmental impact studies can find the cloud behind every silver lining.

Although the revealed preferences of migrants might suggest that a net warming will be beneficial within the industrialized world, to the extent that population has adjusted to existing patterns of climate any change might disrupt place preferences anew. Such a disruption, given the possibility of adaptation, would probably not have severe consequences (Kritz 1990), but it cannot be taken for granted that warming would produce a net gain through its amenity effects.

Public goods

An improved climate, or the repair of a degraded one, has long been one of the classic illustrations in economics of a good that the market cannot adequately provide; Sidgwick (1883) and Meade (1952) cited increased rainfall through afforestation as such a good. Climatic improvement may meet the two formal criteria for a public good: nonrivalry and nonexcludability. But the treatment of climate in these terms—or in more or less equivalent terms as a realm in which externalities are pervasive and significant—is not an uncontroversial one. Coase (1988: 23–4) argued that such situations are better understood as ones of high transaction cost and that an analysis in terms of public goods or externalities strongly implies the need for government intervention while tending to obscure other possibilities that may in practice be at least as efficacious: "inaction, the abandonment of earlier government action, or the facilitating of market transactions."

Most theoretical and empirical work, moreover, is suited to cases where costs and benefits and their distribution are much clearer than they are in global climate change. It is in any case worth noting that commercial rainmaking has long flourished in the United States, both in the so-called prescientific era (before 1946) of weather modification (Spence 1980) and more recently, just as other textbook public goods such as lighthouses (Coase 1974), fertilization by bees (Johnson 1973), and weather forecasting have often been privately provided. Research into the factors that permit private provision of public goods goes back to Olson (1965) and tends to invoke either altruism or the provision of private goods jointly produced with the public one. For weather modification through commercial cloud seeding, a crucial factor appears rather to be the exceptionally low cost of the inputs compared to the possible value of rain produced, despite the high uncertainty as to whether intervention will work. For private weather forecasting, a crucial factor appears to be the better tailoring of the information provided to the needs of the user.

Property regimes

If climate can be understood in consumption terms as a public good, the atmosphere can be represented in property-rights terms as a free access resource. The present understanding of different regimes of control over resources has grown out of the controversial analogy with medieval grazing lands drawn by Hardin (1968) of the *tragedy of the commons*: when resources are not owned privately or controlled by the state, but exist as common property, they will be overexploited to the point of destruction. The current state of the art in social science (e.g., Ostrom 1990, Bromley 1991, 1992) presents a clearer picture of the nature of property rights by distinguishing four different kinds of regimes over resources: private property, common property, state property, and open access. What Hardin and others called common property is now recognized as existing not as any kind of property but under a condition of open access, where the resource has no owner with the right to exclude anyone from use. The term common property is now generally reserved for resources whose use is vested in and controlled by self-governing associations of local users (Ostrom 1992).

A large literature describes common-property systems that have succeeded over long periods in maintaining natural resources such as forests, grazing lands, and fisheries. These cases are frequently invoked as analogues for a possible common-property regime over the global atmosphere or climate (e.g., Stevenson 1990). There are two reasons, however, why they are unlikely to prove directly useful in this role. First, the global atmosphere as a sink for greenhouse gases displays few if any of the characteristics that careful and theoretically informed reviews of the case study literature have been found to be associated with successful common property management by appropriator organizations—notably small size, homogeneity of users, and definite boundaries (Wade 1987, Feeny 1992, Ostrom 1990, 1992). Second, and more fundamentally, although one could characterize the atmosphere as a common pool resource for the disposal of waste gases, it differs importantly from the classic fluid common pools physically most similar to it as groundwater aquifers, fisheries, and oil and gas pools. Whereas overuse of such pools degrades the very resource being used, it is not the capacity of the atmosphere for absorbing carbon dioxide and other greenhouse gases that is undermined by their release in excessive quantities, but the energy and matter it delivers to different uses and users. There is no identity between the users and the losers who are harmed by their activities (leaving aside the enormous uncertainties about the nature and extent of the harm), and hence no such incentive for the users to cooperate in restraining themselves, as exists when their own activities will suffer from the overuse. The regimes where analogues for such a situation are best sought (and which the implied global atmosphere and climate regimes most resemble) are ones of state property rather than common property. Existing studies of the latter are for the most part irrelevant as analogues for global climate change issues.

With these issues to consider, the most promising analogues for further study are ones either of state property (which it is important to distinguish from common property) or of negotiations between states over large common pool resources existing hitherto under a realm of free access—ones of air and water pollution in particular. The development processes of international regimes for the problems of stratospheric ozone depletion, acid rain, atmospheric atomic testing, and regional sea and international river pollution represent the only close historical analogues.

Conclusions and future research avenues

We have confined ourselves in this chapter to considering climate–society analogues for the human dimensions of global climate change. It might be argued that no adequate analogues exist in that realm for the global-scale and unprecedented challenges that climate change may present. Consequently, the more useful analogues might rather be ones of similarly unprecedented and macro-scale challenges of other sorts with which the world or large regions had to cope: major disease outbreaks, major technological innovations, major wars. Certainly, an examination of such episodes as analogues for climate change would be a useful and enlightening exercise. So would the examination of other, lesser nonclimate analogues. Rhodes (1992), for example, advances the concept of *large-scale state policy* adopted from Schulman (1980) as a useful framework, with its own historical and contemporary analogues (the US War on Poverty and space program), for understanding the challenges of climate policy.

Nonetheless, even the restricted field surveyed here offers useful insights and many avenues for more thorough and systematic investigation. Analogies, to be sure, are never perfect and their lessons never clear and incontestable. Yet a review of what we know about past and contemporary climate–society interaction contains rewarding lessons. Social science research on climate has not been extensive, but the work that has been done offers valuable and suggestive lessons by analogy. In particular, its focus on the social dimensions of vulnerability and opportunities as intervening factors between climate changes and consequences that have been experienced in the past can be profitably taken up for use in assessing the human dimensions of future global climate change.

Climate is not the driving force of human affairs that some extreme views occasionally make it out to be, but neither is it a trivial factor. It has often been, and it remains, an important hazard and an important resource for human activities. Climate change or variation has demonstrably been a source of significant stress (and perhaps also significant opportunity) for societies. Yet it has always been only one factor among many; it cannot be dismissed as unimportant, but neither can it be viewed as a sufficient cause of any past or present event. The consequences of a shift in climate are not calculable from the physical dimensions of the shift alone, but require attention to the human dimensions through which they are experienced: to the ways in which humans organize their relations to the biophysical environment and to each other. The impact of climate as a hazard and the importance of climate as a resource vary greatly over time, space, and social group. It follows that predicting the occurrence and degree of a climate change, even quite accurately, is inadequate for deciding how important it is and what, if anything, should be done about it. Should it be decided to do something, altering the characteristics of society may be at least as efficacious in altering the consequences of the climate change as trying to prevent the change might be; even should it not, alterations going on in any case in the characteristics of society will be sure to alter the consequences of the climate changes over time.

References

Abel, W. 1974. *Massenarmut und Hungerkrisen im vorindustriellen Europa*. Hamburg: Paul Parey.

——1976. *Massenarmut und Hungerkrisen im vorindustriellen Europa*, revised edn. Hamburg: Paul Parey.

——1980. *Agricultural fluctuations in Europe from the thirteenth to the twentieth centuries*. London: Methuen.

Abu-Lughod, J. L. 1989. *Before European hegemony: the world systems AD 1250–1350*. New York: Oxford University Press.

Adams, W. M. 1990. *Green development: environment and sustainability in the Third World*. London: Routledge.

——1992. *Wasting the rain: rivers, people and planning in Africa*. London: Earthscan.

Ahuja, D. R. 1992. Estimating national contributions of greenhouse gas emissions: the CSE–WRI controversy. *Global Environmental Change* **2**, 83–7.

Alexandratos, N. 1988. *World agriculture: toward 2000*. London: Pinter (Belhaven, for the UN Food and Agriculture Organisation).

Alexandre, P. 1986. *Climat en Europe au Moyen-age: contribution à l'histoire des variations climatiques de 1000 à 1425*. Paris: Ecole des Hautes Etudes.

Anderson, D. & R. Grove (eds) 1987. *Conservation in Africa: people, policies, and practice*. Cambridge: Cambridge University Press.

Anderson, J. L. 1981. History and climate: some economic models. See Wigley et al. (1981).

Andrews, J. T. & G. Miller 1979. Climatic change over the last 1000 years, Baffin Island, NWT. In *Thule Eskimo culture: an anthropological retrospective*, A. P. McCartney (ed.). Mercury Paper 88, National Museum of Man, Archaeological Survey of Canada, Ottawa.

Andrews, M. & J. T. Andrews 1979. Bibliography of Baffin Island environments over the last 1000 years. In *Thule Eskimo culture: an anthropological retrospective*, A. P. McCartney (ed.). Mercury Paper 88, Archaeological Survey of Canada, National Museum of Man, Ottawa.

Appleby, A. B. 1979. Grain prices and subsistence crises in England and France, 1590–1740. *Journal of Economic History* **39**, 865–88.

——1980. Epidemics and famine in the Little Ice Age [with rejoinder by J. D. Post]. *Journal of Interdisciplinary History* **10**, 643–63.

Arrhenius, S. 1908. *Worlds in the making: the evolution of the universe* [translated by H. Borns]. New York: Harper.

Ausubel, J. H. 1980. Economics in the air: an introduction to economic issues of the atmosphere and climate. In *Climatic constraints and human activities*, J. H. Ausubel & A. K. Biswas (eds). Oxford: Pergamon Press.

——1991a. A second look at the impacts of climate change. *American Scientist* **79**, 210–21.

——1991b. Does climate still matter? *Nature* **350**, 649–52.

Auty, R. M. 1994. Industrial policy reform in six large newly industrializing countries: the resource curse thesis. *World Development* **22**, 11–26.

——1995. Industrial policy, sectoral maturation, and postwar economic growth in Brazil: the resource curse thesis. *Economic Geography* **71**, 257–72.

Bain, D. & H. J. Otway 1979. Comment. *Current Anthropology* **20**, 530.

Barry, R. G., W. Arundale, J. T. Andrews, R. Bradley, H. Nichols 1977. Environmental change and cultural change in the eastern Arctic during the last five thousand years. *Arctic and Alpine Research* **9**, 193–210.

Barry, R. G. & R. J. Chorley 1987. *Atmosphere, weather and climate*, 5th edn. London: Methuen

Barsky, R. B. & J. A. Miron 1989. The seasonal cycle and the business cycle. *Journal of Political Economy* **97**, 503–534.

Baruch, U. 1990. Palynological evidence of human impact on the vegetation as recorded in the Late Holocene lake sediments in Israel. In *Man's role in the shaping of the eastern Mediterranean landscape*, S. Bottema, G. Entjes-Nieborg, W. Van Zeist (eds). Rotterdam: Balkema.

Bassin, M. 1992. Geographical determinism in fin-de-siècle Marxism: Georgii Plekhanov and the environmental basis of Russian history. *Annals of the Association of American Geographers* **82**, 3–22.

Bell, B. 1971. The Dark Ages in ancient history, I: the first Dark Age in Egypt. *American Journal of Archaeology* **75**, 1–26.

——1975. Climate and the history of Egypt: the Middle Kingdom. *American Journal of Archaeology* **79**, 223–69.

Bennett, J. W. & K. A. Dahlberg 1990. Institutions, social organization, and cultural values. See Turner et al. (1990).

Beresford, M. & J. G. Hurst (eds) 1973. *Deserted medieval villages*, 2nd edn. Stroud, England: Alan Sutton.

Beug, H. J. 1967. Contributions to the Postglacial vegetational history of northern Turkey. *Quaternary Palaeoecology* **7**, 349–56.

Bhatia, B. M. 1967. *Famines in India 1860–1965*, 2nd edn. New York: Asia Publishing House.

Bietak, M. 1975. Tell el-Daba II. Der Fundort im Rahmen einer archäologisch–geographischen Untersuchung über das äegyptische Ostdelta. *Denkschriften der Akademie der Wissenschaften, Wien* **4**, 1–236.

Black, R. 1994. Forced migration and environmental change: the impact of refugees on host environments. *Journal of Environmental Management* **42**, 261–77.

Blaikie, P. & H. Brookfield 1987. *Land degradation and society*. London: Methuen.

Blaikie, P., T. Cannon, I. Davis, B. Wisner 1994. *At risk: natural hazards, people's vulnerability, and disasters*. London: Routledge.

Bloom, P. R., M. Pohl, C. Buttleman, F. Wiseman, A. Covich, C. Miksicek, J. Ball, J. Stein 1983. Prehistoric Maya wetland agriculture and the alluvial soils near San Antonio, Río Hondo, Belize. *Nature* **301**, 417–19.

Bohle, H. G., T. Cannon, G. Hugo, F. N. Ibrahim (eds) 1991. *Famine and food security in Africa and Asia*. Bayreuth: Naturwissenschaftliche.

Bohle, H. G., T. E. Downing, M. J. Watts 1994. Climate change and vulnerability: toward a sociology and geography of food insecurity. *Global Environmental Change* **4**, 37–48.

Bonnifield, P. 1981. *The Dust Bowl: men, dirt, and depression*. Albuquerque: University of New Mexico Press.

Botkin, D. 1992. *Discordant harmonies: a new ecology for the twenty-first century*. New York: Oxford University Press.

Bottema, S. 1984. Palynological investigations in Greece with special reference to pollen as an indicator of human activity. *Palaeohistoria* **24**, 257–89.

——1994. Vegetation and climate history in the Near East based upon palynological investigations. Paper presented at the NATO-ARW Conference on "Third millennium BC abrupt climatic change and Old World social collapse", Kemer, Turkey.

Bottema, S. & H. Woldring 1990. Anthropogenic indicators in the pollen record of the Eastern Mediterranean. In *Man's role in the shaping of the eastern Mediterranean landscape*, S. Bottema, G. Entjes-Nieborg, W. Van Zeist (eds). Rotterdam: Balkema.

Boudon, R. 1984. *La place du désordre: critique des théories du changement social*. Paris: Presses Universitaires de France [reissued 1991, Quadrige imprint].

Bowden, M. J., R. W. Kates, P. A. Kay, W. E. Riebsame, R. A. Warrick, D. L. Johnson, H. A. Gould, D. Weiner 1981. The effects of climate fluctuations on human populations: two hypotheses. See Wigley et al. (1981).

Braudel, F. 1979. *Civilization and capitalism, 15th–18th century, III: the perspective of the world.* New York: Harper & Row.

Braun, R., F. Hopkins von, D. Puetz, R. Pandys-Lorch 1993. *Aid to agriculture: reversing the decline.* Washington DC: IFPRI.

Brenner, M., B. Leyden, M. W. Binford 1990. Recent sedimentary history of shallow lakes in the Guatemalan savannas. *Journal of Paleolimnology* **4**, 239–52.

Breuer, G. 1980. *Weather modification: prospects and problems* [translated by H. Morth]. Cambridge: Cambridge University Press.

Briffa, K. R., P. D. Jones, F. H. Schweingruber 1988. Summer temperature patterns over Europe: a reconstruction from 1750 AD based on maximum late-wood density indices of conifers. *Quaternary Research* **30**, 36–52.

Briffa, K. R., T. S. Bartholin, D. Eckstein, P. D. Jones, W. Karlén, F. H. Schweingruber, P. Zetterberg 1990. A 1400-year tree-ring record of summer temperatures in Scandinavia. *Nature* **346**, 434–9.

Bromley, D. W. 1991. *Environment and economy: property rights and public policy.* Cambridge, Massachusetts: Basil Blackwell.

——(ed.) 1992. *Making the commons work: theory, practice, and policy.* San Francisco: ICS Press.

Bryson, R. A. & T. J. Murray 1977. *Climates of hunger: mankind and the world's weather.* Madison: University of Wisconsin Press.

Buechley, R. W., J. Van Brussen, L. E. Truppi 1972. Heat island = death island? *Environmental Research* **5**, 85–92.

Burch Jr, E. S. 1985. *Subsistence production in Kivalina, Alaska: a twenty-year perspective.* Technical Paper 128, Division of Subsistence, Alaska Department of Fish and Game, Juneau, Alaska.

Burton, I. 1992. Regions of resilience: an essay on global warming. See Schmandt & Clarkson (1992).

Burton, I., R. W. Kates, G. F. White 1993. *The environment as hazard,* 2nd edn. New York: Guilford Press.

Butzer, K. W. 1976. *Early hydraulic civilization in Egypt.* Chicago: University of Chicago Press.

——1980a. Civilizations: organisms or systems? *American Scientist* **68**, 517–23.

——1980b. The Holocene lake plain of North Rudolf. *Physical Geography* **1**, 44–58.

——1984. Long-term Nile flood variation and political discontinuities in Pharaonic Egypt. In *From hunters to farmers,* J. D. Clark & S. A. Brandt (eds). Berkeley: University of California Press.

——1990. The realm of cultural-human ecology: adaptation and change in historical perspective. See Turner et al. (1990).

——1994. Toward a new cultural curriculum for the future: a first approximation. In *Re-reading cultural geography,* K. E. Foote (ed.). Austin: University of Texas Press.

Caborn, J. M. 1965. *Shelterbelts and windbreaks.* London: Faber & Faber.

Callendar, G. S. 1938. The artificial production of carbon dioxide and its influence on temperature. *Quarterly Journal of the Royal Meteorological Society* **64**, 223–37.

Caminos, R. A. 1954. *Late Egyptian miscellanies.* London: Oxford University Press.

——1977. *A tale of woe.* Oxford: Griffith Institute, Ashmolean Museum.

Catton Jr, W. R. & R. E. Dunlap 1980. A new ecological paradigm for post-exuberant sociology. *American Behavioral Scientist* **24**, 15–47.

Černy, J. 1933. Fluctuations in grain prices during the 20th Egyptian Dynasty. *Archiv Orientalní* **6**, 173–8.

——1975. Egypt from the death of Ramses II to the end of the twenty-first dynasty. In *Cambridge ancient history* (3rd edn, vol. 2(2)), I. E. S. Edwards (ed.). Cambridge: Cambridge University Press.

Chambers, J. D. & G. Mingay 1966. *The Agricultural Revolution, 1750–1880*. London: Edward Arnold.

Chambers, R. 1989. Editorial introduction: vulnerability, coping and policy. *IDS Bulletin* **21**, 1–7.

Chandler, T. J. 1965. *The climate of London*. London: Hutchinson.

Chang, K. C. 1962. A typology of settlement and community patterns in some circumpolar societies. *Arctic Anthropology* **1**(1), 28–39.

Changnon, S. A. (ed.) 1981. *METROMEX: a review and summary*. Boston: American Meteorological Society.

—— 1992. Inadvertent weather modification in urban areas: lessons for global climate change. *Bulletin of the American Meteorological Society* **73**, 619–27.

Changnon, S. A. , P. T. Schickedanz, F. A. Huff, J. L. Vogel 1977. *Summary of METROMEX*, vol. 1: *weather anomalies and impacts*. Bulletin 62, Illinois State Water Survey, Urbana.

Changnon, S. A. & J. L. Ivens 1981. History repeated: the forgotten hail cannons of Europe. *Bulletin of the American Meteorological Society* **62**, 368–75.

Chapman, G. P. & M. Thompson (eds) 1995. *Water and the quest for sustainable development in the Ganges Valley*. London: Mansell.

Chen, M. A. 1991. *Coping with seasonality and drought*. New Delhi: Sage.

Chen, R. S., E. Boulding, S. H. Schneider (eds) 1983. *Social science research and climate change*. Dordrecht: Reidel.

Clark, P. (ed.) 1985. *The European crisis of the 1590s: essays in comparative history*. London: Allen & Unwin.

Clarke, J. F. 1972. Some effects of urban structure on urban mortality. *Environmental Research* **5**, 93–100.

Clausen, H. B. & C. U. Hammer 1988. The Laki and Tambora eruptions as revealed in Greenland ice cores from 11 locations. *Annals of Glaciology* **10**, 16–22.

Clawson, M. 1966. The influence of weather on outdoor recreation. See Sewell (1966).

Coase, R. H. 1974. The lighthouse in economics. *Journal of Law and Economics* **17**, 357–76.

—— 1988. *The firm, the market, and the law*. Chicago: University of Chicago Press.

Comité Information Sahel 1974. *Qui se nourrit de la famine en Afrique?* Paris: Francois Maspero.

Correia de Andrade, M. 1989. L'intervention de l'Etat et la secheresse dans le Nordeste du Brésil. In *Les hommes face aux secheresses: Nordeste brésilien, Sahel africain*, B. Bret (ed.). Paris: IHEAL.

Courty, M. A. 1994. Le cadre paléogéographique des occupations humaines dans le bassin du Haut Khabour, Syrie du nordest. *Paléorient* **20**, 21–60.

Cronon, W. 1992. A place for stories: nature, history, and narrative. *Journal of American History* **78**, 1347–76.

Crosson, P. R. & N. J. Rosenberg 1993. An overview of the MINK study. *Climatic Change* **24**, 159–73.

Cunha, E. da 1944. *Rebellion in the backlands* [translated by S. Putnam from the original 1902 Portuguese edition]. Chicago: University of Chicago Press.

Culbert, T. P. (ed.) 1973. *The classic Maya collapse*. Albuquerque: University of New Mexico Press.

Culbert, T. P. & D. S. Rice 1990. *Precolumbian population history in the Maya lowlands*. Albuquerque: University of New Mexico Press.

Cunniff, R. L. 1970. *The great drought: northeast Brazil, 1877–1880*. PhD dissertation, University of Texas, Austin.

Currey, B. & G. Hugo (eds) 1984. *Famine as a geographical phenomenon*. Dordrecht: Reidel.

Curschman, F. 1900. *Hungersnöte im Mittelalter*. Leipzig: Teuber.

Cushing, B. 1987. Location-specific amenities, topography, and population migration. *Journal of Regional Science* **21**(2), 74–85.

Dacy, D. C. & H. Kunreuther 1969. *The economics of natural disasters: implications for federal policy*. New York: The Free Press.

Day, J. 1987. *The medieval market economy*. Oxford: Basil Blackwell.

Dekin, A. A. 1969. Paleo-climate and prehistoric cultural interaction in the eastern Arctic. Paper presented at 34th Annual Meeting of the Society for American Archaeology.

——1972. Climatic change and cultural change: a correlative study from eastern Arctic prehistory. *Polar Notes* **12**, 11–31.

Dias, G. M., D. Gross, N. Flowers, A. Mascarenhas, O. Mascarenhas, E. Nunẽs 1986. Drought as a social phenomenon in northeastern Brazil. In *The roots of catastrophe*, R. V. Garcia & P. Spitz (eds). Oxford: Pergamon Press.

Dodds, G. B. 1969. The stream-flow controversy: a conservation turning point. *Journal of American History* **56**, 56–69.

Dotto, L. 1988. *Thinking the unthinkable: civilization and rapid climate change*. Waterloo, Ontario: Wilfred Laurier University Press, for the Calgary Institute for the Humanities.

Dow, K. 1992. Exploring differences in our common future(s): the meaning of vulnerability to global environmental change. *Geoforum* **23**, 417–36.

Downing, T. E. 1990. Monitoring and responding to famine: lessons from the 1984–1985 food crisis in Kenya. *Disasters* **14**, 204–229.

——1991. Vulnerability to hunger in Africa: a climate change perspective. *Global Environmental Change* **1**, 365–80.

Downing, T. E., K. W. Gitu, C. M. Kaman (eds) 1989. *Coping with drought in Kenya: national and local strategies*. Boulder, Colorado: Lynne Rienner.

Drèze, J. 1990. Famine prevention in India. In *The political economy of hunger*, vol. II: *famine prevention*. J. Drèze & A. Sen (eds). Oxford: Oxford University Press.

Drèze, J. & A. Sen 1989. *Hunger and public action*. Oxford: Oxford University Press.

Dumont, R. (with C. Paquet) 1986. *Pour l'Afrique, j'accuse*. Paris: Plon.

Dunbar, M. J. 1970. On the fishery potential of the sea waters of the Canadian north. *Arctic* **23**(3): 150–74.

——1976. Climatic change and northern development. *Arctic* **29**(4), 183–93.

Dunbar, M. J. & D. Thomson 1979. West Greenland salmon and climatic change. *Meddelelser om Grønland* **202**(4), 1–19.

Ekholm, N. 1901. On the variations of the climate of the geological and historical past and their causes. *Quarterly Journal of the Royal Meteorological Society* **27**, 1–61.

Emel, J. & R. Peet 1989. Resource management and natural hazards. In *New models in geography*, R. Peet & N. Thrift (eds). London: Unwin Hyman.

Emmons, D. 1971. Theories of increased rainfall and the Timber Culture Act of 1873. *Journal of Forest History* **15**, 6–14.

Enge, K. & S. Whiteford 1989. *The keepers of water and Earth: Mexican rural social organization and irrigation*. Austin: University of Texas Press.

Farming Systems Research Unit 1994. *Coping with risk and uncertainty in Zimbabwe's communal lands*. Harare: Ministry of Lands, Agriculture and Water Development.

Faulkner, R. O. 1975. Egypt from inception of the Nineteenth Dynasty to the death of Ramses III. In *Cambridge ancient history* (3rd edn, vol. 2(2)), I. E. S. Edwards (ed.). Cambridge: Cambridge University Press.

Feeny, D. 1992. Where do we go from here? Implications for the research agenda. See Bromley (1992).

Feierman, S. 1990. *Peasant intellectuals: anthropology and history in Tanzania*. Madison: University of Wisconsin Press.

Field, J. O. (ed.) 1993. *The challenge of famine: recent experiences, lessons learned*. West Hartford, Connecticut: Kumarian.

Fienup-Riordan, A. 1986. *When our bad season comes: a cultural account of subsistence harvesting and harvest disruption on the Yukon Delta*. Anchorage, Alaska: Alaska Anthropological Society.

Fischer, K. M. A. Frohberg, K. S. Parikh, W. Tims 1991. *Hunger: beyond the reach of the invisible hand*. Laxenburg: IIASA.

Flohn, H. & R. Fantechi 1989. *The climate of Europe, past, present, and future*. Dordrecht: Reidel.
Forsén, J. 1992. *The twilight of the early Helladics*. Jonsered, Sweden: P. Aströms.
Franke, R. W. & B. H. Chasin 1980. *Seeds of famine: ecological destruction and the development dilemma in the West African Sahel*. Montclair, New Jersey: Allanheld & Osmun.
Fuchs, E. 1877. Notes sur l'isthme de Ghabès. *Bulletin de la Société de Géographie* **14**, 248–76.

Gadgil, S., A. K. S. Huda, N. S. Jodha, R. P. Singh, S. M. Virmani 1988. The effects of climatic variations on agriculture in dry tropical regions of India. In *The impact of climatic variations on agriculture*, volume II: *assessments in semi-arid regions*, M. L. Parry, T. R. Carter, N. T. Konjin (eds). Dordrecht: Kluwer.
Galloway, P. B. 1986. Long-term fluctuations in climate and population in the preindustrial era. *Population and Development Review* **12**, 1–24.
Garcia, R. V. 1981. *Nature pleads not guilty*. Oxford: Pergamon Press.
Giri, J. 1983. *Le Sahel demain: catastrophe ou renaissance?* Paris: Editions Karthala.
——1989. *Le Sahel au XXIe siècle*. Paris: Editions Karthala.
Glacken, C. J. 1967. *Traces on the Rhodian shore: nature and culture in Western thought from ancient times to the end of the eighteenth century*. Berkeley: University of California Press.
Glantz, M. H. (ed.) 1987. *Drought and hunger in Africa*. Cambridge: Cambridge University Press.
——(ed.) 1988. *Societal responses to regional climatic change: forecasting by analogy*. Boulder, Colorado: Westview.
——(ed.) 1992. *Climate variability, climate change, and fisheries*. Cambridge: Cambridge University Press.
——(ed.) 1994. *Drought follows the plow: cultivating marginal areas*. Cambridge: Cambridge University Press.
Glantz, M. H. & J. H. Ausubel 1984. The Ogallala Aquifer and carbon dioxide: comparison and convergence. *Environmental Conservation* **11**, 123–31.
Goland, C. 1989. Field scattering as agricultural risk management. *Mountain Research and Development* **13**, 317–38.
Golnarighi, M. & R. Kaul 1995. The science of policymaking: responding to ENSO. *Environment* **37**(1), 16–20, 38–44.
Gore, A. 1992. *Earth in the balance: ecology and the human spirit*. New York: Houghton Mifflin.
Great Plains Committee 1937. *The future of the Great Plains* [House of Representatives Document 144, 75th Congress]. Washington DC: US Government Printing Office.
Greenough, P. R. 1982. *Prosperity and misery in Modern Bengal: the famine of 1943–1944*. Oxford: Oxford University Press.
Gregory, S. 1989. The changing frequency of drought in India, 1871–1985. *Geographical Journal* **155**, 322–34.
Grigg, D. G. 1980. *Population growth and agrarian change: an historical perspective*. Cambridge: Cambridge University Press.
Grove, J. M. 1988. *The Little Ice Age*. New York: Methuen.
Grove, J. M. & A. Battagel 1983. Tax records from western Norway, as an index of Little Ice Age environmental and economic deterioration. *Climatic Change* **5**, 265–82.
Grove, R. H. 1990. Colonial conservation, ecological hegemony, and popular resistance: towards a global synthesis. In *Imperialism and the natural world*, J. M. MacKenzie (ed.). Manchester: Manchester University Press.
——1995. *Green imperialism: colonial expansion, tropical island Edens, and the origins of environmentalism*. Cambridge: Cambridge University Press.
Guichard, F. & M. A. Courty 1994. Comparison of the marine record of the 1650 yr BC Minoan eruption of the Santorini with one of the North I Mesopotamia 2200 yr BC tephra fallout. Abstract, NATO-ARW Conference on Third Millennium BC Abrupt Climatic Change and Old World Social Collapse, Kemer, Turkey.
Gunn, J. W. Folan, J. Eaton, R. Patch 1983. Paleoclimatic patterning in southern Mesoamerica. *Journal of Field Archaeology* **10**, 453–68.

Guterbock, T. M. 1990. The effect of snow on urban density patterns in the United States. *Environment and Behavior* **22**, 358–86.
Gutman, P. S. 1994. Involuntary resettlement in reservoir projects. *Annual Review of Energy and Environment* **19**, 189–210.

Hall, A. L. 1978. *Drought and irrigation in northeast Brazil*. Cambridge: Cambridge University Press.
Halsted, P. & J. O'Shea (eds) 1989. *Bad year economics: cultural responses to risk and uncertainty*. Cambridge: Cambridge University Press.
Hammer, C. U., H. B. Clausen, W. Dansgaard, A. Neftel, P. Kristinsdottir, E. Johnson 1985. Continuous impurity analysis along the Dye 3 deep core. In *Greenland ice core: geophysics, geochemistry, and the environment*, C. C. Langway Jr, H. Oeschger, W. Dansgaard (eds). Washington DC: American Geophysical Union [Geophysical Monograph 33].
Haque, C. E. & M. Q. Zaman 1993. Human responses to riverine hazards in Bangladesh: a proposal for sustainable floodplain development. *World Development* **21**, 93–107.
Hardin, G. 1968. The tragedy of the commons. *Science* **162**, 1243–8.
Harington, C. R. (ed.) 1991. *The year without a summer: world climate in 1816*. Ottawa: Canadian Museum of Nature.
Hazell, P., C. Pomereda, A. Valdés (eds) 1986. *Crop insurance for agricultural development: issues and experience*. Baltimore: Johns Hopkins University Press, for IFPRI.
Heffernan, M. 1990. Bringing the desert to bloom: French ambitions in the Sahara desert during the late nineteenth century – the strange case of "la mer intérieure." In *Water, engineering, and landscape*, D. Cosgrove & G. Petts (eds). London: Pinter (Belhaven).
Heinzelin, J. de 1964. Le sous-sol du temple d'Akasha. *Kush* **12**, 102–110.
Hesse, M. 1966. *Models and analogies in science*. Notre Dame, Indiana: University of Notre Dame Press.
Hewitt, K. 1983. Climatic hazards and agricultural development: some aspects of the problem in the Indo–Pakistani subcontinent. See Hewitt (1983).
——(ed.) 1983. *Interpretations of calamity*. Boston: Allen & Unwin.
Hewitt, K. & F. K. Hare 1973. *Man and environment: conceptual frameworks*. Washington DC: Association of American Geographers.
Hill, A. G. 1990. Demographic responses to food shortages in the Sahel. In *Rural development and population: institutions and policy*, G. McNicoll & M. Cain (eds). New York: Oxford University Press.
Hill, C. V. 1991. Philosophy and reality in riparian South Asia: British famine policy and migration in colonial North India. *Modern Asian Studies* **25**, 263–79.
Hirschman, A. O. 1963. *Journeys towards progress*. New York: Twentieth Century Fund.
——1991. *The rhetoric of reaction: perversity, futility, jeopardy*. Princeton, New Jersey: Princeton University Press.
Hodell, D. A., J. H. Curtis, M. Brenner 1995. Possible role of climate in collapse of Classic Mayan civilization. *Nature* **375**, 391–4.
Holzhauser, H. P. 1984. Zur Geschichte der Aletschgletscher und des Fieschergletschers. *Physische Geographie* **13**, 1–488.
Hufton, O. 1985. Social conflict and the grain supply in eighteenth-century France. In *Hunger and history*, R. I. Rotberg & T. K. Rabb (eds). Cambridge: Cambridge University Press.
Huntington, E. 1917. Maya civilization and climate change. Paper presented at the Nineteenth International Conference of Americanists, Washington DC.
Huq-Husain, S. 1995. The human response to environmental dynamics in Bangladesh. See Chapman & Thompson (1995).
Hurt, R. D. 1981. *The Dust Bowl: an agricultural and social history*. Chicago: Nelson-Hall.
Huss-Ashmore, R. & S. H. Katz (eds) 1989. *African food systems in crisis, part one: micro-perspectives*. New York: Gordon & Breach.

Ingram, M. J., G. Farmer, T. M. L. Wigley 1981. Past climates and their impact on man: a review. See Wigley et al. (1981).

Jacobson, J. 1988. *Environmental refugees: a yardstick of habitability*. Washington DC: Worldwatch Institute.
Jäger, J. & R. G. Barry 1990. Climate. See Turner et al. (1990).
Jahns, S. 1991. *Untersuchungen über die holozane Vegetationsgeschichte von Süddalmatien und Südgriechenland*. Doctoral dissertation, University of Göttingen.
James, W. 1972. The politics of rain control among the Uduk. In *Essays in Sudan ethnography*, I. Cunnison & W. James (eds). New York: Humanities Press.
Jamieson, D. 1988. Grappling for a glimpse of the future. See Glantz (1988).
—— 1991. The epistemology of climate change: some morals for managers. *Society and Natural Resources* **4**, 319–29.
Janssen, J. J. 1975. *Commodity prices from the Ramessid period*. Leiden: Brill.
Jodha, N. S. 1989. Potential strategies for adapting to greenhouse warming: perspectives from the developing world. In *Greenhouse warming: abatement and adaptation*, N. J. Rosenberg, W. E. Easterling III, P. R. Crosson, J. Darmstadter (eds). Washington DC: Resources for the Future.
Johnson, D. B. 1973. Meade, bees, and externalities. *Journal of Law and Economics* **16**, 35–52.
Johnson, K. 1976. *"Do as the land bids": Otomi resource use on the eve of irrigation*. PhD dissertation, Clark University, Worcester, Massachusetts.
Jordan, T. G. 1989. Preadaptation and European colonization in rural North America. *Annals of the Association of American Geographers* **79**, 489–500.

Kahneman, D., P. Slovic, A. Tversky (eds) 1982. *Judgment under uncertainty: heuristics and biases*. New York: Cambridge University Press.
Kammen, D. M., K. R. Smith, A. T. Rambo, M. A. K. Khalil (eds) 1994. Preindustrial human environmental impacts: are there lessons for global change science and policy? *Chemosphere* **29**, 827–1143 [special issue].
Kasperson, J. X., R. E. Kasperson, B. L. Turner II (eds) 1995. *Regions at risk: comparisons of threatened environments*. Tokyo: United Nations University Press.
Kasperson, R. E. & K. Dow 1991. Developmental and geographical equity in global environmental change: a framework for analysis. *Evaluation Review* **15**, 149–71.
Kates, R. W. 1981. Drought in the Sahel: competing views as to what really happened in 1910–1914 and 1968–1974. *Mazangira* **5**, 72–83.
Kates, R. W., J. H. Ausubel, M. Berberian (eds) 1985. *Climate impact assessment: studies of the interaction of climate and society*. Chichester, England: John Wiley.
Kearney, A. R. 1994. Understanding global change: a cognitive perspective on communication through stories. *Climatic Change* **27**, 419–41.
Khong, Y. F. 1992. *Analogies at war: Korea, Munich, Dien Bien Phu, and the Vietnam crisis of 1965*. Princeton, New Jersey: Princeton University Press.
Koerner, R. M. 1977. Devon Island ice cap: core stratigraphy and paleoclimate. *Science* **196**, 15–18.
Kritz, M. 1990. *Climate change and migration adaptations*. Working Report 2.16, Population and Development Program, Department of Rural Sociology, Cornell University.
Kromm, D. E. & S. E. White (eds) 1992. *Groundwater exploitation in the high plains*. Lawrence: University Press of Kansas.
Kupperman, K. O. 1982. The puzzle of the New England climate in the early colonial period. *American Historical Review* **89**, 1262–89.
Kutzleb, C. R. 1968. *Rain follows the plow: the history of an idea*. PhD dissertation, University of Colorado.
Kuznets, S. 1933. *Seasonal variations in industry and trade*. New York: National Bureau of Economic Research [NBER].

Lamb, H. H. 1982. *Climate, history, and the modern world*. London: Methuen.
Landsberg, H. 1973. The meteorologically utopian city. *Bulletin of the American Meteorological Society* **54**, 86–9.
Le Roy Ladurie, E. 1972. *Times of feast, times of famine: a history of climate since the year 1000*. London: George Allen & Unwin.
Le Roy Ladurie, E. & J. Goy 1982. *Tithe and agrarian history from the fourteenth through the nineteenth centuries*. Cambridge: Cambridge University Press.
Lewthwaite, G. R. 1966. Environmentalism and determinism: a search for clarification. *Annals of the Association of American Geographers* **56**, 1–23.
Lindgren, S. & J. Neumann 1981. The cold and wet year 1695—a contemporary German account. *Climatic Change* **3**, 173–87.
Liverman, D. M. 1990. Vulnerability to global environmental change. In *Understanding global environmental change: the contributions of risk analysis and management*, R. E. Kasperson, K. Dow, D. Golding, J. X. Kasperson (eds). ET Program, Clark University, Worcester, Massachusetts.
Lockeretz, W. 1978. The lessons of the Dust Bowl. *American Scientist* **66**, 560–69.
Long, D. R. 1995. Pipe dreams: Hetch Hetchy, the urban west, and the hydraulic society revisited. *Journal of the West* **34**(3), 19–31.
Lowe, J. W. G. 1985. *The dynamics of apocalypse*. Albuquerque: University of New Mexico Press.
Lunden, K. 1974. Some causes of change in a peasant economy. *Scandinavian Economic History Review* **22**, 117–35.

Maass, A. & R. L. Anderson 1978. *. . . and the desert shall rejoice: conflict, growth, and justice in arid environments*. Cambridge, Massachusetts: MIT Press.
Magalhães, A. R. 1992. Understanding the implications of global warming in developing regions: the case of northeast Brazil. See Schmandt & Clarkson (1992).
——1993. Drought and policy responses in the Brazilian Northeast. In *Drought assessment, management, and planning: theory and case studies*, D. A. Wilhite (ed.). Dordrecht: Kluwer.
Magalhães, A. R., H. C. Filho, F. L. Garagorry, L. C. B. Molion, M. da S. A. Neto, C. A. Nobre, E. R. Porto, O. E. Rebouças 1988. The effects of climatic variations on agriculture in Northeast Brazil. In *The impact of climatic variations on agriculture*, vol. 2: *assessments in semi-arid regions*, M. L. Parry, T. R. Carter, N. T. Konjin (eds). Dordrecht: Kluwer.
Magalhães, A. R. & P. Magee 1994. The Brazilian Nordeste (Northeast). See Glantz (1994).
Malin, J. C. 1947. *The grassland of North America: prolegomena to its history*. Lawrence, Kansas.
——1956. The grassland of North America: its occupance and the challenge of continuous reappraisals. In *Man's role in changing the face of the Earth*, W. L. Thomas Jr (ed.). Chicago: University of Chicago Press.
Mathews, J. 1991. A dissenting footnote on p. 45 of *Policy implications of greenhouse warming*. US National Research Council. Washington DC: National Academy Press.
Maunder, W. J. 1986. *The uncertainty business: risks and opportunities in weather and climate*. London: Routledge.
Maxwell, M. 1985. *Prehistory of the eastern Arctic*. New York: Academic Press.
McAlpin, M. B. 1983. *Subject to famine: food crises and economic change in Western India*, 1860–1920. Princeton, New Jersey: Princeton University Press.
McCloskey, D. N. 1976. English open fields as behavior towards risk. *Research in Economic History* **1**, 124–70.
McGovern, T. H. 1981. The economics of extinction in Norse Greenland. See Wigley et al. (1981).
——1991. Climate, correlation, and causation in Norse Greenland. *Arctic Anthropology* **28**(2), 77–100.
McIntosh, C. B. 1975. Use and abuse of the Timber Culture Act. *Annals of the Association of American Geographers* **65**, 347–62.
McPherson, E. G. 1994. Cooling urban heat islands with sustainable landscapes. In *The ecological city: preserving and restoring urban biodiversity*, R. H. Platt, R. A. Rowntree,

P. C. Muick (eds). Amherst: University of Massachusetts Press.

Meade, J. E. 1952. External economies and diseconomies in a competitive setting. *The Economic Journal* **62**, 54–67.

Merton, R. K. 1949. *Social theory and social structure: toward the codification of theory and research.* Glencoe, Illinois: The Free Press.

Meyer, W. B. 1991. Urban heat island and urban health: early American perspectives. *Professional Geographer* **43**, 38–48.

Mitchell, W. P. 1973. The hydraulic hypothesis: a reappraisal. *Current Anthropology* **14**, 532–4.

Montz, B. & E. C. Gruntfest 1986. Changes in American floodplain occupancy since 1958: the experiences of nine cities. *Applied Geography* **6**, 325–38.

Moore, T. G. 1995. Why global warming would be good for you. *The Public Interest* **118**, 83–99.

Mortimore, M. 1989. *Adapting to drought: farmers, famines and desertification in West Africa.* Cambridge: Cambridge University Press.

Müller-Wille, M. 1965. Vor- und frühmittelalterliche Flurwüstungen in Scandinavien. *Zeitschrift für Agrargeschichte und Agrarsoziologie* **13**, 147–74.

Myrdal, G. 1968. *Asian drama: an inquiry into the poverty of nations* [2 volumes]. New York: Pantheon.

Neustadt, R. E. & E. R. May 1986. *Thinking in time: the uses of history for decision makers.* New York: The Free Press.

Nordhaus, W. D. 1993. Reflections on the economics of climate change. *Journal of Economic Perspectives* **7**, 11–25.

Nuttall, M. 1992. *Arctic homeland: kinship, community and development in northwest Greenland.* Toronto: University of Toronto Press.

Olson, M. 1965. *The logic of collective action: public goods and the theory of groups.* Cambridge, Massachusetts: Harvard University Press.

Ominde, S. H. & C. Juma 1991. Stemming the tide: an action agenda. In *A change in the weather: African perspectives on climate change*, S. H. Ominde & C. Juma (eds). Nairobi: ACTS Press.

Ostrom, E. 1990. *Governing the commons: the evolution of institutions for collective action.* New York: Cambridge University Press.

——1992. The rudiments of a theory of the origins, survival, and performance of common-property institutions. See Bromley (1992).

Ostrom, E. & R. Gardner 1993. Coping with asymmetries in the commons: self-governing irrigation systems can work. *Journal of Economic Perspectives* **7**, 93–112.

Parry, M. L. 1978. *Climatic change, agriculture and settlement.* Folkestone, England: Dawson.

——1981. Climatic change and the agricultural frontier: a research strategy. See Wigley et al. (1981).

Parry, M. L. & T. R. Carter 1985. The effect of climate variations on agricultural risk. *Climatic Change* **7**, 95–100.

Parry, M. L., T. R. Carter, N. T. Konjin (eds) 1988. *The impact of climatic variations on agriculture* [2 volumes]. Dordrecht: Kluwer.

Pegeau, D. 1989a. *Sécheresses, desertification et famines: la zone Sahélienne et l'Ethiopie.* Série Notes et Travaux 13, Centre Sahel, Université Laval, Québec.

——1989b. *Sécheresses et famines au Sahel: discours officiels et discours des "experts de la nature."* Série Notes et Travaux 12, Centre Sahel, Université Laval, Québec.

Perry, A. 1993. Climate, greenhouse warming and the quality of life. *Progress in Physical Geography* **17**, 354–8.

Pessoa, D. M. 1987. Drought in northeast Brazil: impact and government response. In *Planning for drought: toward a reduction of societal vulnerability.* Boulder, Colorado: Westview.

Pfister, C. 1984. *Klimageschichte der Schweiz 1525–1860* [2 volumes]. Bern: Haupt.

——1988. Variations in the spring–summer climate of Central Europe from the High Middle Ages to 1850. In *Long and short term variability of climate*, H. Wanner & U. Siegenthaler (eds).

Berlin: Springer.

Picadi, A. C. & W. W. Seifert 1976. A tragedy of the commons in the Sahel. *Ekistics* **43**, 297–304.

Posner, R. A. 1995. *Overcoming law*. Cambridge, Massachusetts: Harvard University Press.

Post, J. D. 1977. *The last great subsistence crisis in the Western world*. Baltimore: Johns Hopkins University Press.

——1985. *Food shortage, climatic variability, and epidemic disease in preindustrial Europe: the mortality peak of the early 1740s*. Ithaca, New York: Cornell University Press.

Ravallion, M. 1987. *Markets and famines*. Oxford: Oxford University Press.

Revelle, R. & H. Suess 1957. Carbon dioxide exchange between atmosphere and ocean and the question of an increase of atmospheric CO_2 during the past decades. *Tellus* **9**, 18–27.

Rhodes, S. L. 1992. Climate change management strategies: lessons from a theory of large-scale policy. *Global Environmental Change* **2**, 205–214.

Rice, D. S. 1993. Eighth-century physical demography, environment, and natural resources in the Maya Lowlands. In *Lowland Maya civilization in the eighth century AD* [a symposium at Dumbarton Oaks, 7–8 October 1989], J. A. Sabloff & J. S. Henderson (eds). Washington DC: Dumbarton Oaks Research Library Collection.

Riebsame, W. E. 1981. *Adjustments to drought in the spring wheat area of North Dakota: a case study of climate impacts on agriculture*. PhD dissertation, Clark University, Worcester, Massachusetts.

——1985. Research in climate–society interaction. See Kates et al. (1985).

——1990. The United States Great Plains. See Turner et al. (1990).

Riebsame, W. E., S. A. Changnon Jr, T. R. Karl 1991. *Drought and natural resources management in the United States: impacts and implications of the 1987–89 drought*. Boulder, Colorado: Westview.

Riney-Kehrberg, P. 1994. *Rooted in dust: surviving drought and depression in southwest Kansas*. Lawrence: University Press of Kansas.

Rocheleau, D. E., P. E. Steinberg, P. A. Benjamin 1994. Environment, development, crisis, and crusade: Ukambani, Kenya, 1890–1990. *World Development* **23**, 1037–1051.

Rogers, P. 1994. Assessing the socioeconomic consequences of climate change on water resources. *Climatic Change* **28**, 179–208.

Root, H. L. 1990. Politiques frumentaires et violence collective en Europe au XVIIIe siècle. *Annales Economies, Sociétés, Civilisations [ESC]* **45**, 167–89.

Rosenberg, N. J. 1986. Climate, technology, climate change, and policy: the long run. In *The future of the North American granary: politics, economics, and resource constraints in North American agriculture*, C. F. Runge (ed.). Ames: Iowa State University Press.

——(ed.) 1993. Towards an integrated impact assessment of climate changes: the MINK study. *Climatic Change* **24**(1–2), 1–173.

Rostlund, E. 1956. Twentieth-century magic. *Landscape* **5**, 23–6.

Rotberg, R. I. & T. K. Rabb (eds) 1981. *Climate and history: studies in interdisciplinary history*. Princeton, New Jersey: Princeton University Press.

Runge, C. F. 1992. Common property and collective action in economic development. See Bronley (1992).

Russell, C. S., D. G. Arey, R. W. Kates 1970. *Drought and water supply: implications of the Massachusetts experience for municipal planning*. Baltimore: Johns Hopkins University Press, for Resources for the Future.

Sabloff, J. A. 1990. *The new archaeology and the ancient Maya*. New York: W. H. Freeman.

Schmandt, J. & J. Clarkson (eds) 1992. *The regions and global warming: impacts and response strategies*. New York: Oxford University Press.

Schneider, S. H. & L. E. Mesirow 1976. *The Genesis strategy: climate and global survival*. New York: Plenum Press.

Schoell, M. 1978. Oxygen isotope analyses of authigenic carbonates from Lake Van sediments. In *The geology of Lake Van*, E. T. Degens & F. Kurtman (eds). Ankara: Mineral Research and

Exploration Institute of Turkey.

Schofield, R. 1985. The impact of scarcity and plenty on population change in England, 1541–1871. In *Hunger and history*, R. I. Rotberg & T. K. Rabb (eds). Cambridge: Cambridge University Press.

Schulman, P. R. 1980. *Large-scale policy making*. New York: Elsevier.

Sen, A. 1981. *Poverty and famines: an essay on entitlement and deprivation*. Oxford: Oxford University Press.

——1990. Food, economics and entitlements. In *The political economy of hunger*, vol. 1: *entitlement and well-being*, J. Drèze & A. Sen (eds). Oxford: Oxford University Press.

Sewell, W. R. D. (ed.) 1966. *Human dimensions of weather modification*. Research Paper 105, Department of Geography, University of Chicago.

Sigdwick, H. 1883. *The principles of political economy*. London: Macmillan.

Slicher van Bath, B. H. 1977. Agriculture in the vital revolution. In *Cambridge economic history of Europe* (vol. 5), E. E. Rich & C. H. Wilson (eds). Cambridge: Cambridge University Press.

Smil, V. 1990. Planetary warming: realities and responses. *Population and Development Review* **16**, 1–29.

Spence, C. C. 1980. *The rainmakers: American "pluviculture" to World War II*. Lincoln: University of Nebraska Press.

Stevenson, G. G. 1990. Common property rights: from Swiss grazing to global environmental change. Paper presented at the First Annual Meeting of the International Association for the Study of Common Property, Durham, North Carolina.

Subbiah, A. R. 1993. Indian drought management: from vulnerability to resilience. In *Drought assessment, management, and planning: theory and case studies*, D. A. Wilhite (ed.). Boston: Kluwer.

Susman, P., P. O'Keefe, B. Wisner 1983. Global disasters, a radical interpretation. See Hewitt (1983).

Sutherland, D. M. C. 1981. Weather and peasantry of upper Brittany, 1780–1789. See Wigley et al. (1981).

Svart, L. M. 1976. Environmental preference migration: a review. *Geographical Review* **66**, 314–30.

Swearingen, W. D. 1987. *Moroccan mirages: agricultural dreams and deceptions, 1912–1986*. Princeton, New Jersey: Princeton University Press.

Tainter, J. A. 1988. *The collapse of complex societies*. Cambridge: Cambridge University Press.

Thompson, G. D. & P. N. Wilson 1994. Common property as an institutional response to environmental variability. *Contemporary Economic Policy* **12**(3), 1021.

Tilly, C. 1975. Food supply and public order in modern Europe. In *The formation of nation states in Europe*, C. Tilly (ed.). Princeton, New Jersey: Princeton University Press.

Tilly, L. A. 1971. The food riot as a form of political conflict in France. *Journal of Interdisciplinary History* **2**, 23–57.

Torry, W. I. 1979. Anthropological studies in hazardous environments: past trends and new horizons. *Current Anthropology* **20**, 517–40.

——1986. Economic development, drought, and famines: some limitations of dependency explanations. *GeoJournal* **12**, 5–18.

Tricart, J. 1994. Les catastrophes naturelles sont-elles un phenomène social? *Annales de Geographie* **557**, 300–315.

Trigger, B. G. 1965. *History and settlement in Lower Nubia*. Publications in Anthropology, Department of Anthropology, Yale University.

Turner II, B. L. 1985. Issues related to subsistence and environment among the ancient Maya. In *Prehistoric lowland Maya environment and subsistence economy*, M. Pohl (ed.). Cambridge, Massachusetts: Peabody Museum.

——1993. Rethinking the "new orthodoxy": interpreting ancient Maya agriculture and environment. In *Culture, form, and place: essays in cultural and historical geography, geoscience and man* (vol. 32), K. Mathewson (ed.). Geoscience Publications, Department of Geography and Anthropology, Louisiana State University, Baton Rouge.

Turner II, B. L., W. C. Clark, R. W. Kates, J. F. Richards, J. T. Mathews, W. B. Meyer (eds) 1990. *The Earth as transformed by human action*. New York: Cambridge University Press.

Turner II, B. L. & K. W. Butzer 1992. The Columbian Encounter and land-use change. *Environment* **43**(8), 16–20.

Turner, M. 1988. Categories and analogies. In *Analogical reasoning: perspectives of artificial intelligence, cognitive science, and philosophy*, C. D. H. Helman (ed.). Dordrecht: Kluwer.

Ullman, E. L. 1954. Amenities as a factor in regional growth. *Geographical Review* **44**, 110–32.

——1967. Geographical prediction and theory: the measure of recreation benefits in the Meramec Basin. In *Problems and trends in American geography*, S. B. Cohen (ed.). New York: Basic Books.

Ungar, S. 1992. The rise and (relative) decline of global warming as a social problem. *The Sociological Quarterly* **33**, 483–501.

US NRC [US National Research Council] (Committee on Science, Engineering, and Public Policy, National Academy of Sciences, National Academy of Engineering, and Institute of Medicine) 1992. *Policy implications of global warming: mitigation, adaptation, and the science base*. Washington DC: National Academy Press.

Utterstrom, G. 1955. Climate fluctuations and population problems in early modern history. *Scandinavian Economic History Review* **3**(1), 3–47.

Van Hise, C. R. 1904. *A treatise on metamorphism*. Washington DC: US Geological Survey.

——1910. *The conservation of natural resources in the United States*. New York: Macmillan.

Van Zeist, W. & S. Bottema 1991. *Late Quaternary vegetation in the Near East*. Wiesbaden: L. Reichert.

Vasari, Y., H. Hyvärinen, S. Hicks (eds) 1972. *Climatic change in Arctic areas during the last ten thousand years* [Acta Universitatis Ouluensis Series A: Scientiae Rerum Naturalium 3, Geologica 1]. Oulu: University of Oulu.

Vibe, C. 1967. *Arctic animals in relation to climatic fluctuations* [Meddelelser om Grønland, Bd 170, Nr 5]. Copenhagen: C. A. Reitzels.

Vries, J. de 1976. *Economy of Europe in an age of crisis*. Cambridge: Cambridge University Press.

——1980. Measuring the impact of climate on history: the search for appropriate methodologies. *Journal of Interdisciplinary History* **10**, 599–630.

——1985. Analysis of historical climate–society interaction. See Kates et al. (1985).

Waddell, E. 1983. Coping with frosts, governments and disaster experts: some reflections based on a New Guinea experience and a perusal of the relevant literature. See Hewitt (1983).

Wade, R. 1987. *Village republics: economic conditions for collective action in South India*. Cambridge: Cambridge University Press.

Warrick, R. A. 1980. Drought in the Great Plains: a case study of research on climate and society in the USA. In *Climatic constraints and human activities*, J. Ausubel & A. K. Biswas (eds). Oxford: Pergamon Press.

——1983. Drought in the Great Plains: shifting social consequences? See Hewitt (1983).

Warrick, R. A. & M. J. Bowden 1981. The changing impacts of drought in the Great Plains. In *The Great Plains: perspectives and prospects*, M. P. Lawson & M. E. Baker (eds). Lincoln: University of Nebraska Press.

Warrick, R. A. & W. E. Riebsame 1983. Societal response to CO_2-induced climate change: opportunities for research. See Chen et al. (1983).

Watts, M. J. 1983. *Silent violence: food, famine, and peasantry in northern Nigeria*. Berkeley: University of California Press.

Weiss, B. 1982. The decline of Late Bronze Age civilization as a possible response to climatic change. *Climatic Change* **4**, 172–98.

Weiss, H. 1994. Late third millennium Mesopotamian socioeconomic collapse. Paper presented at the NATO–ARW Conference on Third Millennium BC Abrupt Climate Change and Old World Social Collapse, Kemer, Turkey.

Weiss, H., M. A. Courty, W. Wetterstrom, F. Guichard, L. Senior, R. Meadow, A. Curnow 1993. The genesis and collapse of third millennium north Mesopotamian civilization. *Science* **261**, 995–1004.

Wenzel, G. W. 1991. *Animal rights, human rights: ecology, economy and ideology in the Canadian Arctic*. London: Pinter (Belhaven).

Wescoat Jr, J. L. 1991. Managing the Indus River basin in light of climate change. *Global Environmental Change* **1**, 381–95.

Wescoat Jr, J. L. & R. Leichenko 1992. *Complex river basin management in a changing global climate: Indus River Basin case study in Pakistan; a national modelling assessment*. Collaborative Paper 5, Center for Advanced Decision Support for Water and Environmental Systems, Boulder, Colorado.

Wescoat Jr, J. L. & J. W. Jacobs 1993. *The evolution of flood hazards programs in Asia: the current situation*. Working Paper 85, Natural Hazards Center, University of Colorado, Boulder.

White, G. F., W. C. Calef, J. W. Hudson, H. M. Mayer, J. R. Sheaffer, D. J. Volk 1958. *Changes in urban occupance of flood plains in the United States*. Research Paper 57, Department of Geography, University of Chicago.

Wigley, T. M. L., M. J. Ingram, G. Farmer (eds) 1981. *Climate and history*. Cambridge: Cambridge University Press.

Wilhite, D. A., N. J. Rosenberg, M. H. Glantz 1986. Improving federal response to drought. *Journal of Climate and Applied Meteorology* **25**, 332–42.

Wilken, G. C. 1972. Microclimate management by traditional farmers. *Geographical Review* **62**, 544–60.

——1987. *Good farmers: traditional agricultural resource management in Mexico and Central America*. Berkeley: University of California Press.

Will, P. E. 1983. Le stockage public des grains en China à l'époque des Qing (1644–1911). *Annales Economies, Sociétés, Civilisations* [ESC] **38**, 259–78.

——1990. *Bureaucracy and famine in eighteenth-century China* [translated by E. Foote]. Palo Alto, California: Stanford University Press.

Wittfogel, K. A. 1957. *Oriental despotism: a comparative study of total power*. New Haven, Connecticut: Yale University Press.

Wong, R. B. 1983. Les émeutes de subsistances en Chine et en Europe occidentale. *Annales Economies, Sociétés, Civilisations* [ESC] **38**, 234–58.

Worster, D. 1979. *Dust bowl: the southern Great Plains in the 1930s*. New York: Oxford University Press.

——1986. *Rivers of empire*. New York: Oxford University Press.

——1992. Grassland follies: agricultural capitalism on the Plains. In *Under western skies: nature and history in the American West*. New York: Oxford University Press.

——1993. *The wealth of nature: environmental history and the ecological imperative*. New York: Oxford University Press.

Wrigley, E. A. & R. S. Schofield 1981. *The population history of England, 1541–1871*. Cambridge, Massachusetts: Harvard University Press.

Zaman, M. Q. 1993. Rivers of life: living with floods in Bangladesh. *Asian Survey* **33**, 985–96.

Zimmermann, E. 1951. *World resources and industries*. New York: Harper.

CHAPTER 5

Integrated assessment modeling

Jan Rotmans & Hadi Dowlatabadi

Contributors
Marjolein B. A. van Asselt, Edward A. Parson, Marco Janssen

The term "integrated assessment" is no longer new and its use is growing rapidly, partly because it has been loosely defined so far. Although many definitions of integrated assessment circulate (Weyant et al. 1996), we have adopted the following definition: integrated assessment is an interdisciplinary process of combining, interpreting, and communicating knowledge from diverse scientific disciplines in such a way that the whole set of cause–effect interactions of a problem can be evaluated from a synoptic perspective with two characteristics (Rotmans & van Asselt 1996):

- It should have added value compared to single disciplinary oriented assessment.
- It should provide useful information to decisionmakers.

This definition of integrated assessment requires that the full range of various causes, mechanisms, and impacts of climate change should be addressed. Integration of just two disciplines, for example, demographics and economics, would not qualify as integrated assessment of climate change; at a minimum, all key policy criteria raised in Article 2 of the Framework Convention on Climate Change have to be addressed (Box 5.1).

Box 5.1 Policy criteria from Article 2 of the Framework Convention on Climate Change

> The ultimate objection of this Convention and any related legal instruments that the Conference of the Parties may adopt is to achieve, in accordance with the relevant provisions of the Convention, *stabilization of greenhouse gas concentrations* in the atmosphere at a level that would *prevent dangerous anthropogenic interference* with the climate system. Such a level should be achieved *within a time frame sufficient to allow ecosystems to adapt naturally* to climate change, to *ensure that food production is not threatened* and to *enable economic development to proceed in a sustainable manner.* (UN 1992) [emphasis added].

Alternatively, integrated assessment can be defined broadly by its assembly of knowledge from a diverse set of sources, relevant to one or more aspects of the climate change issue, for the purpose of gaining insights that would not otherwise be available from traditional, disciplinary research. (These insights could contribute to the scientific community as well as to decisionmakers.)

The discipline-spanning nature of integrated assessment is an important aspect. At the very least, the activity is *multidisciplinary*, encompassing information generated by the full array of disciplines at work in specialized fields of endeavor. When done well, integrated assessment is *interdisciplinary*. That is, the researchers participating in the integrated assessment activity spend enough time learning about the work of the other participants to anticipate the information, scale, and format needs of the other researchers. They are able to see the interconnections of the integrated assessment problems, not simply their own individual research elements. They move beyond the usual cartoon understanding of each other to a point where new understanding of the problem is possible.

Integrated assessment emerged as a new field in climate change research because the traditional reductionist approach to global change research has been unable to meet two significant challenges central to understanding global phenomena. The first challenge is the development of an adequate characterization of the complex interactions and feedback mechanisms among the various facets of global change. Without exception, such feedbacks and interactions are defined away or treated parametrically in reductionist disciplinary research. Scientists and decisionmakers are increasingly aware that the various pieces of the global change puzzle can no longer be examined in isolation. Integrated assessment endeavors to keep track of how the pieces of the puzzle are fitting together, indicating priorities for narrower disciplinary research. The second challenge is that of providing support for public decisionmaking. Integrated assessment offers an opportunity to develop a coherent framework for consideration of multiple objectives of decisionmaking and identification of possible policy criteria.

The issue orientation of integrated assessment research has led to significant progress in interdisciplinary areas. Most of the effort is being expended in building bridges across disciplinary boundaries. In this bridge-building process, new disciplinary challenges are being identified. Resolving these challenges is central to improving researchers' capacity to inform decisionmaking in the future.

From a practical perspective, integrated social, economic, and environmental conditions demand integrated policies. Despite an early history of isolated regulatory initiatives related to air, water, soil, and so on, over the past two decades environmental policies have become increasingly integrated. In Europe, for instance, the European Union has developed integrated environmental policies. In the United States, interdisciplinary research supports the development of environmental impact statements. Integrated assessments make it possible to be better informed in the continued trend to develop more integrated regulatory structures.

This chapter first discusses integrated assessment broadly. Three recent or current integrated assessment efforts are described. The chapter moves on to focus on *integrated assessment modeling*, that is, efforts that are based on linked computer models of different facets of the human–climate system. Models have certain advantages and limitations, and they embody certain frameworks or definitions of the whole system. Indeed, both the strengths and weaknesses of integrated assessment models tend to be related to the simplifications (especially simplified relationships) expressed in the underlying frameworks and coded into the models. Next, the chapter discusses specific issues addressed by integrated assessment models and describes some current models, both macroeconomic models and biosphere process-oriented models. The major findings of the suite of models are then presented, and the chapter ends with a look at the challenges ahead for integrated assessment modelers.

General methods for integrated assessment

Integrated assessment is an iterative, continuing process, where integrated insights from the scientific community are communicated to the decisionmaking community, and experiences and learning effects from decisionmakers form one input for scientific assessment. This complex, intuitive, and value-laden process operates at a variety of levels and scales, so researchers cannot address the process by only one, unique approach. Multiple diverse approaches to integrated assessment are needed, varying from formal and experimental methods (such as models) to heuristic and exploratory methods (such as expert judgment or policy exercises). The divergence of methods employed arises from the uneven state of theory and data across different problem domains covered by integrated assessments, from the differences in problem definition and emphasis, and from different perspectives of the researchers. The many approaches used at this time to address the climate change issue from an integrated viewpoint are all relatively immature. Current integrated assessment research uses one or more of the following methods:

- Computer-aided integrated assessment models can be used to analyze the behavior of complex systems, to show the interrelationships and feedbacks among various issues, to make uncertainties explicit and analyze the accumulation of uncertainties, and to develop and evaluate comprehensive strategies.
- Simulation gaming involves the representation of a complex system by a simpler one with relevant behavioral similarity, and represents complex decision management or policy situations through human participants in roles. Simulation gaming, including the concept of the policy exercise, can be used as an alternative or supplement to formal integrated modeling. Application of those concepts to environmentally related problems is relatively new. See Chapter 2 for a fuller discussion.
- Scenarios can be valuable tools for exploring a variety of possible images of the future. Presently used scenarios, however, are far from integrated; they are often extrapolations of current trends and are based on a limited set of economic and environmental indicators. The main challenge is to

broaden the current set of indicators with social, institutional, and ecological indicators, establishing consistency in assumptions and choices.

- Qualitative integrated assessments are based on a limited, heterogeneous dataset, without using any models. In spite of all expertise and experience built up with respect to qualitative assessment, no underlying generic conceptual framework and consistent method exist.

The selection of specific methods for an integrated assessment depends on the context of the assessment. The simultaneous use of various methods can improve the quality and adequacy of the integrated assessment considerably, enabling analysis and interpretation of the impacts of a wide range of options and strategies.

The advantages of integrated assessment of climate change

Integrated assessment attempts to deal with complex long-term issues surrounded with uncertainties—issues such as global climate change. By doing integrated assessment, researchers can considerably improve the quality and effectiveness of the decisionmaking process with respect to global climate change.

First, integrated assessment can help to put the phenomenon of climate change in the broader perspective of global change, defined as the major factors believed to be important, including all human interventions and alterations. Integrated assessment helps explore the interrelations of global climate change with other global issues, such as stratospheric ozone depletion, land degradation, soil erosion, acidification, and toxification.

Second, integrated assessment can help assess potential mitigative and adaptive responses to climate change. This may be, but does not need to be, in the form of cost–benefit analysis, which compares costs of responses to the cost of impacts they prevent, or a cost-effectiveness analysis that assesses relative effectiveness and cost of different response measures.

Third, integrated assessment can provide a framework in which to structure present scientific knowledge of climate change. In particular, the structuring process of identifying, illuminating, and clarifying current uncertainties is of vital importance. To this end, the different types and sources of uncertainty in the whole cause–effect chain have to be analyzed, as discussed later in this chapter. Based on this identification and classification process, the most important uncertainties have to be compared and ranked. Next, researchers can analyze what kind of uncertainties can (and cannot) be reduced and how. Finally, the integrated uncertainty analysis may indicate how uncertainties propagate through cause–effect interactions.

Fourth, integrated assessment can help in translating the scientific concept of uncertainty into the concept of risk analysis, to assist in decisionmaking under uncertainty. One way of doing this is to relate the concept of uncertainty stemming from disagreement and subjective judgment to the various perspectives people have. This requires implementing various worldviews and favored management styles into integrated assessment studies.

Finally, priorities for climate change research can be set with help of integrated assessment. Integrated assessment helps to identify and prioritize decision-relevant gaps in knowledge. Although disciplinary research is not focused on intersections across research domains or on prioritizing decision-relevant uncertainties and research needs, it can fill the gaps in knowledge. In this sense, integrated assessment supplements disciplinary research.

Perhaps the greatest challenge for integrated assessment is that of gaining credibility. A prerequisite to gaining credibility among the scientific and decisionmaking communities is that a balance be struck between specificity and accuracy, between aggregation and disaggregation, between complexity and simplicity, and between considerations of natural and social processes. As usual, the questions that are to be answered play a central role in the balance struck in the design of integrated assessment, but additional issues, such as transparency (for communication of content), flexibility, and speed (for rapid response to queries) may also influence the design of the framework.

Some investigators eschew integrated assessment, arguing that such approaches are, at best, premature and can lead to inappropriate confidence in questionable or misleading findings. The proponents of integrated assessment argue that the complexity of the issues demands that integrated assessment methods should be used to ensure that key interactions and effects are not inadvertently omitted from the analysis and to highlight areas where new research is needed. In addition, carefully considering uncertainties can be more helpful to decisionmakers in understanding the state of knowledge that is available than if they consider the same issue through individual integration of the disciplinary knowledge base.

Examples of integrated assessment efforts

The notion of integrated assessment has been used for several decades within a broad context, in particular in Europe and North America. In Europe, integrated assessment has its origins in the population–environment, ecological and acidification research of the 1970s, concentrated among other locations at the International Institute for Applied Systems Analysis (IIASA, Austria) and the National Institute of Public Health and Environmental Protection (RIVM, the

Netherlands). With respect to climate assessment, recent large-scale efforts are underway at RIVM, the Stockholm Environment Institute (SEI, Sweden), the University of East Anglia (England), and the Potsdam Institut für Klimafolgenforschung (PIK, Germany).

Recent North American efforts in climate impact assessment date back to the 1970s when concern about the impact of supersonic transport (SST) on stratospheric ozone and ground level ultraviolet levels, and a two-decade decline in global average temperatures prompted speculation about impacts on biota and global cooling. In this early phase, the Climate Impact Assessment Program (CIAP) was launched, which found that the basic scientific knowledge necessary to carry out its mandate was missing. A subsequent workshop, "Environmental and Societal Consequences of Potential Climatic Change," emphasized the importance of understanding the social and economic impacts of climate change, before all climate science uncertainties are resolved. These and other findings of that workshop are strikingly similar to those of more recent studies published in the late 1980s and early 1990s.

Three of the larger integrated assessment projects that have been launched recently in North America and Europe are discussed here. Two of them, the MINK study and the Mackenzie Basin study, are not vertically integrated (i.e., they do not describe a cause–effect chain) but do represent major attempts at systematic integration across impact types and sectors to discern impacts of climate change (horizontal integration). The other, the POLESTAR project, takes account of vertical integration in that it considers causes, mechanisms, and impacts of global change in order to generate future pathways for sustainable development.

The integrated assessment programs mentioned above have chosen to focus on one or more specific regions and their futures, and then brought in a multidisciplinary team of researchers to assess the different possible impacts of future climate change. The programs were designed with different objectives and they describe vastly different sets of regional characteristics. Consequently, their contributions are also different in character.

MINK

The MINK study is a detailed, highly disaggregated regional impact assessment of climate change. This study focused on a four-state region in the United States (*M*issouri, *I*owa, *N*ebraska and *K*ansas). It was funded by the US Department of Energy and conducted and coordinated through Resources for the Future. The study's final reports were published as a series of papers and as a special issue of the multidisciplinary journal *Climatic Change* (Rosenberg et al. 1993).

Impacts on various sectors were assessed—agriculture, forestry, water resources, energy, and the aggregate economy. The study made use of detailed models to assess climate change impacts on different activities in the region. For example, model farms were used to assess impacts for the agricultural sector. Of the many methodological contributions of this program the most innovative are considered to be:

- the use of analog climates (1930s daily data) to simulate future climate change characterized by fluctuations and extreme events
- consideration of intraregional impacts
- consideration of a changing baseline, to synchronize the timing of imposed climate change with demographic and economic change expected over that period
- consideration of an active management strategy responding to a changing environment.

Perhaps the most striking finding of the MINK study is that while climate change impacts could reduce the value of agricultural production by as much as 22 percent, carbon dioxide (CO_2) fertilization could ameliorate the loss to 8 percent, and improved management practices (see pp. 310–311) could lead to a net 3 percent increase in the value of agricultural production. The study is sometimes criticized for failing to consider larger climate perturbations and for failing to resolve highly politicized issues such as water resource management.

Mackenzie Basin Impact Study (MBIS)

This regional impact assessment focuses on a major watershed, the Mackenzie Basin of northwestern Canada. The Mackenzie Basin is the tenth largest river basin in the world, with an approximate area of 1.8 million km^2. This region is sparsely populated (roughly 150000) and has a harsh climate. The study uses four scenarios for climate change, population growth, and socioeconomic trends, with a time horizon of 50 years (Cohen 1993).

This project is distinguished by the large role that national and regional decisionmakers played in defining the central questions being addressed. The study addresses four questions:

- What are the implications of climate change for regional development objectives, and is there a need to alter resource planning?
- Does climate change pose the risk of an increase in resource conflicts?
- What are the major tradeoffs in management response, for example, requirements for changed management strategy in national parks?
- What are the implications of climate change for community management of resources under native land-claim agreements?

The answers to these questions are being studied by many Western and Native scientists. The integration comes into play when the information from physical, biological, and social sciences is combined with the Native scientific know-how—recognizing the importance of climate in the Natives' history and development. The program coordination arises from the central questions being asked, and the four common climate and socioeconomic scenarios. Ideally, each research group will revisit the questions being asked 17 times—once for present-day conditions, and 16 more times for each combination of the climate and socioeconomic scenarios. The program managers will eventually integrate the findings from the various scientists and prepare a coherent regional impact assessment.

POLESTAR

The approach adopted by the POLESTAR project is to try to understand the qualitative interlinkages between the environmental, socioeconomic, political and cultural processes that drive global change, allowing for geographical and sectoral variability. POLESTAR is a generic framework that allows for the construction of future development pathways and for testing these possible future trends against indicators of sustainable development (Raskin et al. 1995). Such an analysis can be done on global, regional, and national levels. More specifically, the POLESTAR framework is a computer-based accounting tool that accommodates a large amount of data. The stepwise procedure works as follows: first, scenarios for population change and development strategies can be developed; then, the resulting changes in availability of the world's resources and in the quality of the environment can be assessed; and, finally, societal responses can be used to explore alternative development pathways.

The framework is built upon other software packages such as the Long-Range Energy Alternative Planning (LEAP) System, the Water Evaluation and Assessment Planning (WEAP) System, the Greenhouse Gas Scenario System (G2S2), and the Coordinated Abatement Strategies Model (CASM). The framework is meant to provide guidance to policymakers, nongovernmental organizations, governments, and industry.

From this brief and general discussion of integrated assessment efforts, we focus in the remaining pages of this chapter on integrated assessment models.

Limitations and possibilities of integrated assessment models

In general, integrated assessment models try to describe quantitatively as much as possible of the cause–effect relationships of a phenomenon and of the crosslinkages and interactions among different issues. More specifically, integrated assessment models of climate change are designed to analyze the phenomenon of global climate change from a synoptic perspective. Although there are some serious attempts being made to construct an integrated model of the Earth's atmosphere, hydrosphere, and terrestrial biosphere (Fisher 1988, Krapivin 1993), it is conceptually and technically far beyond our reach in the foreseeable future to link, let alone integrate, those complex, detailed, and three-dimensional models. Therefore, such integrated assessment models necessarily consist of simpler versions (metamodels, also called reduced-form models) of the more complex or expert models. Where these expert models do not exist, models based on the best available scientific knowledge have to be used.

Metamodels are reformulated, simpler versions of more elaborate and complex aspect-compartment models (expert models) that have been tested, calibrated, validated, and documented in the literature (Rotmans 1990). The reformulation and integration aspects require the definition of a single mathematical concept, resulting in a single mathematical framework that harmonizes aggregation level, temporal and spatial scales, data, and various other characteristics.

The interpretive and instructive value of an integrated assessment model is far more important than its very limited predictive capability. Integrated assessment models of climate change attempt to offer a picture of the processes relevant to global climate change. They are not comprehensive by any means. After all, there are no absolutely reliable models of any of the underlying processes being integrated, and the integration effort involves simplification of these. However, the integration may provide insights about the interactions of these processes and the cumulative implications of the uncertainties about each process. Among the major advantages of such model approaches are the following:

- *Exploration of interactions and feedbacks* Explicit inclusion of systems interactions and feedback mechanisms can yield insights that disciplinary studies cannot offer. Such a model can provide useful indications where new interdisciplinary research would have significant returns. Furthermore, it may be used to estimate the potential magnitude of global climate change and the scale of the interventions necessary to prevent or mitigate symptoms of global climate change.
- *Flexible and rapid simulation tools* The simplified modules in integrated assessment models permit rapid prototyping of new concepts and exploration of their implications. If the interactions among various systems are well characterized, this rapid prototyping may indicate how to validate the new concepts. Furthermore, if the integrated assessment model is being used as a decision-analysis tool, rapid prototyping will permit exploring the implications of the new finding or concept on policy choice and the value of pursuing this new concept (from a policy standpoint). In this way, these models are instruments that can help manage scientific knowledge and insights into the present and future driving forces behind complex social, economic and ecological structures.

- *Counterintuitive results* These results often arise from the interstices of the science elements incorporated in integrated assessment models. Counterintuitive findings are a valuable product of the integration process, and broader scientific credibility is needed to recognize and explore new research pathways thus opened.
- *Tools for communication* Historically, few, if any, opportunities have existed for disciplinary scientists with such broad interests to combine their efforts on a common theme. These models are outstanding means of communication among scientists and exponents of all kinds of disciplines; they may also be used to foster communication among scientists, the public, and policy analysts.

Integrated assessment models have several important limitations and drawbacks:

- *Overly complex structure* This detracts from the pedagogical value of an integrated assessment effort and may even convey the erroneous impression of comprehensiveness and completeness.
- *Unacceptably high level of aggregation* Many of the processes involved in the social and natural systems being modeled in integrated assessment models occur at a micro level, far below the resolution of the models and their formulations. Parameterizations are used to replicate the gross behavior of these processes at the scale and aggregation at which modelers make their calculations. However, the validity of these parameterizations is questionable when nonmarginal changes in underlying conditions are involved.
- *Lack of credibility in disciplinary scientific communities* The very attempt to reproduce the interactions of processes studied by different disciplines is often regarded with suspicion. The integrated assessment modeler is rarely an expert in either discipline, but is trying to build this bridge; both the bridge-building attempt and the credentials of the modeler are grounds for skepticism and resistance.
- *Inadequate treatment of uncertainty* Integrated assessment models involve reduced-form models. The science base is incomplete and uncertain. When reduced-form models are employed to capture some salient aspects of a process, it is important to reflect the uncertainty of the underlying science, as well as the additional uncertainty introduced into the integrated assessment model through development and application of the reduced-form model.
- *Absence of stochastic (random) behavior* Most integrated assessment models are developed using continuous formulation of the underlying processes. However, this is rarely the case in the real world. Climate is a stochastic process, with the most significant impacts arising when

extreme weather events are experienced. Innovations, social movements, and evolution all appear to have a strong element of stochasticity. To the best of our knowledge, few if any of these processes are represented as stochastic events within integrated assessment models. This is a major shortcoming of the current crop of integrated assessment models and may hamper their political acceptance.

- *Limited verification and validation* One of the most vexing aspects of modeling a global system is the absence of a second set of empirical data or any form of counterfactual evidence. The available data are hardly sufficient to adequately characterize the processes being modeled. However, once these data have been used to calibrate models, no data are left to validate the models. At present, the best practitioners have used their models in backcasting exercises in order to parameterize and calibrate key processes. However, short of using only part of the historic data for calibration, modelers have no means to validate the models. Furthermore, even if this practice became commonplace, there is no guarantee that historically validated models will continue to apply in the future. The principle of uniformitarianism (Hutton 1785) may apply to physical systems, but for socioeconomic processes the appropriate framework has yet to be developed. Even if the principle were applied, it offers no guidance for dealing with phenomena outside the bounds of historical experience.
- *Inadequacy of knowledge and methodology* This aspect of the endeavor is not limited to integrated assessment in particular. Climate prediction is far from a solved problem, and dynamic characterizations of processes in social and ecological systems are largely a matter of conjecture. The global climate change problem has by its vast scope forced the application of concepts and heuristics, which, to the best of our knowledge, may be applicable only on smaller (cultural, spatial, and temporal) scales. For example, the notion of a social discount rate applied to valuation of nonmarket impacts of climate change is questionable. Societies set aside wilderness areas such as national parks at implicitly low discount rates. At the same time, investments in education, infrastructure, and research and development seem to indicate alarmingly high discount rates.
- *Modeling formalism may lead to pitfalls* The most significant pitfalls are that policymakers and researchers may treat integrated assessment models as "truth machines," rather than as heuristic tools for developing a better understanding of the issues; and familiarity with particular formalisms (e.g., energy-economics optimization models) may lead to an *availability bias*, where needless restrictions are imposed on how the problem is formulated and solved, or attention is focused on one aspect of the problem while ignoring the rest.

Issues for integrated assessment models

As noted earlier, integrated assessment models of climate change draw from knowledge developed in the relevant disciplinary domains. In modeling the human dimensions of global climate change, researchers draw on knowledge that is discussed in the other chapters of this assessment: from the issue of how demographic transitions occur and the relevance of the population momentum to the importance of social processes in adoption and diffusion of technology. Before delving into the details of each component of integrated assessment models, we discuss how the various elements of integrated assessment models have been treated by the different research teams.

When exploring long-term issues, researchers need to consider large perturbations to human and environmental systems. Unfortunately, the current state of knowledge sheds little if any light on critical issues in the behavior and response of human and environmental systems under these conditions. In effect, the knowledge base is tied to fixed representations of the dynamics of the systems of interest. Furthermore, researchers have little knowledge of the range of perturbations to the current conditions (marginal or gross) over which these fixed models are valid. This paucity of knowledge on which to base long-term projections of the human condition and the global environment is a recurring theme in other chapters of this assessment (e.g., Ch. 3, and Vol. 1, Ch. 5). Nonetheless, integrated assessment models of climate change attempt to shed light on the critical issues by exploring the relevance of different assumptions and modeling strategies.

Ideally, all integrated assessment models of climate change should include all of the elements discussed below. Ideally, every element should be fully interconnected and integrated with the other elements of the models. Just as with the disciplinary research domains, the state of play in integrated assessment is far from ideal. It is tempting to blame the inadequacy of the underlying science. However, few models have achieved even a semblance of balance between representation of the human and environmental systems. In general, the models originating in Europe are typically process based and biased toward a full description of the environmental system, whereas North American counterparts have tended to have an economics or decision analytic bias; these different emphases are reflected in our division of models (see pp. 321–331) into two general classes: macroeconomic and biosphere–climate.

In addition to the issue of imbalance in the models, researchers are far from achieving full integration of the various elements. So far, most of the integrated assessment models have focused only on the aspect of vertical integration. Very few models have addressed the notion of horizontal integration, that is, including crosslinkages and interactions among various pressures, states, and impacts. One of the overall challenges for integrated assessment modeling in the coming decade will be to increase substantially the level of integration within the models.

The lack of integration in current efforts stems partly from the paucity of knowledge and partly from the complexity engendered in developing fully integrated models. For example, a full integration of the notion of technology diffusion and its implications for emissions should also consider the mechanism for such diffusion and the implications for the diffusion of social values and their impact on the desire for children, personal consumption, and environmental quality; the diffusion of institutional systems to help cope with climate extremes; implications for economic growth; and implications for national and international negotiations.

Uncertainty about how to model these issues has plagued past attempts to integrate at this level of coherence. A recent innovation toward the development of more coherence among the elements of integrated assessment models is the use of cultural theory (described in Vol. 1, Ch. 4, and in Ch. 3 of this volume) as a heuristic tool for organizing different models of individual behavior and social interactions. The implication of adopting different cultural perspectives has been explored in the dynamics of demographic modeling (see the discussion later in this chapter).

A final critical element of integrated assessment models comprises exogenous inputs and model structures. All models rely on user-defined inputs at some stage. These user inputs are the expectations about future developments of some or all key driving forces in the models (e.g., economic growth, available technologies, agricultural practice, and value structures). The modelers' expectations are expressed as the dynamics of the human and environmental systems and are reflected in the model structure. In different modeling efforts the boundary between user-defined inputs and modeled structure is set differently. In one model, the emissions trajectory may be exogenously determined; in another, the details of technologies in each sector of the economy are specified to the year 2050 and the emissions are computed internally. From the perspective of coherence within any given integrated assessment framework, it is preferable to perform all analyses internally. To compare models, scientists and decisionmakers must be able to specify certain key trends across the integrated assessment models.

However, another issue deserves attention: the magnitude of errors introduced into an integrated assessment framework through mis-specification of exogenous trends and the model structure. In recent studies of energy-economics models, this issue has been analyzed with some care (Schrattenholzer 1993, Oravetz 1994). It appears that where gross economic, energy, and emissions trends are concerned (over a 30-year time horizon or less), simple models perform almost as well as complex models, but that the errors in model inputs (e.g. in specifying future global emissions) lead to errors larger than structural mis-specification by one half to a whole order of magnitude. On the one hand, this is good news for developers of simple models; on the other hand, this is alarming to those involved in developing models with long time horizons.

Modeling energy-related emissions paths

All models involve specification of some exogenous inputs that drive the future paths of emissions projected. Generally, three methods of projecting future pathways of world emissions can be distinguished:

- exogenous specification of emissions scenarios
- detailed representation of technologies
- aggregate economic modeling.

Many studies specify exogenously a few representative scenarios of emission timepaths, either as a few discretely specified separate futures or as points on a probability distribution of future emissions. If different assessments use common input scenarios, they can standardize their inputs and permit comparison of results. That is the underlying reason for the widespread use of the standard scenarios used by the Intergovernmental Panel on Climate Change (IPCC). These scenarios reflect causal modeling of emissions generated using the Atmospheric Stabilization Framework and the IMAGE 1.0 models (IPCC 1991). (These two models are discussed below.)

The second approach, often called *bottom-up* modeling, requires detailed specification of energy-related and other technologies. In this approach, the present and future probable mixes of technologies in each economic sector are described by their costs, inputs, and outputs, including emissions. The aggregation level may range from broad economic sectors down to individual plants. The advantage of this approach is that it allows specification of particular technical innovations. The disadvantages are that it requires huge numbers of technical coefficients and other data that cannot easily be checked for consistency, and that its abilities to build realistic scenarios of the future diminish over the long term.

The third approach is economic modeling with embedded emission coefficients, projecting future emissions as the outcome of specified production relationships, preferences, and aggregate economic growth. This approach permits the effect of economic policies to be represented, through the dependence of emitting activities on prices and incomes. The aggregation level may range from simple models of the aggregate economy, through aggregate models coupled to more detailed representation of the energy sector, through full dynamic general equilibrium models.

Mixtures of the above three approaches are possible. Some studies combine an aggregate model of the economy with enough technical detail in, for example, the energy or agricultural sector that the impact of introducing or restricting specific technologies can be examined.

Representing land use

Land-use change is among the major proximate causes of global climate change, and climate change is expected to have a major impact on land-use change (Vol. 2, Ch. 2). If the future demand for food at the global level increases by a factor of two to five by the middle of the next century, additional production will put pressure on land that is also experiencing tremendously increased demand for biomass production, commercial wood logging, and urbanization. Other pressures will include demands to preserve wilderness and biodiversity. Expert judgment concerning future development shows us that gains in production are to be realized by intensification rather than extensification and that a diminishing marginal increase in yield per hectare is to be expected unless this intensification is addressed by new technologies, which are not yet in the pipeline. For these reasons, researchers must gain a better understanding of the social, economic, demographic, and cultural driving forces resulting in a continuing global and regional pressure on land and their implications for the biosphere and for society.

In most integrated assessment modeling approaches, land use is poorly represented. Some studies use exogenous series of carbon dioxide (and other greenhouse gas) emissions attributable to land-use changes. Other studies try to model endogenously the role of tropical deforestation within the global biosphere system. So far, even the most advanced attempts to integrate land-use changes have been partial:

- IMAGE 2.0 (Alcamo 1994) models interrelationships among some of the human causes of land-use change and the effects of global climate change on land use and land cover on a 0.5×0.5 grid base
- MiniCAM 2.0 (Edmonds et al. 1996) integrates agriculture and land-use change within an overall global energy–agriculture economic system.

A significant challenge for the future is to include the human dimensions of land-use changes in the integrated modeling efforts.

Representing technological change

Technological change is often credited with being the most fundamental force for change in societies over the past century. It can reasonably be expected to remain a large contributor to societal changes over the coming century. But because technological change is an emergent and multifaceted process (see Vol. 2, Ch. 6), its extent and character are impossible to predict. Although clearly technological change is really endogenous—that is, not an autonomous process but partially socially constructed by policies and choices which can affect its rate and character—the details of these relationships are largely unknown. Technological innovations are not readily adopted by all those who would benefit, and rates of adoption depend on the cultural and institutional context of their implementation, often in the form of a diffusion process.

One approach to representing technological change is to project detailed technology from engineering data, based on detailed assumptions of what technical options will be available, when they are available, how much they cost, and what they emit. Other studies use more compact and aggregate representations of technological change, in the form of input–output models or through the use of an autonomous energy efficiency increase (AEEI).[1] For either approach, varying input–output coefficients or an AEEI, rates of variation can either be specified judgmentally or estimated econometrically from historical data.

The current representation of technology-yielding efficiency in integrated assessment models does not consider any price or regulatory effects; this situation is highly unrealistic. A more realistic representation would be an endogenous representation of technological change, including the appropriate signals influencing technological dynamics.

A further aspect of representing technological change that is important for integrated assessment is the backstop technology. A backstop technology becomes available at a specified future date and provides essentially any quantity of energy at a constant, high marginal cost. Energy-economic models (see Vol. 2, Ch. 4) typically include either or both a fossil and nonfossil backstop technology (e.g., solar electric or nuclear fusion). In long-term model projections, the backstop technology often comes to provide much of the world's energy by the middle of the next century. Consequently, the details of its specification—costs, emissions, and data available—have important effects on outcomes in integrated assessment models.

1. The AEEI is used to represent technological change, usually by a constant factor that indicates improvements in energy efficiency. It is often a model-specific value.

Representing population dynamics

The standard method for including population projections in integrated assessment modeling is to take exogenous scenarios of population growth rates, either global or regional. The three fundamental processes determining population growth and distribution are fertility, mortality, and migration (see Vol. 1, Ch. 2). All three processes are likely to affect, and be affected by, global climate change. In the long term, migration may be highly dynamic and correlated with global climate change. Shifts in population age structure may also have important effects on resource demand. The causality flows of population dynamics should be considered in two directions. Population is a determining factor in global environmental change, but environmental factors also influence population processes. An example of the latter is that declining environmental quality may lead to decreasing food production, which in turn may lead to increased mortality.

Although the fundamental determinants of population dynamics are surrounded with uncertainties, the knowledge and understanding of the driving forces of these basic processes are growing. No present integrated assessment model of climate change takes explicit account of the population–environment dynamics (nor of the internal population dynamics), although the complexity of the population–environment relationship can be addressed only in a broad integrated framework.

A comprehensive approach to population and environment dynamics has to account for population growth and its interrelation with the use of natural and societal resources. During the past two centuries this growth has led to high population densities, in some places leading to deteriorating living standards and also threatening the environment. Given socioeconomic development, the population–environment relationship is affected by the characteristics of the demographic and epidemiological transition: first, an accelerated population growth, then, presumably, the achievement of some form of stability. Indirectly, economic development largely determines population (and health) levels through changes in other socioeconomic sectors, which are mostly concomitant and positive in effect, conceptually described by Niessen & Rotmans (1993).

Representing biogeophysics

For representing the physical, chemical, and biological aspects of the atmosphere, oceans, and terrestrial biosphere in integrated assessment models, a whole family of models is available. These range from simple one-dimensional to complex three-dimensional models. For a variety of reasons, most integrated assessment models contain very simple and inadequate reflections of the complicated biogeophysical processes.

A critical flaw in most integrated assessment models is the representation of the photochemical processes in the atmosphere. Nearly all models treat the atmosphere as one box, which yields globally averaged concentrations of only a limited number of gases, where the photochemical decay processes are modeled simply by specification of fixed atmospheric lifetimes. These model approaches oversimplify the complex reality; they are basically interpretations of the one-, two- and three-dimensional photochemical models. One of the major uncertainties arises from imprecision of photochemical reaction rates. Another major problem is the integration of processes that take place on totally different temporal and spatial scales.

The terrestrial biosphere component is partly represented in the carbon cycle models. These model the cycling of carbon among the atmospheric, oceanic, and biospheric reservoirs. A variety of carbon cycle models exists, from zero-dimensional (such as the reduced-form carbon cycle model of Maier-Reimer & Hasselmann (1987), which is included in many integrated assessment models) to complex, three-dimensional carbon cycle models. A series of global-scale simulation studies using three-dimensional carbon cycle models is presented in Heimann (1993).

The atmosphere–ocean system is often represented by zero- or one-dimensional upwelling box-diffusion models, which fully parameterize the exchange of heat among the land, ocean, and atmosphere boxes. These models use the total change in radiative forcing at the tropopause to calculate global mean temperature changes. One possibility to generate regional instead of global mean climate patterns in integrated assessment models is to use results from general circulation models (GCMs), based on a methodology introduced by Santer et al. (1990) and further refined and illustrated in Hulme et al. (1994). This method normalizes the changes in temperature and precipitation generated by a set of GCMs by the GCM climate sensitivity and then averages these outcomes to obtain composite patterns of changes per degree Celsius of global mean warming. These normalized patterns are then scaled according to global mean temperature changes obtained by simple upwelling box-diffusion climate models. Intermodel differences in these patterns are quantified and used to estimate a range of change patterns, as well as the GCM best guess. The method of producing regional climate change patterns assumes that the spatial pattern of the enhanced greenhouse signal remains constant with time. This is somewhat uncertain and controversial, in particular for the Antarctic regions; more results from transient coupled ocean–atmosphere GCM experiments would be useful to include in this respect.

Other techniques, such as statistical downscaling, can be used to fit grid-based projections to outcomes of simpler one- or two-dimensional climate models. Downscaling techniques can also be applied to refine the relatively coarse climate change patterns derived from GCMs to a finer resolution, which is required for impact (ecosystem) models. These techniques may assume that large-scale changes in mean climate are uniform over heterogeneous terrain and surface attributes.

Modeling ecological impacts

Ecosystem responses to an anthropogenic climate change and accompanying changes in concentrations of greenhouse-related gases can be of two kinds. Existing plants can change their functioning, and the spatial distribution of species can shift. Ecological research is underway to increase understanding of both these phenomena (e.g., Darwin et al. 1996). In plant response studies, scientists have learned about the importance of CO_2 fertilization from atmospheric carbon dioxide increases, and nitrogen (N) fertilization from atmospheric deposition caused by air pollution and increased fertilizer use. Enhancement of photosynthesis, reduction in respiration and increased water-use efficiency resulting from enhanced carbon dioxide concentrations have all been found in laboratory and field experiments (Houghton et al. 1990). However, quantifying the response at the ecosystem level is difficult, because each plant or animal species responds in its own unique way to a changing climate. A sensitivity analysis of a leading plant physiology model suggests that the impact of changed carbon dioxide concentration is greater than the impact of climate change (temperature, precipitation, and photosynthetically active radiation) (Siegel et al. 1995). However, the most advanced global ecosystem modeling efforts continue to seek impacts on ecosystem distributions as a consequence of changes in temperature and precipitation (Smith & Shugart 1993). Thus, it is not even clear if our present characterization of ecosystems will persist.

The traditional Holdridge classification of ecosystem types, based on the climate variables temperature, precipitation, and evaporation, is now widely regarded as inadequate, because it lacks process-based explanation and because it is static. More recent research seeks physiological process-based explanations of the problem of vegetation and climate. Melillo et al. (1993) addressed the question of how changed climate and carbon dioxide concentration will change the productivity and nitrogen cycling of specific types of plants, without examining shifts in their spatial distribution. Prentice et al. (1992) used physiological models (BIOME) to predict what plant types will occur, and which will be dominant, under particular climate conditions. Their modeling of distribution of plant types under present climate (not yet under changing climate) produced better agreement with the observed distribution than has been obtained by traditional methods.

Within the framework of integrated assessment models, the ecosystem response to changing climate is either ignored or poorly modeled. The IMAGE 2.0 model (Alcamo 1994) is an exception to this rule, in the sense that it makes limited use of a modified version of the BIOME model described above (Prentice et al. 1992) and contains a grid-scale terrestrial carbon model, which takes into account climatic parameters, land cover, and atmospheric carbon dioxide concentrations, including feedback processes such as CO_2 fertilization and temperature effects on photosynthesis, respiration, and decomposition.

The ICAM 2 model (Dowlatabadi & Morgan 1995) has adopted a probabilistic model of vegetation cover response to climate change. This model differs from previous efforts in that land cover is statistically estimated using actual vegetation and climate data, yielding a joint multivariate probability of prevalence for each vegetation type, given climate conditions.

Modeling economic impacts

In most impact studies, the main variable that drives the impact functions is the globally averaged change in annual surface temperature, which is, however, demonstrably unimportant in leading to actual impacts. Variables that are loosely related to averaged annual temperature changes—precipitation, sea level, storms, and extremes of droughts or freezes, and thresholds such as the freezing points or the level of dikes and levees—will drive the socioeconomic impacts. Global mean temperature values have been used hand in hand with aggregated impact estimates, since disaggregated impacts require specification of regional climate changes. Although aggregated impact estimates are sometimes based on detailed sectoral analysis (Nordhaus 1991a), they have only illustrative value.

Some analyses classify impacts into market and nonmarket impacts, since they are driven by fundamentally different processes and are expected to depend differently on the time that impacts occur. More detailed treatment of market impacts requires disaggregation by sector. Usually, climate-dependent sectors are chosen as the focus of study, such as agriculture, coastal defense, forestry, and water resources, as well as energy and transport.

However, researchers have deficient knowledge about the climate impacts on these sectors. The uncertainties are enormous, and scientists only know that climate impacts will be part of other social, economic, and environmental changes that may influence society. For example, the world food study of Rosenzweig & Parry (1994) showed that the uncertainties in population projections have at least the same influence on world food supply as climate change uncertainties do (Toth 1994a).

Market impacts estimated by sector must be aggregated to the level of the whole economy. The approaches used in integrated assessment models vary from simple adding up (which assumes that an effect in one sector does not affect any other), to input–output modeling, to general equilibrium modeling, which can follow adjustments through the economy to calculate aggregate welfare loss.

Some integrated assessment studies distinguish between impact estimates for industrialized and less industrialized countries. In industrialized countries, impacts and losses are related mainly to the use of leisure time, to environmental goods and services, and the value of ecosystems. In less industrialized countries, a substantial fraction of population is employed in climate-sensitive sectors (Toth 1994a).

Nonmarket impact estimates are still harder to project and value. These estimates include changes in health and well-being, changes in the pleasure people derive from climate directly, and from the pattern of land use and ecosystems that result from it. So far, only heuristic approaches have been used, and no attempts have been made to disaggregate various forms of nonmarket impacts. An alternative is to define a vector of various measures of valued environmental consequences. For instance, modelers could develop multiattribute utility functions of representative actors; these functions would ideally be defined over uncertain outcomes as well. This strategy has been pursued in ICAM 2 (Dowlatabadi & Morgan 1995) and TARGETS 1.0 (Rotmans et al. 1994a).

Modeling discounting

Economists argue that, for long-term decision problems, future costs and benefits need to be discounted to compare possible long-term strategies with those needed for short-term decision problems (see Ch. 1). Various techniques and methods are used to discount in cost–benefit analyses. In general, two components of the discount rate are distinguished (Schelling 1994). The first component of the discount rate is the time preference for early over later utility. The other component of the discount rate is the rate of change over time of the marginal utility of consumption, based on the expectation that marginal utility of consumption declines with growing per capita consumption. The dilemma with applying the concept of the discount rate in integrated assessment models of climate change is as follows: a high discount rate, between 4 and 10 percent, is consistent with economic theory, but reduces the potential damaging impacts of climate change in the distant future, such that they can be more or less ignored. On the other hand, choosing a low discount rate may be ethically correct but is inconsistent with formulations of other environmental and socio-economic issues (Toth 1994b).

Present discounted net cost and benefit values derived from integrated assessment models are generally known to be very sensitive to the choice of the discount rate. Exactly how sensitive, however, is not very well known, because only a few sensitivity tests for the discount rates in integrated assessment models have been reported in literature so far (Toth 1994b; Edmonds et al. 1997b). The sensitivity experiments that have been performed show that both the appropriate technique and the choice of the discount rate have major impacts on the optimal cost–benefit strategy. Because of the major differences in concepts, techniques, and rates of discounting applied in the various integrated assessment models, a thorough, systematic study is needed to compare the different discount approaches. In this way, the relative contribution of the discount rate can be isolated and its influence can be compared with other important factors in integrated assessment models.

Integrated assessment models

The central focus of this chapter is the integrated assessment modeling effort aimed at gaining a better understanding of the climate change issue. The state-of-the-art of social science thought reflected in the other chapters in this volume is often better expressed and understood in linguistic terms than in formal mathematical expressions. Consequently, there is some tension between those engaged in integrated assessments and those developing integrated assessment models. Some modelers attempt to reflect the vagaries of knowledge by explicitly incorporating them into the model as specific parameters with well-defined uncertainties. However, for many outside the modeling community the explicit definition of the boundaries to the problem, the formalism of mathematical expressions, and the choice of the mathematical workbench are too restrictive and invalidate the whole effort.

At the frontiers of the integrated assessment modeling, however, are attempts to use these heuristic tools to shed light on the new ideas being generated in the social sciences through quantitative analyses of their implications. Examples of such analyses can be found later in this chapter where we discuss the treatment of cultural theory in a model of demographic dynamics, the link between technological change and the policy environment, and the potential tension between modeling at the level of individual decisionmakers and aggregate social behavior.

Current projects in integrated assessment modeling build on a tradition founded in the early 1970s by the Club of Rome (Meadows et al. 1972). Over the past 20 years, many global models have been built (Brecke 1993), all of which were rather complex, highly aggregated and only partially integrated. The next integrated assessment models were developed with a focus on the acid rain issue. The RAINS model, which was developed and used to address the contentious issue of acid rain in Europe, was one of the more successful studies (Alcamo et al. 1990, Hordijk 1991). Despite the tensions that this transboundary problem engendered, the RAINS assessment was part of the process adopted by decisionmakers to arrive at a Europe-wide agreement to control emissions of acid rain precursors. Similar attempts in the United States (e.g., the Acid Deposition Assessment Model) were either not adopted by decisionmakers or were mired in interagency disputes (Rubin et al. 1992).

More recently, the challenge of global climate change has prompted the development of a new class of models. One of the earliest examples of this new class of model is the IMAGE model, developed with support from the government of the Netherlands by Rotmans (1986, 1990). The effort in Europe has continued with the development of the STUGE model (Wigley et al. 1991), which (in a slightly modified form), together with an intermediate version of the IMAGE model, was incorporated in the ESCAPE framework that was developed for the European Community (Rotmans et al. 1994a). A smaller and simpler model, PAGE, was also developed in parallel with the ESCAPE model to answer simple policy questions. The focus of the PAGE model was decision analysis and quantification of key uncertainties (Hope et al. 1993).

Meanwhile, in the United States, the mantle of leadership was assumed by the pioneering work of Nordhaus & Yohe (1983) for the National Academy, an important landmark in integrated assessment modeling. This was followed by the Model of Warming Commitment (MWC) (Mintzer 1987) and the Atmospheric Stabilization Framework (ASF) (EPA 1989). Intercomparison of all of the models mentioned above showed that the overall structure of these models was very similar; models differed mainly in aggregation level. Also, their results were not significantly different (Rotmans 1990). The Electric Power Research Institute (EPRI) has been a key initiator and supporter of integrated assessment modeling in the United States in the 1990s. EPRI's support launched projects at Carnegie Mellon University; Pacific Northwest National Laboratory; and the Massachusetts Institute of Technology.

Development of a new generation of integrated assessment models of climate change is now under way. The latest generation focuses on and benefits from recent findings on ecosystem responses, socioeconomic issues influencing land use, social dynamics, human health impacts, and water resources impacts.

After discussing examples of the frameworks that underlie a macroeconomic-oriented model and a biosphere–climate process-oriented model, respectively, we will describe several currently used integrated assessment models.

Integrated assessment modeling frameworks

At a general level, decisionmakers want to know more about the nature and magnitude of the problem and about appropriate responses. Addressing these issues demands a balance between the simplifications necessary to build a model and consideration of what is relevant in interactions among humans and the environment. For example, this necessitates understanding demographic, institutional, economic, and technological processes, so that relevant information on demographic transition, labor supply and quality, technical change, and other social and economic issues can be included. Also, researchers need to understand and quantify the impact of emissions and land-use change on biogeochemical processes and climate, including the relevant scientific knowledge for modeling the atmospheric fraction and lifetime of various gases and aerosols, their radiative properties, and the response of the climate system to perturbations to Earth's radiative balance. Finally, analysts need to evaluate the impact of the changed environment and climate (as a consequence of anthropogenic emissions and land use) on society in a comprehensive manner, taking into account impacts on market and nonmarket goods.

Building a single model capable of addressing all the nuances of the climate problem is clearly impossible. The price for building any single model of the climate problem is that many issues have to be treated at a very high level of abstraction. Abstractions may negate the value of any results from modeling exercises, despite the learning value of developing the model. This concern is why integrated assessment modeling efforts are increasingly focused on the systematic characterization of model weaknesses and strengths.

Each model relies on a simple, generic framework which can be used as an aide-mémoire for an integrated discussion of climate-related issues, or as a blueprint for a computer model. The framework represents only one characterization of the climate change issue, a characterization based upon a plausible division of the cause–effect chains of global climate change into subsystems. This section discusses two such frameworks, one for the Global Change Assessment Model (GCAM) (Edmonds et al. 1994) and one for the Integrated Model to Assess the Greenhouse Effect (IMAGE) 2.0 (Rotmans et al. 1994b).

The GCAM general framework

In the GCAM, several modeling tools interact to analyze four integrated sets of processes (Edmonds et al. 1994):

- human activities
- atmospheric composition
- climate and sea level
- ecosystems.

The four process sets are shown in boxes (a) through (d) in Figure 5.1. Only a few of the possible interactions are identified in the figure.

In the *human activities* module (a), GCAM provides estimates of environmentally important emissions associated with human activities; consequences of global environmental change, with particular emphasis on human activities; and economic consequences of actions to mitigate and adapt to global environmental change. The GCAM conceptualization of box (a) differs from the usual end-to-end framing of the problem, in which one modeling system generates emissions while another is used to model impacts. In GCAM the human system model that estimates the effects of climate change is also the human system model that generates emissions estimates.

The *atmospheric composition* module (b) provides estimates over time of the concentration of carbon dioxide and of the concentration of other radiatively important gases, including methane, carbon monoxide, nitrous oxide, oxides of nitrogen, sulfuric oxide, volatile organic compounds, and halogenated substances. The principal inputs to this module come from boxes (a) and (d) in the form of annual rates of emission by gas: estimates of anthropogenic emissions from box (a) and estimates of natural sources emissions from box (d).

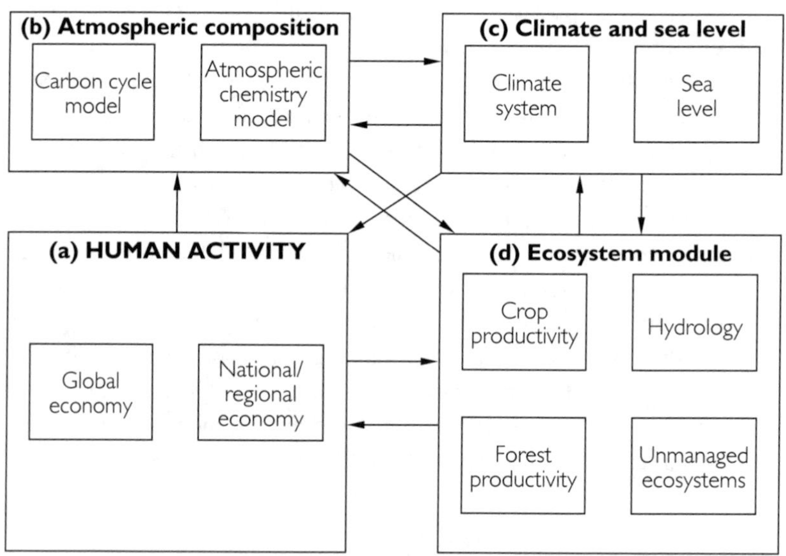

Figure 5.1 GCAM model elements (*source:* Edmonds et al. 1993).

The atmospheric composition module contains two submodules: ocean carbon cycle and atmospheric chemistry. (The terrestrial component of the carbon cycle appears in box (d).) Annual fluxes of carbon into the atmosphere are converted into concentrations of carbon dioxide using the ocean carbon cycle submodule. Other greenhouse-related gases have principal sinks in the atmosphere and therefore their concentrations are determined in the atmospheric chemistry module with supplemental calculations for gases, such as methane, that have terrestrial sinks.

The *climate and sea level* module (c) provides estimates over time of climate-related variables—including temperature, precipitation, solar radiation, cloudiness, and windiness—and sea level. Inputs to this module come primarily from box (b), which provides concentrations of radiatively important gases. Additional input comes from box (d), which generates information on albedo, surface roughness, and surface wetness.

The climate change submodule provides estimates of temperature, precipitation, solar radiation, cloudiness, windiness, and humidity. The computation of global temperature change is accomplished by estimating radiative forcing, equilibrium climate feedback (sensitivity), and dynamic adjustment (principally through ocean thermal lag). These global-scale parameters are distributed to geographic regions via flexible rules that draw on external information sources, such as GCM results. The precipitation regime is developed through a similar process.

The *terrestrial ecosystem* module (d) provides estimates over time of agricultural and forest productivity; water resources (surface flow and groundwater recharge in component watersheds of major river systems); and composition, boundaries, and primary productivity of unmanaged ecosystems.

Crop productivity is a function of both climate variables such as temperature, precipitation and solar radiation, and atmospheric carbon dioxide concentration. The module estimates crop, range, and herbaceous biomass productivities at representative sites; key crops include wheat, corn, rice, soybeans, sorghum, cotton, pasture, and range. In addition, forest productivity is simulated. These productivities are passed to box (a), where demands for and supplies of agricultural products, land, and water are determined within an economic general equilibrium context.

Similarly, module (d) develops estimates of potential surface and groundwater availability for each major agricultural region. In box (a) the water markets will be balanced within large watersheds.

The interfaces and feedbacks among the boxes are very important in representing the interactions of human systems and climate-related systems. Differences of scale—temporal, geographic, and level of aggregation—present continuing challenges, as does deriving regional results from global data.

The IMAGE general framework

The framework underlying the IMAGE 2.0 model differentiates four systems:

- pressure system: the social and economic forces underlying the pressure on the biosphere
- state system: the physical, chemical and biological changes in the state of the biosphere
- impact system: the social, economic and ecological impacts as a result of human disturbance
- response system: human interventions as response to ecological and societal impacts.

Figure 5.2 presents the framework as a simple pressure—state—impact—response diagram that represents many interactions between the human system and the climate system. The linkages between the various subsystems in Figure 5.2 represent processes that are divided into forces, feedbacks and human interventions. Examples of the forces, feedbacks and interventions are presented in the accompanying notes. Figure 5.2 shows that changes unleashed in one subsystem result in a cascade of events that may eventually find their way back to the starting point. More specifically, while demographic and consumption pressures lead to changes in land use and energy consumption, such activities lead to environmental and economic impacts that may play significant roles in the future evolution of demographic and consumption patterns.

The framework of Figure 5.2 represents two dimensions of integration that can be usefully distinguished. First, the vertical integration captures as much as possible of the cause–effect relationships (causal chain) of a phenomenon. Vertical integration closes the pressure—state—impact—response loop, linking a pressure to a state, a state to an impact, an impact to a response, and a responses to a pressure. Second, horizontal integration addresses the cross linkages and interactions among various pressures, among various states, and among various impacts. Total integration means that various pressures are linked to various states, to various impacts and to various responses. The integrated assessment modeling realm contains many hybrid forms of integration, where vertical and horizontal integration routes are mixed, yielding many diagonal interactions.

A vertical integrative approach to population dynamics has to account for population growth and its interrelation with the use of natural and societal resources, fundamentally changing global development. Global climate change may influence the health status of people through heat stress, vector-borne diseases, water-borne bacteriological diseases, and food production. Health effects stemming from changing climate conditions may adversely affect the economy, particularly in less industrialized countries.

Horizontal integration is intended to shed some light on the interrelation-

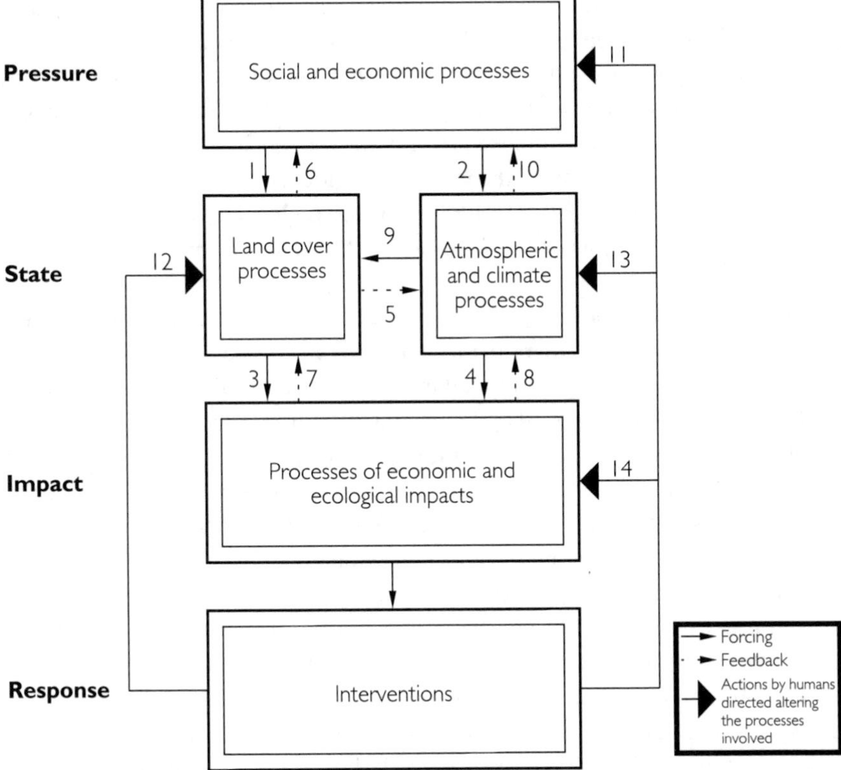

Forces

1. Economic growth, population growth, and human needs and wants lead to demand for land and energy.
2. Economic growth, population growth, and human needs and wants lead to changes in atmospheric composition and climate.
3. Large-scale land-use changes lead to land degradation, erosion and deterioration of ecosystem health, which may have profound economic impacts in the long term.
4. Changed atmospheric composition and climate affect agricultural production and natural ecosystem health on the one hand, and human health, on the other hand.
5. Large-scale land-use changes lead to changes in atmospheric composition and in regional and global climate.

Feedbacks

6. Scarcity in land resources leads to structural shifts in the agricultural sector, and changes in food patterns, urbanization, and migration.
7. Changes in terrestrial ecosystems and in agricultural production lead to shifting land cover and land use.
8. Changes in terrestrial ecosystems lead to changes in atmospheric composition and changes in evapotranspiration and albedo.
9. Climate change leads to altered demand for land resources to maintain "favorable habitats" for humans.
10. Changes in atmospheric and climate processes lead to altered social and economic processes.

Interventions

11. Abatement measures such as reducing emissions of greenhouse gases, (e.g., through introduction of energy taxes).
12. Land-cover maintenance and carbon sequestration policies such as afforestation programs.
13. Geoengineering policies such as release of stratospheric aerosols or pumping fertilizer into the oceans.
14. Adaptation policies such as investments in infrastructure or development of more resilient crops.

Figure 5.2 A simple pressure—state—impact—response diagram for the various elements of the climate change issue.

ships among common pressures, common state changes, and common impacts. An example of the need for horizontal integration is the complex issue of land use, where the overall challenge is to shed some light on the complex dynamics of the interplay among population growth, economic growth, land management, and food supply (pressure factors); the biogeochemical changes in the land system (state dynamics); the impacts on global and regional climate; and the impacts of changing food supply conditions on human health, agriculture, and economics. Analysis of this loop can lay the basis for integrated land and soil management strategies.

Biogeochemical aspects of the climate system are characterized by an interconnected complex of transport mechanisms and transformation processes, many of which are cyclic. Horizontal integration for the climate system means that the global biogeochemical cycles, insofar they are related to climate change, and the interactions and feedbacks among the cycles in the biosphere are taken into account. This can be done by coupling the various compartments—atmosphere, terrestrial biosphere, lithosphere (soils), hydrosphere (oceans, lakes, river basins), and cryosphere—and subsequently integrating the physical, chemical, and biological interactions among the diverse compartments.

The impact system is often researched through computer models. Three types of strongly interrelated impact models can be distinguished: models that describe the effects of anthropogenic multiple stress on ecosystems in terms of ecological succession, structure, and resilience; models that describe the impact of global climate change on human health, both direct and indirect (via the world's food and water supply); and models that specify the market and nonmarket impacts for various sectors, such as the agricultural sector, water management, and coastal defense.

The above described frameworks exemplify formal descriptions of the climate change problem. Their successful integration is a challenge in its own right. However, for policy-motivated integrated assessment, this is only part of the story. In policy research, a decision framework is also needed before relevant issues can be addressed. When considering the climate change problem, decisionmakers can choose from a variety of policy options, varying in their intent to mitigate, adapt to, or research the issue further with the aim to educate. The mechanism each of these policies to be implemented, and the level at which they are implemented, are either simulated or calculated as an optimization problem within integrated assessment models.

Current integrated assessment modeling activities

Without claiming to give a complete description of current integrated assessment models, we give a brief overview of current integrated assessment modeling programs. This overview is partly based on a questionnaire distributed among 17 continuing integrated assessment modeling programs participating in the Energy Modeling Forum's EMF-14 project (see p. 356; also see Vol. 2, Ch. 4). The remaining information has been collected from model documents, scientific papers, and previous overviews. A summary of model attributes is presented in Table 5.1, which offers overview of the basic characteristics of the current generation of integrated assessment models.

Beyond the notion that integrated assessment models should involve an attempt to combine social and natural science descriptions of the climate change problem, the models have little in common. Differing objectives have brought about integrated assessment model designs characteristic of each research group. In general, however, two schools of integrated assessment models are distinguished here:

- *macroeconomic-oriented school,* which represents simple, fully parameterized decision analytic formulations of the climate problem
- *biosphere–climate oriented school,* which represents more comprehensive, process-oriented pictures of the climate problem.

Macroeconomic-oriented models

Macroeconomic-oriented models are often small models that offer the dual benefits of versatility and clarity. They tend to stem from macroeconomic principles and are mostly used for cost–benefit or cost-effectiveness analyses. The insights gained using these smaller models have often guided the development of the more complex modeling efforts. Ideally, the cost–benefit models can be used to inform the initiation and progress of the sequence of decisions and actions related to climate change policy.

The Dynamic Integrated Model of Climate and the Economy (DICE)

The DICE model (Nordhaus 1992, 1994) is a dynamic optimization framework in which the climate change problem has been cast as how a decisionmaker chooses between current consumption, investment in productive capital, and investment to reduce emissions of greenhouse gases. In DICE, population growth and technological change yield productivity growth. Both of these factors of production are exogenously specified and assumed to decline asymptotically to zero.

Table 5.1 Summary characterization of integrated assessment models.

Model	Forcings 0. CO_2 1. Other GHG 2. Aerosols 3. Land use 4. Other	Geographic specificity 0. Global 1. Continental 2. Countries 3. Grids/basins	Socioeconomic dynamics 0. Exogenous 1. Economics 2. Tech. choice 3. Land use 4. Demography	Geophysical simulation 0. Global Δt 1. 1-D Δt, Δp 2. 2-D, Δt, Δp 3. 3-D, climate	Impact assessment 0. Δt 1. Δ sea level 2. Agriculture 3. Ecosystems 4. Health 5. Water	Treatment of uncertainty 0. None 1. Uncertainty 2. Variability 3. Stochasticity 4. Cultural perspectives	Treatment of decisionmaking 0. Optimized 1. Simulated 2. Simulated with adaptive decisions
AIM (Matsuoka et al. 1994, Morita et al. 1994a,b, 1995, Matsuoka et al. 1995	0 1 2 3	2 3	1 2 3 4	1 2	0 1 2 3 5	0	1
CETA (Peck & Teisberg 1991, 1992a,b,c, 1995a,b)	0 1	0	1 2	0	0	1	0
CFUND (Tol 1995)	0 1	1	1	0	0 1 2 3 4	1	0
Connecticut (Yohe 1995, Yohe & Wallace 1996)	0	0	1	0	0	1	0
CSERGE (Maddison 1995)	0	0	1	0	0	1	0
DICE (Nordhaus 1990, 1991a, 1992a,b, 1994)	0	0	1	0	0	1	0
DIAM (Grubb et al. 1995)	0	0	1	0	0	1	0
ICAM-2 (Dowlatabadi & Kandlikar 1995, Dowlatabadi et al. 1995)	0 1 2 3	1 2	1 3 4	1 2	0 1 3	1 2 3	1 2
IMAGE 2.1 (Alcamo 1994)	0 1 2 3	3	0 2 3	2	1 2 3	1	1
MERGE (Manne et al. 1994, Manne & Richels 1995)	0 1	1	1 2	0	0	1	0
MiniCAM (Edmonds & Reilly 1985, Edmonds et al. 1996)	0 1 2 3	2 3	1 2 3	2	0	1	1
MIT (Prinn et al. 1996, Yang et al. 1996)	0 1 2 3	2 3	1	2 3	0 2 3	1	0 1
PAGE (Hope et al. 1993)	0 1	1 2	1	0	0 1 2 3 4	2	1
PEF	0 1	1	0	0	0	2	1
PGCAM (Edmonds et al. 1993)	0 1 2 3	2 3	1 2 3 4	2	0 2 3 5	1	1
TARGETS (Hammitt et al. 1992, Martens et al 1994, Rotmans et al. 1994a, 1995, Hoekstra 1995, Martens 1995, van Asselt et al. 1995)	0 1 2 3 4	0	1 2 3 4	2	1 2 3 4	4	1 2

The single consumer maximizes discounted present value of utility of consumption, subject to a Cobb–Douglas production function that includes a climate damage factor. Emissions per unit output are assumed to decline exogenously at a fixed rate, and can be further reduced by costly emission control measures.

An increasing, convex emission-control cost function is estimated from prior studies, in which reducing emissions 50 percent from the prevailing level at any time costs about 1 percent of the world economy. Current carbon emissions add to atmospheric concentrations via a fixed retention ratio, and realized temperature change is modeled by a two-box model representing the atmosphere (and the mixed-layer upper ocean), and deep ocean. Damage from climate change is a quadratic function of realized temperature change with a 3°C change calibrated to cause a 1.3 percent world GNP loss.

In earlier analyses, Nordhaus estimated the potential impacts of an equilibrium 3°C change on various sectors of the US economy. The sum of his damage estimates indicated a damage level of 0.25 percent of GNP for a 3°C equilibrium climate change. Accounting for linkages or other impacts that may have been overlooked, he judged that 1 to 2 percent of GNP was a plausible upper bound for damages from a climate change of this magnitude. With this research he laid the foundation upon which most subsequent impact analyses have relied.

Recently, two variants of the DICE model have been developed, one with multiple regions and decisionmakers (the Regional Integrated Model of Climate and the Economy, or RICE), another with uncertainty in key parameter values (Probabilistic Integrated Model of Climate and the Economy, or PRICE). RICE, being developed by Nordhaus & Yang (1995), has six or more world regions. In this model, a quasi-convergence of the different economies is assumed. The optimum tax rate is selected so that the world's utility is maximized. Cooperative solutions to RICE are similar to those achieved with DICE. In PRICE (Nordhaus & Popp 1997), a small number of parameters (eight) are assumed uncertain and resolved with an *e*-folding time of 30 years.[2] The major uncertainties in this model are long-run economic growth, the emissions of non-carbon-dioxide greenhouse-related gases, and the extent of cooperation among nations.

The Carbon Emissions Trajectory Assessment (CETA) model

The CETA suite of models was developed by Peck & Teisberg (1992). These models are based on the Global 2100 model developed earlier by Manne and Richels. Global 2100 combined a macroeconomic module of overall economic activity

2. The *e*-folding time is the time for $1/e$, or about 63.2 percent, of a gas to be removed from the atmosphere.

with an energy-technology module. The focus of the framework is to map out optimal paths for energy (in particular electricity) investments in the future. Fuel and technology choices are influenced by resource and technology availability as well as policies which (through taxes) manipulate relative prices of different fuels. In CETA, Peck & Teisberg have added reduced-form carbon cycle, climate change, and stylized impact modules. They considered only one or two global regions, and have extended the time horizon of the model from 2100 to 2450. In several studies Peck & Teisberg have explored the consequences of adopting different damage functions (changing power, dependence on rate of climate change rather than absolute climate change, and damages arising from stochastic extreme events). Their studies have shown consistently that little is gained by early adoption of stringent greenhouse gas abatement strategies.

The Model for Evaluating Regional and Global Effects (MERGE)

MERGE is the integrated assessment model that Manne & Richels have developed with additional input from Mendelsohn (Manne et al. 1994). At the core of this model resides a revised version of the Global 2100 model, now being exercised to the end of the twenty-second century. It embodies a general equilibrium model with five world regions, in which each region's consumer makes both savings and consumption decisions. A simple climate model represents atmospheric lifetimes of carbon dioxide, methane, and nitrous oxide, then calculates global changes in radiative forcing, and equilibrium and realized global average temperature change. Illustrative impact functions are defined separately for market and nonmarket components. The former is modeled as a quadratic function of realized temperature change, fitted to a single point estimate. The latter is estimated as a willingness to pay in each region to avoid a specified temperature change, modeled as a logistic function of regional income; the nonmarket components are, in other words, effectively modeled as a worldwide public good (Manne et al. 1994).

Hammitt

In the simple decision analytic framework developed by Hammitt and his colleagues, a decision about abatement can be made in the short term, when issues are uncertain, or at a future time, when key uncertainties have been resolved (Hammitt et al. 1992, Hammitt & Adams 1994). The model includes a base-case trajectory for emissions of greenhouse-related gases, from which emissions can be reduced by two classes of abatement measures: energy conservation, represented as a low-cost logistic decline in energy intensity; and fuel-switching, represented as the replacement of emitting capital equipment by higher-cost non-emitting equipment. Concentrations are modeled by a linear impulse–response function, and global average temperature by a simple model incorporating energy balance and an upwelling-diffusion ocean. Damages are modeled either by specifying a maximum permissible change in global mean temperature or by hypothesizing a simple convex damage function.

This model has been employed to examine two-period decision problems (i.e., problems for which different decisions can be made in two different phases) with one or two world regions. One study examined a single-actor sequential decision problem, in which current-period abatement decisions are revised in a future period when uncertainty regarding climate sensitivity and maximum temperature has been resolved. Another examined interactive decisions by two world regions, setting abatement strategies independently in the first period while knowing that, in a future period, with more knowledge about sensitivity, they will abate to meet a specified temperature target with a fixed burden-sharing rule. Climate catastrophes have also been explored, with scenarios postulating large releases of methane from de-stabilization of clathrates[3] and collapse of the thermohaline circulation.[4]

Chao

Chao developed the first model to consider explicitly the impacts of episodic climate events in 1992. His concern was that, should climate change lead to extreme and irreversible damages, the appropriate abatement strategy may be different from that found with smooth quadratic damage functions indexed on temperature change. A Poisson model of extreme events was used. His formulation includes quantification and propagation of uncertainties throughout the model (Chao 1995).

Connecticut

The Connecticut model being developed by Yohe fills a critical gap in integrated assessments. Connecticut is a marriage between the early Nordhaus & Yohe (1983) aggregate emissions model and the latest variant of the Nordhaus (1993) DICE framework. In this model, abatement costs are endogenously calculated within an optimization framework with explicit quantification of uncertainties. A two-part energy sector is explicitly incorporated into the production function. Aggregate income production is a function of capital, labor, fossil fuel, and nonfossil fuel inputs. Preliminary findings from the model suggest the need for minimal abatement in the early years.

---

3. Currently, methane is trapped in stable lattice-like configurations in the Earth's crust.
4. Ocean flows are in part a function of both temperature and salt content; water on the surface can become heavier than water beneath it because it is cooler or more salty.

Policy Evaluation Framework (PEF)

The PEF is being developed by the US EPA and Decision Focus (Cohan et al. 1994). The goal of this framework is to provide decisionmakers with the information they will need to formulate climate policies, despite the existence of scientific and socioeconomic uncertainties. PEF encourages exploration of the policy implications of alternative technological, economic, physical, and biological assumptions and scenarios. PEF integrates deterministic parametric models of physical, biological, and economic systems. These models represent greenhouse gas emissions, atmospheric accumulation of these gases, global and regional climate changes, ecosystem impacts, economic impacts, and mitigation and adaptation options. PEF is a two-period decision analytic framework for exploration of climate policy for the United States and the rest of the world. The model has roughly 30 uncertain parameters; with alternative values for these, up to 100000 end-points can be considered.

Model for the Assessment of Greenhouse-gas Induced Climate Change (MAGICC)

MAGICC has been developed by Wigley and colleagues, primarily at the Climatic Research Unit, University of East Anglia, England (Wigley 1994). MAGICC is a set of coupled gas-cycle, climate and ice-melt models that allows determination of the global mean temperature and sea level consequences of user-specified emissions scenarios. MAGICC includes all major greenhouse gases, the effects of sulfate aerosols, and of stratospheric ozone depletion. The MAGICC framework consists of a set of simple models, which are intended to represent the state-of-the-art scientific knowledge in their areas and reproduce the results of more complex models adequately. The model estimates uncertainty ranges resulting from model parameter uncertainties relative to a default scenario.

Biosphere–climate process-oriented models

The more comprehensive integrated assessment models aim at a more thorough description of the complex long-term dynamics of the biosphere–climate system. This dynamic description often includes some of the many geophysical and biogeochemical feedbacks within the system. Some modeling approaches even deal with the biosphere–climate dynamics at a geographically explicit level. However, the socioeconomic system in these models is usually poorly represented. The larger models usually do not serve the purpose of performing cost–benefit or cost-effectiveness analyses, but can provide insights into the intricate interrelationships among the various components of the human system and the biosphere–climate system. Ideally, this can lead to new priority setting in the climate change policy process.

The Integrated Model to Assess the Greenhouse Effect (IMAGE) 2.0

Although IMAGE 2.0 evolved institutionally from the earlier, global average model version, IMAGE 1.0 (Rotmans 1990), it is conceptually and structurally very different from its namesake. The model presents a geographically detailed global and dynamic overview of the linked society–biosphere–climate system, and consists of three fully linked subsystems: the energy–industry system, the terrestrial environment system, and the atmosphere–ocean system (Alcamo 1994). The energy–industry models compute emissions of greenhouse gases in 13 world regions as a function of energy consumption and industrial production. End-use energy consumption is computed from various economic driving forces. The terrestrial environment models simulate the changes in global land cover on a grid scale, based on climatic and economic factors. The roles of land cover and other factors are then taken into account to compute the flux of carbon dioxide and other greenhouse gases from the biosphere to the atmosphere. The atmosphere–ocean models compute the buildup of greenhouse gases in the atmosphere and the resulting zonal average temperature and precipitation patterns. The model includes many important feedbacks and linkages among models in these subsystems.

To provide a long-term perspective about the consequences of climate change, the model's time horizon extends to the year 2100. The time steps of the various submodels vary considerably, from one day to five years. In general, the submodels of IMAGE 2.0 are more process oriented and contain fewer global parameterizations than previous models.

One of the main achievements of the IMAGE 2.0 model is that it is a first attempt to simulate in geographic detail the transformation of land cover as it is affected by climatic, demographic, and economic factors. It links explicitly and geographically (on a grid scale of 0.5° latitude by 0.5° longitude) the changes in land cover with the flux of carbon dioxide and other greenhouse gases between the biosphere and atmosphere, and conversely takes into account the effect of climate in changing productivity of the terrestrial and oceanic biospheres.

The individual submodels and the model as a whole have been calibrated against measurements and other data from 1970 to 1990, assuming initial states of all models in 1970. Submodels with highly dynamic behavior were initialized in 1900 in order to establish their non-equilibrium states in the year 1970. The model was able to reproduce 1970–1990 trends in energy consumption, emissions related to the energy–industry system, terrestrial fluxes of carbon dioxide, and other greenhouse gases to the atmosphere, the buildup of greenhouse gases in the atmosphere, and long-term current climate patterns.

Integrated climate assessment models (ICAM)

ICAM versions 0, 1, and 2 were developed at Carnegie Mellon University, in the Department of Engineering and Public Policy (Dowlatabadi & Morgan 1993). The ICAM model versions have developed increasingly sophisticated and detailed descriptions of the climate change problem, at each stage quantifying the uncertainties in the model components and clarifying where additional research would most contribute to resolution of the climate policy dilemma. This information is then used in the next iteration of the research program to define the disciplinary research needs and the direction of refinements to ICAM.

The ICAM model versions are designed to capture the uncertainties in knowledge about the precursors, processes, and consequences of climate change. The models can be used to simulate abatement activities, adaptation to a changed climate, and geoengineering activities. The development of ICAM 2 has involved updating all previous modules, and developing demographics, fuel market, aerosols, terrestrial ecology, and coastal impacts modules. The spatial and temporal scales have also been refined to five years and seven geopolitical regions. The higher spatial resolution makes it possible to examine gross differences in the magnitude of regional climate change, as well as different economic circumstances and availability of resources to adapt to a changed climate.

ICAM models have been used to show the wide range of possible future emissions, climate conditions, and impacts; the dangers of deterministic modeling with narrow sensitivity studies; the importance of sulfur aerosol forcing in regional policy decisionmaking; the relative importance of decision rules in policy decisionmaking; and the relative contribution of the various parts of the problem in making decisionmaking difficult. Moreover, illustrative runs of ICAM highlight how uncertainties confound the choice of abatement policies, and how key factors may be identified in determining the character of the problem and key uncertainties in making informed judgments.

Massachusetts Institute of Technology (MIT)

At MIT a large integrated model is under development, to be constructed principally by reconciling and joining existing component models. The individual component models are a revised version of the GREEN model to simulate economic activity and anthropogenic emissions of greenhouse gases, a two-hemisphere model of atmospheric chemistry, a variant of the Goddard Institute for Space Studies (GISS) climate model, the terrestrial ecosystems model (TEM) of Melillo et al. (1993), and various impact functions. The integrated model will be computationally demanding, probably precluding full uncertainty analysis. The model will likely be used for analysis of the sensitivity of key outputs to a few major discrete alternatives, either in the form of scenarios or in structural representation of particular submodels.

Activities related to model development include semi-annual policy forums used to keep project researchers in touch with a variety of national and international policymakers, and a forthcoming series of short notes on aspects of global climate change for lay people.

The Global Change Assessment Model (MiniCAM/PGCAM)

The integrated assessment program at the Pacific Northwest National Laboratory (Washington DC) involves an interdisciplinary team with a long and sustained track record in climate-related research. Two integrated assessment models are being developed within the program—MiniCAM and PGCAM. The two models are differentiated by their complexity and specificity.

MiniCAM (Edmonds et al. 1996, 1997b) makes extensive use of reduced-form modules (or metamodels). MiniCAM is designed to be suitable for uncertainty analysis. This framework begins with the Edmonds–Reilly–Barns and agriculture/land use models (Edmonds et al. 1996) for projection of economic activity and emissions of greenhouse gases and sulfate aerosols. The MAGICC model (Wigley 1994) is then used to generate a global temperature response commensurate with the emissions. The SCENGEN model is then used to arrive at regional climate patterns based on the global climate change. The market and nonmarket impacts are expressed in economic terms and follow the formulation proposed in the MERGE 1.5 model of Manne et al. (1994).

PGCAM is a much more complex framework making use of detailed models of human activities. The human activities within this framework are simulated using the Second Generation Model (SGM), a computable general equilibrium model. Twelve regionally specific models have been developed through collaboration with regional experts. The suite of SGM modules is used explicitly to allocate land use and other resources, and estimate anthropogenic emissions. Again, the MAGICC model is used to convert the emissions data to globally averaged temperature and precipitation change, and the SCENGEN model is used to map this change into regional patterns of changed climate according to the output of one or a combination of GCMs. The regional temperature and precipitation fields are employed in detailed regional agriculture (EPIC), ecology (BIOME2 and BIOME3), and hydrology (HUMUS) models in order to assess regional impacts of projected climate change.

MiniCAM has illuminated the importance of sulfur aerosols in emissions mitigation (Edmonds et al. 1994), developed the concepts of "where" and "when" flexibility (flexibility in determining where and when emissions mitigations occur so as to minimize the cost of achieving a specific emissions mitigation goal) (Richels et al. 1996), quantified the relationship between technology and emissions mitigation costs, and explored the relationship among energy-related emissions mitigation, agriculture, and land use.

PGCAM, in contrast, is being employed to examine detailed climatic issues, including the effects of interannual climate variability on crops and fresh water.

Asian–Pacific Integrated Model (AIM)

AIM is a large-scale model for scenario analyses of greenhouse gas emissions and the impacts of global climate change in the Asia–Pacific region (Morita et al. 1995). AIM comprises two main models: the AIM emission model for predicting greenhouse gas emissions and the AIM impact model for estimating the impacts of global climate change. These are linked by the global cycle and climate change models. The AIM emission model is composed of Asia–Pacific country models, which are integrated into a regional model. This in turn is linked to a rest of the world model (six regions), which ensures that interactions among these regional models are consistent. Users specify a variety of global and regional assumptions about such factors as population, economic trends, and government policies, which interact with the regional and country models to provide estimates of energy consumption, land-use changes, and so on. These ultimately lead to future projections of greenhouse gas emissions. The emissions are fed into the global cycle model, which provides a variety of climate change scenarios based on GCM experiments. The various climate change scenarios drive the AIM impact model and generate regional climate impacts estimates. The AIM impacts model then calculates the impact on net primary production—for water supply, agricultural production, wood supplies, and so forth—and then projects higher order impacts on the regional economy.

The Tool to Assess Regional and Global Environmental and Health Targets for Sustainability (TARGETS)

Besides the IMAGE model, a second branch of RIVM's Integrated Assessment Program is the overall integrated assessment framework. TARGETS aims at the analysis of global change and sustainable development from a synoptic perspective (Rotmans et al. 1994a, 1995, Rotmans & de Vries 1996). The model explores the long-term dynamics of the human and environmental system that may shape the Earth system over the next hundred years. The TARGETS framework basically consists of a population and health model, a resources–economy model, a biophysics model, a land model, and a water model.

Each of the submodels consists of linked pressure, state-descriptive, impact and response modules, capturing the vertically integrated cause–effect chain. Coupling the various pressures, states, impacts and responses for the various subsystems underlying the models brings horizontal integration into play. A first version of the TARGETS model has been made operational on a global level, with global datasets. The TARGETS model utilizes aggregated data and processes which are provided by theme-specific integrated models such as the IMAGE 2.0

model and the RAINS model. TARGETS spans 200 years, starting at the end of the preindustrial era (1900) and ending in 2100, with time steps varying from one month to one year.

A unique feature of TARGETS is that the model deals with uncertainties in an explicit but alternative way. This has been realized by introducing multiple model routes, which are reflections of different perceptions of scientific and policy uncertainties, and has been implemented for all submodels of TARGETS. This approach is described later in the chapter.

Calibration and validation of models

With respect to calibration and validation of integrated assessment models, two major problems present difficulties. First, modelers can choose from many definitions and interpretations of the terms "calibration" and "validation." Moreover, complete calibration and validation of simulation models are impossible, because the underlying systems are never closed (Oreskes et al. 1994). Second, calibration and validation of the integrated assessment models as a whole is not possible, as the requisite data and scientific knowledge are not at hand.

To address the first problem, we define calibration as the procedure for comparing the model results with the results of the real system (historical output, such as observational data). The question to answer is how closely the model output approximates the observational data. In spite of the vagueness in the phrase "as close as possible," statistical techniques can be used to quantify the difference between the model output and measured data.

Some models are calibrated over a historical period of 20 years, but their projections tend to reach out 100 years into the future. Although for some model parts it is very difficult to reconstruct the past 100 years (e.g., land-use transformations), where possible submodels should be reconstructed historically over a longer calibration period (Toth 1994a).

Validation is defined here as the procedure for testing the adequacy of a given mathematical model, where two different types are distinguished: practical validation and conceptual validation. Of the two, conceptual validation is the more complex.

Practical validation concerns the validity of the outcomes of the model. In fact, this implies that the outcomes of the model are compared with a new set of observational data, if available, which lie outside the calibration pathway.

Conceptual validation concerns the test of whether the model represents the real system. This implies that the internal structure of the model is evaluated by testing whether the concepts and theoretical laws of the system under consideration are interpreted and represented in a sound way. In practice this means that the model structure, relations, parameters, and dynamic behavior over a chosen historical period reflect the prevailing theoretical insights and the key facts pertaining to that part of reality which the model is supposed to represent. Conceptual validation is often carried out by applying statistical techniques to test the estimates of parameter values, the distribution functions of parameters, and the coherence of relations (the latter mainly by regression and correlation analysis). As a matter of fact, conceptual validation is often problem and domain dependent.

To address the second problem, overall calibration and validation of integrated assessment models is crucially important, because they imply harmonization of temporal and spatial scales, aggregation levels, time steps and data of the individual submodels. Because this is practically impossible, one way to partly overcome this problem is to calibrate and validate individual submodels of integrated assessment models. However, the successful calibration and validation of individual submodels does not guarantee the validity and reliability of the whole integrated assessment model. For example, although numerical weather prediction models are now displaying great accuracy in short-term forecasting, coupled ocean–atmosphere models are far from satisfactory in describing present-day conditions in an internally consistent manner. In social science, similar problems abound when considering distributional issues and collective action.

An important way of validating submodels of integrated assessment models is by intercomparison with expert models, which they are supposed to represent at the meta-level. An example of validating a simple carbon cycle model against observational data and more complex two- and three-dimensional carbon cycle models is presented in Rotmans & den Elzen (1993) and Wigley (1993).

Having validated the submodels, modelers should attempt to (partly) validate the integrated assessment framework as a whole, at least in terms of adequately testing the coherence and internal consistency of the whole model, as well as validating model results for future explorations outside the original validation domain.

Finally, model intercomparison is an important component of validating integrated assessment models. This means not only comparing model results for a specified set of scenarios, but also comparing basic endogenous and exogenous assumptions, and performing thorough sensitivity and uncertainty analyses. As mentioned above, some of these model intercomparison aspects are now being done within the scope of the EMF-14 project (see p. 356).

Enhancing integrated assessment methodologies

Scientific knowledge is established at least partially because researchers have established and accepted methods that have been proven to produce reliable results. In a developing field such as integrated assessment, researchers are in the process of developing methods that will meet these tests for scientific credibility. For a complex interdisciplinary global issue such as climate change, the research community conducting integrated assessments must pay particular attention to the problems involved in representing and accounting for uncertainties, and for the technical problems in dealing with models and issues at different levels of aggregation (from the local to the global).

Treatment of uncertainty

Because integrated assessment models are intended to capture the entire set of cause–effect interactions involved in climate change, such models are prone to accumulate uncertainties. The issue of uncertainty is therefore of crucial importance. The issue should be given more attention in determining the aggregation level of the various submodels and of the whole model and in determining the structure of the model (Toth 1994a). This consideration must be balanced by the basic requirement for integrated assessment modeling to represent and characterize uncertainty in present policy-relevant scientific knowledge.

The clear danger in integrated assessment modeling is that more detailed and disaggregated modeling results will be also more unreliable. Moreover, doing uncertainty analysis for integrated frameworks is rather difficult, not only because of the cumulation of uncertainties, but also because of the different types and sources of uncertainty.

Several approaches to analyze and present uncertainties are possible. One simple way of presenting uncertainties is by specifying a set of future scenarios, where the scenarios selected are expected to span a range of plausible, representative futures. The United Nations and IIASA have adopted this approach for their population projections, and the IPCC for its emissions scenarios. The difficulty with this approach is that, although it offers plausible causal mechanisms for the different trajectories, it gives no information on the likelihood of each outcome.

Some investigators have confused model sensitivity analysis with uncertainty analysis. Sensitivity analysis is a very powerful approach to understanding the character of a model and its response to marginal changes in key variables and parameter values (Iman & Conover 1982, Kleijnen et al. 1990). However, it does not offer any insight about the overall uncertainty in projections regarding the knowledge used to make those projections. For example, although the sensitivity analysis of a simple model (e.g., $Y = a.X^b$) would show *b* to be the parameter to which the output *Y* is more sensitive, *b* may be known to within 10 percent and *a* could be known to within two orders of magnitude. Thus, the uncertainty in *a* is more critical in determining the uncertainty in the projections of *Y*. Sensitivity analysis would be misleading under these circumstances; uncertainty analysis is needed (McRae et al. 1982, Iman & Helton 1985, Helton 1993).

Uncertainty analysis is carried out through sampling the whole range of plausible values for each input. Then statistical tests are performed to examine the relationship between the inputs and outputs. Many of the techniques for this approach have been adopted from computational nuclear physics (Iman & Conover 1982). Many standardized packages for general application were developed (Iman & Conover 1982, Gardner et al. 1983, Henrion & Morgan 1985), and the applications to energy and environmental modeling followed (Dowlatabadi 1984, Iman & Helton 1985, Reilly et al. 1987, Hettelingh 1989).

Uncertainty analysis of complex models is a significant threefold challenge: how to characterize uncertainties, how to sample these uncertainty distributions, and what statistical tests to devise for inference in uncertainty analysis. As models grow more complex, the number of uncertain variables also grows, as does the number of samples needed to generate reliable statistical inference for uncertainty analysis. Advances in both computational methods and heuristic approaches to limiting the number of uncertain parameters are needed to keep pace with the growing complexity of integrated assessment models of global change. (See Vol. 1, Ch. 2 for a method of grouping uncertainties in population projections. For example, high fertility is likely to be associated with high mortality.)

A critical aspect of the treatment of uncertainty in integrated assessment models is the communication of the results to decisionmakers to help them identify the major lacunae in current knowledge and anticipate the unexpected. Therefore, integrated assessment researchers must make uncertainties within integrated assessment models explicit, visible, and tangible. The problem, however, is that none of the above described methods is able to make uncertainties explicit, because that requires a classification of the different sources of uncertainty.

Several attempts have been made to classify the different types and sources of uncertainties in models (see Vol. 1, Ch. 1, and Ch. 4 in this volume). Morgan & Henrion (1990) distinguish three kinds of uncertainty: about empirical quantities, about the functional form of models, and from disagreements among experts. An alternative classification is the distinction of Funtowicz & Ravetz (1989, 1990) in technical uncertainties (observations versus measurements), methodological uncertainties (the right choice of analytical tools), and epistemological uncertainties (the conception of a phenomenon).

Model quantities in integrated assessment models can be characterized as follows:

- empirical quantities: measurable properties of the real-world systems being modeled
- steering variables and parameters: quantities over which the decision-maker exercises direct control
- value variables and parameters: quantities representing preferences of the decisionmakers
- state variables: quantities representing the state of the system
- auxiliary variables and parameters: quantities introduced because of computation or programming rules.

More generally, four thrusts can be discerned in analyzing uncertainty in integrated assessment models:

- characterizing parameter and model uncertainties
- characterizing variability in values and regional and individual decision-making
- exploring decisionmaking under uncertainty and the value of information
- treating the uncertainties in the context of control theory with non-adaptive and adaptive agents.

Parameter uncertainties have been quantified in several models. Indeed, some models have been designed with this as a primary criterion (Hammitt et al. 1992, Hope et al. 1993, Dowlatabadi & Morgan 1993). In general, these models can be used to communicate the level of uncertainty to decisionmakers, all the way from inputs to outputs. The depictions in Figure 5.3 illustrate the range of uncertainties in projection of various key outcomes. The implications of these uncertainties for policy choice are presented in Figure 5.4, where the outcomes are shown to have strong regional variations.

To indicate the degree of uncertainty in projections and the possible role of bias resulting from modeling error, researchers may explore how the results would vary if different model structures were employed to arrive at projections of future states of the world and how those variances would affection valuation of the policy outcomes. A brief summary of the results of exploring model structure uncertainty have been reproduced in Table 5.2. In the top half of this table the structure of the model examined is specified. In the bottom half the outcomes of interest for each region and the world as a whole are recorded. Six different model formulations are explored. The structure of each model is determined by the column entries at the top half of the table; one of two alternative modules is chosen in each row. Only a subset of the possible combinations is reproduced here. The subset chosen illustrates how structural assumptions can systematically change outcomes.

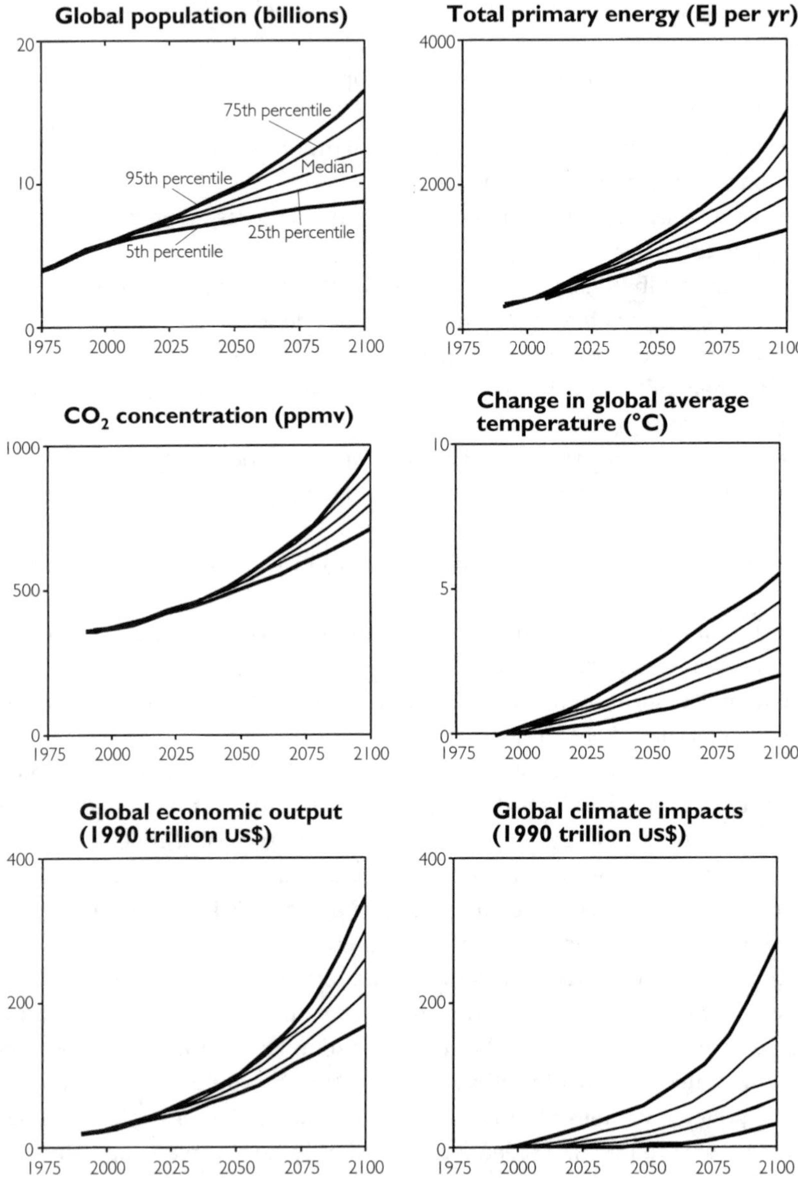

Figure 5.3 Parameter uncertainties when propagated through an integrated assessment model can generate impressions of the accuracy with which specific outcomes such as population growth, energy use, and atmospheric CO_2 concentration may be predicted. It is important to realize that the figures presented above are not predictions, but projections used to communicate the implications of scientific uncertainty on the ability to predict future states of the human and Earth systems. The figures presented above are for a business-as-expected scenario.

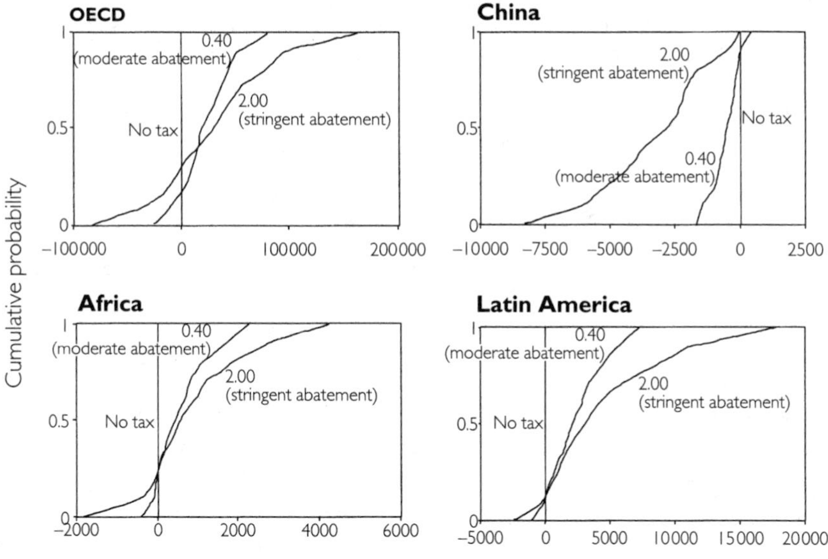

Figure 5.4 If we explore the effects of specific scenarios and translate the uncertainties in the projections into cumulative distribution functions (CDFs) of per capita net discounted utility (in US$), we can illustrate how the different policies fare with respect to one another. Zero means that there was no effect when compared to a no policy case, points along the curve to the left of zero means that action left the regional decisionmaker worse off, points along the curve to the right of zero means that policy action left the decisionmaker better off. The figures presented here were generated using 40 realizations of a model where the key parameter's uncertainty ranges were sampled using a Latin hypercube sampling procedure. Thus, each datum along the CDF is an equiprobable discounted utility (over the period 1990 to 2100) for the specified region.

The outcome used to illustrate variations in model projection is simply the probability that a moderate abatement policy would have a positive payback (note, in Fig. 5.4, the intersection of each policy's cumulative distribution function (CDF); the zero line is the probability that the policy would lead to a loss to the decisionmaker). These probabilities are reported in the lower half of the table for the various regions and the world as a whole. The regions have been arranged so that the regional attraction for moderate climate abatement is in ascending order. Thus, using Model 1, China is least likely and Latin America most likely to benefit from a moderate abatement policy. The models 1–6 have been ordered so that the probability of success (reading from left to right) first rises, and then falls. This general pattern is repeated in all regions, but the magnitude of model structure impact on outcome varies by region. Note that the aggregate outcome exhibits the same trend but without offering any insight

Table 5.2 Probability, as a function of model structures, that a $4.00 per tonne carbon tax that begins in the year 2000 and increases by $4.00 per tonne every five years through the year 2100 will have a positive net present value.

Model alternatives	Six alternative model structures					
Model	1	2	3	4	5	6
Discounting ❑ applied at the same level globally ● based on regional growth per capita	❑	●	●	●	●	●
Technological change ❑ occurs autonomously ● induced by carbon tax	❑	❑	●	●	●	●
Aerosols ❑ radiative effects excluded ● radiative effects included	❑	❑	❑	●	●	●
Adaptation to climate impacts ❑ impacts are permanent ● adaptation occurs after detection	❑	❑	❑	❑	●	●
Oil and gas ❑ reserves exhausted by 2050 ● new reserves will be discovered	❑	❑	❑	❑	❑	●
Region	**Characterization of the likelihood that moderate abatement policy will have a positive net present value**					
China	=	=	=	=	=	=
Eastern Europe and the Former Soviet Union	–	+	+	±	†	=
India and Southeast Asia	±	±	±	–	–	=
Africa	±	±	±	–	–	–
Middle East	±		±	±	–	=
OECD	±	++	++	±	±	–
Latin America	+	+	++	+	+	–
World	–	+	++	±	±	=

Key: = very unlikely; – unlikely; ± even chance; + likely; ++ very likely.

about the significant regional diversity in outcomes. Finally, in some regions (China and Africa) the outcomes are relatively robust with respect to uncertainty in model structure.

The results presented here simply illustrate the impact of model structure on uncertainty. The specific findings depend on the distributional properties of the outcome chosen. Other outcomes with different distributional properties may exhibit a different set of model-structure-induced biases.

For analysis of uncertainty in integrated assessment models, empirical and value quantities are especially important: value parameters are among those that people are most unsure about, and empirical quantities constitute the majority of quantities in models intended for policy analysis. The major sources of uncertainty in empirical quantities are errors in measurements and observations, the chosen modeling approach, and disagreement and subjectivity. Subjective judgment and disagreement among scientific experts are important sources of uncertainty in integrated assessment models. Although much disagreement arises simply from different technical interpretations of the same available scientific evidence, it is regularly complicated by the different perspectives people have. (See Vol. 1, Ch. 1 for a further discussion of built-in structural uncertainties in models.)

Currently available methods are unable to make uncertainties associated with disagreement and subjectivity explicit. Relating the concept of uncertainty with the concept of cultural perspectives, based on cultural theory (Douglas 1978, Thompson et al. 1990, Rayner 1991), van Asselt et al. (1995) arrived at the concept of perspective-based alternative model routes, as a methodology to make uncertainties within the model visible and tangible. In this way, alternative model routes can be created, in which not only parameters but also relationships are varied, according to the bias and preferences of a particular perspective, resulting in alternative model structures.

Aggregation versus disaggregation

One of the critical issues in integrated assessment modeling is that of aggregation versus disaggregation. The level of aggregation within a modeling framework refers to the formulation of the dynamics in the model in terms of level of detail, which is often closely related to the spatial and temporal resolution chosen within the framework. One problem with integrated assessment models is that they consist of a variety of submodels, which have different aggregation levels; for example, they differ in complexity, and spatial and temporal resolution. In many cases these submodels are only linked, not integrated. The different levels of temporal and spatial aggregation in the submodels of an integrated assessment framework results in the model being shaped like an hourglass. The economic–energy models operate in multiyear time steps with large-nation or regional political boundaries. Atmospheric chemistry models operate in small time steps on a small scale, whereas climate models have a relatively coarse spatial resolution (grid-cells of a few degrees) but run at a fine temporal resolution. Finally, ecological impact models require data at fine spatial resolutions (about half a degree), but their time resolution varies greatly, from one day to a season.

Also, to be policy relevant, integrated assessment models need to have different aggregation levels at several points. Policymakers are primarily interested in the decisionmaking aspects of a problem at a scale where they are operating, for instance, a country or political region. This area of focus can be quite small, for instance, a watershed.

Insofar as spatial resolution changes are concerned, statistical downscaling techniques are available as referred to earlier. With regard to temporal resolution changes and changes in dynamics of the model, only heuristic approaches can be used.

The trend in integrated assessment modeling is to move toward greater and greater disaggregation, assuming that such a move yields better models. In general, it is difficult to know when to stop building more detail into an integrated assessment model. With each incremental level of sophistication comes new insight and continued variation in the strategy chosen. However, past decades of model building have shown that small and transparent models are often superior in that they provide similar results to large models faster and offer ease of use. Considering this, various strategies for further improving integrated assessment models can be followed. First, realizing that an integrated assessment framework is as good as its weakest part of the whole model chain, it is much more effective to improve the rather weak or poorly defined model parts, rather than refining and disaggregating the already adequate submodels. Second, a no-regrets modeling strategy is to introduce appropriate region-specific information into submodels, but maintain the ability to run the model at a fairly high level of aggregation (Toth 1994a). Finally, building generic submodels (i.e., models independent of regional or temporal differences) has many advantages. This means that the theories and assumptions must be applicable at different levels of spatial aggregation and for different regions in different periods (Rotmans et al. 1994b).

Building political credibility

Integrated assessment (with and without modeling) contributes in important ways to climate change research, but it also has a unique role to play in informing policy analyses and decisionmaking processes. To improve the political credibility of integrated assessment methods and results, researchers should communicate with other scientific and policymaking communities, enrich and augment communication techniques, and enhance integrated assessment methodologies. These strategies will be discussed in the following section.

Improving the communication process

Ideally, the findings of integrated assessment efforts will inform future policies with long-term contributions to finding the path of future social, technical and economic development. One guide to the successful use of integrated assessment is the RAINS model, which was effectively used in the international acid rain negotiations. Although drawing parallels between the acid rain issue and the much more complex global climate change issue is problematic, some general insights can be gained. Hordijk (1991) and Mermet & Hordijk (1989) have formulated guidelines for developing integrated assessment models for use in international negotiations, based on experiences with the use of the RAINS model in acid rain negotiations in Europe. One of the most important guidelines was that the model should be co-designed by scientists and potential users. This means involvement of the community of stakeholders to establish the model's credibility during its development. Involvement includes discussions on the model's input and outputs, the presentation of the model results, and the level of detail needed for developing alternative strategies. This helps tailor the model to the users' needs. Since this is a continuing process, an intermediary layer of project managers may be established between decisionmakers and modelers.

None of the current generation of integrated assessment models of climate change is being developed in this kind of close conjunction with decisionmakers. This explains why some of the current models are politically naïve, and the model and the decisionmaker together lack political credibility and can offer only limited input to decisionmakers. For example, single-region economic optimization models offer the comparative efficiencies of various strategies, but offer little insight of political value because they do not deal with the distributional aspects of climate policies. This indicates that integrated assessment models should function within the setting of the political arena, where efficiency often takes a back seat to equity. In such a setting, different groups exhibit different levels of risk aversion, they adopt different decision rules, and their utility bundle is composed of different indicators. Only a few of the currently existing integrated assessment models are flexible enough to represent the interests of various parties (through space and time).

Having decisionmakers as early stakeholders in the research program is desirable, but may lead to irresistible pressure for research toward unattainable goals or may mire development efforts in the struggle among conflicting value systems. For example, decisionmakers want to have geographically explicit impacts, which has led many research groups to eschew accurate characterization of what may be projected in favor of precise characterization of impacts with much higher probability of error. Under these circumstances, the modelers need to communicate to decisionmakers the difficulty of attaining such lofty goals. Failing that, they should make clear the magnitude of uncertainties in geographically explicit predictions.

The next generation of integrated assessment models should make use of enhanced integrated assessment concepts, as a result of a continuous consultative process and interfacing with representative groups of decisionmakers. This means, among other things, determining the appropriate level of (dis-)aggregation, making the models actor-oriented by introducing behavioral rules and decisions, deriving consistent and integrated scenarios, and including explicit treatment of uncertainties. The interaction process among model development groups and decisionmakers should curb the demand for the unattainable and prepare decisionmakers for the difficulties they face in selecting strategies when large uncertainties abound.

To gain political credibility, the critical question is how to interact with decisionmakers most effectively. Many different approaches can be adopted. Some groups have chosen to embrace the stakeholders by seeking the active participation of regional decisionmakers in research planning, as in the Mackenzie Basin study (Cohen 1993). Others have developed simulation techniques which engage the decisionmakers in strategic games of pedagogical value to both researchers and decisionmakers—as in the resource management exercises of de Vries et al. (1993). Still others are developing integrated assessment models with the expressed desire to have them be accessible to decisionmakers and their scientific advisors—as in ICAM (Dowlatabadi & Morgan 1993b) and TARGETS (Rotmans et al. 1995). Other large integrated assessment models communicate primarily or exclusively with other researchers and, through them, with decisionmakers.

The final issue to address is where the communication among integrated assessment teams and decisionmakers should take place, or what a suitable communication platform is. One possibility is to develop integrated assessment models that can be run by the decisionmakers on their personal computers. Then a new problem arises: if the models are sufficiently complex to have scientific credibility, few decisionmakers have the time (or inclination) to delve into them deeply, and if they are overly simplified, they may offer useful insights, but their scientific (and thus also political) credibility may be questioned. Another possibility would be to use integrated assessment models within the context of policy exercises, as elucidated below. In this way the models serve to provide guidelines in the background. To facilitate simultaneous and fast decisionmaking, group decision meetings can be organized (computerized Delphi methods).

An effective platform for communication between scientists and high-level policymakers has proven to be German Enquete Meetings. These are carefully prepared and organized debates in the Deutsche Bundestag, where scientists and decisionmakers discuss various prespecified issues directly. Integrated assessment models could assist in setting the agenda for these meetings and could be the means of communication between the scientific and decisionmaking community.

Augmenting communication techniques

This section discusses four techniques or instruments that may ultimately lead to improved communication between the integrated assessment community and the decisionmaking community: the policy exercise concept, the indicator framework, visualization techniques, and scenarios.

Policy exercises

The policy exercise may be defined as a negotiation session in which decisionmakers and policy analysts try to formulate response strategies and are engaged in simulation games where the model is used to evaluate strategies. The policy exercise approach, which is extensively discussed in Chapter 3, is most appropriate for ill-structured complex issues in a situation where no single or ultimate decisionmaking authority can be identified, with many actors operating independently, with many conflicting interests, and with strong influence from external effects (Toth 1988). At RIVM the Global Environmental Strategic Planning Exercise (GESPE) is under development, which aims at the implementation of a learning environment about the potential impacts of anthropogenic climate change in interaction with demographic, agricultural, economic, and resource developments (de Vries et al. 1993).

Indicators

Modelers can improve communication with decisionmakers by designing a framework of indicators. Decisionmakers already have indicators in their lexicon, using them to formulate environmental policies and resulting targets to be achieved. Indicators are pieces of information that help measure changes and progress in decisionmaking. However, indicators can be linked at different scales, sectors, and themes. Modelers can systematically structure the interlinkages among indicators by using integrated assessment models. Using the pressure—state—impact—response framework (see pp. 318–321) as an organizing principle for both models and indicators, we can derive two similar organizing mechanisms, both based on the concept of causality. Linking a set of indicators to an integrated modeling framework can:

- show how the various indicators are interlinked (linkages within the cause–effect chain of an issue—vertical integration—and among different issues—horizontal integration).
- yield insights into the dynamic behavior of indicators (behavioral patterns of social, economic, and environmental systems)
- enable long-term projections to be made for climate change and global change (long-term trends for social, economic, and environmental indicators)

- identify critical system variables and guide the selection of indicators, as well as their aggregation.

A hierarchical set of indicators can be linked to models at various levels of aggregation, from highly aggregated indices to absolute indicators in the form of observed data or statistics. Indicators can then serve as vehicles to communicate model results, and used as the basis for mapping response strategies. Used in this way, an indicator is defined as a characteristic of the status and the dynamic behavior of the system being studied. The dimension and aggregation level of an indicator may vary from a singular, statistics-based variable (absolute indicator) to a multidimensional composite, highly aggregated variable (index).

Within the hierarchical framework of indicators, the various manifestations of indicators will be distinguished, enabling bridge building between the advocates of using highly composite indicators and the traditional statisticians. Linking a framework of indicators to an integrated modeling framework can yield coherent and integrative information that can be generated only by an interconnected framework of indicators, and not by separate indicators. In constructing the hierarchical framework of indicators and indices, modelers can take the following steps: experimentation, selection, scaling, weighing, and aggregation. The various steps can be based upon a combination of expert judgment, Delphi techniques, multicriteria analysis, public opinion polls, value-based decisions and modeling experiments. This requires frequent and intensive interaction between decisionmakers and modelers (Hope et al. 1992, Rotmans et al. 1994a).

Visualization

Because of the level of complexity of the structure of integrated assessment models and the results these models produce, using appropriate visualization techniques is important. Visualization techniques facilitate the presentation of information in a way that corresponds to the way people intuitively perceive images. Such features help to make the model backgrounds, as well as model results, more immediately available and broadly accessible to a wide range of users, who may vary from the general public to decisionmakers. Apart from the traditional and mostly static techniques to visualize information, such as diagrams, graphs, tables and histograms, innovative techniques that allow for an interactive, comprehensive, and dynamic presentation of information can be used. These visualization techniques can help to make the models as transparent as possible, to make the underlying theories as clear as possible, to provide easy-to-use interfaces, and to display uncertainties and complexity of the systems behavior comprehensibly. Effective visualizations can present detailed findings so they can be understood at aggregate levels, surmounting a barrier that may exist with highly abstract and complex messages that need to be made comprehensible to decisionmakers.

Aggregation aims to reduce model results to a preferably one-dimensional form, but visualization enables researchers to represent many dimensions in one picture. On the one hand, these multidimensional representations include more information about linkages and interactions among different components, but, on the other, the resulting pictures may be more complex and need more explanation. Finally, multimedia techniques might lead to a better understanding of model results by decisionmakers.

Scenarios

Scenarios play a key role in assessing the future risks of and potential responses to global change. However, current scenarios suffer from at least two flaws: they rely too heavily on deriving the future from present conditions, and they lack a full range of social science inputs.

First, scenarios are often extrapolations of current trends and conditions, which is an inadequate method for making long-term projections. Such a future pathway may include surprises, but no methodology has yet been developed that enables surprises to be systematically incorporated into scenarios. A more promising alternative than using extrapolation methods is to first determine desirable states, for which the framework of indicators can be used, and then indicate whether and how these states could be reached. Using this method of *backcasting* to develop coherent and consistent response strategies for global change, the techniques of optimization might serve as a helpful guide, which may vary from optimal control theory for smaller integrated assessment models to the use of genetic algorithms for larger integrated assessment models (Robinson 1988, 1990).

Second, current scenarios do not include social, cultural, and institutional developments, and they lack the requisite variety needed to describe possible worlds that are determined by the dynamic interplay among groups with different cultural and institutional perspectives (see Vol. 1, Ch. 4). Most scenarios developed for global change focus on the environmental, demographic, technological, and economic aspects of global change independently. However, taking into account social, cultural, and institutional aspects and their dynamic interactions would give future scenarios more breadth and could thus increase the understanding of potential future developments. As argued by Janssen & Rotmans (1995), there is no fit between the IPCC 1990 and 1992 scenarios and different cultural perspectives. Therefore, a useful contribution of the social sciences to scenario construction would be to select appropriate social, cultural and institutional indicators to account for the diversity of cultural perspectives. Because most indicators to be selected cannot be adequately modeled with the present integrated assessment models, they can serve as a guiding principle for the further improvement and refinement of the current generation of those models.

Major findings

Integrated assessment of climate change is a relatively new endeavor, and development has proceeded at a hectic pace. It is too early to demand very robust conclusions, but some preliminary findings can be identified. These findings fall into two broad categories. The first are findings relevant primarily to decisionmakers. The second are relevant primarily to scientists engaged in integrated assessments and in fundamental research.

Contributions to the policy debate

From the perspective of policy designers and decisionmakers, the critical question is whether the climate problem deserves early and significant attention. Policymakers are concerned about the risks from climate change, the cost and nature of early action, the distribution of costs associated with action, and avoidable losses. No single integrated assessment model answers all of these questions. However, the various assessments shed light on different aspects of the issue. In the collective results from these studies concrete insights can be found. Below, we present findings on severity of the climate change issue, timing of action, factors affecting cooperation, and equity. These findings are used to discuss implications for present-day decisionmaking and future research needs.

Should there be abatement?

The recognition that human activities may disturb the climate system on a global scale is sobering. However, such a recognition does not necessarily call for stringent abatement actions. The question of response actions is contingent on perceived risks of current trends. Two basic approaches have been adopted for answering this question: a physical modeling paradigm (utility maximizing) and an economic modeling paradigm.

Using a physical modeling paradigm, a researcher would set a maximum rate of global mean temperature increase (say of 0.1°C per decade) and a maximum total global mean temperature increase (say of 2°C above preindustrial global mean temperature). Beyond these maximum rates, significant and irreversible damages are incurred by ecosystems. There are three major shortcomings in these targets:

- They are defined in terms of temperature changes, but climate change involves much more than temperature; ecosystems are vulnerable to all variables interacting with one another, not simply to temperature change.
- They are defined in terms of global averages, but large regional variations in temperature are likely.
- They are based on very limited information and do not take into account actual impact mechanisms and the feedbacks and nonlinearities that may exacerbate or ameliorate realized impacts in various regions.

The analytical maximums suggested above will probably be exceeded. Risk assessment calculations show that, in all but one of the IPCC 1992 and 1990 scenarios, the rate and level of global temperature go far beyond such target levels. Thus, these scenarios might all be interpreted as exceeding acceptable climate risk scenarios. The exception is the accelerated policy (AP) scenario, which may be considered as posing a moderate risk from climate change impacts for the next 50 years.

The cost–benefit or utility-maximizing paradigm differs from the physical approach in asserting that environmental thresholds have equivalents in social and economic systems. The equivalence between the two systems is implemented through definition of market and nonmarket values for environmental impacts. Thus, the risks from climate change impacts are balanced against risks from climate policy impacts.

An important aspect of the utility-maximizing paradigm is that resources may be allocated in an optimal manner among different generations. The manner in which this optimality is achieved is by assuming technical progress, leading to increasing levels of service from available resources through time, and an appropriate discount rate. As the nonmarket resources are somehow assigned a value by today's decisionmakers, it is possible to step over the thresholds of irreversible damages to ecosystems. The realization of this possibility is determined by the discount rate chosen by the analyst. Some economists have suggested low discount rates, in the range 0–2 percent per year (Cline 1992). These lead to large impact estimates in the distant future and urge significant action now. Other economists (see Ch. 1) argue that adopting low discount rates is inconsistent with revealed public and private investment decisions. They have adopted higher discount rates. The optimal emissions strategies so calculated balance present-day discounted costs and benefits while violating temperature thresholds. However, although present-day market investment decisions suggest discount rates in the 3–5 percent per year range, public policy decisions such as the creation of national parks and wilderness areas hint at discount rates close to 0 percent for these specific nonmarket goods. Public policy decisions reflect a very wide range of discount rates.

The severity of the climate change issue cannot be established from a physical paradigm because accurate models of environmental impacts have not yet been developed. For example, it is not clear whether the threshold of impacts should be set to avoid loss of ecosystem function, keystone species, indicator species, biodiversity, or individual organisms. The questions faced by advocates of the socioeconomic paradigm are just as vexing. What is the correct discount rate? Do values of decisionmakers stay static through time? Can today's utility function be safely used to apportion utility across many generations? How are physical impacts to be translated into economic or utility losses?

Nonetheless, physical and economic modeling paradigms indicate that continued emissions of greenhouse gases and aerosols influence climate. All models associate adverse impacts with such climate change, and advocate some measure of abatement. However, the severity of the abatement target continues to be controversial.

When should abatement actions be taken?

If the decisionmaker has been persuaded of the severity of the climate issue, the next question asked is, "When should we take action?" Again, the two paradigms (physical and socioeconomic modeling) offer different insights.

Physical models such as IMAGE 1.0 have confirmed that a delay in abatement activity (to the time period 2010 to 2030) leads to a relatively small penalty in climate change commitment. The economic models (Richels & Edmonds 1994) show that such delays can lead to significant cost savings in meeting future abatement targets. The key insights here are that climate change is a function of the change in the stock of greenhouse gases in the atmosphere. The atmospheric stock is roughly 100 times larger than the flow because of anthropogenic activity. Furthermore, mitigation aims to influence the flow rate, and policies aimed at changing the near-term flow of greenhouse gases are likely to be more costly than those aimed at stabilizing the ultimate atmospheric stock. These findings might seem to lead to a noncontroversial consensus about the timing of abatement—but this is not the case.

IPCC Working Group I chose to define its emissions scenarios (consistent with various stabilization levels of atmospheric carbon dioxide) with significant departures from a no-abatement policy trajectory, probably an expensive approach to meeting a concentration target. Indeed, Wigley et al. (1996) put forward four reasons why early efforts at significant mitigation may prove needlessly costly:

- *Positive marginal productivity* Investments in economic development lead to greater resources available for mitigation in the future.
- *Capital stock* Transition to a lower-carbon-intensity economy is cheaper if timed to coincide with replacement of existing capital.
- *Technical progress* Progress will lead to a lower cost of mitigation.

- *The carbon cycle* The carbon cycle removes more carbon dioxide from the atmosphere through time. Thus, a higher near-term emission path may have greater cumulative emissions but the same final level of atmospheric concentration.

However, these observations have sparked a flurry of activity aimed at rebuttal of the position that delaying mitigation may prove cost effective (Pearce 1996).

From a physical modeling perspective, the advisability of a delay in abatement of emissions is based on the assumption of a smooth transition in the carbon cycle and the climate state. There is some evidence to the contrary in the historic record (White 1993), and researchers only have untested hypotheses about what triggered these past events (Broecker 1994). Furthermore, when asked about the possibility of climate state irreversibilities, prominent climatologists give probabilities in the 1 to 10 percent range for such thresholds being crossed at doubled carbon dioxide concentrations (Morgan & Keith 1995). Perhaps the temperature thresholds identified have internalized these issues. However, from the decisionmakers' perspective, the implicit assessment of these risks has significant shortcomings.

The advisability of delayed mitigation from an economic standpoint is based on strong assumptions about economic growth, and progress in research and development. Indeed, the pace of technological progress over the past century bolsters such confidence; however, the slow pace of R&D programs such as fusion energy suggests that we can be fooled into overoptimism. Grubb et al. (1995) have argued that, the longer we delay the abatement activity, the more disruptive and difficult the abatement is likely to become. Their position assumes that decisionmakers have no foresight or are limited in their ability to act on it, and that more stringent mitigation efforts will be required down the road. This is not the Wigley et al. (1996) case, where investments are made with foresight about the future economic, technological, and regulatory milieu. On the other hand, Edmonds et al. (1997a) have shown that none of the concentration ceilings below 750 ppmv could be achieved by policy measures under consideration within the Berlin Mandate process without immediate non-Annex-I actions, whereas all of the ceilings 450 parts per million by volume (ppmv) and higher are potentially achievable. The relevant question is not whether Wigley et al. are incorrect in their insight about timing, but how to provide both a strong signal to decisionmakers that in the future a more stringent abatement strategy will be implemented and also a strategy for controlling mitigation costs.

Is cooperative implementation desirable and achievable?

If climate change poses a severe risk and abatement is needed, another critical question is who should pay for such action. Two factors enter into this issue: the trends in emissions, and regional (better still, national and local) costs and benefits of climate change policy and impacts.

The question of how the mitigation burden should be shared raises three questions:

- Who bears responsibility for abatement?
- Who should shoulder the burden of abatement?
- Does cooperation alter the level abatement sought?

The modeled regional trends in emissions suggest that economic development and energy use will lead to an increasing burden of emissions (and mitigation) outside the Organisation for Economic Cooperation and Development (OECD) countries. Furthermore, concerted action within the OECD is insufficient to significantly slow or halt anthropogenically induced climate change. Thus, the burden of mitigation will increasingly transfer from the shoulders of the presently industrialized nations to regions of rapid growth in industrialization today, such as China and India.

The economic models of burden sharing suggest that low-cost opportunities for mitigation exist in the less industrialized regions of the world today, as well as in more industrialized regions. Thus, total costs are estimated to be lower if industrialized and less industrialized regions jointly implement mitigation strategies. This follows a broad theoretical insight that, where there is diversity in the costs of abatement, flexibility leads to lower economic costs associated with a given emissions or concentration target. Edmonds et al. (1995) have shown that the distribution of emissions rights and degree of trading have profound effects on the regional costs and benefits of participating in various mitigation protocols, with important implications for the political attainability of global mitigation strategies.

However, one of the challenges in modeling economic processes in the less industrialized regions of the world is that substantial informal economies exist, and the dynamics and equilibrium of the economy as represented in Western models of economic activity are incomplete (see Ch. 2). This incomplete characterization of the less industrialized economies may obscure their relative inelasticity to abate greenhouse gas emissions.

Finally, integrated assessments have been used to show that many factors determine the regional nature of costs and benefits of greenhouse gas abatement. Reliance on heavy industry and high dependence on coal leads to high abatement costs. Reliance on rain-fed agriculture and low-lying coastal resources leads to high abatement benefits. Furthermore, regional differences in manifestation of climate change and local modifiers of climate (e.g., anthropogenic aerosols) lead to large ambiguities in the incidence of climate policy costs and benefits. Nonetheless, models such as CFUND (Tol 1995), MERGE 2.0 (Manne & Richels 1995), and RICE (Nordhaus & Yang 1995) all show that cooperation increases the level of abatement and net benefits, but that, when different regions act in their own self-interest, abatement levels and benefits are lower.

In summary, cooperation in abatement may lead not only to lowered costs of mitigation, but also to a higher standard for mitigation and commensurately higher overall benefits from averted climate change and its impacts.

Here, much larger issues of political economy dominate the results obtained using integrated assessment. The treatment of issues such as burden sharing and joint implementation in integrated assessment models may not solve these political problems, but the observations that cooperation will lower costs and increase the level of mitigation effort while yielding even higher benefits can facilitate global accords.

How can decisionmakers grapple with equity issues?

Addressing equity is far less a modeling issue than a matter of allocation of rights. Modeling does not address equity questions directly, but rather explores the likely results of implementing policies intended to be equitable. Less industrialized nations have argued persuasively that the change in radiative forcing of the atmosphere since the mid-nineteenth century is a consequence of the path of development followed by the industrialized countries (see Vol. 1, Ch. 4). In general, current per capita emissions of less industrialized countries are relatively low, and to have room for growth they demand greater latitude in the control of future emissions. Thus, equitable allocations of emission permits tend to allow less industrialized countries more than they need today. Some studies (e.g., Peck & Teisberg 1995, McKibbin & Wilcoxen 1996, Manne & Richels 1996, Harrison & Rutherford 1997) have explored the trade in emissions permits through time. These generally show that the less industrialized countries sell permits in the near future, and later, as they develop a more energy intensive economy, they buy permits back. All such results are predetermined by the user-specified allocation of permits and expectations about the nature and magnitude of future economic growth.

Integrated assessment modeling has shed new light on two equity-related issues: greenhouse gas equivalencies, and the issue of metrics for aggregation and measurement of policy impacts. These are briefly discussed below.

Global warming potentials (GWPs) were proposed by Lashof & Ahuja (1990) as a means of aggregating and comparing the contribution of different greenhouse gases to changes in radiative forcing (see Vol. 2, Ch. 1). However, this approach is a woefully inadequate measure for intercomparison of different greenhouse gas emissions and determination of their profile in the future. These failures arise because a static physical concept has been applied in a dynamic policy domain. Eckaus (1992) first raised the issue that, if impacts occur in the distant future, some form of discounting should be applied to the GWP framework. Den Elzen (1993) showed the importance of the path of historic emissions scenario used, as well as the difference between transient and equilibrium GWPs. Smith & Wigley (1997) raised further issues with the present set of GWPs formulated by the IPCC (Houghton et al. 1992). Finally, Kandlikar (1995) developed an integrated assessment framework in which the dynamics of both the socioeconomic and physical systems are reflected. Kandlikar argues that the so-called equivalence of greenhouse gases is only meaningful in terms of ultimate impacts from emissions of one molecule of this gas versus a molecule of another gas. These impacts are contingent on past emissions, the response of the climate system, and consequent impacts of climate change.

Greenhouse gas intercomparisons calculated with integrated assessment models differ substantially from the GWPs published by the IPCC (Houghton et al. 1992). For a typical time horizon of 100 years, the difference between IPCC GWPs and the equivalencies derived using integrated assessment models can be as high as 80 percent. The consequence of such large differences for international negotiations and efficacy of abatement policies is difficult to overstate. Although the new equivalence schemes are demanding, requiring explicit choice of many factors (i.e., emissions scenario, climate sensitivity, assumed impacts, utility functions, and discount rates), this is also their strength. Using these equivalence schemes forces decisionmakers to consider explicitly the many issues that affect efficacy and advisability of their actions.

Complicating factors: aerosols and others

Perhaps the most interesting of complicating factors for climate policy analysis is the issue of anthropogenic aerosols. Anthropogenic aerosols (most notably sulfates) are emitted in association with fossil fuel combustion (especially coal) and act to reduce radiative forcing. Currently, the magnitude of their negative forcing is thought to be comparable to the positive forcing of greenhouse gases (Charlson et al. 1992). Unlike most greenhouse gases, aerosols have a very short atmospheric lifetime (only a few days). Thus, the flow of aerosols has a radiative effect thought to be comparable to the radiative effect from the change in the atmospheric stock of greenhouse gases (Fig. 5.5). This is said to have led to a masking of the climate change associated with the change in greenhouse gas concentrations since the preindustrial era.

Aerosols introduce a significant complication into the effect of greenhouse gas abatement policies. The point of curtailing carbon dioxide emissions is to limit the change in atmospheric stock of this gas, limiting climate change commitment. However, in the short term, a more significant reduction in the flow of aerosols leads to consequent early unmasking of climate change. The first calculations show that, in the foreseeable future, the increased radiative forcing from changes in sulfur dioxide concentration could more than offset reductions

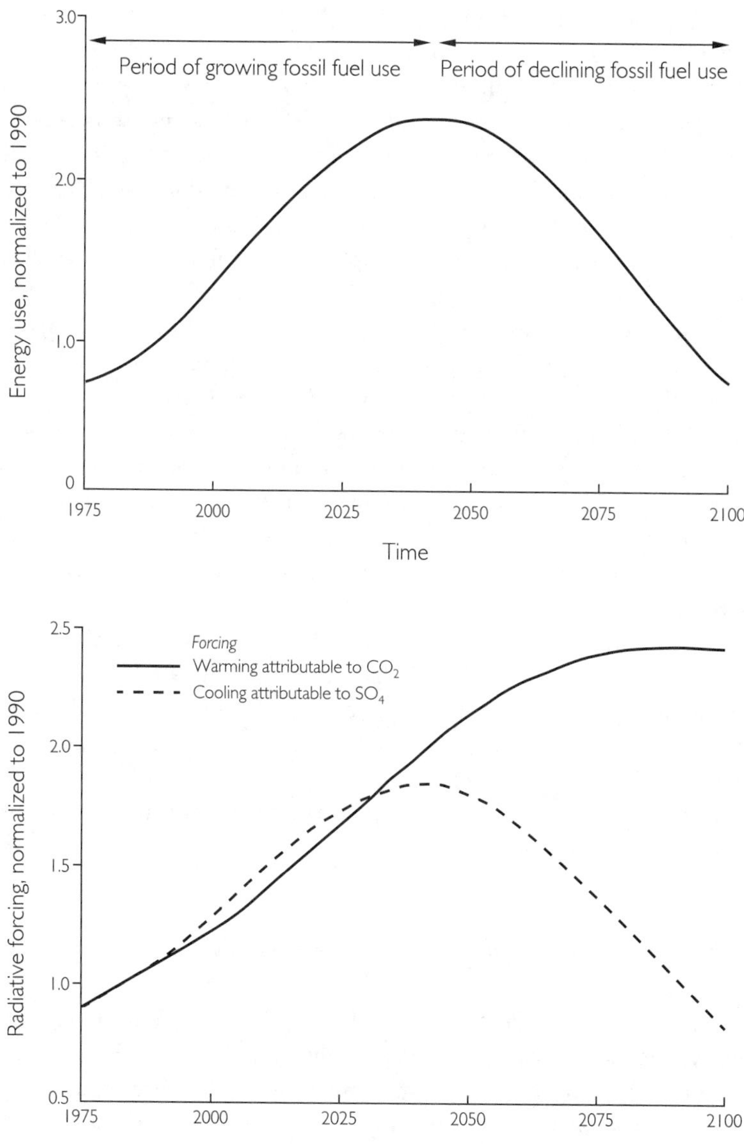

Figure 5.5 Schematic illustration of the difference between response times of climate forcing attributable to $C0_2$ (warming) and sulfate aerosols (cooling) during rising and falling trends in global fossil fuel consumption. A globally averaged forcing caused by SO is not meaningful. Aerosol forcings are regional, and the impact of regionally heterogeneous forcing on dynamics is unknown and likely to be nonlinear (Lal et al. 1995).

in radiative forcing from reduced carbon dioxide emissions (Andreae 1994). Therefore, policies that reduce fossil fuel use are not as effective as a simple greenhouse calculation might imply (Edmonds et al. 1994).

At present, no optimization model has been able to arrive at an acceptable solution to the aerosol problem. This is because none has specified local air pollution penalties associated with sulfur dioxide emissions. In the absence of these, the models opt to increase aerosols to mask climate change.

Some additional insights about the impact of aerosols on climate policy have been obtained using the ICAM 2 model. This model simulates regional climate effects of aerosols. The Northern Hemisphere has much higher anthropogenic sulfate loading. Thus, although aerosols complicate greenhouse gas abatement strategies there, they have negligible affect in the Southern Hemisphere. This same argument holds where different regions in the Northern Hemisphere have different local air-quality measures in place. Thus, the sulfur dioxide impacts in the OECD and China have distinctly different temporal features, leading China to eschew abatement of greenhouse gases until well into the twenty-first century, after local air quality measures have been put into place (Morgan & Dowlatabadi 1996).

Finally, any feature of the problem leading to regional differences in incidence of abatement costs and benefits is a complicating factor. A region's tax, trade, and technology development policies play a significant role in whether the abatement decision will become an opportunity for economic growth or a drain on precious local resources. In general, however, only illustrative cases of these issues have been explored, and the preliminary results are contingent on controversial assertions.

Contributions to the scientific debate

Integrated assessment studies have resulted in identifying critical gaps in disciplinary knowledge, especially when considering long-term dynamics of social, economic, biogeochemical, and climate systems. The absence of key information has led some integrated assessment teams to send scouting parties beyond the frontiers of disciplinary knowledge. Through exploring different possible paradigms, these expeditionary parties have underlined the value of the relevant disciplinary research.

We have discussed many issues where current knowledge is not persuasive and current model structures can lead to systematically biased findings (e.g., the issue of endogenous technological change). Integrated assessments have indicated a need for more focused and concerted disciplinary research in many scientific arenas. Two examples are offered below.

Balancing the carbon budget

To assess the impact of feedback mechanisms within the global carbon cycle, some integrated assessment models have been used to balance the past and present carbon budgets. The surprise here is the number of solutions yielding a balanced historical and present carbon budget. The problem is ill specified, but considering the different modes in which the carbon budget can be balanced has profound implications for the future trajectory of atmospheric carbon dioxide. The same emission pathways can lead to very different atmospheric concentrations of carbon dioxide. In the terrestrial biosphere, the CO_2 fertilization feedback appears to determine the balance and dominates the temperature-related feedbacks, while the net primary feedback seems to counterbalance the soil and respiration feedback effect. Future projections based on the IPCC's *business as usual* 1990 scenario show that the carbon dioxide concentrations calculated with integrated assessment models are about 15 percent lower than the IPCC values. This difference can be explained by the fact that most global carbon cycle models used by the IPCC (Houghton et al. 1990) were unbalanced, and the balanced models do not produce terrestrial fluxes that correspond to observations.

Integrated land-use analysis

First attempts to integrate various aspects of the global land-use problem on a geographically explicit base can be found in the IMAGE 2.0 and MiniCAM 2.0 models. In these models the transformation of land cover is represented as it is affected by climate, demographic, and economic factors. These models link changes in land use and land cover with the flux of carbon dioxide and other greenhouse gases. These models also compute the effects of climate in changing productivity of the terrestrial and oceanic biospheres. Integrating agricultural and land-cover calculations with climate change calculations can provide new insights about shifts in agricultural areas related to climate and the influence that changing land cover has on climate. Preliminary results indicate that policies to mitigate fossil fuel emissions can lead to pressure on unmanaged ecosystems through increased demands for commercial biomass energy (Edmonds et al. 1996). Preliminary results also lend validity to the hypothesis that regional demands for land can serve as a surrogate of regional and local demands driving local land-cover changes, and that land-use rules can be used to represent driving forces of land conversions. Other examples involve the vulnerability of protected areas under shifting vegetation zones, and the consequences for biodiversity and nature conservation. Finally, the model can be used to determine the risks to agricultural productivity as cultivation patterns respond to land-use pressures. These analyses could assist regional policymakers in assessing the seriousness of climate change impacts (Alcamo 1994).

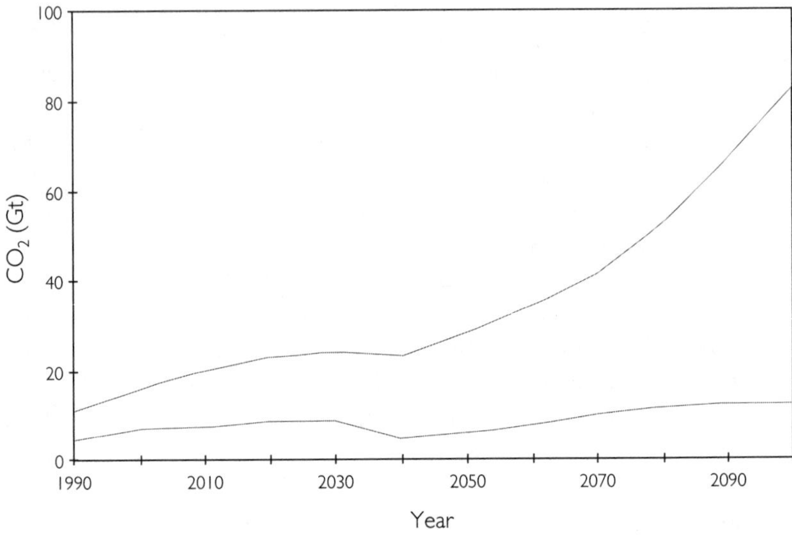

Figure 5.6 The range of global annual CO_2 emissions from the modelers' reference case of EMF-14 (12 models represented).

Quantitative modeling results

Through the efforts of the Energy Modeling Forum (EMF-14) at Stanford University, a model intercomparison of integrated assessments began in January of 1994 (EMF 1994). This exercise brings the community of integrated assessment modelers together, offering them an opportunity to exchange ideas and benefit from informal peer review. Many different scenarios are investigated in this model intercomparison. These scenarios have been designed so that they may be used as diagnostic tools when comparing different models. Here, as a proxy to the volumes of data generated for the EMF-14 exercise, Figure 5.6 presents the envelope of outcomes for carbon dioxide emissions and average global temperature change for the modelers' business as usual reference case. This particular case is selected because it is representative of the best guess of the investigators.

The range of best-guess outcomes is wide enough to span the space of outcomes from significant climate change to compliance with the temperature thresholds. This is a large range of subjective uncertainty; nonetheless, it does not indicate the true range of uncertainties in projections of emissions and temperature change. At present, only a subset of the integrated assessment models are capable of calculating the consequences of parameter and model uncertainties. The range of uncertainties projected with these models when considering parameter uncertainties is comparable to the ranges presented in Figure 5.6. When model structure uncertainties are considered, the ranges are broader still.

Integrated assessment modeling: the challenges ahead

As the integrated assessment process develops and as models become more sophisticated, modelers, policymakers, and other stakeholders will face challenges in building a relevant knowledge base, selecting detail and designing models that reflect reality, using model results with an awareness of their limiting assumptions and partial answers, and establishing integrated assessment as a legitimate and powerful approach to climate change issues.

Scientific knowledge

The problem of having enough knowledge about both natural and social systems is further complicated by a lack of knowledge about the effects and feedbacks within and between systems. Representing important parameters is a basic modeling task, which is made much more difficult by the changing state of knowledge about what is important (see the discussion of aerosols on p. 352).

In the realm of the natural system, scientists seem to be endlessly discovering areas that are crucial to an overall understanding but are poorly understood. For example, the dynamics of the climate system continue to be far from well understood because of a dearth of knowledge about the internal dynamics of this system. The nascent nature of climate science is typified by a continuing stream of surprise findings and disappointment in solving what were once thought to be tractable problems. For example,

- We are still at a loss as to how to model clouds.
- Balancing the carbon cycle remains a challenge, made more difficult with recent evidence of a newly discovered reservoir of organic carbon in the oceans.
- Chlorofluorocarbons, once thought to be the most potent greenhouse gases, are now believed to have a negligible net warming effect.
- Fuel and biomass burning as well as biogenic sources lead to emission of greenhouse gases and aerosols. The former leads to longwave radiation being trapped in the atmosphere and warming. The latter lead to reflection of shortwave radiation. Estimating the magnitude of this cooling effect continues to be a difficult challenge.
- In plant response studies we have learned about the importance of carbon and nitrogen fertilization effect on plants. However, even the first steps

toward an understanding of the ecological consequences of this matter are yet to be completed.

- We have long known about the central role of ocean circulation in the global climate, but new evidence calls into question long-held beliefs on cause and effect in that relationship.

In general, knowledge of key dynamics of social systems is also limited. In addition, the modeling of socioeconomic aspects suffers from a dearth of basic data, in particular outside industrialized countries. Therefore, the models we have developed to describe social dynamics have not been calibrated and validated adequately. The limitations in our knowledge of social dynamics include, but are not limited to the following:

- What brings about health transition (consisting of demographic, epidemiologic, and fertility transition), and how may population changes be predicted over the next century?
- What drives environmentally related human behavior and how may human behavior be predicted over the next century?
- What are the roots and dynamics of technological innovation and diffusion?
- What has led to rapid industrialization in some countries and why have other countries not followed that path?
- What drives processes such as urbanization and migration?
- How are preferences formed and do they evolve through time?
- Can any of the above processes be manipulated through specific initiatives?

How are researchers exploring new ways to realistically represent social systems? One study (Janssen 1995a) focuses on modeling learning and adaptive behavior. The study incorporates a new stream of modeling that has emerged during the past decade, the *complex adaptive systems approach*. Complex adaptive systems are composed of many agents who interact with their environment and can adapt to changes. These systems organize themselves, learn and remember, evolve and adapt. This evolutionary modeling approach is applied in various disciplines and uses a whole range of modeling tools, for example, genetic algorithms. Such tools are used in a case study to model learning and adaptive behavior in social systems.

In an attempt to model interactions among agents and the underlying system, Janssen (1995a) considered many agents having different perspectives consisting of a distinctive worldview and management style. People are assumed to abandon their perspectives in the event of a surprise, that is, when observations or experiences of the world differ from expectations. Agents are further assumed to shift toward worldviews that better explain the observed behavior of the system. Therefore, Janssen simulates this learning and adaptive behavior of agents as a battle of perspectives, using genetic algorithms. A genetic algorithm is a robust problem-solving approach based on the mechanics of the survival of the fittest. After reproduction, crossover, and mutation, the fittest solutions pass on elements of themselves to later generations in an effort to find the most successful solutions. A crucial assumption is that the degree to which the agents' expectations meet measurements determines the fitness of the agents' perspective.

This concept has been applied to the OMEGA integrated assessment framework, which combines the economic part of DICE with the climate part of IMAGE 1.0 (Janssen 1995b, 1996). In the simplified modeling world, the fitness function is only determined by changes in global mean temperature. With this concept in place, an illustrative series of experiments was designed. One such experiment posits a world in which serious global warming may occur due to human intervention in the global Earth's system. In this world, most agents favor a preventive policy. The observed global mean temperature is masked by an additional cooling effect, and this mask falls off in the middle of the next century. Then various agents are confronted with a surprise.

In such a world a cooling surprise would lead to a slowing of emission reductions because now other perspectives will dominate. This results in an additional global mean temperature increase of about 1°C by 2100.

The exploratory experiments show that scanning the future should not be limited to mere extrapolations of our present knowledge, but should include the notion of surprises and the development of flexible strategies to react to surprises.

Obviously, the agents' representations used here are only very abstract images of decisionmakers. However, by considering a set of agents who adopt various perspectives with respect to the climate change problem, modelers will be able to simulate a learning process for the agents and their adaptation of their behavior in terms of policy measures. Janssen did not claim that empirical agents actually learn and adapt in a way that closely resembles the battle of the perspectives. However, some isomorphism may exist between the battle of the perspectives and the ways in which actual agents adapt to their changing environment.

Methodological challenges

A major challenge for integrated assessment modeling is representing uncertainty. To date, most of the integrated assessment models have been run with stochastic sampling of their input parameters. However, only a few models have considered uncertainties in their design. Uncertainty techniques currently available are unable to render various sources and types of uncertainties explicit, provide no systematic and coherent clusters of uncertainties, and fail to explain and clarify uncertainties in a manner understandable to policy-makers. One approach to identify and clarify uncertainties resulting from subjectivity and disagreement among experts is to relate them to the different societal perspectives that people have adopted.

Social science researchers can classify many valid perspectives from which to identify inherent lacunae in the body of scientific knowledge and assess what should be addressed in future integrated assessment models. Therefore, any analysis of uncertainty in integrated assessment models should fully consider many perspectives. The notion of various perspectives implies that each model is regarded as the reflection of the modeler's (or modeling group's) specific perspective. This theme is emerging within the modeling community, although outsiders have pointed to the inherent subjectivity of models (Keepin & Wynne 1984, Funtowicz & Ravetz 1993). Van Asselt & Rotmans (1995) set out to explore the implications of different perspectives in modeling the population issue.

Hitherto, no adequate methods have been available to systematically analyze uncertainty using different perspectives within integrated assessment models. Current techniques of uncertainty analysis used in integrated assessment (e.g., Monte Carlo sampling and probability distribution functions), merely address uncertainty in models stemming from statistical variation, variability, and approximation, but are not capable of analyzing uncertainty growing out of subjective judgment and disagreement among experts. Furthermore, classical methods suffer from the fact that they only address uncertainties in model inputs and neglect the structure of the model itself. Also, estimates of minimum, maximum, and best-guess values used in classical uncertainty analysis are often erroneous or misleading (Frey 1992). Such estimates do not attend to the interactions among multiple, simultaneously occurring uncertainties, precisely those interdependencies and relationships that cannot be ignored in integrated assessment. Current methods thus give decisionmakers no indication regarding the magnitude and the sources of the underlying uncertainties, and such methods therefore fail to translate uncertainty into concepts, such as risk, that dovetail with the experiences, practices, and needs of decisionmakers. At the core of the methodology applied in this example is the notion that subjective judgments and disagreement among experts occur because they have adopted various perspectives.

Therefore, integrated assessment demands new tools, if modelers want to be able to incorporate a variety of perspectives in relation to uncertainty and to translate uncertainty by expressing it in terms of risk. For this purpose van Asselt et al. (1995) introduce the concept of multiple *model routes*, which are chains of biased interpretations of the crucial uncertainties in integrated assessment models. A workable subset of crucial uncertainties is arrived at using a set of selection criteria: magnitude, degree, and time variability.

A basic principle underpinning social science is that biased interpretations are not arbitrary. Van Asselt et al. (1995) set out to use social scientific insights and reasoning with respect to various perspectives as an organizing framework that gives the alternative model routes coherence. Because perspectives can thus be characterized by two dimensions—worldview (i.e., a coherent conception of how the world functions) and management style (i.e., signifying policy preferences and strategies)—perspectives affect both the scenario part and the dynamic part of the model describing the functioning of the world. Model routes, which are themselves combinations of worldviews and management styles, allow the juxtaposition of the favored management style of each perspective with the alternative worldviews. Such experiments teach us what might happen in the event that the adopted worldview fails to describe reality adequately. In this way, uncertainty is a notion that might be usefully deployed by decisionmakers in arriving at their decisions.

Van Asselt et al. (1995) used insights from cultural anthropology, environmental ethics, and sociology of science, to arrive at an aggregated framework of three primary perspectives derived from cultural theory (see Ch. 3, and Vol. 1, Ch.4) . A summarized overview of the main characteristics of the derived stereotypes is set out in Table 5.3.

Table 5.3 Characteristics of perspectives.

	Hierarchist	Egalitarian	Individualist
Myth of nature	Nature perverse/tolerant	Nature ephemeral	Nature benign
Human nature	Sinful	Good and malleable	Self seeking
Type of management	Control	Prevention	Adaptation
Driving value	Stability	Equity and equality	Growth
Attitude to needs/ resources	Rational allocation of resources	Need-reducing strategy	Expand resource base
Risk	Risk accepting	Risk averse	Risk seeking

Source: van Asselt et al. (1995).

The above methodology was applied to the submodels of the TARGETS model (Rotmans & De Vries 1996). The application to the fertility part of the population and health model (Niessenx et al. 1996) illustrates the potency of perspective-based model routes.

The population issue has become the subject of a furious intellectual debate both in the scientific and policymaking communities. Different interpretations of the uncertainties with respect to population dynamics, and the interactions and interdependencies with socioeconomic and environmental processes, underlie the controversy. The perspective-based interpretations summarized

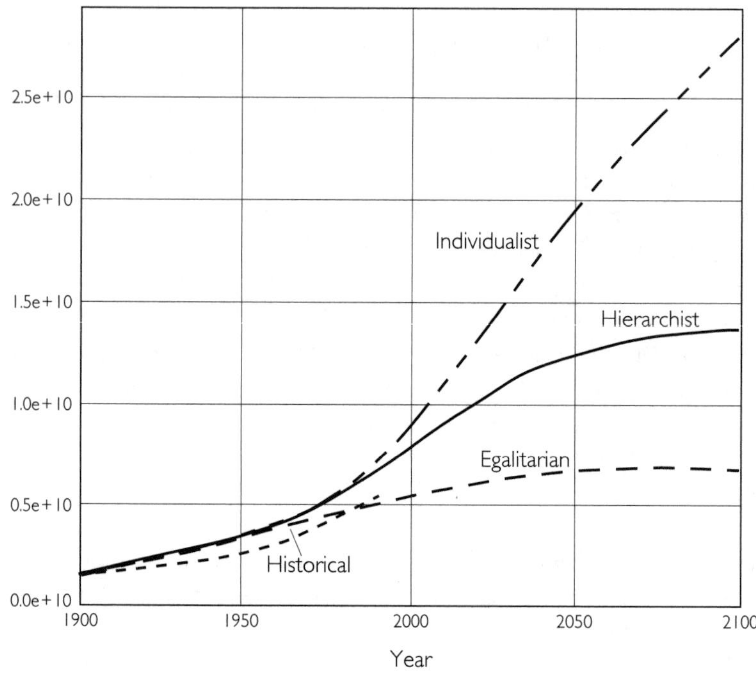

Figure 5.7 Utopian population projections and historical data (source: van Asselt et al. (1995).

in Table 5.4 are used to define alternative values for model quantities and alternative structures to present uncertainties systematically in model relationships.

Population projections associated with the three perspectives are presented in Figure 5.7, together with a comparison using historical data (Bos et al. 1992, UN 1993). The relative similarity in the historical trend suggests that the uncertainties pertaining to the population issue provide enough room for fundamentally differing explanations. The presented projections assume an annual

Table 5.4 Perspective-based interpretation of fertility controversy.

	Hierarchist	Egalitarian	Individualist
Ethical uncertainties	Population growth is a socioeconomic issue	Population growth is an environmental issue	Population growth is resource
Demographic uncertainties	Macro processes determine fertility behavior	Micro and macro processes determine fertility behavior	Micro processes determine fertility behavior
Policy uncertainties	Family planning Abortion is means to create stability	Empowerment General access to abortion	No population policy Legalization of abortion

Source: van Asselt et al. (1995).

economic growth rate of 2 percent. Individualists argue that population growth will decrease in the event of high levels of economic development. An experiment with the individualistic model route assuming a higher economic growth shows stabilization of the world population at lower levels. Preliminary analysis of the preferred management style with the two alternative worldviews (Table 5.5) indicates that a purely egalitarian strategy is relatively risky in terms of egalitarian perception of consequences associated with population numbers surpassing 10 billion people, whereas the hierarchist management style, assuming a carrying capacity of about 15–20 billion people, is more robust in face of uncertainty. Where risks related to decisionmaking under uncertainty are concerned, evaluation of the individualistic management style juxtaposed with the other two worldviews is of less importance, since neither the population size nor population growth is considered to constitute a problem.

Table 5.5 Results of experiments: population numbers in 2100 (billions).

	Management style		
Worldview	Egalitarian	Hierarchist	Individualist
Egalitarian	5	7	8
Hierarchist	15	15	17
Individualist	25	25	25

Source: van Asselt et al. (1995).

The method based on multiple model routes may provide a complementary method useful to uncertainty analysis in integrated assessment models by enabling researchers to render subjective judgment explicit. Using the perspective-based model routes as ways to envisage coherent clusters of various interpretations of the uncertainties in the model, researchers can motivate and explain differences in future projections. The present approach has proved to be a helpful tool to enhance the reflexivity of the modelers, which is at present probably the most important gain. Nevertheless, this methodology is no panacea. Limitations of the methodology reside in the fact that it allows us to do no more than take account of three rather deterministic perspectives, which are related to a controversial theory of institutional culture. Ambiguity in interpreting within the terms of reference of the various perspectives seems unavoidable, and thereby the methodology designed to illuminate subjective judgment requires subjective evaluation in itself.

The presented methodology is only one step in a continuing process of addressing uncertainty and perspectives in integrated assessment models. Implementing multiple model routes is an iterative process, requiring continual readjustment of the qualitative and quantitative descriptions. For the moment, we recognize three major benefits of this research:

- It enhances reflexivity of integrated assessment researchers.
- It at least enables us to consider more than one (hidden) perspective.
- It offers an entrance point for discussion on subjectivity in integrated assessment models.

As demonstrated in the exploratory example above, integrated assessment models should gradually shift from the purely mechanistic perspective to the evolutionary complex systems perspective. This issue of system complexity should not be confused with computational complexity. Whereas the computational complexity of a system arises from the fact that it includes many variables and processes, the dynamics of the system may be simple rather than complex (Pahl-Wöstl 1995). However, we should move forward in the direction of considering the human and environmental systems as strongly interlinked, complex, adaptive systems.

One way to proceed is to develop simple models for specific parts of the human and environmental system with a transparent structure but complex dynamics. Models may then reveal qualitative insights into the functioning of complex systems (Pahl-Wöstl 1995). Based upon this new qualitative knowledge, these simple models can be linked to a larger framework that can be analyzed. In this way a composite framework of simple systems—represented by metamodels—can be built up, which, as a whole, functions as a complex system, showing nonlinear and adaptive (self-learning), perhaps even chaotic, behavior. Incremental changes in conditions of subsystems may then result in considerable changes in the results of the overall system, which may not always be expected beforehand. Following this approach, scientific knowledge of global phenomena can be built up gradually, leading to improved understanding of the fundamental uncertainties in our knowledge of the self-organization of the complex human and environmental system.

From a decision-theoretic perspective, the analytical challenge of developing strategies for response can be recast as a sequence of decisions about what to do. As understanding about the interactions between humans and their environment evolve, the objectives and approaches for climate change mitigation will be revised and refined.

This iterative perspective on climate policy formation does not ask the specific question of which policy is most cost effective, or what level of a carbon tax optimizes social welfare. Instead, the questions relate to how best to manage the coevolution of policy and knowledge. In this paradigm are four interdependent questions:

- What metric(s) of global change should be monitored and targeted for control?
- What should be the target level for the chosen metric of control?
- With what frequency should the goals and objectives be revised?

- How should the goals and objectives be revised?

Cast in this light, the climate policy issue is transformed into a control problem where the usual assumptions about perfect foresight and optimized economic models are cast aside in favor of a framework capable of addressing the more realistic challenges posed by imperfect foresight, stochasticity in environmental indicators, and sequential learning.

We noted above the implications of parameter and model uncertainties for evaluation of policy outcomes. Here, we show the implications of stochasticity and uncertainty on strategic choices for climate policy formation.

In the absence of clear signals about climate change and its impacts, many different control strategies have been suggested. The usual list includes emission limits, atmospheric carbon dioxide concentration limits, and limits on total change in temperature or rate of temperature change. In general, one or more of the relevant metrics will have to be monitored and a control strategy developed to modify policy in order to meet the stated goals.

To date, emissions have been the metric of choice. However, although fossil fuel emissions and chlorofluorocarbons pose little challenge in attribution of the portions resulting from anthropogenic and natural origins, other factors such as stochastic and dynamic properties of the metric also need to be considered. Aiming to limit carbon dioxide emissions is subject to the stochastic nature of random-walk economic activity and significant lags in system response to abatement policy. Thus, the choice of an emission limit is likely to lead to significant problems in monitoring and enforcement. Proponents of permits suggest that permits will ensure that prespecified limits are not exceeded. However, permits require enforcement and may lead to significant fluctuation in the economic burden of abatement from year to year.

Aiming to control temperature change is also questionable. The problem here is fourfold. Temperature exhibits significant periodicity of various timescales. Temperature change is a function of a stock effect from greenhouse gas emissions, in competition with a flow effect from aerosols. Furthermore, the lag in the response of anthropogenic emissions to policy interventions is compounded by uncertainty in the lag of the climate system. Finally, there is significant uncertainty in the sensitivity of the climate system to perturbations in radiative forcing. Hence, development of predictive models of temperature change are plagued with large, and so far irreducible, uncertainties.

Aiming to control atmospheric concentration of carbon dioxide appears to be the most promising control strategy. The task of controlling the stock of a long-lived greenhouse gas through manipulation of its flow is quite straightforward; the only complication arises from the lagged response of emissions to policy intervention. This factor, however, appears to be addressable through appropriate choice of frequency and manner of monitoring and policy response.

Arguing about an appropriate target level for the controlled variable is not useful. Equity in risk aversion, in the face of significant ignorance about the impacts of climate change, determines the subjective target level. Through time, the accumulation of knowledge and evolution of preferences will lead to redefinition of these targets. In the paradigm of sequential learning, the issue that needs to be considered is retention of sufficient flexibility to make such mid-course corrections feasible.

Given institutional inertia, revisions to control will probably not be possible more frequently then every five years. ICAM 2.1 has been used to explore the consequence of this and longer time steps on the control of different metrics of global change. Revisiting the decision less frequently than every five years may lead to a greater propensity for over- or undershooting the target. The key question here is the tradeoff between the administrative and transition costs associated with more frequent adjustments and the imprecision of infrequent control. Where the discussion of control is an important signal to decisionmakers, more frequent adjustments could be greatly beneficial. This is of particular importance where there is cliff-like threshold of impacts or a large tendency to drift away from the target level. Our knowledge about economic activity and emissions of greenhouse gases suggests that return periods longer than 10 years are not desirable. Indeed, for specific near-term targets (e.g., carbon dioxide concentration of 450 ppmv), many combinations of parameter values can lead to rapid drift and require adjustment of controls on a five-year basis.

For various economic and sociological reasons, a good control strategy should satisfy three criteria:

- consistent and steady controls
- simple monitoring and enforcement
- steady approximation to target.

Control requires some predictive capability about the unfettered evolution of the state variable and its response to altered control levels. Both of these factors may evolve through time. An adaptive response strategy involves modification of the control algorithm as new information is revealed. The ICAM framework has enabled different control strategies to be explored. These have ranged from simple *response* models to *adaptive response* models incorporating measures of sensitivity of carbon dioxide emissions to tax (the control variable). In all cases examined, the simple response models outperformed the more complicated models.

Beyond the issues of the metric to monitor (atmospheric concentration of carbon dioxide) and the manner of control (simple quadratic response model, using a time derivative of carbon dioxide concentration), and monitoring and revision of controls on a five-year basis, the learning and control paradigm offers two further insights.

The first insight is that, to understand the system being controlled, modelers must perturb it and observe its behavior. This perturbation has to be such that the propagation of impacts is easy to identify. For example, if a carbon tax is used as the control parameter, modelers need to impose a test tax to understand the system's response. The optimal size for such a tax has been estimated using ICAM and (if implemented in 2000) as about US$15 per tonne of carbon. Furthermore, after the introduction of the test carbon tax, some time is needed to gauge the system response—this we call the initial learning period.

The second insight is about the timing of abatement. The learning aspects of this paradigm impose constraints on when abatement may commence. Unlike the paradigm of optimization models, both a test tax and learning time are needed to learn about and steer a path toward the objective. Thus, the question of delaying abatement also means a delay in learning the dynamics of the system. When the target is close, such delay is inadvisable. Hence, for a 450 ppmv target for carbon dioxide concentration, the economic benefits of a 20-year delay are more than offset by the superior path that can be followed because of the information revealed by earlier action. Furthermore, the longer the delay in abatement, the higher the probability of overshooting the target before being able to manipulate emissions enough to bring concentrations down to the target level. For more distant targets (e.g., 550 ppmv) delay in abatement, of say 30 years, appears to offer the expected economic advantages without placing in jeopardy the search for a cost-effective path to the target.

The challenge of meeting policymakers' needs

Climate change is one of many possible issues that decisionmakers must grapple with. When they formulate policy responses, these are often triggered by extreme events, only rarely by secular trends in key parameters. Furthermore, cost–benefit analysis is only one kind of input policymakers use in making their decisions. Therefore, research that fails to contextualize climate change concerns and which offers only information about cost effectiveness is of only limited use to policymakers. Integrated assessment in general, and models in particular, need to provide timely, relevant analysis at the level of aggregation appropriate to the problem or issue at hand.

When decision points approach or when extreme events bring an issue such as climate change to the fore, policymakers want analytical tools that are as transparent and easy to use as possible (i.e., capable of exploring many possible alternatives quickly), while retaining as much complexity as possible. Past evidence suggests that policymakers look for data on absolute costs and their distribution, that is, who the beneficiaries are.

The overall challenge is to create the right balance between simplicity and complexity, aggregation and disaggregation, stochastic and deterministic behavior, quantitative and qualitative linkages, social and natural sciences, and exogenous and endogenous processes.

Far-from-sufficient scientific knowledge about global climate change precludes modeling all entities, processes, and feedbacks in a quantitative sense. Therefore, researchers need a new class of global, integrated assessment models that, on the one hand, try to capture the essential dynamics of the complex discipline-oriented expert models in metaform (metamodels), but, on the other hand, are intended to promote an understanding of the qualitative interactive linkages, which are poorly understood in a quantitative sense. Using both modeling results and the results of interpretive research can help to provide the balanced analysis needed by decisionmakers at all levels, from international negotiators to firms and households.

Since model results are not the only input to policy considerations, modelers should seek to provide a further level of integration by presenting model results along with results from interpretive research and subjective expert judgment. The combination is a potentially powerful tool. However, experts work in seemingly unsystematic ways, and myriad basic issues in understanding social institutions have never been systematically investigated.

Models should be well documented (most of them are now poorly documented), and descriptions and findings should be published regularly, not only in economics-oriented journals but also in climate-related journals. Further, if exercises to identify critical gaps in disciplinary knowledge are posed as exploratory questions, the pioneering steps of integrated assessment teams can ignite the interest of disciplinary scientists and lead to fruitful collaborations. From these collaborative efforts can emerge a growing consensus about state-of-knowledge issues. The broader, more consensual science base can engender more effective decisionmaking.

As an emerging research approach, integrated assessment is characterized by a diversity in assumptions, methods, problems addressed, and results. To establish authority, integrated assessment models and methods need to be designed to understandable, common standards. Like laboratory procedures, established, well-defined research methods make model results both comprehensible and defensible, as discussed in Volume 1, Chapter 1 of this assessment. To this end, integrated assessment modelers should:

- Develop a common language for external communication. Integrated assessment researchers need to establish common meanings and definitions of often-used but also misused notions, such as integrated assessment, integrated assessment modeling, integration (horizontal versus vertical), exogenous versus endogenous processes, aggregation versus disaggregation, various types and sources of uncertainty, calibration and validation, and discounting.

- Develop and implement minimum scientific standards that must be satisfied by an integrated assessment model, with respect to, for instance, level of integration, level of aggregation, internal consistency, transparency, documentation, numerical stability, and reproducibility.
- Enhance communication with the fundamental research community and with the decisionmaking world to enhance scientific and political credibility. The next generation of models should meet the demands of scientists and decisionmakers adequately, probably resulting in an even greater variety of models addressing the scientific issues and the policy debate at different levels.

Conclusions

Integrated assessment is an issue-oriented research approach that knits together diverse knowledge from many disciplines to focus holistically on climate change processes. Integrated assessment includes model-based systems, simulation gaming, scenario analysis, and qualitative studies. The preceding discussions have presented an overview of the history and philosophy of integrated assessment methods and tools. Several conclusions can be drawn:

- Integrated assessment approaches can help to put climate change issues in the broader perspective of global change, help to identify and evaluate potential mitigative and adaptive strategies, provide a framework in which to structure current scientific knowledge of climate change, translate the concept of uncertainty into risk analysis to aid in decisionmaking, and help to set priorities for new research.
- Integrated assessment models can help explore interactions and feedbacks in Earth and human systems, function as flexible and rapid simulation tools, foster insights (sometimes counterintuitive) that would not be available from a single disciplinary approach, and provide tools for mutual learning and communication among researchers and policymakers.
- Integrated assessment has contributed to the climate change debate in exploring impacts of climate change, mitigation and abatement strategies, issues in cooperative implementation, the likely equity effects of candidate policies, and complicating factors such as aerosols. Models have also provided information on balancing the carbon budget and on various integrated aspects of land use.

- The existing integrated assessment models are unbalanced, have only a very limited level of integration, and therefore need to be improved considerably. In particular, more satisfactory and representative models of social dynamics and ecological systems are needed before integrated assessment models can be made more realistic.
- The treatment of the issue of uncertainty is of crucial importance in integrated assessment models. At present, apart from only a few exceptions, uncertainties are treated poorly in the current generation of integrated assessment models. Two priorities for the near future can therefore be set. The first is to make explicit the various types of uncertainties in integrated assessment models: uncertainties in model structure, parameter values, and structural uncertainties because of disagreement among experts. The second is to quantify the propagation and interdependencies of model uncertainties in the projections of integrated assessment models.
- An overall challenge for the next generation of integrated assessment models is to incorporate insights emerging from new scientific streams such as the areas of complex systems, adaptive behavior, bifurcations, and ignorance about systems. Incorporation of these insights will broaden the scope of integrated assessment frameworks and improve considerably the quality of integrated assessments.
- We do not know how far integrated assessments are from providing the information decisionmakers use. There is a need to examine more carefully the factors that shape policymakers' decisions, and to include policymakers and other stakeholders in design and exercise of the models.
- Integrated assessment models have highlighted significant gaps in disciplinary knowledge needed to address long-term climate change issues. The changing focus of disciplinary research may bring many dividends.
- Integrated assessment modelers should involve modelers from less industrialized countries in every step of the process.

As scientists develop modeling tools that are more open and flexible, policymakers will be able to use the model results and other insights from different integrated assessment approaches to inform decisions that bear on global climate change and on the social context in which climate change issues are to be considered.

References

Alcamo, J. (ed.) 1994. *IMAGE 2.0: Integrated modeling of global climate change*. Dordrecht: Kluwer.
Alcamo, J., R. Shaw, L. Hordijk (eds) 1990. *The RAINS model of acidification: science and strategies in Europe*. Dordrecht: Kluwer.
Andreae, M. O. 1995. Climate effects of changing atmospheric aerosol levels. In *World survey*

of climatology, volume XVI: *future climate of the world – a modelling perspective*, A. Henderson-Sellers (ed.). Amsterdam: Elsevier.

Asselt, M. B. A. van, J. Rotmans, M. den Elzen, H. Hilderink 1995. *Uncertainty in integrated assessment modelling: a cultural perspective based approach*. GLOBO Report Series 9, Report 461502009, National Institute of Public Health and Environmental Protection [RIVM], Bilthoven, the Netherlands.

Bos, E., M. T. Vu, A. Levin, R. Bulatao 1992. *World population projections 1992–1993*. Baltimore: Johns Hopkins University Press.

Brecke, P. 1993. Integrated global models that run on personal computers. *SIMULATION* **60**(2), 140–44.

Broecker, W. S. 1994. An unstoppable superconveyer. *Nature* **367**, 414–15.

Chao, H. P. 1995. Managing the risk of global climate catastrophe: an uncertainty analysis. *Risk Analysis* **15**(1), 69–78.

Charlson, R. J., S. E. Schwartz, J. M. Hales, R. D. Cess, J. A. Coakley, J. E. Hansen, D. J. Hofmann 1992. Climate forcing by anthropogenic aerosols. *Science* **255**, 423–30.

Cline, W. R. 1992. *Global warming: the economic stakes*. Washington DC: Institute for International Economics.

Cohan, D., R. K. Stafford, J. D. Scheraga, S. Herrod 1994. The global climate Policy Evaluation Framework. In *Proceedings of the 1994 A&WMA Global Climate Change Conference*, Phoenix, Arizona, 5–8 April. Pittsburgh: Air & Waste Management Association.

Cohen, S. J. (ed.) 1993. *Mackenzie Basin impact study*. Interim Report 1, Canadian Climate Center, Atmospheric Environment Service, Toronto.

Darwin, R., M. Tsigas, J. Lewandrowski, A. Raneses 1996. *World agriculture and climate change: economic adaptation*. Agricultural Economic Report 703, Economic Research Services, US Department of Agriculture.

Douglas, M. 1978. *Cultural bias*. Occasional Paper 35, Royal Anthropological Institute, London. [Reprinted in *In the active voice*, M. Douglas. London: Routledge & Kegan Paul, 1982.]

Dowlatabadi, H. 1984. *Electricity interchange between integrated systems*. PhD dissertation, University of Cambridge.

Dowlatabadi, H. & M. G. Morgan 1993. A model framework for integrated studies of the climate problem. *Energy Policy* **21**(3), 209–221.

Dowlatabadi, H. & M. Kandlikar 1995. Key uncertainties in climate change policy: results from ICAM-2. Paper presented to the 6th Global Warming Conference, San Francisco, California.

Dowlatabadi, H., M. Kandlikar, C. Linville 1995. Climate change decision making: model & parameter uncertainties explored. Paper presented to the International Society of Bayesian Analysis '95, Oaxaca, Mexico.

Dowlatabadi, H. & M. G. Morgan 1995. *Integrated assessment climate assessment model 2.0, technical documentation*. Department of Engineering and Public Policy, Carnegie Mellon University.

Eckaus, R. S. 1992. Comparing the effects of greenhouse gas emissions on global warming. *The Energy Journal* **13**(1), 25–35.

Edmonds, J. A. 1996. Results from the Snowmass US–China project. Paper presented to the Snowmass Workshop on Integrated Assessment, Snowmass, Colorado.

Edmonds, J. A. & J. M. Reilly 1985. *Global energy: assessing the future*. New York: Oxford University Press.

Edmonds, J. A., H. Pitcher, N. Rosenberg, T. Wigley 1993. *Design for the Global Change Assessment Model*. Laxenburg, Austria: International Institute for Applied Systems Analysis [IIASA].

Edmonds, J. A., M. Wise, C. MacCracken 1994. *Advanced energy technologies and climate change: an analysis using the Global Change Assessment Model (GCAM)*. PNL-9798, Pacific Northwest National Laboratory, Washington DC.

Edmonds, J. A., M. Wise, D. Barns 1995. Carbon coalitions: the cost and effectiveness of energy agreements to alter trajectories of atmospheric carbon dioxide emissions. *Energy Policy* **23**(4/5), 309–336.

Edmonds, J. A., M. Wise, R. Sands, R. Brown, H. Kheshgi 1996. *Agriculture, land use, and commercial biomass energy: a preliminary integrated analysis of the potential role of biomass energy for reducing future greenhouse related emissions* PNNL-11155, Pacific Northwest National Laboratory, Washington DC.

Edmonds, J. A., M. Wise, J. Dooley 1997a. *Atmospheric stabilization and the role of energy technology*. Washington DC: American Council for Capital Formation.

Edmonds, J. A., M. Wise, H. Pitcher, R. Richels, T. Wigley, C. MacCracken 1997b. An integrated assessment of climate change and the accelerated introduction of advanced energy technologies: an application of MiniCAM 1.0. *Environmental Modelling & Assessment*, in press.

Elzen, M. G. J. den 1993. *Global environmental change: an integrated modelling approach*. PhD thesis, University of Maastricht, the Netherlands.

EMF [Energy Modelling Forum] 1994. *Final first round study design for EMF-14: integrated assessment of climate change*. EMF, Terman Engineering Center, Stanford University.

EPA [US Environmental Protection Agency] 1989. Policy options for stabilizing global climate. Draft report to the Congress (D. A. Lashof & D. A. Tirpack (eds)), Office of Policy, Planning and Evaluation, US Environmental Protection Agency, Washington DC.

Fisher, A. 1988. One model to fit all. *MOSAIC* **19**(34), 53–9.

Frey, H. C. 1992. *Quantitative analysis of uncertainty and variability in environmental policy making*. Washington DC: Directorate for Science and Policy Programs, American Association for the Advancement of Science.

Funtowicz, S. O. & J. R. Ravetz 1989. Managing uncertainty in policy-related research. Paper presented to the International Colloquium, "Les experts sont formels: controverses scientifiques et décisions politiques dans le domaine de l'environnement," Arc et Senans, France.

——1990. *Uncertainty and quality in science for policy*. Dordrecht: Kluwer.

——1993. Science for the post-normal age. *Futures* **25**(7), 739–55.

Gardner, R. H., B. Rojder, U. Bergström 1983. *PRISM: a systematic method for determining the effect of parameter uncertainties on model predictions*. Report Studsvik/NW-83/555, Studsvik Energiteknik AB, Nyköping, Sweden.

Grubb, M., T. Chapius, M. H. Duong 1995. The economics of changing course, implications of adaptability and inertia for optimal climate policy. *Energy Policy* **23**(4), 417–32.

Hammitt, J. K., R. J. Lempert, M. E. Schlesinger 1992. A sequential-decision strategy for abating climate change. *Nature* **357**(6376), 315–18.

Hammitt, J. K. & J. L. Adams 1994. The value of international coordination in abating climate change. Paper presented to seminar on "Environmental economics and policy", Kennedy School of Government, Harvard University.

Harrison, G. W. & T. F. Rutherford 1997. *Burden sharing, joint implementation, and carbon coalitions*. Unpublished report, University of South Carolina, Columbia, and University of Colorado, Boulder.

Heimann, M. (ed.) 1993. *The global carbon cycle and its perturbation by man and climate*. EPOC-CT90-0017 (MNLA), Max Planck Institut für Meteorologie, Hamburg.

Helton, J. C. 1993. Uncertainty and sensitivity analysis techniques for use in performance assessment for radioactive waste disposal. *Reliability Engineering and System Safety* **42**, 327–67.

Henrion, M. & M. G. Morgan 1985. A computer aid for risk and other policy analysis. *Risk Analysis* **5**, 195–208.

Hettelingh, J. P. 1989. *Uncertainty in modelling regional environmental systems: the generalization of a watershed acidification model for predicting broad scale effects*. PhD thesis, Free University of Amsterdam.

Hoekstra, A. Y. 1995. *AQUA: a framework for integrated water policy analysis*. National Institute of Public Health and Environmental Protection [RIVM], Bilthoven, the Netherlands.

Hope, C. W., J. Parker, S. Peake 1992. A pilot environmental index for the UK in the 1980s. *Energy Policy* **20**(4), 335–43.

Hope, C. W., J. Anderson, P. Wenman 1993. Policy analysis of the greenhouse effect: an application of the PAGE model. *Energy Policy* **21**(3), 327–38.

Hordijk, L. 1991. Use of the RAINS model in acid rain negotiations in Europe. *Environmental Science and Technology* **25**, 596–603.

Houghton, J. T., J. T. Jenkins, J. J. Ephraums (eds) 1990. *The IPCC scientific assessment*. Cambridge: Cambridge University Press.

Houghton, J. T., B. A. Callander, S. K. Varney (eds) 1992. *1992 IPCC supplement: full scientific report*. Cambridge: Cambridge University Press.

Hulme, M., Z. C. Zhao, T. Jiang 1994. Recent and future climate change in East Asia. *International Journal of Climatology* **14**, 637–58.

Hutton, S. 1785. *The theory of the Earth*. Edinburgh: Royal Society of Edinburgh.

Iman, R. L. & W. J. Conover 1982. A distribution-free approach to inducing rank correlation among input variables. *Communications in Statistics* **B11**(3), 331–4.

Iman, R. L. & J. C. Helton 1985. *A comparison of uncertainty and sensitivity analysis techniques for computer models*. Albuquerque, New Mexico: Sandia National Laboratory

IPCC [Intergovernmental Panel on Climate Change] 1991. *The IPCC response strategies*. Washington DC: Island Press.

Janssen, M. A. 1995a. *The battle of the perspectives*. GLOBO Working Paper 3, National Institute of Public Health and Environmental Protection [RIVM], Bilthoven, the Netherlands.

——1995b. *Optimization of a nonlinear dynamical system for global climate change: a comparative analysis*. GLOBO Working Paper GWP 95-1, National Institute of Public Health and Environmental Protection [RIVM], Bilthoven, the Netherlands.

——1996. *Meeting targets: tools to support integrated assessment modelling of global change*. PhD thesis, University of Maastricht, the Netherlands.

Janssen, M. A. & J. Rotmans 1995. Allocation of fossil CO_2 emission rights: quantifying cultural perspectives. *Ecological Economics* **13**, 65–79.

Kandlikar, M. 1995. Indices for comparing greenhouse gas emissions: integrating science and economics. *Energy Policy* **23**(10), 879–83.

Keepin, W. & B. Wynne 1984. Technical analysis of the IIASA energy scenarios. *Nature* **312**, 691–5.

Kleijnen, J. P. C., G. van Ham, J. Rotmans 1990. Techniques for sensitivity analysis of simulation models – a case-study of the CO_2 greenhouse effect. *Simulation* **58**(6), 410–17.

Krapivin, V. F. 1993. Mathematical model for global ecological investigations. *Ecological Modelling* **67**, 103–127.

Lal, M., U. Cubasch, R. Voss, J. Waskewitz 1995. Effect of transient increase of greenhouse gases and sulphate aerosols on monsoon climate. *Current Science* **69**(9), 752–63.

Lashof, D. & D. Ahuja 1990. Relative contributions of greenhouse gas emissions to global warming. *Nature* **344**, 529–31.

Maddison, D. A. 1995. Cost–benefit analysis of slowing climate change. *Energy Policy* **23**(4/5), 337–46.

Maier-Reimer, E. & K. Hasselmann 1987. Transport and storage of carbon dioxide in the ocean, and in organic ocean-circulation carbon cycle model. *Climate Dynamics* **2**, 63–90.

Manne, A. S., R. Mendelsohn, R. G. Richels 1994. MERGE: a model for evaluating regional and global effects of GHG reduction policies. See Nakicenovic et al. (1994).

Manne, A. & R. Richels 1995. *The greenhouse debate – economic efficiency, burden sharing and hedging strategies*. Unpublished report, Department of Operations Research, Stanford

University.
——1996. The Berlin mandate: the costs of meeting post-2000 targets and timetables. *Energy Policy* **24**(3), 205–210.

Martens, W. J. M. 1995. *Modeling the effect of global warming on the prevalence of schistosomiasis*. GLOBO Report Series 10, Report 461502010, National Institute of Public Health and Environmental Protection [RIVM], Bilthoven, the Netherlands.

Martens, W. J. M., J. Rotmans, L. W. Niessen 1994. *Climate change and malaria risk: an integrated modelling approach*. Report 461502003, National Institute of Public Health and Environmental Protection [RIVM], Bilthoven, the Netherlands.

McRae, G. J., J. W. Tilden, J. H. Seinfeld 1982. Global sensitivity analysis – a computational implementation of the Fourier amplitude sensitivity test (FAST). *Computers and Chemical Engineering* **6**, 15–25.

Matsuoka, Y., T. Morita, H. Harasawa 1994. *Estimation of carbon dioxide flux from tropical deforestation*. CGER-1012-'94, Center for Global Environmental Research, National Institute for Environmental Studies [NIES], Tskuba, Japan.

Matsuoka, Y., M. Kainuma, T. Morita 1995. Scenario analysis of global warming using the Asian Pacific Integrated Model (AIM). *Energy Policy* **23**(4/5), 357–71.

McKibbin, W. J. & P. J. Wilcoxen 1996. *The wrong way to deal with climate change*. Unpublished report, Brookings Institution, Washington DC.

Meadows, D. H., D. L. Meadows, J. Randers, W. W. Behrens 1972. *The limits to growth*. New York: Universe.

Melillo, J. M., A. D. McGuire, D. W. Kicklighter, B. Moore, C. J. Vörösmarty, A. L. Schloss 1993. Global climate change and terrestrial net primary production. *Nature* **363**, 234–80.

Mermet, L. & L. Hordijk 1989. On getting simulation models used in international negotiations. In *Processes of international negotiations*, F. Mautner-Markhof (ed.). Boulder, Colorado: Westview.

Mintzer, I. 1987. *A matter of degrees: the potential for controlling the greenhouse effect*. Washington DC: World Resources Institute.

Morgan, G. M. & M. Henrion 1990. *Uncertainty: a guide to dealing with uncertainty in quantitative risk and policy analysis*. New York: Cambridge University Press.

Morgan, G. M. & D. Keith 1995. Subjective judgments by climate experts. *Environmental Science and Technology* **29**(10), 468A–76A.

Morgan, M. G. & H. Dowlatabadi 1996. Lessons from integrated assessment of climate change. *Climatic Change* **34**, 337–68.

Morita, T., M. Kainuma, H. Harasawa, K. Kai, L. Dong-Kun, Y. Matsuoka 1994. *Asian–Pacific Integrated Model for evaluating policy options to reduce GHG emissions and global warming impacts*. Interim Report, National Institute for Environmental Studies [NIES], Tskuba, Japan.

——1994a. *An estimate of climate change effects on malaria*. Interim Report, National Institute for Environmental Studies [NIES], Tskuba, Japan.

——1995b. *The Asian Pacific integrated model, what can it predict? A collection of AIM simulation results*. Interim Paper IP-95-01, National Institute for Environmental Studies [NIES], Tskuba, Japan.

Nakicenovic, N., W. D. Nordhaus, R. Richels, F. L. Toth (eds) 1994. *Integrative assessment of mitigation, impacts, and adaptation to climate change*. CP-94-9, International Institute for Applied Systems Analysis, Laxenburg, Austria.

Niessen, L. W. & J. Rotmans 1993. *Sustaining health: towards a global health model*. Report 461502001, National Institute of Public Health and Environmental Protection [RIVM], Bilthoven, the Netherlands.

Niessen, L. W., H. Hilderink, W. J. M. Martens, J. Rotmans 1996. *Roads to health: modelling the health transition*. GLOBO Report Series 15 (Report 461502015), National Institute for Public Health and the Environment [RIVM], Bilthoven, the Netherlands.

Nordhaus, W. D. 1990. An intertemporal general equilibrium model of economic growth and climate change. Presented to the workshop on "Economic/energy/environmental modeling for climate policy analysis", Washington DC.

——1991a. To slow or not to slow: the economics of the greenhouse effect. *The Economic Journal* **101**(July), 920–37.

——1991b. A sketch of the economics of the greenhouse effect. *American Economic Review* **81**(2), 146–50.

——1992a. An optimal transition path for controlling greenhouse gases. *Science* **258**, 1315–19.

——1992b. *The "DICE" model: background and structure of a dynamic integrated climate economy.* Unpublished paper, Department of Economics, Yale University

——1993. Rolling the "DICE": an optimal transition path for controlling greenhouse gases. *Resource and Energy Economics* **15**, 27–50.

——1994. *Managing the global commons: the economics of climate change.* Cambridge, Massachusetts: MIT Press.

Nordhaus, W. D. & G. W. Yohe 1983. Future carbon dioxide emissions from fossil fuels. In *Changing climate* [Report of Carbon Dioxide Assessment Committee], US NRC (ed.). Washington DC: National Academy Press.

Nordhaus, W. D. & Z. Yang 1995. RICE: a regional dynamic general equilibrium model of optimal climate-change policy. Unpublished paper, Department of Economics, Yale University.

Nordhaus, W. D. & D. Popp 1997. What is the value of scientific knowledge? An application to global warming using the PRICE model. *Energy Journal* **18**(1), 1–45.

OECD 1993. Environmental indicators: basic concepts and terminology [Background Paper 1, by Group on the State of the Environment]. In *Proceedings of the workshop on indicators for use in environmental performance reviews.* Paris: Organisation for Economic Cooperation and Development.

Oravetz, M. 1994. *Future energy use and Global 2100.* Unpublished paper, Department of Engineering & Public Policy, Carnegie Mellon University.

Oreskes, N., K. Shrader-Frechette, K. Belitz 1994. Verification, validation, and confirmation of numerical models in the Earth sciences. *Science* **263**, 641–6.

Pahl-Wöstl, C. 1995. Complexity, irreducible uncertainties and climate change. Unpublished statement for the Workshop on Integrated Environmental Assessment (IEA), Brussels, May 1995.

Pearce, F. 1996. Sit tight for 20 years, argues climate guru. *New Scientist* **149**, 7.

Peck, S. C. & T. J. Teisberg 1991. *Temperature change related damage functions: a further analysis with CETA.* Palo Alto, California: Electric Power Research Institute [EPRI].

——1992a. *Cost–benefit analysis and climate change.* Palo Alto, California: Electric Power Research Institute [EPRI].

——1992b. *Global warming uncertainties and the value of information: an analysis using CETA.* Palo Alto, California: Electric Power Research Institute [EPRI].

——1992c. CETA: a model for carbon emissions trajectory assessment. *The Energy Journal* **13**(1), 55–77.

——1995. International CO_2 emissions control, an analysis using CETA. *Energy Policy* **23**, 297–308.

——Optimal CO_2 control policy with stochastic losses from temperature rise. *Climatic Change* **31**, 19–34.

Prentice, I. C., W. Cramer, S. P. Harrison, R. Leemans, R. A. Monserud, A. M. Solomon 1992. A global BIOME model based on plant physiology and dominance, soil properties and climate. *Journal of Biogeography* **19**, 117–34.

Prinn, R. H. J., A. Sokolov, C. Wand, X. Xiao, Z. Yang, R. Eckaus, P. Stone, D. Ellerman, J. Melillo, J. Fitzmaurice, D. Kicklighter, Y. Liu 1996. *Integrated global system model for climate policy analysis, I: model framework and sensitivity studies.* Global Change Center, Massachusetts Institute of Technology.

Raskin, P., C. Heaps, J. Sieber 1995. *Polestar system manual*. Stockholm: Stockholm Environment Institute.

Rayner, S. F. 1991. A cultural perspective on the structure and implementation of global environmental agreements. *Evaluation Review* **15**(1), 75–102.

Reilly, J. M., J. A. Edmonds, R. H. Gardner, H. L. Brenkert 1987. Uncertainty analysis of the IEA/ORAU CO_2 emissions model. *The Energy Journal* **8**(3), 1–29.

Richels, R. & J. A. Edmonds 1994. Cost-minimizing paths to CO_2 stabilization. In *Integrative assessment of mitigation, impacts, and adaptation to climate change*, N. Nakicenovic, W. D. Nordhaus, R. Richels, F. L. Toth (eds). CP-94-9, International Institute for Applied Systems Analysis, Laxenburg, Austria.

Richels, R., J. A. Edmonds, H. Gruenspecht, T. Wigley 1996. The Berlin Mandate: the design of cost-effective mitigation strategies. In *Proceedings of the Workshop on Integrating Science, Economics, and Policy*, N. Nakicenovic, W. D. Nordhaus, R. Richels, F. L. Toth (eds). Laxenburg, Austria: International Institute for Applied Systems Analysis.

Robinson, J. B. 1988. Unlearning and backcasting: rethinking some of the questions we ask about the future. *Technological Forecasting and Social Change* **33**, 325–38.

——— 1990. Futures under glass: a recipe for people who hate to predict. *Futures* **22**(9), 820–43.

Rosenberg, N. J., P. R. Crosson, K. D. Frederick, W. E. Easterling, M. S. McKenny, M. D. Bowes, R. A. Sedjo, J. Darmstadter, L. A. Katz, K. M. Lemon 1993. The MINK methodology: background and baseline. In *Towards an integrated impact assessment of climate change: the MINK study*, N. J. Rosenberg (ed.) [reprinted from *Climatic Change* **24**(1–2)]. Dordrecht: Kluwer.

Rosenzweig, C. & M. L. Parry 1994. Potential impact of climate change on world food supply. *Nature* **367**, 133–8.

Rotmans, J. 1986. *The development of a simulation model for the global CO_2 problem* [in Dutch]. Report 840751001, National Institute of Public Health and Environmental Protection [RIVM], Bilthoven, the Netherlands.

——— 1990. *IMAGE: an integrated model to assess the greenhouse effect*. Dordrecht: Kluwer.

Rotmans, J. & M. G. J. den Elzen 1993. Modelling feedback processes in the carbon cycle: balancing the carbon budget. *Tellus* **45B**(4), 301–320.

Rotmans, J., M. B. A. van Asselt, A. J. de Bruin, M. G. J. den Elzen, J. de Greef, H. Hilderink, A. Y. Hoekstra, M. A. Janssen, H. W. Köster, W. J. M. Martens, L. W. Niessen, H. J. M. de Vries 1994a. *Global change and sustainable development*. Report 461502004, National Institute of Public Health and Environmental Protection [RIVM], Bilthoven, the Netherlands.

Rotmans, J., M. Hulme, T. Downing 1994b. Climate change implications for Europe: an application of the ESCAPE model. *Global Environmental Change* **4**(2) 97–105.

Rotmans, J., M. B. A. van Asselt, A. Beusen, M. den Elzen, M. Janssen, H. Hilderink, A. Hoekstra, H. Köster, P. Martens, L. Niessen, B. Strengers, H. J. M. de Vries 1995. *TARGETS in transition*. Bilthoven, the Netherlands: National Institute of Public Health and Environmental Protection [RIVM].

Rotmans, J. & M. B. A. van Asselt 1996. Integrated assessment: a growing child on its way to maturity. *Climatic Change* **34**, 327–36.

Rotmans, J. & H. J. M. de Vries 1996. *Perspectives on global change: the TARGETS approach*. Cambridge: Cambridge University Press.

Rubin, E. S., M. J. Small, C. N. Bloyd, M. Henrion 1992. An integrated assessment of acid deposition effects on lake acidification. *Journal of Environmental Engineering* **118**, 120–34.

Santer, B. D., T. M. L. Wigley, M. E. Schlesinger, J. F. B. Mitchell 1990. *Developing climate scenarios from equilibrium GCM results*. Report 47, Max Planck Institut für Meteorologie, Hamburg.

Schelling, T. C. 1994. Intergenerational discounting. In *Integrative assessment of mitigation, impacts, and adaptation to climate change*, N. Nakicenovic, W. D. Nordhaus, R. Richels, F. L. Toth (eds). CP-94-9, International Institute for Applied Systems Analysis, Laxenburg, Austria.

Schrattenholzer, L. 1993. *The IIASA scenarios of 1981 compared with the IEW results of 1992*. Research

Report RR-93-9, International Institute for Applied Systems Analysis, Laxenburg, Austria.

Siegel, E., H. Dowlatabadi, M. J. Small 1995. Sensitivity and uncertainty analysis of an individual plant model and performance of its reduced form versions: a case study of TREGRO. *Journal of Biogeography* **22**, 689–94.

Smith, S. J. & T. M. L. Wigley 1997. *The policy relevance of global warming potentials*. Boulder, Colorado: National Center for Atmospheric Research.

Smith, T. M. & H. H. Shugart 1993. The transient response of terrestrial carbon storage to a perturbed climate. *Nature* **361**, 523–6.

Thompson, M., R. Ellis, A. Wildavsky 1990. *Cultural theory*. Boulder, Colorado: Westview.

Tol, R. S. J. 1995. *The Climate Fund: sensitivity, uncertainty, and robustness analyses*. Discussion Paper W-95/02, Institute for Environmental Studies, Free University, Amsterdam.

Toth, F. L. 1988. Policy exercises. *Simulation and Games* **19**, 235–76.

——1994a. Practice and progress in integrated assessments of climate change: a review. See Nakicenovic et al. (1994).

——1994b. Discounting in integrated assessments of climate change. See Nakicenovic et al. (1994).

UN 1992. *Framework Convention on Climate Change*. New York: United Nations.

——1993. *World population prospects, the 1992 revision*. New York: United Nations.

Vries, H. J. M. de, T. Fiddaman, R. Janssen 1993. *Strategic planning exercise about global warming*. Report 461502002, GLOBO Report Series 2, National Institute of Public Health and Environmental Protection [RIVM], Bilthoven, the Netherlands.

Weyant, J., O. Davidson, H. Dowlatabadi, J. Edmonds, M. Grubb, E. A. Parson, R. Richels, J. Rotmans, P. R. Shukla, R. S. J. Tol, W. Cline, S. Fankhauser 1996. Integrated assessment of climate change: an overview and comparison of approaches and results. In *Climate Change 1995: economic and social dimensions of climate change*, J. P. Bruce, H. Lee, E. F. Haites (eds) [contribution of Working Group III to the Second Assessment Report]. Cambridge: Cambridge University Press.

White, J. W. C. 1993. Don't touch that dial. *Nature* **364**(6434), 186.

Wigley, T. M. L. 1993. Balancing the carbon budget: implications for projections of future carbon dioxide concentration changes. *Tellus* **45B**(5), 409–425.

——1994. *MAGICC: user's guide and scientific reference manual*. Climatic Research Unit, University of East Anglia.

Wigley, T. M. L. & S. C. B. Raper 1987. Thermal expansion of sea water associated with global warming. *Nature* **330**, 127–31.

Wigley, T. M. L., T. Holt, S. C. B. Raper 1991. *STUGE: an interactive greenhouse model—user's manual*. Climatic Research Unit, University of East Anglia.

Wigley, T. M. L., R. Richels, J. A. Edmonds 1996. Economic and environmental choices in the stabilization of atmospheric CO_2 concentrations. *Nature* **379**, 240–42.

Yang, Z., R. S. Eckaus, A. D. Ellerman, H. D. Jacoby 1996. *The MIT emissions prediction and policy analysis (EPPA) model*. Report 6, MIT Joint Program on the Science and Policy of Climate Change, Massachusetts Institute of Technology.

Yohe, G. 1995. Strategies for using integrated assessment models to inform near term abatement policies for greenhouse gas emissions. In *Proceedings, NATO Advanced Research Workshop on Integrated Assessment of Global Environmental Change: science and policy*. Department of Economics, Wesleyan University, Durham, North Carolina.

Yohe, G. & R. Wallace 1996. Near term mitigation policy for global change under uncertainty: minimizing the expected cost of meeting unknown concentrations. *Environmental Modeling and Assessment* **1**, 47–57.

Sponsoring organizations, International Advisory Board, and project participants

INSTITUTIONAL SPONSORS AND COLLABORATORS

Pacific Northwest National Laboratory (PNNL), USA
US Department of Energy (DOE), USA
Electric Power Research Institute (EPRI), USA
Economic and Social Research Council (ESRC), UK
International Institute for Applied Systems Analysis (IIASA), Austria
National Institute for Public Health and Environment (RIVM), Netherlands
Korean Energy Economics Institute (KEEI), Korea
National Oceanic and Atmospheric Administration (NOAA), USA
Centre for Social and Economic Research on the Global Environment (CSERGE), UK
LOS-Senteret, Norway
Musgrave Institute, UK
Centre for the Study of Environmental Change (CSEC), UK
Potsdam Institute for Climate Impacts Research (PIK), Germany
Swiss Federal Institute for Environmental Science and Technology (EAWAG), Switzerland
Commonwealth Scientific and Industrial Research Organization (CSIRO), Australia
Research Institute of Innovative Technology for the Earth (RITE), Japan

THE INTERNATIONAL ADVISORY BOARD

Dr Francisco Barnes
The Honorable Richard Benedick
Professor Harvey Brooks
Professor the Lord Desai of St Clement Danes
Professor George Golitsyn
Pragya Dipak Gyawali
The Honorable Thomas Hughes
Dr Jiro Kondo
Dr Hoesung Lee
Professor Tom Malone
The Honorable Robert McNamara
Professor Richard Odingo
Professor Thomas Schelling

PACIFIC NORTHWEST NATIONAL LABORATORY

Steering Committee

Chester L. Cooper
James A. Edmonds
Elizabeth Malone
Steve Rayner
Norman J. Rosenberg

Support staff

Allison Glismann
Laura Green
Suzette Hampton
Jenniffer Leyson
K Storck

AUTHORS, CONTRIBUTORS, AND PEER REVIEWERS

W. Neil Adger, *University of East Anglia, UK*
Ahsan Uddin, Ahmed *Bangladesh Centre for Advanced Studies, Bangladesh*
Mozaharul Alam, *Centre for Advanced Studies, Bangladesh*
W. B. Ashton, *Pacific Northwest National Laboratory, USA*
Marjolein van Asselt, *University of Maastricht, the Netherlands*
Viranda Asthana, *Jawaharlal Nehru University, India*
Tariq Banuri, *Sustainable Development Policy Institute, Pakistan*
Richard Baron, *International Energy Agency, OECD, France*
Igor Bashmakov, *Center for Energy Efficiency, Moscow*
Richard E. Benedick, *World Wildlife Fund, Conservation Foundation, USA*
Wiebe Bijker, *University of Limburg, the Netherlands*
Daniel Bodansky, *University of Washington School of Law, USA*
Larry Boyer, *George Washington University, USA*
Judith Bradbury, *Pacific Northwest National Laboratory, USA*
Harvey Brooks, *Harvard University, USA*
Katrina Brown, *University of East Anglia, UK*
Ian Burton, *Atmospheric Environment Service, Canada*
Frederick H. Buttel, *University of Wisconsin, Madison, USA*
Karl W. Butzer, *University of Texas at Austin, USA*
Robin Cantor, *Law and Economics Consulting Group, USA*
Bayard Catron, *George Washington University, USA*
Florian Charvolin, *Centre National de la Recherche Scientifique, France*
Chipeng Chu, *Stanford University, USA*
Chester L. Cooper, *Pacific Northwest National Laboratory, USA*
Robert Costanza, *University of Maryland, USA*
Edward Crenshaw, *Ohio State University, USA*
Pierre Crosson, *Resources for the Future, USA*
Margaret Davidson, *NOAA Coastal Services Center, USA*
Ogunlade Davidson, *University of Sierra Leone, Sierra Leone*
Robert Deacon, *University of California at Santa Barbara, USA*
Ota de Leonardis, *University of Milan, Italy*
Meghnad Desai, *London School of Economics, UK*
Mary Douglas, *University of London, UK*
Hadi Dowlatabadi, *Carnegie Mellon University, USA*
Thomas E. Downing, *University of Oxford, UK*
Otto Edenhofer, *Technical University of Darmstadt, Germany*
James A. Edmonds, *Pacific Northwest National Laboratory, USA*
Paul N. Edwards, *Stanford University, USA*
Paul Ekins, *Birkbeck College London, UK*
Mohammad El-Raey, *University of Alexandria, Egypt*
Aant Elzinga, *University of Gothenburg, Sweden*
Shirley J. Fiske, *National Oceanic and Atmospheric Administration, USA*
Silvio O. Funtowicz, *Joint Research Center, European Commission, Italy*
Erve Garrison, *University of Georgia, USA*
Des Gasper, *Institute of Social Studies, the Netherlands*
Luther P. Gerlach, *University of Minnesota, USA*
Peter Gleick, *Pacific Institute, USA*
George Golitsyn, *Russian Academy of Science, Russia*
Dean Graetz, *Commonwealth Scientific and Industrial Research Organisation, Australia*
Philip C. R. Gray, *Research Center Julich, Germany*
Wayne Gray, *Clark University, USA*
Michael Grubb, *Royal Institute of International Affairs, UK*
Arnulf Grübler, *International Institute for Applied Systems Analysis, Austria*
Howard Gruenspecht, *US Department of Energy, USA*
Simon Guy, *University of Newcastle upon Tyne, UK*

Dipak Gyawali, *Royal Nepal Academy of Science and Technology, Nepal*
Peter M. Haas, *University of Massachusetts, Amherst, USA*
Bruce Hackett, *University of California, Davis, USA*
Nick Hanley, *University of Stirling, UK*
Russell Hardin, *New York University, USA*
Shaun Hargreaves-Heap, *University of East Anglia, UK*
Susanna B. Hecht, *University of California, Los Angeles, USA*
Gerhart Heilig, *International Institute for Applied Systems Analysis, Austria*
Edward L. Hillsman, *Oak Ridge National Laboratory, USA*
Frank Hole, *Yale University, USA*
Leen Hordijk, *Wageningen Agricultural University, the Netherlands*
John Houghton, *US Department of Energy, USA*
Hiliard Huntington, *Stanford University, USA*
Saleemul Huq, *Bangladesh Centre for Advanced Studies, Bangladesh*
Evert van Imhoff, *Netherlands Interdisciplinary Demographic Institute, the Netherlands*
Helen Ingram, *University of Arizona, USA*
Alan Irwin, *Brunel University, UK*
Saiful Islam, *Global Challenge Network, Germany*
Henry D. Jacoby, *Massachusetts Institute of Technology, USA*
Carlo C. Jaeger, *Swiss Federal Institute for Environmental Science and Technology, Switzerland and Darmstadt University of Technology, Germany*
Dale Jamieson, *Carleton College, USA*
Marco Janssen, *National Institute of Public Health and the Environment, the Netherlands*
Sheila S. Jasanoff, *Cornell University, USA*
Craig Jenkins, *Ohio State University, USA*
Denise Jodelet, *Ecole des Hautes Etudes en Sciences Sociales, France*
N. S. Jodha, *World Bank, USA*
Andrew Jordan, *University of East Anglia, UK*
Tae Yong Jung, *Korean Energy Economics Institute, Korea*
Hélène Karmasin, *Institut für Motivforschung, Austria*
Rick Katz, *ESIG/NCAR, USA*
René Kemp, *University of Limburg, the Netherlands*
Willett Kempton, *University of Delaware, USA*
Richard Klein, *National Institute for Coastal and Marine Management, the Netherlands*
Rob Koudstaal, *Resource Analysis, the Netherlands*
Chunglin Kwa, *University of Amsterdam, the Netherlands*
Denise Lach, *Oregon State University, USA*
W. Henry Lambright, *Syracuse University, USA*
Bruno Latour, *Ecole Nationale Supérieure des Mines, France*
Stephen Leatherman, *University of Maryland, USA*
Harro van Lente, *KPMG Inspire Foundation, the Netherlands*
Ronnie D. Lipschutz, *University of California, Santa Cruz, USA*
Diana Liverman, *University of Arizona, USA*
Ragnar Löfstedt, *University of Surrey, UK*
Janice Longstreth, *Waste Policy Institute, USA*
Michael Lovell, *Wesleyan University, USA*
Sven B. Lundstedt, *Ohio State University, USA*
Urs Luterbacher, *Graduate Institute of International Studies, Geneva, Switzerland*
Wolfgang Lutz, *International Institute for Applied Systems Analysis, Austria*
Loren Lutzenhiser, *Washington State University, USA*
Michael Lynch, *Brunel University, UK*
F. Landis MacKellar, *International Institute for Applied Systems Analysis, Austria*
Antonio Maghalães, *Ministry of Planning, Brazil*
Elizabeth L. Malone, *Pacific Northwest National Laboratory, USA*
Tom Malone, *Sigma Xi, USA*
Gavan McDonnel, *University of New South Wales, Australia*
Jacqueline McGlade, *Warwick University, UK*
Tom McGovern, *City University of New York, USA*
Douglas McLean, *University of Maryland, USA*
A. J. McMichael, *London School of Hygiene and Tropical Medicine, UK*
Judith Mehta, *University of East Anglia, UK*
Robert Mendelsohn, *Yale University, USA*
William B. Meyer, *Clark University, USA*

Rob Misdorp, *International Centre for Coastal Zone Management, the Netherlands*
Elena Milanova, *Russian MAB UNESCO Committee, Russia*
Clark A. Miller, *Cornell University, USA*
Vinod Mishra, *East–West Center, USA*
Ronald B. Mitchell, *University of Oregon, USA*
Emilio Moran, *Indiana University at Bloomington, USA*
Tsuneyuki Morita, *National Institute for Environmental Studies, Japan*
Peter Morrisette, *Institute of Behavioral Science, USA*
Han Mukang, *University of Beijing, China*
Dwijen Mullick, *Centre for Advanced Studies, Bangladesh*
Nebojsa Nakicenovic, *International Institute for Applied Systems Analysis, Austria*
Steven Ney, *Technical University, Vienna, Austria*
Robert J. Nicholls, *University of Middlesex, UK*
David Norse, *University College London, UK*
Richard Odingo, *University of Nairobi, Kenya*
Jackton B. Ojwang, *University of Nairobi, Kenya*
Steve Olson, *University of Rhode Island, USA*
Brian O'Neill, *Environmental Defense Fund, USA*
Hans Opschoor, *Free University of Amsterdam, the Netherlands*
Timothy O'Riordan, *University of East Anglia, UK*
John O. Oucho, *University of Nairobi, Kenya*
Edward A. Parson, *Harvard University, USA*
Matthew Paterson, *University of Keele, UK*
David Pearce, *University College London, UK*
Sanjeev Prakash, *Eco-Tibet, India*
Martin Price, *University of Oxford, UK*
Atiq Rahman, *Bangladesh Centre for Advanced Studies, Bangladesh*
Kal Raustiala, *Harvard Law School, USA*
Jerome R. Ravetz, *Research Methods Consultancy, UK*
Steve Rayner, *Pacific Northwest National Laboratory, USA*
John Reilly, *US Department of Agriculture, USA*
Ortwin Renn, *Academy for Technology Assessment and University of Stuttgart, Germany*
John Richards, *Duke University, USA*
Kenneth R. Richards, *University of Indiana, Bloomington, USA*
Richard Richels, *Electric Power Research Institute, USA*
Arie Rip, *University of Twente, the Netherlands*
James Risbey, *Carnegie Mellon University, USA*
John Robinson, *University of British Columbia, Canada*
Richard Rockwell, *Inter-University Consortium for Political and Social Research, USA*
Eugene A. Rosa, *Washington State University, USA*
Luiz Pinguelli Rosa, *Federal University of Rio de Janeiro*
Adam Rose, *Pennsylvania State University, USA*
Norman J. Rosenberg, *Pacific Northwest National Laboratory, USA*
Jan Rotmans, *University of Maastricht, the Netherlands*
Ian Rowlands, *University of Waterloo, Canada*
Paul Runci, *University of Maryland, USA*
Vernon W. Ruttan, *University of Minnesota, USA*
Robert Sack, *University of Wisconsin, USA*
Colin Sage, *Wye College, UK*
Paul Samson, *International Green Cross, Switzerland*
Gerrit Jan Schaeffer, Energy Research Centre, the Netherlands
Thomas Schelling, *University of Maryland, USA*
Jurgen Schmandt, *University of Texas, Austin, USA*
Michiel Schwarz, *Independent Consultant/ Researcher, the Netherlands*
Michael J. Scott, *Pacific Northwest National Laboratory, USA*
Galina Sergen, *University of New South Wales, Australia*
Elizabeth Shove, *University of Lancaster, UK*
P. R. Shukla, *Indian Institute of Management, India*
Udo Simonis, *Science Centre, Berlin*
Jim Skea, *University of Sussex, UK*
Eugene Skolnikoff, *Massachusetts Institute of Technology, USA*
Paul Slovic, *Decision Research, USA*
Youba Sokona, *ENDA–TM, Senegal*
Zofia Sokolewicz, University of Warsaw, Poland

Clive Spash, *University of Stirling,* UK
Bertram I. Spector, *Center for Negotiation Analysis,* USA
Daniel Spreng, *Swiss Federal Institute of Technology, Switzerland*
Detlef Sprinz, PIK-*Potsdam Institute for Climate Impact Research, Germany*
George Stankey, *Oregon State University,* USA
Nico Stehr, *University of British Columbia, Canada*
Paul Stern, *National Academy of Science and Engineering,* USA
Astri Suhrke, *Chr. Michelson Institute, Norway*
Uno Svedin, *Swedish Council for Planning and Coordination of Research, Sweden*
Thanh-dam Truong, *Institute of Social Studies, the Netherlands*
Michael Thompson, *Musgrave Institute,* UK *and* LOS-*Senteret, Norway*
Peter Timmerman, *International Federation of Institutes of Advanced Studies, Canada*
B. L. Turner II, *Clark University,* USA
Lando Velasco, CANSEA, *Philippines*
Pier Vellinga, *Free University of Amsterdam, the Netherlands*
Hugh Ward, *University of Essex,* UK
Tom Webler, *Antioch College,* USA
Peter Weingart, *University of Bielefeld, Germany*
George W. Wenzel, *McGill University, Canada*
James L. Wescoat, *University of Colorado at Boulder,* USA
Lee Wexler, *International Institute for Applied Systems Analysis, Austria*
John Weyant, *Stanford University,* USA
John Whalley, *University of Western Ontario, Canada*
Harold Wilhite, *University of Oslo, Norway*
Donald J. Wuebbles, *University of Illinois,* USA
Brian Wynne, *University of Lancaster,* UK
Kenji Yamaji, *University of Tokyo, Japan*
Yukio Yanigisawa, *Research Institute of Innovative Technology for the Earth, Japan*
Steven Yearley, *University of York,* UK
Shira Yoffe, *Pacific Northwest National Laboratory,* USA
Gary Yohe, *Wesleyan University,* USA

Contents of Volumes 1–4

Index of names

Note This index includes the names of all authors of works with more than two authors. Thus, a name may appear in the index and be represented by "et al." on the page referred to in the text.

Subject index